Definitive MPLS Network Designs

Jim Guichard

François Le Faucheur

Jean-Philippe Vasseur

Cisco Press

800 East 96th Street
Indianapolis, IN 46240 USA

Definitive MPLS Network Designs

Jim Guichard

François Le Faucheur

Jean-Philippe Vasseur

Copyright© 2005 Cisco Systems, Inc.

Published by:
Cisco Press
800 East 96th Street
Indianapolis, IN 46240 USA

Printed in the United States of America   1 2 3 4 5 6 7 8 9 0

First Printing March 2005

Library of Congress Cataloging-in-Publication Number: 2003116497

ISBN: 1-58705-186-9

Warning and Disclaimer

This book is designed to provide information about MPLS network designs. Every effort has been made to make this book as complete and accurate as possible, but no warranty or fitness is implied.

The information is provided on an "as is" basis. The author, Cisco Press, and Cisco Systems, Inc. shall have neither liability nor responsibility to any person or entity with respect to any loss or damages arising from the information contained in this book or from the use of the discs or programs that may accompany it.

The opinions expressed in this book belong to the author and are not necessarily those of Cisco Systems, Inc.

Trademark Acknowledgments

All terms mentioned in this book that are known to be trademarks or service marks have been appropriately capitalized. Cisco Press or Cisco Systems, Inc. cannot attest to the accuracy of this information. Use of a term in this book should not be regarded as affecting the validity of any trademark or service mark.

Feedback Information

At Cisco Press, our goal is to create in-depth technical books of the highest quality and value. Each book is crafted with care and precision, undergoing rigorous development that involves the unique expertise of members of the professional technical community.

Reader feedback is a natural continuation of this process. If you have any comments about how we could improve the quality of this book, or otherwise alter it to better suit your needs, you can contact us through e-mail at feedback@ciscopress.com. Please be sure to include the book title and ISBN in your message.

We greatly appreciate your assistance.

Corporate and Government Sales

Cisco Press offers excellent discounts on this book when ordered in quantity for bulk purchases or special sales.

For more information, please contact U.S. Corporate and Government Sales, 1-800-382-3419, corpsales@pearsontechgroup.com.

For sales outside the U.S., please contact International Sales at international@pearsoned.com.

Publisher	John Wait
Editor-in-Chief	John Kane
Executive Editor	Brett Bartow
Cisco Representative	
Cisco Press Program Manager	
Production Manager	
Acquisitions Editor	
Development Editor	And
Project Editor	Marc
Copy Editor	Gayle Johnson
Technical Reviewers	Bruce Davie
	Xavier Vinet
	Raymond Zhang
	Javier Achirica
	Patrice Bellagamba
	William Copeland
Team Coordinator	Tammi Barnett
Book/Cover Designer	Louisa Adair
Compositor	Mark Shirar
Indexers	Larry Sweazy
	Tim Wright

CISCO SYSTEMS

Corporate Headquarters
Cisco Systems, Inc.
170 West Tasman Drive
San Jose, CA 95134-1706
USA
www.cisco.com
Tel: 408 526-4000
    800 553-NETS (6387)
Fax: 408 526-4100

European Headquarters
Cisco Systems International BV
Haarlerbergpark
Haarlerbergweg 13-19
1101 CH Amsterdam
The Netherlands
www-europe.cisco.com
Tel: 31 0 20 357 1000
Fax: 31 0 20 357 1100

Americas Headquarters
Cisco Systems, Inc.
170 West Tasman Drive
San Jose, CA 95134-1706
USA
www.cisco.com
Tel: 408 526-7660
Fax: 408 527-0883

Asia Pacific Headquarters
Cisco Systems, Inc.
Capital Tower
168 Robinson Road
#22-01 to #29-01
Singapore 068912
www.cisco.com
Tel: +65 6317 7777
Fax: +65 6317 7799

Cisco Systems has more than 200 offices in the following countries and regions. Addresses, phone numbers, and fax numbers are listed on the **Cisco.com Web site at www.cisco.com/go/offices.**

Argentina • Australia • Austria • Belgium • Brazil • Bulgaria • Canada • Chile • China PRC • Colombia • Costa Rica • Croatia • Czech Republic
Denmark • Dubai, UAE • Finland • France • Germany • Greece • Hong Kong SAR • Hungary • India • Indonesia • Ireland • Israel • Italy
Japan • Korea • Luxembourg • Malaysia • Mexico • The Netherlands • New Zealand • Norway • Peru • Philippines • Poland • Portugal
Puerto Rico • Romania • Russia • Saudi Arabia • Scotland • Singapore • Slovakia • Slovenia • South Africa • Spain • Sweden
Switzerland • Taiwan • Thailand • Turkey • Ukraine • United Kingdom • United States • Venezuela • Vietnam • Zimbabwe

About the Authors

Jim Guichard, CCIE No. 2069, is a system architect at Cisco Systems, with a primary focus on MPLS/ IP Layer 2 and Layer 3 VPN technologies. During the last eight years at Cisco, and previously at IBM, he has been involved in the design, implementation, and planning of many large-scale WAN and LAN networks. Using the experience gained from these deployments, he continues to provide valued assistance to many of the larger Cisco service provider customers. His previous publications include *MPLS and VPN Architectures,* Volumes I and II, published by Cisco Press. He has also filed several patents in the area of MPLS.

François Le Faucheur is a system architect at Cisco Systems working in product development in the area of IP QoS and MPLS. He has worked for several telecom carriers in France and Australia on the development of enhanced services on ATM, Frame Relay, SMDS, and IP. He has an engineering degree in real-time data processing from the Ecole Centrale de Paris. He edits and coauthors many IETF specifications in the areas of MPLS and QoS, such as MPLS support of Differentiated Services, DiffServ-aware MPLS TE, and MPLS/BGP-based IPv6 VPNs. He has also filed several patents in the areas of MPLS and QoS.

Jean-Philippe Vasseur is system architect at Cisco Systems where he works on IP/MPLS architecture specifications, focusing on IP, TE, and network recovery. He holds an engineering degree from France and an M.S. from the SIT (New Jersey, USA). Before joining Cisco, he worked for several service providers in large multiprotocol environments. He is an active member of the IETF, co-chair of the IETF PCE (Path Computation Element) Working Group and coauthored several IETF specifications. He is a regular speaker at various international conferences and is involved in various research projects in the area of IP and MPLS. He has also filed several patents in the area of IP and MPLS and is the coauthor of *Network Recovery.*

About the Technical Reviewers

Bruce Davie, Ph.D., has been with the IOS Technologies Division (ITD) since joining Cisco Systems in 1995 and was awarded recognition as a Cisco Fellow in 1998. He leads an architecture group that is currently working on the development of MPLS and QoS capabilities for IP networks. In addition, he is leading a cross-company effort to create a common QoS and MPLS architecture across the Cisco product line. He has more than 15 years of networking and communications industry experience. He is also an active participant in both the IETF and the Internet Research Task Force and is a senior member of the IEEE. He has a bachelor's degree in engineering from Melbourne University and a Ph.D. in computer science from the University of Edinburgh.

Xavier Vinet is a network architect within IP Network Engineering at Equant, specializing in engineering and the implementation of international Equant MPLS networks. For the past eight years, he has also been involved in designing the Internet and MPLS VPN domestic networks of France Telecom. He has a telecom engineering degree.

Raymond Zhang is a senior network architect for INFONET, responsible for global IP backbone infrastructure and routing architecture planning and its evolutions. His current main areas of interest are large-scale backbone routing, traffic engineering, performance and traffic statistical analysis, MPLS-related technologies, multiservice QoS, IPv6, and multicast. He is an active member of IETF and has contributed to several drafts in the areas of MPLS TE, Inter-AS traffic engineering, and others. He has a master of engineering degree from CUNY.

Javier Achirica works in business development in the enterprise services division of Telefonica. He has been involved in the design and deployment of IP networks for ten years, in both corporations and national and international carrier IP networks in different areas of Telefonica, setting up networks in more than 12 countries. He's also active in the most relevant standardization organizations. He earned a degree in physics from the University of Valladolid in Spain and an MBA from the Instituto de Empresa in Madrid, Spain.

Patrice Bellagamba is a consulting engineer at Cisco Systems with a role as technology specialist in the usage of MPLS for large enterprises in EMEA. He has more than 22 years of experience in networking, with 13 years in IP and six years in MPLS and QoS, mainly in design and services for service providers and large enterprises. He holds an engineering degree from Supelec in France.

William Copeland has 15 years of experience in the networking industry and is currently one of the chief architects of MCI's MPLS VPN network.

Dedications

To my wife, Sadie, and my children, Aimee and Thomas. Thanks for your patience and support once again.   *—Jim*

To my adorable children, Lucas and Cylia.   *—François*

To my parents, my wife, Brigitte, and my two daughters, Manon and Eleonore.   *—Jean-Philippe*

Acknowledgments

This book benefited from the contributions of many people.

First, a very special thanks to our technical reviewers—Bruce Davie, Xavier Vinet, and Raymond Zhang—for their constructive, valuable suggestions and thorough reviews. We also want to thank Javier Achirica and Bill Copeland for their technical reviews of specific chapters, as well as Patrice Bellagamba for his significant contributions and technical review of Chapter 6.

We also want to express our gratitude to all the people who kindly shared some of their experiences with us on particular detailed aspects of this book, including Jeff Apcar, Rajiv Asati, Sandeep Bajaj, Jean-Marc Barozet, Magdeleine Bourgoin, Jaudelice Cavalcante de Oliveira, Anna Charny, Christophe Charrier, Denis Churlet, Sukrit Dasgupta, Jaak Defour, Maurice Duault, Denys Dumas, Bertrand Duvivier, John Evans, Don Heidric, Eric Levy-Abegnoli, Olivier Mercier, Pascal Paris, Keyur Patel, Marc Rapoport, and Dan Tappan.

Special thanks go to our wonderful editing team, especially Andrew Cupp, Brett Bartow, and Michelle Grandin.

Finally, this book could not have been written without the continuous support and patience of our families and dearest.

This Book Is Safari Enabled

The Safari® Enabled icon on the cover of your favorite technology book means the book is available through Safari Bookshelf. When you buy this book, you get free access to the online edition for 45 days.

Safari Bookshelf is an electronic reference library that lets you easily search thousands of technical books, find code samples, download chapters, and access technical information whenever and wherever you need it.

To gain 45-day Safari Enabled access to this book:

- Go to http://www.ciscopress.com/safarienabled
- Complete the brief registration form
- Enter the coupon code OJRC-IB1P-4J4B-SFPN-VK0C

If you have difficulty registering on Safari Bookshelf or accessing the online edition, please e-mail customer-service@safaribooksonline.com.

Contents at a Glance

Contents

Chapter 2   Technology Primer: Quality of Service, Traffic Engineering, and Network Recovery   49

Command Syntax Conventions

The conventions used to present command syntax in this book are the same conventions used in the IOS Command Reference. The Command Reference describes these conventions as follows:

- **Bold** indicates commands and keywords that are entered literally as shown.

- *Italic* indicates arguments for which you supply actual values.

- Vertical bars (|) separate alternative, mutually exclusive elements.

- Square brackets ([ ]) indicate an optional element.

- Braces ({ }) indicate a required choice.

- Braces within brackets ([{ }]) indicate a required choice within an optional element.

Foreword

MPLS has established itself as one of the fundamental technologies in the data networking world. Given the way networks are evolving, it is becoming clear that future data networks will have to carry a variety of service types, ranging from voice and video to reliable high-bandwidth data exchange. Since such networks are extremely critical to businesses, the availability of these networks has to be extremely high, combined with very low convergence time in case of failures. They also should offer differentiated quality of service. Fortunately, MPLS is a technology that has arrived and is ready to meet all those challenges. Needless to say, any network professional who aspires to participate in the future of data networks must be well versed in this technology.

MPLS is a technology that provides a Layer 2 connection-oriented transport mode through a Layer 3 network. This seemingly straightforward mechanism is so powerful that it has changed the data networking industry in profound ways. To unravel the applicability of MPLS, it is important to take a quick trip to the pre-MPLS IP world and discuss the impact of MPLS.

IP as a technology is ubiquitous and powerful, but IP routing has some fundamental constraints. Each node involved in transporting an IP packet from source to destination makes its own routing decision based on the information carried within the packet header. IP routing protocols ensure that routers have consistent routing tables; otherwise, packets may loop or may never get delivered. Though the per-hop nature of IP routing decisions provides resiliency, it has two fundamental constraints. First, since traffic always uses the shortest path to the destination, critical links can get overloaded. Secondly, a public-domain IP node cannot route a private IP packet since the routing entry for a destination address must be unique and private IP space does not satisfy that requirement.

To circumvent these constraints, two design principles were widely prevalent prior to MPLS. On one hand, service providers had an ATM or Frame Relay-based Layer 2 infrastructure underlying the IP network to engineer IP traffic over long paths. This approach allowed for more optimal utilization of network resources. On the other hand, enterprise networks, which used the public network as transport, had to build elaborately tunneled virtual private networks with endpoints on their own premises. The enterprise routers then handled the entire complexity of the VPNs. Of course, traditionally expensive Layer 2 data networks or pure TDM networks were other options available to build enterprise networks.

But the advent of MPLS technology has taken away these shackles. Since MPLS provides a connection-oriented end-to-end Layer 2 transport mode independent of the shortest IP path, service providers have been quick to realize that the functionality of the underlying Layer 2 (ATM or Frame Relay) infrastructures could be handed over to IP routers, which would use MPLS technology to provide the same service. This MPLS approach enables service providers to eliminate an entire set of Layer 2 switches, allowing them to be more competitive and to offer cheaper Internet services. Moreover, since the MPLS control plane largely utilizes the existing IP routing control plane, MPLS, as a new technology, has minimal overhead. The MPLS label-switched paths also are resilient against failures and have the ability to carry the information necessary to enforce quality of service within the backbone. Thus, MPLS has become a huge boon to Internet backbone service providers.

Since MPLS provides a Layer 2 path through the IP infrastructure, it was just a matter of time before the realization that effective virtual private networks could be built using the same technology as the transport mechanism. When an IP packet rides within an MPLS label-switched path, the backbone IP routers do not need to look into the IP header of the packet. This design has given rise to MPLS-based Layer 3

VPNs (L3VPNs), which has moved the VPN complexity from the enterprise world to the service provider. Thus, a brand new service offering for service providers has emerged that has made enterprise networks more efficient.

The introduction of Layer 3 VPNs has been followed by another realization: If the IP backbone is agnostic to the content of the MPLS packets, why not use it for transporting frames from lower layers? This has ushered in services like Layer 2 VPNs (L2VPNs), Virtual Private LAN Service (VPLS), and Virtual Private Wire Service (VPWS). This opaqueness of the payload also has encouraged usage of MPLS label-switched paths as a multicast delivery mechanism. Now service providers can offer newer services and enterprise networks can operate their infrastructure more efficiently.

This book comes as a boon to professionals who want to understand the power of MPLS and make full use of it. As with any technology, understanding the protocols themselves is one thing, and understanding the applicability of these protocols is another. The authors have wisely chosen a format with multiple in-depth design studies showing applications of MPLS technology. The initial chapters thoroughly explain the operations of the protocols themselves before presenting the individual design studies. The applicability of MPLS itself is quite broad, and hardly any single source can explain the tricks of optimizing network designs in each application. This book, indeed, can be that single source.

I recommend this book to any network professional who is instrumental in architecting, designing, or troubleshooting MPLS-based data networks. The knowledge gathered here will enrich your understanding of MPLS and serve as a solid foundation for future technology education.

Enjoy the ride.

Parantap Lahiri
Manager, IP Network Infrastructure Engineering, MCI

Introduction

The last few years have seen the pace of Multiprotocol Label Switching (MPLS) deployments accelerate in all regions of the globe. MPLS is now a mature technology ready for prime time and able to meet the challenges of 21st century networks. Various factors have driven the adoption of this technology. Initially it provided a scalable architecture through which to deliver Layer 3 Virtual Private Networks (VPNs). More recently, with the surge of multimedia traffic (such as telephony and video) carried on the IP/MPLS backbone, the need for traffic engineering, fast recovery, and differentiated quality of service (QoS) has become apparent. Migration of existing Layer 2 services onto an IP/MPLS infrastructure has also garnered much interest. New MPLS applications such as ATM and Ethernet pseudowire services and Virtual Private LAN Service (VPLS) have emerged to round out a very broad portfolio of MPLS-related services and technologies.

Given the widespread acceptance of the technology, MPLS has been integrated into a large set of very diverse service provider environments, including national telcos, IXCs, ILECs, CLECs, RBOCs, global service providers, and ISPs. The success of the Layer 3 VPN service offered by these operators is such that it is generally the benchmark for enterprises to evaluate and build their intranet solutions over. In addition, some large- and medium-sized enterprises are now also building and operating their own private MPLS infrastructures.

The ability to combine Layer 2 and Layer 3 VPNs, traffic engineering, fast recovery, and tight QoS and to derive the benefits of each has led to the adoption of MPLS as the basis for the next-generation multiservice networks. These networks carry not only Internet best-effort data traffic but also mission-critical data, telephony, and video. They also deliver VPN, multicast, and IPv6 services and transport ATM, Ethernet, and Frame Relay traffic. This is facilitated by the fundamental decorrelation built into MPLS between application-related functions and transport functions. This allows multiservice MPLS networks to be architected with flexible edge devices that are customer-aware and application-nimble, attached to a high-performance, high-availability core infrastructure that is application- and customer-unaware.

Network planners and architects have various sources to turn to when seeking information on the concepts and protocols involved in specific facets of MPLS, such as VPN, QoS, and traffic engineering. However, no single source illustrates how to actually design a network that combines those optimally for a specific environment and provides details on the latest technologies, services, and design techniques. The variety of environments and requirements found in production networks makes it difficult to provide a single set of one-size-fits-all design recommendations. The set of services to be offered by various network operators often vastly differs from one environment to another. For instance, one network operator may have to support multicast traffic within the Layer 3 VPN service. A second may need to offer a rich set of classes of service to address all the application requirements presented to it. A third may have to support IPv6 services. Another may have to trunk ATM switches over the packet network. Also, economic challenges greatly differ between network operators. Whereas one may own fiber and transmission assets and can easily overprovision its network, another may lease its network capacity and thus be pressured to strictly optimize bandwidth usage and make use of MPLS traffic engineering techniques in the core.

To complicate matters, restoration requirements may be quite different. One network may target subsecond restoration times. Another network trunking Public Switched Telephony Network (PSTN) traffic may require extremely fast convergence on the order of tens of milliseconds.

Another consideration is that although some deployments involve a single autonomous system, others involve multiple operators or force an operator's backbone to be split into multiple autonomous systems for operational, size, or historical reasons. Most features require very different designs, depending on whether they span a single autonomous system, multiple autonomous systems from a single provider, or multiple providers.

Also, because of their specificities, different networks hit different scalability barriers and need different features or design alternatives to overcome these limitations.

Finally, some MPLS technologies are closely intertwined and need to be designed together to operate in perfect synergy. DiffServ, DiffServ-aware MPLS traffic engineering, and MPLS Fast Reroute are excellent examples of features that need to be combined very thoughtfully because they tightly interact with each other.

With so many considerations to take into account when designing a network, the possibilities may appear endless or overwhelming to a service provider or an enterprise moving over to an MPLS network.

Definitive MPLS Network Designs aims to address these concerns. It provides you with a series of detailed design studies showing you how to combine key techniques and MPLS-related technologies at the heart of IP/MPLS networks. The design studies present designs of fictitious operators (as opposed to a blueprint for actual designs of existing commercial network operators or enterprises). Each design is representative of existing real-world network designs that have been deployed or are about to be deployed.

Throughout the various design studies, sample configurations are given for illustrative purposes. Specific autonomous system numbers and/or public IP address blocks are used as references (these addresses are not attributed to any particular network operator). If these numbers were to be provided to any operator in the future, the design studies would not refer by any means to those operators.

Each design study is based on a set of characteristics and objectives common to a given profile of network operators that deploy MPLS today (such as an Interexchange Carrier (IXC), a global provider, an enterprise, and so on) and discusses all the corresponding design aspects. However, the design aspects presented in the context of one operator profile to address a given set of requirements may be applicable in other environments sharing these requirements. Therefore, this book contains different combinations of ideas that, when taken as a whole, provide a reusable design toolkit.

How This Book Is Organized

Not every network architect has in-depth knowledge of all the technologies involved in today's networks. Therefore, the first two chapters provide a comprehensive overview of all the technologies used in the various design studies. They focus on the essential concepts, protocols, and more-recent developments. Chapter 1 focuses on the technologies that have the most impact at the edge of the network: Layer 3 VPN, multicast VPNs, IPv6, and pseudowire. Chapter 2 is devoted to QoS, MPLS traffic engineering, and network recovery technologies that are an integral part of modern core networks.

The remaining chapters present a series of design studies. Each one is based on a specific network that is hypothetical but that is very representative of a profile of service providers and enterprise networks running MPLS today.

Each design study chapter has four parts. First, the authors describe the network environment, including the set of supported services, network topology, POP structure, transmission facilities, basic IP routing design, and possible constraints. Next, the objectives that influenced the design are identified. These can include optimizing bandwidth usage, supporting seamless VPN service through a partner service provider, trunking the existing ATM infrastructure over the MPLS core, and offering a rich set of QoS guarantees. Then, each design study details all aspects of the network design, covering VPN, QoS, traffic engineering, network recovery, and, where applicable, multicast, IPv6, and pseudowire. The chapter ends by listing a number of lessons that can be drawn from the design study. This way, all types of service providers and enterprises can adapt aspects of the design solutions to meet their individual network environment and objectives.

Chapter 3 describes a data and long-distance voice service provider in the U.S. (an IXC) that owns fiber and transmission facilities nationwide. In particular, this design study covers Layer 3 VPN design, QoS design based on an overengineered core, and fast recovery over unprotected DWDM transmission facilities.

Chapter 4 describes the design of a national telco deploying a multiservice backbone over which multiple services have been migrated (such as IPv4 Internet and IP VPN services). This network is also used to trunk the domestic public telephony traffic and to introduce new services (such as IPv6 Internet and Carrier's Carrier). Also, this chapter details the use of shared PE routers in which all services are offered on the same devices: a rich CoS offering on the access and QoS/Fast Reroute for telephony traffic in the core.

Chapter 5 describes an international service provider with many POPs all around the globe. This service provider relies on interconnection with regional service providers and establishes tight agreements with them to provide a seamless service for its customers. Also, it has deployed virtual POPs (VPOPs) to establish a point of presence in a particular country without extending its own core network to reach the corresponding parts of the world. The company takes advantage of interprovider MPLS traffic engineering LSPs that offer guaranteed bandwidth and fast recovery through another provider's IP/MPLS network. This chapter contains a detailed design discussion of inter-AS Layer 3 VPNs, including the single-operator case, multioperator case, and multicast. It also describes extensive traffic engineering aspects related to bandwidth optimization, including DiffServ-aware traffic engineering in combination with a rich set of QoS mechanisms. You'll also read about transport of ATM traffic onto traffic engineering LSPs and the VPOP design and its associated traffic engineering, restoration, and QoS operations in an inter-AS environment.

Finally, Chapter 6 describes a large enterprise (a group of banks) relying on Layer 3 VPN services to control communications within and across subsidiaries in an environment where mergers, acquisitions, and expansion in other countries are common. In particular, this design covers the operation of a private international MPLS core in conjunction with branch connectivity provided by other Layer 3 MPLS VPN and Frame Relay service providers. You'll read about the use of IPSec for secure communication across a subset of users with strict security requirements, and QoS over a mix of fast and relatively low-speed links. The chapter also details how a managed voice service operates within this enterprise Layer

3 MPLS VPN design. You'll also see how a telephony service provider uses the Layer 3 MPLS VPN technology inside its own network to offer managed telephony services to multiple customers.

References Used in This Book

Throughout this book you will see references to other resources. These are provided in case you want to delve more deeply into a subject. Such references appear in brackets, such as [L2VPN]. If you want to know more about this resource, look up the code in the "References" appendix to find out specific information about the resource.

Who Should Read This Book

The target audience for this book includes the following networking professionals:

- Network architects

- Network designers

- Network engineers

- Technical managers

- Telecommunications professors and instructors

- Technical consultants

- Students

Those preparing for the MPLS portion of the CCIP or CCIE Service Provider Cisco certification also can greatly benefit from this book.

CHAPTER 1

Technology Primer: Layer 3 VPN, Multicast VPNs, IPv6, and Pseudowire

As described in the introduction to this book, numerous technologies, when combined, make up today's integrated MPLS/IP networks. Clearly very few people have a complete grasp of all these technologies and how they interact. However, a general understanding of each is necessary to gain the most value from the design studies in this book. Therefore, our aim within the first two chapters is to provide a high-level overview of the relevant technologies. This first chapter focuses on the technologies that have the most impact at the edge of the network. It concentrates on Layer 3 VPN, multicast VPNs, IPv6, and pseudowire.

It is not the intention of this chapter to provide all the technical details for each technology. Rather, this chapter focuses on the essential aspects as well as more-recent developments of these technologies. It also gives useful references to various books, IETF drafts, RFCs, and so forth that you can check if you're interested in more technical details.

References Used in This Book

Throughout this book you will see references to other resources. These are provided in case you want to delve more deeply into a subject. Such references appear in brackets, such as [L2VPN]. If you want to know more about this resource, look up the code in the "References" appendix to find out specific information about the resource.

MPLS VPN Services in MPLS/IP Networks

A number of technologies provide Virtual Private Network (VPN) solutions. We define such solutions as those that can deliver private network access for many subscribers of the service across a shared infrastructure. One such technology used to provide these services is Multiprotocol Label Switching (MPLS).

MPLS may be used to deliver VPN solutions at either Layer 2 (as described in [L2VPN] and [VPLS]) through the use of Pseudowire technology or Layer 3 (as described in [2547bis]) of the OSI Reference Model. All solutions allow a network operator to deliver a private service over a shared IP network.

A private network delivered over a shared infrastructure is not a new concept. Indeed, these services have been in existence for a long time. The Frame Relay and Asynchronous Transfer Mode (ATM) technologies provide Layer 2 service. IP tunneling (either Generic Routing Encapsulation [GRE] or IP Security [IPSEC-ARCH]) provides Layer 3 service over an IP network.

During the late 1990s, only about 2 percent of Enterprise networks obtained Layer 3 VPN service from a service provider. The rest opted for Layer 2 transport services (primarily Frame Relay) and either a managed or unmanaged router service. The managed solution called for the operator of the network to provision and manage the customer premises equipment at the end of the transport circuit, whereas the unmanaged service simply provided a circuit to the customer on which that Enterprise installed routers and built their own VPN routing infrastructure.

However, over time, each of the aforementioned technologies suffers from scaling issues to varying degrees, especially when applications demand any-to-any connectivity (an example of which is voice over IP [VoIP]). When you select a VPN solution, the factors that determine its ultimate scaling properties are a key criterion. Evaluation of each technology should take into consideration the following points:

- How much design, provisioning, and configuration are necessary for each new VPN
- How provisioning and configuration scale with the number of VPN sites
- How customer routing scales (how many adjacencies are needed)
- How backbone routing scales (how many adjacencies and how much state)
- How the service scales for the end customer
- What type of services are required within a VPN

Splitting the different technologies into the two broad categories of *overlay* and *network-based VPN* can help you make such an evaluation. It is clear that an overlay arrangement does not scale to the size and number of client connections typically needed today. This is primarily because of the need to provision an individual connection from each site to every other site (so as to provide any-to-any connectivity) and the need to run routing adjacencies across these connections (an $O(n)$ problem, where n is the number of sites). When contrasted with a network-based solution, where each site needs only a connection to its locally attached PE router (an $O(1)$ problem, where 1 is a constant), it is easy to see that the network-based category is more appropriate for this environment. Therefore, the trend as we move into the 21st century is to deploy a network-based Layer 3 VPN solution. This is where the MPLS VPN architecture based on [2547bis] really shines.

This architecture provides complete isolation between different end-customer network domains, both within the service provider core network and at the edge routers that provide the interface to the VPN service. It also provides the ability to reduce the amount of routing state that core routers within the service provider backbone network need to hold to meet the scalability requirements and ensure optimal service delivery. This was not true of earlier attempts at providing network-based Layer 3 VPNs. Examples included shared routers, in which multiple customers attached to the same edge routers and access lists were used to isolate them, and dedicated routers, in which each customer had his or her own edge router interface into the service provider network.

This section reviews from a high level the basic [2547bis] architecture (called the Layer 3 MPLS VPN architecture from this point on) and all its necessary components. We will also look at how this technology is progressing across autonomous system boundaries. For more detailed technical information, refer to [2547bis], [MP-BGP], [MPLS-VPN-Vol1], and [MPLS-VPN-Vol2] as additional resources.

Layer 3 MPLS VPN Network Components

Several network components are defined within the Layer 3 MPLS VPN architecture. These components perform different functions within the overall architecture framework and are used in combination to constitute a Layer 3 VPN service.

Figure 1-1 summarizes each of the network components used in the Layer 3 MPLS VPN architecture:

- **Provider network (P-network)**—The core MPLS/IP network administered by the service provider. Two P-networks are illustrated to show how different autonomous systems may be connected.

- **Provider router (P-router)**—An MPLS/IP router deployed within the P-network with no edge service attachments.

- **Provider edge router (PE-router)**—A service provider edge router that provides VPN end-customer attachment and service delivery.

- **Autonomous system boundary router (ASBR-router)**—A service provider autonomous system edge router that provides attachment to an adjacent autonomous system that belongs to either the same or a different operator.

- **Customer network (C-network)**—A customer network administered by the end user attached to the Layer 3 MPLS VPN service.

- **Customer edge router (CE-router)**—A customer router that provides a gateway between the C-network and the P-network. The CE-router may be administered by the end user (and thus belong to the C-network) or may be managed by the service provider.

Figure 1-1 *Layer 3 MPLS VPN Network Components*

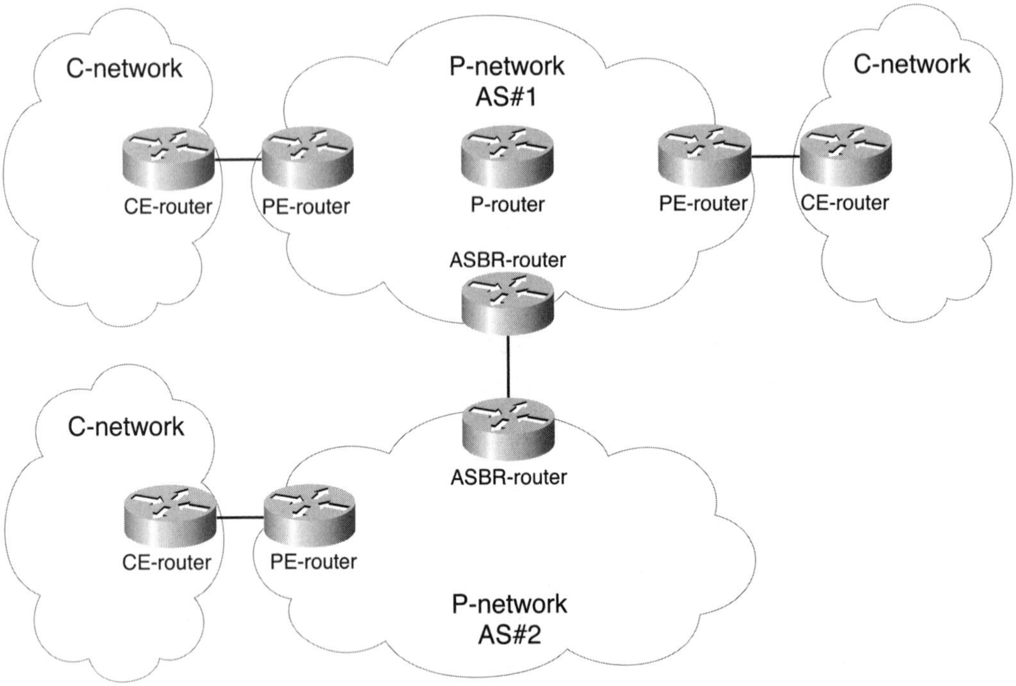

Separation of Routing State at PE Routers

Because each PE router needs to support multiple end customers, separation of routing state between these customers is mandatory. This separation is achieved by storing routing information in customer-specific Virtual Routing/Forwarding instances (VRFs). A VRF may be visualized as a separate virtual router instance within a physical router. It consists of the following structures:

- An IP packet forwarding and routing table
- A set of interfaces that use the forwarding table
- A set of rules that control the import and export of routes to and from the VPN-specific routing table
- A set of routing protocol peers that inject routes into the VPN-specific routing table

Without this separation it would be possible for one VPN customer to gain access to another customer's private network. The VRFs also provide a mechanism whereby each customer can use his or her own registered IP address space, or private addresses from the [PRIVATE] space, without concern that his or her routing information might clash with another customer of the service provider, or the service provider infrastructure itself. Figure 1-2 shows how a PE router separates routing information via VRFs.

Figure 1-2   *Routing Separation with VRFs*

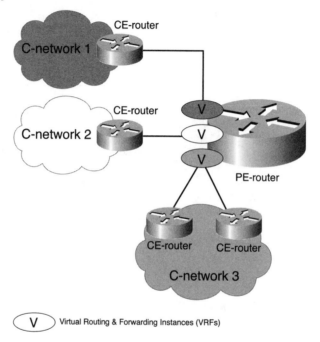

In Figure 1-2, each customer site attaches to the service provider PE router by way of one or more CE routers (which incidentally may also be a switch) and some form of attachment circuit (Frame Relay, ATM, Ethernet, and so on). It is possible for multiple customer sites to attach to the same PE router and therefore the same VRF (as is the case with C-network 3 in Figure 1-2). Each PE router interface that faces a customer site wanting to belong to a given VPN is associated with the VRF that corresponds to that VPN. This is so that the PE router can determine which VPN customer can be reached via which interface(s).

Customer-to-Service Provider Routing Exchange

As soon as the CE router has physical connectivity with the PE router, it must be able to exchange routing information with the service provider. This may be achieved through static configuration. In this case a dynamic routing protocol is unnecessary, because static routes provide all the necessary IP forwarding information. However, for customers who do not want to use static routing (for example, because of dual-homing requirements or a large number of routes that cannot be summarized), the Layer 3 MPLS VPN architecture specifies the ability to exchange routing information using a dynamic routing protocol such as Border Gateway

Protocol version 4 (BGP-4), Open Shortest Path First (OSPF), Enhanced Interior Gateway Routing Protocol (EIGRP), or Routing Information Protocol version 2 (RIPv2). A PE-router can run multiple dynamic routing protocols concurrently, as illustrated in Figure 1-3.

Figure 1-3   *PE-CE Routing Protocol Exchange*

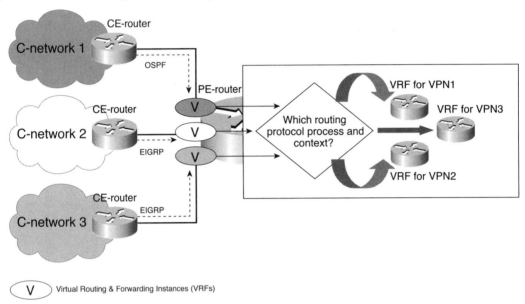

Because many VPN customers may be connected to a single PE router, each running one of the dynamic routing protocols (or static routing), the PE router must be able to know which routing protocol update came from which VPN client. This functionality may be called the *routing context,* and each routing protocol process at the PE router may run multiple contexts, each belonging to a separate VPN. This is illustrated in Figure 1-3, where both C-network2 and C-network3 run EIGRP and the PE router can determine which VRF should be populated with which routes based on the context.

Label Allocation at the PE Router

As discussed in the later section "Forwarding of Layer 3 MPLS VPN Packets," a PE router relies on labels attached to incoming packets from the backbone network, or from an attached customer site in the case of the Carrier's Carrier service (covered in the later section "Carrier's Carrier Architecture"), to perform forwarding. Therefore, for each route received from a locally attached customer site, the PE router may allocate a separate label—a label that represents the entire VRF—or it may allocate a single label to represent several routes from the same source attached to that VRF. The label allocation policy is driven by how the customer attaches to the Layer 3 MPLS VPN service. If a customer has a single connection into its local PE router, allocation of a different label for each prefix has little benefit and increases the number of resources required at the PE router to store the forwarding state. Therefore, allocating a single label that represents the gateway (that is, the CE router through which the routes can be reached) is appropriate in this case. On the other hand, a customer who wants to use the Carrier's Carrier architecture, where label switching is extended across the PE-CE link toward the customer site, must use a single label per prefix to maintain the Label-Switched Path (LSP) between source and destination endpoint.

Advertisement of VPNv4 Routes Across the IP/MPLS Backbone

Having received local routing information from attached customer sites, either via a dynamic routing protocol or through static configuration by the service provider, a PE router advertises the routing state to other PE routers in the network for subsequent distribution to remote customer sites in the same VPN.

Because multiple customers may use the same IP address space (which typically happens if they are using the addresses from [PRIVATE]), to avoid overlap within their service boundaries, the service provider needs to be able to distinguish between different customer routes. This is achieved through the creation of VPNv4 prefixes at the PE routers using extensions to BGP-4 (as detailed in [MP-BGP]) before the routes are advertised into the core network. VPNv4 prefixes are constructed by prepending a 64-bit *route distinguisher* to the IPv4 address, as shown in Figure 1-4. This ensures global uniqueness for each VPN route within the service provider backbone.

Figure 1-4   *VPNv4 Address Format*

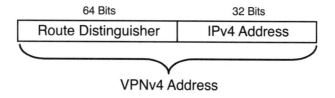

A number of different formats for the route distinguisher are possible, as shown in Figure 1-5. It should be noted that the route distinguisher value may differ at each PE router, even for the same VPN, because its purpose is to uniquely distinguish between IPv4 routes, not to identify a given VPN.

BGP-4 was initially created to advertise only IPv4 prefix information and therefore could not be used to advertise the VPNv4 routes created by the PE routers. Therefore, BGP-4 was extended, via Multiprotocol BGP (MP-BGP) [MP-BGP], to allow it to carry routes from multiple address families, including VPNv4 routes that belong to the VPN-IPv4 address family. The ability to use this particular address family is indicated during BGP capabilities exchange between two MP-BGP peers during their initial session startup.

Figure 1-5   *Route Distinguisher Formats*

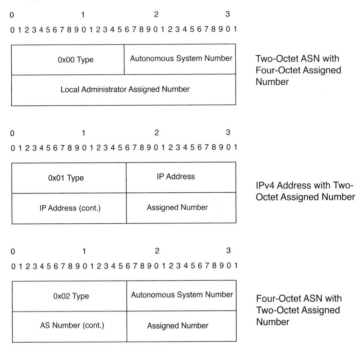

If routes from a given VRF were statically configured or learned through an Interior Gateway Protocol running on the PE-CE links, they must be redistributed into MP-BGP. This redistribution must be explicitly configured. As soon as the customer routes are present in the MP-BGP table, they are advertised within the VPN-IPv4 address family, either directly between PE routers or via route reflectors.

The redistribution process performs a number of tasks. The first is to translate a given IPv4 prefix in the VRF to a subsequent VPNv4 route in the backbone. The PE router also assigns the relevant export tags (called *route targets,* as discussed in the next section) and rewrites the BGP next-hop attribute to one of its interface addresses. It also sets all the necessary BGP attributes, such as local preference, MED, communities, and so forth). Finally, a label is assigned for each prefix (which may or may not be a unique value, as discussed in the preceding section). The resulting update is ready for transmission to other PE routers or route reflectors.

Import of Remote Routing Information into VRFs

After receiving an MP-BGP routing update, a PE router needs to determine into which VRF(s) the routes contained in the update should be placed. This is defined by the import policy in the receiving PE routers' VRFs and is locally configured in each VRF. As mentioned earlier, each update will have been tagged by the advertising PE router with one or more extended community attributes (defined in [EXTCOM]) known as route targets. The route target tells the receiving PE router into which VRFs the routes should be imported based on the local configuration. The format of the route target is shown in Figure 1-6.

Figure 1-6   *Route Target Formats*

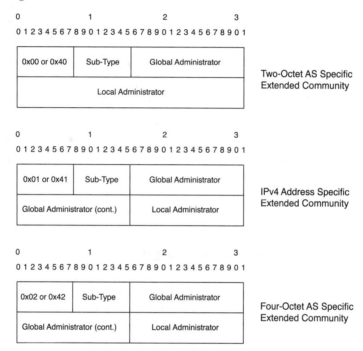

The use of route targets provides a very flexible approach to the creation of different VPN topologies. For example, if a customer needs connectivity within his or her own intranet, the same route target value may be used at each PE router to which the customer is attached. However, if extranet connectivity is required, a route target may be allocated to represent the extranet. Alternatively, the service provider may choose to import multiple route target values to build the VPN.

Another typical topology is a central-site extranet. In this case multiple end customers might need connectivity to a central service (provided by their Layer 3 MPLS VPN operator or some other division within their own corporation) but have their own networks protected from other clients. This type of topology can be achieved by allocating a different route target for the central site and a per-customer route target for each remote site.

Figure 1-7 reviews all the components discussed so far. It shows the CE→PE→PE→CE route and label distribution.

Figure 1-7 *End-to-End Control Plane Packet Flow*

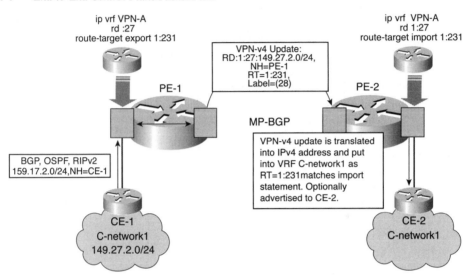

Forwarding of Layer 3 MPLS VPN Packets

As soon as the control plane setup between PE routers has taken place (as described in the previous sections) and some form of tunneling between PE routers is available (such as an MPLS label-switched path or IP tunnel), the service provider can forward customer packets across the IP/MPLS backbone and deliver them to the correct remote site.

Layer 3 MPLS VPN packet forwarding across an MPLS-enabled backbone is implemented via label switching with a two-level label stack imposed on the original IP datagram by the ingress PE router. It is also possible to restrict the label stack to one level by using IP tunneling techniques such as Layer 2 Tunneling Protocol version 3 (described in [L2TPv3]) or GRE in the backbone.

The outer label in an MPLS environment may be assigned by one of three different protocols: Label Distribution Protocol (LDP), Tag Distribution Protocol (TDP), or Resource Reservation Protocol Traffic Engineering (RSVP-TE). When LDP or TDP is used to allocate the outer label, each service provider router allocates a local label for all the routes in its routing table (except those learned via BGP-4). These label/prefix bindings are exchanged between directly connected neighbor routers using the LDP/TDP protocol (the details of this exchange may be found in [LDP]). When RSVP-TE is used between PE routers, the LDP protocol is not needed, and the outer label is instead the label allocated by RSVP-TE to represent the traffic-engineered tunnel interface. (You'll read more about RSVP-TE in the next chapter beginning with the section "Traffic Engineering.")

When a two-level label stack is used (which is typical for the Layer 3 MPLS VPN service), the outer label in the stack corresponds to the label assigned to the IP address of the remote PE router (the BGP next hop for a given remote VPN prefix). The inner label in the stack represents the label assigned to the customer route itself by the originating (egress) PE router. This is essentially the *VPN label*.

NOTE   There are cases where a larger label stack is necessary, such as when RSVP-TE tunnels exist in the network core. In this case a stack of {RSVP-TE, LDP, VPN} may be present while traversing the tunnels.

In the case of an MPLS-enabled backbone, the outer label is generally removed by the penultimate hop router before the packet is delivered at the egress PE router. This process is called *penultimate hop popping*. This functionality does not occur if IP tunneling is used in the backbone; instead, the IP encapsulation must be removed by the egress PE router. Penultimate hop popping behavior has the added benefit of preventing a two-stage lookup at the egress PE router.

Regardless of whether MPLS or IP tunneling is used in the backbone, the egress PE router needs to forward any incoming packets from the backbone network based on a lookup of the VPN label. This is achieved by performing a lookup of the label within the Label Forwarding Information Base (LFIB). The label is thus removed and the packet is forwarded based on information contained in the LFIB. Figure 1-8 illustrates this process.

Figure 1-8   *Layer 3 MPLS VPN Packet Forwarding*

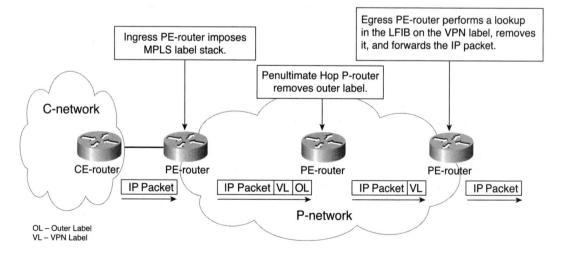

OL – Outer Label
VL – VPN Label

Remote Access to the Layer 3 MPLS VPN Service

Many different options are available to connect remote users to a Layer 3 MPLS VPN service. Chapter 2 of [MPLS-VPN-Vol2] provides technical and configuration details for most of these options. However, the following remote-access solutions are some of the most common:

- Dial-in access via Layer 2 Tunneling Protocol (L2TP) Virtual Private Dialup Network (VPDN)

- Dial-in access via direct Integrated Services Digital Network (ISDN)

- DSL access using Point-to-Point Protocol over Ethernet (PPPoE), Point-to-Point Protocol over ATM (PPPoA), and VPDN (L2TP)

Dial-in Access Via L2TP VPDN

The VPDN solution provides dial-in access via a Public Switched Telephone Network (PSTN) or ISDN. This concept uses a tunneling protocol (such as L2TP) to extend the dial connection from a remote user and terminate it on an L2TP network server (LNS), which in this context is called a Virtual Home Gateway (VHG).

Figure 1-9 shows a high-level example of the VPDN concept.

Figure 1-9 *Dial-in Using the VPDN Concept*

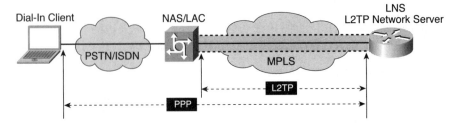

Dial-in Access Via Direct ISDN

Direct ISDN access does not require the use of any tunneling protocol from the remote client to a Layer 3 MPLS VPN PE router, unlike the previous VPDN solution. Instead, a PPP link is established over the ISDN B channel directly to the PE router. The PE router obtains the remote client's credentials using CHAP and then forwards them to a RADIUS server for authentication. Upon successful authentication, the RADIUS server returns configuration parameters for the client (such as VRF name, IP address pool, and so forth). The PE router then creates a virtual-access interface for the PPP session based on local configuration and the information returned by the RADIUS server. The user CHAP authentication process then finishes, and the remote user is afforded access to the relevant VPN.

Figure 1-10 shows the direct ISDN access solution.

Figure 1-10   *Direct ISDN Connectivity*

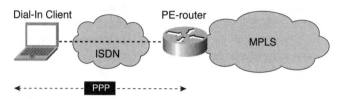

DSL Access Using PPPoA or PPPoE and VPDN (L2TP)

Digital Subscriber Line (DSL) access is provided by terminating DSL connections using the L2TP VPDN architecture or via a direct connection to a PE router. This provides the infrastructure for large-scale DSL termination. Figure 1-11 shows the DSL connectivity option using the L2TP VPDN solution.

Figure 1-11   *DSL Connectivity Using PPPoE or PPPoA*

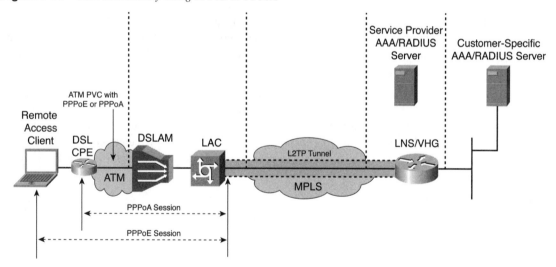

As shown in Figure 1-11, a remote-access client may access his or her Layer 3 MPLS VPN environment using PPPoE (if the CPE acts as a bridge) or PPPoA (if the CPE acts as a router). RFC 1483 routed (PPPoA) and bridged (PPPoE) encapsulation is used, and an L2TP tunnel is built from the receiving NAS/LAC to one of the LNSs within the service provider point of presence (POP).

Carrier's Carrier Architecture

The initial Layer 3 MPLS VPN service consisted of the architecture detailed in the previous sections and was primarily targeted at providing Layer 3 network-based VPN services to customers with a limited amount of IP routing information (because of their relative size in terms of regional and global reach). With restricted routing information, the service provider PE routers could scale to a large number of end customers. This model is still the primary delivery vehicle for Layer 3 MPLS VPN services today.

However, over time larger customer deployments have been requested, including large Enterprises and Internet service providers (ISPs), as well as other VPN providers, that want to obtain IP-based any-to-any connectivity. This requirement has been driven in part by the desire of these customers not to have to build their own Layer 2 network, but instead to use the Layer 3 MPLS VPN network for transport. With the reduction in infrastructure costs and the added benefit of full any-to-any connectivity, this service is very attractive.

Although the service is attractive for large Enterprises and other carriers for the reasons already noted, it comes at a considerable cost, in terms of scale, to the operator of the Layer 3 MPLS VPN network. For example, consider an ISP as the customer of this service. It might want to exchange full Internet routes (some 155,000+ routes) between its sites. Because the Layer 3 MPLS VPN service requires that customer routing state be stored at the PE routers and be distributed to other PE routers within its control, this presents a significant scaling problem at the edge of the network, not to mention the route distribution load offered to the control plane within the service provider network.

As a trade-off to provide connectivity for customers with large routing requirements, and as a complement to the regular Layer 3 MPLS VPN services for other VPN or non-VPN carriers that want to obtain basic IP connectivity, the Carrier's Carrier architecture was introduced. This architecture allows for the direct exchange of customer routes between their own sites and the use of the Layer 3 MPLS VPN backbone as pure IP "transport" between these sites. Figure 1-12 illustrates this concept.

Figure 1-12   *Carrier's Carrier Architecture*

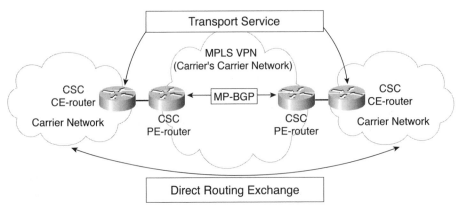

The Carrier's Carrier architecture classifies routes as either *internal* or *external*. Internal routes are those that the service's client exchanges with the Layer 3 MPLS VPN provider. These typically are the BGP next hops of any of its external routes but may also be the addresses of internal services it wants to make available to other parts of its network. External routes are those that it exchanges directly between its own sites using BGP-4 or MP-BGP (IPv4 or VPNv4).

NOTE   The exchange of VPNv4 routes between the sites of a carrier network that uses the Carrier's Carrier architecture is commonly called *hierarchical VPNs*. You will see an example of this type of service in Chapter 4, "National Telco Design Study."

In Figure 1-12, you can see that several new network elements are introduced with the Carrier's Carrier architecture:

- **Carrier Supporting Carrier (CSC) PE router**—The same as a normal PE router, except that it provides MPLS-to-MPLS label forwarding rather than IP-to-MPLS label imposition, as with the normal Layer 3 MPLS VPN service.

- **CSC CE router**—The same as a normal CE router, except that it runs a label distribution protocol with the PE router. This may be LDP or BGP-4 (with some extensions to carry label information, as detailed in [BGP+Label]).

- **Carrier network**—The network of the carrier that is obtaining VPN services from the MPLS VPN Service Provider. This network may or may not be enabled to run MPLS switching functionality, either with LDP, TDP, or RSVP-TE.

- **Carrier's Carrier network**—The Layer 3 MPLS VPN network that provides Carrier's Carrier functionality at its PE routers for attached Carrier networks.

Because all external routing information is exchanged directly between the customer sites, there is no need for the service provider that provides Carrier's Carrier services to carry the routes at its PE routers. If you consider the ISP example of 155,000+ Kbps routes, removing the requirement to carry these routes substantially reduces the amount of routing state held by the PE routers. However, because the BGP-4 next-hop addresses for these routes will be within the customer routing space, these addresses need to be exchanged with the Carrier's Carrier service provider so that an end-to-end packet-forwarding path can be achieved.

Packet Forwarding with Carrier's Carrier

Because only internal routes are exchanged between the CSC CE routers of the carrier network and the CSC PE routers of the Carrier's Carrier network, the CSC PE routers no longer carry any customer external routing information and therefore can't forward IP packets toward those destinations. The result is that the CSC PE routers must be able to forward packets using a label directed toward the BGP next hop of those destinations. In this way the CSC CE-routers can establish an end-to-end LSP between themselves, and the Carrier's Carrier network simply label-switches traffic between them. This LSP may be established by running the LDP protocol (or BGP-4, which can carry labels along with the IPv4 prefix [BGP+Label]) between the CSC CE routers and CSC PE routers. All these elements are shown in Figure 1-13.

Figure 1-13   *Internal/External Route Exchange*

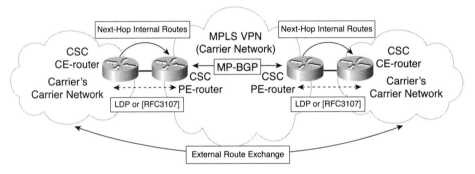

Having exchanged all the internal and external routing information, an end-to-end LSP may be established between the CSC CE routers. Figure 1-14 shows the LSP creation between two customer sites for traffic sent toward subnet 196.1.1.0/24. OL refers to the outer label, and VL refers the VPN inner label.

Figure 1-14   *LSP Between CSC Customer Sites*

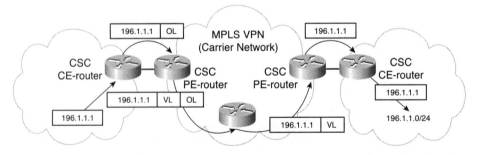

NOTE   In some cases the carrier sites may also be running MPLS label switching. This certainly is the case if hierarchical VPNs are in place, as you will see in Chapter 4. This does not affect the overall packet forwarding scheme details in this section. It simply means that the LSP used to establish an end-to-end LSP between carrier sites is extended beyond the CSC CE routers.

A more detailed analysis of the Carrier's Carrier architecture may be found in [VPN-ARCH-Volume-2].

Layer 3 MPLS VPN Services Across Autonomous System Boundaries

As Layer 3 MPLS VPN services have become more popular, the need to provide connectivity across different autonomous system boundaries has become a reality. Large Enterprise customers are often multinational and, because of their geography, might not always be able to get full VPN connectivity through a single service provider. Even if connectivity can be achieved via a single service provider infrastructure, the topology of the network may be split into multiple autonomous systems. Therefore, the Layer 3 MPLS VPN service needs to expand beyond a single autonomous system.

Inter-autonomous system connectivity may be achieved in a number of ways. [2547bis] defines them as follows:

- (A) VRF-to-VRF connections at the autonomous system boundary
- (B) Multiprotocol external BGP redistribution of labeled VPNv4 routes from an AS to a neighboring AS
- (C) Multihop external BGP redistribution of labeled VPNv4 routes between source and destination autonomous systems, with external BGP redistribution of labeled IPv4 routes from an AS to a neighboring AS

These three connectivity models are often referred to as options A, B, and C. Options A and B generally are used between two different operators, although A is by far the most widely deployed. Therefore, they normally are associated with *inter-provider connectivity*. Option C, on the other hand, is generally used between different autonomous systems of the same operator and therefore is normally associated with *inter-AS connectivity*. Option B is also appropriate for inter-AS connectivity, although with more limited scalability characteristics when compared with Option C.

NOTE   To avoid confusion between the terms inter-provider and inter-AS, we will use inter-AS for all future references.

Inter-AS Back-to-Back VRFs (Option A)

This model assumes direct connectivity between PE routers of different autonomous systems. The PE routers are attached via multiple physical or logical interfaces, each of which is associated with a given VPN (via a VRF). Each PE router therefore treats the adjacent PE router like a CE router, and the standard Layer 3 MPLS VPN mechanisms are used for route distribution within each autonomous system. Figure 1-15 provides an example of this model.

Figure 1-15 *(Option A) Inter-Provider*

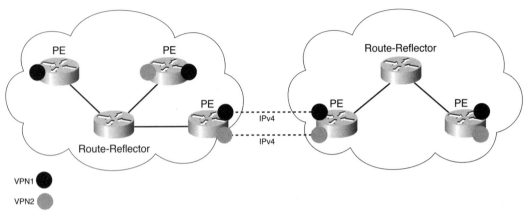

This model has become popular for connectivity between different VPN providers because each autonomous system is essentially isolated from the other. This provides better control over routing exchanges and security between the two networks. This model offers other advantages (as you will see in the design studies later in this book), although it is considered the least scalable of all the inter-AS connectivity options.

Inter-AS VPNv4 Exchange (Option B)

This model allows Autonomous System Boundary Routers (ASBR routers) to use external MP-BGP to advertise VPNv4 routes between autonomous systems. The receiving ASBR router then distributes the VPNv4 routes into the local autonomous system.

External MP-BGP provides the functionality to advertise VPNv4 prefix/label information across the service provider boundaries. The advertising ASBR router replaces the two-level label stack (which it uses to reach the originating PE router and VPN destination in the local AS) with a locally allocated label before advertising the VPNv4 route. This is necessary because the next-hop attribute of all routes advertised between the two service providers is reset to the ASBR router peering address, so the ASBR router becomes the termination point of the LSP for the advertised routes. To preserve the label-switching path between ingress and egress PE routers, the ASBR router must allocate a local label that may be used to identify the label stack of the route within the local VPN network. This newly allocated label is set on packets sent toward the prefix from the adjacent service provider. This inter-AS model is illustrated in Figure 1-16.

Figure 1-16   *(Option B) Inter-AS*

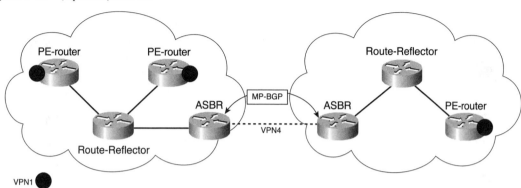

This model is also popular from a theoretical perspective for connectivity between different service providers because it again isolates both autonomous systems but with the added advantage that it scales to a higher degree than Option A. However, this model has a number of security and QoS considerations, as you will see in the design studies.

Inter-AS VPNv4 Exchange Between Route Reflectors (Option C)

This model combines external MP-BGP exchange of VPNv4 routes between route reflectors of different autonomous systems with the next hops for these routes exchanged between corresponding ASBR routers. Because route reflectors of different autonomous systems will not be directly connected, multihop functionality is required to allow for the establishment of the external MP-BGP sessions. The exchange of next hops is necessary because the route reflectors do not reset the next-hop attribute of the VPNv4 routes when advertising them to any adjacent autonomous systems. The reason for this is that they do not want to attract the traffic for the destinations that they advertise. They are not the original endpoint—just a relay station between the source and destination PE routers.

The PE router next-hop addresses for the VPNv4 routes are exchanged between ASBR routers. The exchange of these addresses between autonomous systems can be accomplished by redistributing the PE router /32 addresses between the two autonomous systems or by using [BGP+Label], which lets you run BGP-4 with label information between the ASBR routers. Figure 1-17 shows this model.

Figure 1-17 *(Option C) Inter-AS*

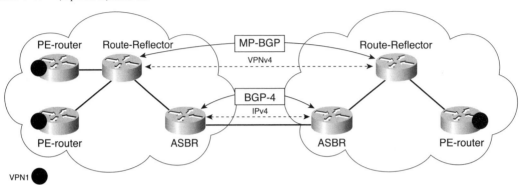

This model normally is deployed only when each autonomous system belongs to the same overall authority, such as a global Layer 3 MPLS VPN provider with autonomous systems in different regions of the world. However, Option B is equally suited for this purpose and is indeed also deployed in networks where autonomy between different regions is desired.

A more detailed analysis of the Carrier's Carrier architecture, as well as all the inter-autonomous system connectivity models, may be found in [MPLS-VPN-Vol-2].

Multicast VPNs

This section quickly reviews the basic components of IP Multicast and then looks at how multicast can be provided to customers using a Layer 3 MPLS VPN service.

IP Multicast provides a mechanism for transporting data from a single source to many recipients (called *receivers*). This is in contrast to IP Unicast, in which a packet is sent from a single source to a single recipient. The destination address of a multicast packet is taken from the Internet Assigned Numbers Authority (IANA) 224.0.0.0–239.255.255.255 address block, and each address refers to a multicast group. In other words, multiple endpoints may belong to the group and receive traffic addressed to the group address. This is similar in concept to broadcast, except that it is restricted to members of a group rather than to all hosts on a given subnet, as is the case with broadcast.

A multicast source, such as a server delivering a multicast-capable application, transmits multicast packets using the multicast group address, and receivers listen for traffic that is addressed to the group of which they are members. These packets are forwarded across the network using a distribution tree. Each network element in the path from source to receiver(s) is responsible for replicating the original packet at each branch of the tree. Only a single copy of the original packet is forwarded across any particular link in the network, thus creating an efficient distribution tree for many receivers. There are two different types of distribution trees: source trees and shared trees.

Source Distribution Multicast Trees

A source tree allows a source host of a particular multicast group to be located at the "root" of the tree while the receivers are found at the ends of the branches. Multicast packets travel from the source host down the tree toward the receivers. Multicast forwarding state is maintained for the source tree using the notation {S, G}, where S is the source IP address and G is the group.

Figure 1-18 shows a source tree in which host 172.27.69.52 sends multicast packets down the tree to destination group 239.192.0.7. The {S, G} state for this multicast stream is therefore {172.27.69.52, 239.192.0.7}.

Figure 1-18   *IP Multicast Source Tree*

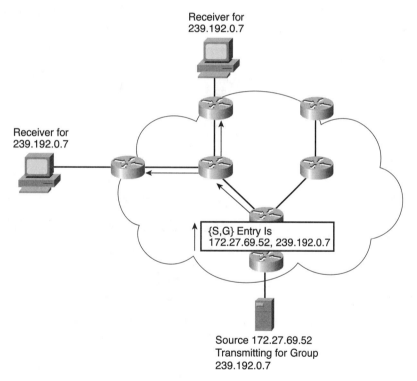

Source trees are also sometimes called Shortest Path Trees (SPTs) because the path between source and receivers is the shortest available path. This means that a separate source tree is present for every source that transits multicast packets to a given group, and therefore {S, G} state for each {Source, Group} exists in the network. Therefore, even though source trees provide the most optimal routing, it is at a price—additional multicast state within the network.

A receiver on a source tree must know the source of the tree—that is, its IP address. To join the source tree, a receiver must send an explicit {S, G} join to the source (the local router actually sends this on behalf of the receiver).

IP Multicast Shared Trees

Shared trees have the root of the tree at a common point somewhere in the network. This common point is called the rendezvous point (RP) and is where receivers join so as to learn about active sources. Multicast sources transmit their traffic to the RP. When receivers join a group on the shared tree, the RP forwards packets from the source toward the receivers. In this way the RP is effectively a go-between where source and receiver come together.

Multicast forwarding entries for shared trees use a different notation, {*, G}, where * represents any source. Figure 1-19 shows a shared tree for group 239.192.0.7.

Figure 1-19 *IP Multicast Shared Tree*

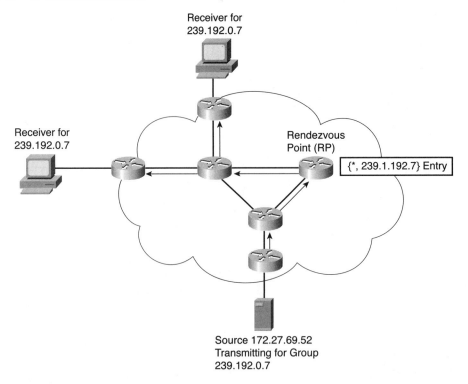

Shared trees are not as optimal as source trees because they do not follow the shortest path. Instead, all traffic from the source travels via the RP toward the receivers. However, the amount of state held in the network is less because the $\{*, G\}$ notation removes the requirement for specific $\{S, G\}$ entries. A further difference is that shared trees do not require the receivers to know the IP address of a particular multicast source. The only address needed by the receivers is that of the RP.

The shared tree shown in Figure 1-19 is a unidirectional tree. However, IP multicast also supports bidirectional trees, in which traffic may travel up and down the tree. This type of tree is useful when the tree has a large number of sources. Not all traffic needs to pass through the RP, because it can travel up and down the tree.

Protocol-Independent Multicast (PIM)

Clearly IP Multicast needs a mechanism that can create a multicast routing table based on some discovery mechanism. The most common protocol in use today is Protocol-Independent Multicast (PIM). PIM uses the unicast routing table to check whether a multicast packet has arrived on the correct inbound interface, a process called Reverse Path Forwarding (RPF). This check is independent from the routing protocol because it bases its decisions on the unicast routing table contents.

PIM comes in two flavors: Dense Mode (PIM-DM) and Sparse Mode (PIM-SM).

PIM Dense Mode (PIM-DM)

PIM-DM has proven to be a pretty inefficient mode of operation, because it is based on the assumption that every subnet in the network has at least one receiver for a given $\{S, G\}$ group. This clearly is not normally the case.

Because of this assumption, PIM-DM floods all multicast packets to every part of the network. Each router that does not want to receive the multicast traffic is required to send a prune message back up the tree to prevent the traffic from being sent to it. Branches to which no receivers are attached are thus pruned from the tree.

PIM Sparse Mode (PIM-SM)

PIM-SM is far more efficient than PIM-DM because it does not rely on flooding to distribute multicast traffic. PIM-SM uses a pull model in which it transits traffic toward a given receiver only if specifically asked to do so. This requires an explicit join for the given multicast group. Initially all receivers join the RP on the shared tree but can join a source tree based on bandwidth thresholds that are defined in the network. This has the advantage of moving the receiver onto the optimal path to the source of the multicast traffic.

Source-Specific Multicast (SSM)

Source-Specific Multicast (SSM) is a fairly recent development worthy of discussion. You will see its use in this book's design studies. This mode of operation relies on the fact that the IP address of a given source for a particular multicast group is known before any join is sent from the receiver. (The source is learned via an out-of-band mechanism such as Internet Group Management Protocol version 3 [IGMPv3], IGMPv3lite, or URL Rendezvous Directory [URD].) Therefore, a source tree is always built when using SSM, so shared trees and rendezvous points are not required when running SSM. This has the advantage of providing optimal routing between source and receiver without having to first discover the source from the RP.

Multicast Support Within a Layer 3 MPLS VPN

Reviewing the basic functionality of IP multicast highlights an issue for the operator if it wants to extend that service to it Layer 3 MPLS VPN customers; this issue is one of scale. Given the amount of multicast state that might be generated by each VPN customer, the service provider backbone P network would need to be engineered so that it could distribute and store all the IP multicast information for each customer. A further issue could involve IP address conflict between different customers.

IP tunneling (such as GRE) is one method of eliminating the customer multicast state from the P network because the IP tunnels are overlaid across the MPLS/IP network. This also prevents the service provider from having to run any IP Multicast protocols in the P network, because all packets are sent as unicast. However, this approach has several disadvantages, including a full mesh of IP tunnels between CE routers. Also, nonoptimal multicast packet forwarding is achieved and bandwidth is wasted because of the replication of packets across all IP tunnels. Furthermore, the number of tunnels introduces an operational and management overhead that is very difficult to control.

Another more scalable approach is documented in [mVPN], which introduces the concept of *multicast domains,* in which CE routers maintain PIM adjacencies with their local PE router instead of with all remote CE routers. This is the same concept as deployed with the Layer 3 MPLS VPN service, where only a local routing protocol adjacency is required rather than multiple ones with remote CE routers. Within a multicast domain, an end customer can maintain his or her existing multicast topology, configurations, and so on and transition to a multicast service provided by the Layer 3 MPLS VPN operator. In this model P routers do not hold any customer-specific multicast trees but instead hold a single group for that VPN, regardless of the number of multicast groups deployed by the end customer. Regardless of which multicast mode the service provider is using (PIM-SM, PIM-DM, SSM, and so on), the amount of state in the P network can be determined and is not dependent on the specifics of a given customer multicast deployment.

Multicast Domains

The concept of a multicast domain is realized by a set of multicast-enabled VRFs that can send multicast traffic between them. This means that if a given CE router sends IP multicast packets toward its local PE router, that PE-router can deliver the multicast traffic to all interested parties at remote CE routers. The multicast-enabled VRFs are called *mVRFs*.

A multicast domain essentially maps all customer multicast groups within a given VPN into a single unique global multicast group within the P network. The service provider administers this global multicast group. The mapping is achieved by encapsulating the original multicast packet in a GRE packet whose destination address is a multicast group known globally within the service provider P network, and it is associated with the given multicast domain. The source of the GRE packet is the ingress PE router through which the multicast packet first entered the Layer 3 MPLS VPN network. Therefore, a set of VPN customer multicast groups can be mapped into a single {S, G} or {*, G} entry in the service provider P network.

The P network is responsible for building a default multicast distribution tree (called the default MDT) between PE routers for each multicast domain it supports. The unique multicast group in the P network is called an *MDT group*. Every mVRF belongs to a default MDT. Figure 1-20 illustrates the multicast group concept and shows two separate VPNs, each with its own multicast group within the service provider P network.

Figure 1-20   *Multicast Domains for VPN Multicast*

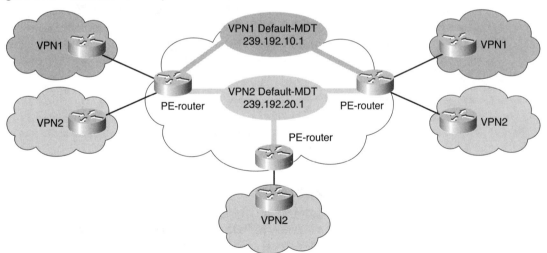

mVPN PIM Adjacencies

Various PIM adjacencies are formed within an mVPN environment. The first adjacency is held within each VRF that has multicast routing enabled. This adjacency runs from PE router to CE router. The customer multicast routing information, which is created by each PIM instance, is specific to the corresponding mVRF.

In addition to the PE-CE adjacency, the PE router forms a PIM adjacency with any remote PE routers that hold mVRFs that belong to the same multicast domain. This PIM adjacency is accessed via a Multicast Tunnel Interface (MTI), which uses GRE encapsulation, and is used as the transport mechanism between mVRFs. This PIM adjacency is necessary to exchange multicast routing information contained in the mVRFs and specific to customers attached to the said mVRF.

The last PIM adjacency to be created is within the global PIM instance—that is, the PIM instance that runs in the service provider P network. The PE router maintains global PIM adjacencies with each of its IGP neighbors (P routers in most cases). The global PIM instance is used to create the MDTs used to connect mVRFs.

All these adjacencies are shown in Figure 1-21.

Figure 1-21   *mVPN PIM Adjacencies*

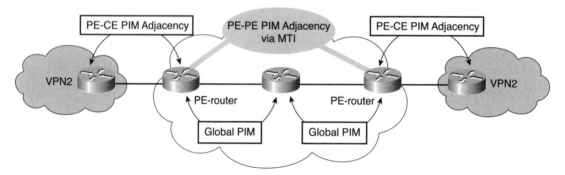

Multicast Forwarding with mVPN

Having established all the necessary state for a given multicast domain, forwarding of multicast traffic can be divided into two categories: packets from the C network (C packets) received at the PE router interface associated with a given mVRF, and packets from the P network (P packets) received from other PE routers via a global multicast interface.

When C packets are received at a PE router, the following events take place:

1 A C packet arrives via a VRF interface that is associated with a given mVRF.

2 The C packet is replicated based on the contents of the outgoing interface list (olist) for the {S, G} or {*, G} entry in the mVRF. The olist may contain interfaces that are multicast-enabled within the same mVRF, in which case the packets are forwarded using normal multicast procedures. The olist also may contain a tunnel interface (MTI) that connects it to the multicast domain for the customer VPN.

3 If the olist contains a tunnel interface, the multicast packet is encapsulated using GRE. The packet's source is set to the BGP peering address of the PE router. The destination address is set to the MDT group address associated with the customer VPN.

4 The IP precedence value of the C packet is copied to the P packet.

5 The C packet is considered a P packet in the global multicast routing instance.

6 The P packet is forwarded through the P network using standard multicast procedures. P routers are thus unaware of any multicast VPN activity and treat the P packets as native multicast packets.

After the P packet is sent to the P network at the ingress PE router, the following events take place:

1 The P packet arrives at the egress PE router interface in the global multicast domain.

2 The P packet {S, G} or {*, G} entry is determined within the global multicast routing table.

3 The P packet is replicated out of any P network interfaces that appear in the olist of the {S, G} or (*, G) entry.

4 If the {S, G} or {*, G} entry has the Z flag set (signifying that multicast packets are received or transmitted on an MTI, this indicates to the receiving PE router that this is an MDT group packet and therefore must be de-encapsulated to reveal the original C packet.

5 The destination mVRF of the C packet is determined from the MDT group address in the P packet. The incoming MTI interface is resolved from the MDT group address.

6 The C packet is presented to the target mVRF, with the appropriate MTI interface set as the incoming interface. The RPF check verifies the tunnel interface as valid. In other words, packets with this source are expected to arrive via the MTI interface.

7 The C packet is treated as a native multicast packet in the VPN network. The C packet is replicated to all multicast-enabled interfaces in the mVRF that appear in the olist for the {S, G} or {*, G} entry.

All this activity is shown in Figure 1-22.

Figure 1-22 *mVPN Multicast Packet Forwarding*

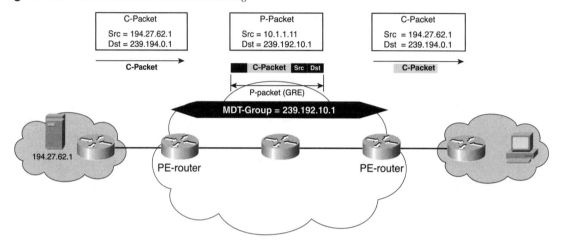

Figure 1-22 shows a source with IP address 194.27.62.1 transmitting to multicast group 239.194.0.1 within the customer VPN. When the multicast C packets from this source arrive at the ingress PE router, a P packet is created by encapsulating the C packet using GRE. The source IP address of the P packet is set to 10.1.1.11 (the BGP peering address of this PE router), and the destination address is set to 239.192.10.1 (the MDT group for this VPN in the P network).

IPv6 Over MPLS Networks

IP version 6 (IPv6) is a new version of IP designed to replace IP version 4 (IPv4), which is currently deployed and used extensively throughout the world. IPv6 benefits are mainly a result of its much larger addressing space, which is required to cope with the Internet expansion and with the explosion of Internet-capable appliances.

As of early 2004, about two-thirds of the total IPv4 address space had been allocated. Increasingly stricter allocation policies have significantly curbed the rate of address allocation to the point where it is unlikely that the entire IPv4 address space will be fully allocated in the foreseeable future. However, in the face of the growing number of devices requiring IP connectivity, such policies have forced widespread use of address conservation techniques such as the use of private addresses along with Network Address Translation (NAT) devices. NAT dynamically maps many private addresses into a small number of public addresses, typically at the network edge between private networks and the public Internet. A further address-saving technique is on-demand allocation of IP addresses from a shared pool to devices that do not require permanent connectivity. Although these address-conservation techniques have reduced the address allocation requirements in the past few years, they are incompatible with a number of fundamental new evolution trends on the Internet:

- **Peer-to-peer applications**—Although most applications in the past were based on client/server architecture, many applications developed recently rely on a peer-to-peer architecture. This includes VoIP, open file-sharing applications such as Napster, and gaming applications. Although these can be made to work through NAT, this entails a significant operational cost and requires application-specific handling within the NAT device.

- **Explosion of Internet-enabled devices**—Although PCs are the key devices requiring IP connectivity, many other types of devices now also need Internet connectivity, such as mobile phones, portable entertainment devices, personal digital assistants, and home and industrial appliances.

- **"Always-on" connectivity**—Because of the advancement and multiplication of access technologies, such as broadband and wireless, many devices now enjoy "always-on" connectivity.

This results in renewed pressure for a much more generous address allocation policy, which only IPv6 can offer.

Because IPv6 is now gaining acceptance, service providers have been asked by their customers, or will be asked in the coming years, to offer IPv6 services.

After providing an overview of IPv6, the following sections discuss the deployment options available to service providers that currently operate an IPv4 MPLS backbone, particularly the IPv6 Provider Edge (6PE) and IPv6 VPN Provider Edge (6VPE) approaches. 6PE allows for global IPv6 reachability service, and 6VPE allows for IPv6 VPN service over a pure IPv4 MPLS/IP backbone.

Overview of IPv6

IPv6 was designed in the early 1990s within the Internet Engineering Task Force (IETF). It is composed of a whole suite of protocols and procedures. The key topics of IPv6 are presented in the following sections.

IPv6 Header

The base IPv6 protocol is specified in [IPv6]. The key changes in the protocol header from IPv4 to IPv6 are as follows:

- The size of the network address field is quadrupled to 16 bytes, affording theoretically $3.4 * 10^{38}$ addressable nodes, which provides more than enough globally unique IP addresses for every network device on the planet.

- The header format is simplified through the use of fixed-length fields and daisy chaining of optional headers (between the fixed IPv6 header and the transported data).
- The IP header checksum is removed.
- Support for hop-by-hop segmentation is removed.
- Alignment on 64-bit boundaries is achieved.

Figure 1-23 compares the IPv4 header and the IPv6 header.

Figure 1-23 *Comparison of IPv6 and IPv4 Headers*

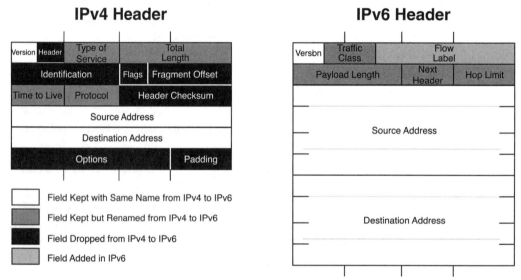

IPv6 Addressing

[ADDR-ARCH] specifies IPv6 address representation and addressing architecture.

IPv6 addresses, which are 128 bits long, are represented as a series of eight 16-bit fields separated by colons. Each 16-bit field is represented as four hexadecimal characters. 200A:1234:00CD:0000:0000:005C:7F3C:E34B is an example of an IPv6 address.

To allow more concise representation, one occurrence of a successive 16-bit field equal to 0000 can be represented by a double colon, and leading 0s in each 16-bit field can be omitted. Thus, the address just mentioned can be represented more concisely as 200A:1234:CD::5C:7F3C:E34B.

For prefix representation, the same prefix notation as IPv4 is used. For example, 200A:1234:00CD::/48 designates a 48-bit IPv6 prefix.

The most important address types are as follows:

- **Global unicast addresses**—These are unicast addresses that are globally assigned. They are identified by the 3-bit prefix 001.

- **Link-local unicast addresses**—These are unicast addresses for local communication between devices on the same link and are used during autoconfiguration and when no routers are present. They are identified by the 10-bit prefix 1111111010 (or, equivalently, FE80::/10).

- **Multicast addresses**—These are identified by the 8-bit prefix 11111111 (or, equivalently, FF00::/8).

- **IPv4-mapped IPv6 addresses**—These represent the addresses of IPv4 nodes as IPv6 addresses. They are identified by the prefix ::FFFF/96.

- **Anycast addresses**—These address a packet to the nearest of a set of hosts. Anycast addresses can be allocated from any of the unicast address types.

- **Unique local IPv6 unicast addresses**—These are unicast addresses that are globally unique and are intended for local communications, usually inside a site. They are not expected to be routable on the global IPv6 Internet. Those are specified in [UNIQ-LOCAL].

As with global IPv4 addresses, the global IPv6 unicast addresses are structured in a hierarchical manner that allows efficient aggregation of prefixes for routing in the IPv6 Internet. IANA has allocated a prefix range to each Regional Internet Registry (RIR). In turn, the RIRs have defined a coordinated allocation policy [IPV6RIR] to allocate a subset of their own prefix range to entities requesting IPv6 addresses, such as an ISP. In turn, the ISP allocates a subset of its prefix ranges to end users, who then allocate different prefixes from that range to their network links.

Neighbor Discovery and Autoconfiguration

A lot of care has been put into the design of IPv6 to minimize configuration and facilitate plug-and-play operations. To that end, the neighbor discovery protocol (see [IPv6-DISC]) allows IPv6 hosts and routers on a link to dynamically discover or exchange the relevant information local to that link. The functions supported by neighbor discovery include the following:

- **Prefix discovery**—IPv6 hosts discover the set of address prefixes on the link.

- **Parameter discovery**—IPv6 nodes learn link parameters such as the link MTU.

- **Address autoconfiguration**—IPv6 nodes automatically allocate an IPv6 address to an interface.

- **Address resolution**—IPv6 nodes determine the link-layer address of destinations on the link (equivalent to ARP for IPv4).

- **Handling of unreachability issues**—IPv6 nodes detect neighbor unreachability as well as duplicate addresses. IPv6 hosts can be instructed to redirect their traffic to a better first-hop router.

Address autoconfiguration is supported in IPv6 through both a stateless mechanism and a stateful mechanism. With IPv6 stateless address autoconfiguration (see [AUTO-CONF]), an IPv6 host can automatically generate its unique interface addresses by combining an interface identifier that uniquely identifies the interface on the link (for example, using an IEEE MAC address) and the prefix advertised by the routers for that link. With the IPv6 stateful address autoconfiguration, IPv6 hosts can communicate with a server using Dynamic Host Configuration Protocol for IPv6 (DHCPv6; see [DHCP-IPv6]) to obtain configuration information such as IPv6 addresses.

Graceful renumbering of hosts is supported in IPv6 via the assignment of multiple addresses to an interface and the concept of address lease lifetime, allowing smooth phasing out of old addresses.

IPv6 Routing

Because IPv6 forwarding is also based on a longest match on variable-length prefixes, IPv6 routing is very similar to IPv4 routing, except for the requirement to handle the increased address size of IPv6.

All the routing protocols commonly used today for IPv4 have been extended to support IPv6 routing. RIP has been extended by [RIP-IPv6] to support IPv6. This is called RIPng or RIPv6. IS-IS has been extended in [ISIS-V6] to simultaneously support IPv4 and IPv6 routing in an integrated manner. On the other hand, OSPFv3, specified in [OSPF-IPv6], supports IPv6 routing only. Where both IPv4 and IPv6 routing are required, OSPFv3 needs to run in "ships in the night" mode for IPv6 routing at the same time as OSPFv2 for IPv4 routing. [BGP-IPv6] specifies how Multiprotocol-BGP (MP-BGP) is used to support IPv6 interdomain routing.

IPv6 Quality of Service

Quality of service (QoS) in IPv6 is the same as in IPv4 and also relies on the Differentiated Services model (see [DIFF-ARCH]) or the Integrated Services model (see [INT-SERV]) along with RSVP signaling (see [RSVP]). As described in the section "The IETF DiffServ Model and Mechanisms" in Chapter 2, the Traffic Class field initially defined in the IPv6 header has been superseded to convey the Differentiated Services field.

The IPv6 header also contains a Flow Label field initially intended for QoS applications. Its actual use is still under discussion and is now receiving much less attention because of the wide acceptance of the Differentiated Services model for QoS.

IPv6 Security

Security is very similar in IPv6 and IPv4 because most of the network layer security components, such as the IPSec architecture (see [IPSEC-ARCH]), are equally applicable to IPv4 and IPv6.

Deploying IPv6 Over an MPLS Network

Many migration approaches are available to a service provider to add IPv6 services to its current service portfolio. However, those need to be assessed in the corresponding light when the operator is already running IPv4 MPLS in the network core. For example, an IPv4 MPLS core is likely to be the underpinning infrastructure for very significant revenue-generating services (such as MPLS VPN services) as well as for transit of key overlay networks (such as PSTN trunking or ATM trunking). Therefore, it is of paramount importance that the migration to IPv6 services avoid introducing risks of instability in the multiservice core. Also, a number of advanced MPLS features may be deployed in the core, such as traffic engineering, fast reroute, and MPLS QoS. The IPv6 migration approach must not disturb operations of these features for the IPv4 traffic and should allow the IPv6 traffic to benefit from them. Finally, where the installed equipment has very high MPLS forwarding performance, it may be desirable for the IPv6 migration approach to take advantage of MPLS forwarding for IPv6 traffic.

The most obvious approach for introducing IPv6 services is of course to upgrade the whole network to support IPv6 routing and forwarding natively. Although this approach is the most intuitive and clearly offers very scalable support of global IPv6 connectivity, service providers running an IPv4 MPLS network often do not retain that approach, at least in the short-to-midterm, for the following reasons:

- They prefer to avoid (or at least postpone) the corresponding introduction of native IPv6 in the core network, which involve risks and costs that can be avoided with other approaches.

- This approach does not allow MPLS features deployed in the core, such as FRR, TE, and MPLS QoS, to be immediately picked up by the IPv6 traffic.

- It requires high-performance native IPv6 forwarding on all the installed equipment, as it doesn't take advantage of MPLS forwarding.

- It is not easily extendable to enrich the IPv6 connectivity services to MPLS VPN services.

Another possible migration approach is to use IPv6 over IPv4 tunneling. This involves creating IPv4 tunnels on CE routers and run IPv6 routing on top of these tunnels. This uses simple well-known techniques and requires absolutely no upgrade in the backbone (not even on PE routers). And because tunneled IPv6 traffic automatically benefits from the VPN isolation of the IPv4 MPLS VPN service, such a tunneling approach from CE router to CE router is deployed by some service providers as a way to kick-start an IPv6 service with fast time to market. However, deploying IPv6 services using this approach entails custom design, configuration, and operations. Also, this approach suffers from the usual scalability challenges of tunneling techniques (creating and managing tunnels, as well as routing, from every CE router to every other CE router). For these reasons, operators are looking at other approaches to support large-scale production IPv6 services.

Pseudowire technology, discussed later in the section "Layer 2 Services and Pseudowires", allows ATM circuits, Frame Relay circuits, port-to-port Ethernet, or VLAN connections to be emulated over an IPv4 MPLS backbone. These can in turn be used to interconnect IPv6 routers, eventually resulting in IPv6 connectivity supported over an IPv4 MPLS network. Like the IPv6 over IPv4 tunneling approach, this approach avoids any IPv6 upgrade to the core but also comes with comparable scalability challenges because the corresponding mesh of circuits needs to be provisioned across the IPv6 devices. Like IPv6 over IPv4 tunneling, this approach has been used by some service providers for early introduction of IPv6 services.

Finally, the 6PE and 6VPE approaches specified in [6PE] and [6VPE], respectively, allow support of global IPv6 reachability services and IPv6 VPN services over an IPv4 MPLS backbone. These approaches have proven very attractive to operators running an IPv4 backbone because

- They do not require any upgrade to P routers, hence preserving the backbone stability and minimizing operational costs.

- They allow very gradual deployment by upgrading only the PE routers offering the IPv6 services (and where route reflectors are used, either upgrading those or deploying a separate mesh of route reflectors for IPv6).

- They are very scalable because they rely on the same single-sided provisioning model as the MPLS VPN architecture, whereby adding a new site involves only configuration on the attachment port for that particular site.

- They take advantage of MPLS forwarding in the core and its very high performance.

- They ensure that the IPv6 traffic automatically benefits from the advanced MPLS features that may be deployed in the core, such as FRR, TE, and MPLS QoS.

IPv6 Provider Edge (6PE)

The Layer 3 MPLS VPN architecture presented earlier in this chapter introduces a fundamental paradigm. This paradigm is the routing and transport of IPv4 VPN traffic transparently over an IPv4 MPLS core that remains entirely unaware of these IPv4 VPN routes and that remains aware of only the operator's internal IPv4 routes. This is achieved by combining the following:

- Hierarchical routing, in which the core network establishes IPv4 PE-to-PE connectivity while IPv4 VPN reachability is advertised only between the PE routers transparently over the core

- Tunneling of IPv4 VPN packets through the core from PE router to PE router in IPv4 MPLS LSPs so that the core does not need any IPv4 VPN awareness

The 6PE solution uses this same transparent routing and transport paradigm to achieve global IPv6 reachability over an IPv6-unaware IPv4 MPLS backbone. The key difference obviously is that the reachability information advertised among PE routers via MP-BGP is no longer IPv4 VPN prefixes but rather IPv6 prefixes. So the PE routers become dual-stack (meaning that they run IPv4 and IPv6) and are called 6PE routers. They support IPv6 (and typically also IPv4) on access interfaces but still support only IPv4 and IPv4 MPLS on the core-facing interfaces.

P routers remain IPv6-unaware and run the usual IPv4 routing and IPv4 label distribution. This architecture is illustrated in Figure 1-24.

Figure 1-24   *6PE Architecture*

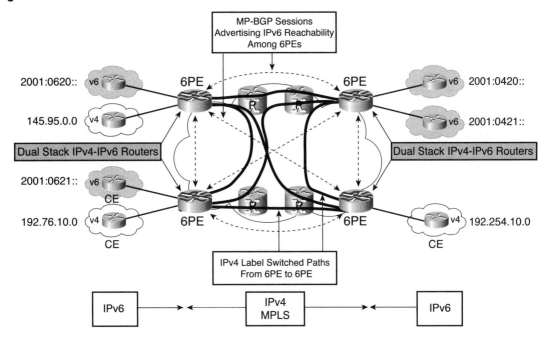

One way to look at the 6PE solution is to consider that the IPv4 MPLS core effectively carries the traffic of one additional VPN, whose traffic and address space happen to be IPv6. Just as in the case of IPv4 VPNs, the core routers remain unaware of the routes that belong to that particular VPN. Note, however, that this special "VPN" does not involve the route-control mechanisms of [2547bis] (such as VRFs, route distinguishers, and route targets), because the routing and forwarding tables of IPv6 are naturally separated from those of IPv4.

From a control plane perspective, the following steps take place before IPv6 communication can happen from a source IPv6 site connected to a 6PE router (called the *ingress 6PE router*) to an IPv6 destination located in another IPv6 site also connected to a 6PE router (called the *egress 6PE router*):

  1 Reachability of the IPv4 address of the egress 6PE router loopback interface is advertised in the core network via the IPv4 IGP to all P routers and to all other 6PE routers (see Step 1 in Figure 1-25).

Figure 1-25   *6PE Control Plane Operations*

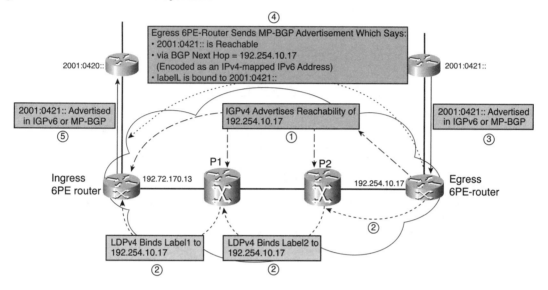

2   Labels are distributed in the core to all P routers and 6PE routers for this IPv4 loopback address through the usual IPv4 label distribution techniques, such as the LDP protocol. In particular, this results in establishing IPv4 connectivity from the ingress 6PE router to the egress 6PE router in the form of an IPv4 LSP (see Step 2 in Figure 1-25).

3   The 6PE routers run MP-BGP among each other using the labeled IPv6 address family. Because the core supports only IPv4, the MP-BGP sessions run over an IPv4 stack. Upon learning reachability toward the destination IPv6 prefix (for example, via an IPv6 routing protocol running with the IPv6 CE router, as in Step 3 of Figure 1-25, or via configuration of an IPv6 static route), the egress 6PE router advertises reachability for this prefix to all other 6PE routers using MP-BGP, as in Step 4 of Figure 1-25. Because the core provides IPv4 connectivity only among 6PE routers, when advertising the IPv6 reachability, the egress 6PE router must convey to other 6PE routers its IPv4 address as the BGP next hop. However, the BGP protocol specifications assume that the BGP Next Hop field is of the same address family as the reachability information (IPv6 in that case). As discussed, the IPv6 addressing architecture defines the IPv4-mapped IPv6 address format precisely for the purpose of representing the address of an IPv4 node as an IPv6 address. Thus, the IPv4 address of the egress 6PE router is encoded in the BGP Next Hop field as an IPv4-mapped IPv6 address. A label is also advertised by the egress 6PE router for the IPv6 prefix. Finally, the egress 6PE router populates an entry in its LFIB for this label/prefix that indicates how to forward the packets received with that label. Depending on the label allocation policy, this might be to pop the label and forward to the next hop interface to the destination, or it might be to pop the label and perform a lookup in the IPv6 forwarding information base.

4   After running the usual BGP route-selection algorithm, the ingress 6PE router populates its IPv6 forwarding information base with an entry for the advertised IPv6 prefix that indicates that a packet destined for that IPv6 prefix

— Is to be encapsulated using MPLS with a label stack whose bottom label is the label advertised in MP-BGP for the IPv6 prefix and whose top label is the label advertised in the core for the IPv4 loopback address of the egress 6PE router that is the BGP next hop for that IPv6 prefix

— Is to be forwarded to the interface on the IPv4 shortest path to the egress 6PE router

5   If a routing protocol is used between the source site and the ingress 6PE router, the ingress 6PE router advertises the reachability of the IPv6 prefix in that routing protocol, as in Step 5 in Figure 1-25.

IPv6 communication can now take place over the IPv4 MPLS backbone. When the ingress 6PE router receives an IPv6 packet, it performs a lookup on the destination IPv6 address in its IPv6 forwarding information base that matches the entry populated by the control plane, as just discussed. Thus, the ingress 6PE router pushes a label stack in front of the IPv6 packet with a bottom label that is the one advertised in MP-BGP for the IPv6 prefix and with a top label that is the one advertised by the core label distribution protocol for the BGP next-hop IPv4 loopback address. The 6PE router finally forwards that labeled packet toward the core on the next-hop interface to the egress 6PE router.

The P routers perform regular IPv4 label-switching operations, resulting in the swapping of the topmost label (or the popping of that label on the penultimate router if PHP is used).

Finally the packet is received by the egress 6PE router. Where PHP is used in the core, the packet is received with a single label, which is the label advertised in MP-BGP for the IPv6 prefix. Otherwise, the egress 6PE router first pops the IPv4 label, thereby exposing the label advertised in MP-BGP. When performing a lookup in its label information base for that label, the egress 6PE router finds the entry populated by the control plane, which tells it how to properly forward that packet.

Packet forwarding at every hop is illustrated in Figure 1-26. In this example, PHP is used and MP-BGP allocates a separate label to each IPv6 prefix so that the packet can be label-switched by the egress 6PE router without requiring an IPv6 lookup.

You can see that IPv6 devices in the IPv6 sites are unaware that IPv6 packet forwarding occurs over MPLS in the core; they operate in their regular IPv6 way. Similarly, P routers in the MPLS core are unaware that the MPLS packets they are switching actually carry IPv6 traffic.

As with the MPLS VPN architecture, the 6PE routers can run a full mesh of MP-BGP sessions for exchange of IPv6 reachability or can use the usual BGP scaling techniques, such as route reflectors.

Figure 1-26   *6PE Data Plane Operations*

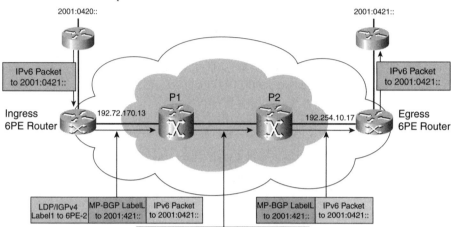

The 6PE approach can operate across multiple autonomous systems. One such scenario is where the 6PE solution is localized within each autonomous system. In this case, the ASBRs of these autonomous systems exchange regular IPv6 reachability information (perhaps without even being aware that the other network uses the 6PE approach). Another scenario is where the 6PE solution spans multiple autonomous systems. In that case, the labeled IPv6 reachability information is exchanged between the route reflectors (or directly between the 6PE routers) of the different autonomous systems. At the same time, labeled IPv4 routes for the 6PE routers' loopback addresses are exchanged between the ASBRs of the different autonomous systems to ensure that the 6PE routers can be reached across the different autonomous systems via IPv4 LSPs.

IPv6 VPN Provider Edge (6VPE)

In addition to IPv6 global connectivity services that can be offered by the 6PE approach, service providers are asked by their customers to offer IPv6 VPN services. The prime driver for such IPv6 VPN services is the exact same need for isolation of end users' intranets as sought with IPv4 VPN services. The 6VPE approach combines the "IPv6 handling" of 6PE with the "VPN handling" of IPv4 MPLS VPNs (described earlier, in the section "MPLS VPN Services in MPLS/IP Networks") to support such IPv6 VPN services over an IPv4 MPLS backbone.

The salient extensions to the 6PE approach are as follows:

- Use of a different address family in MP-BGP defined for the 6VPE purpose, which is the VPN-IPv6 address family (Address Family Identifier AFI = 2 for "IPv6", Sub Address Family Identifier SAFI = 128 for "labeled VPN"). A VPN-IPv6 address is a 24-byte entity, beginning with an 8-byte route distinguisher (RD) and ending with a 16-byte IPv6 address. The role and encoding of the RD is exactly as with IPv4 VPNs.

- Use of the VRF concept of the Layer 3 MPLS VPN architecture, in which each VPN has a separate set of routing and forwarding tables, along with all the associated mechanisms to control import and export of routes into and out of VRFs, including tagging of routes with route targets.

The 6VPE approach yields the same benefits as the 6PE approach. For example, as with 6PE, only the PE routers that actually connect IPv6 VPN services need to be upgraded to support IPv6 and the 6VPE functionality. Thus, the service provider can also introduce IPv6 VPN services without any upgrade or configuration changes on the core routers.

Also, because the 6VPE approach relies on the very same mechanisms as Layer 3 MPLS VPN for IPv4, the service provider can offer the end user the exact same VPN service and features for IPv6 as for IPv4, making the IPv6 VPN service much simpler to understand and integrate within the customer intranet.

Finally, the service provider can rely on the exact same set of Operations, Administration, and Maintenance (OAM) tools to support both the IPv4 and IPv6 VPN service, thus dramatically reducing operational costs.

Layer 2 Services and Pseudowires

Traditionally, the components of data networks consisted of a number of layers, each providing a well-defined service to the layers above them. At the *Transport layer,* service providers could deploy optical equipment (such as SDH/Sonet/xWDM) and copper (xDSL, E1, T1) technologies to present leased-line services. Above this layer, *Transmission services* were deployed (X.25, Frame Relay, ATM, and so on). These provided virtual leased line or virtual circuit (VC) services. The last layer, the *Network layer,* provided IP services such as Internet access and network-based Layer 3 VPNs. Today, most routers can bypass the transmission layer and obtain services directly from the transport equipment.

Due to the high demand for Layer 3 services, the capabilities in terms of capacity on routers have outstripped those at Layer 2, where most providers have deployed OC-12 links in their ATM backbones but OC-48 or even OC-192 in their IP/MPLS network. Because of this, these same providers are considering using the bandwidth available on their IP networks to deliver Layer 2 services. This is indeed what has happened in the recent past with the introduction of pseudowire technology based on MPLS.

Pseudowire technology provides all the mechanisms to emulate a Layer 2 transport service over an IP/MPLS infrastructure.

Pseudowire Network Components

Several components are used to create pseudowire services, each of which is described in [pwe3-req]. These different elements provide different functions:

- **Attachment Circuit (AC)**—The physical or virtual circuit attaching a CE device (either a Layer 2 switch or router) to a PE router. The AC may be a Frame Relay VC, Ethernet port, Ethernet VLAN, ATM VC, ATM VP (virtual path), HDLC circuit, PPP, and so on.

- **Pseudowire (PW)**—A connection between two provider edge (PE) devices that connects two ACs of the same type or different types. This element carries the actual Layer 2 traffic from the AC by encapsulating it in MPLS.

- **Pseudowire edge (PE) equipment**—Service provider edge equipment (switch or router) that provides end-customer attachment and service delivery.

- **Tunnel Label-Switched Path (LSP)**—Where MPLS is used in the core, the pseudowire architecture [see pwe3-cp] relies on an LSP (called the tunnel LSP) in each direction between two pseudowire-capable edge devices. An MPLS label identifies the tunnel LSP and is used to carry one or multiple pseudowires between a given pair of ingress and egress PE devices. Tunnel LSPs may be created by distributing labels automatically using LDP or BGP with label distribution, by deploying traffic-engineered tunnels between PE devices, or by setting static labels along the path between the source and destination PE devices.

- **Directed LDP session**—This targeted LDP session runs between PE devices that provide pseudowire services. The session is used to signal pseudowire setup and status.

- **Virtual circuit label**—The pseudowire Forwarding Equivalence Class (FEC) provides a unique locally assigned label for each AC. These labels are signaled across the directed LDP session to the appropriate remote PE device.

- **Pseudowire identifier (PWid)**—Each pseudowire is identified through a unique identifier (32 bits).

Some of these components are shown in Figure 1-27.

NOTE   Figure 1-27 shows that multiple pseudowires may be carried across the tunnel LSP. A single tunnel LSP is adequate because the virtual circuit label identifies the individual pseudowires.

Figure 1-27 *Pseudowire Network Components*

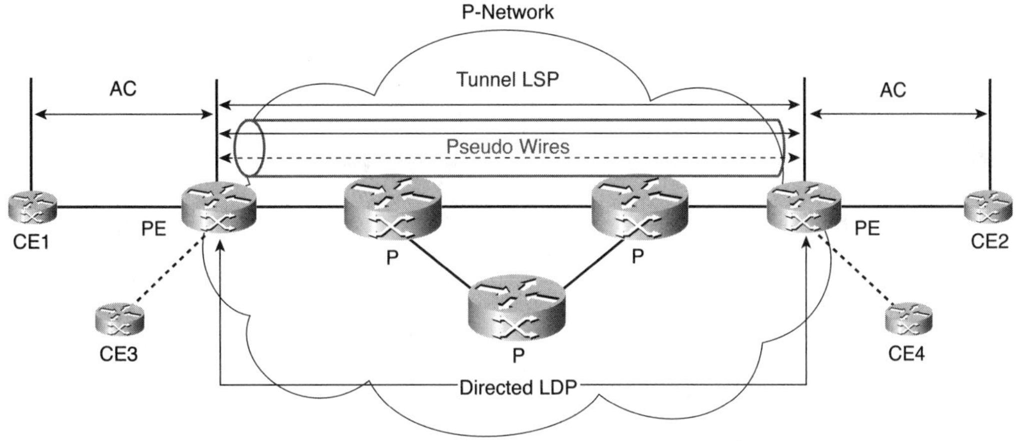

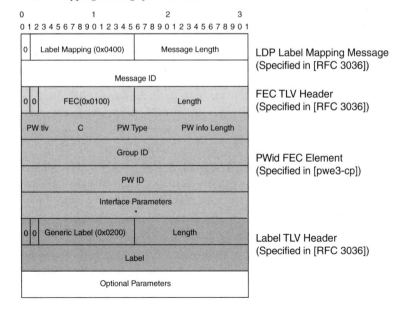

Pseudowire Forwarding Equivalent Class

Pseudowire setup is signaled between PE devices using LDP downstream unsolicited mode across a directed session. As illustrated in Figure 1-28, an LDP label mapping message is used to convey the information for a given pseudowire. It contains a FEC TLV, a label TLV, and optional parameter TLVs (if necessary).

Figure 1-28 *LDP Label-Mapping Message for Pseudowire*

As shown in Figure 1-29, the FEC TLV contains a PWid FEC element that identifies the pseudowire circuit associated with the advertised label.

Figure 1-29 *PWid FEC Element*

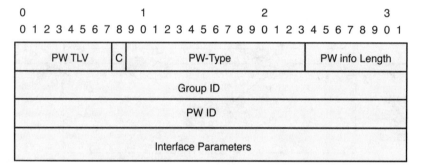

C: ControlWord (1 bit)—Control word present if bit set.
PW-Type (15 bits)—Type of VC e.g FR, ATM, VLAN, Ethernet, PPP, HDLC.
PW Info Length (8 bits)—Length of PWID field and interface parameters.
Group ID (32 bits)—Represents a groups of PWs.
PW ID (32 bits)—Connection identifier used in conjunction with the PW-type to
               identify a particular PW. The PW ID and the PW type must be the
               same at both endpoints.
Interface Parameters (Variable)—Edge facing interface parameters, such as MTU.

Pseudowire Creation and Signaling

There are several ways that two attachment circuits may be cross-connected to establish a pseudowire circuit between them. [pwe3-cp] describes the use of automatic discovery and automatic configuration. However, the most common method at this time is manual configuration through the router's command-line interface (CLI).

Using this method, the operator must initially establish the attachment circuits at each of the PE routers through which the pseudowire will connect. Having established the local attachment circuits, a pseudowire connection may be configured, including the endpoints of the directed LDP session, unique PWid, and so forth.

If a directed LDP session between the ingress and egress PE routers already exists, signaling of the pseudowire may take place using this existing session. However, if one does not exist, it is created based on the endpoint parameters (such as IP addresses) specified in the pseudowire setup configuration.

After receiving the LDP label mapping message, each PE router can match the PWid information and therefore establish the connection. The label carried within the message for this pseudowire is set on all packets flowing for this circuit between ingress and egress PE routers.

This sequence of events is shown in Figure 1-30.

Figure 1-30   *Pseudowire Signaling and Setup*

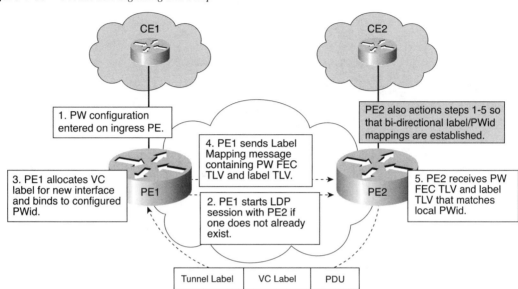

Pseudowire Encapsulation

Depending on the service type (ATM, Frame Relay, Ethernet, and so on), different encapsulations are used. They are defined in [pwe3-atm], [pwe3-fr], [pwe3-eth], and [pwe3-sonet]. In addition to this encapsulation, a control word (32-bit entity) may be carried. It provides additional information for a given service. For example, the control word is used with Ethernet encapsulation to ensure sequencing. With Frame Relay, the control word contains protocol control information such as Forward Explicit Congestion Notification (FECN), Backward Explicit Congestion Notification (BECN), Discard Eligibility (DE), and so forth, as well as sequencing.

Pseudowire Packet Flow

After the pseudowire is successfully established, each Layer 2 Protocol Data Unit (PDU) that enters the PE router on an incoming attachment circuit associated with the pseudowire is sent to the pseudowire.

Figure 1-31 shows how the Layer 2 packet is carried across the MPLS network with an inner label (called the *VC label* and shown as VL in the figure) that identifies the pseudowire, and an outer label (shown as OL in the figure) that identifies the tunnel LSP between the ingress and egress PE routers.

Figure 1-31 *Pseudowire Packet Flow*

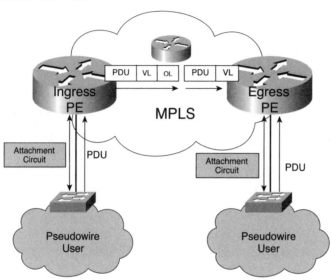

Technology Primer: Quality of Service, Traffic Engineering, and Network Recovery

Quality of service (QoS), traffic engineering, and network recovery technologies are an integral part of today's networks. Each is used extensively in the network's core as well as at its edge (in the case of QoS). Therefore, this chapter's aim is to provide a high-level overview of each of these technology areas.

As in the previous chapter, it is not our intention to provide all the technical details for each technology. References to the resources listed in the "References" appendix are included in brackets so that you can obtain more detailed information.

Quality of Service in MPLS Networks

QoS ensures that packets receive appropriate treatment as they travel through the network. This helps applications and end users have an experience that is in line with their requirements and expectations and with the commitments contracted by the customer with the network operator.

This section first discusses traffic requirements and Service Level Agreements (SLAs). Then it covers mechanisms available to enforce QoS in the network. It finishes by discussing QoS design approaches on the edge and in the core involving different combinations of these QoS mechanisms.

Traffic Requirements and Service Level Agreements

A number of relevant metrics characterize traffic requirements, as discussed in the following sections.

Application Requirements

As with other statistical multiplexing networks such as Frame Relay and ATM, when you're trying to characterize the effect that an MPLS/IP network has on a data stream, it is natural to consider the following metrics:

- Which packets arrive and which do not. This characterizes packet loss.

- Out of the packets that did arrive, how long did it take them to get there, and did this time vary? This characterizes packet delay and delay variation.

- When is such service available? This defines service availability.

The IP Performance Metric Working Group (IPPM) of the Internet Engineering Task Force (IETF) has developed formal specifications for these metrics.

If a given packet arrives at its destination measurement point and does so within a "reasonable" time (meaning that it is still useful to the application), the packet is not lost (see [IPPM-LOSS]). Otherwise, it is considered lost. Loss in a network may be caused by packets being dropped from a device's egress queue when this queue builds up too much because of congestion and packets have to be discarded. We will revisit this topic in more detail in the section "Core QoS Engineering." For now, it is worth pointing out that packet discard as a result of queue buildup may happen even in networks that are engineered so that their average load is well below link capacity. This happens because significant bursts may still occur at very short intervals that are relevant to queue operations. Loss can also be caused by packets being black-holed while routing is in the process of reconverging after a topology change.

Delay through a network can be characterized via the one-way delay or the round-trip time.

For a given packet, the one-way delay (see [IPPM-OWDELAY]) is the amount of time between when the last bit of the packet is transmitted by the source measurement point and when the first bit of the packet is received at the destination measurement point.

The round-trip delay (see [IPPM-RTDELAY]), more commonly called the round-trip time (RTT), is the amount of time between when the last bit of the packet is transmitted by the source measurement point and when the first bit of the packet is received at the source measurement point, after it has been received and immediately sent back by the destination measurement point.

The delay variation between two packets (see [IPPM-DELVAR]) is the difference between the one-way delay experienced by these two packets.

In advanced high-speed routers, the switching delay is of the order of tens of microseconds and is therefore negligible. Thus, the one-way delay in a network is caused by three main components:

- **Serialization delay at each hop**—This is the time it takes to clock all the bits of the packet onto the wire. This is very significant on a low-speed link (187 milliseconds (ms) for a 1500-byte packet on a 64-kbps link) and is entirely negligible at high speeds (1.2 microseconds for a 1500-byte packet on a 10-Gbps link). For a given link, this is clearly a fixed delay.

- **Propagation delay end-to-end**—This is the time it takes for the signal to physically propagate from one end of the link to the other. This is constrained by the speed of light on fiber (or the propagation speed of electrical signals on copper) and is about 5 ms per 1000 km. Again, for a given link, this is a fixed delay.

- **Queuing delay at each hop**—This is the time spent by the packet in an egress queue waiting for transmission of other packets before it can be sent on the wire. This delay varies with queue occupancy, which in turns depends on the packet arrival distribution and queue service rate.

In the absence of routing change, because the serialization delay and propagation delay are fixed by physics for a given path, the delay variation in a network results exclusively from variation in the queuing delay at every hop. In the event of a routing change, the corresponding change of the traffic path is likely to result in a sudden variation in delay.

The availability characterizes the period during which the service is available for traffic transmission between the source and destination measurement points (usually as a percentage of the available time over the total measurement period).

Although many applications using a given network may each potentially have their own specific QoS requirements, they can actually be grouped into a limited number of broad categories with similar QoS requirements. These categories are called classes of service. The number and definition of such classes of service is arbitrary and depends on the environment.

In the context of telephony, we'll call the delay between when a sound is made by a speaker and when that sound is heard by a listener as the mouth-to-ear delay. Telephony users are very sensitive to this mouth-to-ear delay because it might impact conversational dynamics and result in echo. [G114] specifies that a mouth-to-ear delay below 150 ms results in very high-quality perception for the vast majority of telephony users. Hence, this is used as the design target for very high-quality voice over IP (VoIP) applications. Less-stringent design targets are also used in some environments where good or medium quality is acceptable.

Because the codec on the receiving VoIP gateway effectively needs to decode a constant rate of voice samples, a de-jitter buffer is used to compensate for the delay variation in the received stream. This buffer effectively turns the delay variation into a fixed delay. VoIP gateways commonly use an adaptive de-jitter buffer that dynamically adjusts its size to the delay variation currently observed. This means that the delay variation experienced by packets in the network directly contributes to the mouth-to-ear delay.

Therefore, assuming a delay budget of 40 ms for the telephony application itself (packetization time, voice activity detection, codec encoding, codec decoding, and so on), you see that the sum of the VoIP one-way delay target and the delay variation target for the network for high-quality telephony is 110 ms end to end (including both the core and access links).

Assuming random distribution of loss, a packet loss of 0.1–0.5 percent results in virtually undetectable, or very tolerable, service degradation and is often used as the target for high-quality VoIP services (see [SLA]).

For interactive mission-critical applications, an end-to-end RTT on the order of 300–400 ms is usually a sufficient target to ensure that an end user can work without being affected by network-induced delay. Delay variation is not really relevant. A loss ratio of about 0.5–1 percent may be targeted for such applications, resulting in sufficiently rare retransmissions.

For noninteractive mission-critical applications, the key QoS element is to maintain a low loss ratio (with a target in the range of 0.1–0.5 percent) because this is what drives the throughput via the TCP congestion avoidance mechanisms. Only loose commitments on delay are necessary for these applications, and delay variation is irrelevant.

Service Level Agreement

A Service Level Agreement (SLA) is a contractual arrangement between the operator and the customer formalizing the operator's commitments to address the customer-specific QoS traffic requirements.

SLAs offered by operators typically are made up of the following elements:

- **Traffic Conditioning Specification (TCS)**—This identifies, for each class of service (CoS) and each site, the subset of traffic eligible for the class of service commitment. For example, for a given site this may indicate the following:

  - VoIP traffic from that site up to 1 Mbps is to receive the "Real-Time" class QoS commitments, and VoIP traffic beyond that rate is dropped.

  - SAP traffic up to 500 kbps is to receive the QoS commitment from the "Mission-Critical" class, and the SAP traffic beyond that rate is transmitted without commitment.

  - The rest of the traffic is to receive the QoS commitments of the "Best-Effort" class.

- **Service Level Specification (SLS)**—This characterizes the QoS commitments for each class using the delay, delay variation, loss, and availability metrics discussed previously.

- **SLS reporting**—These are reports made available to the user by the operator that characterize the QoS actually observed in the network.

- **Commercial clauses**—This specifies what happens if the QoS commitments are not met. It may include financial credit whose amount is computed based on the actual deviation from the commitments.

SLS commitments are statistical and the corresponding SLS reporting is based on active measurement. Sample traffic is injected into the network between measurement points, recording the QoS metrics (delay/jitter/loss) actually experienced by these samples. The SLS must specify

- How a single occurrence of each metric is measured

- What series of samples the metric is measured on and at what frequencies the series are generated

- How statistics are derived based on the measured metric over the sample series

Multiple statistics can be defined, such as percentiles, median, and minimum, as done in [IPPM-OWDELAY]. However, because SLS must be kept simple enough for easy communications between operator and customers, and because the tighter the commitment, the harder it is for the operator to meet it, SLS offered today generally focuses on an average of the measured metric over a period of time, such as a month.

The SLS must also indicate the span of the commitment. With unmanaged CE routers, this is from POP to POP. With managed CE routers, this is most commonly based on a point-to-cloud model. The SLS commitments are expressed separately over CE-to-POP, POP-to-POP, and POP-to-CE. However, with some classes, such as VoIP, it may sometimes be based on a point-to-point model so that SLS commitments may be expressed as CE-to-CE. This provides a more accurate end-to-end QoS indicator for the end user than the concatenation of commitments over multiple segments. These two models are illustrated in Figure 2-1.

Figure 2-1 *Point-to-Cloud and Point-to-Point SLS Models*

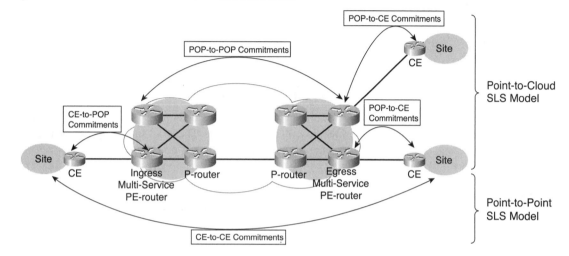

For example, an SLS may indicate that the commitments for the "Real-Time" class of service are that one-way delay, delay variation, and loss are less than 50 ms, 25 ms, and 0.25 percent, respectively, as measured from POP to POP over a series of samples generated every 5 minutes and averaged over a one-month period.

QoS Mechanisms

The previous sections showed that the prime QoS metrics are delay, delay variation, and loss. We can also observe that the delay (excluding its component imposed by serialization and propagation), the delay variation, and the loss all result purely from egress queuing (in the absence of topology change). This explains why the QoS mechanisms we will now discuss are all fundamentally designed to contribute in different ways to reducing egress queue occupancy for traffic requiring high QoS.

Mechanisms that accelerate network recovery after topology changes, and hence that reduce the loss and delay variation induced in such situations, are discussed in the "Core Network Availability" section.

The Fundamental QoS Versus Utilization Curve

Fundamental queuing theory (see [QUEUING1] and [QUEUING2]) teaches that, if you consider a queuing system, the queue occupancy and the steady state depend on the actual arrival distribution and on the service pattern. But if you define the utilization as the ratio between the average arrival rate and the average service rate, you observe that, on high-speed links, regardless of those distributions, the following points are true:

- If the utilization is greater than 1, there is no steady state, and the queue keeps growing (or packets keep getting dropped when the queue limit is reached), and QoS is extremely bad.

- If the utilization is sufficiently less than 1, the queue occupancy remains very small, and QoS is very good.

- As the utilization increases toward 1, queue occupancy increases and QoS degrades in a way that is dependent on the packet arrival distribution.

Therefore, the fundamental QoS versus utilization curve looks like Figure 2-2. This curve is a fictitious one intended to show the general characteristics. The exact shape depends on multiple parameters, including the actual arrival distribution, which is notoriously hard to characterize in IP networks.

Figure 2-2   *The Fundamental QoS Versus Utilization Curve*

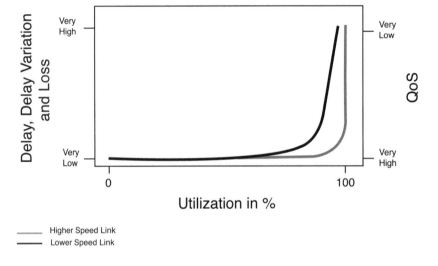

This explains why controlling QoS of a given flow through a network is primarily about controlling the utilization in the actual queue used by this flow at every hop traversed by that flow. (To a lesser extent, it is also about controlling the traffic arrival distribution for a given average arrival rate.)

As with other technologies involving statistical multiplexing (such as ATM or Frame Relay), the utilization in an IP network can be controlled at every hop for a flow in three ways:

- **Capacity planning**—By adjusting the link's bandwidth or the share of link bandwidth allocated to a particular queue, the operator can increase the service rate so that the utilization on that link/queue is sufficiently low for a given traffic arrival rate.

- **Data path mechanisms**—By handling different classes of traffic in different queues and by scheduling these queues with different priorities and service rates, it is possible to enforce a different utilization for each class, depending on its respective QoS requirements.

- **Control plane mechanisms**—By modifying a flow's path, it is possible to find a path where the utilization is lower at every hop than on the regular shortest path first (SPF) path (or in fact is lower than a desired level when constraint-based routing is used).

The fundamental data path mechanisms used in MPLS/IP networks are those of the Internet Engineering Task Force (IETF) DiffServ model and the extensions to MPLS for the support of DiffServ.

The control plane mechanisms used in MPLS/IP networks are IGP metric tuning, MPLS traffic engineering (MPLS TE), and DiffServ-aware MPLS Traffic Engineering (MPLS DS-TE), which are described later in this chapter in the sections "Traffic Engineering" and "DiffServ-Aware MPLS Traffic Engineering." Their characteristics of interest from a QoS perspective are briefly compared in Table 2-1.

Table 2-1 *Control Plane Mechanisms for QoS*

	IGP Tuning	Traffic Engineering	DiffServ-Aware MPLS Traffic Engineering
Mode	Connectionless	Connection-oriented	Connection-oriented
Constraints	Optimize on a single metric	Optimize on one of multiple metrics. Satisfies multiple arbitrary constraints, including an aggregate bandwidth constraint.	Optimize on one of multiple metrics. Satisfies multiple arbitrary constraints, including a per-class bandwidth constraint.
Admission Control	No	On an aggregate basis. Can be used to limit aggregate utilization.	On a per-class basis. Can be used to independently limit the utilization for each class.

The IETF DiffServ Model and Mechanisms

The objective of the IETF DiffServ model is to achieve service differentiation in the network so that different applications, including real-time traffic, can be granted their required level of service while retaining high scalability for operations in the largest IP networks.

Scalability is achieved by

- Separating traffic into a small number of classes.

- Mapping the many applications/customer flows into these classes of service on the edge of the network so that the functions that may require a lot of state information are kept away from the core. This mapping function is called traffic classification and conditioning.

It can classify traffic based on many possible criteria, may compare it to traffic profiles, may adjust the traffic distribution (shape, drop excess), and finally may mark a field in the packet header (the Differentiated Services or DS field) to indicate the selected class of service.

- Having core routers that are aware of only the few classes of services conveyed in the DS field.

You can ensure appropriate service differentiation by doing the following:

- Providing a consistent treatment for each class of service at every hop (known as the per-hop behavior [PHB]) corresponding to its specific QoS requirements

- Allowing the service rate of each class to be controlled (by configuring the PHB) so that the utilization can be controlled separately for each class, allowing capacity planning to be performed on a per-class basis

These key elements of the DiffServ architecture are illustrated in Figure 2-3.

Figure 2-3 *The DiffServ Architecture*

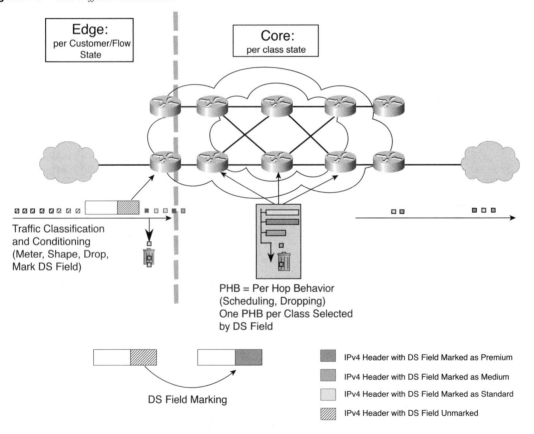

DiffServ is a flexible model. It is up to each operator to decide how many classes of service to support, which PHBs to use, which traffic conditioning mechanisms to use, and how to allocate capacity to each PHB to achieve the required QoS for each class of service.

Observe that DiffServ operates in an orthogonal manner with routing. DiffServ operates purely in the data path and can be used in conjunction with any current and future routing technology. This is why it can be easily combined with IGP routing, MPLS TE, or MPLS DS-TE.

The IPv4 Type of Service (ToS) field (and the IPv6 Traffic Class field) have been superseded. The corresponding 6 most significant bits have been redefined as the Differentiated Services field (DS field; see [DS-FIELD] and [DIFF-TERM]). The remaining 2 bits are used for Explicit Congestion Notification (ECN; see [ECN]).

The DS field is used at the edge of the network by the traffic classification and conditioning function to encode the Differentiated Services Codepoint (DSCP) value. This value is used at every hop by DiffServ routers to select the PHB that is to be experienced by each packet it forwards.

The 3 most significant bits of the superseded IPv4 type of service octet are used to represent the Precedence field, which was intended for use in a more limited but similar way to the DS field. The DS, DSCP, and Precedence fields are illustrated in Figure 2-4.

Figure 2-4   *The DS Field and DSCP*

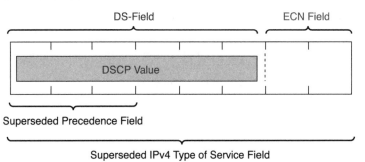

The traffic classification and conditioning functional block is typically located at the service boundary between the customer and the service provider or between two service providers. It is applied on every incoming packet. It identifies the subsets of traffic that need to receive the various differentiated services (classification) and prepares each such traffic subset for entrance into the DiffServ core (conditioning). Clearly, the traffic classification and conditioning policy is highly customizable to reflect the various specific customer requirements and service classes offered by the operator.

The traffic classification stage can take into account any field in the packet header. For example, it may simply look at the DS field if traffic has already been marked upstream. Classification may also consider transported protocols (such as SMTP, HTTP, and so on) or source and destination IP address (such as of application servers) or may even perform deep packet inspection. This can include identifying particular types of transactions within a customer application or identifying web requests to particular URLs. Traffic classification is used to steer the various packet flows toward the appropriate traffic conditioning stage.

An instance of traffic conditioning is composed of an arbitrary subset of the following elements: meter, marker, shaper, and dropper.

The meter can be used to compare the classified stream against a contracted traffic profile, determining for each packet whether that packet is in-profile or out-of-profile. This information is passed to the following element. A traffic profile is usually based on a token bucket with a specified rate burst size. The marker sets the DS field of the packet header, possibly taking into account the result of the meter.

The shaper delays some packets of the classified stream to bring that stream into compliance with a specified traffic profile before it enters the DiffServ core. The dropper discards some packets of the classified stream (for example, the out-of-profile packets identified by the meter). This is called *policing* .

We pointed out previously that queue occupancy depends on utilization as well as traffic arrival distribution (in other words, do packets arrive in big bursts, or are they relatively well spaced over time?). You see that, in addition to their role of enforcing contracted SLS at network boundaries, shaping and policing are mechanisms that affect the traffic arrival distribution by smoothing traffic on its entrance into the network, therefore contributing to lower queue occupancy.

Figure 2-5 provides a logical view of the traffic classifier and conditioner.

Figure 2-5   *The DiffServ Traffic Classifier and Traffic Conditioner*

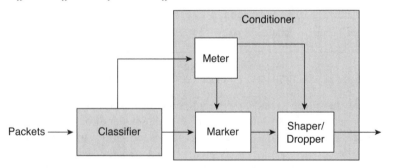

A PHB simply characterizes the externally observable forwarding behavior of a DiffServ router to the corresponding traffic stream. PHBs may be specified in terms of the share of resources allocated to them (such as the fraction of link bandwidth, buffers, and priority in accessing those) or in terms of observable relative QoS characteristics (such as level of delay/jitter and level of loss).

The IETF has specified a number of PHBs. The most important ones are the Default PHB, the Expedited Forwarding (EF) PHB, and the Assured Forwarding (AF) PHB groups.

The Default PHB corresponds to the common, best-effort forwarding behavior available in all routers (that aren't running DiffServ) for standard traffic whose responsibility is simply to deliver as many packets as possible as soon as possible. This PHB is intended for all traffic for which no special QoS commitments are contracted.

The EF PHB (see [EF]) is intended to support low-loss, low-delay, and low-jitter services. The EF PHB guarantees that its traffic is serviced at a rate that is at least equal to a configurable minimum service rate (regardless of the offered load of non-EF traffic) at both long and short intervals. Configuring the minimum service rate higher than the actual EF load arrival rate allows the EF queue to remain very small (even at short intervals) and consequently lets the EF objectives be met.

[AF] (with terminology updates in [DIFF-TERM]) specifies forwarding of packets in one of four AF classes. Within each AF class, a packet is assigned one of three levels of drop precedence. Each corresponding PHB is known as AFij, where i is the AF class and j is the drop precedence. Each AF class is allocated a certain number of resources, including bandwidth. Forwarding is independent across AF classes. Within an AF class, packets of drop precedence p experience a level of loss lower than (or equal to) the level of loss experienced by packets of drop precedence q, if p < q. Packets are protected from reordering within a given AF class regardless of their precedence level. To minimize long-term congestion in an AF queue, active queue management (such as Random Early Detection [RED] [see RED]) is required with different thresholds for each drop profile.

The AF PHB groups are intended to address common applications that require low loss as long as the aggregate traffic from each site stays below a subscribed profile and that may need to send traffic beyond the subscribed profile with the understanding that this excess traffic does not get the same level of assurance.

For backward compatibility with the legacy use of the Precedence field, [DS-FIELD] defines a set of PHBs called the class selector PHBs (CS0 to CS7), each with a DSCP value where the 3 most significant bits reflect a former precedence value and the 3 other bits are set to 0. For example, CS7 corresponds to a DSCP field of 111000.

Table 2-2 lists the recommended DSCP value for each PHB, along with the value of the Precedence subfield.

Table 2-2 *DSCP and Precedence Values*

DSCP in Binary	DSCP in Decimal	Precedence	PHB
000000	0	0	Default
001000	8	1	CS1
001010	10	1	AF11
001100	12	1	AF12

continues

Table 2-2   *DSCP and Precedence Values (Continued)*

DSCP in Binary	DSCP in Decimal	Precedence	PHB
001110	14	1	AF13
010000	16	2	CS2
010010	18	2	AF21
010100	20	2	AF22
010110	22	2	AF23
011000	24	3	CS3
011010	26	3	AF31
011100	28	3	AF32
011110	30	3	AF33
100000	32	4	CS4
100010	34	4	AF41
100100	36	4	AF42
100110	38	4	AF43
101000	40	5	CS5
101110	46	5	EF
110000	48	6	CS6
111000	56	7	CS7

PHB definitions do not specify any particular implementation mechanisms. To instantiate a particular PHB, the network administrator activates, and tunes, an appropriate combination of specific packet-scheduling mechanisms and active queue management mechanisms supported by the DiffServ router.

Priority Queuing (PQ) and Class-Based Weighted Fair Queuing (CBWFQ) are examples of packet scheduling mechanisms commonly implemented on DiffServ routers.

PQ provides absolute priority to packets in that queue relative to any other queue so that packets from other queues are served only when there is currently no packet to serve in the priority queue. For packets in the priority queue, the impact of traffic from any other queue on delay and delay variation is the smallest possible. If the packet arrives in the priority queue when it is not empty, the impact is null. If the packet arrives in the priority queue when it is empty, the worst-case additional delay is equal to the time it takes to finish servicing a packet from another queue that may already be in transmission. Thus, the delay and delay variation offered by PQ are the lowest achievable and are virtually unaffected by the presence of traffic in other queues and their respective load. This is why PQ is the ideal mechanism to implement the EF PHB.

CBWFQ supports a set of queues and services each queue at least at a specified minimum rate when the queue is not empty and there is some congestion on the link so that queues are actually contending. CBWFQ implementations may also support a configurable maximum rate for each queue and a configurable share of the minimum bandwidth currently unused by other queues to be allocated to the considered queue.

RED and Weighted Random Early Detection (WRED) are examples of active queue management mechanisms commonly implemented on DiffServ routers that can be used instead of tail dropping. Tail dropping is the simplest packet-discard mechanism. It drops any packet as soon as the corresponding queue occupancy reaches a certain fixed queue size.

RED maintains a moving average of the queue occupancy and defines a minimum and maximum threshold. When the moving average is below the minimum threshold, no arriving packets are discarded. When the moving average is above the minimum threshold and below the maximum threshold, a random subset of arriving packets is discarded. When the moving average is above the maximum threshold, all arriving packets are dropped. This discarding is intended to trigger congestion avoidance mechanisms in Transmission Control Protocol (TCP) when congestion occurs. The randomness discard is intended to avoid the possible synchronization of TCP's cyclic behavior across all senders so that the mean queue depth, and therefore the delay, should normally remain close to the minimum threshold.

WRED is an extension to RED that supports configuration of different minimum thresholds, maximum thresholds, and drop probability curve between the thresholds, for different subsets of traffic sharing the same queue but subject to different drop probability commitments. WRED is commonly used to implement the multiple drop precedences within each AF class. Figure 2-6 shows sample WRED drop profiles for the AF11, AF12, and AF13 PHBs that could be applied in the queue handling the AF1 class.

Figure 2-6   *Sample WRED Profiles for the AF1 Class*

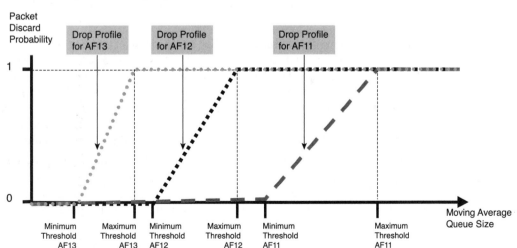

MPLS Support of DiffServ

With respect to DiffServ, the objective of MPLS is simply to allow the exact same DiffServ service to be transparently offered to end users when all, or parts of, the network run MPLS. In an IP network, DiffServ core routers identify the PHB to apply to a given packet by looking at the DS field in the IP header. However, in an MPLS network, the IP header is encapsulated behind the MPLS header so that the DS field is not directly visible to Label Switch Routers (LSRs). Therefore, the PHB to be applied to a packet must be conveyed to the router by some other means.

Each label stack entry in the MPLS header contains a 3-bit EXP field that was put aside in [MPLS-STACK] for future use. This field is shown in Figure 2-7.

Figure 2-7 *MPLS Header and Exp Field*

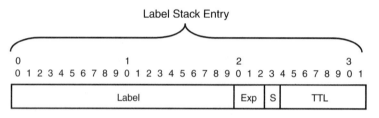

[MPLS-DIFF] specifies how DiffServ is supported over MPLS and how the EXP field can be used for that purpose. Two methods for conveying the PHB to be applied to a packet by routers are defined:

- **Use of E-LSP**—Traffic from up to eight PHBs, which can span multiple DiffServ classes (for example, the Default PHB and EF and two AF classes) can be carried on a single E-LSP. The mapping between the EXP values and the PHBs normally relies on a preconfigured mapping, but this mapping can also be explicitly signaled at Label-Switched Path (LSP) establishment. The router's selection of both the queue and, where applicable, the drop precedence depends on the EXP field. The use of an E-LSP to transport traffic from the EF PHB and from the AF1 class is illustrated in Figure 2-8.

- **Use of L-LSP**—An L-LSP carries only a single DiffServ class (for instance, Default, EF, or one AF class). The router selects the queue from the label. The EXP field is used only when applicable to select the drop precedence. Use of two L-LSPs for separate transport of traffic from the EF PHB and from the AF1 class is illustrated in Figure 2-9.

Figure 2-8   *E-LSP Example for EF and AF1*

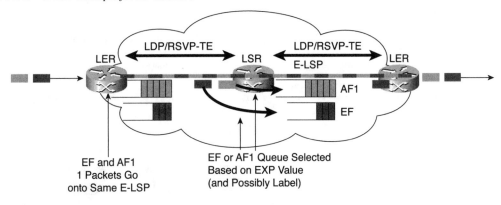

E-LSP established via
label distribution protocol
(LDP or RSVP-TE).

Figure 2-9   *L-LSP Example for EF and AF1*

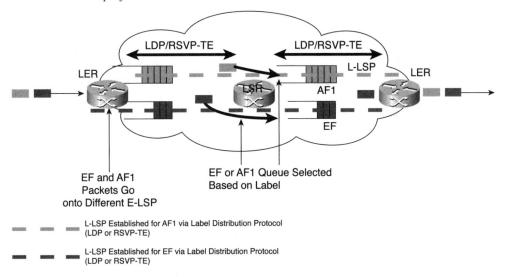

As illustrated in Figure 2-10, at the boundary between the IP and MPLS network, the Label
Edge Router (LER) first identifies the PHB to apply to an incoming IP packet and then selects
the outgoing LSP based on the packet destination and, possibly, on the PHB. Finally, the LER
sets the EXP field to indicate the PHB to be applied.

Figure 2-10 *DiffServ Label Edge Router*

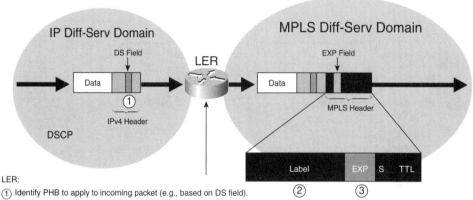

LER:
① Identify PHB to apply to incoming packet (e.g., based on DS field).
② Pick the label which supports the right FEC and the right PHB.
③ Mark the EXP field to reflect the PHB.

When the LER identifies the PHB to apply to an incoming packet, it relies on a traffic classification stage similar to the one described earlier in the context of DiffServ for IP. Hence, the PHB may simply be derived from the content of the DS field in the received IP header or may be based on any other field in the IP header.

[MPLS-DIFF] specifies the signaling extensions to LDP (see [LDP]) and RSVP-TE (see [RSVP-TE]) for setup, maintenance, and teardown of E-LSPs and L-LSPs. However, E-LSPs relying on predefined mapping between EXP values and PHBs do not require the use of any of these signaling extensions because by definition the necessary information is preconfigured.

Even though the way to convey the PHB to a router is different in an MPLS network compared to an IP network, the actual PHBs applied are strictly the same (Default, EF, AFij, and so on). They can be instantiated via the exact same packet scheduling and active queue management mechanisms. No MPLS-specific scheduling mechanism (such as per-label queuing) is involved in supporting DiffServ over MPLS. Consequently, a pure DiffServ service supported over an MPLS cloud is indistinguishable from the DiffServ service supported over an IP network. Note, however, that a DiffServ service over MPLS may be enhanced via additional MPLS mechanisms such as TE or DS-TE.

Production deployment of DiffServ over MPLS today uses E-LSPs with preconfigured mapping between EXP values and PHBs. (The exception is label switching-controlled ATM MPLS networks, where only L-LSPs are applicable because the EXP field is invisible to ATM-LSRs.) This allows for very simple deployment in the core with very smooth introduction, because no resignaling of LSPs is required when deploying DiffServ. This involves only reconfiguring the PHBs on routers so that they can classify packets based on the EXP values in the MPLS header to apply the necessary PHB. L-LSPs may be used in the future, if and when more than eight PHBs are needed in the MPLS core.

Combining Tools to Support SLA

Capacity planning, DiffServ, DiffServ over MPLS, and control plane mechanisms such as TE and DS-TE (which are presented in detail in the "Traffic Engineering" and "DiffServ-Aware MPLS Traffic Engineering" sections) may be combined to control traffic utilization and in turn control QoS. The following section examines how this is achieved.

Core QoS Engineering

To help understand the challenge involved in core QoS design, we must briefly discuss the time scale of traffic distribution. Operators closely monitor the traffic utilization on their links with a typical measurement period of about 5 to 10 minutes. This provides excellent information on traffic trends over the day, week, or month.

However, the time scale at which it is important to understand traffic distribution to be able to apply queuing theory or perform a simulation to predict queue occupancy (and therefore QoS) is on the order of the millisecond.

The challenge is that, as of today, the traffic characteristics of large traffic aggregates in an IP core at small time scales are not well understood. In other words, it is difficult to estimate the small time scale distribution of packets that have to be queued on a link simply by knowing the long-term utilization. Two main schools of thought can be identified:

- One suggests that traffic tends to smooth with aggregation so that traffic aggregates can be considered smooth and Markovian, so M/M/1 queuing theory applies. See [QUEUING1] or [QUEUING2] for an introduction to the M/M/1 model and associated formulas.

- The other suggests that traffic does not smooth with aggregation and that traffic aggregates are bursty and self-similar. Therefore, limited theoretical results are available to characterize queue occupancy.

Depending on their assumptions about aggregate traffic characteristics, papers on the subject conclude different values for what is the maximum large time scale utilization that can be achieved on core links to maintain specific levels of QoS (say, for VoIP) (see, for example, [TRAFFIC1], [TRAFFIC2], [TRAFFIC3], and [TRAFFIC4]). However, it is more and more widely accepted that very high peak utilizations at a large time scale may be achieved on very high-speed links while maintaining very good delay/jitter/loss characteristics (more than 90–95% on OC-48 and OC-192). On lower-speed links, the maximum utilization that can be achieved while offering very good QoS is significantly lower, suggesting that enforcing an aggregate maximum utilization across all traffic to ensure high QoS for just a subset of the traffic (such as VoIP) may involve more significant bandwidth wastage.

To determine the maximum utilization to enforce in a given network to achieve a given level of QoS, network operators use a combination of theoretical analysis, simulation, heuristics based on real-life observation, and safety margin.

In light of this relationship between the utilization measured at a large time scale and QoS performance levels, we see that selecting a QoS design for the core is mainly a trade-off between

- Capital expenditure involved in link/port capacity increase
- Operational expenditure involved in deploying QoS mechanisms (engineering, configuration, monitoring, fine-tuning, and so on)
- Level of QoS performance targeted

In other words, it is a trade-off between throwing bandwidth at the QoS problem and throwing mechanisms at the QoS problem.

Where provisioning extra link capacity doesn't involve significant capital expenditure or lead time and only very high-speed links are used, it is generally not worth enforcing different maximum utilization per class. Therefore, aggregate capacity planning is the most effective approach. Thus, operators in such environments rely exclusively on capacity planning for both normal operations and failure situations. They may compensate for the inherent shortcomings of capacity planning (such as unexpected traffic growth or unanticipated failure) through an additional safety margin. A typical example of capacity planning policy is to maintain an aggregate maximum utilization below 40–50 percent in the normal case and below 70 percent in failure situations. Alternatively, to mitigate the capacity planning shortcomings, some operators resort to the use of MPLS Traffic Engineering to remove local congestion by redistributing the traffic load to avoid having to factor in an excessive safety margin, which could result in significant overengineering and bandwidth wastage.

Other operators believe that although capacity planning is the key tool, DiffServ can ideally address its shortcomings. In the face of an unplanned situation or event, the capacity planning rules may be breached for some period of time. DiffServ can easily be used to ensure that the resulting degradation affects only some classes (for example, best effort) and has no noticeable impact on important classes (such as VoIP).

Finally, some other networks may use lower-speed links (for example, DS-3 or OC-3) in their core so that the maximum utilization that can be achieved for different classes is significantly different, meaning that aggregate capacity planning would result in significant capacity wastage. Also, in some parts of the world, link bandwidth increase may represent significant capital expenditure or long lead times. In these cases, extensive use of DiffServ even in the absence of failure is likely to be the most cost-effective approach. In that case capacity planning is performed on a per-class basis. Where fine or very fine optimization of link utilization is sought, TE or DS-TE can complement DiffServ and capacity planning through their constraint-based routing and admission-control capabilities so that traffic load is optimally redistributed on links.

Edge QoS Engineering

The network edge is where the boundary between the customer and the network operator lies. Hence, when DiffServ is used in the network, all the traffic classification and conditioning functions necessary to reflect the SLA traffic conditioning specification must be deployed on the edge (on the PE router and/or on the CE router).

Because they are dedicated to a single customer and run right to his or her premises, access links generally cannot be easily provisioned to sufficient speeds to ensure that congestion will never occur. Thus, the access links are often the most stringent bottlenecks in the end to end path. For this reason, finer grain QoS is usually supported on the access links with a higher number of classes of service. Multiple PHBs/queues corresponding to the offered classes of service are typically activated on CE routers and PE routers on the access links.

Also, because the serialization delay on low-speed access links can be high for long packets, fragmentation and interleaving mechanisms may be used to allow packets from real-time flows, such as VoIP, to be transmitted without waiting for complete transmission of a long packet.

Because of the significant serialization delays and because small queue occupancy has a bigger impact on QoS metrics on low-speed links, the QoS metrics provided in the SLS on the access are dependent on the access speed. They also involve (for the classes of service with high QoS commitments) strict traffic conditioning such as policing, shaping, or noncommitments for traffic exceeding an agreed-upon traffic profile.

QoS Models

In summary, the design models discussed for MPLS networks can be referred to as N/M/P, where

- N is the number of queues on access
- M is the number of queues in core
- P is the number of TE/DS-TE class types, where
  - 0 means that MPLS TE is not used
  - 1 means that MPLS TE is used
  - 2 (or more) means that DS-TE is used with two (or more) class types

The most common QoS models are listed in Table 2-3.

Table 2-3 *QoS Design Models in MPLS Networks*

QoS Model	Edge	Core Data Path	Core Control Plane
1/1/0	No DiffServ	No DiffServ	No TE
N/1/0	DiffServ with N classes	No DiffServ	No TE
N/1/1	DiffServ with N classes	No DiffServ	TE
N/M/0	DiffServ with N classes	DiffServ with M classes	No TE
N/M/1	DiffServ with N classes	DiffServ with M classes	TE
N/M/P	DiffServ with N classes	DiffServ with M classes	DS-TE

For example, USCom, described in Chapter 3, "Interexchange Carrier Design Study," uses the 1/1/0 QoS model (or the 3/1/0 model if the customer selects the corresponding access option). Telecom Kingland, described in Chapter 4, "National Telco Design Study," deployed the 4/3/1 model. Globenet, described in Chapter 5, "Global Service Provider Design Study," relied on the 5/3/0 model in North America and on the 5/5/2 model in other parts of the world. Eurobank, described in Chapter 6, "Large Enterprise Network Design Study," selected the 1/6/0, 3/6/0, and 6/6/0 models (depending on their access links).

Traffic Engineering

The notion of traffic engineering has existed since the first networks were invented. It relates to the art of making efficient use of network resources given a network topology and a set of traffic flows. In other words, the fundamental objective of traffic engineering is to route the traffic so as to avoid network congestion and increase the network's ability to absorb the maximum amount of traffic. To meet such an objective, you can use several traffic engineering techniques, one of which is MPLS-based traffic engineering.

The best way to introduce MPLS Traffic Engineering (called simply MPLS TE in this section) is to start with the well-known illustration called "the fish problem."

IP routing relies on the fundamental concept of destination-based routing. As shown in Figure 2-11, as soon as the two traffic flows originated by routers R1 and R6 towards R5 reach router R2, they follow the same IGP shortest path because IP packets are routed by default based on their destination IP address. In this example, the two flows follow the path R2–R3–R4–R5. If the sum of traffic from these two flows exceeds the network capacity along this path, this inevitably leads to network congestion. This congestion can be avoided by routing some of the traffic along the other available path (R2–R7–R8–R4, where some spare capacity is available).

Figure 2-11 *The Fish Problem*

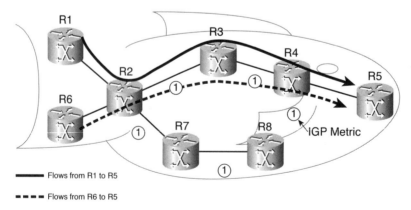

In such a simple network, it is easy to adjust the IGP metrics so as to load-balance the traffic across the two available paths (which normally must have equal cost). However, networks are obviously significantly more complex, and IGP metric optimization is not that simple and does not always provide the level of granularity required. That being said, this is one of the possibilities for traffic-engineering an IP network. Another option is to employ MPLS Traffic Engineering, which provides a rich set of features with a very high granularity to efficiently traffic-engineer an MPLS/IP network.

This section first reviews the set of constraints (also called *attributes*) of a TE LSP. Then the method for computing the TE LSP path obeying the set of constraints is discussed, followed by an overview of the signaling aspects to set up a TE LSP. Finally, you will see the method used to route traffic onto TE LSPs.

MPLS Traffic Engineering Components

The fundamental idea of MPLS TE is to use a Traffic-Engineered Label-Switched Path (TE LSP or tunnel) to forward the traffic across the network by taking into account a set of constraints and the network topology and resources available with the objective of making efficient use of the network.

In short, the TE LSP attributes (constraints) determine the desired characteristics of the LSP (between its source and destination).

The traffic engineering LSP attributes are

- Destination
- Bandwidth
- Affinities
- Preemption
- Protection by Fast Reroute
- Optimized metric

Destination

The source of the TE LSP is the headend router where the TE LSP is configured, whereas its destination must be explicitly configured. Note that the source of a TE LSP must also be explicitly specified in case the TE LSP path is computed by some offline tool.

Bandwidth

One of the attributes of a TE LSP is obviously the bandwidth required for the TE LSP. Several methods can be used to estimate the bandwidth requirement. The most obvious way is to obtain a traffic matrix between the routers involved in a mesh of TE LSPs. This can be achieved by means of various tools such as NetFlow (see [MPLS-MGT] for more details on network management solutions). It is also worth mentioning that some more recent inferring techniques rely on the measurement of link utilization to compute the traffic matrix. However, such methods usually just provide estimates whose accuracy is variable and that vary greatly with the network topology.

The traffic flow pattern between two points is rarely a constant and is usually a function of the time of day, not to mention the traffic growth triggered by the introduction of new services in the network or just an accrued use of existing services. Hence, it is the responsibility of the network administrator to determine the bandwidth requirement between two points and how often it should be reevaluated. You can adopt a very conservative approach by considering the traffic peak, X percent of the peak or averaged bandwidth values. After you determine the bandwidth requirement, you can apply an over/underbooking ratio, depending on the overall objectives. Another approach consists of relying on the routers to compute the required bandwidth based on the observed traffic sent to a particular TE LSP. The TE LSP is set up with a predetermined value (which can be 0), and the router keeps monitoring the amount of traffic sent to the destination on the TE LSP. On a Cisco router, such a capability is called auto-bandwidth. It provides high flexibility by means of several configurable parameters: the sampling frequency (the frequency at which the bandwidth is sampled), the LSP resize frequency, and the minimum and maximum values that a TE LSP size can take. For example, the router can sample the amount of traffic sent every 30 minutes, select the peak value from among a set of samples, and resize the TE LSP no more frequently than once a day with the constraint of always being between 30 Mbps (the minimum value) and 200 Mbps (the maximum value). This provides high flexibility for the network administrator, who can determine the most appropriate trade-off between reactiveness (adapting the demand to the actual bandwidth requirement) and network stability (how often a TE LSP should be resized).

Affinities

A 32-bit flag field that must match the set of links a TE LSP traverses represents affinities. In a nutshell, this can be seen as a coloring scheme (with up to 32 colors). Each link of the network can also have up to 32 colors. It might be desirable in certain circumstances to ensure that a TE LSP exclusively traverses links of specified colors. For the sake of illustration, consider a network with a mix of terrestrial and satellite links. They mainly differ by their propagation delays (which are significantly higher for the satellite links). Hence, the network administrator may decide to color those links (by setting up a specific bit of the 32-bit affinity field). For a TE LSP that carries sensitive traffic for which a short propagation delay is desired, the constraint of avoiding links marked with this specific color can be enforced. Conversely, it is also possible to impose the constraint of selecting links that have a specific color. Any combination is possible, offering a high degree of flexibility.

Preemption

The notion of preemption refers to the ability to define up to seven levels of priority. In the case of resource contention, this allows a higher-priority TE LSP to preempt (and, consequently, tear down) lower-priority TE LSP(s) if both cannot be accommodated due to lack of bandwidth resources on a link.

For example, suppose that a TE LSP T1 of priority X1 cannot be set up along a specific path because of three other TE LSPs—T2, T3, and T4—which respectively have lower priorities X2, X3, and X4, where X2, X3, X4 < X1. Because T1 has a higher priority, it can preempt any TE LSP of a lower priority to accommodate its bandwidth requirements. Details related to the preemption schemes and algorithms to determine the set of preempted TE LSPs can be found in [PREEMPT]. Note that a low preemption number indicates a high preemption (preemption 0 corresponds to the highest priority).

A network administrator can have different motivations for using multiple preemptions in the network. For the sake of illustration, we can mention two typical uses of multipreemption schemes. First, you can ensure that the most important/critical TE LSPs take precedence over other less-important and less-critical TE LSPs in case of resource contention. (For example, voice TE LSPs should be able to preempt data LSPs in case of contention provoked by unexpected traffic growth or network failure.) Second, this lets you circumvent the effect of bandwidth fragmentation in distributed path computation environments. (When the bandwidth is fragmented, it is always more challenging to find a path for larger TE LSPs; hence, they can be configured with a higher priority.)

It is worth noting that because multiple preemptions are available, this implies that an announcement of the available bandwidth on a per-preemption basis should occur. In other words, for each pool of bandwidth, a set of eight available bandwidth values is advertised. For example, consider a link L with 100 Mbps of reservable bandwidth traversed by three TE LSPs:

- T1 with a bandwidth of 10 Mbps and a preemption of 1
- T2 with a bandwidth of 20 Mbps and a preemption of 3
- T3 with a bandwidth of 15 Mbps and a preemption of 5

If you make the assumption of a single pool of bandwidth, the corresponding router advertises the following set of available bandwidth for the link:

- Available bandwidth for preemption 0 = 100 Mbps
- Available bandwidth for preemption 1 = 90 Mbps
- Available bandwidth for preemption 2 = 90 Mbps
- Available bandwidth for preemption 3 = 70 Mbps
- Available bandwidth for preemption 4 = 70 Mbps
- Available bandwidth for preemption 5 = 55 Mbps
- Available bandwidth for preemption 6 = 55 Mbps
- Available bandwidth for preemption 7 = 55 Mbps

For example, 55 Mbps of bandwidth is available for the TE LSPs having a preemption of 5, 6, or 7, whereas TE LSPs with a preemption of 3 or 4 can have up to 70 Mbps and a TE LSP with a preemption of 0 can get 100 Mbps. Of course, in this example if a headend router decides to signal a TE LSP of preemption 3 for 65 Mbps, the TE LSP T3 is preempted to accommodate the higher-priority TE LSP.

Protection by Fast Reroute

MPLS Traffic Engineering provides an efficient local protection scheme called Fast Reroute to quickly reroute TE LSPs to a presignaled backup tunnel within tens of milliseconds (see the "Core Network Availability" section). Such a local protection scheme can be used for some TE LSPs requiring fast rerouting on network failure and is signaled as a TE LSP attribute. In other words, it is possible when setting up a TE LSP to explicitly require the protection by Fast Reroute for the TE LSP whenever Fast Reroute is available on the traversed router. This lets you define different classes of recovery in which some TE LSPs are rerouted according to the normal MPLS Traffic Engineering procedures (as discussed later in this section) and other TE LSPs benefit from fast recovery by means of Fast Reroute. Some additional parameters are detailed in the "Core Network Availability" section.

Optimized Metric

The notion of shortest path is always related to a particular metric. Typically, in an IP network, each link has a metric, and the shortest path is the path such that the sum of the link metrics along the path is minimal.

MPLS TE also uses metrics to pick the shortest path for a tunnel that satisfies the constraints specified. MPLS TE has introduced its own metric. When MPLS TE is configured on a link, the router can flood two metrics for a particular link: the IGP and TE metrics (which may or may not be the same).

To illustrate a potential application, consider the case of links having different bandwidth and propagation delay characteristics. Given this, it might be advantageous to reflect each property by means of a different metric. The IGP metric could, for instance, reflect the link bandwidth, whereas the TE metric would be a function of the propagation delay. Consequently, the IETF specification named [SECOND-METRIC] proposed to have the ability to specify the metric that should be optimized when computing the shortest TE LSP path. On a Cisco router, when a TE LSP is configured, the metric to optimize can also be specified. For instance, the shortest path for a TE LSP carrying voice traffic could be the path offering the shortest propagation delay. Conversely, the path computed for TE LSPs carrying large amounts of data traffic would be determined with the objective of traversing high-speed links. Note that the current Constraint Shortest Path First (CSPF) implementation tries to compute the shortest path based on one of the two metrics (IGP or TE). Dual-metric optimization is an NP-complete problem that would make the path computation significantly more CPU-intensive.

Hierarchy of Attributes (Set of Ordered Path Option)

As you saw previously, when configuring a TE LSP, a set of attributes are specified that must be satisfied when computing the TE LSP path. But what happens if no path satisfying the set of constraints can be found? The answer is straightforward: the TE LSP is not set up. The solution is to relax the constraint that cannot be satisfied and retry at regular intervals to see whether a path satisfying the preferred set of attributes can be found.

The Cisco MPLS TE implementation provides such functionality in a very granular fashion. For each TE LSP, the network administrator can specify multiple sets of attributes with an order or preference. For instance, the most preferred set of attributes could be to get 50 Mbps of bandwidth, a specific affinity constraint (such as avoid all the "red" links), and a preemption of 5. If not all of these constraints can be specified, the user can decide to simply relax the affinity constraint or reduce the bandwidth, for instance. This provides great flexibility to ensure that the TE LSP can always be established along with an important control on the hierarchy among the set of constraints. (For instance, first relax the affinity constraint and then reduce the bandwidth as a last resort, or try to reduce the bandwidth first.)

A good common practice consists of always explicitly configuring a fallback option with no constraint. In such a case the TE LSP path is identical to the IGP shortest path, and the TE LSP could always be set up, provided that some connectivity exists between the source and the destination. Furthermore, the multiple sets of attributes can be ordered by preference, with the ability for the headend router to regularly try to reoptimize a TE LSP to find a path that satisfies a preferred set of attributes. For instance, suppose that a TE LSP is configured with 10 Mbps of bandwidth with a fallback option of 1 Mbps. The TE LSP is successfully set up along the path R1–R2–R3–R4–R5. If the link R3–R4 fails and no other path offering a bandwidth of 10 Mbps can be found in the network, the headend router tries to find a path with 1 Mbps of available bandwidth. Then, when a reoptimization is triggered, the headend router first tries to evaluate whether a path for 10 Mbps can be found.

TE LSP Path Computation

There are two options for computing a TE LSP path: *offline* and *online path computation*. With offline path computation, an offline tool is used to compute the path of each TE LSP, taking into account the constraints and attributes (such as bandwidth, affinities, optimized metrics, preemption, and so on), the network topology, and resources. Because the computation is simultaneously performed for all the TE LSPs in the network, offline tools try to achieve a global network optimization with multiple criteria such as maximum link utilization, minimized propagation delay, and so on, and with the objective of maximizing the amount of traffic the network can carry. This can be achieved thanks to the global view of the network characteristics and traffic demands. Then the TE LSP paths are downloaded on each corresponding headend router.

The second path computation method relies on *distributed path computation*, whereby each router is responsible for computing the path(s) of the TE LSP(s) it is the headend for. No central server computes the TE LSP's path in the network. A very well-known algorithm for computing the TE LSPs is the CSPF algorithm(s). Although a multitude of variants exist, it is worth describing its most commonly used version variant. CSPF computes the shortest path(s) (in a similar fashion as the SPF algorithm used by link-state protocols such as OSPF and IS-IS) that satisfies the set of specified constraints. For instance, all the links that do not satisfy the bandwidth requirement or the affinity constraint (if present) for the TE LSP in question are pruned from the network topology. Then the Dijkstra algorithm computes the shortest path over the resulting subgraph.

We could probably devote an entire book to the respective strengths and weaknesses of each approach. In a nutshell, online path computation is more dynamic, more reactive to network and traffic changes, and more robust (it does not rely on a single centralized server) because of its distributed nature. It also yields less-optimal paths. In contrast, the offline approach usually allows for a higher degree of optimality at the price of less dynamicity, scalability, and increased management overhead.

MPLS TE IGP Routing Extensions

The path computation module needs to learn the available bandwidth on each link to compute a TE LSP path. This is achieved via specific routing protocol extensions, as defined in [OSPF-TE] and [ISIS-TE]. Each link is originally configured with reservable bandwidth (which may or may not be equal to the actual link speed if the network administrator is willing to make any under/oversubscription). As TE LSPs are set up and torn down, the amount of reserved bandwidth varies on each link and is reflected by the IGP. Note that the available bandwidth is provided for each preemption level.

Of course, it would be undesirable to flood a new IGP Link-State Advertisement (LSA) each time the available bandwidth changes. Hence, a nonlinear threshold mechanism is used such that small changes do not trigger the flooding of an IGP LSA update. The downside of such an approach is the potential inaccuracy between the available bandwidth flooded by the IGP and the actual reservation state. Consequently, a headend router may compute a path even though the required bandwidth is not actually available at some hop. In this case, the router that can't accommodate this request rejects the TE LSP set up and immediately triggers the flooding of an IGP LSA update to inform the headend router (and all the routers in the network) of the actual reservation state. The headend router in turn computes a new TE LSP path, this time taking into account up-to-date information.

The threshold scheme is made nonlinear to ensure more frequent updates (closer thresholds) as the available bandwidth for the link gets closer to 0. Ensuring more accurate bandwidth reservation states allows the operator to reduce the risk of unsuccessful TE LSP setup. In practice, such a scheme works extremely well and provides a very efficient trade-off between IGP flooding frequency and up-to-date reservation state dissemination.

Note also that the receipt of an IGP LSA reflecting a bandwidth reservation state never triggers a routing table computation. It is worth mentioning that even in large networks the IGP overhead related to the announcement of the reservable bandwidth along with other TE-related links attributes does not affect the IGP scalability.

Signaling of a Traffic Engineering LSP

As soon as the TE LSP path is computed, the next step is to set up the TE LSP. The signaling protocol for MPLS TE is RSVP-TE, which actually relies on RSVP with some extensions specific to MPLS TE (see [RSVP-TE]). RSVP-TE uses the RSVP messages defined in [RSVP] to set up, maintain (refresh), signal an error condition, and tear down a TE LSP. These messages are Path, Resv, Path Error, and Resv Error. Each message contains a variable set of objects. As mentioned earlier, several new objects in addition to the existing objects defined for IPv4 flows have been specified for use by MPLS TE. Those objects are related to TE LSP attributes such as the computed path (also called ERO), bandwidth, preemption, Fast Reroute requirements, and affinities, to mention a few.

When initiating a TE LSP setup, the headend router starts sending an RSVP Path message that specifies the TE LSP attributes. The Path message is processed at each hop up to the final destination. Then, on the reverse path, RSVP Resv messages are sent to the headend router. Each hop along the path checks whether the TE LSP constraints can effectively be satisfied. If they can, each router sends a Resv message to its upstream neighbor along the TE LSP path to confirm the successful setup. Note that it also provides the label to be used for the corresponding TE LSP. This messaging sequence is shown in Figure 2-12.

Figure 2-12   *The Steps of Setting Up a TE LSP*

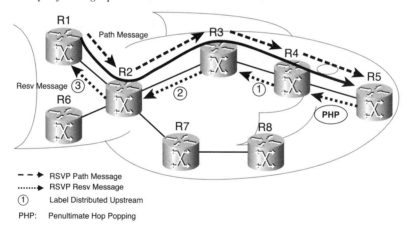

After a TE LSP is set up, it must be maintained by successive refreshes of the corresponding state (RSVP is a soft-state protocol). Each router sends a Path message downstream and a Resv message upstream for each active TE LSP at a regular configurable interval. The different routers operate in an asynchronous fashion. An interesting optimization (called *refresh reduction*) that drastically reduces the refresh overhead has been proposed in [REFRESH-REDUCTION]. The basic principle consists of sending a limited amount of information to refresh a TE LSP state instead of resending the complete Path and Resv messages. Moreover, it is worth mentioning that the ability to transmit RSVP messages in a reliable fashion has been added to RSVP and is also defined in [REFRESH-REDUCTION].

Handling errors is obviously part of the RSVP signaling set of procedures. Hence, when a TE LSP experiences a failure that triggers a teardown (and consequently the removal of the corresponding control and data plane states), a set of RSVP messages is sent both upstream and downstream to the triggering router. Such conditions can be provoked by insufficient resources upon signaling, network element failures (link, node), preemption of a TE LSP by a higher-priority TE LSP, and so on.

NOTE TE LSPs are unidirectional. Bidirectional TE LSPs have been defined in [GMPLS] but generally are undesirable and unnecessary in the context of packet networks. Indeed, they require finding a path that satisfies the constraints in both directions, which may not always be possible. Such an additional constraint may also impose a nonoptimal path. Unidirectional TE LSPs are much more suitable to packet networks and are more in line with the fundamental asymmetrical nature of data networks and IP routing.

No routing adjacency is established over TE LSPs. In contrast to other technologies (such as ATM, which also is used for traffic engineering purposes), TE LSPs confer to MPLS TE a significantly higher scalability.

Routing onto a Traffic Engineering LSP

After the TE LSP has been successfully set up, the last step is to determine the set of traffic that must be carried onto the TE LSP. The first method to route traffic onto a TE LSP is to configure a static route where the static route points to a TE LSP instead of a "regular" physical interface. Note that recursive static routes can also be configured. In this case, a static route points to an IP address, which for instance can be the loopback interface address of a BGP next hop. Consequently, each IPv4 or VPNv4 (in the context of Layer 3 MPLS VPNs) route announced by the BGP next hop would use the TE LSP without having to configure a static route per announced prefix.

Another mechanism known as *Autoroute on Cisco routers* (other router vendors have proposed similar mechanisms) allows the headend router to automatically take into account the TE LSP in its routing table computation. It always prefers a TE LSP to the IGP shortest path to reach the TE LSP destination and any destination downstream to the TE LSP's tail-end. Detailed references for the Autoroute feature can be found in [AUTOROUTE].

Solving the Fish Problem

Going back to the previous example illustrated in Figure 2-11, consider the following set of assumptions. All the links have a metric of 1 and a capacity of 10 Mbps. The flows' bandwidth requirements, (R1,R5) and (R6,R5), are 8 Mbps and 7 Mbps, respectively. Suppose that R1 first computes a path for its TE LSP of 8 Mbps. It selects the shortest path satisfying the set of constraints (in this simple example, the only constraint is bandwidth), which is R1–R2–R3–R4–R5 (the shortest path cost satisfying the bandwidth constraint). After the TE LSP has been successfully set up, the IGP reflects the available bandwidth on each link. Then R6 computes its TE LSP path requiring 7 Mbps of bandwidth and determines that the shortest path offering 7 Mbps of available bandwidth is R6–R2–R7–R8–R4–R5. This lets you avoid congestion on the links R2–R3 and R3–R4, which cannot accommodate the sum of the two traffic flows. This is illustrated in Figure 2-13.

Figure 2-13 *A Path Computed by the Headend Router R6 That Satisfies the Bandwidth Requirement*

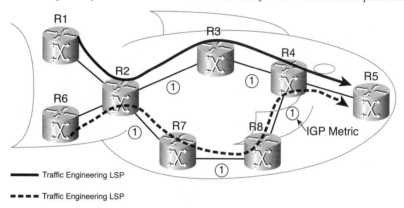

TE LSP Deployment Scenarios

Figure 2-14 illustrates different scenarios involving TE LSPs.

Figure 2-14   *Various Deployment Scenarios Involving MPLS TE*

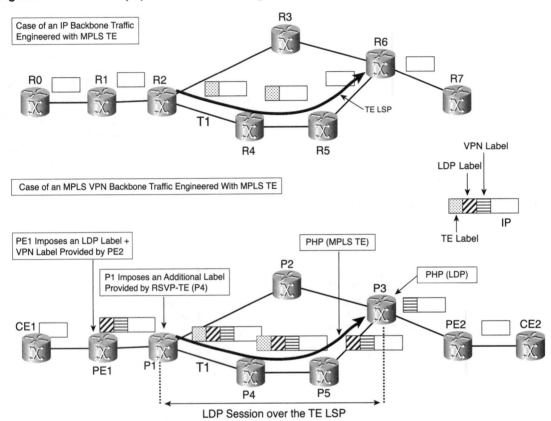

The following explains the two deployment scenarios shown in Figure 2-14:

- **IP backbone traffic engineered with MPLS TE**—In Figure 2-14, consider an IP packet sent from R0 to R7, and observe the different steps that occur in the forwarding path. The IP packet is first IP-routed from R0 to R2, where it is forwarded to T1, a TE LSP from R3 to R6. In this example, a label provided by RSVP-TE is pushed by R2, the headend of the T1 TE LSP. Then the packet is label-switched according to the labels distributed by RSVP-TE to the penultimate hop, R5, which removes the RSVP-TE label (an operation called Penultimate Hop Popping (PHP)). The IP packet then is finally IP-routed to its final destination, R7.

- **Layer 3 MPLS VPN backbone traffic engineered with MPLS TE**—This scenario is slightly more complicated. In addition to the labels usually required by MPLS VPN (the LDP and BGP labels), an additional label corresponding to the TE LSP is pushed onto the label stack as the traffic is forwarded onto the TE LSP by the TE LSP headend router. In Figure 2-14, an IP packet is sent by the CE router. Upon receiving the IP packet, the PE router determines the VRF and pushes a two-label stack. This label stack corresponds to the BGP label provided by the PE router, which advertises the destination prefix for the VPN in question plus the LDP label to reach the destination PE router. The packet is then label-switched until it reaches P1. At this point, the headend router P1 pushes an additional label corresponding to the TE LSP. It is worth mentioning that the LDP label is swapped and the remote LDP peer P3 provides the corresponding label. Why is an LDP session required between the headend and the tail-end of the TE LSP (P1 and P3 in this example)? As you saw in the previous example, a PHP operation is performed by the penultimate hop of the TE LSP. Hence, without an LSP session between the headend and tail-end of the TE LSP, the TE LSP tail-end router (P3 in this example) would receive a packet with an unknown BGP label instead of receiving an LDP label and would just drop the packet (or forward it using what it believes to be the correct forwarding entry, thus causing a traffic black hole).

NOTE	In the case of a TE LSP established between PE routers, there is no need for any LDP session. Hence, two labels are imposed on the IP packets received from the CE routers—the BGP label and the RSVP-TE label.

Reoptimizing a Traffic Engineering LSP

Network state keeps changing. Links and nodes fail and recover; new TE LSPs are set up while others may be torn down. Consequently, for any TE LSP, a more optimal path may appear in the network. It is then highly desirable to detect the existence of such a path and reoptimize a TE LSP along a better path when it becomes available. Consider the example shown in Figure 2-15.

Figure 2-15 *Reoptimizing a TE LSP*

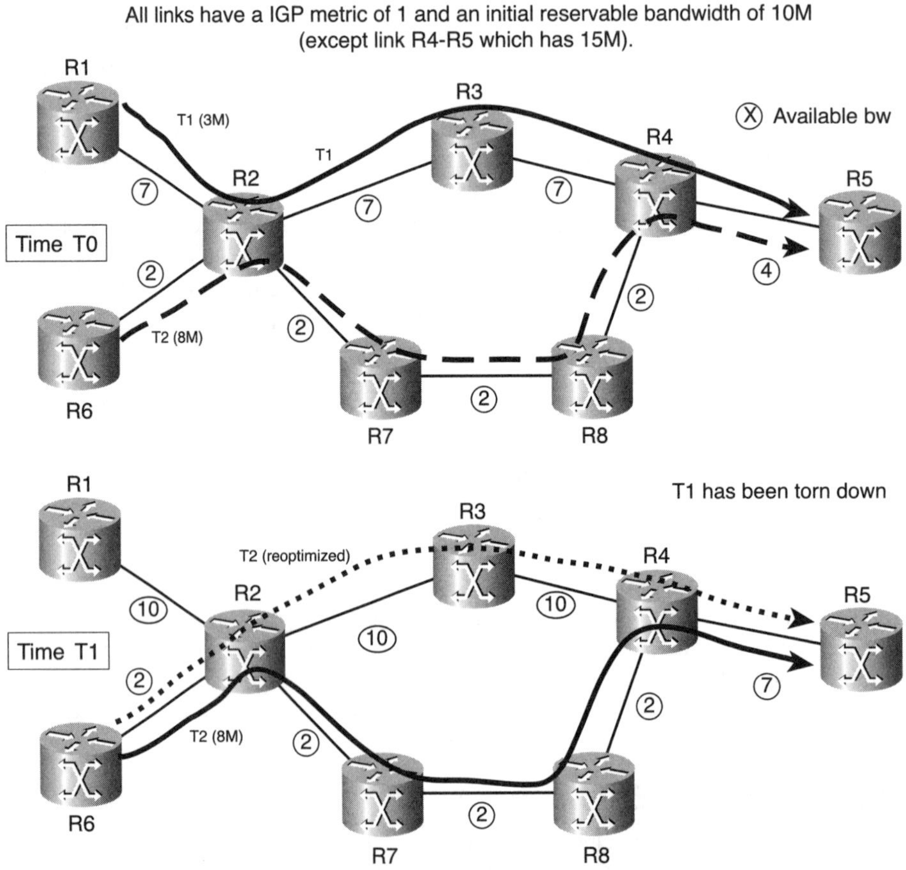

All links have a IGP metric of 1 and an initial reservable bandwidth of 10M
(except link R4-R5 which has 15M).

In Figure 2-15, all the links have a cost of 1 and an initial reservable bandwidth of 10 Mbps, except the link R4–R5, which has 15 Mbps of reservable bandwidth. Suppose that the first TE LSP to be signaled is T1 between R1 and R5 (for 3 Mbps), which follows the shortest path, obeying the bandwidth constraint, of R1–R2–R3–R4–R5. Immediately following this event, R6 signals the TE LSP T2 (for 8 Mbps), which follows the shortest path offering 8 Mbps of bandwidth, which is R6–R2–R7–R8–R4–R5. Hence, at time t0, both T1 and T2 are up and running. At time t1, the TE LSP T1 is torn down, which frees up 3 Mbps of bandwidth along the path R1–R2–R3–R4–R5. When a reoptimization evaluation process is triggered by R6, it determines that a more optimal (shortest) path exists between R6 and R5 (the path R6–R2–R3–

R4–R5), and it reroutes the TE LSP along this more optimal path. This illustrates the concept of reoptimization. There are several important aspects to highlight:

- **Nondisruptive reoptimization**—A key property of MPLS TE is its ability to reoptimize a TE LSP along a more optimal path *without any traffic disruption* . Hence, the headend router should not tear down the "old" LSP and then reestablish it along a more optimal path. Instead, the headend router first establishes the new TE LSP (which belongs to the same session as the old TE LSP). As soon as that new TE LSP is successfully set up, the old TE LSP is torn down. This is known as the *make-before-break* mechanism, a property that was not really available (implemented) with other Layer 2 protocols such as ATM.

- **Avoid double booking**—If you carefully observe Figure 2-15, you will notice that after T1 has been torn down, the available bandwidth on the link R4–R5 is 7 Mbps, which is not enough to accommodate the second occurrence/LSP of T2 (along the more optimal path). So how can R6 set up the LSP along the path R6–R2–R3–R4–R5 without first tearing down the TE LSP, because the make-before-break procedure appears to have both LSPs active at the same time? The answer is that T2 is reoptimized with the option of sharing the bandwidth with the old LSP of T2. In other words, when the new LSP of T2 is signaled, the router R4 sees that it shares the bandwidth with the old LSP (thanks to RSVP's Share Explicit option). Hence, no double booking occurs (R4's call admission control does not count the bandwidth twice). Similarly, when computing the path for the reoptimized TE LSP, the headend (R6 in this example) knows that the available bandwidth to reoptimize T2 is the current network reservation state plus the bandwidth that will be freed up by the current LSP for T2.

An important aspect of any MPLS TE network design relates to the reoptimization triggers. How often and when should a TE LSP be evaluated for reoptimization? A Cisco router has several reoptimization triggers:

- **Manual reoptimization**—A command is issued on the headend router that triggers a reoptimization evaluation for each TE LSP the router is the headend for. If a better path is found, the TE LSP is reoptimized according to the make-before-break procedure.

- **Timer-based reoptimization**—A reoptimization timer is configured on the headend router. Upon expiration, the headend tries to reoptimize each TE LSP it is the headend for.

- **Event-driven reoptimization**—In some cases, it may be desirable to trigger a reoptimization upon the occurrence of a particular event, such as the restoration of a link in the network. Indeed, if a link is restored in the network, some TE LSPs may benefit from that new link to follow a more optimal path. When configured, each time a new link is advertised as newly operational, this triggers the evaluation of any potential reoptimization. It is worth noting that this should be handled with some care to avoid network instability. Let's consider the case of an unstable link. This would have the effect of constantly attracting new TE LSPs, which would then fail and be reoptimized again, creating some very undesirable network instability and consequently traffic disruption. This explains why such a trigger should always be used in conjunction with a dampening mechanism at the interface or IGP level to avoid network instabilities in case of unstable links or routers.

MPLS Traffic Engineering and Load Balancing

Load balancing is undoubtedly a key aspect of traffic engineering. It refers to the ability to share the traffic load between two routers across multiple paths. In IP routing, those N paths must have equal costs (except in the case of Enhanced Interior Gateway Routing Protocol [EIGRP]), and the share of traffic between those N paths is also equal. More accurately, two methods exist to perform IP load balancing—per-packet and per-destination. With per-packet load balancing, the load-balancing algorithm leads to a strict equal share across the N path because the traffic (on a per-packet basis) is balanced in a round-robin fashion. With per-destination load balancing, a hash algorithm on several IP fields (such as the source and destination IP addresses) is used to ensure that all the packets that belong to the same flow always follow the same path (thus avoiding reordering of packets that belong to the same flow). Consequently, the load between the N paths may not be exactly equal.

The reason why traffic can be load-shared only between equal-cost paths in IP routing is to avoid the formation of routing loops. Indeed, without any further IGP routing enhancements, if the packets were distributed among unequal-cost paths, some packets would be sent back to some routers along their path.

In contrast, MPLS TE offers a higher degree of flexibility. First, a headend router can set up multiple TE LSPs to a particular destination, which may follow paths with unequal costs. This does not introduce any routing loops because packets are label-switched along all the TE LSP paths in accordance with the path explicitly signaled at LSP setup time. Second, the multiple TE LSPs may have different characteristics. For instance, if two TE LSPs are established between R1 and R2, each having a bandwidth of 10 Mbps and 20 Mbps, the headend router (R1) shares the load between the two LSPs proportional to their respective bandwidth (twice more packets are sent to the TE LSP with 20 Mbps of bandwidth). Note that some router implementations allow the operator to override this sharing ratio by configuration. It is worth mentioning that the usual traffic load-balancing techniques available for IP (per-packet and per-destination) equally apply to MPLS TE.

MPLS Traffic Engineering Forwarding Adjacency

By default, a headend router does not advertise any of its TE LSPs within its self-generated LSA/LSPs. This implies that its TE LSP(s) do not influence the routing decisions of other routers. Under some circumstances it is desirable to adopt different behavior and allow a router to advertise in its LSA/LSP the existence of a TE LSP. In other words, the headend advertises a TE LSP as a "physical" link even though no routing adjacency has been established over the TE LSP. Consequently, any router receiving the headend router's LSA/LSP takes the TE LSP into account in its SPF calculation. In this case, we usually say that the TE LSP is advertised as a forwarding adjacency (FA). This is a TE LSP attribute configured just like any other LSP attributes on the headend router. Figure 2-16 illustrates forwarding adjacency.

Figure 2-16 *Forwarding Adjacencies*

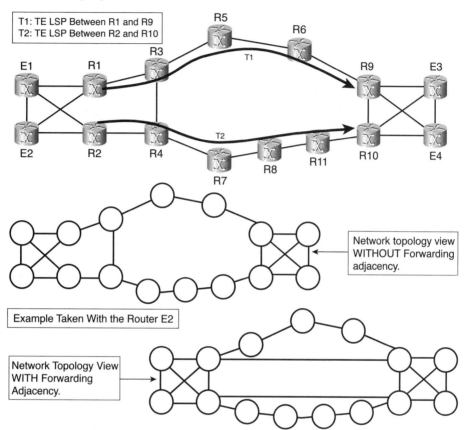

Other parameters are associated with a forwarding adjacency. One is the metric, because the TE LSP is advertised as any other "regular" link. Another one is the timer to control how long the TE LSP can be in a down state before reflecting this state in the LSA/LSP. Indeed, consider the TE LSP T1 from R1 to R9 that follows the path R1–R3–R5–R6–R9. If configured as a forwarding adjacency, R1 advertises T1 as a "regular" link between R1 and R9. If a failure occurs along T1's path (for instance, the link R6–R9 fails), T1 also fails. One option is to immediately reflect the topology change in the LSA/LSP (the link R1–R9 no longer exists). However, it is usually desirable to wait for a period of time, because T1 is likely to be restored by a recovery mechanism. You will see in the "Core Network Availability" section that a local protection mechanism such as MPLS TE Fast Reroute would recover T1 within 50 ms. Hence, if T1 reflects the failure of the TE LSP without waiting, this would lead to advertising two IGP LSA/LSPs in a very short period of time. This would trigger two consecutive routing table updates on each router in the network. This explains why it may be desirable to wait for a period of time before advertising the FA as down. The amount of time usually varies according to the network design and network recovery mechanism that is in place.

NOTE   To consider a link during SPF, a router always checks that the link is advertised in the LSA/LSP of both ends. For instance, in Figure 2-16, when E1 computes its SPF, before considering the link R1–R9 (TE LSP configured as a forwarding adjacency), it checks whether the link is advertised in both the R1 and R9 LSA/LSPs. This is known as the double connectivity check. Hence, it requires that a TE LSP is also configured between R9 and R1 as a forwarding adjacency because TE LSPs are unidirectional.

In the case of a large number of TE LSPs configured on a headend router as forwarding adjacencies, this may significantly increase the size of the router's LSA/LSP. That being said, this is not a real issue in practice.

There are two ways to advertise a TE LSP as a forwarding adjacency:

- **As an IP link**—In this case, the TE LSP is seen by other routers as a regular IP link, without any traffic engineering capability.

- **As a traffic engineering link**—This implies that the headend router must advertise the TE LSP as a link with traffic engineering characteristics such as reservable bandwidth, affinities, and so on.

In the first case, the other routers may use the TE LSP in their SPF computation to route their IP traffic. In the second case, if the TE LSP is advertised as a TE link, the other routers could also take the forwarding adjacency into account in their CSPF calculation to route their own TE LSP because they see the forwarding adjacency as a regular TE link. This introduces the notion of a hierarchical TE LSP—that is, a TE LSP routed within other TE LSPs.

Forwarding adjacencies may be useful in some network designs. A typical example is when load balancing must be achieved between PE routers. Consider the typical case of various POPs interconnected via long-distance links and made up of a set of PE routers dual-attached to two P routers. Between each pair of PE routers are several IGP paths that can all be used to load-balance the traffic across those paths if and only if they have an equal IGP path. Note that this applies to both the case of IP (without MPLS) and MPLS Traffic Engineering (unless exactly one TE LSP is set up per available path, which is usually hard to achieve). Thus, one solution consists of computing the set of link metrics such that all the paths between each pair of PE routers have an equal cost. However, this is virtually impossible to achieve and is likely to be inefficient in terms of bandwidth usage if the network is made up of links with disparate link bandwidths.

Another solution relies on the use of forwarding adjacencies. As shown in Figure 2-16, a full mesh of TE LSPs is set up between the P routers, which are configured as FA and announced as FA (links) with a fixed metric. This way, every PE router (such as E2 in Figure 2-16) sees every other PE router at an equal IGP path cost via every possible path, provided that the link costs between PE routers and P routers are themselves equal.

Of course, such a design requires some analysis in terms of parameter settings (in particular, for the timers related to the TE LSP's liveness). It also increases the size of the IS-IS LSP and OSPF LSA (Type 1) because each headend router now advertises each TE LSP it is the headend for as a physical link. This may lead to an increase in each IS-IS LSP/OSPF LSA size and consequently the Link-State Database (LSDB) size. Moreover, some careful analysis must be done to study the traffic routing in the network because the network view of each router no longer reflects the actual network topology.

Automatic Meshing of a Mesh of TE LSPs

A quite common deployment scheme of MPLS Traffic Engineering, which is illustrated in several case studies in this book, consists of setting up a mesh of TE LSPs between a set of routers. Depending on the network size and the decision to deploy MPLS TE between the core or edge routers, the number of routers involved in a mesh can range from a few routers to tens or even a few hundred. Furthermore, because TE LSPs are unidirectional, a mesh of N routers implies the configuration of N − 1 TE LSPs per headend. The total number of TE LSPs in the network is then N * (N − 1) TE LSPs. For instance, a mesh of 50 routers requires the configuration of 2,450 TE LSPs. Such a configuration task can be eased by using scripts but is still undoubtedly cumbersome and subject to configuration errors. Moreover, adding a new member to the mesh requires not only the configuration of N new TE LSPs (one to each existing router of the mesh) but also one additional TE LSP on each of the N routers terminating on the new member of the mesh. Consequently, having some mechanisms automating the creation of meshes of TE LSP is extremely useful. In a nutshell, such functionality consists of several components:

- **Discovery process**—The first task is to discover the routers that participate in the mesh. IGP extensions have been proposed in [OSPF-TE-CAPS] and [ISIS-TE-CAPS] that allow a router to announce its mesh group membership. (As you will see in several case studies, having multiple TE meshes might be required. Hence, the generalized notion of mesh groups has been introduced.) Thus, a router first announces the set of mesh groups it belongs to (this set may obviously be reduced to one). Note also that mesh groups may or may not overlap. In other words, the set of routers that belong to mesh group M1 may fully or partially intersect with the set of routers that belong to mesh group M2.

- **TE template**—For each mesh group a router belongs to, the network administrator configures a set of attributes that apply to all the TE LSPs of the specific mesh group. Note that because bandwidth may vary for each destination, an elegant solution consists of using the auto-bandwidth mechanism described earlier.

- **Automatic TE LSP setup**—As soon as a router has discovered all the routers that participate in the mesh group(s) it belongs to, it starts establishing the required TE LSPs.

DiffServ-Aware MPLS Traffic Engineering

As explained in the section "Quality of Service in MPLS Networks," DiffServ (introduced in [DIFF-ARCH]) and MPLS DiffServ (covered in [MPLS-DIFF]) define QoS mechanisms in the data path (such as how to schedule different traffic streams in different queues) independently of how traffic is routed in the network. Conversely, MPLS TE defines how traffic aggregates may be routed into a network independently of the QoS mechanisms that may be deployed and hence how traffic may actually be scheduled at every hop. Consequently, although MPLS TE and DiffServ can be deployed simultaneously in a given network, they remain unaware of each other so that MPLS TE performs constraint-based routing and admission control on an aggregate basis across all DiffServ classes. DiffServ-aware MPLS Traffic Engineering (DS-TE) is an extension to MPLS TE to make it aware of DiffServ. It allows the benefits of constraint-based routing and admission control to be applied separately, and hence more accurately, to different classes of services (or to different sets of such classes with similar requirements).

With DS-TE, separate MPLS TE tunnels are established for different DiffServ classes of service (or for different sets of classes of service). Then, when performing constraint-based routing for these tunnels, the resources actually available to the corresponding class(es) of service can be taken into account (as opposed to the aggregate link bandwidth). Also, the specific attributes of the class(es) of service can be enforced (as opposed to attributes that are common to all the classes of service). It is also possible to enforce separate engineering constraints for the different classes of traffic. For example, one of the DS-TE requirements identified by service providers (see [DSTE-REQ]) for networks carrying a significant amount of voice over IP traffic is to be able to limit the total VoIP load below a certain percentage of the link bandwidth. This helps control the delay and jitter for this traffic while filling the rest of the link with traffic which is less delay- and jitter-sensitive.

Thus, the objective of DS-TE is to allow support of applications with very tight QoS requirements without relying on overengineering.

The next section reviews how DS-TE extends the MPLS TE components introduced earlier. Like TE, the DS-TE extensions are purely in the control plane. DS-TE relies on MPLS DiffServ in the data path (either E-LSPs or L-LSPs, as defined in the "Quality of Service in MPLS Networks" section) and does not introduce any additional QoS mechanisms.

Bandwidth Constraints Model

A key objective of DS-TE is to be able to enforce different bandwidth constraints on different types of traffic. We define a class type (CT) as the set of DS-TE LSPs that share the same set of bandwidth constraints. DS-TE supports up to eight CTs (CT0 to CT7).

A bandwidth constraints model defines the relationships between CTs and bandwidth constraints (BC0 to BC7). Three bandwidth constraints models are currently specified and supported by the DS-TE protocol extensions: the Russian Dolls Model (RDM) (see [DSTE-RDM]), the Maximum Allocation Model (MAM) (see [DSTE-MAM]), and the Maximum Allocation Model with Reservation (MAR) (see [DSTE-MAR]).

With RDM, the bandwidth constraints apply on CTs in a nested manner. For example, assuming that three CTs are in use:

- All LSPs from CT2 use no more than BC2.
- All LSPs from CT1 and CT2 together use no more than BC1.
- All LSPs from CT0, CT1, and CT2 together use no more than BC0.

With MAM, each bandwidth constraint applies independently to each CT, whereas the MPLS TE maximum reservable bandwidth constitutes an aggregate bandwidth constraint across all CTs. For example, assuming again that three CTS are in use, with MAM:

- All LSPs from CT2 use no more than BC2.
- All LSPs from CT1 use no more than BC1.
- All LSPs from CT0 use no more than BC0.
- All LSPs from CT0, CT1, and CT2 together use no more than the maximum reservable bandwidth.

The RDM and MAM models are illustrated in Figure 2-17 with three class types.

Figure 2-17   *RDM and MAM Bandwidth Constraint Models for DS-TE*

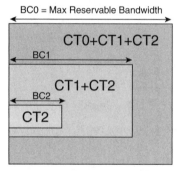

Russian Dolls Model (RDM)

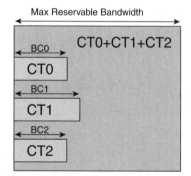

Maximum Allocation Model (MAM)

A single bandwidth constraints model must be used everywhere in a given DS-TE cloud.

The nested bandwidth constraints of RDM in the control plane match well the commonly used DiffServ bandwidth allocation policy in the data path which schedules real-time class with absolute priority, and then allocates most of the remaining bandwidth to the next priority class, and then most of the remaining bandwidth to the next class, and so on. For this reason, RDM can achieve very high link utilization while simultaneously guaranteeing quality of service to the various DiffServ classes. Also, through the use of preemption, RDM can guarantee that each CT will be granted a desired amount of bandwidth. Thus, RDM is often the bandwidth constraints model of choice in DS-TE deployments.

MAM may be attractive when simpler administrative bandwidth allocation policies (such as individually limiting each CT) are sought or when multiple classes are scheduled independently with comparable priorities in bandwidth allocation. However, MAM generally cannot achieve very high link utilization while simultaneously guaranteeing quality of service to all classes.

MAR is based on MAM, but with extensions aimed at addressing the limitation of MAM that we just mentioned. To that end, with MAR, class types are actually allowed to exceed their bandwidth constraints in the absence of contention but revert to them when contention across class types occurs. However, MAR brings significant additional complexity, and its applicability is not yet well understood.

Extensions to the Traffic Engineering LSP Attribute

DS-TE adds one TE LSP attribute, which is the class type. In accordance with the bandwidth constraints model in use, this determines the bandwidth constraints that are applicable to that DS-TE LSP.

Extensions to TE LSP Path Computation

The exact same algorithm for path computation can be used for DS-TE. The only difference is that the algorithm needs to take into account the bandwidth available to the particular combination of the preemption level and the CT of the TE LSP under consideration.

Extensions to Traffic Engineering IGP Routing

With DS-TE each link can be configured with up to eight bandwidth constraints.

Recall that the IGP has been extended for MPLS TE to advertise up to eight values of available bandwidth—one for each of the eight preemption levels. DS-TE simply generalizes these eight values as now advertising the available bandwidth for an arbitrary combination of preemption and class type. Thus, a given DS-TE network can only support a maximum of eight active combinations of preemption and CTs. For example, a DS-TE network may use eight CTs with one preemption level for each, or four CTs with two preemption levels for each, but it cannot use five CTs with two preemption levels for each.

Extensions to TE LSP Signaling

DS-TE specifies one additional RSVP object to convey the TE LSP class type during RSVP-TE signaling. In particular, this allows admission control to take into account the corresponding bandwidth constraints.

Further details on the IGP and RSVP-TE extensions for DS-TE can be found in [DSTE-PROTO].

NOTE   All the DS-TE extensions are backward-compatible with regular TE, which behaves as a particular case of DS-TE in which a single CT is used with eight preemption levels. This allows smooth migration from regular TE deployments to DS-TE.

Routing onto DiffServ-Aware TE LSPs

As with TE LSPs, static routes and recursive static routes to BGP next hops can be used to steer traffic onto DS-TE LSPs. This can be done when traffic of different classes of service is destined for different prefix ranges. An example is when the voice traffic terminates in trunk voice gateways that are connected to dedicated LANs configured with specific prefix ranges.

For dynamic routing over DS-TE LSPs, the mechanism discussed earlier that dynamically routes traffic over TE LSPs needs to be extended to perform such routing on a per-class of service basis. It also must be able to take into account the suitability of tunnels to carry each class of service. For example, Cisco supports a CoS-Based Tunnel Selection (CBTS) feature that extends the autoroute feature to dynamically route and forward traffic to DS-TE tunnels on a per-prefix/per-class of service basis depending on the classes of service that tunnels are configured as eligible to carry.

Example of DS-TE Deployment

The canonical example of DS-TE deployment is where separate meshes of tunnels are built for voice and data traffic. The voice TE LSPs and data TE LSPs can then be engineered specifically against the respective quality of service requirements of voice and data traffic. For example, the operator may use the RDM model to ensure that the voice load stays below 50 percent of the link capacity (to control delay and jitter for voice and to ensure that the rest of the traffic is allocated sufficient bandwidth) while the aggregate load across both voice and data is limited to 100 percent of the link capacity. Also, the path for each voice TE LSP is computed by taking into account only the voice load. It may be optimized on a metric reflecting propagation delay, with a high preemption level to ensure that voice TE LSPs are as close as achievable to their shortest path and that they can be protected by Fast Reroute. As shown in Figure 2-18, such a DS-TE deployment ensures that, whenever possible, the voice traffic follows the path resulting in minimal delay (the upper path in the figure), while the data traffic follows the path offering the necessary bandwidth (the lower path in the figure).

Figure 2-18 *Sample DS-TE Deployment for Voice and Data*

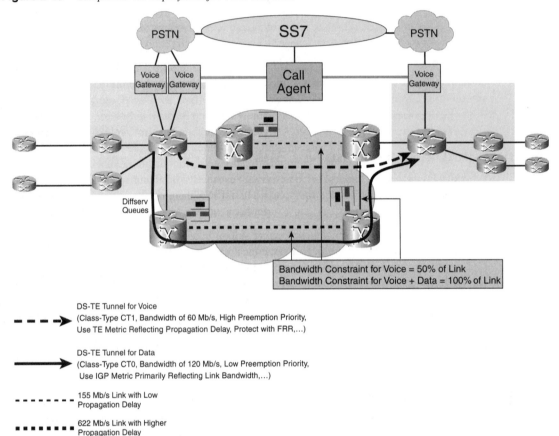

MPLS Traffic Engineering in the Context of Multiarea and Multi-AS

You have seen that in a distributed path computation environment the headend router is responsible for computing the TE LSP path, taking into account the TE LSP attributes and network topology and resource information provided by the IGP. Note that the headend router is also responsible for reoptimization should a better path appear in the network. However, what happens if the headend and tail-end routers reside in different IGP areas or autonomous systems? There are several issues to sort out.

The first issue is *path computation* because the headend and tail-end routers do not reside within the same IGP area. Because of this, the headend does not have the required information to compute an end-to-end path satisfying the set of constraints. There are two possible solutions:

- Per-area/AS path computation
- Path computation element

The per-area/AS path computation solution consists of configuring a set of hops that the TE LSP must traverse. (We usually call these "loose hops" because they only loosely specify the path; the router hops between the loose hops are not specified.) The loose hops are the Area Border Routers (ABRs) and Autonomous System Boundary Routers (ASBRs) in the case of interarea and inter-AS MPLS TE, respectively. Note that this is a minimum requirement; the network administrator may decide to specify additional hops.

For example, consider Figure 2-19. It depicts the situation of a TE LSP from R1 (in area 0.0.0.1) to R10 (in area 0.0.0.2), assuming OSPF for illustration purposes. The per-area path computation just mentioned works as follows: The network administrator configures a few loose hops, such as ABR1, ABR3, and R10. R1 (the headend router in this example) first computes the path in area 0.0.0.1 because it has all the required information (the path is R1–R2–R3–ABR1). Then R1 calls RSVP-TE to signal the TE LSP by means of an RSVP Path message. Instead of specifying the complete path to the destination, this message contains a set of strict hops (within area 0.0.0.1) and loose hops (outside area 0.0.0.1). Note that by strict hops we mean a set of hops directly connected to each other. Upon receiving the RSVP Path message, ABR1 determines that the next hop is a loose hop (ABR3 in this example). In fact, this is explicitly signaled in RSVP (a flag specifies whether that hop is a loose hop). Hence, ABR1 computes the shortest path satisfying the set of constraints in its own area (the backbone area 0.0.0.0) to reach ABR3 by running CSPF and taking into account the topology and resource information pertaining to area 0.0.0.0. The same process is then performed by ABR3 to reach R10. Note that a similar path computation solution applies equally to a TE LSP spanning multiple autonomous systems. This provides a simple approach that does not require any additional routing or signaling extensions beyond [RSVP-TE]. If ABR1 or ABR3 cannot find a path that satisfies the set of constraints, another combination of loose hops can be selected.

Although quite simple, the downside of such an approach is that it cannot guarantee the computation of the shortest path end to end. Indeed, if you study Figure 2-19, you see that R1, ABR1, and ABR3 all compute the shortest path to the next loose hop that satisfies the set of constraints. However, the resulting end-to-end path is not in this case the shortest path end to end. In this example, the shortest path (assuming that it satisfies the set of constraints) is R1–R4–ABR2–R6–R7–ABR4–R10. This is one of the main weaknesses of this approach. Another limitation is related to the ability to compute diversely routed paths between a pair of routers. With such a path-computation approach, the idea is to start computing the first path, record the set of visited routers, and signal the second path by indicating the set of hops to avoid to guarantee path diversity. Such a two-step approach may lead to situations where no solution can be found even though a solution exists. This is inherent in the fact that both paths are not computed simultaneously.

Figure 2-19 *Inter-AS MPLS Traffic Engineering*

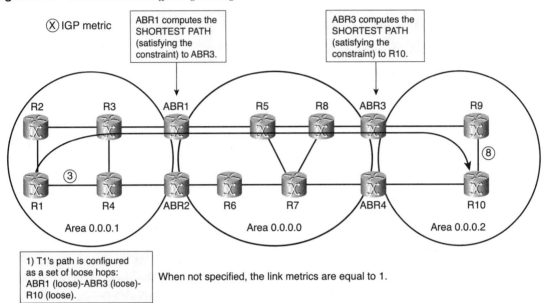

The path computation element is another solution that has been proposed to address the shortcomings of the previous approach and compute an optimal (shortest path) interarea/AS TE LSP path. Such a path-computation technique is described in detail in [INTER-AREA-AS]. Note that PCE-based TE LSP path computation techniques are discussed in the IETF PCE Working Group (see [PCE]). It relies on a router's ability to send a path-computation request to a Path Computation Element (PCE), which can be an ABR in the case of interarea MPLS TE or an ASBR for inter-AS MPLS TE. In a nutshell, the requesting router sends the request to a dynamically discovered (by means of IGP extensions) PCE attached to its local area or AS and referred to as the headend PCE. If the destination of the TE LSP belongs to an area the headend PCE is attached to, the PCE can compute the shortest path to the destination because it has the required information (indeed, the PCE has the network topology and resource information for both areas). Otherwise, the headend PCE relays the request to another PCE, which in turn computes all the shortest paths obeying the set of constraints from every ABR in the tail-end area to the TE LSP destination. Upon receiving the set of computed paths, the headend PCE can compute a shortest path end to end and return it to the requesting headend router. The PCE solution is recursive backward and relies on distributed path computation. It allows for the computation of end-to-end shortest paths and diverse paths if they exist. A detailed example is provided in Chapter 5 in the context of Inter-AS TE LSPs used to interconnect virtual POPs.

The next issue to consider is *TE LSP reoptimization*. Handling reoptimization in the context of interarea/AS MPLS TE is slightly more challenging than in the case of a flat IGP area. Indeed, how does the headend router detect that a more optimal (shortest) path exists if it happens to be in another area/AS?

One approach might be to systematically try to resignal any interarea/AS TE LSP without knowing beforehand whether a more optimal path exists. If it turns out that one of the ABRs can find a better path, the TE LSP follows the better path. However, such a solution has the drawback of systematically resignaling the interarea/AS TE LSP (which implies RSVP processing, new label allocation, and so forth) even if no better path exists.

Hence, a solution (available on Cisco routers) has been proposed in [LOOSE-PATH-REOPT]. It allows the headend to be informed of the existence of a more optimal path in some downstream area/AS, either after having explicitly sent an inbound request or by means of explicit notification from the ABR that has detected the presence of a better path. In the former case, the headend router simply sets a specific bit in the RSVP Path message that triggers the reevaluation of the existing path on each node whose next hop is defined as a loose hop (for instance, ABRs 1 and 3 in Figure 2-19). If a better path (than the current path) exists, the ABR notifies the headend router, which in turn performs a reoptimization. If no better path exists, the ABR stays silent. Furthermore, the ABR also can explicitly notify the headend router of the existence of a better path without being explicitly polled by the headend.

If PCE-based path computation is used, the reoptimization process is similar to a regular path computation request, except that the existing path is provided to the PCE. (This is necessary because the PCE might be stateless and does not keep state related to existing TE LSPs. Therefore, providing the relevant information related to the existing TE LSP, such as the current path, bandwidth, and so on, lets you avoid double-booking the bandwidth.)

With both methods, as soon as the headend router is informed of the existence of a better path and decides to reoptimize a TE LSP, the corresponding TE LSP rerouting that follows is similar to the intra-area case. The rerouting is performed by means of the non-traffic-disruptive make-before-break procedure.

The case of an inter-AS TE LSP has several commonalities with interarea MPLS TE in terms of path computation, reoptimization, and so on. The IETF defined the set of requirements for inter-AS MPLS Traffic Engineering in [INTER-AS-TE-REQS]. In this section, we will just highlight the most significant specificities of inter-AS MPLS TE.

The first specificity of inter-AS TE is related to the existence and nonvisibility of the inter-ASBR links. In most situations, autonomous systems are interconnected by non-IGP-enabled inter-ASBR links (the routing protocol in use is usually BGP-4). Hence, a headend router does not have the visibility of the ASBR links and in particular the TE link characteristics such as bandwidth, affinities, and so on.

One obvious solution is to use the per-AS path computation approach described earlier and specify all the ASBRs as loose hops. However, in the case of an inter-AS TE LSP, this requires configuring quite a significant number of hops (such as ASBR1, ASBR3, ASBR5, ASBR7, and R9 for an inter-AS TE LSP from R1 to R9 in Figure 2-20). You also have to configure a potentially large number of combinations of loose hops on the headend router to handle the case of LSP setup failure. Furthermore, having the visibility of the inter-ASBR would allow the headend to make a more efficient path computation.

Figure 2-20 *Nonvisibility of the Inter-AS TE Links*

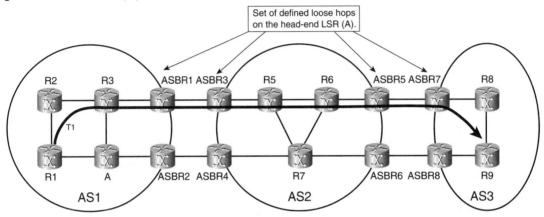

For example, suppose that the link ASBR1–ASBR3 does not meet the bandwidth requirement of T1. Because R1 (the headend in this example) does not know the state of that link, it may try to signal the TE LSP across that link. In this case, ASBR1 would reject the TE LSP (by returning an RSVP Path Error). R1 would then try another combination of loose hops. Hence, a more efficient solution implemented on Cisco routers consists of flooding inter-ASBR link state, although no IGP routing adjacency is established between the two ASBRs. This allows a reduction in the number of ASBRs that are required to be configured as loose hops and improves the path computation efficiency. This is illustrated in Figure 2-21.

Figure 2-21 *Flooding of Inter-AS links*

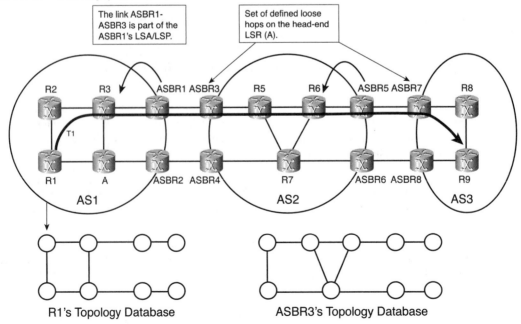

Thanks to this capability, T1 can be configured with the following simplified sets of loose hops: ASBR3–ASBR7–R9 or ASBR4–ASBR8–R9.

The second key aspect and requirement in the case of inter-AS MPLS TE deployed between autonomous systems belonging to different companies (also called interprovider) is the need for policy control at AS boundaries. Indeed, it is desirable to deploy some policy control functions on ASBRs to enforce the agreement between autonomous systems. More specifically, the policy control module ensures that the total amount of bandwidth consumed by the inter-AS TE LSPs does not exceed some agreed-upon value. It may also be desirable to check various TE LSP attributes such as the preemption value and the number of TE LSPs.

Finally, an important aspect to highlight in the case of PCE-based inter-AS TE path computation is the requirement to use consistent metrics across multiple autonomous systems. Indeed, as explained previously (and as described in detail in Chapter 5 by means of an example), the end-to-end shortest path is computed thanks to a recursive backward algorithm that relies on the computation of path segments by each PCE for its own domain. Consequently, this requires that each PCE use comparable metrics to compute an end-to-end shortest path. A common practice is to use a common scheme to compute the TE metric across the various autonomous systems traversed by the inter-AS TE LSPs.

Core Network Availability

This section discusses how you can improve network availability by means of various network recovery mechanisms, which allow for the rerouting of the affected traffic along an alternate path.

Network recovery mechanisms are available at various layers (optical, SONET/SDH, MPLS/IP, and so on). A detailed reference on this topic is [NET-RECOV]. However, this section focuses on the recovery techniques provided by IP routing and MPLS Traffic Engineering.

When electing a particular network recovery mechanism (or sometimes a set of mechanisms), you should first determine the overall objectives in terms of network availability. Such objectives are usually driven by the application requirements. For instance, the requirement in terms of availability for ATM traffic carried over MPLS is undoubtedly significantly more stringent than for the Internet traffic. Moreover, even for a specific application such as VoIP, the requirements may vary from one service provider to another. Indeed, consider a network carrying VoIP traffic. If the objective is to ensure that a voice call will not be dropped in case of a network element failure, a convergence time of several seconds (usually about 2 seconds, although such a value greatly depends on the tolerance of the VoIP gateway's signaling protocol) is perfectly acceptable. On the other hand, if the service provider wants to offer VoIP service that can tolerate any network element failure without any noticeable degradation for the user, the recovery mechanism must be able to reroute the traffic within a few tens of milliseconds along a backup path offering stringent QoS guarantees. This highlights the fact that the objectives must first be clearly established so as to come up with the most appropriate network recovery design.

After you have determined the network recovery objectives, you should evaluate the various available network recovery mechanisms while keeping in mind various criteria. The convergence time is obviously the first one that comes to mind. How much time is required to reroute the traffic upon a network element failure? This is clearly a critical aspect to consider, but certainly not the only one. The following are a few other important aspects:

- **The scope of recovery**—Determines whether the recovery mechanism can handle link failure, Shared Risk Link Group (SRLG) failure, or node failure. As a reminder, the concept of SRLG relates to the notion of multiple links sharing a common resource whose failure would provoke all the links to fail simultaneously. For example, consider the case of multiple links routed across the same fiber. A fiber cut would imply the failure of all the links. We say that they share the same SRLG.

- **QoS during failure**—Does the alternate path (usually called a backup path) provide an equivalent QoS?

- **Network overhead**—This relates to the number of extra state required in the network by the recovery mechanism.

- **Cost**—There is a very wide range of network recovery mechanisms whose costs vary by several orders of magnitude. For instance, an optical 1+1 protection mechanism, although very efficient in terms of rerouting time and QoS along the backup path, requires additional equipment for the traffic replication and some extra bandwidth dedicated to protection (actually as much bandwidth as the protected bandwidth). On the other hand, other recovery mechanisms such as IP are usually cheaper both in terms of extra equipment and network resources (of course, they may not provide the same level of performance).

- **Network stability**—Does the network recovery under some circumstances (such as when very fast recovery is required) potentially lead to network instability when faced with frequent path changes?

This list is not meant to be exhaustive. It simply provides some of the most important aspects to evaluate when considering a network recovery mechanism. These different aspects are illustrated throughout this book in the various case studies.

In some cases, it might be desirable to elect to use a combination of recovery mechanisms, although such an option requires some extra care to avoid race conditions between recovery mechanisms and double protection, which may lead to a lack of optimality in terms of backup resources. For instance, a common approach consists of combining SONET protection with fine-tuning Interior Gateway Protocol (IGP) rerouting.

Protection Versus Restoration

There are actually two families of network recovery mechanisms—protection and restoration. A protection mechanism relies on the precomputation (and signaling) of a backup (alternate) path before any failure. In contrast, a restoration mechanism requires the computation of the backup path only after the failure has occurred; in other words, the backup path is computed on the fly. In terms of convergence time, protection mechanisms are usually faster but also require more network overhead because extra state is required.

Local Versus Global Recovery

This other characteristic of a network recovery mechanism relates to the location of the node in charge of redirecting the traffic along a backup path. A recovery mechanism is said to be local when the node immediately upstream of the failure is responsible for rerouting the traffic should a failure occur. Conversely, with a global recovery mechanism, such as the default rerouting mode of MPLS TE, described in this section, the headend of the affected TE LSP is in charge of the rerouting.

You will see various network recovery mechanisms: IP routing (restoration), MPLS TE headend reroute (global restoration), MPLS TE path protection (global protection), and MPLS TE Fast Reroute (local protection).

Before describing the recovery mechanisms involved in IP routing and MPLS Traffic Engineering, it is worth introducing the notion of a recovery cycle. It can be used to describe the different steps involved in any network recovery procedure (see Figure 2-22).

Figure 2-22   *The Recovery Cycle*

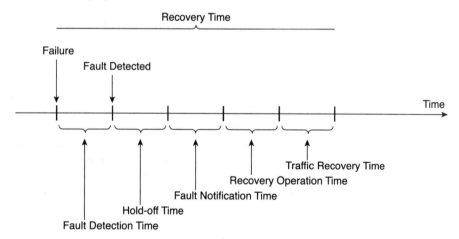

The first phase of the recovery process is failure detection. Its duration is a function of various parameters such as the Layer 1 or 2 protocol in use, the keepalive mechanisms (when required in some environments), and so on. You will see various illustrations of the mechanisms involved and typical failure detection times in the various cases studies. Typically, the failure detection time can range from a few milliseconds to several seconds or even tens of seconds in some cases.

As soon as the fault is detected, it might be desirable to wait for a certain amount of time (the hold-off time) before triggering any action. For instance, this can be the case when IP routing is used in conjunction with optical protection. As soon as the fault is detected, IP waits for a configurable period of time to maximize the chance that the optical layer will recover from the fault. If the fault has not been cleared after the hold-off period, the recovery mechanism is activated.

The next phase is called fault notification. It may take some time to signal the fault to the node that can reroute the traffic onto an alternate path. In the example of local recovery, the fault notification time is, of course, null. Conversely, with a global recovery mechanism, the fault notification has to be propagated upstream of the failure to the node responsible for the rerouting, which may take a nonnegligible amount of time.

The two final steps are related to the traffic recovery itself and depend on the recovery mechanism in use. In a nutshell, they refer to the actual operation of rerouting the traffic.

Network Recovery with IP Routing

Over the years, several routing protocols have been designed. Two major families of routing protocols exist: distance vector protocols (such as Routing Information Protocol [RIP] and EIGRP) and link-state routing protocols (such as Open Shortest Path First [OSPF] and Intermediate System-to-Intermediate System [IS-IS]).

This section focuses on link-state protocols such as OSPF and IS-IS because they have been deployed in most service provider networks because of their superiority in terms of scalability, optimality, and convergence properties.

Link-state routing protocols rely on the concept of a Link-State Database (LSDB)—a collection of Protocol Data Units (PDUs) called Link-State Advertisements in OSPF (see [OSPFv2]) and Link-State Packets in IS-IS (see [ISIS])—that describes some part of the overall network topology and IP address reachability. (This section uses the generic term LSA for both OSPF and IS-IS.) Each router is responsible for originating one or more LSAs (depending on whether we refer to IS-IS or OSPF) and the collection of all the LSAs originated by each router constitutes the LSDB. In contrast to the distance vector protocols, each router running a link-state routing protocol has a complete view of the network topology through its LSDB. Then an algorithm known as the Dijkstra algorithm allows for the computation of the Shortest Path Tree (SPT), according to a specific metric, from the computing router (the tree root) to every reachable node in the network. Finally, based on this SPT, each node builds its routing table, which contains the shortest path to each reachable IP prefix in the network.

A crucial aspect of link-state routing is of course to guarantee the synchronization of all the routers' LSDBs within a routing domain. This is of the utmost importance to avoid routing loops (because routers with different views of the network topology may make inconsistent routing decisions, leading to a routing loop). Such a lack of synchronization between LSDBs can occur during transient states for a temporary period, as illustrated later in this section.

Although OSPF and IS-IS differ in many respects, they are quite similar as far as the recovery aspects are concerned. Thus, this section applies equally to OSPF and IS-IS.

Let's start with the situation during steady state. As shown in Figure 2-23, in steady state, all the routers have an identical LSDB. The Hello protocol is used between neighboring routers to check that each neighbor is "alive" by means of short messages exchanged at regular intervals (we usually say that a router maintains routing adjacencies).

Figure 2-23   *Link-State Routing Protocols*

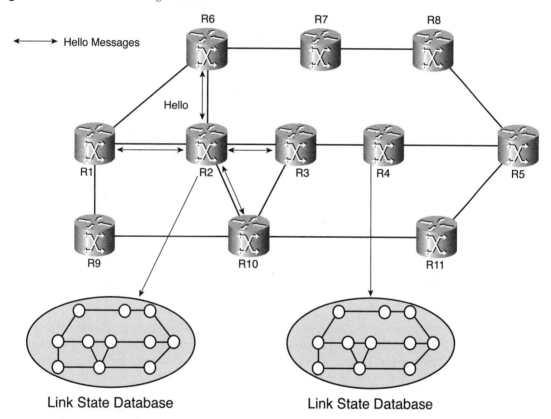

Given the steady state, we can describe the major steps of the IP routing recovery cycle upon failure. For the sake of illustration, consider the case of a failure of the link R4–R5, as shown in Figure 2-24.

Figure 2-24 *Mode of Operation of IP Routing Upon Failure*

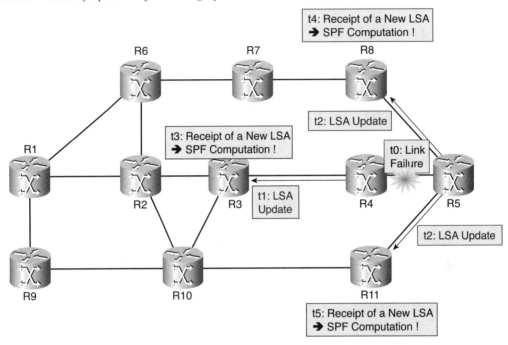

At time t0, a failure occurs (for example, the link R4–R5). As with any recovery mechanism, the first phase is detecting the failure. As already pointed out, the fault detection time is a function of many factors, such as the underlying Layer 1 or 2 protocol, the tuning of the Hello message frequency, and so on.

A router's detection of the failure (R4 and R5 in this example) triggers the creation of a new LSA reflecting the topology change. However, it may be useful to delay the origination of this LSA for propagation to other routers (the notion of hold-off timer, described earlier in this section). The delay between the triggering of an LSA and the origination of the LSA is usually a dynamic function in modern router implementations. Later you will see the set of mechanisms used to control the LSA origination frequency and why such a dynamic timer scheme is so useful. When the LSA origination timer expires (at time t1 on R4 and time t2 on R5 in this example), the LSA is flooded throughout the network such that each router can reflect the topology change in its LSDB and recompute its routing table.

Suppose that R3 receives R4's LSA at time t3. R3 first checks whether the received LSA is "new" (whether it reflects a network topology change or just an LSA refresh). If the LSA signals a topology change, a new routing table calculation is triggered (usually called an SPF computation). Similar to the case of the LSA origination, there is a timer between an SPF and its execution. Indeed, in the case of multiple simultaneous failures (such as a node failure, which can result in the failure of many of its connected links), a node receives multiple new

LSAs (for example, from every neighbor of the failing resource). Hence, waiting for some time before computing the SPF may be a good idea so as to get the most accurate new topology before computing the new routing table. The reason why it is desirable to have a dynamic timer will become clear through the various case studies.

NOTE   The timing shown in this example is given for the sake of illustration. Different sequences of events could occur. (For instance, the router R8 could receive R5's LSA before R3 receives R4's LSA.)

For a link failure, although two LSAs are systematically originated, one by each end of the failed link, the receipt of one LSA is sufficient to exclude that link for SPF computation. Indeed, before considering a link in its SPT, a router always checks that the link is announced by both ends of the link (this is called a two-way connectivity check).

The LSA flooding process is reliable. The receipt of an LSA must always be acknowledged. The nonreceipt of an acknowledgment triggers the resending of the LSA.

Upon receipt of R4's LSA, R3 recomputes a new routing table so as to reroute the traffic accordingly. For instance, the traffic from R1 to R5 in this case is rerouted along the path R3–R10–R11–R5. Consider a slightly different network topology without any link between R3 and R10. In such a situation, the first node that can reroute the traffic from R1 to R5 is R2. This highlights the importance of R4's LSA being quickly flooded by R3 (before computing its own SPF) with minimal delay, because the rerouting node is now several hops upstream from the failure. Thus, speeding up the LSA propagation is of the utmost importance so as to increase the convergence time. This involves trying to limit the processing delay on each node by means of various router internal mechanisms. This provides the appropriate priority to the LSA flooding process and potentially the use of QoS mechanisms to reduce the queuing delays experienced by LSA packets.

As soon as a new LSA or set of new LSAs is received, each router starts an SPF computation, which is actually made up of two components: the SPT computation and the routing table update (where the shortest path for each prefix is computed). Of course, there are no simple rules for computing the SPF duration because it depends on many factors, such as the network size and topology, the number of IP prefixes in the network, and so on. But to give an order of magnitude, an optimized SPT computation rarely exceeds a few tens of milliseconds in a large network with hundreds of routers. On the other hand, the routing table computation is usually on the order of several hundreds of milliseconds for networks with a few thousand IP prefixes. An interesting optimization of SPF called Incremental SPF (iSPF) allows for a drastic reduction of the SPT and routing table computation time in many failure circumstances by selectively recomputing the SPT only in the parts of the topology where it is necessary.

The final step consists of updating the Forwarding Information Base (FIB) residing on the line cards in the case of a distributed routing architecture. Note that this last step may require some time (which could be on the order of a few hundreds of milliseconds in the case of large FIBs).

Use of Dynamic Timers for LSA Origination and SPF Triggering

As previously mentioned, dynamic timers are used to control both the origination of an LSA and the triggering of SPF computation. Any recovery mechanism has the goal of trying to provide fast restoration of a network element affected by a failure that requires fast reaction to such failure events. In the example of IP routing, you saw that a router detecting a loss of a routing adjacency provoked by a link or neighbor node failure originates a new LSA reflecting the network topology change. Such an LSA is flooded throughout the network, and every router receiving this new LSA consequently triggers a new routing table calculation. To decrease the overall convergence time, it is desirable for every router connected to the failed resource to quickly originate a new LSA and for every router receiving such a new LSA to quickly trigger an SPF computation. But this requires some caution so as to protect the network from unstable network elements. Consider the case of a "flapping" link. If a new LSA is quickly originated at each link state change, this would unavoidably result in frequent IGP LSA updates and SPF triggering on every router in the network, potentially leading to network instability. Thus, the solution to this problem is to use a dynamic timer to quickly react to simple failures but also dampen the LSA origination and SPF triggering if frequent network state changes occur in the network. The algorithm used on a Cisco router to dynamically compute such a timer is based on exponential back-off with three parameters used by the router. (Example 2-1 is given for the IS-IS LSP origination but applies equally to the SPF triggering.)

Example 2-1 *Exponential Back-Off*

```
!
router isis
lsp-gen A B C
```

Parameter B in Example 2-1 specifies in milliseconds how long the router detecting the loss of adjacency for the first time waits before originating a new LSP. If a second state change occurs, the router waits for C milliseconds. If a third state change happens, the router waits for 2 * C, and then 4 * C, and so on up to a maximum of A seconds. At this stage, the delay between the origination of two LSPs is A seconds if the link keeps flapping. Then if the link stays in a stable state for 2 * A seconds, the router returns to the original behavior. This is illustrated in Figure 2-25.

Figure 2-25   *Exponential Back-Off Algorithm for LSA Origination*

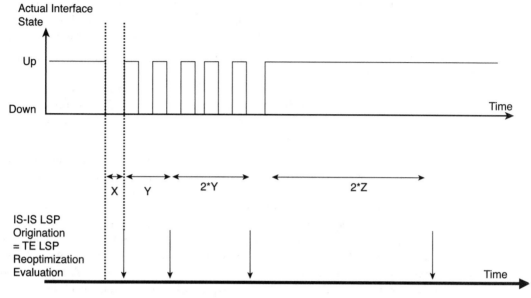

Exponential Back-Off Algorithm for LSA Origination

A similar algorithm is used for SPF triggering.

Such an exponential back-off algorithm allows for quick reaction while preserving network stability in case of unstable network elements. Several examples of parameter setting for both LSA origination and SPF triggering are provided throughout this book.

Computing the Convergence Time with IP Routing

You have seen the different steps that occur during the IP recovery process. As soon as the failure is detected, each neighboring router of the failed resource originates a new LSA after a timer has elapsed. Each LSA is reliably flooded throughout the network. Finally, each node receiving a new LSA (reflecting a topology change) triggers an SPF computation after another timer has also elapsed. Consequently, the total convergence time depends on quite a long list of factors: the routing timer settings, the network topology and number of prefixes, and so on. Several examples are provided in various case studies, but we'll give you an order of magnitude, with some careful design rules. Rerouting times on the order of 1 second can be achieved in very large networks but require some nonnegligible engineering work. Also, you should keep in mind two important aspects inherent in IP routing:

- **Lack of predictability**—All the routers of course eventually converge, but the exact event timing is hard to predict.

- **Transient routing loops**—Because the flooding of a new LSA takes some time, at some point the various routers in the network may have unsynchronized LSDBs. Hence, having different views of the network topology, they may make routing decisions leading to loops. That being said, these loops are temporary and are cleared as soon as all the routers converge.

As explained earlier, it may be desirable to wait for a certain period of time before flooding an LSA or computing an SPF. For instance, when flooding a new LSA, it may be desirable to wait for some time to expire in case another lower-layer recovery mechanism can restore the failed resource. When computing an SPF, in case of a node failure, several LSAs are originated. Hence, waiting before computing the SPF increases your chances of getting an accurate LSDB before computing a new routing table.

To protect the network from instability caused by a flapping network resource, a dynamic timer is desirable. The case of an unstable link is a good example. Without a dynamic LSA origination timer, both R4 and R5 would constantly originate new LSAs that would in turn generate some potentially nonnegligible routing control updates and would also trigger new routing table computations on each node—which, of course, is highly undesirable. Hence, a back-off mechanism has been designed to quickly react (originate the new LSA) when a link first fails and then slow down the LSA origination if the link flaps. The algorithm (available on Cisco routers) used by the back-off mechanism has three parameters: T1, T2, and T3. T1 specifies how long a router that has detected a link failure (more precisely, a loss of routing adjacency) waits before originating a new LSA. If a second state change occurs, the router waits for T2 before originating a new LSA. If the link keeps flapping, the period between successive LSA originations doubles at each change, up to a maximum value of T3. If the link remains in a stable state for 2 * T3, the router reverts to the original behavior. Such an algorithm allows for fast reaction upon single failure while protecting the network in case of unstable resources. A similar algorithm can be used for the SPF calculation, which also provides an efficient mechanism for fast convergence while protecting the router from some misbehaving router(s) or some major network instability conditions.

A common misperception is that IGPs converge in tens of seconds. This section has shown that in reality this can be reduced to 1 to 2 seconds with appropriate tuning. Furthermore, IP routing inherently provides backup bandwidth sharing. Indeed, no resource is reserved beforehand should a resource fail. Hence, the available bandwidth can be used to reroute any traffic upon failure. On the other hand, subsecond rerouting time is much more difficult to achieve. Other network recovery mechanisms are probably more suitable for such requirements. Moreover, guaranteeing equivalent QoS in case of network failure is also quite challenging.

Network Recovery with MPLS Traffic Engineering

MPLS Traffic Engineering provides a full spectrum of network recovery mechanisms. We will first review the default recovery mode (called MPLS TE reroute) based on global restoration, and then path protection (global protection), and finally MPLS Fast Reroute (local protection). Each mechanism differs in its ability to meet various recovery requirements such as rerouting times, scope of recovery, ability to provide equivalent QoS during failure, required amount of extra state, and so on. Depending on its requirements, a service provider then can elect the appropriate MPLS TE recovery mechanism.

MPLS TE Reroute

MPLS TE reroute, the default mode of network recovery of MPLS Traffic Engineering, is a global restoration mechanism:

- **Global**—The node in charge of rerouting a TE LSP affected by a network element failure is the headend router.

- **Restoration**—When the headend router is notified of the failure, a new path is dynamically computed, and the TE LSP is signaled along the new alternate path (assuming one can be found). For the sake of exhaustiveness, it is also possible to precompute or preconfigure an alternate path. Be aware that before any failure occurs, you should determine a path that is fully diverse from the active one, because you won't know about a failure beforehand.

Consider the example shown in Figure 2-26. A TE LSP T1 is initially set up along the path R1–R2–R3–R4–R5. The link R3–R4 fails. After a period of time (the fault detection time), the router R3 (and the router R4) detects the failure. Again, this period of time essentially depends on the failure type and the Layer 1 or 2 protocol. If you assume a Packet over SONET (PoS) interface, the fault failure detection time is usually on the order of a few milliseconds. In the absence of a hold-off timer, the router upstream of the failure immediately sends the failure notification (RSVP-TE Path Error message) to the headend router (R1 in this example).

Figure 2-26   *MPLS Traffic Engineering Reroute (Global Restoration)*

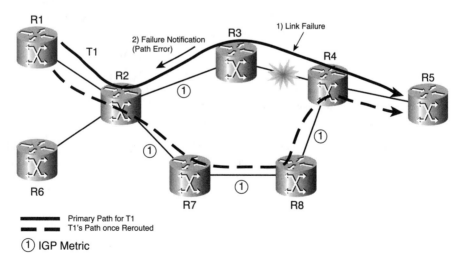

3) New Path Computation
4) Signaling of the New LSP
5) Update of the Routing Lable Entry

As soon as R1 is notified of the failure experienced by T1, it immediately triggers the computation of a new path (CSPF) for T1. (Even if the IGP LSA update has not been received yet, R1 prunes the link R3–R4 from its local traffic engineering database before recomputing a new path.) After the new path is computed, the new TE LSP is signaled along the newly computed shortest path obeying the set of constraints (R1–R2–R7–R8–R4–R5 in this example).

Accurately quantifying the time required to perform the set of operations just described is particularly difficult because of the many variables involved. These include the network topology (and hence the number of nodes the failure notification and the new LSP signaling messages have to go through and the propagation times of those through fiber), the number of TE LSPs affected by the failure, CPU processor on the routers, and so on. That being said, we can provide an order of magnitude. On a significantly large and loaded network, the CSPF time and RSVP-TE processing time per node are usually a few milliseconds. Then the propagation delay must be taken into account in the failure notification time as well as in the signaling time. So, on a continental network, MPLS TE headend rerouting would be on the order of hundreds of milliseconds.

MPLS TE Reroute is undoubtedly the simplest MPLS TE recovery mechanism because it does not require any specific configuration and minimizes the required amount of backup state in the network. The downside is that its rerouting time is not as fast and predictable as the other MPLS TE recovery techniques that are discussed next. Indeed, the fault first has to be signaled to the headend router, followed by a path computation and the signaling of a new TE LSP along another path, if any (thus with some risks that no backup path can be found, or at least with equivalent constraints).

MPLS TE Path Protection

Another network recovery mechanism available with MPLS TE is path protection. The principle is to precompute and presignal a TE LSP used as a backup in case the primary TE LSP is affected by a network element failure. The backup LSP path can be dynamically computed by the headend (by CSPF) or by means of an offline tool.

Consider the network shown in Figure 2-27. The backup LSP has to be diverse (which means it should not use any of the same facilities, such as links, as the protected TE LSP) because the fault location by definition is unknown beforehand. Multiple schemes offer various degrees of diversity and thus protect against different scopes of failure. Figure 2-27 shows an example of a backup path offering link diversity and a backup path offering node diversity.

Compared to MPLS TE reroute, path protection is obviously faster because it does not require computation of an alternate TE LSP path and resignaling of the new TE LSP before starting to reroute the traffic along the backup path. On the other hand, such a network recovery suffers from a lack of scalability because it requires doubling the number of TE LSPs in the network. Hence, creating a full mesh of TE LSPs between 50 routers with path protection requires the configuration of 4900 TE LSPs instead of 2450. Moreover, if some guarantees are required in terms of bandwidth along the backup paths, this implies extra bandwidth reservation, which cannot be used for other primary TE LSPs. Finally, the constraint of end-to-end path diversity may lead to following some nonoptimal paths in case of network failure.

Figure 2-27   *MPLS Traffic Engineering Path (Global Protection)*

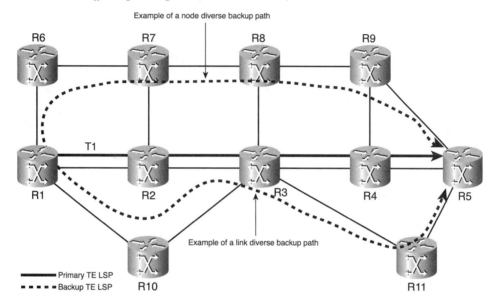

MPLS TE Fast Reroute

MPLS TE Fast Reroute, a local protection mechanism, is by far the most widely deployed MPLS TE recovery mechanism. It relies on the presignaling of backup tunnels at each node, which are used to locally reroute all the TE LSPs affected by a network failure. To protect a facility such as a link, SRLG, or node, the set of relevant routers must be configured. The set of required backup tunnels may be configured manually (in which case their paths are statically configured) or by means of automatic mechanisms (details of such mechanisms are seen in several case studies).

Consider the network shown in Figure 2-28. At each hop, a backup tunnel is configured that follows a diverse path from the protected facility. (In this case, the facility is links, but you will see that Fast Reroute can also be used to protect against SRLG and node failure.) Figure 2-28 illustrates the use of Fast Reroute to protect the link R2–R3.

Figure 2-28 *MPLS Traffic Engineering Fast Reroute (Link Protection)*

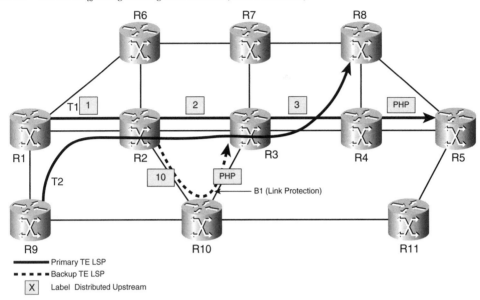

Mode of Operation Before Failure

We will now review the steps required to use MPLS TE Fast Reroute before any failure occurs.

As shown in Figure 2-28, a backup tunnel B1 from R2 to R3 is signaled before any failure. It protects all the TE LSPs that cross the link R2–R3 (such as T1 and T2). At this point, it is worth mentioning that the eligibility of a TE LSP to benefit from Fast Reroute along its path can be configured on a per-TE LSP basis and can be explicitly signaled in RSVP-TE. (Indeed, it may be desirable to protect only a selected subset of TE LSPs by means of Fast Reroute, based on various availability requirements.)

In this example, two TE LSPs traverse the link R2–R3. We will focus on the TE LSP T1. T1 is signaled along the path R1–R2–R3–R4–R5. (The corresponding labels distributed by RSVP-TE [Resv messages] are shown in Figure 2-28.) When the T1 LSP is first signaled, each LSR along the path determines whether the TE LSP is asking to be protected by Fast Reroute. If T1 is signaled with such a property, every router tries to select a backup tunnel to protect the TE LSP should a link fail. In the case of T1, R2 (also called a Point of Local Repair [PLR]) selects B1 as the backup tunnel to be used in case of failure of the link R2–R3. Each PLR selects a backup tunnel that meets the requirement to intersect the protected TE LSP on some downstream node (called the Merge Point [MP])—R3 in this example. RSVP-TE signaling lets you specify more parameters related to Fast Reroute, such as any requirement for bandwidth protection (in other words, whether a backup tunnel offering an equivalent QoS is required). We will revisit this aspect later.

Mode of Operation During and After Failure

Upon a link failure (the link R2–R3 in Figure 2-28), the first step of the recovery cycle is the failure detection by the PLR (R2). As already pointed out, depending on the failure detection mechanism in use, this can range from a few milliseconds (PoS alarms) to a few tens or hundreds of milliseconds. Various failure-detection mechanisms are examined in the case studies. As soon as the failure is detected, the PLR triggers the following set of actions:

- Each protected TE LSP (for which a backup tunnel was selected before the failure) enters "protection active" mode. In this mode the regular label-swap operation is performed, followed by a label push and the immediate redirection of the traffic along the backup tunnel path. In other words, each protected TE LSP is encapsulated onto the selected backup tunnel and then is label-switched along the backup tunnel path until it reaches the MP (R3). For instance, in this example, the label is first swapped by the PLR R2 from 1 to 2 (as in the steady state), the label 10 is then pushed onto the label stack, and the rerouted traffic is sent to R10. Note that R10 does not see any specific change here (no state related to the rerouted TE LSP is created on the LSR along the backup tunnel path). R10 performs a regular operation (PHP) and sends the traffic to R3. Finally, R3 receives a labeled packet with the label value 2 (as in steady state) but from another interface, which does not pose any problem with global label space allocation platforms such as routers. A regular label-swap operation is performed by R3 (from 2 to 3) followed by a PHP performed by R4 until the IP packet is delivered to the TE LSP destination, R5.

- Because the path followed by a rerouted TE LSP may no longer be optimal end-to-end, a notification is sent by the PLR to the headend router of a rerouted TE LSP. In turn, the headend router triggers a nondisruptive reoptimization by means of the make-before-break procedure explained in the section "Reoptimization of a Traffic Engineering LSP."

- As soon as local rerouting occurs, the PLR must refresh the set of rerouted TE LSP onto the backup tunnel. Indeed, RSVP-TE is a soft-state protocol; hence, the state of each TE LSP must be regularly refreshed. You already saw that refreshes are performed by sending RSVP-TE Path and Resv messages (downstream and upstream, respectively). This also applies to a rerouted TE LSP. Consequently, for each TE LSP rerouted onto a backup tunnel, the PLR must keep refreshing the TE LSP state by sending Path messages to the downstream neighbor onto the backup tunnel. (Note that those RSVP-TE Path messages are label-switched from the PLR to the MP, so they are not seen by any intermediate node along the backup path. This explains why the rerouted TE LSPs do not create any additional state along the backup path.) It is also important to mention that in some cases the headend router may not be able to reroute the affected TE LSP. In this case, the rerouted TE LSP stays in this mode until a reoptimization can occur. This highlights the need to refresh the state of such locally rerouted TE LSPs. Several additional details are related to the signaling procedures when Fast Reroute is triggered; they are described in [FRR].

But why should the state be refreshed downstream if its respective headend router will eventually quickly reoptimize the TE LSPs? There are two reasons. First, depending on the RSVP-TE timer setting and the event sequence timing, the state for the rerouted TE LSP may time out before the headend router has had time to effectively reoptimize the affected TE LSP end to end. Another reason might be the impossibility for the headend router to find an alternate path obeying the set of required constraints. In such a case, an implementation should maintain the rerouted TE LSP in its current state (along the back tunnel) to avoid TE LSP failure, until a more optimal path can be found.

The situation as soon as Fast Reroute has been triggered (also called *during failure*) is shown in Figure 2-29.

Figure 2-29   *Mode of Operation for MPLS Traffic Engineering (Link Protection)*

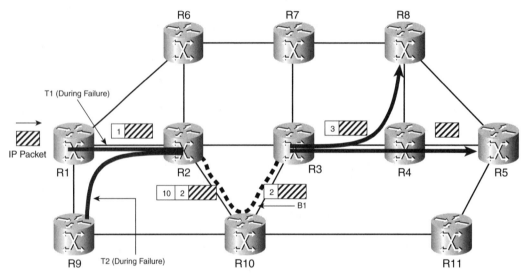

Note that the labels depicted in this diagram just correspond to the TE LSPT1 but a similar operation is performed for the TE LSP T2.

The Fast Reroute mode of operation has been described using the example of link protection, but the use of Fast Reroute is not limited to link protection. It also protects TE LSPs from node failure. This is illustrated in Figure 2-30.

The objective now is to protect a TE LSP from a node failure. In the example, the solution is to presignal a backup tunnel bypassing the node to protect (also called the next-next hop [NNHOP] backup tunnel). Therefore, you would signal a backup tunnel B2 from the PLR (R2) to the MP (which is the PLR's next-next hop—R4 in our example). As soon as the PLR detects a node failure, the exact same principle is applied, and the affected TE LSPs (that follow the path R2–R3–R4) are rerouted onto B2.

Figure 2-30   *MPLS Traffic Engineering Fast Reroute (Node Protection)*

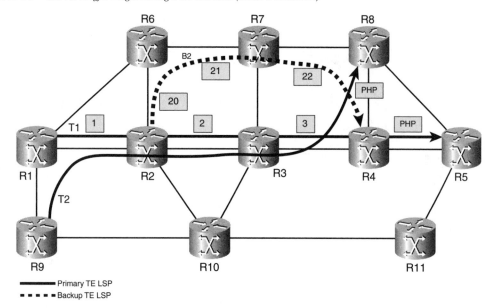

Primary TE LSP
Backup TE LSP

One additional issue must be solved. In the regular RSVP-TE mode of operation, the labels are distributed in the upstream direction (from the tail-end router to the headend router) on a hop-by-hop basis. For instance, R4 binds the label 3 to R3, R3 distributes the label 2 to R2, and R2 distributes the label 1 to R1. Note that R2 does not know (and, at steady state, R2 does not need to know) which label is used between R3 and R4. It only requires the label expected by R3. You saw in the previous example that when Fast Reroute is triggered, the PLR first performs the regular label-swap operation. So applying the same set of rules, the PLR (R2) would perform a label-swap operation (1 to 2) and then push the label 20, which would be swapped along B2's path (20→21, 21→22) before a PHP is performed by the backup tunnel penultimate hop, R8. But then R4 receives label 2 even though it expects to receive label 3. This shows that in case of an NNHOP backup tunnel, the PLR must in fact swap the incoming label to the label value that the MP expects (3 in this example).

This is achieved by means of RSVP-TE extensions that allow the various crossed routers along a TE LSP path to be recorded, along with the corresponding allocated labels. Thanks to this extension, which uses the RSVP-TE Route Record Object (RRO), the PLR can unambiguously determine the label expected by the MP. Therefore, it can trigger the appropriate label-swapping operation before pushing the backup label and redirecting the rerouted TE LSP onto the appropriate outgoing interface.

The complete sequence of operations in case of Fast Reroute used for node protection is shown in Figure 2-31.

Figure 2-31 *Mode of Operation for MPLS Traffic Engineering Fast Reroute Node Protection*

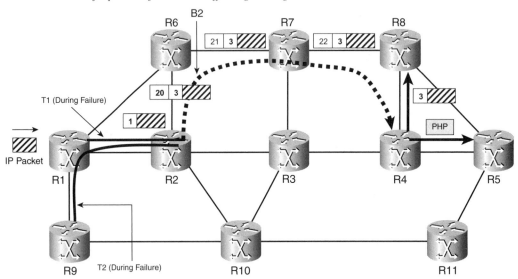

Note that the labels depicted in this diagram just correspond to the TE LSP
T1 but a similar operation is performed for the TE LSP T2.

━━━━ Primary TE LSP
■ ■ ■ ■ Backup TE LSP

It is interesting to note how the PLR detects a node failure as opposed to a link failure. This is actually quite a difficult problem, because when a node power supply fails, for instance, its attached links also fail. So how does the PLR tell a link failure from a node failure? It can't (although some mechanisms [not yet available] have been proposed). Consequently, to be on the safe side, the PLR always makes the assumption of a node failure if both next-hop and next-next-hop backup tunnels are configured.

Number of NNHOP Backup Tunnels Required by Fast Reroute Backup

The minimum number of backup tunnels required on a given PLR to protect a node equals the number of next-next hops. Indeed, going back to our example, three backup tunnels are required on R2 to protect all the TE LSPs against a node failure of R3:

- An NNHOP backup tunnel starting on R2 and terminating on R4 to protect the TE LSPs that follow the path R2–R3–R4

- An NNHOP backup tunnel from R2 to R7 to protect the TE LSP following the path R2–R3–R7

- An NNHOP backup tunnel from R2 to R10 to protect the TE LSPs following the path R2–R3–R10

We mentioned earlier that MPLS TE Fast Reroute can also protect against SRLG failure. MPLS TE Fast Reroute can be used to protect TE LSPs from SRLG failure by simply taking into account the SRLG membership (flooded by the IGP) of each link when computing the backup tunnel's path.

Backup Tunnel Path Computation

A multitude of path computation algorithms can compute the backup tunnel paths that can either be distributed or centralized. As already pointed out, the set of objectives largely dictates the algorithm complexity.

For example, the requirement can be to just find a path disjoint from the facility (such as link, SRLG, or node) to protect. In this case, the algorithm is quite straightforward. On the other hand, if additional constraints, such as bandwidth protection, bounded propagation delay increase, and so on, must also be satisfied, this leads to a usually nonlinear increase in algorithm complexity. In this category, algorithm efficiency is usually measured in terms of required backup capacity, among other criteria.

Indeed, one of the objectives of any recovery mechanism is to minimize the required number of resources dedicated to backup. If some guarantees are required along the backup path, in terms of bandwidth, delays, and so on, this implies the reservation by the backup tunnel of network resources such as bandwidth. With respect to such guarantees, a relatively common objective is to protect against single network element failure. (Note that in the case of an SRLG, such a network element can itself be composed of multiple links. This might be the case when several optical lambdas are multiplexed over a single fiber by means of technology such as Dense Wavelength Division Multiplexing [DWDM] and thus are all part of the same SRLG.) When such an assumption is considered acceptable (usually referred to as the *single failure assumption*), you can make an interesting observation. If two backup tunnels protect independent resources, because it is assumed that those two resources will not fail simultaneously, this also means that the two backup tunnels will never be active at the same time. Hence, the required amount of backup bandwidth is not the sum of their bandwidth on every link they share, but simply the largest of their respective bandwidth. Support for this concept of bandwidth sharing by the backup path computation algorithm allows for a significant reduction in the amount of required backup bandwidth under the single-failure assumption.

Backup Tunnel Load Balancing

This refers to the ability to presignal more than one backup tunnel between a PLR and an MP when protecting a single network element (that is, a set of four next-hop backup tunnels to protect a single link). Why? There could be several reasons for such a design, but the most common one is the inability to find a path for a single backup tunnel that satisfies the necessary constraints. For instance, consider the case of an OC-192 link for which the operator requires full bandwidth protection. In other words, a backup tunnel must be computed that provides an equivalent QoS (which can usually be reduced to the constraint of finding a path offering equivalent bandwidth). It just might not be possible to find such a path.

One solution would be to signal multiple backup tunnels (for instance, four 2.5-Gbps backup TE tunnels) such that the sum of their bandwidth equals the bandwidth of the protected facility (for example, an OC-192 link). Hence, a PLR has several backup tunnels to protect a given facility. As soon as a TE LSP requesting protection is signaled, the PLR selects one backup tunnel from among the set of candidates (the set of backup tunnels that satisfy the TE LSP requirements). It is important to highlight that for each TE LSP, a single backup tunnel is selected (this is why the term *load balancing* requires some clarification). You don't use multiple backup tunnels to protect a single TE LSP upon failure to avoid packet reordering. The packets of a single flow would follow different paths. This could lead to packet reordering, especially if the backup tunnel's paths have different characteristics, such as bandwidth and/or propagation delay. Sophisticated algorithms are needed on the PLR to perform an efficient backup tunnel selection to tackle the usual well-known challenges. One challenge is packing problems (for a set of TE LSPs, how to choose a set of backup tunnels to satisfy the maximum number of requests). Another challenge is smart mapping (for example, map different sets of primary TE LSPs with different attributes onto different backup tunnels with the corresponding property).

This might be seen as a simple and elegant solution, but it comes at the cost of some additional overall complexity and requires configuration of more backup tunnels.

Revertive Versus Nonrevertive

When is a newly restored link reused? There are actually two situations to consider.

First is the case of TE LSPs locally rerouted by Fast Reroute. If the link is restored before its headend router reoptimizes the TE LSP, you could envision letting the PLR revert the TE LSP to the original path. However, such an approach (also called local reversion) has several drawbacks. But in case of a flapping link, it would result in constantly switching the traffic from one path to another, which would lead to recurring traffic disruptions if no dampening algorithm were used. Hence, the Fast Reroute specification (see [FRR]) recommends global revertive mode, whereby the decision to revert to the newly restored link is entirely driven by the headend router.

The second situation is when the TE LSP is reoptimized by the headend along a more optimal path and the link is then restored. It is again the decision of the headend router to reoptimize any of its TE LSPs along this path. (Several considerations can be taken into account, such as the reoptimization frequency and the gain in terms of path optimality.)

Fast Reroute Summary

Fast Reroute has enjoyed great success thanks to its ability to provide SONET-like recovery times (provided that the link failure can be quickly detected, such as by means of PoS alarms, which is usually the case on backbone links). And thanks to its local protection nature, the Fast Reroute convergence time is highly optimized and deterministic. The rerouting node is immediately upstream of the failure (there is no fault notification time), and the backup path is signaled before the failure (backup paths are not computed on the fly). On the other hand, Fast Reroute requires the establishment of a potentially nonnegligible number of backup tunnels. You will see later in this book that several techniques and tools are available to facilitate the deployment of Fast Reroute and automate the creation of backup tunnels. In terms of complexity, as already pointed out, the backup tunnel path algorithm complexity and its management is a function of the set of requirements.

In summary, MPLS TE Fast Reroute is an efficient local protection mechanism that provides tens of milliseconds of convergence time. In addition, MPLS TE Fast Reroute can meet stringent recovery requirements such as bandwidth and propagation delay protection by means of more sophisticated backup tunnel path computation algorithms.

CHAPTER 3

Interexchange Carrier Design Study

USCom is a fictitious nationwide data and long-distance voice service provider in the U.S. that provides connectivity between local exchanges in different geographic regions. It also facilitates inter-Local Access and Transport Area (LATA) services (as described in the Federal Communications Commission [FCC] Telecommunications Act of 1996), as well as a complete portfolio of data services. USCom may be classified as an Interexchange Carrier (IXC) that owns its fiber and transmission facilities as well as a Layer 2 switching infrastructure (ATM and Frame Relay) spanning its service footprint.

NOTE   A LATA in the U.S. determines where a Local Exchange Carrier (LEC) can transmit traffic and where an IXC is required to carry traffic between LATAs. A state may have several LATAs. A few LATAs cross state boundaries.

This chapter discusses the current USCom MPLS network design, its evolution, and how USCom characteristics and objectives influenced the corresponding design decisions that were made.

USCom's Network Environment

USCom has been offering Internet access for many years to other service providers (wholesale), Enterprises, and small/medium business customers. It currently has an installed base of more than 35,000 Internet ports. These Internet ports are supported on 350 Internet edge routers (called Internet access provider edge [PE] routers) located in their 100 Points of Presence (POPs) that are situated across the country. Internet connectivity is obtained via transit providers, private peering sessions, and connections in major cities to various Network Access Points (NAPs).

USCom has also had great success with its Layer 3 Multiprotocol Label Switching (MPLS) VPN service (which is based on the architecture described in [2547bis]) since its inception in 2002. Acceptance of the service has grown throughout USCom's customer base. Currently some 12,500 VPN ports are installed across the country, and this number is growing considerably on a monthly basis. The customer-managed customer edge (CE) routers are connected via 255 Layer 3 MPLS VPN PE routers hosted in USCom's various POPs. Note that PE routers are dedicated to either the Internet or Layer 3 MPLS VPN access. Given the success of this offering, USCom plans to add 6000 customer access links per annum, although based on the current trend this figure is considered conservative. Total traffic volume, which includes both Internet and VPN, is expected to grow at approximately 30 percent per annum.

References Used in this Book

Throughout this book you will see references to outside resources. These are provided in case you want to delve more deeply into a subject. Such references will appear in a bracketed code, such as [L2VPN]. If you want to know more about this resource, look up the code in this book's appendix and you can find out specific information about the resource.

USCom owns fiber across the country and is running a long-distance optical core based on dense wavelength division multiplexing (DWDM) technology. This translates to availability of raw high-speed links (OC-48 (2.488 Gbps) and OC-192 (10 Gbps)) for provider router (P router) and PE router interconnection, at relatively low cost and provisioning time. USCom can activate additional capacity by enabling additional wavelengths (lambdas) in a relatively short time frame. USCom takes advantage of this to enforce an overengineering policy for core router links.

The high-speed core links are provided to routers as native lambdas straight from the DWDM equipment without any intermediate SONET Add/Drop Multiplexer (ADM). (Note that SONET framing is in use between the routers and the DWDM equipment.) These links do not benefit from any protection at the optical level. Some links interconnecting P routers and PE routers are provided through a SONET infrastructure overlaid over the optical infrastructure. The SONET links are protected by means of SONET protection provided by Bidirectional Line Switch Rings (BLSRs) with four fibers, also called BLSR/4. (See [NET-RECOV] for more details on SONET-SDH recovery mechanisms.)

Intra-POP connectivity is achieved via Packet over SONET (PoS) or switched Gigabit Ethernet. Because of the relatively low cost of switched Gigabit Ethernet technology and the negligible cost of fibers within a premises, USCom also maintains an overengineered intra-POP capacity.

Access from CE router to PE router for both Internet and Layer 3 MPLS VPN connectivity is provided via Frame Relay, ATM, leased line, or SONET. Each of these physical (or logical) links is dedicated to a single CE router. These links involve a significant cost that typically precludes simple overengineering and mandates tight dimensioning. Access speeds range from 64 kbps to OC-48.

The USCom nationwide backbone POP topology, interconnected through OC-48 and OC-192 links, is illustrated in Figure 3-1.

Figure 3-1 *USCom Nationwide Topology*

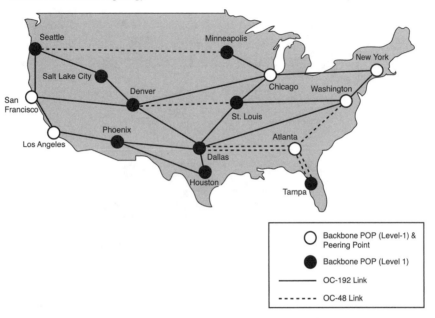

The USCom network is structured into three levels of POPs. Each POP is classified as either a backbone (Level 1), medium (Level 2), or small (Level 3) facility. The level depends on the density of the customer access and combined traffic throughput requirements. All routers are operated as a single autonomous system, with American Registry for Internet Numbers (ARIN) assigned AS number 32765. USCom has been assigned the 23/8 IP address space. The company uses this for its internal infrastructure as well as customer allocation.

Level 1 POPs are the backbone POPs (as shown in Figure 3-1) comprising the high-capacity backbone P routers dedicated to long-distance transit and interconnection of lower-level POPs to this long-distance transit backbone. PE routers providing Internet and Layer 3 MPLS VPN services from these major locations are also deployed, as well as some additional P routers acting as an aggregation layer inside the POP for these PE routers. Aggregation P routers reduce the number of IGP adjacencies that have to be maintained by the backbone P routers to two, because each core P router has to peer with only two aggregation P routers (in addition to the other core P routers in the backbone) instead of with all the PE routers in the POP (whose number can be fairly high, and growing, in a Level 1 POP).

Each Level 1 POP has two backbone P routers that interconnect via OC-48, dual OC-48, or OC-192 links to the rest of the backbone network. They also interconnect with lower-level POPs using either OC-3 (155.52 Mbps) or OC-48 links. Each backbone P router is connected to both local aggregation P routers via a point-to-point OC-48 link. Each PE router (and there may be several) is connected to both aggregation P routers via OC-3 PoS links. There are currently 15 Level 1 POPs, the structure of which is illustrated in Figure 3-2.

Figure 3-2 *USCom Level 1 POP Design*

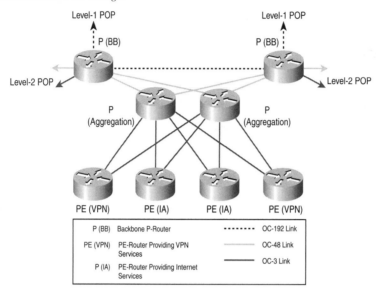

The Level 2 POPs are composed of P routers that connect to the Level 1 POPs, or another Level 2 POP, via OC-3 or OC-48 links, and the PE routers in medium access locations. Each PE router is connected to both backbone P routers via redundant switched Gigabit Ethernet (using two separate Gigabit Ethernet switches). There are currently 25 Level 2 POPs, the structure of which is illustrated in Figure 3-3.

Figure 3-3 *USCom Level 2 POP Design*

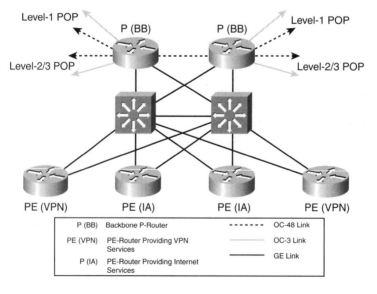

The Level 3 POPs are composed of PE routers in remote locations and P routers that connect to Level 2 POPs via OC-3 links. There are currently 60 Level 3 POPs, the structure of which is illustrated in Figure 3-4.

Figure 3-4   *USCom Level 3 POP Design*

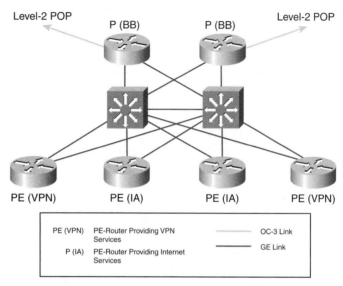

Several years ago, USCom deployed a SONET network providing OC-3 links. These links are protected at the SONET layer by the protection mechanisms provided by four-fiber BLSRs. These allow recovery from any link failure, with some special conditions specified by the SONET standard, within 60 ms. USCom satisfies all the conditions, including ring distance limited to 1200 km, less than 16 SONET stations, and ring in idle state before protection. Figure 3-5 shows the protected OC-3 links provided by the four-fiber BLSRs and used between Level 1 and Level 2/3 POPs. Because these links are protected and stable, USCom decided to use them in the core network without any changes.

NOTE   The use of SONET protection covers only the case of a link failure within the SONET network but not an IP router interface failure (sometimes considered a link failure) or a router failure. On the other hand, USCom considers router interface failures and router failures rare enough that they are acceptable and do not the use of additional recovery mechanisms such as Automatic Protection Switching (APS).

Figure 3-5   *Protected OC-3 Links Provided by Four-Fiber BLSRs*

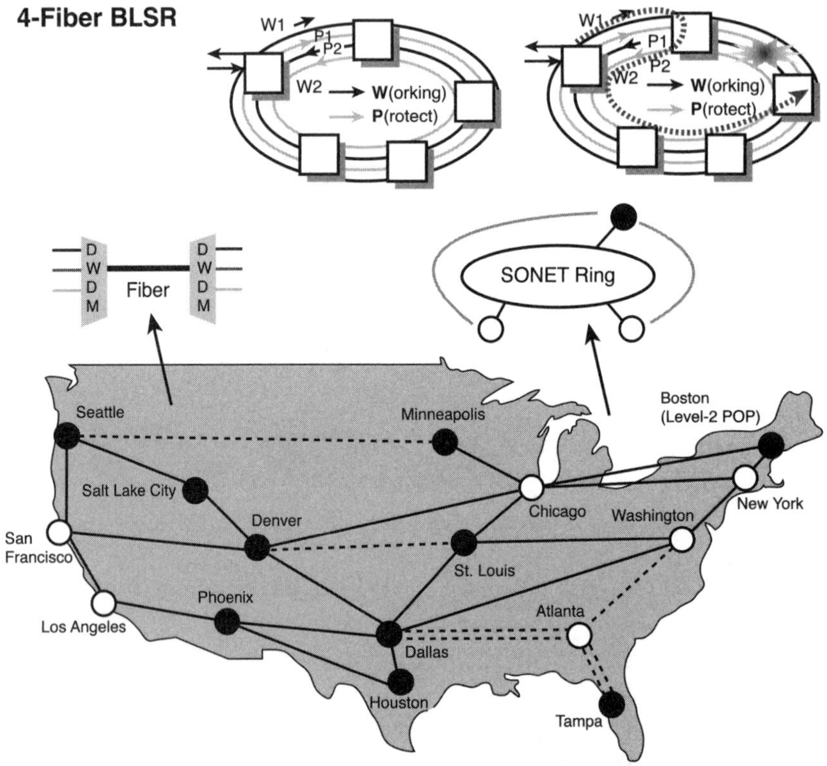

Figure 3-5 also shows that the USCom optical network uses DWDM technology, allowing the multiplexing of tens of light paths over a single fiber. Note that USCom has deployed Coarse Wave Division Multiplexing (CWDM) equipment in some metro areas, offering a lower degree (4) of multiplexing. The DWDM equipment lets the company provide 1+1 optical protection. Such a protection scheme relies on specialized optical equipment performing traffic bridging along the primary and secondary light paths, each of which follows diverse paths. Upon a link failure, such as a fiber cut or optical equipment failure, the receiving side quickly detects the failure and switches the traffic received from the primary light path to the secondary. This type of mechanism, usually qualified as "single-ended," is undoubtedly efficient because it does not require any extra signaling mechanisms or coordination between the sender and receiver (just the receiving side performs the switching function). Hence, the rerouting time is very fast (a few milliseconds). Moreover, a strictly equivalent quality of service (QoS) is guaranteed upon a network element failure because the secondary path is identical to the primary path (although it might be longer to be diverse from the primary path). On the other hand, this requires dedicating half of the fiber capacity for backup recovery. Furthermore, such a protection scheme implies that additional optical equipment needs to be purchased.

Hence, USCom decided to use all the network bandwidth to route the primary traffic and rely on some upper-layer protection mechanisms (see the section "Network Recovery Design") to offer equivalent rerouting time at significantly lower costs. All the light paths provided to the IP/MPLS layer for inter-Level 1 links and Level 1-to-Level 2 links therefore are unprotected. This is perfectly in line with the previously described core network overengineering strategy adopted by USCom.

Although DWDM offers the ability to provide high bandwidth in a very cost-effective fashion, it has a downside. Multiple links share some common resources and equipment whose failure may impact several links. This is called Shared Risk Link Group (SRLG), and the production design should take it into account.

Putting all this information together, you can see from Figure 3-6 how connectivity is typically achieved from a Level 3 to a Level 2 to a Level 1 POP.

Figure 3-6   *Inter-POP Connectivity Within the USCom Network*

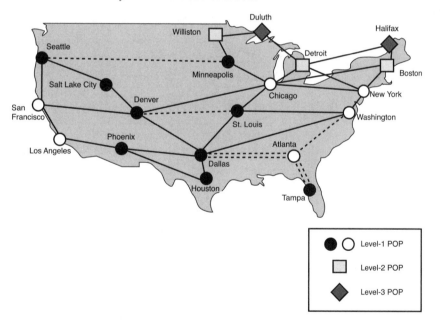

Table 3-1 summarizes the various types of links used in the USCom network, along with their main characteristics and localization.

Table 3-1   *Link Types and Characteristics in the USCom Backbone*

Link Type	Speed	Protection	Localization
OC-192 DWDM	10 Gbps	None	Level 1 POP-Level 1 POP
OC-48 DWDM	2.5 Gbps	None	Level 1 POP-Level 1 POP Level 1 POP-Level 2 POP
OC-48 SONET	2.5 Gbps	SONET protection	Level 1 POP-Level 2 POP Level 2 POP-Level 2 POP
OC-3 SONET	155 Mbps	SONET protection	Level 2 POP-Level 3 POP
Gigabit Ethernet	1 Gbps	None	Intra-Level 2 POP Intra-Level 3 POP

During the past several years, USCom has gathered various network failure statistics; they are summarized in Table 3-2. These statistics have been used to assess USCom's design requirements for its backbone network.

Table 3-2   *Link Failure Statistics Within the USCom Network*

Failure Type	Link/Router Type	Occurrence	Duration
Link failure	OC-3 SONET links	On average once a day in the network	From a few seconds to several days (fiber cut)
Link failure	OC-48 and OC-192 links	Unknown	Unknown
Router interface failure	Edge+core	Negligible	A few hours
Router failure (such as power supply, router software failure with traffic impact)	Edge+core	Once every two months	Variable
Router reboot (planned failure)	Edge (IA and VPN PE routers)	Once every six months	10 minutes
Router reboot (planned failure)	Core	Once a year	10 minutes

USCom's Network Design Objectives

USCom's objectives for its network design include the following considerations:

- Ensure that the Layer 3 MPLS VPN design can cope with current scale requirements as well as the predicted growth of this service over the coming years.

- Enrich the Layer 3 MPLS VPN service with quality of service commitments, allowing it to be marketed as the service of choice for enterprises that want to converge their data/voice/video networks onto a single multimedia intranet.

- Offer high-availability commitments to VPN users without additional capital expenses.

The following sections review the design elected by USCom, as well as the corresponding rationale behind the routing, Layer 3 MPLS VPN, QoS, traffic engineering, and network recovery. A final section points out a number of lessons that can be drawn from the USCom design.

Routing and Backbone Label Forwarding Design

All networks, whether they span whole continents or just a group of geographic regions, present design challenges that must be addressed by the network architects. Some issues are easier to tackle than others, and certain services present unique challenges. This section reviews how USCom decided to deploy its internal and external IP routing, and also how it decided to organize its Layer 3 MPLS VPN service.

We have established that USCom operates a national backbone infrastructure that spans the continental U.S. This network must support a number of different services, including Internet access and Layer 3 VPN service. During the initial Layer 3 VPN deployment, USCom decided to deploy MPLS technology to support the architecture specified in [2547bis]. This architecture provides a network-based VPN service. It was discussed in detail in Chapter 1, "Technology Primer: Layer 3 VPN, Multicast VPNs, IPv6, and Psuedowire."

Having deployed MPLS for this service, USCom also felt that it was the right technology to support fast rerouting (FRR) capability (which you'll read about in the "Network Recovery Design for Link Failures" section). Clearly, the network will need to support even more new services in the future, so USCom's selection of MPLS as its primary technology allows the company to support existing and future service requirements.

Label Distribution Protocol (LDP) is used within the backbone to allow label switching from one edge of the USCom network to the other. However, at this point in time, only the Layer 3 VPN traffic is label-switched, leaving the Internet traffic to be forwarded by normal IP forwarding procedures. The rationale behind the decision to separate VPN forwarding from standard IP forwarding was driven primarily by the desire to continue operating the Internet network in the exact same way as before Layer 3 VPN services were introduced. This avoided any changes in configuration, monitoring, troubleshooting, or any other operational procedures that were in place for Internet traffic. In addition to this, a number of technical challenges exist if Internet traffic is label-switched, including how the existing IP tools (such as NetFlow) might behave, and how network events such as denial of service (DoS) attacks can be tracked and resolved. Chapter 5, "Global Service Provider Design Study," shows how these issues can be overcome and the USCom plan to introduce these new technologies in the future.

From an internal routing perspective, USCom runs Intermediate System–to-Intermediate System (IS-IS) as its Interior Gateway Protocol (IGP), which carries the loopback interface addresses of the PE routers (IP and VPN PE routers) as well as internal link addresses. The number of internal routes is approximately 3000. USCom does not expect to have more than 1000 routers in the IS-IS routing domain within the next two years. Hence, the IS-IS network is a flat Level 2 network that avoids having to manage the complexity of multiple levels of hierarchy.

USCom measured that the flooding activity on the existing network was perfectly reasonable. The Shortest Path First (SPF) computation time was calculated on the order of 100 ms (usually closer to 60 ms), not including the routing table updates. If at some point in the future the number of IS-IS routers has to be drastically increased because of the activation of IS-IS on various edge devices such as the ADSL or Dial access routers, USCom might consider splitting the network into multiple levels (each POP would be the Level 1 hierarchy). This would be necessary to also preserve the network convergence times. (A detailed analysis of these aspects appears in [NET-RECOV].)

Separation of Internet and Layer 3 MPLS VPN Services

From a forwarding perspective, Layer 3 VPN traffic is separated from Internet traffic, where VPN traffic is label-switched across the USCom network and Internet traffic is IP-routed/forwarded. The PE routers serving VPN and Internet customers are also separate. This is primarily because the Internet service has been deployed for a number of years and USCom wanted to deploy the new Layer 3 MPLS VPN service as a separate project, without concern that it might affect the existing customer base.

The backbone network infrastructure is addressed from the 23.49.0.0/16 block. This includes all P routers, PE routers (whether Internet or Layer 3 VPN), and any other equipment within the USCom network. The P router and core-facing interfaces on the Internet and Layer 3 VPN PE routers take their addresses from the 23.49.0.0/21 range (providing IP addresses 23.49.0.1–23.49.7.254).

The Internet PE routers and IPv4 route reflectors (RRs) take their loopback interface addresses from the 23.49.8.0/22 range (providing IP addresses 23.49.8.1–23.49.11.254).

The Layer 3 MPLS VPN PE routers and VPNv4 RRs (used for the MPLS VPN service) take their loopback interface addresses from the 23.49.16.0/22 range (providing IP addresses 23.49.16.1–23.49.19.254). This block is large enough to address 1022 devices. If the service increases above this amount, the 23.49.20.0/22 range is made available.

Each Layer 3 MPLS VPN PE router has a loopback interface configured; it is used as the source address for all Multiprotocol BGP (MP-BGP) peering sessions. Likewise, each Internet access PE router has a loopback interface assigned; it is used as the source address for all IPv4 BGP-4 peering sessions.

USCom also evaluated using one of the private IP address blocks from the [PRIVATE] range for its internal infrastructure. The use of private addresses provides some protection from the Internet because it is not a routable address space. Therefore, the internal USCom network would theoretically be hidden from the outside. However, locally attached customers could still access the network—for example, by sending traffic via a default route to USCom. Therefore, the advantages of using private address space are mitigated. Also, a future acquisition of another company might present some integration challenges, so the use of private addresses for the design was rejected.

Because the Internet PE routers and Layer 3 MPLS VPN PE routers are separate, and because USCom chose to forward only VPN traffic through label switching, forwarding separation needs to occur at the LDP level. The default behavior of the LDP protocol when executing in frame-based mode is to create and distribute label bindings for every IGP learned or local (static or connected) prefix. This is unnecessary in the USCom network because only the VPN traffic is to be label-switched, and all Internet traffic is to be routed and will never need any of the allocated label space. Therefore, only the MPLS VPN PE router loopback interface addresses (255 currently) require label bindings, because they are the only destinations to which traffic is forwarded through label switching. Example 3-1 shows how LDP filtering is achieved.

Example 3-1   *Filtering Label Binding for PE Router Loopback Interfaces*

```
no tag-switching advertise-tags
tag-switching advertise-tags for ldp-pe-filter
!
ip access-list standard ldp-pe-filter
 ! Main IP VPN PE-router loopbacks
 permit 23.49.16.0 0.0.3.255
 ! Reserved IP VPN PE-router loopback block
 permit 23.49.20.0 0.0.3.255
```

NOTE   Example 3-1 also shows that USCom has added the 23.49.20.0/22 address range to the filter. This range currently is not used in the deployed network. It is held in reserve in case the existing 23.49.16.0/22 address block becomes exhausted. Rather than updating the filter on all routers in the future, USCom chose to permit this block from Day 1 of the design.

NOTE   It is worth mentioning that LDP filtering needs to be activated on all the routers in the network, including the P routers, not just the PE routers. This prevents label space from being allocated unnecessarily throughout the network. It also prevents the forwarding of Internet traffic using label switching.

In the future, USCom may also decide to label-switch its Internet traffic. This may be achieved by either removing the LDP filtering (the configuration of which is shown in Example 3-1) or updating the LDP filter to include the Internet PE router loopback interface addresses.

Internet Service Route Reflection Deployment

The USCom RR design for Internet service is fairly typical. It follows the network's physical topology (for loop avoidance), as shown in Figure 3-7. (Only core POPs with external peering points are shown in the figure even though the design is relevant to all Level 1 POPs.) Each Level 1 POP has two Internet RRs (the backbone P routers). All Internet PE routers peer locally and are clients of these devices. All Level 1 POP RRs are fully meshed at the BGP-4 level. The aggregation P routers are also clients of these RRs.

Figure 3-7   *Placement of IPv4 Route Reflectors for Internet Service*

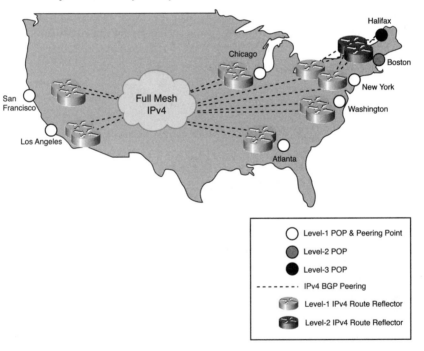

A second level of RR hierarchy is deployed between the Level 1 and Level 2 POPs. Each Level 2 POP has two RRs (which again are the exiting backbone P routers); these are clients of their nearest Level 1 POP RRs. Every Internet PE router within a Level 2 POP is a client of the local Level 2 RRs. Each Level 3 POP Internet PE router and backbone P router peers with its nearest Level 2 POP RRs (once again following the network's physical topology).

Figure 3-8 shows how the IPv4 BGP peerings are arranged between different levels of POPs and the placement of the RRs within those POPs. Note that this figure provides the typical topology, although in some cases the Level 2 POP RRs may peer with different Level 1 POPs. (In other words, one RR peers with a different Level 1 POP than the other RR within the Level 2 POP.) This depends on the RR's geographic location in the overall topology.

Figure 3-8   *IPv4 POP-to-POP BGP Route Reflection*

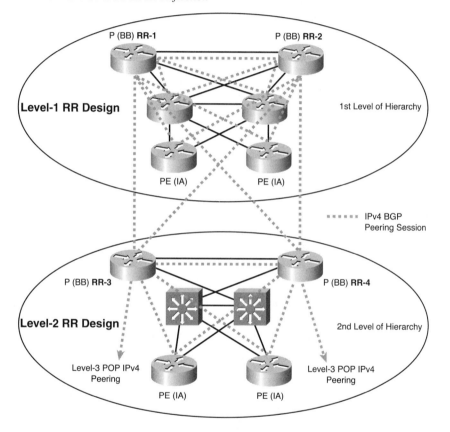

The global IPv4 BGP table currently contains approximately 155,000 Internet routes.

Layer 3 MPLS VPN Service Design Overview

USCom's Layer 3 MPLS VPN service is designed to target the growing number of organizations that are outsourcing their information technology to a third-party service provider. It also targets organizations that want to move away from a traditional overlay Layer 2 VPN model (such as Frame Relay or ATM). This trend is primarily driven by cost reductions for the end customer and the ability to receive additional services in a scalable manner, such as QoS and multicast. In many cases a hub-and-spoke topology, which is common if the environment is Frame Relay-based, is no longer sufficient to meet the end users' application requirements. The ability to use an infrastructure that inherently provides any-to-any connectivity is very attractive from an availability, scale, and service deployment perspective. The initial service offering addresses only the "unmanaged" market, where USCom provides network connectivity for the end user but the end user maintains control over their own routing. However, the design positions USCom to offer "managed" service, where it manages the end-user equipment, in the future.

USCom uses all 100 POPs to provide its Layer 3 MPLS VPN service. Customer access is via Frame Relay, ATM, leased line, and PoS. Access speeds range from n * DS0 (64 kbps) to OC-3 (low- to medium-speed) and from OC-3 to OC-48 (high-speed).

The current network deployment has 255 PE routers; this may be considered a dense deployment in the U.S. These are spread around all 100 POPs, with an average of two in each Level 3 POP, three in each Level 2 POP, and six in each Level 1 POP. However, PE routers are deployed based on customer demand at each location; therefore, the average numbers do not necessarily correspond to the actual deployed topology. For example, 30 of the Level 3 POPs currently have only one PE router deployed rather than two. On the other hand, the New York POP, which is a Level 1 facility, has ten PE routers, which is more than the average.

USCom initially defined two different types of customers who may access the national Layer 3 MPLS VPN service, as described in the following list. Note that Internet connectivity is considered a separate service and therefore is not bundled with the VPN service:

- **VPN intranet**—This customer requires connectivity between internal sites for the creation of an intranet. No extranet connectivity is provided. However, if the evolution of the USCom network introduces any central services (such as web hosting, firewalls, and so on), the customer is eligible for connectivity to these services.

- **VPN extranet**—This customer requires connectivity between internal and external partner sites for the creation of an extranet.

USCom breaks its VPNs into three categories—small, medium, and large—as described in Table 3-3. These categories are based on the customer's size as measured by the number of sites in the VPN. Current statistics show that 500 VPNs are deployed, with a combined total of 12,500 VPN sites, representing ten large VPNs, 200 medium VPNs, and 290 small VPNs. The VPN sites represent 62,500 total VPNv4 routes in the network.

Table 3-3   *IP VPN Categories*

VPN Category	Number of Sites	Percentage of Total Sites	Number of Prefixes in VPN	Percentage of Total Customers
Small VPN	2 to 10	15 %	Ones to tens	58%
Medium VPN	11 to 200	45%	Tens to hundreds	40%
Large VPN	201 to thousands	40%	Hundreds to thousands	2%

As you can see, although the majority of VPN customers fall within the small VPN category, they represent only 15 percent of the total number of sites. Only 2 percent of customers fall within the large VPN category, but they represent 40 percent of the total number of sites.

PE Router Basic Engineering Guidelines

Configuring a new Layer 3 MPLS VPN customer requires a set of engineering guidelines that is flexible and easy to implement from a centralized management system. A number of common attributes need to be configured for each new customer. These are outlined in Chapter 1 and can be summarized as follows:

- Definition and configuration of the Virtual Routing/Forwarding instance (VRF)
- Definition and configuration of the Route Distinguisher (RD)
- Routing protocol context and/or static routing configuration
- Import/export policies
- Interaction between the backbone control plane and the VRF
- Configuration and association of customer-facing router interfaces with previously defined VRFs
- Quality of service (QoS) policies

The values chosen for each VRF attribute, as well as specifics of the routing protocol context, vary from VPN customer to customer. However, because a number of default attributes can be assumed, the provisioning system needs only to provide a template that can accept different values on a per-customer basis. Most commercially available provisioning systems today have default templates for configuring these attributes.

In most cases, the PE-CE links used for the Layer 3 MPLS VPN service have their IP addresses allocated from the USCom IP address space. However, on an exception basis, customer address space is sometimes used. The decision to use customer address space is primarily driven by the customer's size and topology and whether the customer's address space can be summarized into convenient blocks. If customer address space is used, USCom requires that it be a globally assigned block and not from the private range so as to avoid any potential address range clash with other VPN customers.

In all cases, USCom uses the Interface Group MIB (see [IF-MIB]) to monitor the status of the physical PE-CE links. This is achieved by polling the *IfOperStatus .ifIndex* object, the details of which are specified in [IF-MIB].

USCom will not provision more than 15 percent of the total access links of any given customer onto a single PE router. This will help prevent a large percentage of the VPN from losing connectivity in the event of a PE router hardware failure or planned maintenance. Although USCom has not reached the scaling limits on any of its PE routers, it has decided to apply an upper boundary to the total number of Layer 3 MPLS VPN customer accesses per PE router. This is driven by a number of factors, including the type of access device (such as the router's size and capability), traffic throughput requirements, additional service requirements (such as QoS), and so on. Table 3-4 provides an overview of USCom's engineering rules in this space for two of its router platforms. USCom will stop adding customers on each platform if any of the hard limits is reached.

Table 3-4   *PE Router Sizing Rules*

Engineering Parameter Limits	Platform 1 Limits	Platform 2 Limits
USCom IGP routes	3000	3000
Number of iBGP/eBGP peers	350	2000
Number of VRFs	200	1000
Total VRF routes	60,000	300,000
Average number of sites per VRF	3	3
Average number of routes per VPN	300	300
Total CE connections per PE	600	3000

Table 3-4 also shows that because the typical average number of sites per VRF per platform is 3, this translates into a total number of CE connections per PE of 600 and 3000.

VRF Naming Convention

When choosing a name for a given VPN VRF, it is important to remember that the network operations staff will use the name to troubleshoot connectivity problems for the VPN. Several naming conventions might be adopted. USCom chose to use a representation of the name followed by an abbreviation of the customer name, starting with a VRF name of V101 and incrementing it by 1 for each new VPN deployed. This allocation scheme is shown in Table 3-5.

Table 3-5   *VPN Name Allocation Scheme*

Customer Name	VRF Name
U.S. Post Office	V101:USPO
SoccerOnline International	V102:SoccerOnline
BigBank of Massachusetts	V103:BigBank
<Next customer>	V104 and so on

Route Distinguisher Allocation

The *route distinguisher (RD)*, as described in [2547bis], is an 8-byte entity that lets the MPLS VPN architecture uniquely identify a particular route within the operator's backbone network. The structure of the RD depends on the type specified in the first 2 bytes of the attribute.

USCom chose to use its autonomous system number plus a uniquely defined number specific to a given VPN customer. Figure 3-9 shows the format of the RD chosen by USCom.

Figure 3-9   *Route Distinguisher Format*

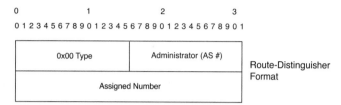

In theory, several schemes are available when choosing an RD allocation method. The main ones can be summarized as follows:

- **Use a unique RD for every VPN**—A unique RD for each VPN is the easiest option to deploy because every PE router uses the same value for a given VPN customer. However, deploying this scheme prevents the operator, which has VPNv4 route RRs in its topology (which is typically the case; USCom has such a topology), from offering load-balancing services to customers who are dual-homed to the Layer 3 MPLS VPN service. This is because the VPNv4 routes cannot be guaranteed to be unique. Therefore, certain paths may be unavailable to the PE routers that will perform the load balancing, because the RRs will advertise only the "best" path.

- **Use a unique RD for each VPN on a per-PE basis**—A unique RD may be allocated to each VPN at each PE router, although the value may be different between PE routers for a given VPN. In this case the operator can provide load-balancing services when RRs are deployed. This is because the VPNv4 routes can be guaranteed to be unique within the MPLS backbone. Note that such a scheme requires a little more memory space to store the additional VPNv4 routes.

- **Use a unique RD for each VPN on a per-interface/per-PE router basis**—A unique RD may be allocated for each VRF on a per-interface basis. The advantage is that a particular site within a VPN can be identified based on the RD value of any route originated by that site. However, other methods are available to achieve the same aim, such as use of the *site of origin (SoO)* attribute, which is much less resource-consuming. The format of this attribute can be found in [EXTCOM].

USCom chose to use a unique RD per VRF (the second option), because it required load-balancing services for a number of VPN customers with dual-homed CE routers. Although this scheme requires additional memory at the PE routers, the ability to provide load balancing when RRs are deployed was necessary to address USCom customer requirements. The range of RDs available is 32765:1 through 32765:4,294,967,295, which is way beyond what USCom will ever require.

NOTE   Traffic load balancing and its implications for the service provider backbone network are
                discussed in more detail in the section "Load Balancing Support" in Chapter 4, "National Telco
                Design Study."

Route Target Allocation for Import/Export Policy

Selecting a route target for each VPN is necessary to specify that VPN's specific import/export
policies. [EXTCOM] specifies three main formats that may be used for the route target
extended-community attribute.

USCom chose to use the two-octet AS format with its own AS number, 32765, as the ASN
portion of the community. Use of any customer AS numbers was rejected in the design because
the possibility of conflicting numbers was apparent if any VPN customers were using private
AS numbers from the [64512–65535] range.

Route target values 32765:[1–100] were reserved for future use, so values 32765:101 through
32765:65535 are available for VPN customer allocation. This fits nicely with USCom's VRF
naming convention, in which it maps the VRF name to the number in the route target. For
example, BigBank of Massachusetts, whose VRF name is v103:BigBank, uses a default route
target value of 32765:103.

NOTE   Some VPN customers may require the use of more than one route target per VRF. An example
                is a topology in which the spoke sites require connectivity to a central service. This type of
                topology is often called central services or hub and spoke. The mapping of the VRF name with
                the route target cannot be used in this case.

Basic PE Router Configuration Template

Example 3-2 provides the basic PE router configuration template used by USCom.

Example 3-2   *PE Router Configuration Template*

```
hostname USCom.cityname.PErouter-number
!
ip vrf vpn-name
 rd 32765:1-4294967295
 route-target export 32765:101-65535
 route-target import 32765:101-65535
!
interface Loopback0
 description ** interface used for BGP peering **
 ip address 23.49.16.0/22 range address and network mask
!
```

PE Router Control-Plane Requirements

One of the most significant challenges for any Layer 3 network-based VPN service is distributing customer-specific routing information between edge routers and achieving this in a scalable manner. As the service grows, more and more VPN routes need to be advertised using the backbone control-plane infrastructure. The amount of information could become significant as the service becomes more and more successful.

Although USCom's future expansion projections for its Layer 3 MPLS VPN service do not indicate any kind of saturation point in terms of routing information capacity, it is clear that over time, as the service matures, the design of the backbone control-plane infrastructure will be critical.

The current network deployment has 255 PE routers providing Layer 3 MPLS VPN services. With this number of PE routers, and the requirement to carry an ever-expanding VPNv4 address space, USCom chose to deploy VPNv4-specific RRs (the details of which are discussed in section "VPNv4 Route Reflector Deployment Specifics") to help scale the distribution of routes. RRs help scale the network infrastructure in a number of ways. You will see in other chapters that additional functionality may be added to further increase this scaling. However, USCom chose to use RRs primarily to ease the network's operational complexity as the number of MP-BGP TCP sessions required by the PE routers into the backbone could be reduced to two (one to each RR), as opposed to every other PE router in the network.

Each PE router is required to maintain at least two MP-BGP peering sessions into the USCom backbone network. These sessions will be used to exchange VPNv4 prefix information with other PE routers via the VPNv4 RRs. Two sessions are necessary for redundancy in case an RR fails or connectivity to that RR becomes unavailable.

PE Router Path MTU Discovery

In Cisco IOS, by default, all PE routers have Path MTU Discovery [see PMTU] disabled. This means that the default TCP Maximum Segment Size (MSS) is used for all TCP sessions. This default normally is based on the outgoing interface MTU size minus the IP header/options and TCP header/options (for a total of 40 bytes). For example, for an Ethernet interface with an MTU of 1500 bytes, the MSS is calculated as 1460.

BGP on Cisco routers uses a default MSS value of 536 bytes regardless of the outgoing interface type. The problem with this small value is that BGP signaling information sent across a given BGP session needs to be segmented into a much higher number of packets, substantially increasing convergence times. However, [PMTU] provides a mechanism in which the PE router can discover the optimum MSS to use for its BGP sessions, and therefore reduce the number of messages generated. USCom enables [PMTU] on all its VPN PE routers, and VPNv4 RRs, using the configuration shown in Example 3-3.

Example 3-3 *PE Router PMTU Configuration Template*

```
hostname USCom.cityname.PErouter-number
!
ip tcp path-mtu-discovery
```

VPNv4 Route Reflector Deployment Specifics

Two tools are available to assist in the scaling of the TCP sessions required to support the VPNv4 address family for Layer 3 MPLS VPN service—*confederations* and *route reflectors*. USCom chose to deploy RRs in its Layer 3 MPLS VPN design; these are completely separate from the RRs used for its Internet service. This separation provides improved convergence times, as well as scalability in terms of CPU and hardware memory requirements. USCom did not have a requirement to deploy confederations, because its service requirements did not necessitate multiple sub-autonomous systems to split the MP-BGP topology.

While reviewing the needs of the Layer 3 MPLS VPN service from a control-plane perspective, it was clear that the rules for RR deployment were different from those followed for the Internet service, because the VPN traffic would be label-switched rather than routed. The primary difference between label switching and IP forwarding within the backbone network is that label switching allows the RRs to be deployed outside the packet-forwarding path, because the forwarding decision for a given packet is made at the edge of the network rather than on a hop-by-hop basis. This paradigm is a little different from the typical Internet design used for IPv4 route distribution, in which the common practice is to place the RRs so that they follow the network's physical connectivity. This type of design avoids any forwarding loops that could be caused by bad route placement. Figure 3-10 shows what can happen if these rules are not followed when forwarding IP traffic natively instead of via label switching.

Figure 3-10 *Forwarding Loop with Incorrectly Designed IPv4 Route Reflection*

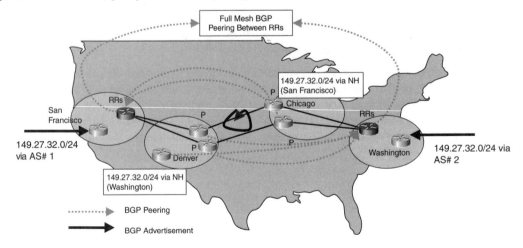

Figure 3-10 shows that the Denver POP believes that 149.27.32.0/24 can be reached via a Washington next-hop address, whereas the Chicago POP believes it can be reached via a San Francisco next-hop address. This is clearly a bad design, because both POPs should peer with their geographically closest RRs. In this case, packets loop between Chicago and Denver.

This issue is eliminated when packet forwarding is achieved through label switching (or IP tunneling), because the packets' original destination IP address is no longer examined in the network core.

Deployment Location for VPNv4 Route Reflectors

The Internet RR topology described previously is not well suited to the Layer 3 MPLS VPN service because the topology assumes that all RRs will carry the same set of routes. This may not be necessary, or even desirable, for the VPN service, because not all PE routers will need the same set of routes. Hence, it would not scale as well as a partitioned VPN RR design, which may become necessary for a large-scale VPN topology. Another drawback of this Internet topology for the VPN service is that it introduces a number of BGP hops that increase the convergence delay for routing updates. This may be detrimental to the Layer 3 MPLS VPN SLA, and therefore the topology of the VPNv4 RRs is a little different, as shown in Figure 3-11.

Figure 3-11 *VPNv4 Route Reflector Deployment*

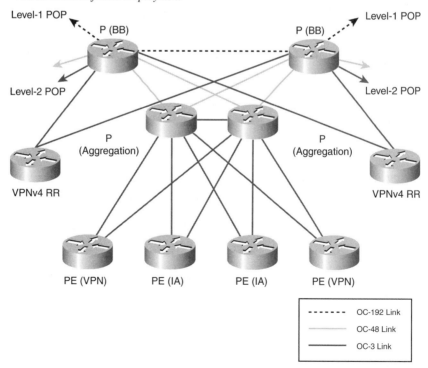

The VPNv4 RRs are deployed only within Level 1 POPs and are connected directly to both core backbone P routers via OC-3 links. The topology does not follow the network's physical path; this is unnecessary because of the deployment of LDP in the backbone. Level 2 and Level 3 POPs do not house any RRs but instead peer directly with their local Level 1 POP. All VPNv4 RRs peer within a full mesh.

The initial deployment has VPNv4 RRs in six locations: San Francisco, Los Angeles, Denver, Chicago, New York, and Washington. Each PE router has peering sessions with a pair of RRs that are within its local regional vicinity. For example, a PE router in Boston may peer with an RR in New York and another in Chicago. A maximum of 200 peering sessions has been defined within the engineering deployment guidelines for the RRs. Although the currently deployed hardware could support more than this number, USCom has validated only up to 200 peering sessions within its labs. Because the current network has 255 existing VPN PE routers, and each PE router peers to local RRs based on geography, no RR within the topology has close to this maximum number of peering sessions.

USCom takes advantage of *update groups,* which are enabled by default in the level of Cisco IOS it is running on its routers. Therefore, USCom can dynamically build groups of MP-BGP peering partners that have the same outbound policy. The update group does not consider the extended communities used by the PE routers for import/export policy; therefore, all the PE routers belong to the same group. This provides the ability to build one MP-BGP update (instead of one per PE router) and to replicate it to all members of the update group. This functionality provides improved performance at the RRs. Each RR, just like the PE routers, also uses [PMTU].

The design of the control plane must provide the ability for all Layer 3 MPLS VPN PE routers to learn routes from the centralized VPNv4 RRs. Ideally each PE router should peer based on geography as much as possible, and to different Level 1 POPs. This is useful so that a particular Level 2/3 POP does not lose all routing information in the event of a catastrophic failure within a given Level 1 POP, such as a complete power outage.

Figure 3-12 illustrates the topology of the VPNv4 RRs. It shows that the Boston Level 2 POP peers to both the Chicago and New York Level 1 POPs to provide geographic redundancy. All PE routers within a Level 1 POP (for example, the New York POP) peer to their local RRs, because a local power failure would mean that they would not be able to maintain a peering session with another Level 1 POP because all connectivity would be lost. Therefore, there is little point in following the same design rule as the Level 2/3 POPs.

Figure 3-12   *Physical Topology of VPNv4 Route Reflection*

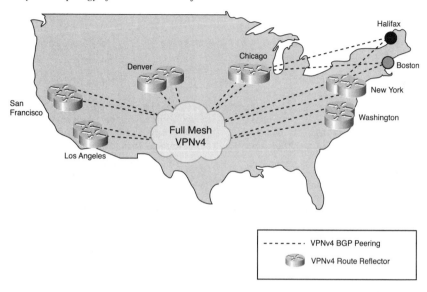

Preventing Input Drops at the VPNv4 Route Reflectors

Each RR has an interface-level queue, referred to in Cisco IOS as the *input hold queue,* that may not by default be large enough to prevent input drops at the interface. Dropping TCP packets reduces the protocol's efficiency and causes retransmissions to occur. This behavior can slow down the convergence of MP-BGP at the VPNv4 RRs. For this reason, USCom tunes the queue value using the following algorithm:

Input hold queue = (TCP window size / mss) * number of MP-BGP peers
where TCP window size is the TCP window size for the MP-BGP session, mss is the TCP maximum segment size, and number of MP-BGP peers is the number of route reflector clients.
The window size (sndwnd) and mss (max segment size) values can be found using the **show ip bgp neighbor** command in Cisco IOS.

PE Router and Route Reflector VPNv4 MP-BGP Peering Template

USCom uses the template shown in Example 3-4 for the VPNv4 MP-BGP configuration of the PE routers and RRs.

Example 3-4   *PE Router and Route Reflector VPNv4 BGP Configuration Template*

```
! PE-router configuration
hostname USCom.cityname.PErouter-number
!
ip tcp path-mtu-discovery
```

continues

Example 3-4   *PE Router and Route Reflector VPNv4 BGP Configuration Template (Continued)*

```
!
interface Loopback0
 description ** interface used for BGP peering **
 ip address 23.49.16.0/22
!
router bgp 32765
 no bgp default ipv4-unicast
 neighbor 23.49.16.0/22 address-for-1st-RR remote-as 32765
 neighbor 23.49.16.0/22 address-for-1st-RR update-source Loopback0
 neighbor 23.49.16.0/22 address-for-1st-RR remote-as 32765
 neighbor 23.49.16.0/22 address-for-1st-RR update-source Loopback0
 ..
 !
 address-family vpnv4
 neighbor 23.49.16.0/22 address-for-1st-RR activate
 neighbor 23.49.16.0/22 address-for-1st-RR send-community extended
 neighbor 23.49.16.0/22 address-for-1st-RR activate
 neighbor 23.49.16.0/22 address-for-1st-RR send-community extended
 ..
 exit-address-family

! VPNv4 Route Reflector configuration
hostname USCom.cityname.RRrouter-number
!
interface Loopback0
 description ** interface used for BGP peering to RR-clients **
 ip address 23.49.16.0/22 range address and network mask
!
router bgp 32765
 neighbor 23.49.16.0/22 address-1st-PE-router remote-as 32765
 neighbor 23.49.16.0/22 address-1st-PE-router update-source Loopback0
 ..
 !
 address-family vpnv4
 neighbor 23.49.16.0/22 address-1st-PE-router activate
 neighbor 23.49.16.0/22 address-1st-PE-router route-reflector-client
 neighbor 23.49.16.0/22 address-1st-PE-router send-community extended
 ..
 exit-address-family
```

PE-CE Routing Protocol Design

As discussed in Chapter 1, various routing protocols (and static routing) are available for connectivity between the CE routers and PE routers. When assessing the requirements for the Layer 3 MPLS VPN service design, the set of routing protocols to offer was evaluated. The initial deployment of the service included static routing and BGP-4 support only on the PE-CE links. However, RIPv2 was added fairly shortly afterwards to provide service to customers who were unable to run BGP-4, such as those with PE-CE links backed up via ISDN to a Network Access Server (NAS).

USCom avoids using RIPv2 as much as possible because of its periodic update behavior and the implications of this on the PE routers' CPU cycles. For customers who require RIPv2, USCom configures **flash-update-threshold 30** to prevent Flash updates from being sent before the regular periodic updates. Flash updates send new routing information as soon as something changes in the customer topology and therefore can increase CPU requirements substantially during customer routing instability events. Also, USCom imposes the use of BGP-4 for dual-attached sites to avoid having to configure RIP tagging for loop prevention.

Static Routing Design Considerations

VPN sites that are single-homed to the USCom network may use static routing. However, this depends on the number of routes (a low number is mandatory, usually no greater than 5) and whether these routes are likely to change on a regular basis. Static routing is particularly suitable if route summarization is easily achievable for the set of routes that can be reached for a particular VPN site. In the majority of cases, only a few routes can be accessed via a single-homed site, such as a local /24 LAN segment, so static routing is adequate.

Clearly static routing does not provide any dynamic rerouting capability. Although static routing provides good stability while requiring minimal router resources, USCom actively encourages its larger Enterprise customers to run a dynamic routing protocol. The overhead of managing static routing in this case is considerable, especially at the central sites, where route summarization is often impossible.

In many cases, even if the customer has only a single connection to the Layer 3 MPLS VPN service, if the customer takes Internet service from somewhere else within the site, whether from USCom or some other Internet service provider, it is likely that the customer will follow a default route toward the Internet exit point. This means that the CE router needs to have *all* the relevant static routes from the VPN pointing toward the PE router. An appropriate addressing scheme that allows some summarization simplifies the configuration exercise but nevertheless is prone to errors and typically is avoided.

For stability reasons, USCom prefers to configure the static routes with the **permanent** keyword. This prevents the static routes from being withdrawn in MP-BGP in the event that a PE-CE link flaps or fails. The downside of this design decision is that traffic continues to be attracted toward the failed link, even if the PE router is unable to forward traffic from other sites across the link. However, because the customer site is single-homed, the added backbone stability is preferred over the suboptimal (unnecessary) packet forwarding.

Current statistics show that approximately 40 percent of USCom's PE-CE connections use static routing.

PE-CE BGP Routing Design Considerations

50 percent of VPN PE-CE connections use external BGP (eBGP). This is the protocol of choice for USCom, because it is used to dealing with this protocol (with experience from the Internet service), and it can easily add policy on a per-VPN basis. Some end users are already familiar with the BGP protocol and have been running it within their network before migrating to the VPN service, although this is normally restricted to large Enterprises. Also, many of these end users already subscribe to an Internet service and therefore are familiar with how the protocol is used. Therefore, standardizing on BGP is an obvious choice.

To protect the PE routers, every customer BGP-4 peering session is configured to accept only a maximum number of prefixes. This is achieved through the use of the **neighbor maximum-prefix** command on each PE-CE BGP peering session. USCom also uses *route dampening* (with the same set of parameters) for all its customers who attach to the VPN service via external BGP. This is stringently applied to all customers because route flaps (constant routing information changes) can cause instability in the control plane of the USCom network. The policy applied for dampening is as follows: Any route that flaps receives a *penalty* of 1000 for each flap. A *reuse limit* of 750 is configured so that a route, once suppressed, can be readvertised when the limit reaches 750. After a period of 15 minutes (the *half-life time*), the total value of the accumulated *penalty* is reduced in value by 50 percent. If the accumulated penalty ever reaches a *suppress limit* of 3000, MP-BGP suppresses advertisement of the route regardless of whether it is active.

Both of these parameters are configured using the template shown in Example 3-5.

Example 3-5   *Restricting the Number of Prefixes on PE-CE BGP Links Template*

```
router bgp 32765
  address-family ipv4 vrf vrf-name
   neighbor 23.50.0.6 remote-as customer-ASN
   neighbor 23.50.0.6 activate
   neighbor 23.50.0.6 maximum-prefix 100
   no auto-summary
   no synchronization
   bgp dampening route-map vpn-dampen
   exit-address-family
 !
route-map vpn-dampen permit 10
 set dampening 15 750 3000 60
```

NOTE   USCom uses the same set of dampening parameters for all eBGP PE-CE peering sessions. It also uses a route map for ease of provisioning. The parameters contained in the route map are inherited by all customer accesses that use external BGP.

The maximum prefix setting is determined at service provisioning time. It differs from customer to customer.

| **NOTE** | USCom currently does not tune any of the BGP timers to decrease convergence times. |

PE-CE IGP Routing Design Considerations

In recent months USCom has seen an increase in the number of customers requesting either OSPF or EIGRP support on their PE-CE links. These customers typically have large, and often complex, IGP topologies.

A number of benefits may be gained by running IGP on the PE-CE links:

- The service provider MPLS VPN network may be used for WAN connectivity while remaining within the customer's IGP domain. This provides a "drop and insert" approach to migrating the existing network onto the new infrastructure.

- A relatively seamless routing domain from the attached customers' perspective may be obtained. This avoids the extra costs associated with staff retraining to support an additional routing protocol such as BGP-4.

- IGP fast convergence enhancements can be deployed, especially in the case of multihomed sites, which may be useful in the case of a PE router or PE-CE link failure.

- External routes can be prevented within the IGP topology.

- IGP routing metrics can be maintained across sites, and the USCom network can remain transparent to the end user from a routing perspective.

- In the presence of customer back-door links (direct connectivity between customer sites, such as via leased lines), superior loop-avoidance and path-selection techniques can be used, such as sham links (OSPF) and site of origin (EIGRP).

A provider could offer a specific routing protocol as the only choice to avoid the costs associated with provisioning, maintaining, and troubleshooting different routing protocols. However, such an offering might force the VPN customers to compromise their design requirements and would ultimately hurt the provider through restriction of its customer base. If multiple routing protocol choices are to be offered on the PE-CE links, it is important to carefully consider the convergence characteristics (which are important to the VPN customer) and the service's scalability (which is important to both VPN customer *and* service provider).

USCom chose to offer RIPv2, EIGRP, and OSPF, all of which are provided on a restricted basis (in terms of the number of sites permitted to attach to a given PE router for each protocol). These restrictions are currently set at 25 for each protocol, although this figure is not a hard rule. It depends on the specific customer attachment needs (such as the number of routes and so forth) and is monitored to obtain more deployment experience. The IGPs are configured on a per-customer basis. The complexity of the configuration is driven by the complexity of the attached customer topology.

Specifics of the OSPF Service Deployment

USCom currently has two large customers who run OSPF on their PE-CE links. A number of features are included in the service provider design at the PE routers to support these customers.

A different OSPF process ID is used for each VPN. By default the same process ID is used for the VPN on all PE routers that have attached sites for that VPN. This is important. Otherwise, the OSPF routes transported across the MPLS VPN network are inserted as external routes (Type 5 LSAs) at a receiving OSPF site. This is typically undesirable because externals are by default flooded throughout the OSPF domain. Using the same process ID causes the PE router to generate interarea (Type 3 LSAs) routes instead, which are not flooded everywhere and therefore are bounded.

USCom uses the following command for *all* OSPF deployments. It protects the PE router from a large flood of Link-State Advertisements (LSAs) from any attached CE router.

```
[no] max-lsa maximum [threshold] [warning-only] [ignore-time value]
   [ignore-count value] [reset-time value]
```

Restricting the number of LSAs at the PE router is important because it protects the OSPF routing process from an unexpectedly large number of LSAs from a given VPN client. That might result from either a malicious attack or an incorrect configuration (such as redistributing the global BGP-4 table into the customer OSPF process).

Using this functionality, the PE routers can track the number of non-self-generated LSAs of any type for each VPN client that runs OSPF on the PE-CE links. When the maximum number of received LSAs is exceeded, the PE router does not accept any further LSAs from the offending OSPF process. If after 1 minute the level is still breached, the PE router shuts down all adjacencies within that OSPF process and clears the OSPF database.

USCom leaves the threshold, ignore time, ignore count, and reset time at their default values of 75 percent, 5 minutes, 5, and 2 times ignore time, respectively. Because only two OSPF clients exist at this time, the maximum LSA count is set to 10,000. USCom will continue to monitor this as new OSPF deployments arrive so as to optimize the default value.

Each router within an OSPF network needs to hold a unique identifier within the OSPF domain. This identifier is used so that each router can recognize self-originated LSAs and so that other routers can know during routing calculation which router originated a particular LSA. The LSA common header has a field known as the *advertising router* . It is set to the originating router's router ID.

The router ID used for the VRF OSPF process within Cisco IOS is selected from the highest loopback interface address within the VRF or, if no loopback interface exists, the highest interface address. This may be problematic if the interface address selected for the router ID fails, because a change of router ID is forced, and the OSPF process on the router must restart, causing a rebuild of the OSPF database and routing table. This clearly may cause instability in the OSPF domain. Therefore, USCom allocates a separate loopback address for each VRF that has OSPF PE-CE connectivity. This address is used as the router ID as well as for any sham links that may be required.

Specifics of the EIGRP Service Deployment

USCom found that a number of large Enterprise customers requested EIGRP connectivity with their PE routers. This protocol is widely deployed within Enterprise networks. Therefore, USCom felt that offering support for this protocol was a "service portfolio" differentiator. USCom deploys a number of features at the PE routers to support this protocol.

Automatic summarization is disabled as a matter of course for all EIGRP customers. The default behavior is for this functionality to be enabled. However, because the MPLS VPN backbone is considered transparent, USCom uses the **no auto-summary** command to disable it.

To support external routes within a customer EIGRP domain, a default metric of 1000 100 255 100 1500 is used, but this may be changed on a per-customer basis.

USCom supports the EIGRP site-of-origin (SoO) cost community. This community attribute is applied automatically at the point of insertion (POI) (the originating PE router) when an EIGRP route is redistributed into MP-BGP. Supporting this functionality allows USCom to support back-door links within a customer EIGRP topology by affecting the BGP best path calculation at a receiving PE router. This is achieved by carrying the original EIGRP route type and metric within the MP-BGP update and allowing BGP to consider the POI before other comparison steps.

USCom also supports the SoO attribute. This is configured by default for every site that belongs to a given EIGRP customer. This feature allows a router that is connected to a back-door link to reject a route if it contains its local SoO value. Example 3-6 shows this default configuration.

Example 3-6   *EIGRP SoO Attribute Configuration Template*

```
interface Serial 1/0
 ip vrf forwarding vrf-name
 ip vrf sitemap customer-name-SoO
!
route-map customer-name-SoO permit 10
 set extcommunity soo per-customer-site-id
 exit
```

USCom protects the PE routers from saturation of routing information by using the maximum-prefix feature. The following shows the syntax of this command:

```
maximum-prefix maximum [threshold] [warning-only]
    [[restart interval] [restart-count count] [reset-time interval] [dampened]]
```

At this point in time the default values for *threshold,* **restart**, **restart-count**, and **reset-time** are used. These values are 75 percent, 5 minutes, 3, and 15 minutes, respectively.

NOTE   It is worth noting that running an IGP between the PE router and the CE router requires some significant extra configuration for USCom.

IP Address Allocation for PE-CE Links

USCom decided within its design that it would allocate the PE-CE link IP addresses from one of its registered blocks. This allows more flexibility in determining a filtering template that can be applied to all PE routers so that unwanted traffic can be dropped at the edge. It also avoids any conflicts with customers' IP address space, because many will have selected IP addressing from the [PRIVATE] private ranges.

The block of addresses chosen for this purpose is taken from the 23.50.0.0/16 address block. Because the customer access routers are unmanaged, each PE-CE link is assigned a 255.255.255.252 network mask that allows two hosts. For example, 23.50.0.4/30 provides IP addresses 23.50.0.5 and 23.50.0.6 with which to address the PE-CE link of a given VPN customer. These addresses are redistributed into MP-BGP so that they are available within the VPN for troubleshooting purposes.

NOTE	USCom also decided to allow customer address space for the PE-CE links. However, this would be on an exception basis, and the IP addresses must be from a registered block.

Controlling Route Distribution with Filtering

Each PE router within the USCom network has finite resources that are distributed between all services that are offered at the edge. Because many VPN clients will access the network via the same PE routers, USCom would like to be able to restrict the number of routes that any one customer can carry within its routing table. This is achieved by applying the maximum routes command to all VRFs, as shown in Example 3-7.

Example 3-7   *Maximum Routes Configuration Template*

```
hostname USCom.cityname.PErouter-number
!
ip vrf vpn-name
 rd 32765:1-4294967295
 route-target export 32765:101-65535
 route-target import 32765:101-65535
 maximum routes maximum-#-of-routes {warning-threshold-% | warning-only}
```

USCom considered what values should be set within this command. It noticed that if the value of the limit imposed were set too low, valid routes would be rejected, causing a denial of service for some customer locations. Also, USCom noted that the **maximum routes** value must be able to cater to all types of routes injected into the VRF, including static routes, connected routes, and routes learned via a dynamic protocol. USCom decided to start with a **maximum routes** limit that was set for each VRF to be 50 percent more than the actual number of routes in steady state, with a warning at 20 percent more than the actual number of routes in steady state.

NOTE   When a link-state IGP, such as OSPF, is run on the PE-CE links, restricting route input to the VRF does not stop the link-state database from being populated. Therefore, additional protection mechanisms are required. These are discussed in the "Specifics of the OSPF Service Deployment" section earlier in this chapter.

USCom decided not to use any filtering for customer route distribution during its initial deployment of the Layer 3 MPLS VPN service. Because of this, all RRs carry the same set of routes, and each PE router relies on the Automatic Route Filtering (ARF) feature to ignore any routing updates that contain routes that are not locally imported into any attached VRFs.

Security Design for the Layer 3 MPLS VPN Service

Security of the network infrastructure is one of the most important considerations when designing any robust network. [ISP-security] provides an excellent overview of security best practices for ISP networks. Most of the material presented is also relevant to the USCom Layer 3 MPLS VPN service, because it presents basic router security tips, and USCom already follows these for its Internet service.

Although the Layer 3 MPLS VPN service separates customer routing from backbone routing, existing tools such as traceroute provide a method of revealing the core topology of the USCom network from within a customer VPN. Because of this, USCom chose to disable this behavior through the use of the **mpls ip propagate-ttl forwarded** command throughout the network. This command is discussed in detail in Chapter 13 of [VPN-Arch-Volume-1]. It basically has two effects: It propagates the IP TTL into the label header, and it propagates the label TTL into the IP header (where the packet exits the MPLS backbone). By disabling the TTL propagation (via the **no mpls ip propagate-ttl forwarded** command), USCom can hide its internal infrastructure from the output of any customer-initiated traceroutes that are sourced from within a Layer 3 VPN. This command, however, does not protect any of the Internet PE routers because packets are IP-forwarded rather than label-switched toward the Internet. Therefore, USCom has a policy of not advertising the IP address blocks used for its internal infrastructure toward the Internet. It also applies packet filters toward these addresses at the external-facing interfaces of the Internet PE routers.

Although the core addressing is hidden from traceroute through the use of the **no mpls ip propagate-ttl forwarded** command, the same cannot be guaranteed for the subnet used for PE-CE circuit addressing. DoS attacks can always be performed if the VPN client knows one or more of the IP addresses of the PE router. This is easy to determine through the use of the **traceroute** command. Visibility of PE router circuit information could allow the VPN client to intrude or perform DoS attacks on the PE router.

If the CE router is managed, which is not the case for USCom in its initial deployment, the PE router circuit address can be hidden by a filter that prevents it from being redistributed into the customer network. In addition, various inbound filters can be applied at the PE router to restrict CE router access; this is what USCom has adopted for its unmanaged service. Example 3-8 shows the filter template chosen for deployment.

Example 3-8 *PE-CE Link Filter Template*

```
ip access-list extended PE-CE-Filter
 permit icmp host CE-host-address host PE-router-PE-CE-link-address
 permit bgp host CE-interface-address host PE-interface-address
 deny ip any 23.49.0.0 0.0.255.255
 permit ip any any
```

The first line of the access list (the second line of Example 3-8) permits ICMP packets such as pings to be sent from the VPN customer to the directly connected PE router interface. Allowing such packets is useful for the customers, because they can perform diagnostics and management activity. The second line permits the BGP routing protocol to exchange routes by allowing communication between the CE router and PE router interface addresses. If a VPN customer is using a different protocol, this needs to be explicitly allowed within the filter.

The third line of the access list blocks any IP packets that are addressed to a destination within the USCom backbone network. The last line permits all other IP traffic to pass-through the PE router.

Quality of Service Design

The quality of service (QoS) marketed by a service provider and actually experienced by its customer base, is a key element of customer satisfaction. This is particularly true because most customers have already migrated, or soon will migrate, their mission-critical applications, as well as their voice and video applications, to IP services. In turn, this means that QoS is a key element of service provider competitiveness and success in the marketplace for both Internet and Layer 3 MPLS VPN services.

The levels of performance offered as part of Internet services in some parts of the world (such as the U.S.) have increased tremendously in recent years. This section discusses the Internet SLA that USCom offers in such a context. It also reviews the Layer 3 MPLS VPN SLA that USCom offers. Its objective is to allow customers to successfully carry all their mission-critical applications, as well as converge their data, voice, and video traffic. Finally, this section presents the design, both in the core and on the edge, deployed by USCom to meet these SLAs.

SLA for Internet Service

USCom offers an SLA for its Internet service. This SLA is made up of availability commitments, as well as performance commitments, as summarized in Table 3-6.

Table 3-6   *USCom Internet SLA Commitments*

SLA Parameter	SLA Commitment
Service availability (single-homed, no backup)	99.4%
Mean Time To Repair (MTTR)	4 hours
POP-to-POP Round-Trip Time (RTT)	70 ms
POP-to-POP Packet-Delivery Ratio (PDR)	99.5%

The availability commitments are provided to each Internet site. They are characterized by service availability of 99.4 percent (for a single-homed site attached via a leased line and without dial/ISDN backup) and an MTTR of 4 hours. Higher-availability commitments are offered with optional enhanced access options such as dial/ISDN backup and dual homing. Service availability is defined as the total number of minutes in a given month during which the Internet site can transmit and receive IP packets to and from the USCom backbone, divided by the total number of minutes in the month. USCom calculates service availability and MTTR based on trouble ticket information reported in the USCom trouble ticketing system for each site and customer.

Because USCom does not manage the Internet CE routers, the performance commitments of its Internet SLA are not end-to-end (not site-to-site). Instead, they apply POP-to-POP. The performance commitments are made up of an RTT of 70 ms and a PDR of 99.5 percent, which apply between any two POPs.

Using active measurements and averaging, USCom computes the POP-to-POP RTT and PDR. Dedicated devices located in every POP are used to generate two sets of sample traffic every 5 minutes to every other POP. The first sample traffic is a series of ten ICMP ping packets, which the sample traffic source uses to measure RTT. The second sample traffic is a series of ten UDP packets. The sample traffic destination uses them to measure the PDR (the ratio of received sample packets divided by the total number of transmitted sample packets). The worst RTT value measured over every hour is retained as the "worst hourly value." These "worst hourly values" are then averaged over the day, and the daily averages are averaged over the month. This yields the monthly average RTT value to be compared against the 70-ms SLA commitment specified in Table 3-6.

SLA for the Layer 3 MPLS VPN Service

Several considerations influenced the SLA definition of the Layer 3 MPLS VPN service. The first was the need to offer QoS levels that allow VPN customers to converge their data, voice, and video applications onto a common infrastructure. The second was the fact that it is relatively easy and cheap for USCom to "throw bandwidth" at the QoS problem in the core (from POP to POP). As discussed in the next section, the most attractive approach for USCom to offer the appropriate QoS to all traffic of all application types, including the most demanding applications such as voice, was to offer indiscriminately the highest required QoS to all the traffic. In turn, this means that the SLA needed to specify only a single set of POP-to-POP performance commitments that were applicable to all traffic.

USCom handles all traffic the same way in the core and does not allocate more resources to some types of traffic over others. Therefore, there is no need for the company to charge differently depending on the mix of traffic types from the customer or to limit the rate at which some traffic types from a given customer site might enter the network. This results in a very simple service for both USCom and the customer in which the customer can transmit as much traffic as he wants, of any traffic type, without USCom's having to know or even care about it. In turn, this means that the service charge for a Layer 3 MPLS VPN site is a flat fee that depends only on the site's port access speed.

The next consideration was the fact that, unlike in the core, "throwing bandwidth" at the QoS problem on the access links (CE-to-PE and PE-to-CE links) is not easy or cheap for USCom. This is primarily because these links are dedicated to a single customer and need to be provisioned over access technology where capacity is usually still scarce or at a premium. This means that congestion is to be expected on some of the CE-to-PE and PE-to-CE links. Therefore, prioritization mechanisms (such as differentiated services) are required on these links to protect the high QoS of the most demanding and important applications.

The final main SLA consideration was the fact that USCom does not manage the CE routers that access the Layer 3 MPLS VPN service. This means that prioritizing traffic onto the CE-to-PE links, and the resulting QoS experienced by various applications on this segment, is entirely under the control of the customer (because such mechanisms have to be performed by the device that transmits onto the link) and conversely is entirely out of USCom's control. In turn, this means that USCom cannot offer any SLA performance commitment for the CE-to-PE segment. This does not mean that QoS cannot be achieved on that segment. Instead, it recognizes that such QoS is under the customer's operational domain and thus is the customer's responsibility.

Similarly, USCom does not restrict in any way the proportion of each traffic type that a CE router can send, nor does it restrict which remote VPN site this traffic is destined for. Therefore, USCom has no way of knowing, or controlling, how much traffic will converge onto a remote PE router for transmission to a given CE router on the corresponding PE-to-CE link. In addition, sizing of the corresponding PE-to-CE link is under the customer's control. Thus, although USCom manages the upstream device on the PE-to-CE link, it cannot offer any SLA performance commitment on the PE-to-CE link either.

To help illustrate this point, imagine that a given customer has a VPN containing five sites—S1, S2, S3, S4, and S5—each of which is connected to its respective PE router via a T1 link. Imagine that S1, S2, S3, and S4 all transmit 500 kbps worth of voice traffic destined for S5. The egress PE router that attaches to S5 receives 2 Mbps of voice traffic destined for S5. It is clear that no matter what scheduling/prioritization mechanism may be used on the link to S5 by this PE router, and leaving aside any other traffic, trying to squeeze 2 Mbps of voice traffic onto a T1 link will result in poor QoS, at least on some voice calls (if not all).

However, the upstream end of the PE-to-CE link (the PE router itself, where prioritization and differentiation have to be implemented to offer appropriate QoS to the various applications on that segment) is not in the customer operational domain. So, unlike the CE-to-PE link case, the customer is not in a position to implement the required mechanisms independent of USCom to ensure that the right QoS is provided to all applications on the PE-to-CE link.

To ensure that the customer can achieve QoS on the PE-to-CE link in cases where that link may become congested, USCom decided to offer a service option (the "PE-to-CE QoS" option) whereby USCom would activate on the PE-to-CE link a fixed set of DiffServ per-hop behaviors (PHBs) that the customers can use as they see fit. Using this service offering, by properly sizing the PE-to-CE link, by controlling the amount of traffic for a given type of application (such as voice) sent from and to a given CE router, and by triggering the appropriate PHB made available by USCom for that type of traffic, the customer can ensure that the required QoS is provided to important applications. To trigger the appropriate PHB for a given packet, the customer simply needs to mark the packet's DS field in the IP header according to the Differentiated Services Codepoint (DSCP) values specified by USCom for each supported PHB. This marking must be performed at the ingress VPN site (on the ingress CE router) so that the DS field is already marked when the egress PE router applies the PHB during transmission of the packet onto the PE-to-CE link (after forwarding takes place and the MPLS header is popped). This is described in detail in the "QoS Design on the Network Edge" section.

The "PE-to-CE QoS" service option is marketed with a flat fee corresponding to the value-add provided to the end user and reflecting the extra processing load on the PE router. This option is kept very simple, without any customizable parameters.

For each application to experience the required QoS end-to-end, the corresponding requirements must be met on every segment of the traffic path—that is, within the ingress VPN site, from the ingress CE router to the ingress PE router, from USCom POP to POP, from egress PE router to egress CE router, and finally within the egress VPN site. The following summarizes how the USCom SLA performance commitments play out across each segment of the end-to-end path:

- **POP-to-POP**—USCom offers arbitrarily to all traffic (independent of its application type and/or actual requirements) SLA performance commitments across the backbone (from POP to POP). This is compatible with the most stringent requirements of any application (including voice).

- **CE-to-PE link**—USCom provides no SLA performance commitments on this segment. It is the customer's responsibility to ensure that the QoS required by the various applications is offered appropriately. The customer may achieve this by ensuring that the

CE-to-PE link is sufficiently overengineered for the total aggregate load or by deploying DiffServ mechanisms on the ingress CE router, including classifying traffic into separate DiffServ classes and applying the corresponding PHBs.

- **PE-to-CE link**—USCom provides no SLA performance commitments on this segment. However, as a service option, USCom can take the responsibility of applying DiffServ PHBs. It is then the customer's responsibility to use these PHBs, in combination with traffic control on ingress CE routers and capacity planning for the PE-to-CE link, to ensure that the QoS required by the different applications is provided on that segment.

- **Layer 3 VPN sites**—Because this is entirely out of the USCom realm of operation, USCom leaves it to the customer to ensure that the right QoS is offered inside the VPN. The customer may achieve this by overengineering the VPN site network (that is, via switched Gigabit Ethernet technology) and/or deploying DiffServ within the VPN Site.

These SLA points are illustrated in Figure 3-13.

Figure 3-13 *USCom VPN SLA Performance Commitments and Customer Responsibility*

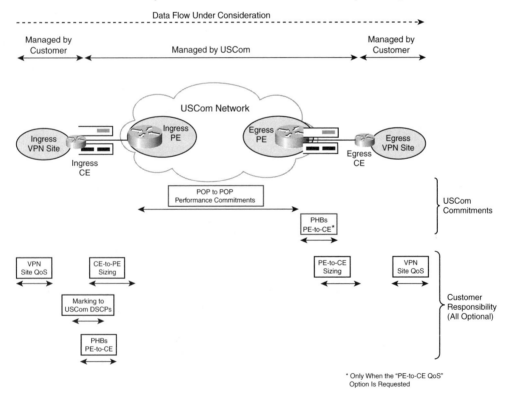

As with the Internet SLA, all the performance commitments apply POP-to-POP. The RTT and PDR commitments provided in the Internet SLA are appropriate for any multimedia application, so those are also used in the Layer 3 MPLS VPN SLA. However, because the performance commitments must meet the QoS requirements of all applications, including real-time/VoIP, a jitter commitment is added in the VPN SLA to the RTT and PDR commitments.

NOTE   Because in the core no distinction is made between Internet traffic and VPN traffic, Internet traffic experiences the same performance level as VPN traffic. Nonetheless, USCom elected to include only the jitter commitment in the VPN SLA. The first reason for this is that USCom's service of choice for customers running real-time traffic is the Layer 3 MPLS VPN service. The second reason is that it is possible that, in the future, it will become more economical for USCom to deploy some DiffServ differentiation in the core and prioritize real-time traffic over other traffic so that very low POP-to-POP jitter may no longer be provided to all traffic by default.

As with the RTT and PDR, USCom uses active measurement and averaging to compute the jitter. The same series of sample traffic of ten UDP packets sent every 5 minutes that is used to measure the packet delivery ratio is also used to measure the jitter. Note that the sample source and sample destination do not need to synchronize their internal clocks because jitter can be computed by the destination only using its local timestamp on packet arrival and analyzing the variation over the known transmitted interpacket interval. The worst value measured over every hour is retained as the "worst hourly value." These "worst hourly values" are then averaged over the day, and the daily averages are averaged over the month.

Table 3-7 lists the Layer 3 MPLS VPN SLA commitments.

Table 3-7   *USCom Layer 3 MPLS VPN SLA Commitments*

SLA Parameter	SLA commitment
Service availability (single-homed, no backup)	99.4%
Mean Time To Repair (MTTR)	4 hours
POP-to-POP Round-Trip Time (RTT)	70 ms
POP-to-POP Packet-Delivery Ratio (PDR)	99.5%
POP-to-POP jitter	20 ms
Optional "PE-to-CE QoS"	Optional support of three PHBs on the PE-to-CE link

When unable to meet the commitments listed in Table 3-6 over the one-month measurement period, USCom offers refunds to its VPN customers in the form of service credits. The SLA specifies how the service credits are computed, depending on the observed deviation from the commitment for each SLA parameter.

QoS Design in the Core Network

This section presents the QoS design USCom deployed in the core network to support the Internet SLA and the Layer 3 MPLS VPN SLA performance commitments described in the previous sections. As discussed in the section "USCom's Network Environment," thanks to its DWDM optical infrastructure, and thanks to the use of Gigabit Ethernet switching within its POPs, USCom can enforce an overengineering policy. Therefore, it can maintain a low aggregate utilization everywhere in the core without incurring any excessive additional capital expenditure. USCom elected to take full advantage of this by

- Relying exclusively on aggregate capacity planning and overengineering to control QoS in the core and not deploying any DiffServ mechanisms or MPLS Traffic Engineering. This results in simpler engineering, configuration, and monitoring of the core.

- Pushing this overengineering policy approach further so that, in most cases, the aggregate utilization is kept low even during a single link, node, or SRLG failure. In turn, this ensures that QoS is maintained during most failures. (Protection against SRLG failure is discussed later, in the "Network Recovery Design" section.)

- Factoring in a safety margin when determining USCom's maximum utilization for capacity planning purposes to compensate for the shortcomings of capacity planning. This is discussed in the "Core QoS Engineering" section of Chapter 2, "Technology Primer: Quality of Service, Traffic Engineering, and Network Recovery."

Thus, USCom is adhering to the 1/1/0 model (or 3/1/0 model when the PE-to-CE QoS option is used) presented in the "QoS Models" section of Chapter 2.

The maximum distance between any two POPs in the USCom network is 4000 km. Assuming 25 percent of extra distance to cope with a longer actual physical route and additional distance when transiting via intermediate POPs, the one-way maximum distance is 5000 km and the round-trip maximum distance is 10,000 km. Assuming a 5-ms per 1000 km of light propagation delay through fiber, the maximum round-trip propagation delay in the USCom network is 50 ms.

NOTE   USCom's optical network is quite dense so that the IP topology is generally congruent with the underlying optical topology. This is why only 25 percent of extra distance is factored in when computing the maximum one-way distance.

The SLA RTT commitment of 70 ms leaves 20 ms of round-trip queuing delay. Assuming a maximum of 12 hops in one direction, such a round-trip queuing delay is safely met if the delay at each hop is kept below 0.8 ms. In fact, the round-trip queuing delay is likely to be significantly better than 20 ms because delay commitment is statistical in nature and therefore does not accumulate linearly. However, USCom uses the simpler linear rule because exact accumulation formulas are not strictly known, and estimate functions are quite complex.

Similarly, the SLA jitter commitment of 20 ms can be safely met if the jitter is kept below 0.8 ms at every hop, which is all the more true if the queuing delay itself is bounded at 0.8 ms, as identified to meet the RTT commitment.

USCom determined through mathematical analysis and simulation of aggregate queuing through a single hop and by applying an empirical safety margin that the per-hop queuing delay requirement can be safely met with a maximum aggregate utilization of 70 percent for any of the link speeds used in its core. In other words, USCom characterized the shape of the QoS versus utilization curve (discussed in the section "The Fundamental QoS Versus Utilization Curve" in Chapter 2) for its particular environment and various core link speeds.

This analysis also indicated that the level of loss caused by excessive queue occupancy under such conditions would be well below what is necessary to achieve the SLA's packet delivery ratio (in fact, it would actually be negligible). However, the packet delivery ratio also accounts for other causes of loss, such as those due to failures and routing reconvergence.

Based on this, USCom specified its capacity planning policy whereby additional core capacity is provisioned whenever

- The measured link utilization exceeds 40 percent in the absence of any failure in the network.

  or

- The link utilization exceeds 70 percent in the case of a single failure of a link, node, or SRLG.

Clearly, this policy ensures that POP-to-POP performance commitments are met because the link utilization is significantly below the maximum aggregate utilization in the absence of failure and is below or equal to the maximum aggregate utilization in the case of a single failure.

To enforce this policy, USCom monitors link utilization at 10-minute intervals on every link. When the utilization reaches 40 percent, an alarm is triggered. If this level is reached in the absence of failure and is not caused by any exceptional event, additional capacity is provisioned.

Also, USCom uses a network engineering and simulation tool with "what-if" analysis capabilities. On a regular basis, the measured maximum utilization figures for all links are fed into the tool. The tool then determines what the maximum utilization would be on all links should any link, node, or SRLG fail. If this exceeds 70 percent and cannot be reduced by adjusting IS-IS metrics (without redirecting excessive traffic onto another link), additional capacity is provisioned.

NOTE   USCom has identified a small number of nodes and SRLGs in the current network whose single failure would result in a load on other links possibly exceeding 70 percent. This means the performance could possibly be somewhat degraded should any of those actually fail. But because such failure scenarios are very rare and affect performance only during the duration of the failure, it is very unlikely that they would prevent USCom from meeting its SLA commitments over its one-month period. Thus, USCom decided that these few exceptions to the capacity planning rules were tolerable.

It is therefore clear that as long as USCom can enforce its high overengineering policy (based on the capacity planning rule of keeping utilization on all links below 40 percent in the absence of failure and below 70 percent in the presence of failure), the SLA performance commitments can be met without deploying any additional QoS tools in the core network, such as MPLS DiffServ or MPLS Traffic Engineering.

Because the DWDM optical core is currently far from reaching capacity limitations (that is, all lambdas used on a given fiber), the link provisioning lead time is only a few weeks. Because traffic growth on the USCom backbone is relatively steady and free from huge spikes (as shown in Figure 3-14), USCom felt it will indeed be able to enforce its overengineering policy, at least in the next one to two years. Thus, USCom has not yet deployed MPLS DiffServ or MPLS Traffic Engineering. However, if in the longer term enforcing the high overengineering policy becomes difficult, USCom will then consider such technologies.

Figure 3-14   *USCom Utilization and Traffic Growth*

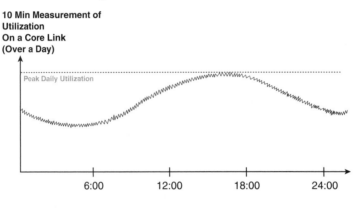

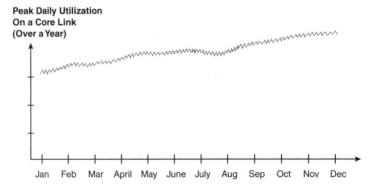

In summary, although USCom offers tight POP-to-POP SLA commitments for Internet and Layer 3 MPLS VPN traffic, its core QoS design is very simple. It relies entirely on capacity planning, with enforcement of a high overengineering policy applied on an aggregate basis to all traffic. It does not involve any additional QoS mechanism in the core network.

QoS Design on the Network Edge

This section presents the QoS design deployed by USCom on the customer-facing interfaces of the PE routers. Because USCom does not implement any differentiated service in the core network and does not care about the mix of traffic classes received from a CE router, no QoS mechanism is configured on the ingress of the PE routers for both Internet customers and Layer 3 MPLS VPN customers.

On the egress side of the PE router, by default no QoS mechanisms are activated. However, if the Layer 3 MPLS VPN customer requests the PE-to-CE QoS option, a fixed QoS service policy is applied on the egress side of the PE router that activates three DiffServ PHBs.

Because USCom does not perform any QoS mechanism on the ingress side of the PE router or in the core, the Precedence field (or even the full Differentiated Services field) of an IP packet is carried transparently through the USCom network. Its value at the time of transmission by the egress PE router onto the PE-to-CE link (that is, after popping of the complete MPLS header) is unchanged from when the packet was transmitted by the customer ingress CE router. Therefore, USCom can use the Precedence field in the IP header as the classification criteria to apply the PHBs on the PE-to-CE link. To control which packets receive what PHB, the customer just has to mark the Precedence field on the ingress CE router (or upstream of it) in accordance with the Precedence-to-PHB mappings defined by USCom and specified in Table 3-8.

NOTE	The ability to transparently transport the Differentiated Services field of the IP header over a Layer 3 MPLS VPN service provider network without modifying the value set by the customer is often called the QoS transparency feature.

Table 3-8   *Precedence-to-PHB Mapping for the PE-to-CE QoS Option*

Precedence Values	PHB[*]	Targeted Traffic
0, 1, 2, 3	BE	Best-effort traffic
4, 6, 7	AF41	High-priority traffic
5	EF	Real-time traffic

[*]See the section "The IETF DiffServ Model and Mechanisms" in Chapter 2.

For example, the customer could configure its CE router to

- Set the Precedence field to a value of 5 when sending a VoIP packet to the CE-to-PE link.

- Set the Precedence field to a value of 4 when sending an Enterprise Resource Planning (ERP) packet to the CE-to-PE link.

- Set the Precedence field to a value of 0 when sending other packets to the CE-to-PE link.

The result of this configuration is that when USCom transmits packets to the PE-to-CE link, it applies the EF PHB to the voice packets, the AF41 PHB to the ERP packets, and the BE PHB to the rest of the traffic. This effectively allows the customer to ensure that its applications are prioritized as it sees fit on the PE-to-CE link in case of congestion on that link.

Note that the customer would also probably configure its CE router to apply some custom PHBs on the CE-to-PE link to manage potential congestion on the CE-to-PE link. This set of custom PHBs does not have to be the same as the ones applied by USCom for the PE-to-CE QoS option, but it must be consistent with it, and its DS-field-to-PHB mapping must be consistent with the one from USCom. For example, the customer could decide to perform finer differentiation and activate a set of four PHBs with the Precedence-to-PHB mappings shown in Table 3-9.

Table 3-9   *Sample Precedence-to-PHB Mapping for Custom CE PHBs*

Precedence Values	PHB	Targeted Traffic
0, 1, 2	BE	Best-effort traffic
3	AF31	High-priority noninteractive traffic
4, 6, 7	AF41	High-priority interactive traffic
5	EF	Real-time traffic

End-to-end QoS operation when the PE-to-CE QoS option is not used, and when it is used by a customer, are illustrated in Figures 3-15 and 3-16, respectively.

NOTE   Because Precedence values of 6 and 7 are set aside for network control (including IP routing) and network administration (including some network management traffic), some service providers apply preferential treatment inside their network to traffic marked with these Precedence values to guarantee the stability of their core. For example, as explained in the "Quality of Service Design" section in Chapter 4, Telecom Kingland schedules its internal control, management, and routing traffic inside a dedicated queue completely separate from the queue used for customer traffic. To make sure customer traffic does not interfere with their own network control or network administration traffic, such service providers either drop traffic sent by customers with a Precedence field set to 6 or 7 or remark it to a different value so that it does not map to the same MPLS EXP value as their own Precedence 6 and 7 traffic. However, because USCom does not enforce any traffic differentiation in its core, it decided to accept, as is, traffic from customers with Precedence set to 6 or 7 and to schedule those as high-priority traffic in its PE-to-CE QoS option (as shown in Table 3-8). Should USCom deploy preferential treatment of its network control or network administration traffic inside its core in the future, it would have to ensure that customer traffic cannot interfere with this preferential treatment. (For example, USCom would have to remark the Precedence or impose on such customer traffic an EXP value different from the one it uses for its network administration and control traffic.)

Figure 3-15   *End-to-End QoS Operations Without the PE-to-CE QoS Option*

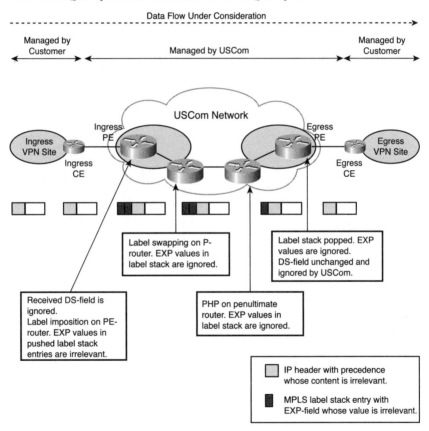

Figure 3-16 *End-to-End QoS Operations with the PE-to-CE QoS Option*

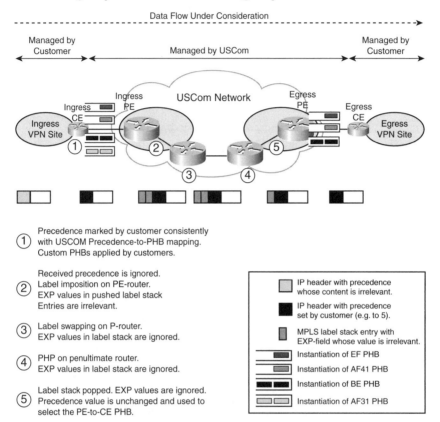

① Precedence marked by customer consistently with USCOM Precedence-to-PHB mapping. Custom PHBs applied by customers.

② Received precedence is ignored. Label imposition on PE-router. EXP values in pushed label stack Entries are irrelevant.

③ Label swapping on P-router. EXP values in label stack are ignored.

④ PHP on penultimate router. EXP values in label stack are ignored.

⑤ Label stack popped. EXP values are ignored. Precedence value is unchanged and used to select the PE-to-CE PHB.

☐	IP header with precedence whose content is irrelevant.
■	IP header with precedence set by customer (e.g. to 5).
▪	MPLS label stack entry with EXP-field whose value is irrelevant.
▭	Instantiation of EF PHB
▭	Instantiation of AF41 PHB
▭	Instantiation of BE PHB
▭	Instantiation of AF31 PHB

USCom elected to perform classification for the PE-to-CE QoS based on Precedence rather than the full DS field because it offers the end customer the flexibility to perform traffic marking either on the Precedence field or on the full DS field. For example, if the customer elected to mark VoIP packets with the DS field set to the EF DSCP (101110), these packets would be classified by the egress PE router appropriately because the first 3 bits of the packet's DS field, which constitute the Precedence field, are set to 101, which is Precedence 5.

Because USCom wanted to support a simple fixed set of PHBs for the PE-to-CE QoS option without any customizable parameters, it selected a versatile set of PHBs, as shown in Table 3-10, and a versatile PHB instantiation intended to be suitable for typical customer needs.

Table 3-10   *PHB Instantiation for the PE-to-CE QoS Option*

PHB	Instantiation
EF	Priority queue with 40% of the link bandwidth allocated.
	In the absence of congestion, bandwidth is not limited.
	In the presence of congestion, bandwidth is limited to 40% (excess is dropped) to protect the mission-critical applications expected to be handled by the AF41 PHB.
AF41	Class queue with most of the remaining bandwidth allocated (50% of the link bandwidth). This ensures strong prioritization of AF41 over BE.
	In case of contention across all classes, this queue is granted 50% of the link bandwidth. However, this queue is not limited to 50%. It can use more if the other queues are not currently using their allocated bandwidth.
	Random Early Detection (RED), as discussed in the section "The IETF DiffServ Model and Mechanisms" of Chapter 2, optimizes performance for TCP traffic, which is expected to be common in this class.
BE	Class queue with remaining bandwidth allocated (10% of the link bandwidth).
	In case of contention across all classes, this queue is granted 10% of the link bandwidth. However, this queue is not limited to 10%. It can use more if the other queues are not currently using their allocated bandwidth.
	Random Early Detection (RED) optimizes performance for TCP traffic, which is expected to be common in this class.

Example 3-9 illustrates how USCom configures PHB instantiation using Cisco IOS Modular QoS CLI (MQC) and applies it as the egress service policy of a PE router for a PE-to-CE link (see [QoS-CONF] and [QoS-REF] for details on how to configure QoS on Cisco devices using MQC). Note that the service policy is applied on the ATM1/0/0.100 and ATM1/0/0.101 interfaces because the PE-to-CE QoS option has been requested for the corresponding attached site. Expressing bandwidth as a percentage of the link bandwidth (rather than in absolute values) in the policy map is extremely convenient. It allows the use of a single policy map on all physical and logical interfaces regardless of their actual link speed.

Example 3-9   *Egress Service Policy for the PE-to-CE QoS Option*

```
ip vrf v101:USPO
 description VRF for US Post Office
 rd 32765:239
 route-target export 32765:101
 route-target import 32765:101
!
ip vrf v102:SoccerOnline
 description VRF for SoccerOnline International
 rd 32765:240
 route-target export 32765:102
 route-target export 32765:102
!
ip vrf v103:BigBank
 description VRF for BigBank of Massachusetts
```

continues

Example 3-9 *Egress Service Policy for the PE-to-CE QoS Option (Continued)*

```
 rd 32765:241
 route-target export 32765:103
 route-target import 32765:103
 !
interface ATM1/0/0.100 point-to-point
 description ** BigBank_Site2 with PE-to-CE QoS option
 ip vrf forwarding v103:BigBank
 ip address 23.50.0.17 255.255.255.252
 pvc 10/50
  vbr-nrt 1200 1000 2
  encapsulation aal5snap
  service-policy out policy-PE-CE-QoS
 !
interface ATM1/0/0.101 point-to-point
 description ** SoccerOnline_Site1 International with PE-to-CE QoS option
 ip vrf forwarding v102:SoccerOnline
 ip address 23.50.0.9 255.255.255.252
 pvc 10/60
  vbr-nrt 1500 1500 3
  encapsulation aal5snap
  service-policy out policy-PE-CE-QoS
 !
interface ATM1/0/0.102 point-to-point
 description ** US Post Office_Site10 without PE-to-CE QoS option
 ip vrf forwarding v101:USPO
 ip address 23.50.0.13 255.255.255.252
 pvc 10/50
  vbr-nrt 1200 1000 2
  encapsulation aal5snap
 !
class-map class-PrecHigh
  match precedence 4 6 7
class-map class-PrecVoice
  match precedence 5
 !
policy-map policy-PE-CE-QoS
  class class-PrecVoice
   priority percent 40
  class class-PrecHigh
   bandwidth percent 50
   random-detect
  class class-default
   bandwidth percent 10
   random-detect
```

In summary, the USCom QoS edge design is very simple: By default, no QoS mechanism is activated on the PE routers. When a customer selects the PE-to-CE QoS option, a fixed service policy is applied in the egress direction onto the PE-to-CE link in order to instantiate a traditional set of three PHBs targeted at real-time, mission-critical, and best-effort applications.

Traffic Engineering Within the USCom Network

As established earlier in the "QoS Design in the Core Network" section, one of the fundamental network design rules adopted by USCom is the overprovisioning of available network resources, hence ensuring bounded link utilization in the core. This implies the following:

- Sufficient bandwidth must be provisioned in the core optical network.

- The metrics used by IGP (IS-IS in the case of USCom) must be computed so as to efficiently balance the traffic load in the core. In other words, traffic engineering is achieved through manipulating the IGP metrics. To ensure that link utilization remains below 40 percent in the absence of failures at all times, USCom decided to develop an internal tool that computes a set of IS-IS metrics that are used to traffic-engineer the network. The tool is run on a regular basis (approximately every 6 months) to accommodate some traffic growth. It is triggered by the monitoring of link utilization in the network by the USCom management system.

NOTE   It is worth mentioning that changing the IGP metrics is not a completely cost-free operation. It requires some nonnegligible work for the network operations staff. Indeed, each IS-IS link metric must be changed individually to give the network time to converge before changing another IS-IS metric. Moreover, although transient states may lead to temporary congestion, as already stated in the section devoted to the network QoS design, this is unlikely to impact the overall SLA because it is averaged over a period of one month. Furthermore, such changes are performed during maintenance windows. Another constraint added to the IGP metric computation tool is to keep the link utilization below 70 percent in the case of a single link, node, or SRLG failure. In the case of the USCom network, this was an achievable objective in most cases.

Network Recovery Design

Network recovery is undoubtedly a key component of the overall network design because it impacts the network availability of the various service offerings and consequently the SLAs presented by USCom. In particular, USCom had an objective to offer high availability for both the Layer 3 MPLS VPN and Internet services. USCom's existing customers clearly required network availability for its VPN traffic equivalent to that given by the regular Layer 2-based network (Frame Relay, ATM, and so on). As far as the Internet traffic was concerned, although the requirements of this service are usually less stringent, USCom decided to arbitrarily provide high network availability to both the Layer 3 MPLS VPN and Internet traffic. As specified earlier in the SLA section, a network availability of 99.4 percent is guaranteed for both types of traffic.

Before determining its network recovery design, USCom had to consider several objectives and network design constraints, such as the required network availability, the failure scope coverage (link/SRLG/node failure), the requirement for covering single versus multiple failures, the traffic rerouting time, QoS during failure, and single versus multiple class of recovery (CoR). Other criteria, such as the operational constraints and cost aspects, were also taken into account.

Network Availability Objectives

When considering the network failure scope, USCom had a requirement that the network be able to survive any single failure, including the failure of an SRLG (which is considered a single failure). In terms of rerouting time, the goal was to provide a 50-ms convergence time upon an inter-POP link or SRLG failure.

NOTE   A link failure can be provoked by a fiber cut or optical equipment failure.

As mentioned in the "USCom's Network Environment" section, although a very limited set of data was available for the newly deployed optical network, USCom expected that link failures would be by far the most common failure scenario (90 percent of the failures were expected to be link failures). Consequently, the objective was to provide a rerouting time similar to SONET (60 ms) in case of link and SRLG failures only.

Because the USCom network was designed to engineer customer traffic flows based on the computed set of IS-IS metrics, link utilization does not exceed 40 percent during steady state and 70 percent during a single link/SRLG failure. Because of this, QoS can be guaranteed during failure (along the backup path) without the requirement of any type of DiffServ deployment in the core network. Hence, the only objective that USCom had in the design was to provide a backup path and to implement fast recovery (50 ms) upon link and SRLG failure. Based on this design, the rerouted traffic flows should not suffer from QoS degradation.

In terms of class of recovery, USCom decided to provide equivalent network availability to all traffic without any discrimination between types. In other words, both the Internet and Layer 3 MPLS VPN traffic should benefit from the same rerouting time objectives.

Operational Constraints on Network Recovery Design

One of USCom's key objectives was to carefully minimize the network management complexity for all service offerings. The adoption of a new technology, such as MPLS Fast Reroute, could not be justified if the cost of such an implementation unreasonably increased the network management complexity. Although such criteria might be somehow subjective, trying to keep the network as simple as possible was a clear objective, and it is reflected in the resulting network design.

Cost Constraints for the Network Recovery Design

Obviously USCom could have selected from a large set of network recovery mechanisms to be able to reach its particular network availability objectives. Every mechanism has some benefits and drawbacks in terms of efficiency, complexity, scalability, scope of recovery, and so on (as discussed in the Chapter 2 section "Core Network Availability"). For USCom, the cost of the chosen network recovery strategy to meet the set of objectives for network availability was of the utmost importance and had to be kept as low as possible. In particular, the purchase of additional equipment at any layer (optical or IP/MPLS) was to be avoided if at all possible.

Network Recovery Design for Link Failures

SONET link failures are handled at the SONET layer. In the case of the optical links, USCom decided to deploy unprotected light paths and MPLS-based Traffic Engineering Fast Reroute (FRR) to provide 50-ms rerouting time upon link and SRLG failure for every unprotected light path. An important objective was to keep the operation as simple as possible. Moreover, the only constraint to be taken into account as far as the backup tunnel path was concerned was the SRLG diversity. Indeed, as pointed out in the "Traffic Engineering Within the USCom Network" section, thanks to the in-house IGP metric computation tool, the network was designed such that any recovery path offers an acceptable QoS during failure.

USCom elected to pursue the following MPLS Traffic Engineering Fast Reroute design for each light path that is to be protected:

- Configuration of a one-hop unconstrained primary TE Label-Switched Path (LSP)
- Dynamic configuration of an SRLG diverse next-hop (NHOP) backup tunnel

Before reviewing each of these aspects, it is useful to revisit the definitions of the terms one-hop, NHOP, and next-next hop (NNHOP).

As shown in Figure 3-17, a one-hop TE LSP is defined as a TE LSP that starts on router X and terminates on router Y, where Y is a direct neighbor of X. The signaling aspects of such a TE LSP are identical to any other TE LSP. The forwarding is different because it does not require any additional MPLS labels. Indeed, when a packet is sent to a one-hop TE LSP, no additional label is pushed (because of the penultimate hop popping operation).

Figure 3-17   *One-Hop, NHOP, and NNHOP TE LSP*

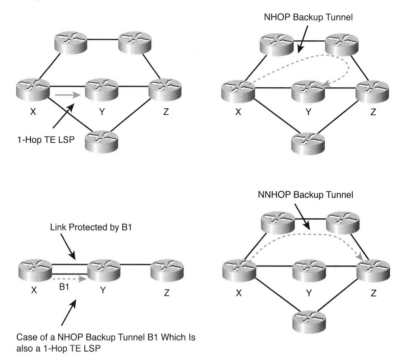

An NHOP backup tunnel simply refers to the fact that a backup tunnel originating on router X terminates on a direct neighbor of X (router Y in Figure 3-17). As shown in Figure 3-17, such a backup tunnel can be a one-hop tunnel if it protects a link via another parallel link or a multihop backup tunnel.

An NNHOP backup tunnel is a backup tunnel that originates on router X and terminates on router Z, where Z is one of X's neighbor's neighbors.

If you review each of these elements in more detail (along with the corresponding parameter tuning), you can see that configuration of a one-hop unconstrained primary TE LSP is possible because MPLS Traffic Engineering is just used with the aim of providing Fast Reroute protection. A single one-hop primary TE LSP is required so as to carry all the traffic routed through the link in question. (This is ensured because the TE LSP does not have any constraint, so its path just follows the IS-IS shortest path.) The use of such a primary one-hop TE LSP allows for the automatic protection of all the IP prefixes routed by the IGP along the same link that the one-hop tunnel follows.

Dynamic configuration of an SRLG diverse NHOP backup tunnel is made possible by flooding SRLG-related information within the IGP, as specified in [ISIS-GMPLS] and [OSPF-GMPLS]. In turn, this allows every router acting as a Point of Local Repair (PLR) to dynamically and automatically compute an NHOP backup tunnel path, SRLG diverse from the protected link (a path that does not have any SRLG in common with the protected link). USCom decided to make use of such technology to reduce the management complexity.

Figure 3-18 shows an example of SRLG (the links St. Louis–Chicago and St. Louis–Washington share SRLG 1). It also illustrates an example of a one-hop unconstrained primary TE LSP and NHOP SRLG diverse backup tunnel for the St. Louis–Washington OC-192 link.

Figure 3-18 *USCom MPLS Traffic Engineering Fast Reroute Design*

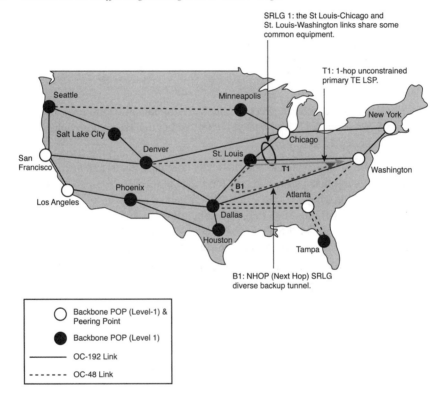

In this example, the router in St. Louis has to compute an SRLG diverse path for the backup tunnel B1 that will be used to protect the link St. Louis–Washington.

| NOTE | The USCom team in charge of managing the optical layer provided all the information related to the design shown in Figure 3-18 (in particular, the SRLG membership). |

The first step in deploying this design is to configure the SRLG membership on each router. This information is then flooded throughout the network by means of the relevant IS-IS extensions. Example 3-10 provides the necessary Cisco IOS configuration used by USCom for this process.

Example 3-10 *Configuration of SRLG Membership*

```
hostname USCom.StLouis.P1
!
interface POS0/0
 description ** St Louis - Washington OC-192 link
 mpls traffic-engineering srlg 1
!
interface POS1/0
 description ** St Louis - Chicago OC-192 link
 mpls traffic-engineering srlg 1
```

In addition, each router has been configured to automatically configure and set up a one-hop unconstrained primary TE LSP and an NHOP SRLG diverse backup tunnel for each protected link (the unprotected light path).

Example 3-11 illustrates how to automatically configure and set up unconstrained one-hop TE LSPs to each neighbor. These TE LSPs terminate at the IP address that is connected to each next-hop neighbor. They are fast-reroutable (protected by means of Fast Reroute). They do not have any other constraints such as bandwidth, affinities, and so on. This is because the aim of these TE LSPs is to use MPLS TE Fast Reroute as a fast local protection mechanism as opposed to using MPLS TE to effectively perform some traffic engineering functions.

Example 3-11 *Automatic Configuration of the One-Hop Primary Unconstrained TE LSP*

```
hostname USCom.StLouis.P1
!
mpls traffic-engineering auto-tunnel primary onehop
```

NOTE On a Cisco IOS router, additional commands allow the operator to tune other parameters.

NOTE As discussed in the Chapter 1 section "Forwarding of Layer 3 MPLS VPN Packets," the property of penultimate hop popping (PHP) consists of removing the TE LSP label at the penultimate router. Consequently, as pointed out, in the case of a one-hop tunnel, when PHP is in use, no label is added because the headend router is also the penultimate hop. Consequently, when one-hop tunnels are used for protection, as in the USCom network, no additional label is required when forwarding to a one-hop tunnel.

Example 3-12 shows the configuration that triggers the setup of one SRLG diverse backup tunnel per protected interface.

Example 3-12 *Automatic Configuration of NHOP SRLG Diverse Backup Tunnel*

```
hostname USCom.StLouis.P1
!
mpls traffic-engineering auto-tunnel backup nhop-only
mpls traffic-engineering auto-tunnel backup srlg exclude
```

Referring back to Figure 3-18, given the previous configuration, all traffic routed to the St. Louis–Washington link according to the IS-IS routing table is carried to the primary tunnel, T1.

As shown in Figure 3-19, the router in St. Louis has an NHOP backup tunnel B1 configured to protect any fast reroutable TE LSP traversing the protected link St. Louis–Washington. Hence, upon a failure of the St. Louis–Washington link, T1 is rerouted to B1 within a few tens of milliseconds. Consequently, in the case of a failure of this link, all the traffic routed to the link is rerouted along the path followed by the backup tunnel B1. In a second step occurring right after the rerouting, the primary tunnel T1 is reoptimized by the PLR in St. Louis along a more optimal path. Because T1 is unconstrained, that path corresponds to the IS-IS shortest path along the new topology, as shown in Figure 3-19.

In the case of a link failure, the design selected by USCom guarantees a traffic restoration time within a few tens of milliseconds. This meets USCom's rerouting time requirements.

NOTE   Thanks to the IGP network engineering rules, the IS-IS metrics can be computed by the USCom in-house IGP metric computation offline tool. The path followed by the backup tunnel and dynamically computed by each router in the network is guaranteed to offer an acceptable QoS to all traffic.

NOTE   Because the TE LSPs are unidirectional, one one-hop unconstrained primary TE LSP and one NHOP SRLG diverse backup tunnel are required in each direction to fully protect a link with MPLS TE Fast Reroute.

Figure 3-19 *MPLS Traffic Engineering Mode of Operation in the Case of the St. Louis–Washington Link Failure*

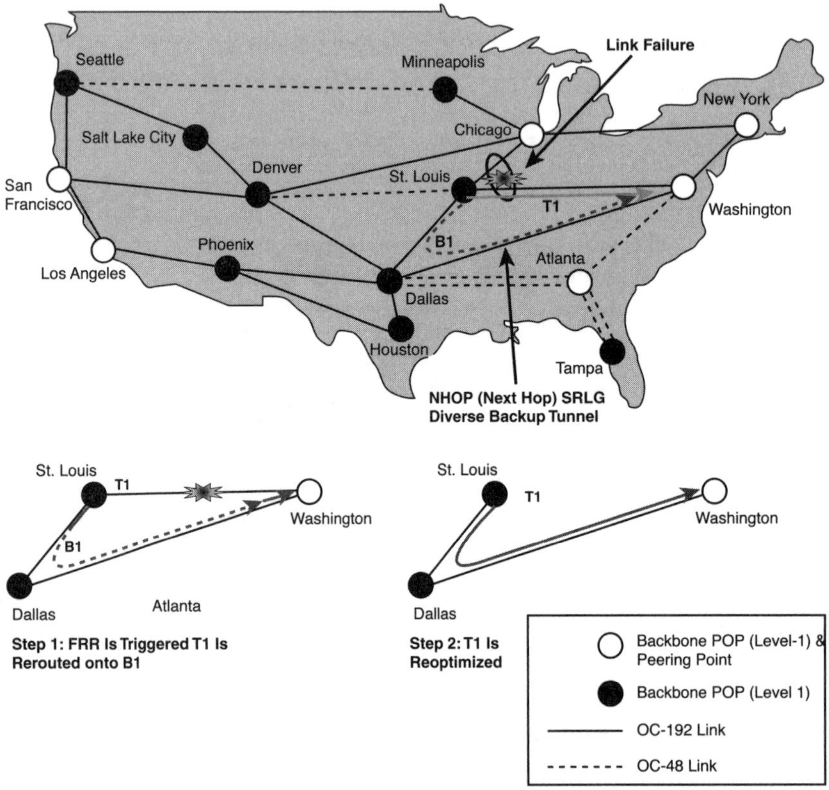

Prefix Prioritization Within the USCom Network

When FRR is triggered, the fast reroutable traffic engineering LSP T1 is immediately rerouted to the selected backup tunnel. At a lower level of detail, this means that all the IP prefixes routed by means of T1 (shown in Figures 3-17 and 3-18) must have their forwarding entries updated to reflect the path change. Upon failure detection, MPLS TE Fast Reroute is triggered by the PLR. This operation consists of updating the forwarding entry for each affected IP prefix in a serialized fashion. Consequently, some prefixes are rerouted faster than others. (Note that the total rerouting time for all prefixes still occurs within a very short period.) USCom adopted an interesting design solution that consists of giving a higher priority to important prefixes so that they get rerouted before less-important prefixes.

NOTE   Note that this is just an optimization, but it may be useful in large networks such as USCom, which has more than 3,000 IS-IS prefixes.

Given the Layer 3 MPLS VPN service offered by USCom, and the desire to maintain the same level of service for its Internet customers, USCom chose to use prefix prioritization during the FRR process. To ensure that IP and VPNv4 traffic is restored first in the case of a link failure, the IP addresses that represent a BGP next hop (a loopback from either an Internet or Layer 3 MPLS VPN PE router) were chosen for prioritization. This optimizes the reroute of these services, because these addresses are used by recursive resolution to reach all IP and VPNv4 prefixes advertised by the USCom PE routers. IP addresses of internal links, such as those between P routers, were considered less important, or at least did not require such a stringent convergence time.

NOTE   It is worth observing that the Internet traffic is IP-routed in steady state (because of LDP label filtering). During failure the traffic is label-switched along the backup tunnel and then the primary multihop TE LSP.

This prioritization is achieved using the configuration shown in Example 3-13.

Example 3-13 *Configuration of Prefix Prioritization*

```
hostname USCom.StLouis.P1
!
mpls traffic-engineering fast-reroute acl prefix-priority
!
ip access-list standard prefix-priority
 permit 23.49.16.0 0.0.1.255
 permit 23.49.20.0 0.0.1.255
 permit 23.49.10.0 0.0.1.255
```

NOTE   In Example 3-13, the subnets 23.49.16/24, 23.49.20/24, and 23.49.10/24 represent the main and reserved Layer 3 MPLS VPN PE router loopbacks and the Internet PE router loopback addresses, respectively.

NOTE   The configuration of such prefix prioritization triggers an FRR database sorting function that ensures that the important prefixes are rerouted first.

Temporary Loop Avoidance

The MPLS TE Fast Reroute design elected by USCom allows the company to meet its 50-ms rerouting time objective in case of link failure, but it requires a bit of extra work to be entirely satisfactory. By their very nature, IGP link-state protocols may lead to temporary loops during network convergence. (Until all the routers have synchronized their Link-State Database [LSDB] and have converged, a loop-free state cannot be guaranteed.) By default, the knowledge of a TE LSP is kept local to the router that is the headend for that TE LSP. The FRR design chosen by USCom does not escape this rule (the TE LSP [T1] is not visible to any other router in the USCom network). The consequence of this upon a link/SRLG failure is that the router in St. Louis locally reroutes all the traffic traversing the St. Louis–Washington link. After a period of time (determined by the IS-IS timer tuning, discussed later in this chapter), both the routers in St. Louis and Washington originate a new IS-IS LSP that reflects the new network topology and, in particular, the loss of adjacency between those two routers. The IS-IS LSP is then flooded throughout the network, and each router triggers a new routing table calculation.

IP routing is distributed, so the sequence of events is not deterministic. In particular, although the Dijkstra algorithm guarantees the computation of a loop-free path during steady state, this may not be the case during network convergence, when the routers' LSDB may not be synchronized.

To help illustrate this point, consider the following sequence of events:

- **Time t0**—The St. Louis–Washington link fails. (More precisely, the interface connecting the link to Washington fails on the router in St. Louis.)

- **Time t1**—The router in St. Louis detects the failure and triggers a local reroute by means of MPLS Fast Reroute. IS-IS originates a new IS-IS LSP and recalculates its routing table and forwarding database (note that MPLS Fast Reroute and IS-IS operate independently).

- **Time t2**—The router in Chicago receives the newly originated IS-IS LSP and recalculates its routing table and forwarding database.

During the time interval (t2–t1), the LSDBs of the routers in St. Louis and Chicago are not synchronized with each other. Assume that the IS-IS link metrics have been computed by the in-house tool such that

- The shortest path from Chicago to Washington is Chicago–St. Louis–Washington (in the absence of failure).

- In case of failure of the St. Louis–Washington link, the shortest path from St. Louis to Washington is via Chicago and New York.

During t2–t1, a temporary loop appears between the St. Louis and Chicago routers for the traffic sent from Chicago to Washington. This happens because during t2–t1, the St. Louis router sends the traffic for Washington back to the Chicago router, as shown in Figure 3-20.

Figure 3-20   *Temporary Loop Effect During IS-IS Network Convergence*

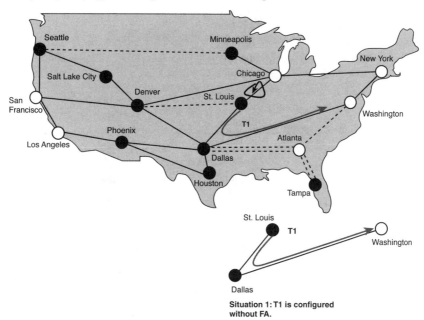

Forwarding Adjacency for Loop Avoidance

The solution to this problem is to configure the primary tunnel T1 as a forwarding adjacency (FA). Configuring a primary TE LSP as an FA has the effect of flooding the TE LSP as an IP link within the IGP. This means that as long as the TE LSP is operational, the node in St. Louis advertises T1 as a physical link in its IS-IS LSP. Consequently, when the physical link St. Louis–Washington fails, T1 is rerouted and then reoptimized along the path St. Louis–Dallas–Washington. T1 is still advertised in the IS-IS LSP originated by the St. Louis node as a physical link. Hence, upon link failure, no new IS-IS LSP is advertised, and the other routers in the USCom network do not detect any network topology change. (Of course, this requires configuring the FA with the same cost as the primary link it traverses.) This avoids the undesirable temporary loop effect just described. This process is illustrated in Figure 3-21.

Figure 3-21   *Avoiding the Temporary Loop with Forwarding Adjacency*

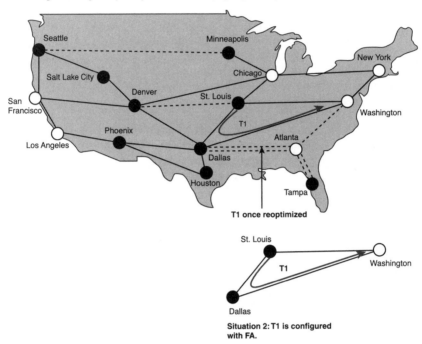

The advantage of using a forwarding adjacency is that any temporary loop during network convergence can be avoided. Moreover, in the case of a temporary failure of a few seconds, FA prevents the generation of two network convergence sequences throughout the network (which impacts hundreds of routers in the case of USCom).

As with all design choices, there are trade-offs. In the case of a forwarding adjacency, some failures such as fiber cuts may last for several days or even weeks, although USCom has not yet gathered a significant optical failure history. In such a case, the path followed by the traffic routed across the St. Louis–Washington link may follow a nonoptimal path for a long period of time because IS-IS is unaware of any topology changes. For instance, the traffic following the path Denver–St. Louis–Washington would actually follow the path Denver–St. Louis–Dallas–Washington, because the router in Denver does not actually see the failure of the link St. Louis–Washington. However, the path Denver–Dallas–Washington might have been more optimal. This is because T1 is still advertised as a physical link; hence, the other routers do not see any network topology change. In the USCom case, this was not considered an issue, because the network is overprovisioned. Therefore, the backup path, although potentially not optimal for some period of time, still provides the required QoS guarantees. Moreover, USCom has a monitoring system capturing the SNMP traps. Therefore, a procedure can be put into place to detect link failures and potentially deconfigure forwarding adjacencies on some primary tunnels if the failure lasts too long, such as in the case of a fiber cut. Of course, the deconfiguration of forwarding adjacency triggers an IGP convergence and is equivalent to the previous case where temporary loops occur.

Reuse of a Restored Link

An important consideration in the USCom FRR design was the reuse of a restored link after failure. Once a link is restored, a couple of strategies can be put into place:

- Reuse the restored resources as soon as possible.
- Wait for a period of time before reusing the link to maximize the network stability.

A multitude of link failure profiles are possible. For example, a link can fail and then be reliably restored (an up-down effect caused by a temporary network element failure, such as a laser desynchronization). On the other hand, a link can become unstable, experiencing a set of successive failures (in other words, the link is flapping). In such cases, waiting for a period of time before reusing a link helps determine whether it is safe to reuse the link. A flapping effect is highly undesirable; it can generate network instabilities, triggering storms of LSP flooding, SPF computation on each router, and so on. To solve such issues, multiple techniques can be used, such as back off and dampening. These can be implemented at various layers (such as the interface level, IGP, MPLS Traffic Engineering, and so on). In a nutshell, the key idea is to dampen the use of a link that suffers from instabilities to preserve network stability.

Various back-off/dampening algorithms have been designed (based on accumulated penalties such as BGP dampening, exponential back off, and so on). In the case of MPLS Traffic Engineering, on a Cisco router, the triggering of the TE LSP reoptimization always drives the reuse of a link. When a router tries to reoptimize a TE LSP path by means of a CSPF algorithm, it first determines whether a more optimal path other than the path currently in use can be found. If it can, the TE LSP is gracefully rerouted along the more optimal path. A Cisco router has various configurable reoptimization triggers that can be individually activated and deactivated:

- **Timer-based trigger**—Every (Tr) seconds, a headend router attempts to reoptimize its set of TE LSPs.
- **User-triggered**—Reoptimization forced by the user.
- **Link-up**—Each time the IGP signals a link, every router tries to see whether its set of TE LSPs can benefit from that new link.

USCom therefore had to make a decision regarding the following trade-offs:

> Reuse a restored link as soon as possible to quickly alleviate some congestion, but with the potential risk of generating network instability
> or
> Wait for a period of time before reusing a restored link whose state does not change

Because the USCom backbone is overprovisioned, the immediate reuse of a restored link was not considered a priority when compared to preserving network stability. Hence, USCom decided to be conservative in the reuse of a restored link. It would rely on IS-IS to declare the link operational according to the IS-IS back-off mechanism, described in the Chapter 2 section "Use of Dynamic Timers for LSA Origination and SPF Triggering." No TE LSP reoptimization is triggered on a link-up event. On the traffic engineering side, USCom decided to use the timer-based approach, with a timer value of 15 minutes. Hence, every 15 minutes, a router tries to see whether the link is restored so as to reoptimize the one-hop unconstrained primary TE LSP along the link. As soon as a link is restored, in the worst case, the TE LSP is rerouted to it in 15 minutes.

NOTE   Note that even if the IS-IS adjacency is reestablished across the restored link, the traffic routed between the two routers according to the computed routing table is steered to the TE LSP. This means that the traffic traverses the restored link only when the TE LSP is reoptimized along that path.

Multiple Failures Within the USCom Network

When assessing its multiple-failure requirements, USCom found that the only cause of concern was multiple failures provoked by the failure of an SRLG. Such a situation is handled by the design because every backup tunnel path is dynamically computed to be "SRLG diverse" from the protected link. (The links visited along the backup tunnel path do not share any SRLG with the link protected with FRR.) Any other case of multiple failures (such as an SRLG failure followed by the failure of another link that does not belong to the failed SRLG) was not considered a requirement because of the low probability of multiple simultaneous failures of independent elements. It is worth pointing out that the USCom network could survive double failures without experiencing a disconnected network but would not have any guarantee in terms of rerouting times and QoS during those multiple failures.

Link Failure Detection Within the USCom Network

The main challenge when protecting links in a switched environment (such as the intra-POP Gigabit Ethernet links) is quickly detecting a link failure. In the case where two routers are interconnected via a direct Gigabit Ethernet link, in only a few milliseconds the neighbor can detect a link failure caused by a fiber cut or a router interface failure. On the other hand, if the routers are interconnected by means of an intermediate Layer 2 switch, as in the case of the USCom Level 3 switched POP, this presents the challenge of link failure detection, because it requires the use of a fast hello (keepalive) protocol. Indeed, consider the following two cases:

- Two routers connected by a direct PoS or Gigabit Ethernet link. The failure of the link or one of the router interfaces is quickly detected by means of the alarms provided by Layer 1 or 2.

- Two routers connected by means of a Layer 2 switch. In this case, the failure of the link or router interface is seen only by the switch and the router connected to the failed element. Hence, the routing neighbor of the router attached to the failed element cannot detect such failures other than with a hello protocol between the two routers.

Because router interface failures are pretty rare and intra-POP links also very rarely fail, USCom decided not to protect these intra-POP links and to just rely on the IS-IS convergence.

Node Failures Within the USCom Network

When assessing the requirements for protection against node failure within the network, USCom chose to differentiate between the case of planned router maintenance and unplanned router failure.

Planned Router Maintenance

A software or hardware upgrade may require a router to be taken out of operation for a period of time (typically 10 minutes on average in USCom's case, as indicated in Table 3-2). In this case, for the core routers, USCom adopted the approach of setting up the IS-IS overload bit of the router in question via an administrative procedure. This has the effect of triggering a network-wide IS-IS convergence (rerouting) of the traffic around the router in question. As soon as the network has fully converged, the upgrade can finally take place without any traffic disruption. Such an approach is particularly suited to the USCom environment. The network overengineering rules are such that the network does not experience any congestion, even in such circumstances as a single network element failure. After the router has been reloaded, the original link metrics are restored.

In the case of the planned router maintenance of edge routers (Layer 3 MPLS VPN and Internet PE routers), things are quite different. USCom considered three scenarios:

- **Internet customer sites that are dual-attached**—Before upgrading the Internet PE routers, USCom relies on a script to automatically increase the MED value for all the BGP routes announced to the set of affected CE routers. This allows each CE router to smoothly reroute its traffic to the second PE router it is connected to; this avoids any traffic disruption. The actual PE router maintenance takes place 5 minutes after the BGP routing changes.

- **VPN customer sites that are dual-attached**—This could be two colocated CE routers connected to two different Layer 3 MPLS VPN PE routers or a single CE router connected to two different Layer 3 MPLS VPN PE routers. A similar procedure is applied to the case of dual-attached CE routers if BGP is used as the routing protocol between CE router and PE router. No particular measure is taken for other routing protocols or the CE routers using static routing.

- **Internet and VPN customer attached to a single PE router**—In this case, USCom handles the router maintenance, which inevitably provokes some traffic disruption, during a maintenance period.

In all these cases, USCom managed to get a maintenance period window of 4 hours on the first Sunday of every month from 3 a.m. to 7 a.m.

Unexpected Router Failures

USCom noted that several types of router failures have highly variable effects on data forwarding. These effects can vary from the traffic being black-holed to absolutely no consequences on the traffic, depending on the router platform, failure types, and so on.

Two examples are provided in the next section to illustrate how the USCom IS-IS design met the requirements of unexpected router failures:

- The case of a power supply failure at a core router
- The case of a router failure that does not trigger any link failure, or the failure cannot be detected by the neighbors

Convergence of IS-IS

When designing the tuning of IS-IS from a convergence perspective, USCom had the objective of providing a convergence of 5 seconds in the case of a router failure or intra-POP link failure (when Layer 2 switches are used to interconnect routers). Link failures were considered outside the scope of IGP tuning because MPLS Traffic Engineering Fast Reroute covers them. This convergence time includes detection of the failure, propagation of the topology change, and local convergence (computing a new routing table).

Of course, a number of IS-IS parameters come into play when tuning IS-IS for faster convergence. As mentioned in Chapter 2's "Core Network Availability" section, the IGP convergence time is basically made up of three main components:

- The failure detection time
- The flooding of the new IS-IS LSP reporting a topology change
- The routing table computation on each router (SPF algorithm, Routing Information Base (RIB) update, and so on)

IS-IS Failure Detection Time

When a router failure occurs, also implying multiple link failures (such as a power supply failure), the SONET or light path link failure is detected within tens of milliseconds. On the other hand, as mentioned, the case of a link or a router failure within a switched POP (Level 3) requires a hello protocol. USCom decided to set the IS-IS hello frequency to 1 second (one IS-

IS hello message [IIH]Drew, I changed back to parenthesis since this does not refer to a reference but to the name of the hello messages. Thanks. is sent to every adjacent neighbor every second). Note that in the USCom network topology the maximum number of adjacent neighbors stays within a very reasonable limit (less than 30). Hence, sending an IS-IS Hello message every second to each neighbor is not of concern. The Hold timer is set to 3 seconds. If no IS-IS message is received during this period, the routing adjacency is declared down.

Flooding of New IS-IS LSPs

The flooding of new IS-IS LSPs is basically a function of the LSP origination time (discussed later in this section), the propagation delay, and the processing time at each router hop. In the USCom network, because the optical network is pretty dense, the worst-case propagation delay from coast to coast is 50 ms. Based on several internal tests, USCom determined that the worst-case processing delay of an IS-IS LSP even on a pretty heavily loaded router would rarely exceed 10 ms. This calculation supposes that the flooding of the newly received IS-IS LSP always occurs before the triggering of the new SPF.

NOTE   Note that the ability to systematically flood an LSP before triggering an SPF may not exist on some router platforms but is quite important to limit the convergence time of any link-state routing protocol. Indeed, upon receiving a new LSP (an LSP reflecting a topology change), a router should always first flood the LSP instead of triggering an SPF and then flooding the LSP.

Furthermore, every router has to be configured to ensure that the queuing delay experienced by the IS-IS control messages is bounded and negligible so it won't severely impact the total convergence time. It is of the utmost importance to provide a high priority to the IS-IS control messages. This applies to hello messages to avoid losing a routing adjacency in case of congested links (not in the case of USCom, however). It also ensures a quick LSP update because hello messages may reflect a topology change (if the LSP is not a refresh), which is required to quickly converge to reroute the traffic to alternate paths. Because IS-IS control messages do not rely on IP, internal mechanisms need to ensure that IS-IS messages get the relevant precedence over other user traffic.

NOTE   The serialization delay on a link from OC-3 to OC-192 of an IS-IS LSP is not a significant factor in the overall IS-IS convergence.

Based on the previous flooding time analysis, USCom determined that the total flooding time should never exceed 200 ms. (This is the time to originate the new IS-IS LSP plus the total propagation delay between the originating routers and the routers where the traffic is rerouted along an alternate path by IS-IS.)

Routing Table Computation on Each Node

The final component of the IS-IS convergence to consider is the routing table computation time, which is itself made up of two components:

- The SPF computation
- The routing table computation and update to router line cards (in the case of a distributed router architecture)

Some testing on the USCom network showed that the SPF computation time was 100 ms, and the complete routing table update was 500 ms.

IS-IS Configuration Within the USCom Network

Example 3-14 provides the configuration of the St. Louis P router shown in Figure 3-1 to achieve the IS-IS convergence objective of 5 seconds upon a node failure. Similar configurations are adopted for all the routers in the network.

Example 3-14 *Fast IS-IS Configuration*

```
hostname USCom.StLouis.P1
!
interface pos0/0
 isis hello-interval 1
 isis hello-multiplier 3
!
router isis
 lsp-gen 5 50 20
 spf-interval 5 50 20
 prc-interval 5 50 20
```

NOTE   The hello interval and hello multiplier must be configured on each interface that is associated with the IS-IS process.

Considering the syntax lsp-gen A B C, USCom decided to set B to 50 ms so that every router would get a chance to detect all the possible local failures (caused by SRLG failure) before originating a new IS-IS LSP. Indeed, upon SRLG failure, multiple local links may fail, and these failures might not be detected simultaneously. Thus, the 50 ms of waiting time before originating the new IS-IS LSP provides an accurate network topology state. If a second failure occurs, the router originates a second LSP after 20 ms (C = 20).

This also applies to the triggering of the SPF. In the syntax spf-interval A B C, B is set to 50 ms. This gives a chance, in case of an SRLG failure, to receive all the IS-IS LSPs reflecting the new topology and consequently the SRLG failure before triggering a new (second) SPF. See the section "Core Network Availability" in Chapter 2 for an explanation of the various IS-IS tuning parameters.

To help illustrate the outcome of the IS-IS parameter settings, consider two extremes:

- **The case of a power supply failure at a core router**—In this case the links attached to the router will also likely fail, which will provide a fast failure indication to the neighbors of the failing routers. Each neighbor originates a new IS-IS LSP that is flooded throughout the network, and each router converges. In such a case, the failure is detected before the expiration of the hold-time timer. The propagation delays and SPF/RIB computation time are such that the objective of 5 seconds total convergence time is easily met.

- **The case of a router failure that does not trigger any link failure, or the failure cannot be detected by the neighbors**—For the sake of illustration, two situations should be considered:

  — A router fails, with impact on traffic forwarding, but the attached links do not fail.

  — A router fails, with impact on traffic forwarding. Its attached links also fail, but its neighbors cannot detect these failures. Typically this is the case with a switched POP.

In these two situations, the failure detection occurs by means of the IS-IS adjacency maintenance procedure—hence, within 3 seconds (until the hold-time timer expires). This still provides 2 seconds for the neighbors of the failing router to originate their new IS-IS LSP, for the new LSP(s) to be flooded throughout the network, and finally for all the nodes to converge. Hence, this guarantees that the 5-second rerouting time objective is also met with the previously mentioned IS-IS parameter tuning. Note that only a subset of the routers is required to converge for the impacted traffic (traffic routed through the failing router) to be restored.

It is worth mentioning that other router failures do not affect data forwarding, such as a control plane failure on a distributed platform. In such failures, if the control plane cannot be restored within 3 seconds (the value of the hold-time timer), the IS-IS neighbor declares a loss of adjacency, and IS-IS converges (the traffic is rerouted around the failing router). However, the user traffic is unaffected because the alternate paths offer an equivalent QoS in the case of USCom.

It is worth noting that an edge router failure always has an impact on the traffic originated by locally attached CE routers as well as the traffic to those sites. USCom decided not to initially implement any high-availability (HA) functionality on the Internet or Layer 3 MPLS VPN PE routers, but this will be assessed at a later stage. Hence, this applies to any type of router failure. Because the customer sites are out of the realm of the USCom operation (they are unmanaged), the customers, depending on the routing protocol in use and their parameter settings, control the convergence time.

Design Lessons to Be Taken from USCom

A number of observations can be made from USCom's design decisions:

- Straightforward engineering rules such as structured VRF naming conventions, route distinguisher/route target allocation schemes, and well-defined configuration templates allow for a simpler Layer 3 MPLS VPN service deployment.

- Operation of the Internet service can be kept exactly as before deployment of the Layer 3 MPLS VPN service by separating forwarding of Internet and VPN traffic in the core. VPN traffic is carried over MPLS LSPs, while Internet traffic remains forwarded as IP traffic.

- PE router protection techniques, such as limiting the number of routes within a VRF or restricting the number of prefixes received from a given client, should be a mandatory part of the Layer 3 MPLS VPN service deployment.

- Simple tuning of certain router parameters, such as the input hold-queue and Selective Packet Discard (SPD), can considerably enhance convergence of the BGP control plane.

- Route reflectors should be deployed to help scale the number of BGP TCP sessions required at the PE routers.

- Enabling path MTU discovery at the PE routers and route reflectors allows the TCP protocol used by BGP to run more efficiently, thus providing better convergence times.

- Where core bandwidth is plentiful/cheap/quick to provision, the core QoS design can rely on pure overengineering to maintain QoS during single failures and to achieve a good SLA that satisfies mission-critical and multimedia applications. This is a low operational expenses (opex) design because of simpler engineering, configuration, monitoring, troubleshooting, and fine-tuning. This is usually an attractive avenue for "facilities-owned" operators with an optical infrastructure.

- Even when no QoS mechanism is supported in the core, and unmanaged CE routers are deployed, it is a good idea to offer an optional QoS mechanism on egress PE routers. Doing so provides added value for customers because it manages congestion on the last weak link in the chain (the first weak link, the CE-PE link, can be managed by the customer anyway) and does not add significant complexity to the design.

- A network can follow a simple design to be able to offer a 50-ms convergence time upon link or SRLG failure by means of MPLS Traffic Engineering Fast Reroute, at a minimal cost in terms of opex and capital expenditure (capex). Such backup tunnels can be automatically configured and set up with minimal configuration.

- Node failures may be covered by minimal IGP tuning to obtain a few seconds of rerouting time upon a router failure that affects data forwarding. USCom might consider more-aggressive IS-IS parameter settings if it has to increase its network availability in the future.

CHAPTER 4

National Telco Design Study

Telecom Kingland (TK) is a fictitious Internet service provider (ISP) based in the imaginary country of Kingland. It is representative of an incumbent telecommunications service provider in Europe or Asia. Such providers are often called *telcos* . These providers used to provide services to the national regulated markets and were owned by their respective governments, operating predominantly as a monopoly. In the face of deregulation of the national markets, and the opening of those markets to competition, telcos have been undergoing drastic changes. These changes include partial or complete privatization, rationalization of assets and operational expenses (opex), and internal reorganizations that help the telcos offer competitive services and prices in this new landscape.

Because of their common history, many telcos exhibit similar characteristics. They typically have a very broad service portfolio covering all telecommunications services, including fixed telephony, mobile telephony, and data. They generally have complete nationwide geographic coverage with a very dense service footprint, and they own fibers and transmission facilities. Despite increasing competition, they typically have retained a significant market share in their domestic markets.

To support all the new services that have emerged over the years, many telcos have deployed a plethora of overlay and parallel networks. Today, they are seeking significant cost reductions through the migration of many services onto a next-generation multiservice packet-based backbone network. TK identified such a migration as a key strategic direction. To that end, TK evolved its packet core as a nationwide multiservice network over which multiple existing services (such as IPv4 Internet and Layer 3 MPLS VPN services) have been migrated. This network is also used for Public Switched Telephone Network (PSTN) trunking and the introduction of new services (such as IPv6 Internet).

The vision underpinning this network integration is a very strong separation between the core network, which is designed as a high-performance, high-quality, service-independent infrastructure, and the edge network, which is designed to be multiservice-capable and feature-rich.

The objective of this chapter is to discuss the specifics of the IP/MPLS network design chosen by a particular network operator, illustrative of a national telco. This chapter shows how the characteristics and objectives of this type of operator influenced the design decisions that were made and also discusses the design evolutions.

Telecom Kingland Network Environment

As with all typical telcos, TK owns fiber links throughout the country. It has deployed an extensive Synchronous Digital Hierarchy (SDH) infrastructure over these fiber facilities in addition to its older time-division multiplexing (TDM) infrastructure. All SDH links are protected. TK offers leased-line services from 64 kbps to 2 Mbps over its TDM network and from 2 Mbps to STM-16 (2488.32 Mbps) over the SDH network organized in a large set of rings.

In more recent years, TK deployed a dense wavelength division multiplexing (DWDM) infrastructure that allows it to provision DWDM links between Points of Presence (POPs) at low cost and with short lead times (on the order of a few days) by activating additional wavelengths. These raw DWDM links are supported at STM-16 (2.5 Gbps) and STM-64 (10 Gbps) rates and are not protected by the DWDM layer.

X.25, Frame Relay, and ATM services have also been offered for many years. These are carried over a completely separate ATM core network. Frame Relay and ATM services are available from a large number of Layer 2 POPs throughout the country.

In line with its strategic direction, TK evolved its core packet network into a nationwide core ready for multiservice integration. We call this core the Multiservice Packet Core (MPC).

The MPC is made up of

- 6 Level 1 POPs
- 50 Level 2 POPs

The Level 1 POPs provide transit across the country (large city-to-large city connectivity). They are connected to each other using unprotected STM-64 DWDM links in a partial mesh that is based on geography and traffic requirements.

Each Level 2 POP is connected to two Level 1 POPs using unprotected STM-16 DWDM links, except for a few smaller Level 2 POPs that are connected to the two backbone P routers of the closest Level 1 POP via protected STM-1 (155 Mbps) SDH links. Also, instead of being connected to two Level 1 POPs, a few Level 2 POPs are connected to two other Level 2 POPs that provide transit toward the Level 1 POPs. Figure 4-1 illustrates this connectivity.

The MPC is a pure core network and is made up of P routers only. Services are provided to end customers via edge devices (such as PE routers and access servers), which can be located in any of the MPC's 56 POPs. The MPC provides transit across all these edge devices as well as IP connectivity to external networks such as the public Internet.

TK has been offering Internet access services for many years, as well as Layer 3 MPLS VPN services for more than 4 years. TK has an installed base of more than 15,000 dedicated Internet ports and more than 30,000 dedicated Layer 3 MPLS VPN ports grouped into more than 2400 VPNs. Remote access via PSTN/ISDN as well as digital subscriber line (DSL) is also offered for both Internet and Layer 3 MPLS VPN services.

Figure 4-1   *Telecom Kingland Multiservice Packet Core Topology*

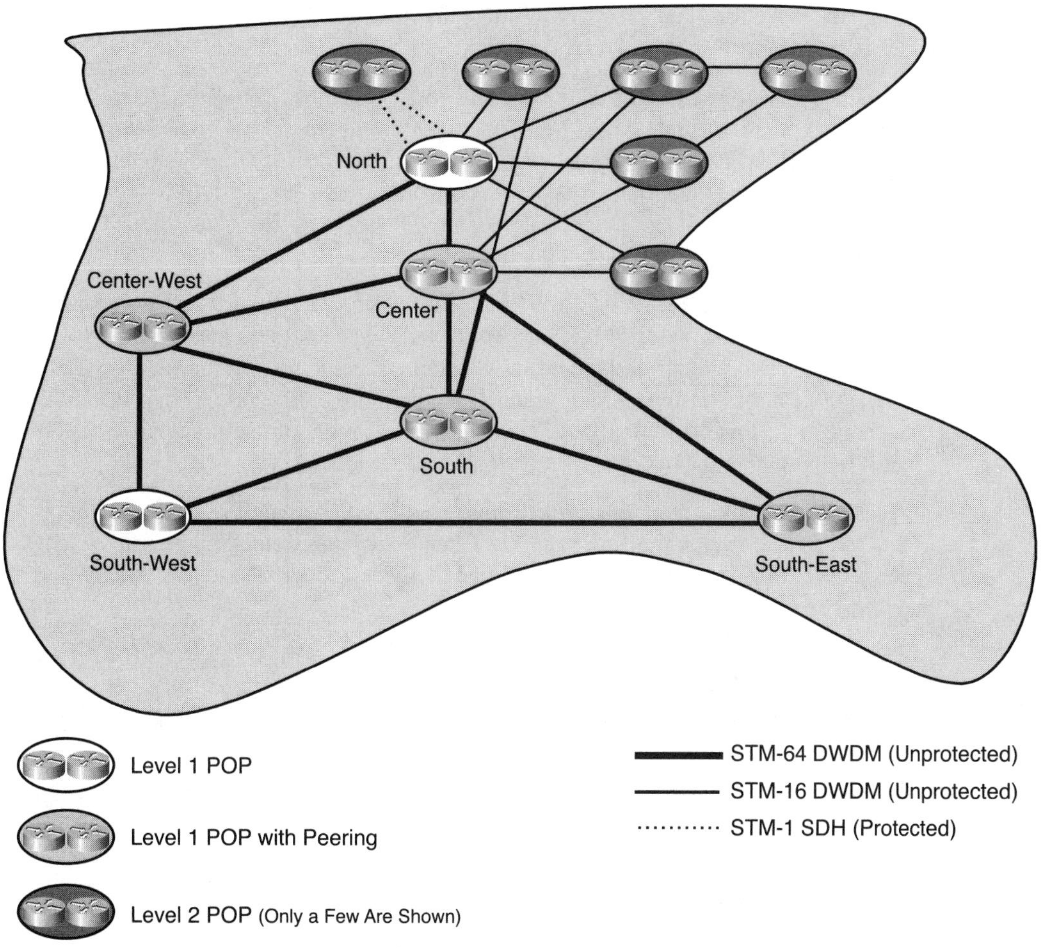

TK elected to connect both the Internet and the Layer 3 MPLS VPN dedicated ports to the same set of shared PE routers. There are 450 such PE routers, which we call multiservice PE routers (mPE routers). These mPE routers are spread over the 56 POPs and are connected locally to the MPC P routers.

The Layer 3 MPLS VPN service is enriched with support of three classes of service (CoSs), support of Multicast within the VPNs, and support of voice VPNs. A Carrier's Carrier (CsC) option is also offered to a few large customers with special requirements such as an extremely large number of routes or the need to manage VPN membership themselves (for example, because of regular and frequent membership changes). All these additional services are also offered on the same mPE routers.

TK also supports remote access to the Internet for wholesale customers, such as the group within TK that offers Internet access to residential and small office/home office (SOHO) customers, as well as other ISPs. TK has more than 90,000 narrowband dial ports (PSTN/ISDN) and several million broadband users over DSL.

The MPC P routers, as well as all the edge devices connecting users (such as mPE routers and access servers), are operated as a single autonomous system (32764). The Interior Gateway Protocol (IGP) is Open Shortest Path First (OSPF), which is structured into multiple areas to cope with the large number of routers. This network is made up of 3000 IGP routes, more than 150,000 Internet routes, and more than 120,000 VPNv4 routes (which are carried at the mPE routers/VPNv4 route reflectors, but not at the P routers).

Internet and Layer 3 MPLS VPN services are also offered in many countries outside Kingland using the TK International IP/MPLS network (which is an autonomous system separate from the national network). Currently there are 40 international POPs, but this number is expected to grow significantly over the coming years. The international network is connected to the MPC backbone in the Level 1 POPs. This network carries a subset of the more than 120,000 VPNv4 routes found within the national MPC.

A Class 4 telephony switch replacement was recently completed. It also takes advantage of the MPC to carry telephony transit traffic. The Class 4 switches (telephony transit switches) have been removed from the network and replaced by soft switches. These soft switches are made up of the following:

- **Voice over IP media gateways**—VoIP media gateways (also called *VoIP trunk gateways*) connect the Class 5 switches (the telephony switches connecting subscribers) via TDM interfaces, packetize the voice calls, and route the corresponding IP packet streams onto the MPC network.

- **Call agent**—The call agent participates in the telephony signaling protocol (Signaling System No. 7; see [SS7]). It controls the VoIP gateways via a media gateway control protocol, as covered in [MEGACO] or [MGCP].

This telephony transit logical architecture is illustrated in Figure 4-2.

References Used in this Book

Throughout this book you will see references to other resources. These are provided in case you want to delve more deeply into a subject. Such references appear in brackets, such as [L2VPN]. If you want to know more about this resource, look up the code in the "References" appendix to find out specific information about the resource.

Figure 4-2   *Telecom Kingland Telephony Transit Logical Architecture*

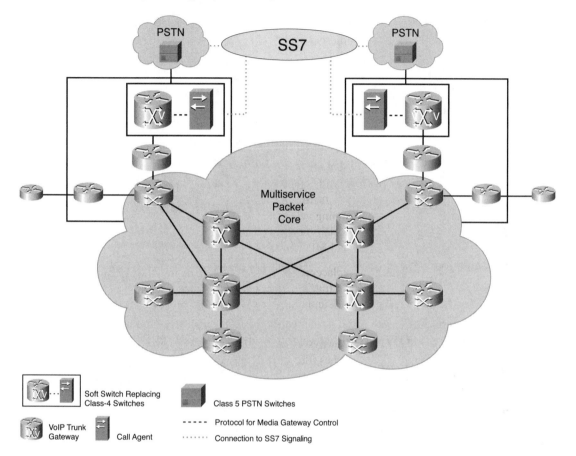

This voice transit approach offers very significant cost reductions. First and foremost, operational expenses have been reduced significantly because of lower site costs incurred by the much more compact technology of modern soft switches as compared to legacy Class 4 switches. Also, as illustrated in Figure 4-3, a reduction in the number of ports and transmission capacity is achieved. It results from the migration from a mesh topology (where every Class 4 switch had to have separate dedicated connections with every other Class 4 switch with which it was tandem switching) to a cloud topology (where each soft switch only needs to be connected to the MPC locally). Moreover, for voice traffic TK can take advantage of lower bandwidth costs per kbps that can be achieved through multiplexing over the very high-speed MPC.

Figure 4-3   *Cloud Topology for Telephony Transit*

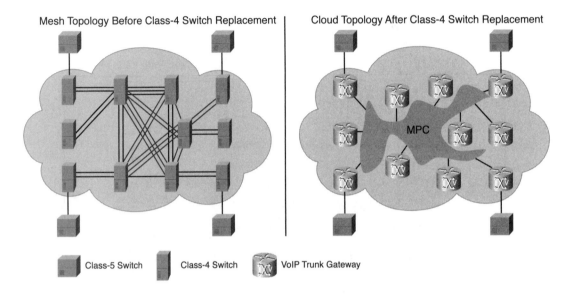

A total of 64 VoIP trunk gateways are currently deployed. There are four gateways in each of the six Level 1 POPs and two gateways in 20 of the 50 Level 2 POPs.

Because Kingland was an early adopter of IPv6, TK introduced an IPv6 Internet access service to its portfolio a year ago to meet customer demand. TK is also planning to introduce an IPv6 VPN service next year.

Telecom Kingland POP Structure

Each Level 1 POP is composed of two backbone P routers that are connected to several other Level 1 POPs via STM-64 links and that support the STM-16 connections to Level 2 POPs.

In four of the six Level 1 POPs, the P routers are also connected to gateways providing external connectivity such as Internet peering points and gateways to TK's international network.

Each Level 2 POP is made up of two backbone P routers, which support STM-16 connectivity to two Level 1 POPs (or, in a few cases, support STM-1 connectivity to two different P routers of the same Level 1 POP).

Both Level 1 and Level 2 POPs host the edge devices providing customer connection to the MPC. For Enterprise services (as opposed to residential services and wholesale services), this includes the following:

- mPE routers (offering IPv4 Internet and Layer 3 MPLS VPN services) that are connected to the two P routers via STM-1 links (or via STM-16 for a few high-speed mPE routers in Level 1 POPs).

- Network Access Servers (NASs) and Broadband Access Servers (BASs) supporting remote access to Internet and Layer 3 MPLS VPN services. These devices are separate from the ones used for wholesale services because they offer a higher grade of service imposing different operational practices (such as reduced maintenance windows) and different design rules (such as lower port oversubscription). The NAS and BAS for Internet access are connected to the P routers via dual Gigabit Ethernet switches. The NAS and BAS for access to the Layer 3 MPLS VPN service are connected via dual Gigabit Ethernet switches to the mPE routers.

For wholesale services, the edge devices include a very large number of NASs and BASs also connected to the P routers via dual Gigabit Ethernet switches. The backbones from operators using TK's NAS/BAS wholesale services are connected to the MPC via SDH or Gigabit Ethernet for Internet peering.

For PSTN trunking, the VoIP trunk gateways are dual-attached to two telephony PE routers (also called *PE-PSTN*) by multiple STM-1 links. In turn, these telephony PE routers are attached to the two P routers in the POP by local STM-16 links.

The Level 1 and Level 2 POP designs are shown in Figures 4-4 and 4-5, respectively.

Figure 4-4 *Telecom Kingland Level 1 POP Design*

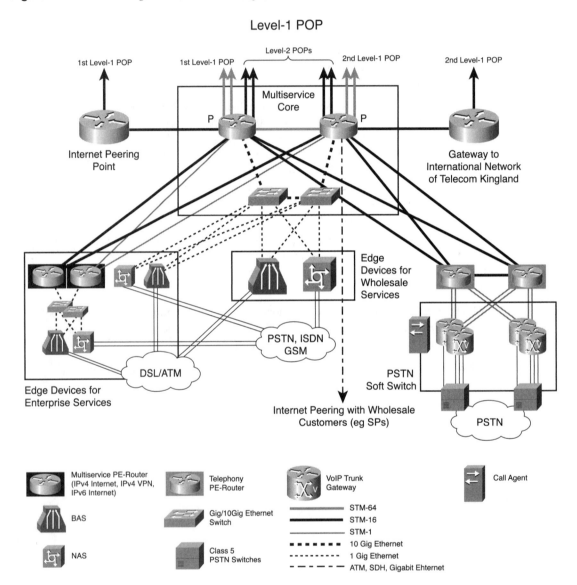

Figure 4-5   *Telecom Kingland Level 2 POP Design (a Case of POP with PSTN Trunking)*

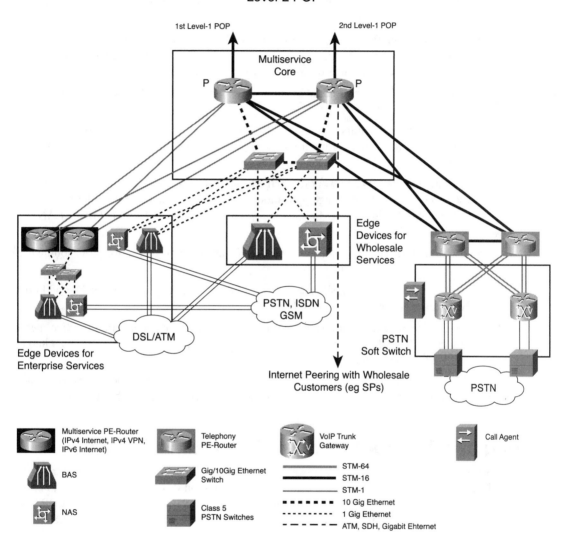

Level-2 POP

Telecom Kingland Design Objectives

The architecture and design of the TK network was greatly influenced by the following objectives:

- The next-generation network should align with the TK strategic vision of a packet-based, highly resilient, multiservice core. This core network should be surrounded by sophisticated edge devices offering feature-rich services.

- All existing IP Services should be supported on multiservice edge devices interconnected via the MPC network.

- Additional cost benefits should be realized through migration of PSTN trunking over the MPC network while ensuring the same quality of service as with the former PSTN network.

- Ensure that the MPC network offers the level of service required by all the existing IP services, the PSTN trunking application, and any anticipated future services, such as pseudowire (including ATM pseudowire), Layer 2 VPNs, and Virtual Private LAN Service (VPLS).

- Achieve the necessary quality of service while avoiding excessive overprovisioning in the core to control bandwidth costs.

- Achieve the necessary resilience without additional capital expenses (such as additional equipment for protection of DWDM links).

- Maximize the core's stability and performance by removing application-/service specific-functions from the core wherever possible. For example, turn the MPC network into an IPv4 BGP-free zone.

The rest of this chapter discusses the design TK selected to meet these objectives, from the viewpoints of routing, VPN, QoS, traffic engineering, network recovery, and IPv6.

Routing and Backbone Label-Forwarding Design

The backbone of the TK domestic network supports MPLS label switching of all Unicast traffic. The labels are assigned and distributed using Label Distribution Protocol (LDP) and RSVP-TE (Resource Reservation Protocol Traffic Engineering). TK chose not to deploy any LDP filters (unlike USCom in the previous chapter). Therefore, both Internet and Layer 3 MPLS VPN traffic is label-switched.

Because all Unicast traffic is label-switched, and because TK does not provide a native IP Multicast service, the IPv4 BGP address family is not required to be deployed on the P routers in the MPC. This facility allows TK to run an Internet-free core network, although MP-BGP is still required to distribute the VPNv4 routes created by the Layer 3 MPLS VPN service.

NOTE	You will see in the later section, "mVPN Service Application," that TK provides Multicast services to its Layer 3 MPLS VPN customers only. This is an additional service provided within the customer's VRF. It uses the mVPN technology that was reviewed in the "Multicast VPNs" section of Chapter 1, "Technology Primer: Layer 3 VPN, Multicast VPNs, IPv6 and Pseudowire."
	When using this technology, as each Multicast packet is encapsulated using [GRE] with a source address of the ingress mPE router, the RPF checks performed on Multicast packets are always an mPE router loopback interface address rather than the original source address within the customer VPN. Because these mPE router loopback addresses are distributed by the IGP, no additional functionality is necessary to successfully perform the RPF checks.
	On the other hand, if TK supported a global IP Multicast service, RPF vector functionality would be necessary (as you will see in Chapter 5, "Global Service Provider Design Study"). This functionality allows an RPF check to be performed on a route's BGP next hop rather than that route's originator.

Removing the BGP IPv4 address family from the core of the domestic network had several implications that needed to be addressed:

- **Service provisioning**—Many of the existing scripts that were currently used to provision the edge and core routers needed to be changed to remove any redundant BGP configuration such as IPv4 address family sessions at the P routers.

- **Fault detection**—A failure in the packet forwarding path needed to be detected and subsequently repaired. Unlabeled IP packets could no longer be forwarded within the core because of the removal of IPv4 routes from the P routers.

- **Security**—The tools used to identify attack threats, such as IP Source Tracker, no longer work within the network's core because the P routers forward only MPLS packets, not IP packets.

- **Troubleshooting**—The Network Operations staff needed to understand how to troubleshoot an MPLS core network as opposed to a pure IP environment.

However, an Internet-free core also has a number of advantages:

- The amount of routing state stored locally on P routers is greatly reduced, thus decreasing the memory and processor usage.

- The BGP IPv4 address family peering mesh can be substantially reduced because only the edge routers need to carry IPv4 BGP routes.

- Stability of the core network is likely to be enhanced because it is no longer aware of external routes. For example, an external route flap can no longer affect a P router because this router does not carry external routes.

- Market perception of increased security of an Internet-free private core can be taken advantage of even though it is possible to secure the core network without removing the IPv4 address family.

TK believed the benefits of an Internet-free core outweighed the migration's complications and addressed the implications pointed out previously in the following way: As part of the migration, all the existing provisioning scripts were modified to correctly configure both the edge mPE routers and the core P routers. Most of this exercise involved removing the BGP configuration on the P routers rather than additional commands and reconfiguring the mPE routers to peer with IPv4 address family route reflectors (RRs) located in the Level 1 POPs.

Clearly denial of service (DoS) attacks are a concern for any network operator. Before migrating the core network to MPLS switching, TK used the IP Source Tracker tool to identify the source of any suspected DoS attacks. When a specific destination was suspected of being under attack, TK enabled IP Source Tracker on its routers so that each line card could create a Forwarding Information Base (FIB) entry for the destination address and collect information about traffic flow to the tracked destination. This data was then observed periodically to identify the source of the attack.

With its transition to an Internet-free core, TK was forced to push this functionality to the mPE routers because these were the only devices in the network that used the FIB to forward IP packets (IP Source Tracker works in conjunction with the FIB). All MPLS packets are forwarded using the Label Forwarding Information Base (LFIB) rather than the FIB and therefore are not subject to tracking with the currently available IP Source Tracker feature.

When a DoS attack is suspected, either within a VPN or via the global Internet, TK enables IP Source Tracker on the egress mPE router through which the attack is suspected. Then TK examines the output to determine the source IP address of the attack. The company then can identify the ingress mPE router by examining the identified source address within the BGP table at the egress mPE router. Note that without MPLS forwarding in the core network, the mPE router has no way of identifying the entry point for the attack. Its next hop for the source may not actually be the router through which the packet entered the network.

With respect to forwarding fault detection and troubleshooting, LSP liveliness is determined through the use of LSP-ping (see [LSP-PING]). This functionality allows pings to be initiated using the Cisco Service Assurance Agent (SAA) to test that a particular LSP is functioning correctly. If a failure is detected, TK uses LSP Traceroute (also documented in [LSP-PING]) to identify the point of failure within the network and then takes corrective action. The SAA and LSP-ping functionality are initiated from the mPE routers.

In terms of control plane fault detection for LDP and MPLS Traffic Engineering, in case a Traffic Engineering LSP or LDP LSP fails, TK uses the regular set of troubleshooting features available on the P routers. This allows for extensive detail on the TE/LDP LSP's operational state (CLI **show** and **debug** commands, SNMP traps related to TE/LDP, and IGP TE extensions).

IGP-LDP synchronization functionality (enabled using the global **mpls ldp sync** command) is also deployed. This allows the IGP to stay synchronized with the LDP protocol so that packets are not forwarded across a given link until both the IGP and LDP protocols have converged. Lack of coordination between the IGP and LDP may result in packet loss in two situations:

- On link-up when the IGP adjacency starts, the router may begin forwarding traffic on the link before LDP label exchange between the link peers has finished. This causes traffic loss of the label-switched packets because no LSP is yet available along the preferred path (determined by the IGP).

- If an LDP session is lost but the IGP adjacency is not, the router may continue forwarding traffic using the link associated with the LDP session in preference to alternative paths with fully synchronized LDP sessions. That would lead to the same undesirable effect as just mentioned.

Packet loss in these situations may be reduced by means of synchronizing the LDP protocol with the IGP. On a link-up event, if an LDP session is already operational, the IGP brings up an adjacency as normal. However, if an LDP session is not operational, the following occur:

- If the LDP neighbor can be reached, the IGP delays sending hellos until either the LDP session is operational or a hold-down timer expires.

- If the LDP neighbor cannot be reached, the IGP starts sending hellos.

- When the IGP adjacency is up, and before the LDP session is fully operational, the router initially announces reachability to the link using IGP's maximum metric. This prevents any traffic from being forwarded along the corresponding link.

- When the LDP session is successfully established, the router announces the link using the normal configured metric for the link, allowing traffic to use the link.

If at some point in the future the LDP session subsequently fails after the IGP advertises the configured link metric, the following actions occur:

- The IGP again starts advertising its maximum metric for the link.

- When the LDP session returns, the IGP resumes advertising the configured link metric.

Shared-Edge Internet and Layer 3 MPLS VPN Services

As mentioned, the edge of the TK domestic network consists of mPE routers that provide a variety of services, including Internet and Layer 3 MPLS VPN. The MPC's P routers are shared for transport of all services.

The implication of running shared services on the same edge routers was evaluated for the design. Clearly security of the P network and edge was of paramount importance, as was network scaling. The Chapter 5 section "Layer 3 MPLS VPN Security and Scalability" provides details of how these challenges can be met and overcome, so these design aspects are not covered in this chapter.

Internet Service: Route Reflection Deployment

A further positive implication of removing the BGP IPv4 address family from the P routers is that the Internet RRs may follow a design similar to the VPNv4 route reflection. This is because packets are no longer IP-forwarded in the core and need not follow the network's physical topology (as explained in the previous chapter). Hence, TK chose to deploy RRs for its Internet service using a centralized model but kept the IPv4 RRs separate from those used for VPNv4 routes. The main reason for separation was control-plane convergence; TK did not want contention between the two services during a failure.

As shown in Figure 4-6, each Level 1 POP has two RRs serving the IPv4 address family. Each mPE router within a Level 2 POP peers with the two RRs closest to it. Each mPE router within a Level 1 POP peers with the local RRs.

Figure 4-6   *IPv4 Route Reflector Connectivity*

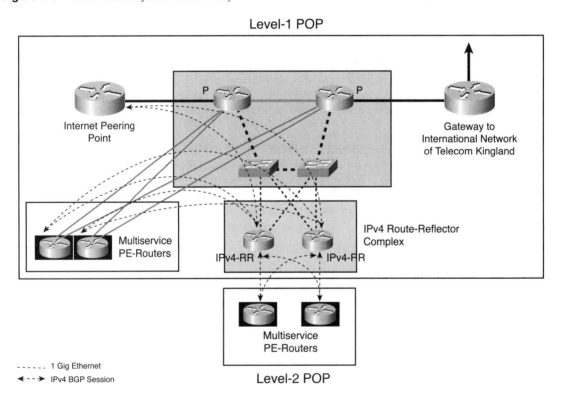

Layer 3 MPLS VPN Service: Design Overview

TK's drivers for introducing a network-based Layer 3 VPN service were similar to those for USCom, as discussed in the preceding chapter. However, the Layer 3 MPLS VPN technology found traction earlier in Kingland. Therefore, TK's network services portfolio is a little more mature, with more VPN sites and several additional services already deployed.

Many drivers forced early adoption of this technology in Kingland as well as other countries in this region. At the time (circa 1998), many new service providers were emerging, challenging the incumbent providers. One way for these new operators to differentiate themselves from the incumbents was to provide additional services above and beyond the traditional Frame Relay/ATM services. TK quickly followed suit and introduced an MPLS-based VPN service that it marketed aggressively. A further reason for the accelerated growth of this technology was that Kingland had a long history of providing managed services (for example, Frame Relay services were managed more often than not). Therefore, it was easier for TK to use Layer 3 MPLS VPN technology to interconnect the CE routers. The historic predominance of managed VPN services also explains why today the vast majority of Layer 3 MPLS VPN customers in Kingland continue to have a managed service.

Because of the maturity of the TK Layer 3 MPLS VPN service, a wide range of customer profiles are targeted, including small and medium businesses (SMBs), teleworkers, Enterprises (small through large), ISPs, and so forth. The design selected for this service is similar in many ways to the one selected by USCom. For example, all the existing POPs are used for Layer 3 MPLS VPN services and offer a wide range of access speeds. The edge of the network is a little different, however, because TK chose to run both Layer 3 MPLS VPN and Internet services from its mPE routers.

TK currently has 450 mPE routers deployed. TK services a total of 2400 VPN domestic clients, with a combined total of 100,000 VPNv4 routes (including remote-access clients). In addition to these customers, the international network has 360 VPN customers. The domestic network offers a Carrier's Carrier service (described later in this chapter) that has five customers, increasing the number of VPNv4 routes carried in the TK backbone to 120,000 (about 18,000 for the international network and about 2000 for the Carrier's Carrier service).

NOTE   Interprovider connectivity is described in the next chapter. Therefore, the TK international network is not described in this chapter.

TK has defined four different types of service offerings that are available to both domestic and international customers:

- **Intranet VPN**—This customer requires connectivity between internal sites for the creation of an intranet. This customer may access TK-owned central services.

- **Extranet VPN**—This customer requires connectivity between internal and external partner sites for the creation of an extranet.

- **Intranet + Internet**—This is an intranet customer that also requires Internet connectivity. Note that Internet service is bundled along with Layer 3 MPLS VPN as a service package.

- **Remote-access VPN**—This is an intranet customer connected via dial, ISDN, or DSL. Note that this service is bundled with the intranet Layer 3 MPLS VPN service.

Moreover, several VPN categories are defined. They help identify the size and scope of the attached customer. These categories are based on collation of statistics gathered by TK over a number of years, as shown in Table 4-1.

Table 4-1   *IP VPN Categories*

VPN Category	Number of Sites	Percentage of Total Sites	Number of Prefixes in VPN	Percentage of Total Customers
Domestic Type-1	2 to 10	17.5%	Ones to tens	66%
Domestic Type-2	11 to 200	28%	Tens to hundreds	16%
Domestic Type-3	201 to thousands	39.5%	Hundreds to thousands	1%
International	10 and over	10%	Hundreds to thousands	16.75%
Carrier's Carrier	50 to 500	5%	Hundreds	.25%

Multiservice PE Router Basic Engineering Guidelines

The engineering guidelines governing the addition of VPN clients to the Layer 3 MPLS VPN service are similar to those used by USCom in the preceding chapter. However, because the edge routers are shared between different services, additions to these basic guidelines are necessary so that scale and security are maintained. Chapter 5 contains the details of all the necessary scale and security features for overlapping services.

All services are provisioned from a centralized management system. A number of default templates, such as the ones discussed in the preceding chapter, are used.

TK allocates a /32 IP address to each customer CE router that it manages so that it can access and monitor this device from its Network Operations Center (NOC). This address is taken from a TK allocated address block. It is exported from the customer VRF using a unique route-target value that is used solely by the management VPN. The PE-CE links are addressed from a different TK registered public address block and are not redistributed into an attached customer's IGP. This allows TK to use the same IP address block on every PE-CE link, thus saving TK thousands of addresses.

Customer VRF Naming Convention

Unlike the USCom design, TK decided not to use a representation of a customer name for the VRF name. Instead, it chose to use the real customer name (noting that the maximum length of the name in Cisco IOS is 32 characters). The same name is used for a given customer on all PE routers that attach sites of that customer. TK preferred this approach because it felt this was more intuitive for the operations staff, because they did not need to cross-reference a representative name to a real customer name. This made the name easier to use while troubleshooting connectivity problems.

RT/RD Allocation Schemes

TK chose to use its autonomous system number (32764) within the route distinguisher/route target format. It also chose to use a unique RD per VRF and per PE router (as described in the preceding chapter). This approach has a cost in terms of memory consumption but is required for the design because TK has multiple load-balancing requirements (as you will see in the "Load-Balancing Support" section).

The route-target range 32764:[1-100] is reserved for special use, such as network management and future (as yet unknown) service requirements. The remaining route-target range is available for customer allocation. By default, one unique RT per VPN is allocated to each customer.

Network Management VPN

A management VPN is used to connect to and manage the CE routers. The management VPN imports all the relevant CE router /32 addresses that are allocated by TK. To achieve this, TK evaluated several different options:

- **Option 1**—The PE router that connects to the LAN where all the network management equipment is located imports routes that carry the route-target values that correspond to the export route-target values used for a given customer VPN. The mPE router attaching to the remote customer sites imports routes that carry the route-target value that corresponds to the export route-target value configured in the management VRF.

- **Option 2**—The PE router that connects to the management LAN is configured with a single import/export route-target pair that each customer VRF also has configured in addition to its customer-specific route-target values.

- **Option 3**—The CE router /32 loopback interface addresses are advertised using a unique route-target value that only the management VPN imports.

TK chose to use Option 3 because it had the least overhead in terms of provisioning and also provided much better isolation of the network management system (NMS) because only the CE router addresses are known to the NMS. The NMS reachability information is not redistributed from the CE router into the customer IGP, and customer routes are not known by the NMS. The template shown in Example 4-1 is used for each VRF.

Example 4-1   *PE Router Configuration Template for Network Management VPN*

```
ip vrf vrf-name
 rd 32764:customer-and-PE-router-specific-value
 export map Network_Management
 import route-target 32764:10
 import route-target 32764:customer-specific-value
 export route-target 32764:customer-specific-value
!
access-list 10 permit customer-CE-address
route-map Network_Management permit 10
 match ip address 10
 set extcommunity rt 32764:11 additive
```

This configuration template causes the CE router addresses to be advertised with the customer route-target value (so that the CE router addresses are accessible from within the VPN for troubleshooting purposes), as well as the network management route-target 32764:11. The network management route target value is taken from the reserved range that TK uses to import into its network management VPN. An additional import statement covering route-target value 32764:10 is also added so that the network management address can be imported into the VRF for two-way connectivity. This address is not redistributed into the customer IGP at the CE router.

Load-Balancing Support

TK uses a different RD value for each VRF provisioned at the mPE routers. Because TK uses VPNv4 RRs, the use of a unique RD is necessary to support its load-balancing capabilities. The reason for this is that the combination of an RD and IPv4 address constitutes a VPNv4 address, and MP-BGP considers matching addresses comparable within the BGP best path calculation. For example, a VPNv4 prefix of 32764:101:10.1.1.1 originated from an mPE router in the Center-West Level 1 POP would be comparable to a VPNv4 prefix of 32764:101:10.1.1.1 originated from an mPE router in the South-East Level 1 POP. An RR in the Center Level 1 POP therefore receives the same prefix twice but chooses a best path based on the normal BGP selection process and readvertises only that best path to other mPE routers. The result of this is the loss of a given path to a receiving mPE router in another POP, which would prevent it from performing any sort of load balancing. This is illustrated in Figure 4-7.

Figure 4-7   *Path Selection at a VPNv4 Route Reflector*

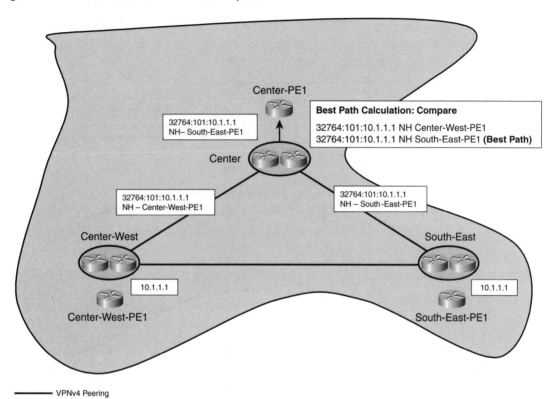

Center-PE1

32764:101:10.1.1.1
NH– South-East-PE1

Best Path Calculation: Compare

32764:101:10.1.1.1 NH Center-West-PE1
32764:101:10.1.1.1 NH South-East-PE1 **(Best Path)**

Center

32764:101:10.1.1.1
NH – Center-West-PE1

32764:101:10.1.1.1
NH – South-East-PE1

Center-West   South-East

10.1.1.1   10.1.1.1

Center-West-PE1   South-East-PE1

——— VPNv4 Peering

Figure 4-7 shows that a customer VPN network is dual-attached to mPE routers South-East-PE1 and Center-West-PE1. It advertises reachability for 10.1.1.1/32 to both mPE routers with the same metric. The mPE router Center-PE1 only receives the path via South-East-PE1 and therefore cannot load-balance traffic using the Center-West-PE1 path. To rectify this situation, a different RD may be used at each mPE router (which is the solution chosen by TK). Therefore, as shown in Figure 4-8, both paths can be received by the Center-PE1 mPE router.

Getting the different routes to the mPE routers through the RRs is only part of the problem. To successfully provide load balancing of traffic toward the 10.1.1.1/32 destination over both available paths via mPE routers South-East-PE1 and Center-West-PE1, TK chose to use iBGP multipath functionality to ensure that the mPE routers use multiple routes.

Figure 4-8   *Different RD Usage for Load-Balancing Support*

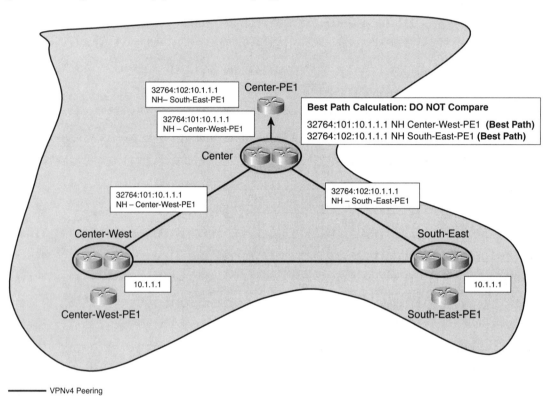

iBGP Multipath Support for VPNv4

The normal operation of MP-BGP is to install a single best path into the routing table. However, this behavior can be changed using the maximum-paths number-of-paths command, which allows up to 16 different paths. MP-BGP uses the best-path algorithm to select one of the available paths as the best path; this path is inserted into the routing table. However, because of the maximum-paths configuration, the other additional paths may also be inserted into the routing table. All these entries can then be used to provide unequal-cost load balancing on a per-source/destination pair basis.

TK limits the number of maximum paths based on a given customer requirement, which is typically only two different paths. The reason is that each extra path requires additional memory and processing at the mPE router, so tight controls on the deployment of this functionality are necessary. TK charges extra for load balancing support because it is considered an additional service above and beyond the basic connectivity to an MPLS-based VPN.

eiBGP Multipath Support for VPNv4

TK also provides an eiBGP multipath service. This support is similar in functionality to iBGP multipath. It is deployed in the TK network for multihomed sites that require load balancing of traffic from the core. The key difference with this feature is that it can take into consideration both internal MP-BGP and external BGP paths from within a VRF for load-balancing purposes. The maximum-paths eibgp number-of-paths command is used to enable this feature on a per-customer basis.

mPE Router Control-Plane Requirements

TK follows the same set of control-plane recommendations as specified in the preceding chapter. This includes the use of path MTU discovery (see [PMTU]), input queue tuning, and Selective Packet Discard (SPD) tuning. In addition, TK also selected a centralized route reflection design with a single level of hierarchy. However, as stated earlier, the IPv4 and VPNv4 reflection is kept separate.

VPNv4 Route Reflector Placement

TK uses its six Level 1 POPs to house its VPNv4 RRs. Each Level 1 POP has two RRs, and a limit of 300 MP-BGP peering sessions is imposed on each reflector. This limit is based on internal TK testing. It does not represent the theoretical maximum number of peering sessions that the RRs could handle.

Each mPE router in a Level 1 POP has redundant MP-BGP peering sessions with the two RRs located in the local Level 1 POP. mPE routers in Level 2 POPs have redundant RR connections to two separate Level 1 POPs. Figure 4-9 shows the RR connectivity in a Level 1 POP.

Figure 4-9 *VPNv4 Route Reflector Connectivity*

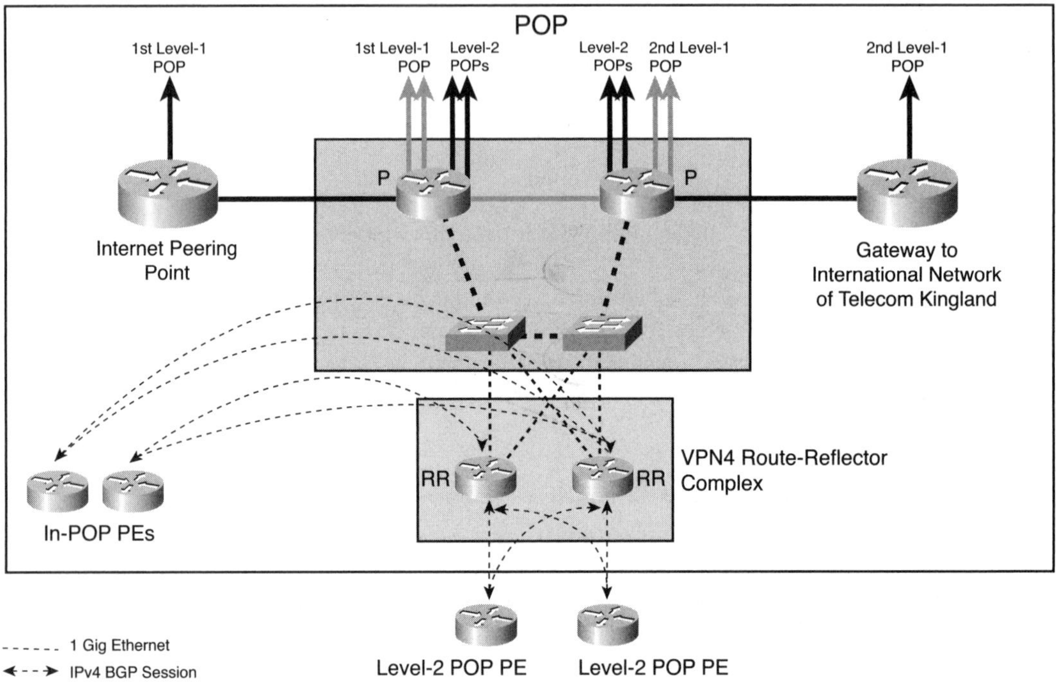

A full mesh of MP-BGP peering is deployed between all the RRs, as shown in Figure 4-10.

PE-CE Routing Protocol Design

TK offers a service similar to the one discussed in the preceding chapter in terms of static routing and BGP-4 on the PE-CE links. However, because TK manages the CE routers, it is more able to use static routing for the large number of single-attached customer sites, whose sole routing requirement is to advertise their local LAN subnet. Typically a default route pointing toward the mPE router is configured at the CE router, and the LAN subnet is configured as a static route in the VRF at the mPE router. If a site requires more than a small set of subnet advertisements, or if it learns a default route locally via another service provider, or if it needs load-balancing support, BGP-4 is the protocol of choice.

Figure 4-10   *Peering Between VPNv4 Route Reflectors*

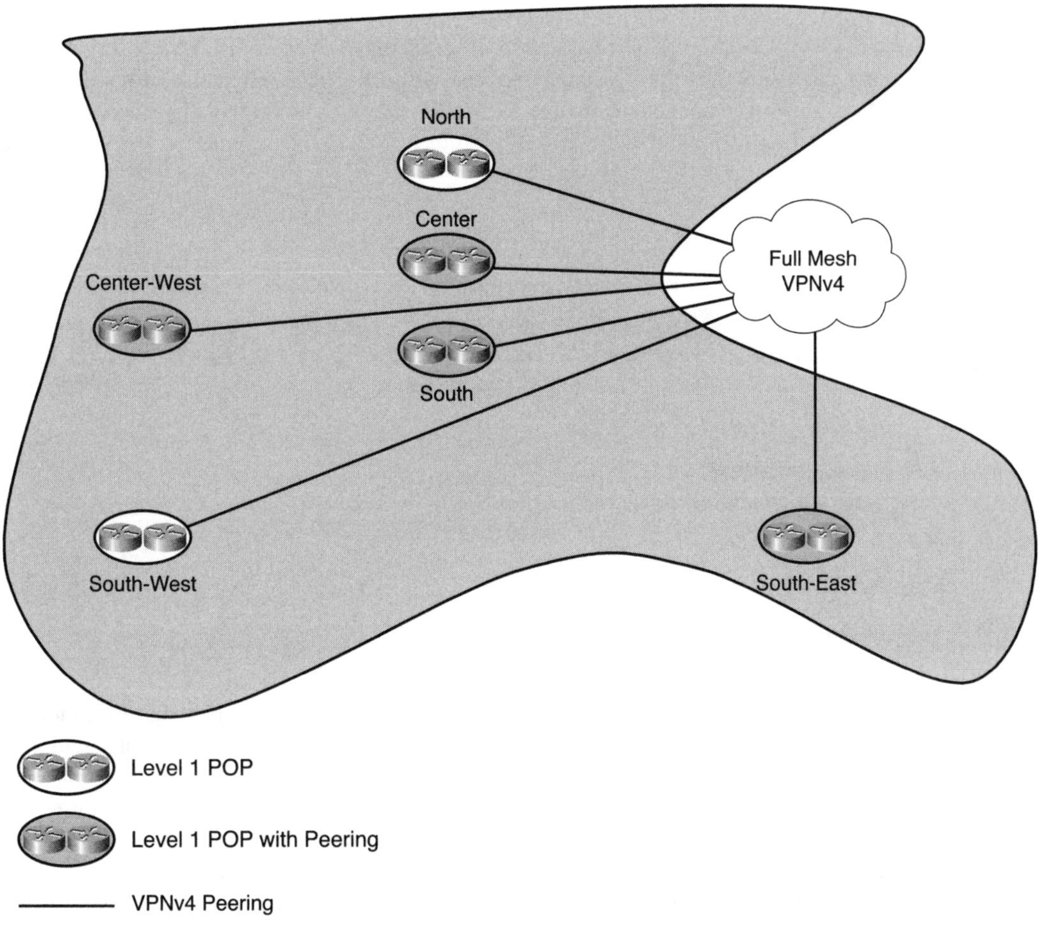

Carrier's Carrier Service

With an established Layer 3 MPLS VPN service, TK has attracted a wide variety of customer types, each with different characteristics and profiles. However, some customer requirements could not easily be met using TK's existing service. Primarily, the following two were not straightforward to address:

- Hierarchical VPNs
- Large customers with substantial routing information

The main issue with supporting these two services is scale, especially the memory requirements placed on the mPE routers.

Hierarchical VPNs allow a TK customer to offer its own Layer 3 MPLS VPN service while using a single VPN over the TK backbone for transport service. They also provide autonomy for the customer to manage and change VPN/VRF membership at will. This concept is illustrated in Figure 4-11.

Figure 4-11   *Hierarchical VPNs Concept*

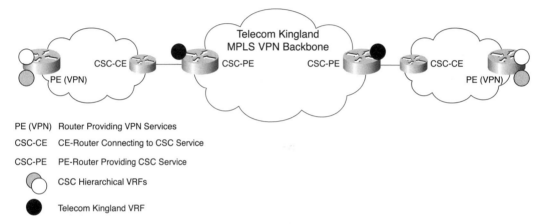

PE (VPN)   Router Providing VPN Services

CSC-CE   CE-Router Connecting to CSC Service

CSC-PE   PE-Router Providing CSC Service

⊘   CSC Hierarchical VRFs

●   Telecom Kingland VRF

The next requirement to consider is large customers with substantial routing information. A small number of customers wanted to carry between 5000 and 10,000 IGP routes within their Layer 3 MPLS VPN. Although the existing deployed hardware could easily handle this number of routes at the mPE routers, TK felt that architecturally the basic service was not optimal if the number of this type of customer were to grow. Because of this requirement, as well as the hierarchical VPN requirement, TK decided to use the Carrier's Carrier architecture (which was briefly described in Chapter 1) to service the needs of these customers.

As with the standard Layer 3 MPLS VPN service, TK manages the CSC-CE router on the customer's behalf. This provides some benefits in terms of routing protocol filtering and QoS control over the links between the CSC-CE router and CSC-PE router.

Because BGP-4 is the preferred PE-CE routing protocol on the existing Layer 3 MPLS VPN service, TK decided to continue using this protocol for the Carrier's Carrier service, with the extensions provided by [BGP+Label]. These extensions allow MPLS labels to be carried along with the BGP routes. Therefore, an additional label distribution protocol, such as the one covered in [LDP], was deemed unnecessary. Static routing was ruled out because of the number of expected next-hop router addresses exchanged across the PE-CE links.

Use of the Carrier's Carrier architecture is restricted to selective mPE routers. This is primarily because new software is required on the edge routers because [BGP+Label] technology appeared in router software after the initial Layer 3 MPLS VPN deployment. Figure 4-12 shows the basic Carrier's Carrier models supported by the design.

Figure 4-12 *Carrier's Carrier Connectivity Models*

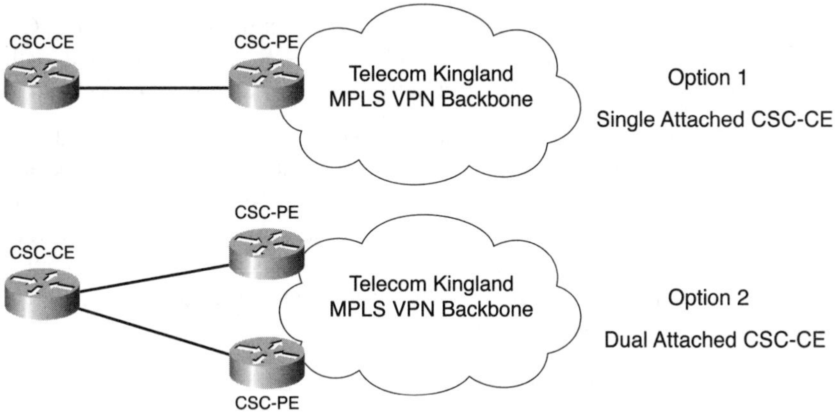

Load-Balancing Support with Carrier's Carrier

Load balancing of traffic across the Carrier's Carrier service is supported in the design, but only within the TK Layer 3 MPLS VPN backbone (that is, between CSC-PE routers). This facility is achieved by use of the iBGP multipath feature at the CSC-PE routers when more than one path is available for a given end-customer destination. Figure 4-13 shows a topology where this feature may be useful.

Figure 4-13 *BGP Multipath for the Carrier's Carrier Service*

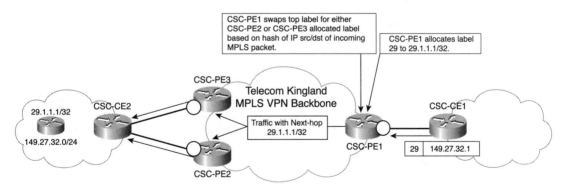

In this case traffic may be load-balanced across the TK backbone between the two egress CSC-PE routers, CSC-PE2 and CSC-PE3. As with the regular Layer 3 MPLS VPN service, this is achieved through the combined use of different RDs for the same VRF on CSC-PE2 and CSC-PE3. The two paths are advertised to CSC-PE1 by the RRs, and as iBGP multipath functionality is configured on CSC-PE1 it can select more than one path toward the next hop 29.1.1.1/32.

Figure 4-13 shows that CSC-PE1 receives packets that contain an MPLS label that points toward a given next-hop address located in another customer site. CSC-PE1 swaps this label for the VPN label received for 29.1.1.1/32 from either CSC-PE2 or CSC-PE3. Then it pushes on the LDP label used in the TK backbone to reach the corresponding CSC-PE router. Load balancing is achieved by performing a hash function on the IP source/destination in the incoming MPLS packets. The result of this hash function provides a result whereby one of the next hops to reach 29.1.1.1/32 may be selected.

The Carrier's Carrier service is enabled using a configuration template, which is shown in Example 4-2.

Example 4-2   *Carrier's Carrier Configuration Template*

```
address-family ipv4 vrf vrfname
 neighbor CSC-CE-address remote-as remote-asn
 neighbor CSC-CE-address activate
 neighbor CSC-CE-address send-label
```

NOTE   If the same autonomous system number is used in multiple sites of the same customer attached to the Carrier's Carrier service, as with the regular Layer 3 MPLS VPN service, an additional command is needed. This command enables AS override so that the CSC-mPE router replaces the customer AS number with the AS number assigned to TK. The syntax of the additional command is **neighbor** *CSC-CE-address* **as-override**.

To restrict the number of routes that the CSC-CE router sends to the CSC-PE router, filtering is performed during the redistribution of the customer IGP routes into the [BGP+Label] BGP process. This filtering ensures that only the next-hop addresses of the customer PE routers (if using the hierarchical VPN service) or customer peering routers (if using the standard Carrier's Carrier service) are advertised to the CSC-PE routers. TK configures this filtering based on the information provided by the CsC customer.

Large Carrier's Carrier Customer Attachment Example

The largest customer attached to the TK Carrier's Carrier service is Kingland Technology, which has 1000 sites. 630 of these sites are remote offices that connect via an IGP (EIGRP in this case) to their nearest regional sites. In addition to the remote sites, Kingland Technology has 350 regional sites and 20 core sites. The regional sites are connected to the TK Carrier's

Carrier service via the Level 2 POPs, and the core sites are connected to the six Level 1 POPs. The remote sites are directly connected to a regional site or central site. The routers in the remote sites advertise reachability information to the CSC-CE routers through EIGRP.

Each TK Level 1 POP has on average three connections from Kingland Technology. These connections are serviced using three separate mPE routers. The Level 2 POPs have on average six connections, which are serviced using two separate mPE routers. Figure 4-14 shows this connectivity model.

Figure 4-14   *Kingland Technology Connectivity to Telecom Kingland*

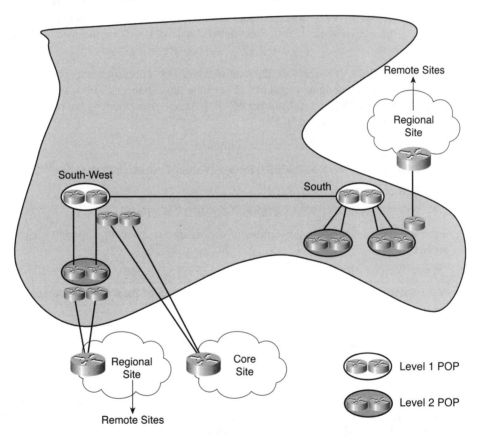

With this topology, Kingland Technology can run its own internal routing and outsource the advertisement of this information between its sites to TK. To support this configuration, TK runs an internal multihop BGP-4 mesh across the Kingland Technology regional and core sites. The RRs used to exchange this information are kept within the Kingland Technology core sites. Each CSC-CE router runs redundant BGP-4 sessions with the RRs within its nearest core site.

Kingland Technology has a total of 10,000 routes. However, these routes have only 370 next hops because the remote sites can be reached through the CSC-CE router of a central or regional site. By running multihop BGP-4 between the CSC-CE-routers, only these 370 CSC-CE router addresses need to be exchanged with TK's Layer 3 MPLS VPN service. The 10,000 routes are hidden from TK's MPC network.

Remote Access to the Layer 3 MPLS VPN Service

Many different options are available to connect remote users to a Layer 3 MPLS VPN service. Chapter 2 of [MPLS-VPN-Vol2] provides technical and configuration details for most of these options. This section doesn't cover these details. Instead, it looks at the specific design options that TK chose.

For Layer 3 MPLS VPN services, the deployed network currently has more than 5000 remote-access users, who belong to a total of 625 separate remote-access VPNs. With an average of eight routes per VPN, the total number of VPNv4 routes generated by the remote-access solution set is approximately 5000.

TK provides three main remote-access solutions:

- Dial-in access via L2TP Virtual Private Dialup Network (VPDN)
- Dial-in access via direct ISDN
- DSL access using PPPoE or PPPoA and VPDN (L2TP)

Table 4-2 breaks down how the number of sites is spread across the different remote-access services.

Table 4-2   *Remote Access to MPLS VPN Service Breakdown*

VPN Category	Number of Sites	Percentage of Total Remote-Access Sites
Dial-in via L2TP	3500	70%
ISDN	50	1%
DSL	1450	29%

To support the Layer 3 MPLS VPN remote-access services, TK has a separate set of Network Access Server (NAS) devices in each Level 1 and Level 2 POP. They are connected to the mPE routers via Gigabit Ethernet. To support the dial-in services, TK has deployed 12 L2TP network servers (LNSs), two in each Level 1 POP, and it limits the maximum number of L2TP sessions to 1000 for each device.

Dial-In Access Via L2TP VPDN

To provide dial-in access via the PSTN or ISDN, TK chose to use the VPDN design that was discussed in Chapter 1 in the section "Remote Access to the Layer 3 MPLS VPN Service." This concept uses a tunneling protocol (such as L2TP) to extend the dial connection from a remote user and terminate it on an LNS, which in this context is called a Virtual Home Gateway (VHG).

TK supports connection speeds of up to 56 kbps for dialup via the PSTN and 64 kbps/128 kbps for dialup via the ISDN.

Figure 4-15 shows a high-level example of the VPDN concept.

Figure 4-15   *Dial-In Using the VPDN Concept*

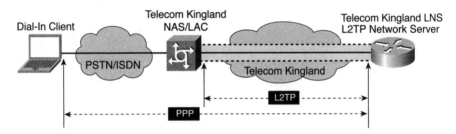

Using this infrastructure, a remote client may dial in to any of the TK Level 1/Level 2 POP NASs. After RADIUS authentication, the remote client can be tunneled to one of the 12 LNSs for access to their Layer 3 MPLS VPN environment. Figure 4-16 provides a more detailed topology specific to TK.

Dial-In Access Via Direct ISDN

TK provides a direct digital ISDN service to some of its customers. This service is deployed by attaching a primary rate ISDN connection to an mPE router. TK currently has six of these connections, one in each Level 1 POP. The primary interface is housed in one of the existing mPE routers, as shown in Figure 4-17.

Figure 4-16   *Dial-In Using VPDN—Telecom Kingland Design*

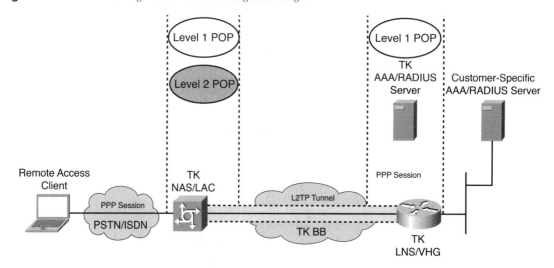

Figure 4-17   *Level 1 Direct ISDN Connectivity*

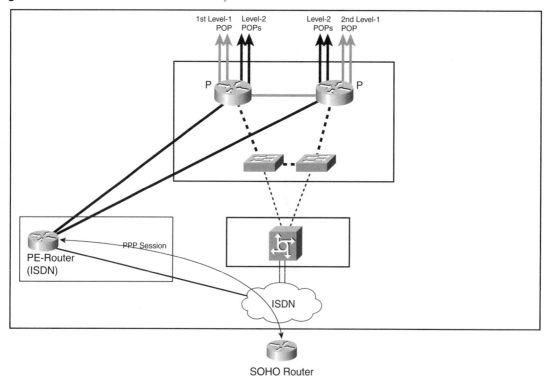

Direct ISDN access does not require the use of any tunneling protocol from the remote client to the TK mPE router. Instead, a PPP link is established over the ISDN B channel directly to the mPE router. The mPE router obtains the remote client's credentials using CHAP; it then forwards the credentials to the TK RADIUS server for authentication. Upon successful authentication, the RADIUS server returns configuration parameters for the client (such as VRF name, IP address pool, and so forth). The mPE router then can create a virtual-access interface for the PPP session based on local configuration and the information returned by the RADIUS server. The user CHAP authentication process then can finish, and the remote user is given access to the relevant VPN.

DSL Access Using PPPoE or PPPoA and VPDN (L2TP)

DSL access is provided to business clients by terminating DSL connections using the L2TP VPDN architecture rather than a direct connection onto an mPE router. This provides the infrastructure for large-scale DSL termination, with access speeds up to 1.2 Mbps. Figure 4-18 shows the DSL connectivity option.

Figure 4-18   *DSL Connectivity Using PPPoE or PPPoA*

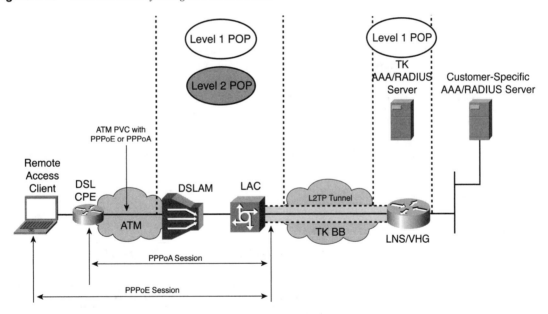

As shown in Figure 4-18, a remote-access client may access its Layer 3 MPLS VPN using PPPoE (if the CPE acts as a bridge) or PPPoA (if the CPE acts as a router). RFC 1483 routed (PPPoA) and bridged (PPPoE) encapsulation is used, and an L2TP tunnel is built from the receiving NAS/LAC to one of the LNSs in the TK Level 1 POPs.

mVPN Service Application

The basic Layer 3 MPLS VPN service offered by TK provides IPv4 Unicast connectivity only. When the Unicast service was initially deployed, there was little demand for Multicast support. What demand there was was met by deploying point-to-point [GRE] tunnels between customer CE routers. From a long-term perspective, TK realized that this approach clearly was not scalable, primarily because of packet replication requirements at the CE routers, the lack of packet replication in the core, and the management and number of IP tunnels required between customer sites. (Packet replication would be more optimal, especially for high-rate Multicast sources of traffic.) However, this approach provided a solution for the few customers that needed Multicast support.

Over time, TK's VPN customers requested more Multicast services. Therefore, TK chose to deploy Multicast services within a customer VPN on the MPC network but not on the international network. The solution chosen was based on the mVPN model that was discussed in Chapter 1.

Multicast Address Allocation

Multicast support within a VPN does not imply that TK should advertise the Multicast addresses used to the IP Multicast community at large. For this reason, TK chose to use the organization local-scope Multicast address block (see [local-scope]), 239.192.0.0/14, for its mVPN service offering. This provides a usable address range of 239.192.0.0 through 239.195.255.255. These addresses are used for the Multicast domains (default-MDT) and any associated data MDTs.

Within the initial Multicast design, the address range 239.192.0.1 through 239.192.15.254 is reserved for default MDTs, yielding a maximum of 4096 Multicast VPNs. This number was considered adequate for the short to medium term. If further addresses are needed in the future, a new range of 239.192.16.0/20 will be used and therefore is reserved.

Address blocks 239.192.32.0/20, 239.192.48.0/20, and 239.192.64.0/20 are reserved for data MDTs. Table 4-3 summarizes the Multicast address allocation.

Table 4-3 *Multicast Address Allocation Scheme*

Address Block	Service Allocation	Current Usage
239.192.0.0/20	mVPN default MDT	Currently in use
239.192.16.0/20	mVPN default MDT	Reserved
239.192.32.0/20	mVPN data MDT	Currently in use
239.192.48.0/20	mVPN data MDT	Reserved
239.192.64.0/20	mVPN data MDT	Reserved

Multicast Routing Protocol Support

The backbone Multicast routing protocol chosen for the design is PIM-SM. PIM-SM is used on all P router to P router links. If an mPE router provides Multicast services (and not all mPE routers within the MPC do), its PE-P or PE-PE link(s) are also enabled for PIM-SM. PIM-SM is not enabled on any edge device that does not provide Multicast services (so Multicast services cannot be offered on those devices).

PIM-SM is used for the default MDT for any Multicast VPNs. This default MDT carries any Multicast control traffic generated for a given Multicast VPN. However, PIM-SSM is used for any data MDTs that are created for these VPNs. This provides a more optimal path for the traffic, and it does not require registration/join with the rendezvous point (RP), but rather directly with the source.

To reduce the amount of state carried at the edge of the network, the default SPT threshold is set to infinity on all mPE routers. The SPT threshold specifies when a leaf router should join the shortest path source tree for the specified group. Note that the normal default setting in Cisco IOS is 0, which would mean that an immediate join is sent toward a given source after the first Multicast packet from that source is received. Because PIM-SM is only used for the default MDTs, setting the SPT threshold to infinity ensures that all Multicast control traffic flows via the rendezvous point. This has the advantage of reducing the amount of {S, G} state at the mPE routers. The disadvantages are that a nonoptimal routing path is used, and a very robust RP in terms of switching/replication capabilities is required.

Group-to-RP mappings for the default MDTs are distributed using the bootstrap router (BSR) capability. This provides an automatic distribution mechanism of Multicast groups and indicates which RP should be joined. Candidate BSRs (C-BSRs) originate bootstrap messages that contain a priority field. This is used to select which C-BSR router becomes the elected C-BSR.

All the previously described capabilities are illustrated in Figure 4-19. Example 4-3 provides the basic configuration template for this design.

Figure 4-19 *Backbone Multicast Design*

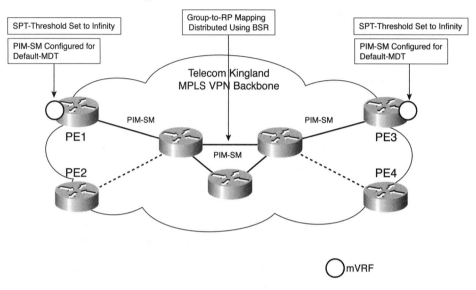

Example 4-3 *mVPN Configuration Template for PE Routers*

```
ip multicast-routing vrf vrfname
ip vrf vrfname
 mdt default default-MDT-for-this-VPN
!
ip pim spt-threshold infinity group-list MDT-range
!
ip access-list standard MDT-range
 permit 239.192.0.0 0.0.15.255
```

Rendezvous Point and BSR Design for PIM-SM

Because PIM-SM is used in the backbone network, rendezvous points are needed. This is because PIM-SM operates by default over a unidirectional shared tree whose root is the rendezvous point. Last-hop routers join this tree when they have receivers that are interested in receiving traffic for a given Multicast group. Therefore, all mPE routers that have Multicast-enabled VPNs join the shared tree by sending a join toward the RP for each Multicast domain.

Placement of the RPs generally depends on the location of Multicast receivers, the amount of traffic that will flow via the RP, and the location of the Multicast senders. Because TK only uses PIM-SM for the default MDTs in its Multicast VPN service, the location of senders and receivers is of less importance because PIM-SSM is used to directly join the source of any data MDTs. Therefore, TK decided to deploy an RP in four of the six Level 1 POPs and to allow each of these to be C-BSRs also.

Because each of the Level 1 POPs has both P routers and mPE routers, consideration was given as to which of these devices might perform the RP and BSR functionality. The mPE routers were considered, but because they were already providing edge functionality for various services, TK thought it was inappropriate to burden them with additional control-plane functionality. The P routers were also rejected, because their main purpose was considered to be switching packets rather than control-plane activity (hence the Internet-free core design you saw earlier). Therefore, the final design decision was that the RPs/BSRs would be standalone routers that attach directly to the core P routers, as shown in Figure 4-20.

Figure 4-20   *Rendezvous Point POP Design*

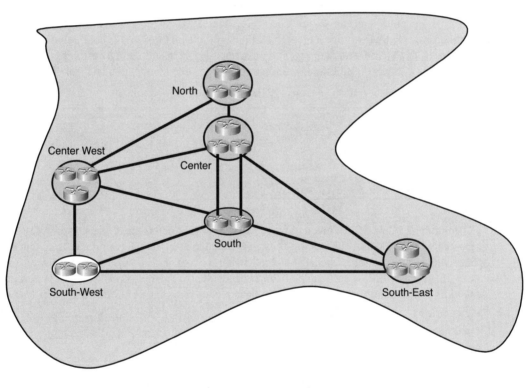

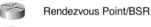 Rendezvous Point/BSR

Level 1 POP With RP

Use of Data-MDTs in the mVPN Design

The default behavior for a PE router receiving a Multicast packet on an mVRF interface is to forward the packet using the default MDT. This means that all PE routers that have joined the default tree receive the Multicast traffic, regardless of whether they have interested receivers. In such situations a PE router simply drops the Multicast traffic, but this is clearly suboptimal. Therefore, the mVPN architecture allows for the creation of data MDTs on a per-customer basis. Data MDTs are created based on predetermined bandwidth limits and receipt of traffic matching the limits from locally attached customer sources. Only PE routers that have interested receivers for the group will join the data MDT.

TK selected to use the default MDT for customer and backbone control traffic only (such as customer-specific joins and so on). Therefore, data MDTs are used within the design for any Multicast traffic that exceeds a predefined threshold. (This threshold is configured as 1 Kbps, which essentially causes a data MDT to be created for each source in a customer mVPN.) Example 4-4 shows the additional commands that are added to the template from Example 4-3.

Example 4-4   *mVPN Configuration Template for Data MDTs*

```
ip vrf vrfname
 mdt data data-MDT-from-range-allocated-to-mVPN threshold 1
!
ip pim ssm range Data-MDT
!
ip access-list standard Data-MDT
 permit 239.192.32.0 0.0.15.255
```

The number of data MDTs given to a particular mVPN is determined on a customer-by-customer basis. TK uses the mdt log-reuse command in each mVRF configuration so that it can receive a syslog message whenever a data MDT is reused. This helps over time to determine how many data MDTs a particular customer needs. It also balances core Multicast state against sending traffic to mPE routers that do not have receivers for a given Multicast group.

PIM-SSM rather than PIM-SM is used to signal data MDTs. This allows each mPE router to join the source of a given customer Multicast group directly rather than via an RP.

Restricting Multicast Routing State at mPE Routers

Because mPE router memory is a finite resource, TK decided to restrict the number of Multicast routes allowed in a given mVRF. Multicast routes are called *m*routes. They are used in the forwarding path and are specific to a given customer Multicast domain.

The mroutes are restricted through the use of the **ip multicast vrf** *vrfname* **route-limit** command. TK generates a warning when a 60 percent threshold of the maximum configured mroutes is reached. The maximum number of mroutes differs depending on the customer requirements. However, for ease of management, TK chose to use a default value of 300. The company might change this value as it gains more experience with its customer requirements.

Quality of Service Design

On the access links, TK supports three user-visible classes of service (CoSs) as part of its Layer 3 MPLS VPN service:

- VPN Real-Time
- VPN Premium
- VPN Standard

Each of these is supported by a separate queue on the access links between CE routers and mPE routers. TK also supports a fourth queue on the access links for a user-hidden CoS that handles routing traffic between CE routers and mPE routers.

A single CoS is supported on the access for the Internet service. It is identical to the Standard CoS of the Layer 3 MPLS VPN service.

In the network's core, TK decided to schedule all the VPN traffic, regardless of its CoS, in a single queue also used for Internet traffic. The reasons are detailed in the "QoS Design in the Core Network" section (including the fact that thanks to its DWDM infrastructure, TK can fairly easily provision additional bandwidth to keep aggregate load low). This queue is called the default queue (DF). However, a separate queue optimized for real-time operations, the Expedited Forwarding queue (EF), is used to transport telephony transit traffic. Finally, a third queue, the Assured Forwarding 3 queue (AF3), is dedicated to the transport of control traffic that is essential to network operations. This comprises the internal routing traffic (OSPF and MP-BGP traffic), some management traffic (such as Telnet), the MPLS signaling traffic (LDP, RSVP-TE) and the telephony signaling traffic from the PSTN soft switches.

Table 4-4 details the mapping between each type of traffic, the DSCP values, the queues on the access links, the EXP/DSCP values in the core, and the queues in the core.

Table 4-4   *Mapping of Classes, DSCP, EXP, and Queues*

Class of Service	DSCP on Access	Queue in Access	EXP/DSCP in Core	Queue in Core
VPN Real-Time	46 (EF)	EF	EXP=5	DF
VPN Premium	18 (AF21) in contract 20 (AF22) out of contract	AF2	EXP=2	
VPN Standard and Internet	0	DF	EXP=0	
VPN edge routing	48 (precedence 6)	AF3	—	—
Telephony transit	32 (precedence 4)	—	EXP=4	EF
Telephony transit signaling	24 (precedence 3)	—	EXP=3	AF3
Core control (routing, management, signaling)	—	—	DSCP=48 EXP6	

For example, the VPN Real-Time CoS from the Layer 3 MPLS VPN service is marked with DSCP 46 on the access links between CE routers and mPE routers. It uses the EF queue on these links, but in the core it is marked with EXP 5 and scheduled into the DF queue.

Layer 3 MPLS VPN and Internet SLA

TK offers QoS commitments over the core (POP to POP) to all Layer 3 MPLS VPN and Internet customers.

In the core, a single level of commitment is provided to all classes of service of the Layer 3 MPLS VPN service as well as for the Internet traffic. These commitments are shown in Table 4-5.

Table 4-5   *Telecom Kingland POP-to-POP SLA Commitments*

SLA Parameter	SLA Commitment
POP-to-POP round-trip time	35 ms
POP-to-POP jitter	5 ms
POP-to-POP loss	0.2%

On the access link, the customer can decide for each VPN site the percentage of access bandwidth allocated to the Real-Time CoS and to the Premium CoS. However, TK offers the Real-Time CoS only if the access rate is at a minimum 256 kbps and is limited to a maximum of 33 percent of the access rate. The customer selects a single percentage for each CoS that applies to both directions of the access link.

A web interface is offered to the users of the Layer 3 MPLS VPN service. They may directly configure, or reconfigure, the percentage allocated to the Real-Time and Premium CoS, as well as the classification criteria for identifying the traffic belonging to each CoS.

Policing is performed on the CE router for the traffic sent by the end user to the VPN Real-Time and Premium CoSs. Traffic sent to the VPN Real-Time CoS in excess of the selected percentage is dropped to protect the rest of the real-time traffic from delay and jitter degradation. Traffic sent to the VPN Premium CoS in excess of the selected corresponding percentage is remarked as "out of contract." This way it can be subject to selective discard should there be congestion in the AF2 queue, thus protecting the rest of the VPN premium traffic from loss. Also, if in the future TK introduces differentiated treatment of the VPN classes of service in the core, the "out of contract" marking could also be used in the core to apply selective discard to this subset of the VPN premium traffic.

Only a single CoS is supported on the Internet access service, which is the same as the Layer 3 MPLS VPN Standard CoS. 100 percent of the access rate of an Internet service is effectively always allocated to the Standard CoS.

As explained in the "Edge QoS Engineering" section of Chapter 2, "Technology Primer: Quality of Service, Traffic Engineering, and Network Recovery," on lower-speed links, even small queue occupancies have a significant impact on delay. The effect varies considerably and has many parameters, such as the actual link speed, the maximum packet size, the maximum load compared to the service rate for each queue, and so forth. Some of these are outside TK's control. Therefore, TK does not offer standard SLAs to Layer 3 MPLS VPN and Internet customers over the access links. Instead, it takes responsibility for configuring the DiffServ mechanisms for the three CoSs on the access link but it leaves it to the customer to use these mechanisms appropriately to achieve the desired level of QoS.

However, at the request of some customers, TK has worked to establish specific custom SLAs for the access links. For example, Table 4-6 lists the specific commitments for each CoS on the access provided as part of such a custom SLA. This custom SLA is built on a number of assumptions. These include a maximum packet size of 66 bytes in the real-time queue, a limit of 33 percent of link speed for the Real-Time CoS, a maximum load of 50 percent for the premium traffic, and the use of fragmentation and interleaving on lower-speed links and short access links (so that propagation on the access links is negligible). To establish these delay figures, TK first ran simulations that computed the 99.9 percentile delay for a perfect queuing system under these assumptions. Then TK factored in the expected deviations of the actual implementation from such a perfect queuing system. For example, this includes the effect of the transmit buffer (known on Cisco devices as the transmit ring). This is further discussed in the later section "QoS Design on the Network Edge for Layer 3 MPLS VPN and Internet."

Table 4-6   *Sample Custom Per-CoS VPN SLA on Access*

CoS	SLA Parameter	SLA Commitment
VPN Real-Time (in contract)	One-way delay	Access speed-dependent: 256–512 kbps: 30 ms 1–2 Mbps: 15 ms 34–155 Mbps: 5 ms
	Loss	0.1%
VPN Premium (in-contract)	One-way delay	Access speed-dependent: 64–128 kbps: 250 ms 256–512 kbps: 125 ms 1–2 Mbps: 60 ms 34–155 Mbps: 25 ms
	Loss	0.1%
VPN Standard	Bandwidth	All bandwidth unused by the VPN Real-Time and VPN Premium classes can be used by the VPN Standard class

QoS Design in the Core Network

As described previously, TK opted to handle separately the telephony traffic, the Internet/Layer 3 MPLS VPN traffic, and the control traffic in the core of the network. This allows TK to isolate the three types of traffic from one another and to apply different capacity planning policies and different sets of QoS mechanisms to each.

For the telephony transit traffic, TK wanted to provide optimum delay and jitter even under failure situations, including catastrophic failure situations such as multiple simultaneous failures or complete POP failure. To that end, TK combined the following mechanisms:

- Use of strict priority queuing for the EF queue to achieve optimum delay and jitter in a short time.

- Use of MPLS Traffic Engineering to transport the telephony transit traffic over tunnels that are constraint-based routed and limited by configuration to keep the telephony transit traffic load under 40 percent on any link. TK deemed this sufficiently low to bound the delay, jitter, and loss through the MPC to the required levels for telephony transit traffic.

- Separate capacity planning for the telephony traffic (which is well-known and closely monitored) to make sure that link capacity is such that

  — In the absence of failure, the tunnels carrying the telephony traffic all follow their shortest path. The telephony traffic load is less than 20 percent of link capacity.

  — Under all targeted failure situations, including catastrophic failure scenarios, all the tunnels should fit (using a path that may or may not be the shortest path) while satisfying the constraint of keeping the load under 40 percent of link capacity.

The details of the MPLS Traffic Engineering design for the telephony traffic can be found in the "MPLS Traffic Engineering Design" section.

For Internet and Layer 3 MPLS VPN traffic, it is relatively easy and inexpensive for TK to provide additional capacity in the core when needed through the activation of additional wavelengths on its DWDM infrastructure. Also, the QoS targets are not as stringent as for telephony. For these reasons, TK elected to rely on only capacity planning to achieve appropriate QoS for that class of traffic. To that end, a capacity planning policy is followed to trigger provisioning of additional link capacity whenever one of the following is true:

- The aggregate load across all traffic (including not just Layer 3 VPN and Internet traffic but also telephony transit) reaches 45 percent of the link capacity, in the absence of failure, as determined by the monitoring of interface counters.

- The aggregate load across all traffic would reach 85 percent of the link capacity should one of the links, SRLGs, or nodes fail. This is determined by a centralized simulation tool that collects current network topology and traffic matrix information and assesses the theoretical load on all links resulting from failure situations.

The "Core QoS Engineering" section of Chapter 2 characterized the relationship between the maximum utilization at a large time scale and the experienced QoS levels. In accordance with this approach, TK determined that such a capacity planning policy ensures that the Layer 3 MPLS VPN and Internet POP-to-POP SLA specified previously can be met in normal situations as well as during expected failures.

For control traffic, TK allocates 2 percent of the link capacity to the corresponding queue. In the absence of failure, as well as under planned failures, the control traffic could have been handled appropriately in the default queue because capacity planning aims to keep aggregate load under 85 percent. However, in the face of catastrophic failure scenarios or combinations of factors resulting in breach of the capacity planning rules (such as a combination of unexpected Internet/VPN traffic growth and a failure), the link could enter a congested state. Use of a separate queue for the control traffic ensures that, in such situations, the control traffic (including routing and telephony signaling) is unaffected by overall congestion. This protects both the stability of the MPC and the stability of the telephony transit traffic.

With respect to the QoS models presented in the "QoS Models" section of Chapter 2, TK follows a 4/3/1 model because it deploys four queues on the access and three queues in the core and uses traffic engineering (TE) with a single class type. (In other words, TK uses regular MPLS Traffic Engineering but it does not use DiffServ-aware MPLS Traffic Engineering.)

Figure 4-21 illustrates the interfaces where TK applies the various QoS service policies in its network. In particular, it shows that TK applies a core egress policy to reflect the core QoS design presented previously on all the P router interfaces as well as on the core-facing interfaces of the mPE routers.

Figure 4-21 *Telecom Kingland Service Policies for QoS*

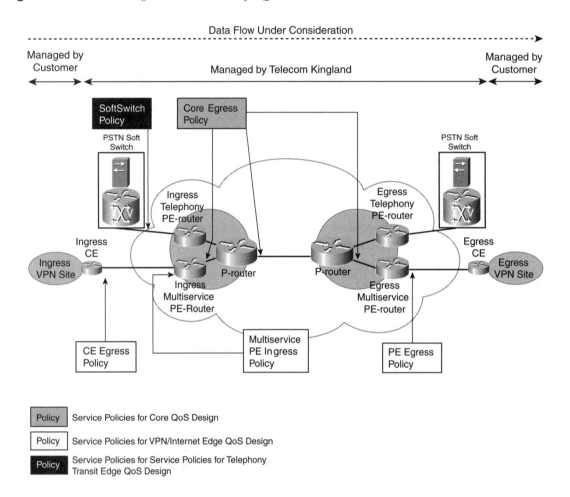

This core egress policy is detailed in Example 4-5 for the case of an STM-16 core link.

Example 4-5 *Core QoS Egress Service Policy in Telecom Kingland for STM-16 Links*

```
int pos0/0
 service-policy output Core-QoS-policy
!
class-map match-any class-Telephony
 match mpls exp 4
!
class-map match-any class-Control
 match dscp 48
 match mpls exp 6
```

Example 4-5 *Core QoS Egress Service Policy in Telecom Kingland for STM-16 Links (Continued)*

```
 match mpls exp 3
!
policy-map Core-QoS-policy
 class class-Telephony
  priority percent 55
  queue-limit 4092
 class class-Control
  bandwidth percent 2
  queue-limit 417
 class class-default
  bandwidth percent 43
  random-detect
  random-detect exponential-weighting-constant 14
  random-detect 1344 8958 1
  queue-limit 17916
```

Telephony transit traffic is classified based on the EXP value of 4 in accordance with the QoS mapping listed in Table 4-4. It is scheduled using the DiffServ EF PHB with strict priority queuing. As explained previously, MPLS Traffic Engineering is used to ensure that the load of telephony traffic is maintained below 40 percent of link capacity, even under failure situations. Thus, TK does not strictly need to police the traffic going into the EF queue. However, the company decided to activate a policer with the following characteristics:

- It is a conditional policer. This means that policing is effective only if there is congestion on the link (in other words, if the sum of traffic across all the CoSs exceeds the link rate and packets need to be buffered before transmission on the link).

- It is configured at a "lenient" rate of 55 percent of link capacity to leave very significant headroom beyond the maximum expected load of 40 percent. This lets TK cope with a possible transient surge of telephony traffic load during the short time interval following a failure. During this time, primary MPLS TE tunnels carrying telephony traffic are fast-rerouted over a backup tunnel, and these primary tunnel paths have not yet been reoptimized. See the "Backup Tunnel Constraints" section for a detailed explanation of this load surge and its duration.

You can see that TK expects to never actually effectively police the telephony transit traffic in normal situations as well as during failure. The policing is configured only as a safety measure to ensure that the telephony transit traffic can never hog all the link bandwidth, even under a completely unpredicted combination of events that would starve the rest of the traffic, including the control traffic, and possibly bring the network down.

The control traffic is classified based on the following:

- DSCP value of 48 (which corresponds to precedence 6), because Cisco routers automatically set the DSCP to this value when generating routing packets (OSPF, BGP) as well as other essential control traffic (LDP, RSVP-TE, Telnet)

- EXP value of 6, for routing packets that are MPLS encapsulated over the core, such as MP-BGP packets
- EXP value of 3, for telephony transit signaling traffic (SS7)

The control traffic is granted 2 percent of the total link which represent 50 Mbps.

The DF queue carrying the rest of the traffic is allocated all the remaining bandwidth—that is, 43 percent of the link bandwidth. As explained previously, TK ensures by capacity planning that the aggregate load across all traffic is kept below 85 percent, even during targeted failure. This means that the DF queue is expected to always operate with low queue occupancy, which is necessary to satisfy the tight POP-to-POP SLA commitments that TK offers to Internet and Layer 3 MPLS VPN traffic. Still, as a safety measure in case the DF queue fills up under special circumstances (such as a combination of multiple failures and exceptional traffic growth), TK activated Random Early Detection (RED) (see [RED]) in the DF queue. This facilitates smooth adjustment of TCP traffic load (which is dominant in the DF queue) to the available capacity during these special circumstances. It also keeps the delay in the DF queue at reasonable levels and avoids global synchronization of TCP flows.

RED maintains a moving average of the queue occupancy. It also defines a minimum and maximum threshold and a maximum probability denominator, which together control the random discard of packets. TK followed recommendations for fine-tuning RED parameters on high-speed links. These recommendations allow high link utilization while minimizing queue occupancy and avoiding global synchronization of TCP flows. They resulted in TK's adopting the RED drop profile shown in Figure 4-22 and discussed here.

Figure 4-22   *RED Drop Profile for the DF Queue in the Core*

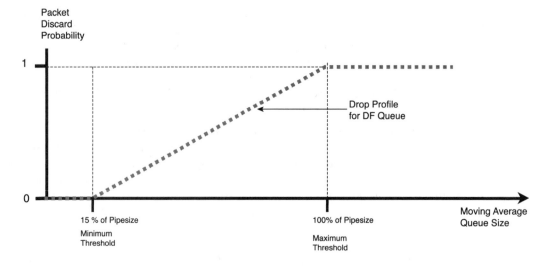

On Cisco routers, the moving average is computed as follows:

$$\text{average} = (\text{old\_average} * (1 - 2^{-n})) + (\text{current\_size} * 2^{-n})$$

Hence n, which is the exponential weighting constant, controls how fast or slowly the moving average tracks the current queue size. The objective is for the average queue size to filter out the short-term variations in queue occupancy (thus avoiding drastic swings in the face of short time scale traffic burstiness). It does this while reacting fast enough to significant queue variations corresponding to long-term queue buildup to trigger random drop early enough.

If n is too high, the average queue occupancy varies very slowly after the current queue size varies. In case of traffic load increase, this could result in the queue's filling up and reverting to tail drop before random drop is activated. Similarly, as soon as the traffic load has decreased, this could result in random drop continuing to drop packets unnecessarily long after the congestion has disappeared.

Conversely, if n is too low, the average queue occupancy reacts very quickly to variations in current queue size. This could result in overreaction of RED and frequent unnecessary dropping of traffic.

TK configured n such that

$2^{-n} = 10 / B$
where B = queue-bandwidth / (MTU * 8)
and MTU = 1500 bytes

In the case of the DF queue, 43 percent of the link bandwidth is allocated to the queue. So, on STM-16 links, B = 89583 packets. Hence, TK configured the exponential weighting constant to 13 for the DF queue on STM-16 links.

The minimum threshold should be set high enough to maximize link utilization. It also should be set low enough to ensure that random drop kicks in early enough to start slowing down some TCP sources when needed. If it's set too low, packets will get dropped unnecessarily, and traffic will be prevented from using the link capacity. If it's set too high, the queue will fill up before random drops get a chance to slow down some sources.

The difference between the minimum threshold and the maximum threshold needs to be high enough to allow the random dropping behavior to avoid global synchronization of TCP sources. But if the maximum threshold is too high, random drop may not slow down enough sources, thus allowing the queue to fill up.

The maximum probability denominator controls the proportion of dropped packets. The drop probability grows linearly from 0 (no drop), when the average queue occupancy equals the minimum threshold, to 1 divided by "maximum probability denominator" (one packet is discarded every "maximum probability denominator" packets), when the average queue occupancy equals the maximum threshold.

TK selected the following settings:

- The minimum and maximum thresholds are set to 15 percent and 100 percent, respectively, of the pipe size, where

  pipe size = RTT * queue-bandwidth / (MTU * 8)

- The maximum probability denominator is set to 1

Thus, on STM-16 links, and assuming a 100-ms RTT, TK uses a minimum threshold of 1344 and a maximum threshold of 8958 for the DF queue.

NOTE   RED and Weighted Random Early Detection (WRED) operations depend on many parameters, such as the mix of TCP and non-TCP traffic, the flows' RTTs, and each flow's reaction to traffic drop. Therefore, fine-tuning these operations is a difficult task that depends on the actual environment. Thus, TK monitors RED/WRED operations in its network to assess whether parameter adjustments are necessary for best performance.

Finally, TK decided to limit the instantaneous queue size of each of the three queues. When the queue size reaches this limit, all subsequent packets are dropped. This ensures that buffers can never be hogged by a particular queue that receives an unexpected and excessive amount of traffic. In turn, this avoids buffer starvation on line cards and protects other queues and interfaces. Finally, it places a hard bound on delay and jitter through that hop.

For the EF queue, the queue limit is configured so that it corresponds to an absolute worst delay through that hop of 3 ms for the real-time traffic. On an STM-16 link where up to 55 percent of link bandwidth can be used by the EF queue, and assuming a packet size of 126 bytes (because TK uses G.711 codecs at a 10-ms sampling interval, which means a payload of 80 bytes plus an IP/UDP/RTP header of 40 bytes and a PPP header of 6 bytes), this means an EF queue limit of 4092 packets. For the control traffic queue, the queue limit is set so that up to 100 ms worth of traffic can be buffered. On an STM-16 link where 2 percent of the link bandwidth is allocated to this queue, this represents 417 packets (assuming a packet size of 1500 bytes). Because random early detection is used inside the DF queue, all packets get dropped as soon as the moving average for the queue size reaches the maximum threshold. However, because of the lag between the instantaneous queue size and its moving average, it is possible that the instantaneous queue fills up beyond the maximum threshold before the random drop is effective. To limit the instantaneous queue size without interfering with random early detection, TK configured the queue limit to be twice that of the maximum threshold.

Some of the routers in TK's network have a distributed architecture. These routers comprise multiple line cards that support the various interfaces and that are interconnected inside the router by an internal switch fabric. A packet that is received on a given line card and that needs to be forwarded to an interface attached to another line card transits through the switch fabric. The switch fabric on TK's routers is nonblocking so that its sustained throughput is higher than the combined throughput of all interfaces. Therefore, there will not be any sustained contention across ingress line cards needing to send their packets across the fabric. However, because of possible synchronization of traffic bursts across multiple line cards or in some scenarios of DoS attacks, it is conceivable that packets on an ingress line card may have to be buffered for short periods of time before being transmitted across the fabric. Thus, to ensure the highest possible QoS, TK also deployed a QoS policy on the ingress line cards to handle buffering toward the switch fabric. On the Cisco routers used by TK, this is referred to as activating a "To-Fab" QoS policy. The To-Fab QoS policy deployed by TK is very similar to the egress QoS policy discussed earlier. It ensures that the telephony traffic is handled with strict priority and that some percentage of the bandwidth is allocated to the control traffic. Note that this policy is effectively applied to each virtual output queue on every ingress line card.

NOTE   Assume that an ingress line card simply maintained a single queue toward the fabric for transmission of all traffic toward all egress line cards, in case traffic to a given egress line card had to be held. (For example, this might happen because the egress line card had already used up more than its fair share of fabric bandwidth.) In that case, all traffic behind would get held, even if it were destined for different egress line cards that are entitled to use fabric bandwidth. This is called *head-of-line blocking* . To prevent head-of-line blocking and avoid any wastage of fabric bandwidth, the Cisco routers used by TK maintain, on every ingress line card, a separate virtual queue for traffic going to each different egress line card. The To-Fab QoS policy applies to each of these virtual output queues.

Figure 4-23 illustrates the virtual output queues toward the switch fabric. Thus, it shows the application points for the To-Fab QoS policy applied by TK in its routers that have a distributed architecture. The figure also shows the application of the core egress QoS policies on the egress interfaces.

Figure 4-23 *To-Fab QoS Policy Over Virtual Output Queues*

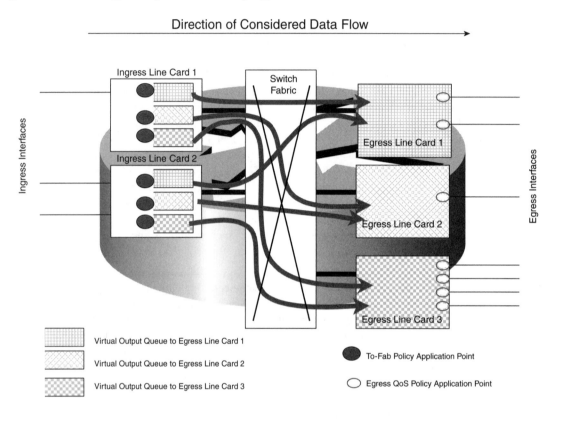

Guaranteeing quality to the telephony transit traffic was the highest-priority objective for the core QoS design deployed by TK. This motivated the decision to handle the telephony transit completely separately in the core from any other traffic. However, more-critical voice applications and services are starting to be offered as native VoIP services. Also, the MPC link capacity keeps increasing to cope with data traffic that is growing at a much faster pace than the total voice and telephony traffic. Finally, the Class 4 switch replacement project is demonstrating daily that the MPC can reliably satisfy the demanding QoS requirements of telephony. For these reasons, TK will be investigating possible evolutions to the QoS core design. This may include handling the Real-Time VPN CoS jointly with the telephony transit traffic so that it also benefits from the same absolute quality of service as telephony. It may also include handling the premium traffic separately from the standard VPN and Internet traffic in the core. In that case the in-contract premium traffic would be given strong preferential treatment over the out-of-contract premium traffic through the use of WRED.

QoS Design on the Network Edge for Layer 3 MPLS VPN and Internet

As illustrated in Figure 4-21, enforcing the edge QoS design involves applying different QoS service policies at different points:

- **CE egress QoS policy**—Responsible for performing detailed traffic classification (including custom classification), marking to the TK DSCP values, metering and policing the contracted rate for each CoS, and enforcing the PHBs for each CoS to manage link bandwidth from the CE router to the mPE router.

- **PE ingress QoS policy**—Responsible for mapping DSCP values to EXP values and hence controlling the mapping of traffic classes into the core queues.

- **PE egress QoS policy**—Responsible for metering and policing contracted rates and for enforcing the PHBs for each access CoS to manage the link bandwidth from the mPE router to the CE router.

CE Router Egress Policy

Consider a VPN site with Frame Relay access at 256 kbps. The user has requested that 33 percent of this access bandwidth be allocated to the Real-Time CoS (to accommodate three simultaneous voice calls using G.729 with 20-ms packetization time, each requiring 26.4 kbps). The user also wants 50 percent to go to the Premium CoS. Figure 4-24 illustrates the hierarchy between the physical interface bandwidth, aggregate access rate, and minimum bandwidth guaranteed to each CoS.

NOTE   The percentage of bandwidth that TK allocates to the Routing CoS depends on the access speeds and on whether the number of prefixes dynamically advertised on the access link is small, medium, or large. TK has precomputed a value for each combination so that the estimated time to advertise all the prefixes is on the order of a few seconds.

Figure 4-24 *Hierarchy of Bandwidth Commitments*

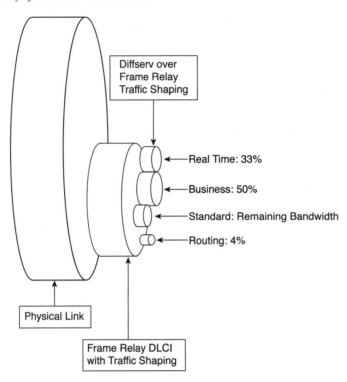

Example 4-6 presents the corresponding CE egress QoS policy template. Each component of this template is discussed next.

Example 4-6 *CE Egress QoS Service Policy Template for a VPN Site with Three CoSs*

```
interface serial0/0
 tx-ring-limit 2
 frame-relay traffic-shaping
!
interface serial0/0.1 point-to-point
 ip address CE-PE-link-subnet CE-PE-link-subnet-mask
 frame-relay interface-dlci 100
 class map-class-CE-to-PE-256
!
!identifies Routing Traffic
access-list 110 permit tcp any eq bgp any
access-list 110 permit tcp any any eq bgp
!identifies SAA Traffic
access-list 111 permit ip any IP-address-of-SAA-shadow-router mask
!identifies Premium traffic
access-list 112 permit ip any host 10.10.20.1
!
```

Example 4-6   *CE Egress QoS Service Policy Template for a VPN Site with Three CoSs (Continued)*

```
class-map match-any class-RealTime
 match ip dscp 40
 match ip dscp 46
!
class-map match-all class-RealTime-without-SAA
 match class class-RealTime
 match not ip access-group 111
!
class-map match-any class-Premium
 match ip dscp 24
 match ip access-group 112
!
class-map match-all class-Premium-without-SAA
 match class class-Premium
 match not ip access-group 111
!
class-map match-any class-Routing
 match ip access-group 110
!
policy-map police-RealTime-without-SAA
 class class-realTime-without-SAA
   police cir percent 33 bc 20 ms conform-action set-dscp-transmit 46
     exceed-action drop
!
policy-map police-Premium-without-SAA
 class class-Premium-without-SAA
   police cir percent 50 conform-action set-dscp-transmit 18
     exceed-action set-dscp-transmit 20
!
policy-map CE-to-PE-QoS-policy
 class class-RealTime
  priority
  service-policy police-RealTime-without-SAA
 class class-Premium
  bandwidth percent 50
  random-detect dscp-based
  random-detect exponential-weighting-constant 3
  random-detect dscp 18 11 33 1
  random-detect dscp 20 4 11 1
  service-policy police-Premium-without-SAA
 class class-Routing
  bandwidth percent 4
  set ip dscp 48
 class class-default
  bandwidth remaining percent 100
  set ip dscp 0
!
map-class frame-relay map-class-CE-to-PE-256
 frame-relay cir 256000
 frame-relay mincir 256000
 frame-relay bc 2560
 frame-relay be 0
```

continues

Example 4-6 *CE Egress QoS Service Policy Template for a VPN Site with Three CoSs (Continued)*

```
frame-relay fragment 320
service-policy output CE-to-PE-QoS-policy
!
rtr responder
!
```

The functional components of this CE egress policy and their respective ordering are illustrated in Figure 4-25.

Figure 4-25 *CE Egress Policy Functional Components*

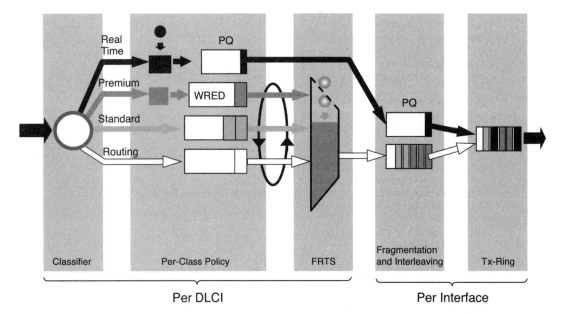

The first component is the classifier, which identifies which packets belong to which CoS. You can see in Example 4-6 that the customer indicated that

- The real-time traffic must be classified based on a premarked DSCP of 46 (EF) and 40 (precedence 5).

- The premium traffic must be classified based on a premarked DSCP of 24 (precedence 3) and based on a destination IP address of 10.10.20.1.

The routing traffic is identified by matching the TCP port numbers that identify the BGP protocol.

The next component is a per-CoS policy composed of separate policing, marking, and scheduling (or a subset of those) for each CoS. TK enforces systematic policing on the Real-Time class to its contracted rate instead of conditional policing (which would drop traffic only if there were congestion). This delivers a service that is perceived by end users as highly predictable. The Real-Time class can always properly carry a given number of voice calls (and never more). This is opposed to a service in which the number of voice calls that can be properly carried varies depending on what happens in other classes. This would be the user perception if conditional policing were used. In Example 4-6, the burst tolerance configured in the real-time policer is set to 20 ms, which is large enough to accommodate the simultaneous burst of one packet from each of the three targeted simultaneous calls. (The packet size with G.729-20-ms calls is 66 bytes so that the maximum burst could be 3 * 66 = 198 bytes, which fits within 20 ms at a rate of 33 percent of 256 kbps.)

With respect to scheduling, the VPN Real-Time CoS is given strict priority over any other traffic to achieve optimum delay and jitter. The queues for the VPN Premium CoS and the Routing CoS are allocated a minimum bandwidth guarantee of 50 percent and 4 percent, respectively. The Standard CoS is allocated the remaining bandwidth. Note that these bandwidth settings are minimum guarantees that each queue gets in case of contention across the multiple queues. But if any of the queues is not using its minimum guarantee, the other queues can use the leftover bandwidth and consequently use more than their minimum guarantee. WRED is used in the VPN Premium queue to avoid global synchronization of TCP flows and to enforce selective dropping of out-of-contract premium traffic over in-contract premium traffic in case of congestion in the premium queue. For fine-tuning of the WRED profile to apply on the in-contract traffic, TK followed rules optimized for RED operations over lower speeds (as encountered in the access):

- The exponential weighting constant n is such that

  $2^{-n} = 1 / B$, where B = bandwidth / (MTU * 8)

  and MTU = 1500 bytes

- The minimum and maximum thresholds equal 100 percent and 300 percent of B, respectively.

- The maximum drop probability is set to 1.

With an access rate of 256 kbps and 50 percent of bandwidth allocated to the premium queue, B = 11, n = 3, the minimum threshold = 11, and the maximum threshold = 33.

For the WRED profile to apply to the out-of-contract traffic, TK applied more-aggressive minimum and maximum thresholds of 30 percent and 100 percent of B, respectively (hence, 4 and 11).

These WRED drop profiles for the premium queue are illustrated in Figure 4-26.

Because the Frame Relay access rate (CIR) for this customer is 256 kbps, the CE router is configured to perform Frame Relay traffic shaping at the corresponding rate. The per-CoS policy described previously is effectively applied to packets being buffered by the Frame Relay traffic shaping. As illustrated in Figure 4-25, TK takes advantage of the optimization of the Frame Relay traffic shaping (FRTS) implementation on Cisco routers. This ensures that the real-time packets coming from the strict priority queue bypass the Frame Relay traffic shaper, which avoids any delay and jitter that could have been introduced by shaping.

Figure 4-26   *WRED Drop Profiles in the Premium Queue on Access*

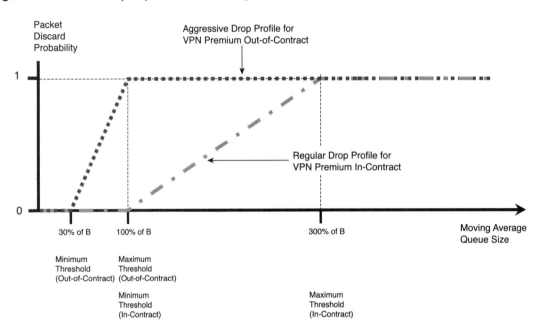

On low-speed links, the serialization time of long packets is very significant. For example, it takes about 23 ms to transmit a 1500-byte packet at 512 kbps. Therefore, if a real-time packet is elected for transmission by the scheduler immediately after the transmission of such a long packet is initiated, the voice packet has to wait for those 23 ms of serialization time. Because this compromises the targeted delay commitments for the Real-Time CoS, TK decided to use fragmentation and interleaving mechanisms on the access links. These mechanisms fragment long packets and allow interleaving of real-time packets between fragments of the long packets. The actual mechanisms used are FRF.12 Frame Relay fragmentation (see [FRF.12]) in the case of Frame Relay access and the segmentation mechanism built into Multilink PPP (see [MLPPP]) (but used on a single link) in the case of PPP access links. In Example 4-6, you see that FRF.12 fragmentation is activated with a fragment size of 320 bytes (which represents 5 ms on a 512-kbps interface). Note that in the case of Frame Relay, the rate that is meaningful for computing the serialization time of a packet or fragment is actually the rate of the underlying physical interface (not the PVC CIR), because this rate dictates the serialization time. Although reducing the fragment size further and further would reduce the delay and jitter of the voice traffic accordingly, it would also increase the processing impact in similar proportions. Thus, trade-offs are necessary. This is why TK selected a fragment size of 320 bytes in that case.

For implementation reasons, after the router scheduler has selected the next packet to be transmitted on the wire, this packet is handed over for actual transmission to the framing and transmission logic via a small buffer. The role of this buffer is to ensure that the transmission logic is supplied with an uninterrupted flow of packets to transmit (assuming that there are indeed packets to transmit). Therefore, no transmission cycle is wasted in accessing packets at transmission time; hence, line-rate transmission can be achieved. On Cisco routers this buffer is called the transmit ring (or Tx-ring for short). Because this buffer is a pure first-in, first-out (FIFO) buffer, a real-time packet just selected by the scheduler for transmission has to wait until the packets already in the Tx-ring buffer are transmitted before it is transmitted. Thus, the Tx-ring effectively adds an additional delay and jitter component that is equal to the time it takes to empty a full Tx-ring. Although Cisco routers automatically adjust the size of the Tx-ring buffer depending on the interface speed, the operator can further fine-tune it if needed. Reducing its size reduces the delay and jitter introduced by the Tx-ring buffer. However, Cisco recommends reducing the Tx-ring only when needed to satisfy specific delay/jitter requirements. Cisco also recommends never reducing it below two packets; otherwise, the router may no longer be able to achieve line rate transmission. As you can see in Example 4-6, TK elected to reconfigure its size to two packets. Because fragmentation is also used and limits the fragment size to 320 bytes (which represents 5 ms at a 512-kbps interface rate), the Tx-ring now introduces a maximum delay and jitter of only 10 ms.

As discussed in the "SLA Monitoring and Reporting" section that follows, TK uses Cisco SAA active measurement to monitor the QoS actually experienced in each CoS over the access links. This involves traffic samples being generated by an SAA shadow router in the POP toward the CE router and then being sent back to the SAA shadow router by the CE router. To perform measurement for each CoS, separate samples are generated for each CoS with the corresponding DSCP marking. To make sure these samples experience the same QoS as the real-time traffic and the in-contract premium traffic, TK needs to make sure the samples are not dropped by the Real-Time CoS policer or marked as out-of-contract by the Premium policer. This is why TK uses hierarchical policies with a parent policy applying the scheduling policy to all the traffic of a given CoS and with a child policy underneath to police only the subset of traffic that is not SAA traffic. Hierarchical policies are ideally suited to this sort of application because they allow the application of a service policy to a class that is itself part of a higher-level policy. This effectively allows for the definition of nested policies.

mPE Router Ingress Policy

Because TK manages the CE routers and thus can trust them to perform accurate classification, marking, and policing, the mPE routers do not need to perform those functions on input interfaces connecting the CE routers.

The default behavior of Cisco PE routers is to copy the 3-bit Precedence field of the IP header into the 3-bit EXP field of any MPLS label stack entry pushed on a packet received from the CE router. Because this default behavior achieves exactly the EXP value mapping desired by TK and listed in Table 4-4, TK does not need to activate any DSCP-to-EXP mapping function on the mPE routers. In fact, the DSCP and EXP values were actually selected by TK to that end.

Altogether, this means that no input policy is generally required for QoS purposes on the mPE routers on interfaces attaching VPN sites or Internet sites. This is a great benefit. It can be achieved in the case of managed CE routers because the number of service policies and associated QoS actions on an mPE router could be very large considering the number of CE routers it supports.

However, TK applies input policies in a number of situations. First, on every interface supporting Internet peering, TK activated an input policy that remarks the DSCP of all the received packets to DSCP=0 to make sure that traffic received from the Internet is handled appropriately in its network. Also, in some cases, very low-cost CE routers that cannot perform policing are used. Then, TK activates an input policy on the mPE router to perform the policing function there and to enforce the respective contracted rate of the VPN voice and VPN Premium CoS. Finally, more-recent platforms are being deployed as mPE routers in TK's network. They can perform aggregate input policing on all customer-attaching interfaces without performance impact. Therefore, TK is considering applying such input policies that perform per-CoS policing and validation of DSCP marking as a security measure. This will protect TK's network from potential tampering or replacement of the managed CE routers on the customer premises.

Suppose in the future TK decides to offer differentiated treatment to the Premium VPN CoS in the core and wants to preferentially discard the premium traffic that is out-of-contract over the premium traffic that is in-contract in case of congestion. Separate EXP values would have to be used in the core. In this case, TK would have to activate an input service policy on the mPE routers supporting Layer 3 MPLS VPN customers. This would map the in-contract DSCP value of 18 (AF21) and the out-of-contract DSCP value of 20 (AF22) to two different EXP values, because the default mapping currently maps both to the same EXP value of 2. An alternative approach would be to select other DSCP values for in-contract and out-of-contract. Those values would be automatically mapped to different EXP values through the default mapping (for example, DSCP 16 and DSCP 8, which respectively map by default into EXP 2 and EXP 1). The latter approach would have the advantage of not requiring any marking action on the mPE routers.

Now suppose in the future TK extends its offerings to unmanaged services for Layer 3 MPLS VPN or Internet access whereby TK does not manage the CE router. Input policies performing policing and remarking over the interfaces supporting such customers would be needed on the mPE routers. Examples of such input policies for unmanaged Internet and Layer 3 MPLS VPN services can be found in the "PE Router Ingress Policy" section of Chapter 5.

mPE Router Egress Policy

TK applies an egress QoS policy on the mPE router to manage the link toward the CE router that is very similar to the CE router egress QoS policy. The main difference is that classification can be performed directly on the DSCP values because all the traffic has already been classified and marked by the ingress CE router.

QoS Design on the Network Edge for Voice Trunking

The telephony soft switches used by TK are configured so that the media streams generated by the VoIP trunk gateways (the packets carrying the packetized voice) are all marked with DSCP value 32. The telephony signaling traffic to be transported over the packet backbone is marked with DSCP value 24.

QoS Design on the Network Edge for Layer 3 MPLS VPN CsC

TK supports the three user-visible CoSs (Real-Time, Premium, and Standard) as well as the Routing CoS to manage possible congestion on the access links of the Carrier's Carrier (CsC) service (the links between the CSC-mPE routers and the CSC-CE routers). In the core, the CsC traffic is handled in exactly the same way as the rest of the VPN traffic and benefits from the same SLA commitments.

Because TK manages the CSC-CE routers, it implements an egress service policy on the link toward the CSC-mPE router. It is similar to the service policy applied on regular VPN CE routers, but with a few adjustments to cope with the fact that all the end-user traffic is label-switched (as opposed to IP-routed) between the CSC-CE router and the CSC-mPE router:

- Classification for the Real-Time CoS and the Premium CoS is performed based on the EXP value in the topmost entry of the MPLS label stack after label imposition (or label swapping in the case of hierarchical VPNs) by the CSC-CE router. Real-time traffic is identified by EXP value 5 and premium traffic by EXP value 2.

- While the real-time traffic is policed (with dropping of the excess), the premium traffic is not policed on the CSC-CE router. TK currently uses a single EXP value (of 2) for the premium traffic in the MPC, and no EXP value is defined to identify the out-of-contract premium traffic. If in the future TK enhances the QoS design to support differentiated treatment of in-contract and out-of-contract premium traffic in the MPC, a second EXP value will be defined and could be used by policing on the CSC-CE router to mark out-of-contract traffic.

- Customer-specific classification is not supported. It is up to the end customer to make sure the packets reach the CSC-CE router with the appropriate marking. Because TK relies on the default EXP marking behavior on the CSC-CE router, this means real-time packets must arrive with a DSCP value whose 3 precedence bits are set to 5 (or with an EXP value of 5 in the case of hierarchical VPN). Also, premium packets must arrive with a DSCP value whose 3 precedence bits are set to 2 (or with an EXP value of 2 in the case of hierarchical VPN).

- The BGP routing traffic between the CSC-CE router and the CSC-mPE router is classified via the same IP access list as with regular VPN CE routers because the BGP traffic exchanged between the CSC-CE router and the CSC-mPE router is not encapsulated in MPLS.

- The rest of the traffic has its EXP value remarked to 0.

Figure 4-27 illustrates the location where the CsC service policies are applied as well as marking in DSCP and EXP fields for packets belonging to the Real-Time CoS.

Figure 4-27 *CsC QoS Service Policies*

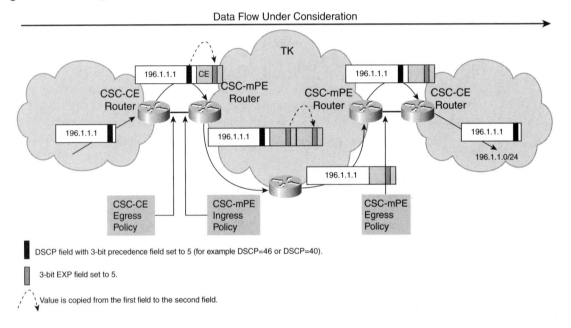

DSCP field with 3-bit precedence field set to 5 (for example DSCP=46 or DSCP=40).

3-bit EXP field set to 5.

Value is copied from the first field to the second field.

As with the regular Layer 3 VPN service, TK does not need to actually activate any input QoS service policy on the CSC-mPE routers because

- TK manages the CSC-CE routers and can trust its marking.
- The default behavior of the CSC-mPE router achieves the right EXP marking for packets transmitted toward the core (because it copies the EXP value from the topmost entry of the incoming label stack into the swapped label entry and any pushed label entry).

Again, because of the MPLS encapsulation of all end-user traffic, the egress service policy applied on the mPE router over the link to the CE router is specific to the CsC service. This policy is the mirror image of the egress QoS policy applied on the CSC-CE router and just described.

SLA Monitoring and Reporting

TK performs ongoing active measurement using Cisco Service Assurance Agent (SAA) to establish actual performance and to report to its Layer 3 MPLS VPN and Internet users against SLA performance commitments.

NOTE	Cisco SAA is an embedded performance-monitoring agent in Cisco IOS software that performs active measurement. This means that it generates synthetic packets mimicking various types of packets of interest (for example, short voice packets marked as belonging to the Real-Time CoS or longer TCP packets marked as belonging to the Premium CoS). It also measures the actual performance metrics experienced by these packets when transiting the network (from one SAA agent to another SAA agent), such as delay, jitter, and loss. A router can behave as an SAA generator or an SAA responder, which only responds to SAA probes sent by the generator. An SAA agent can generate probes and perform corresponding measurements at regular intervals. Measurement results can be collected via the command-line interface (CLI) or SNMP. An SAA agent can also generate events asynchronously when measured performance levels cross certain configured thresholds.

As illustrated in Figure 4-28, SAA shadow routers are deployed in every POP, while the SAA responder function is activated on CE routers.

Figure 4-28   *Telecom Kingland SLA Measurement*

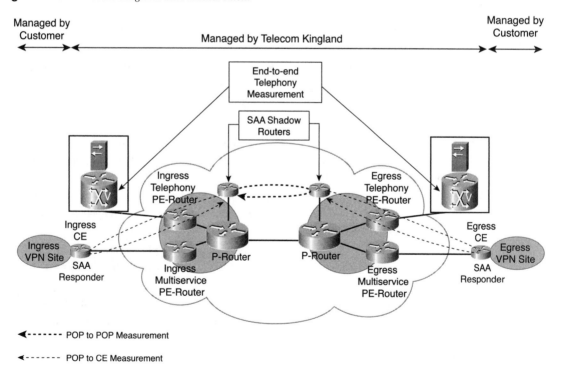

Each SAA shadow router performs ongoing measurements between itself and every other SAA shadow router at 2-minute intervals. The corresponding traffic samples are generated with a DSCP value of 0 so that they get mapped to EXP 0 and get treated as Layer 3 MPLS VPN and Internet traffic in the core. These measurements are used to compute a POP-to-POP matrix of round-trip time, jitter, and loss.

SAA shadow routers also perform ongoing measurements between themselves and CE routers at 5-minute intervals. Separate measurements are performed for each user-visible CoS, each using a DSCP value of 46, 18, or 0 and a packet size of 64 bytes, 128 bytes, and 128 bytes, respectively. These measurements are used to compute a one-way delay (by dividing the round-trip time in half) and a loss for a given site.

Actual performance values are computed in the following ways:

- Ten sample packets are generated at every measurement interval.
- All measurements in a given sample are averaged into a "sample value."
- The sample values are averaged over the hour into an "hourly value."
- The worst hourly value of the day is retained as the "daily value."
- The daily values are averaged over the month into a "monthly value."

Based on these computed values, TK provides a number of SLA reports to its customers through a web interface that includes the following:

- **Real-time POP-to-POP report**—This provides the POP-to-POP matrix of current hourly values for round-trip time, jitter, and loss.
- **Real-time site report**—This provides, for a given VPN site and for each CoS, the current hourly values for one-way delay and loss.
- **Monthly POP-to-POP report**—This provides the POP-to-POP matrix of monthly values for round-trip time, jitter, and loss for comparison against the POP-independent values committed in the VPN and Internet SLA.
- **Monthly site report**—This provides, for a given VPN site and for each CoS, the monthly values for one-way delay and loss, as well as the number of bytes and packets transmitted in each direction and the site availability for the month.

To control the end-to-end quality of service experienced by telephony transit traffic, TK also performs separate end-to-end active measurement from VoIP gateway to VoIP gateway for delay, jitter, and loss.

RTP Control Protocol (RTCP) (see [RTP]) lets TK monitor the quality of service experienced by the voice media stream over the Real-Time Protocol (RTP) (see [RTP]) by performing ongoing measurement of some statistics (packet loss, jitter) during a voice call. Such statistics are collected by the telephony VoIP trunk gateways in TK's network and then recorded as part of the Call Detail Record (CDR) established for every phone call and collected by a central server for applications such as billing. TK developed an application that accesses the CDR QoS statistics on the server and analyzes them to confirm operations within the targeted QoS objectives.

MPLS Traffic Engineering Design

As part of the overall MPC network design, TK conducted a detailed study to determine how it might provision sufficient network capacity to avoid congestion on any core link during steady state and under network element failure.

Moreover, as discussed in the "Quality of Service Design" section, to bound the delay, jitter, and loss to the levels required by telephony transit traffic, TK wanted to strictly enforce that the load of telephony traffic always be kept below 40 percent on any link and under any circumstances (including failure). Consequently, TK decided to deploy MPLS TE so that PSTN voice traffic could be constraint-based-routed across the MPC network and be subject to a call admission control limit of 40 percent on any link.

MPLS TE is deployed to carry only PSTN traffic. Therefore, all other traffic (such as Internet, Layer 3 MPLS VPN, and so forth) is label-switched across the MPC using the labels allocated by the LDP process and consequently follows the OSPF shortest path.

A full mesh of TE LSPs is set up between all the PE-PSTN routers (which connect the VoIP gateways, as illustrated in Figures 4-3 and 4-4). There are two TE LSPs between any two PE-PSTN routers residing in Level 1 POPs. There is a single TE LSP between any two PE-PSTN routers when at least one of them resides in a Level 2 POP (detailed reasoning for this design is provided later).

To differentiate between a Level 1 and Level 2 PE-PSTN, a naming convention for the routers was chosen in which the router's name begins with PE-PSTN1 for Level 1 and PE-PSTN2 for Level 2.

Setting the Maximum Reservable Bandwidth on Each MPC Link

To enable the TE design TK chose, each link in the MPC needed to be configured with a maximum reservable bandwidth value. This value indicates how much of the link bandwidth may be reserved for traffic engineering purposes. It can be configured to any value, regardless of the actual link speed. For example, an STM-1 link with 155 Mbps of total bandwidth may be configured with 310 Mbps of maximum reservable bandwidth. Therefore, the router may signal TE LSPs for up to 310 Mbps, which provides a bandwidth overbooking factor of 2. Conversely, the operator may choose to advertise a smaller value than the actual link speed to limit the amount of traffic carried on the link. This is the design elected by TK. Each link is configured with a maximum reservable bandwidth equal to 40 percent of the link speed. This guarantees that the bandwidth of TE LSPs established through a link for PSTN traffic never exceed 40 percent of that link bandwidth. For instance, an OC-192 link between two Level 1 POPs is configured with a reservable bandwidth equal to 0.4 * 10 Gbps = 4 Gbps. This configuration is shown in Example 4-7. It is used as a template for all OC-192 interfaces. (Similar templates exist for all the different link speeds in the MPC.)

Example 4-7 *OC-192 Configuration Template*

```
interface pos3/0
 ip rsvp bandwidth 4000000
 !
```

TE LSPs Bandwidth

One of the most challenging aspects of any MPLS TE design is obtaining a traffic matrix to appropriately configure the bandwidth of the TE LSPs. That said, in the case of the PSTN network, TK had very good knowledge of the existing public voice traffic matrix, which it acquired by means of various monitoring tools available on its telephony network during the past two decades. Because of this, several dimensioning rules have been applied to determine the initial size of the TE LSPs.

For inter-POP traffic, the traffic peak is multiplied by a factor of 0.9 to take into account the fact that the peaks do not occur simultaneously between each POP. Such dimensioning is considered conservative. TK observed that during the less-active periods the traffic could be as little as one-sixth to one-tenth of the peak and that each peak period rarely exceeded a few hours every day. Hence, the TE LSPs are sized based on 90 percent of the busiest hours.

Furthermore, the voice traffic during the weekends is generally significantly less than during weekday hours. Thus, during the weekend the observed PSTN traffic load is significantly less than the reserved bandwidth.

Although the PSTN voice traffic is relatively stable, the mobile voice traffic increases at a nonnegligible rate. The required bandwidth for the PSTN traffic can easily be derived from the number of calls that can be accepted by the VoIP gateways and by applying the inter-PSTN-POP traffic dimensioning rule just specified. However, the IP traffic generated by the mobile voice traffic must also be considered. Thus, TK decided to resize each TE LSP bandwidth once every two months. For each TE LSP, an external script collects the related SNMP data (number of bytes transmitted on each TE LSP) every hour. This allows for the collection of a very accurate traffic matrix and tracking of the traffic growth. Once every two months, each TE LSP is resized up if the observed peak value exceeds the configured bandwidth value by 5 percent for more than 5 percent of the samples. Similarly, each TE LSP is also resized down if the observed peak value is 90 percent or less than the configured bandwidth for more than 95 percent of the samples.

Path Computation

A dynamic CSPF algorithm is used to compute the shortest path for each TE LSP satisfying its constraints. (This is limited to the bandwidth constraint, except for TE LSPs between PE-PSTN1 routers where both the bandwidth and the affinity constraints must be satisfied, as discussed later.) Note that because the MPC network contains a limited number of TE nodes, the CSPF computation time is negligible (on the order of a few milliseconds). The choice to run CSPF on the TE LSP headends was made (as opposed to an offline path computation approach) for its ability to cope more rapidly with network element failures.

TE LSPs Between PE-PSTN1 Routers

The voice traffic between major cities in Kingland is significantly higher than between smaller cities. Therefore, TK decided to adopt a slightly different design for the TE LSPs between the PE-PSTN1 routers in Level 1 POPs than for the TE LSPs between PE-PSTN1 routers and PE-PSTN2 routers in Level 2 POPs. Because the TE LSPs between PE-PSTN1 routers are larger than the other TE LSPs, the design involves splitting the traffic over two TE LSPs.

The rationale behind this is that as the ratio between LSP size and link maximum reservable bandwidth increases, the likelihood of not being able to find a path satisfying the bandwidth constraint also increases, especially in failure scenarios. Hence, to minimize that risk, TK decided to load-balance the traffic between each pair of PE-PSTN1 routers across multiple TE LSPs (two in this case). Moreover, these TE LSPs are configured with a higher preemption (priority) than the TE LSPs between PE-PSTN1 and PE-PSTN2 routers as well as the TE LSPs between PE-PSTN2 routers, because (even after a split) they are still significantly larger. This circumvents the well-known issue of bandwidth fragmentation that can occur when using a distributed CSPF for the TE LSP path computation. Indeed, with distributed CSPF, there is no synchronization between routers. Each router computes the path for the set of TE LSPs it is the headend router for. Consequently, in some cases, bandwidth fragmentation may occur whereby a larger TE LSP cannot be routed because of some other smaller TE LSPs that were previously routed. RSVP-TE defines a multipriority scheme in which a TE LSP of priority X can preempt a TE LSP of priority Y if X < Y (a lower number reflects a higher priority). This preemption scheme can be used to help solve the bandwidth fragmentation problem.

For the sake of illustration, consider the example shown in Figure 4-29 (where just a limited number of TE LSPs are represented for simplicity). The following characteristics can be observed:

- All the links are configured with a maximum reservable bandwidth of 4 Gbps (roughly 40 percent of STM-16).

- A TE LSP T1 of 1.8 Gbps is established between PE-PSTN2-1 and PE-PSTN2-4. Another TE LSP T2 of 1.5 Gbps is established between PE-PSTN2-2 and PE-PSTN2-3.

- The links cw1–sw1 and cw2–s1 have 2.8 Gbps and 2.9 Gbps of available bandwidth, respectively (because of other established TE LSPs across those links not represented in the figure).

Figure 4-29 *Bandwidth Fragmentation Solved by a Multipriority Scheme*

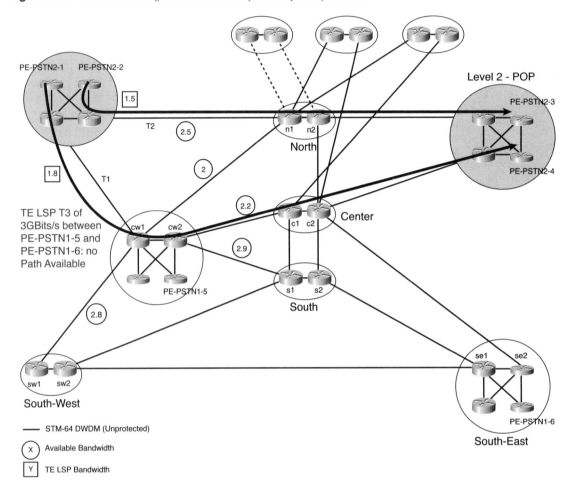

Given the situation shown in Figure 4-29, no path could be found for a TE LSP of 3 Gbps between PE-PSTN1-5 and PE-PSTN1-6. In this situation the bandwidth is said to be "fragmented" because although the necessary bandwidth is available collectively across the multiple possible paths, it is not available on any one path. The solution is to displace T1 (the tunnel between PE-PSTN2-1 and PE-PSTN2-4 in Figure 4-29) to free up some bandwidth for T3 (the tunnel between PE-PSTN1-5 and PE-PSTN1-6), which could in turn be routed. Hence, in situations such as the one just described, T3 would preempt T1 and would in this case follow the path PE-PSTN1-5–cw2–c1–c2–s2–PE-PSTN1-6. After being preempted, the TE LSP T1 would in turn be rerouted onto a different path without any manual intervention.

This also illustrates why the PSTN traffic between two PE-PSTN1 routers is split onto two TE LSPs instead of one. Doing so limits their size and consequently increases the probability of finding a path for a TE LSP. (Indeed, smaller TE LSPs are less likely to provoke bandwidth fragmentation.) Because these LSPs are still significantly larger than the TE LSPs between PE-PSTN2 and the TE LSPs between PE-PSTN1 and PE-PSTN2, they are configured with a higher preemption priority to benefit from the preemption mechanism just described.

The resulting TE LSP placement is shown in Figure 4-30.

Figure 4-30 *Situation After Preemption and Rerouting of a Lower-Priority TE LSP*

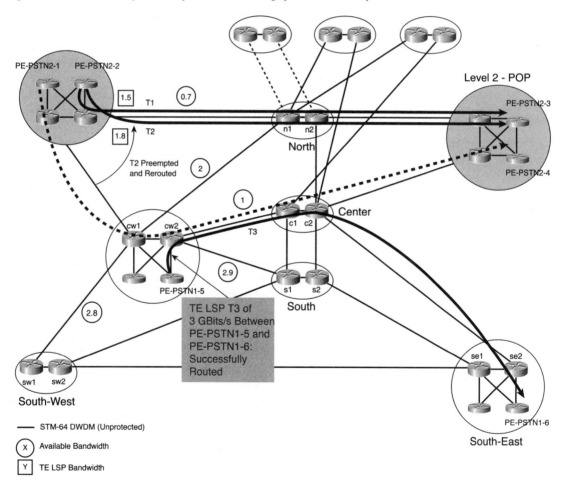

Of course, such a multipriority scheme does not provide an absolute guarantee that bandwidth fragmentation will never occur, but it limits the risk of its occurrence.

TK ran several CSPF simulations with a random TE LSP placement. These simulations showed an extremely low risk of bandwidth fragmentation, with such an approach combining the splitting of the large TE LSPs and a multipriority scheme.

Establishing two TE LSPs between a pair of PE-PSTN routers has some other interesting properties. Provided that those LSPs are diversely routed, the impact of a single failure can be limited to a smaller proportion of the traffic between two POPs and consequently two cities.

The second positive consequence is that establishing two TE LSPs can be used to achieve more even load distribution across links. In the TK design, MPLS TE ensures that no more than 40 percent of the link speed is used by the PSTN traffic on every link. In some circumstances, it is conceivable that some links carry 30 percent of the traffic whereas other links carry only 10 percent. Although such a situation meets the TK objectives, achieving more-optimal load balancing is always desirable. This can be done when traffic is split across multiple TE LSPs. The only downside of such a strategy is the increase in the number of TE LSPs in the network. In the case of TK, such an increase is perfectly acceptable because it concerns only the TE LSPs between PE-PSTN1 routers. Thus, the number of TE LSPs is increased by $12 * 11 = 121$ additional LSPs.

The solution to achieve such load balancing is to apply the concept of affinities defined by MPLS TE. In a nutshell, the idea is to use a 32-bit mask to indicate up to 32 link properties and use them as input constraints to be satisfied by a TE LSP so as to achieve a particular objective. In the example of the MPC network, the design between the VoIP gateways and the P routers residing in the Level 1 POPs is highly symmetric. Each VoIP gateway is dual-attached to two PE-PSTN1 routers that are themselves dual-attached to two P routers in the Level 1 POP. Hence, the idea is to use a color scheme for the link between PE-PSTN1 and the P routers and for the link between the P routers in the Level 1 POPs. Doing so load-balances the TE LSPs between each pair of PE-PSTN1 routers. This concept is shown in Figure 4-31.

Figure 4-31 shows that two TE LSPs (T1 and T2) are configured between PE-PSTN1-1 and PE-PSTN1-3. As just mentioned, the objective is to ensure that T1 and T2 are diversely routed when possible. Thus, three shades (light gray, medium gray, and dark gray) are used for the links between PE-PSTN and the P routers and the P routers of the same Level 1 POP. This ensures that T1 and T2 traverse a different P router to exit the source POP and to enter the destination POP. The OSPF metric of the links between the P routers has been computed such that two TE LSPs between a disjoint pair of P routers are always diversely routed end-to-end in steady state. Note that the affinity constraint is relaxed in case a PE-PSTN is incapable of finding a feasible path satisfying those constraints, which could occur in case of failure.

Figure 4-31   *Three-Color Scheme for Load-Balancing TE LSP Between Level 1 POPs*

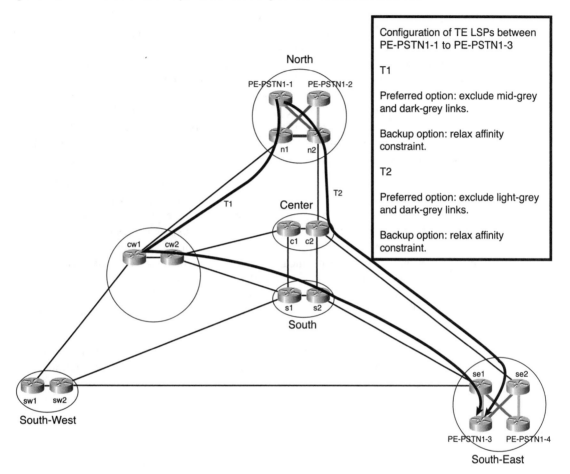

TE LSPs Between PE-PSTN1 and PE-PSTN2 Routers or Between PE-PSTN2 Routers

The design of the TE LSPs between two PE-PSTNs that do not both reside in a Level 1 POP is quite straightforward. There is only one TE LSP between a pair of such PE-PSTNs (no load balancing is required), and the only constraint that must be satisfied is bandwidth (no coloring scheme).

Reoptimization of TE LSPs

Capacity planning rules for the MPC network are such that there is enough capacity so that all the TE LSPs very easily follow the IGP shortest path (or the shortest path satisfying the color constraints where those are used) in steady state. (In fact, in steady state the voice load is expected to remain below 20 percent on every link.) In other words, only in the case of link/SRLG/node failure might some TE LSPs be rerouted along a non-shortest path to guarantee that the maximum amount of PSTN traffic on any link does not exceed 40 percent of the actual link speed. Furthermore, TK decided to have TE LSPs of a fixed bandwidth size (as opposed to resizing TE LSPs frequently, an example of which appears in Chapter 5). Thus, the only case when TE LSPs should be reoptimized is upon network element restoration, upon TE LSP resizing, or upon the addition of a link or node—none of which happens very frequently.

The MPC network is a national network with relatively short propagation delays (the propagation delay between two POPs never exceeds 15 ms, regardless of the path). Therefore, a TE LSP routed over a non-IGP shortest path does not experience significantly higher propagation delay compared to the OSPF shortest path. Thus, even when a TE LSP should be reoptimized (because a shorter path satisfying the constraints exists), the need for reoptimization should not be very critical. This is because the non-IGP shortest path offers propagation delays close to the IGP shortest path (a critical parameter for the voice traffic). Note that in some networks, the path followed by a TE LSP may experience significantly higher propagation delays than the IGP shortest path. However, this is not the case with the MPC national network.

Considering the various aspects mentioned here, TK decided to trigger a reoptimization once every 10 minutes. In this way, every headend router determines whether a more optimal (shorter) path can be found for each of its TE LSPs. If a more optimal path can be found, the TE LSP is reoptimized along the new path in a nondisruptive fashion using a make-before-break approach. Note that the CSPF computation for each TE LSP does not incur any CPU spikes considering the low number of TE LSPs per headend router. This also means that a TE LSP may follow a nonoptimal path for at most 10 minutes if a more optimal path exists because of the restoration or addition of a network element (such as a link or node).

MPLS Traffic Engineering Simulation

Before deploying MPLS Traffic Engineering, TK decided to conduct some CSPF simulations. Several objectives were set for these simulations:

- Dimensioning of the network should be such that all the TE LSPs follow their OSPF shortest path (subject to the color constraints, if any) in steady state.

- The average PSTN load on every link should be below 20 percent in the absence of failure.

- The maximum number of TE LSPs per midpoint should be determined. Each TE LSP consumes some memory on each router it traverses. Hence, it's important to determine the maximum number of TE LSPs a node has to support both in steady state and under failure.

Furthermore, because RSVP-TE is a soft-state protocol, each TE LSP must be refreshed at a regular interval. Hence, the number of TE LSPs per midpoint has implications for the parameter settings of RSVP-TE and the potential need to use techniques such as refresh reduction (see Chapter 2 for details). The maximum number of TE LSPs per midpoint is discussed further in the next section.

- The longer path that is necessary to satisfy the bandwidth constraint under failure conditions affects propagation delay. This impact should be studied.

- Ensure that a path satisfying the TE LSP constraints can be found under any conditions (including the case of double failures).

The results of the CSPF simulations confirmed TK's expectations. During steady state, 100 percent of the TE LSPs follow the shortest path (or the shortest path satisfying the color constraints), and the maximum voice load on any link is below 20 percent. On the other hand, in the case of some SRLG failures, or node failure in a Level 1 POP, several TE LSPs are routed along a longer path. This meets the objective of not exceeding 40 percent of the PSTN traffic on every link. The propagation delay along those longer paths still meets the voice delay requirements.

TE Scaling Aspects

When analyzing the scaling properties of MPLS TE, several important variables must be considered:

- **Total number of TE LSPs**—There are a total of six Level 1 POPs and 20 Level 2 POPs, with two PE-PSTN routers per POP. This leads to a total of (51 * 52) + (12 * 11) (because there are two LSPs between each pair of PE-PSTN1s) = 2784 TE LSPs. Strictly speaking, the total number of TE LSPs is not the most important scalability criterion as compared to the number of TE LSPs each router would have to manage (as headend and midpoint router). However, the total number of TE LSPs is interesting from a management, monitoring, and provisioning point of view.

- **Number of TE LSPs per headend router**—The maximum number of TE LSPs per headend router is (2 * 11) + 40 = 62 for the PE-PSTN1 routers and 51 for the PE-PSTN2 routers. This number can be considered very low; indeed, modern routers can easily handle a few thousand TE LSPs as headend.

- **Number of TE LSPs per midpoint router**—This is important data to consider, because it can represent a nonnegligible proportion of the total number of TE LSPs in the network, especially in sparsely connected core networks. Hence, running a simulation to evaluate the worst-case scenario (the most loaded router in terms of the number of TE LSPs to support) both in steady state and under various failure scenarios is quite useful. In the case of the MPC network, an analysis showed that under a single failure scenario, in worst-case conditions, the most loaded router would have to handle 25 percent of the total number of TE LSPs—roughly 700 TE LSPs. Again, this does not pose a problem, because most of the routers currently support tens of thousands of TE LSPs as midpoint.

In conclusion, TK felt that the MPC MPLS TE design did not pose any scalability concerns.

Use of Refresh Reduction

TK chose not to activate refresh reduction in its network, considering that the number of RSVP-TE sessions per midpoint router was not substantial.

Provisioning the Mesh of TE LSPs

TK developed a set of scripts to automate the provisioning of the TE LSPs between the PE-PSTN routers.

Monitoring

The monitoring of the MPLS TE network is, of course, of the utmost importance so as to adjust the TE design if necessary. TK decided to gather the following set of information for each TE LSP in the network:

- **Number of reroutes caused by network element failures**—This provides information about the link and node availability. A script then performs events correlation to deduce the root cause of each failure because a single failure can affect multiple TE LSPs.

- **Number of reroutes caused by reoptimization**—TK uses SNMP traps sent by the headend router to the network management system upon reoptimization.

- **PSTN load on every TE LSP**—TK monitors the actual PSTN load carried over any TE tunnel by collecting counters such as the number of bytes transmitted over the TE tunnel interface every hour. This information is used to adjust the TE LSP bandwidth when needed.

- **Link utilization by the PSTN traffic versus bandwidth reservation**—Such data is particularly interesting so as to determine the LSP sizing strategy—particularly in terms of statistical gain across the multiple POP-to-POP voice aggregates. Indeed, if it turns out that the sum of reserved bandwidth for the TE LSPs is always significantly above the actual PSTN traffic load on every link (the EF queue load), TK could readjust the formula used to compute the TE LSP bandwidth. The strategy adopted by TK consists of gathering the relevant SNMP values or variables (via scripts) for the link utilization, EF queue utilization, and total amount of bandwidth reservation for a few selected links.

- **Voice traffic pattern**—The traffic pattern (traffic fluctuation) is a key element in any MPLS Traffic Engineering design. It helps you determine the adequate bandwidth for each LSP. The traffic's burstiness is highly relevant in this case. For example, suppose that a very flat traffic pattern exists. In this case, the bandwidth estimate is quite straightforward. Conversely, in the case of very bursty traffic, sizing of the TE LSPs based on the peak load might not be optimal. It might cause some TE LSPs to follow a longer path in case of failure. (At steady state, the MPC network is dimensioned such that most TE LSPs follow their shortest OSPF path.) To study the traffic pattern, TK decided to write some scripts that would gather the amount of traffic sent on a few selected TE LSPs at a high frequency (every 5 minutes). By combining the traffic pattern data with the proportion of TE LSPs that would not follow their OSPF shortest path, TK can potentially readjust its TE LSP bandwidth size computation formula.

Last Resort Unconstrained Option

The MPC network is designed to survive any single failure. In other words, any TE LSP should be able to find an alternate path if a single network element fails. That said, a safe approach is to configure a last-resort option for each TE LSP whereby no constraint is specified to cope with any unexpected event—in particular, multiple-failure cases.

On a Cisco router, this can be achieved by means of LSP attributes. For each TE LSP, an ordered list of constraints can be specified. The headend router tries to find a path satisfying the preferred set of constraints; if no path is found, the next preferred set of constraints is tried, and so on. Hence, a safe and recommended approach is to configure a last-resort option whereby the TE LSP is configured without any constraint (no affinity, 0 bandwidth, and so on). This guarantees that in any case the headend router can always find a path to the destination, provided that there is still some connectivity to the destination. In this case the TE LSP path is no different from the OSPF path.

On TE LSPs between two PE-PSTN1 routers that use color constraints, the last-resort unconstrained option is used after the backup option, which relaxes the color constraints but not the bandwidth constraints.

Network Recovery Design

The requirements in terms of network availability significantly differ between the PSTN traffic and the rest of the traffic. A convergence time of a few seconds is perfectly tolerable and in line with the SLAs for the Internet and Layer 3 MPLS VPN traffic. However, the objective is to provide a convergence time of a few tens of milliseconds to the PSTN traffic in case of a single link, SRLG, or node failure (similar to the availability provided with TK's former SDH infrastructure). Note that the PSTN traffic must also be rerouted within a few tens of milliseconds in case of a node failure in the MPC network. This was not possible with TK's previous PSTN network. Indeed, the links were protected with SDH. But in the case of Class 4 voice switch failure, all the voice calls were dropped, and the communication had to be reestablished. There was no possibility for a voice call to survive a node failure. That said, note that a Class 4 voice switch failure was extremely rare.

Network Recovery Design for the Internet and Layer 3 MPLS VPN Traffic

With an objective of a few seconds for the Internet and Layer 3 MPLS VPN traffic in case of failure, aggressive OSPF timer tuning clearly was not required. Thus, TK decided to choose conservative OSPF protocol tuning.

Failure Detection Time

By default, OSPF is configured with a 10-second hello interval and a 40-second RouterDeadTimer on most of the commercial router platforms. Because both the NAS and BAS devices are connected by means of Layer 2 switches, the default configuration does not meet the requirements of a few seconds in case of failure. The OSPF hello protocol must be used for failure detection; there is no lower-layer fast failure detection mechanism, as in the case of SDH and DWDM links.

NOTE   The case of point-to-point Gigabit Ethernet interfaces without intervening Layer 2 switches is quite different. Upon fiber cut, a loss of signal (LoS) is quickly detected, making tuning the OSPF hello interval unnecessary. But in the case of TK, Layer 2 switches are used to reduce the number of required ports. Consequently, the failure of a link or port would not be detected by equipment connected behind the Layer 2 switch.

The hello frequency has been set to 1 second with a RouterDeadTimer of 3 seconds. This effectively means that in worst-case failure scenarios the failure is detected within 3 seconds. The configuration template for these changes is shown in Example 4-8.

Example 4-8   *OSPF Timer Configuration Template*

```
interface pos3/0
 ip ospf hello-interval 1
 ip ospf dead-interval 3
!
```

On the other hand, on SDH and DWDM links (which represent the vast majority of the links in the MPC network), network failures are detected within a few milliseconds.

LSA Generation

As soon as the failure has been detected and reported to the OSPF process, the first step is to originate a new LSA to inform the other routers of the topology change. As mentioned in Chapter 2, the challenge is to quickly originate a new LSA so as to improve the IGP converge time while preserving the network stability in case of unstable network resources (such as a link flap). To that end, modern routers provide dynamic mechanisms such as the exponential back-off algorithm described in Chapter 2. TK elected to use the configuration shown in Example 4-9.

Example 4-9   *OSPF LSA Origination Configuration*

```
router ospf 1
 timers throttle lsa all 0 40 5000
```

The variables shown in Example 4-9 can be defined as follows:

- 0 ms is how long a router waits before originating its LSA after it first detects the topology change (the failure in this case).

- 40 ms is how long the router waits before advertising a second LSA if another topology change is detected. TK decided to set this variable to 40 ms (as opposed to 0 ms) because of the presence of SRLGs in its network. Indeed, in case of an SRLG failure, multiple link failures occur. Waiting for 40 ms increases the chance that a router will capture an accurate view of the new network state before originating a new LSA.

- 5000 ms is the maximum delay between two consecutive LSA originations according to the exponential back-off algorithm described in Chapter 2.

Failure Notification Time

For the traffic to be rerouted along an alternate path if a failure occurs, the LSA originated by the node that detects the failure must first be received by the rerouting router, which might be several hops away from the failure. Thus, this period (usually called the failure notification time) is the sum of the propagation, queuing, and processing delays along the path between those two nodes. Note that the processing delay may be optimized by means of various mechanisms on some router platforms, but this component of the failure notification time is considered sufficiently small not to require any further tuning.

TK conducted some studies that showed that the failure notification time in worst-case conditions in its network (considering the high degree of meshing and low propagation delays) rarely exceeded 100 ms. This is negligible considering the overall goal of a few seconds of total convergence time.

SPF Triggering

Similar to the LSA origination case, on a Cisco router an exponential back-off mechanism can be used for the SPF triggering. TK chose the configuration shown in Example 4-10.

Example 4-10 *Exponential Back-Off Configuration*

```
router ospf 1
 timers throttle spf 50 50 10000
```

The variables shown in Example 4-10 can be defined as follows:

- 50 ms is how long a router waits before triggering an SPF computation after it receives the first topology change notification (the new LSA). The motivation for waiting for 50 ms before triggering a new SPF is to increase the chance of receiving all the LSAs in case of an SRLG failure so as to compute a new routing table that captures the actual network state.

- 50 ms is how long the router waits before triggering a second consecutive SPF.

- 10000 ms is the maximum delay between two consecutive SPFs according to the exponential back-off algorithm described in Chapter 2.

NOTE   On modern routers the SPF complexity is usually close to n * log(n), where n is the number of routers in the network. Algorithm complexity characterizes the SPF duration time. TK measured the SPF duration in its network and found that it was always less than 40 ms. Thus, using SPF computation optimization such as incremental SPF was not required.

RIB and FIB Updates

The RIB and FIB update times are, of course, highly hardware-dependent, but TK measured that those times were systematically less than 0.5 seconds in its network on any router platform.

OSPF Design Conclusions

TK's OSPF design clearly allows for rerouting times on the order of a few seconds. This is in line with TK's objective for the Internet and Layer 3 MPLS VPN traffic in case of failure. It is also worth mentioning that in case of failure of the inter-POP links (SDH and DWDM), significantly faster rerouting times can be achieved (about 1 second) thanks to the ability to quickly detect the failure. The worst-case scenario is a failure within a POP caused by the requirement of relying on OSPF to detect the failure (which is 3 seconds in the case of the elected design).

In case of link, SRLG, or node failure, congestion may occur. The congestion is handled by the DiffServ mechanisms that are in place to protect traffic according to its respective importance thanks to appropriate queuing. That said, based on capacity planning, the OSPF metrics have been computed to limit the likelihood of degraded service that would impact the traffic SLA should a single failure occur in the MPC network.

Network Recovery Design for the PSTN Traffic

Because the PSTN traffic must be rerouted within a few tens of milliseconds in case of link, SRLG, or node failure, and because such traffic is routed to TE LSPs, the most appropriate network recovery mechanism is undoubtedly MPLS TE Fast Reroute.

Failure Detection

A key aspect to consider when choosing a network recovery strategy is the network element failure detection time. It might represent a nonnegligible part of the overall rerouting time. In the case of the MPC network, TK decided to exclusively use SDH and DWDM alarms reported in case of link failure by its SDH and DWDM equipment. Because of this, a link failure is usually detected within a few milliseconds.

It is worth elaborating on the case of a router failure, because the P routers of the MPC network are all based on a distributed architecture. This has the advantage that in case of a control-plane failure, the traffic does not suffer from any traffic disruption, so the failure detection time does not matter as much. In the case of a control-plane failure, it is sufficient to rely on the expiration of the RouterDeadTimer (3 seconds) and subsequent failure of the routing adjacency to trigger a reroute for the IP traffic because traffic is not affected in the meantime. Note that for the PSTN traffic routed to TE LSPs, as soon as their respective headend router is informed of the control-plane failure, the TE LSPs are rerouted along another path, avoiding the failed router. Similar to the previous case, the traffic remains unaffected by the control-plane failure. Note that this does not require any specific mechanism and should be considered the default behavior of a distributed architecture platform. That said, note that this assumes that the route processor does not reboot, for example. In that case, upon reloading its software, the route processor may update its line card's control-plane processor, which may lead to traffic disruption. The failure case considered here is a simple route processor failure, such as a hardware failure.

NOTE   The case of PE-PSTN node failure is studied later in this section.

The case of a power supply failure results in the failure of all the router-attached links. Similarly, a line card failure provokes the failure of all its links. Consequently, such failures are equivalent to link failures in terms of triggering network rerouting.

Set of Backup Tunnels

Two types of backup tunnels must be provisioned in the MPC network. The first type is next-hop (NHOP) backup tunnels, which protect the PSTN traffic from the failure of a link or SRLG. The second type is next-next-hop (NNHOP) backup tunnels, which protect the PSTN traffic from a node failure (such as a hardware node failure that affects both the control and forwarding planes).

Backup Tunnel Constraints

The first constraint a backup tunnel path must meet is to be diversely routed from the protected facility.

In the case of an NHOP backup tunnel, the backup tunnel path must be diverse from the link under protection. If the link belongs to an SRLG, the backup tunnel must be diversely routed from the SRLG the protected link belongs to. In other words, the backup tunnel must not traverse any link that shares one or more SRLGs with the protected link. An SRLG failure would provoke the failure of both the protected link and the backup tunnel used to protect that link.

A more optimal solution would be to have a backup tunnel protect the link and another backup tunnel protect the SRLG. Thus, in case of failure, the Point of Local Repair (PLR) would select the appropriate backup tunnel. Furthermore, the same concept could be applied to the case of overlapping SRLGs. Instead of having one backup tunnel SRLG that is diverse from all the SRLGs the protected link belongs to, you could have one backup tunnel per SRLG. Unfortunately, this is not a viable option because a router acting as a PLR cannot differentiate a link from an SRLG failure. Hence, when a link belongs to an SRLG, the NHOP backup tunnel must systematically be SRLG-diverse. This important concept requires some additional explanation. Consider Figure 4-32, which shows the set of SRLGs in the MPC network.

Figure 4-32 *Telecom Kingland SRLG Membership*

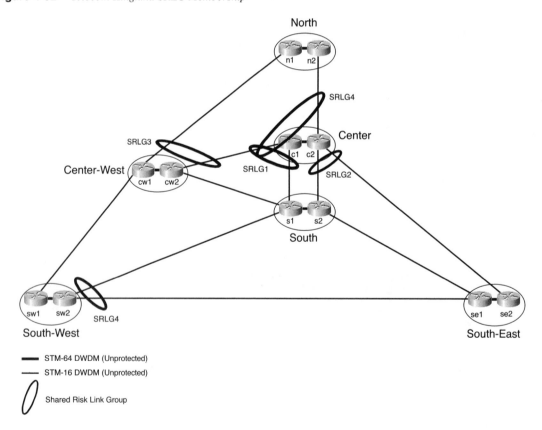

SRLG3 is made up of the links cw2–c1 and cw1–n1. The router cw2 in the Center-West POP that is attached to link cw2–c1 cannot differentiate a failure of the link cw2–c1 (because of an interface failure on the router c1, for instance) from a failure of SRLG3. In both cases, this results in a failure of the link cw2–c1, which is locally detected by cw2. Hence, when computing the path of an NHOP backup tunnel protecting the link cw2–c1, the constraint of having an NHOP backup tunnel that is SRLG-diverse from the link is required. In other words, each time a link belongs to an SRLG, the NHOP backup tunnel protecting against a failure of that link must be SRLG-diverse because of the inability to tell a link from an SRLG failure.

Some research has been conducted to design mechanisms that would identify the cause of such failures before the reroute of a TE LSP were triggered. (This way, several backup tunnels with different constraints would be computed, and the appropriate backup tunnel would be used upon link or SRLG failure.) Such mechanisms rely on the receipt of additional IGP LSAs, potentially in combination with a probing mechanism. The problem with this approach is that it leads to an increase in the overall complexity of the design and the rerouting times. Thus, using a single set of backup tunnels whose path is SRLG-diverse to protect against both link and SRLG failure is the most appropriate choice for TK. Note that this may potentially lead to a less-optimal backup tunnel path. However, this was not an issue in the case of the MPC network, considering the density of the network and the fact that the link propagation delays are not very high.

The second backup tunnel constraint is related to the provisioning of a backup tunnel that provides an equivalent QoS during fast-rerouted periods (during the time that the primary TE LSP is locally fast-rerouted onto its backup tunnel and thus before it is reoptimized by its headend router). This therefore implies that a backup path offering an equivalent bandwidth should be followed.

A possible approach to resolving this constraint (called bandwidth protection) is to compute the backup tunnel path so as to guarantee equivalent bandwidth to all protected tunnels during fast-rerouted periods. Such an approach, to be efficient in terms of required backup capacity, usually requires the use of sophisticated backup tunnel path computation algorithms (which take advantage of the fact that backup tunnels protecting independent facilities can share the backup capacity) in conjunction with additional backup tunnel-selection algorithms at each PLR. These algorithms are based on various criteria to intelligently "pack" the primary TE LSP to their respective backup tunnel while minimizing the problem of bandwidth fragmentation.

Because of the complexity of this approach, TK first analyzed a simpler approach. It was based on the use of zero-bandwidth backup tunnels (computed with CSPF) to evaluate the QoS consequences of various failure scenarios on the PSTN traffic. With such an approach, the backup tunnels just follow the IGP shortest path satisfying the link/SRLG/node-diversity constraint, but without any additional bandwidth constraint. This drastically simplifies the Fast Reroute design. The results of this study showed that in the worst case of an SRLG or node failure, the total proportion of PSTN traffic on any link would never exceed 50 percent during the fast-reroute time. This included the PSTN traffic carried on the primary TE LSP not affected by the failure and the PSTN traffic coming from the rerouted TE LSP (affected by the failure) to the backup tunnel. The DiffServ mechanisms deployed by TK ensure that the PSTN traffic (independent of whether it is carried over a primary TE LSP or is fast-rerouted into a backup

TE LSP) is prioritized and queued in the EF queue. Hence, during the fast-rerouted period (which will not exceed a few hundred milliseconds), the PSTN traffic still receives an appropriate QoS satisfying the SLA requirements. Therefore, although the constraint of not exceeding 40 percent of PSTN traffic on any single link may not be satisfied upon certain failure scenarios for a very short period, TK elected to use the simple approach of zero-bandwidth backup tunnels. The potential QoS degradation would not be noticeable and would last only a very short time, until the headend router reoptimization (see the section, "Period of Time During Which Backup Tunnels Are in Use").

Backup Tunnel Design Between Level 1 POPs

One of the objectives of the TK design is to protect any TE LSP from link, SRLG, or node failure. To achieve this aim, one NHOP SRLG-diverse backup tunnel is required per protected link, and one NNHOP SRLG-diverse backup tunnel per next-next hop. To illustrate this Fast Reroute design, you should consider the example of the cw2–c1 link attached to the router in the Center-West POP.

Protecting the cw2–c1 link requires that an NHOP backup tunnel path be computed that is SRLG-diverse from the link. You can do this by manually considering each link in the network, the SRLG membership, and so on, explicitly configuring the backup tunnel path. This also can be done automatically by each router.

TK opted for an automatic computation and configuration of the backup tunnels. To that end, each router in charge of computing a backup tunnel path for each of its neighbors must be aware of the SRLG memberships of all the links (such as the fact that the links cw2–c1 and c1–s1 belong to the same SRLG). The Internet Engineering Task Force (IETF) has specified some IGP extensions to flood the SRLG membership. In the case of OSPF, [OSPF-GMPLS] defines several new sub-TLVs carried in the link TLV (Type 2) that provide additional link characteristics. One of them is the SRLG membership (sub-TLV 16). On a Cisco router, the SRLG membership of a given link is configured only once on that link, as indicated in Example 4-11. Then it is automatically flooded by means of OSPF to the other routers in the same OSPF area (because the opaque LSA used for MPLS Traffic Engineering extensions has a Type 10).

Example 4-11   *SRLG Membership Configuration*

```
interface POS3/0
 mpls traffic-engineering srlg 1
```

Following the configuration of Example 4-11, on each link, the set of SRLGs the link belongs to is configured. Then the SRLG membership is passed to OSPF and flooded throughout the area (TE LSA—opaque LSA Type 10). Figure 4-33 shows the OSPF SRLG sub-TLV format.

Figure 4-33   *OSPF SRLG Sub-TLV Format*

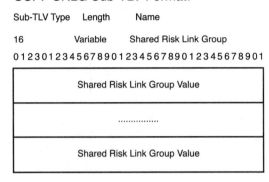

OSPF SRLG Sub-TLV Format:

Sub-TLV Type	Length	Name
16	Variable	Shared Risk Link Group

0 1 2 3 0 1 2 3 4 5 6 7 8 9 0 1 2 3 4 5 6 7 8 9 0 1 2 3 4 5 6 7 8 9 0 1

Shared Risk Link Group Value

....

Shared Risk Link Group Value

Such OSPF extensions allow each router to automatically learn about the SRLG membership. Note that more than one SRLG can be specified for each link. For instance, this is the case with link cw2–c1, which belongs to both SRLG 1 and SRLG 4. Such a situation is called overlapping SRLGs.

Each router is then configured to automatically establish an NHOP SRLG-diverse backup tunnel for each of its attached links where a routing adjacency has been established. It also establishes an NNHOP SRLG-diverse backup tunnel for each of its next-next-hop neighbors.

On each router, configure the following for automatic SRLG-diverse backup tunnel path computation and provisioning:

```
mpls traffic-engineering auto-tunnel backup srlg exclude preferred
```

This does the following:

- Automatically configures NHOP and NNHOP backup tunnel(s)
- Ensures that the backup tunnels are SRLG-diverse when possible

This command triggers the following set of actions:

- By examining its OSPF topology database, each router first determines its set of links where a routing adjacency is established. For each link, an SRLG-diverse NHOP backup tunnel path is computed and presignaled, provided that at least a primary TE LSP traverses the protected link (if no TE LSP exists, there is no need to instantiate a backup tunnel).

- The router then determines its set of next-next hops and configures for each of them an SRLG-diverse NNHOP backup tunnel, provided that at least a primary TE LSP follows this protected section.

Figure 4-34 provides examples of NHOP and NNHOP backup tunnels.

Figure 4-34   *Example of NHOP and NNHOP Backup Tunnels*

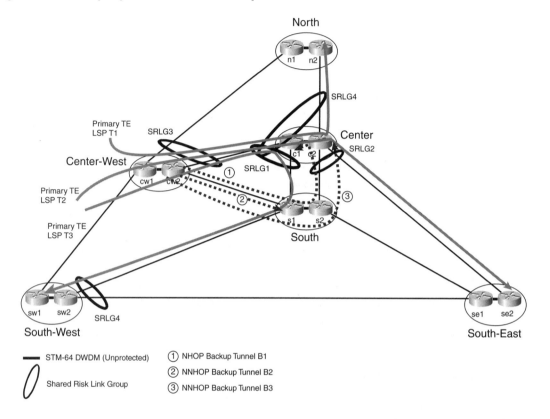

Figure 4-34 shows that for the link cw2–c1, the PLR cw2 computes the shortest path for the NHOP backup tunnel B1. This protects against a failure of the link cw2–c1 that not only avoids the link cw2–c1 but also any link having an SRLG in common with that link (the link c1–s1 in this case). Hence, the resulting path for B1 (assuming that all the links have an equal cost) is cw2–s1–s2–c2–c1.

The second step for cw2 is to compute an NNHOP SRLG-diverse backup tunnel path for each next-next-hop neighbor, should the node c1 fail. (Note that this is done only if at least one primary TE LSP follows the protected path.) The set of next-next-hop neighbors is made up of c2 and s1. Therefore, in this case, two NNHOP backup tunnels are computed and established by cw2 as follows:

- **B2**—This follows the path cw2–s1, which is used to reroute all the primary TE LSP(s) (such as T3) that follow the path cw2–c1–s1 in case of failure of the node c1.

- **B3**—This follows the path cw2–s1–s2–c2. This path is used to protect all the primary TE LSPs (such as T1 and T2) that follow the path cw2–c1–c2 in case of failure of the node c1.

NOTE   Although both NHOP and NNHOP backup tunnels are configured, the only TE LSPs that are rerouted onto an NHOP backup tunnel in case of a link/SRLG failure are the TE LSPs that terminate on the next hop. Other TE LSPs are systematically rerouted onto their NNHOP backup tunnel. This is because a PLR cannot differentiate a link failure from a node failure. Consider the case of the failure of the link cw2–c1 or a node power failure of c1. Both of these result in a failure of the link cw2–c1. Thus, in the case of the failure of the link cw2–c1, the PLR router cw2 has to assume a node failure to be on the safe side. If it turns out that the problem was a link failure, the TE LSPs potentially might have to be rerouted onto a longer backup tunnel path. (This is because the path of an NNHOP backup tunnel is usually longer than the path the traffic would have followed if rerouted via the NHOP backup tunnel.) This is preferable to rerouting onto the NHOP backup tunnel if the failure was in fact a node failure. Some schemes (based on probing) have been proposed to distinguish a link failure from a node failure. The idea is to send a probe message to the NHOP backup tunnel right after the occurrence of a link failure. This allows the PLR to determine whether the next-hop neighbor is alive. If a response is received, the failure is just a link failure; otherwise, the failure is a node failure. Given this, the designer has two choices:

- Make the assumption of a link failure and switch back to the NNHOP backup tunnel if the PLR determines that the node is a node failure.

- Make the assumption of a node failure and switch back to the NHOP backup tunnel (potentially offering a more optimal backup path) if the failure is characterized as a link failure.

In the first mode, the rerouted TE LSPs follow a more optimal path. In case of a node failure, the traffic disruption is significantly longer because it requires some time for the PLR to determine that the failure was in fact a node failure. In the second mode, the path in case of link failure is potentially slightly longer, but the rerouting time is always minimized. The drawback of a potentially less-optimal backup path for a limited period of time (until the rerouted TE LSP is reoptimized along a more optimal path) is limited compared to the advantage of always minimizing the traffic disruption. Therefore, most of the current implementations have elected the second mode without any mechanism to switch back to the NHOP backup tunnel if the failure is a link failure. Indeed, it would take some time for the PLR to characterize the failure. The time during which the rerouted TE LSPs would be rerouted onto the NHOP backup tunnel would then become very limited.

The ability to keep track of the SRLG membership is of the utmost importance. Therefore, TK maintains a database of the MPC links' SRLG memberships that is populated by the team in charge of the network infrastructure. For example, such an SRLG membership could occur because the team in charge of the transport network decided to reroute some optical light paths along another route. Consequently, this may lead to changes in terms of SRLG membership.

Each time an SRLG membership is modified in the database, an alarm is triggered. This tells the team in charge of the MPC IP/MPLS network to reconfigure the SRLG membership accordingly on the relevant links. Note that on a Cisco router, a change in SRLG membership configuration is automatically detected by all the routers in the network. They all trigger the recomputation of their set of backup tunnels to ensure the backup tunnel path SRLG diversity.

Note that such SRLG membership has no impact on the primary TE LSPs. It potentially impacts only the backup tunnels.

Relaxing the SRLG Diversity Constraint

In some situations the constraint of computing an SRLG-diverse backup tunnel path might keep the PLR from finding a solution. Indeed, in some networks where overlapping SRLGs are very common, there might be some regions of the network where an SRLG-diverse backup tunnel could not be found and still a backup tunnel could be useful to protect against interface and router failures. This is not the case with the MPC network. In steady state, an SRLG backup tunnel can always be found. That said, the inability to find an SRLG-diverse backup tunnel could still occur in case of multiple failures. (Note that in case of multiple failures, the QoS objectives may no longer be reached, but at least it could be useful to still be able to have a backup tunnel after the first failure has occurred if a second failure occurs.) Consider the case of a first failure of SRLG2, as shown in Figure 4-35.

If SRLG2 fails, for instance, no SRLG-diverse path exists for an NNHOP backup tunnel between cw2 in the Center-West POP and c2 in the Center POP. However, such a backup tunnel is required to reroute TE LSPs following the path cw2–c1–c2 should the node c1 fail (double failure case).

This is why the SRLG diversity constraint should be relaxed in this particular case. (This is achieved by adding the keyword **preferred** to the configuration of the automatic backup tunnel, as discussed earlier in this section.)

Figure 4-35   *Relaxation of the SRLG Diversity Constraint*

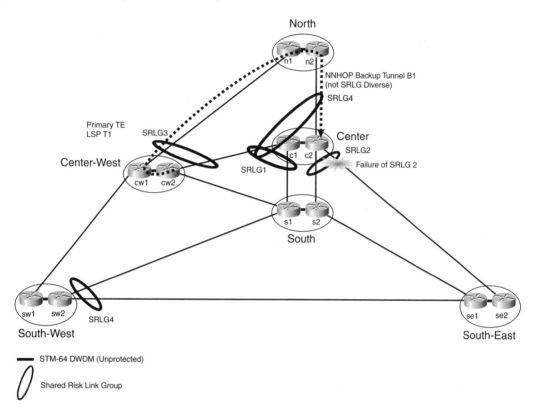

Design of the Backup Tunnels Between Level 2 and Level 1 POPs

Because exactly two links connect a Level 2 POP to a Level 1 POP, TK ensured that they do not share any SRLG with any other link. (Otherwise, a single SRLG failure would result in isolating a POP, which is unacceptable.) The same design as for the Level 1 POP case applies here, with the additional simplification of not having to deal with any SRLG. Each router is configured to automatically compute the required set of NHOP and NNHOP backup tunnels. The only constraint is diversity from the protected section (link or node). This is shown in Figure 4-36. NHOP back tunnel B1 protects against failure of link x2–c1, and NNHOP backup tunnel B2 protects against failure of c1 for tunnels transiting c1 and s1.

Figure 4-36 *Backup Tunnel Design Between Level 2 and Level 1 POPs*

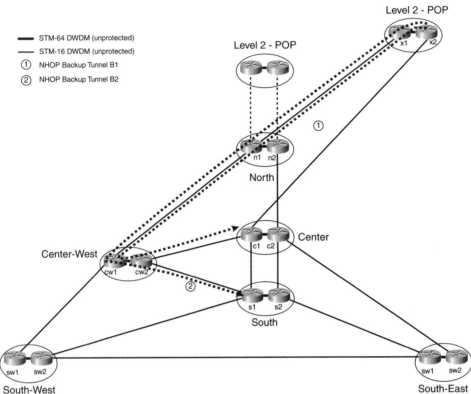

Period of Time During Which Backup Tunnels Are in Use

MPLS TE Fast Reroute (FRR) is a temporary mechanism. The protected TE LSPs are locally rerouted by the node immediately upstream of the failure (the PLR) until they get rerouted along a potentially more optimal path by their headend router. In the case of the MPC network, TK conducted some analysis to approximate the period during which a TE LSP would be rerouted to its backup tunnel in case of a network element failure. This was particularly important because the decision had been made to use zero-bandwidth backup tunnels.

Consider Figure 4-37. Upon a failure of the link cw2–c1, a primary TE LSP T1 (between PE-PSTN2-1 and PE-PSTN2-4) would be locally rerouted to the NNHOP backup tunnel B3 within a few tens of milliseconds. Extensive lab testing established that such local fast rerouting would take 60 ms in the worst case. This includes the time to detect the failure and effectively reroute all the TE LSPs to their respective backup tunnels. Then an RSVP Path Error message is sent to the headend router PE-PSTN2-1 to notify it of the local reroute. Such an RSVP message must be processed by each intermediate hop before it is forwarded toward the headend. The receipt of such a notification by the headend router immediately triggers the computation of a new path for T1. The path computation in the case of the MPC network was less than 2 ms. Because a headend router can potentially have multiple affected TE LSPs, to compute the worst-case reoptimization time, the CSPF duration must be multiplied by the maximum number of affected TE LSPs (less than 62, which is the maximum number of TE LSPs per headend router).

Figure 4-37   *Estimation of the Time During Which a Backup Tunnel Is Active*

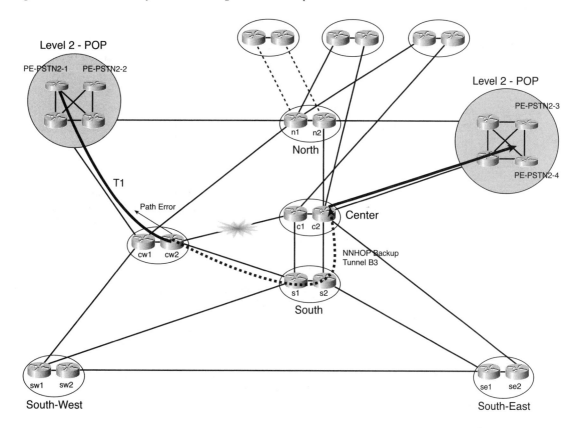

The last component to be added is the signaling delay of a new TE LSP. It is made up of the sum of the propagation delays along the links plus the queuing and processing delays at each intermediate hop. Because the MPC network is a national network, the propagation delay across the whole network is limited to 15 ms. Moreover, the signaling messages are processed in an AF3 queue, as mentioned in the section "Quality of Service Design." Hence, the queuing delay along each hop is negligible.

Finally, the processing delay at each hop was estimated to be at most 10 ms. Consequently, because the maximum number of visited hops is ten, the round-trip signaling time is always less than [10 * 10 (processing delay) + 15 ms (propagation delay)] * 2 (in each direction), which equals 230 ms. Consequently, the maximum amount of time necessary to reroute a TE LSP at the headend router after a failure is 469 ms:

(10 * 10 ms) + 15 ms (time for the headend to receive the RSVP Path Error message notifying it of the failure)
+ 62 * 2 ms (time to recompute the new path)
+ 230 ms (round-trip signaling time)
= 469 ms

This means that in the very worst-case scenario, upon a link, SRLG, or node failure, a TE LSP would be rerouted to its backup tunnel within 60 ms. It would use the backup tunnel for a period of 469 ms before being reoptimized by its headend router. Note that in reality this time typically is significantly shorter for most TE LSPs. (The preceding computation uses the very worst case of a TE LSP following a ten-hop path, a very remote failure, and the improbable case of a headend router having to reroute all its TE LSPs affected by the failure.)

Configuration of a Hold-Off Timer

The need for a hold-off timer was explained in Chapter 2. However, as a reminder, when network recovery schemes are available at multiple layers (optical, SONET-SDH, IP/MPLS), it is desirable to introduce some delays at each layer before triggering the recovery to give a lower-layer network recovery mechanism a chance to recover the fault.

The MPC network has two link types:

- **Unprotected STM-16 and STM-64**—In the case of the unprotected link, no such hold-off timer is required. As soon as the fault is detected, the network recovery mechanism is triggered (IP routing and MPLS TE Fast Reroute).

- **Protected STM-1 links (by SDH) between some Level 2 and Level 1 POPs**— Conversely, in the case of the protected STM-1 links, it is desirable to wait for a period of time before triggering MPLS TE Fast Reroute. This way, in case of link failure, the SDH layer tries to recover the fault. If, after some timer X has elapsed, the fault is not recovered, this means that the SDH layer could not recover the affected resource. The inability of the SDH layer to recover the affected link can be because of an SDH equipment failure or because the fault is outside the SDH layer protection scope (for example, in the case of a router or router interface failure). TK determined that the SDH recovery time in its network was bounded to 80 ms (based on its SDH ring size, number of Add/Drop Multiplexers (ADMs), and so on). Hence, TK decided to set the hold-off timer to 100 ms.

NOTE   The activation of such a timer has the following consequence: In case of a router interface failure or a router failure, the MPLS TE Fast Reroute time is increased by 100 ms.

On a Cisco router, the hold-off timer can be configured via the use of the **carrier-delay** command (configured on each interface), as shown in Example 4-12.

Example 4-12 *Configuration of Carrier Delay*

```
interface pos3/0
 carrier-delay ms x (where x is the timer value)
!
```

Failure of a PE-PSTN Router

The case of a PE-PSTN failure is shown in Figure 4-38.

Figure 4-38 *PE-PSTN Node Failure*

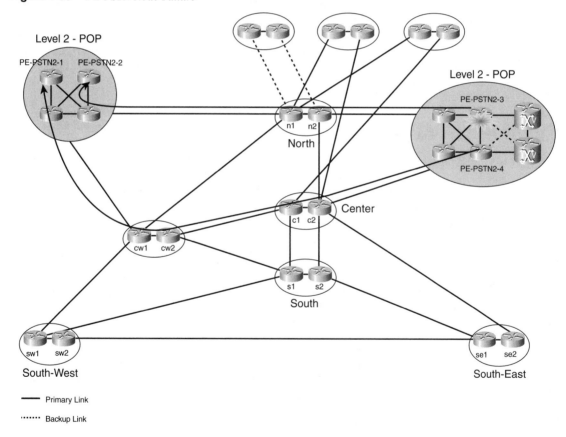

In steady state, a VoIP gateway routes all its traffic to a single PE-PSTN (via static routing). Upon failure of this primary PE-PSTN, the VoIP gateway reroutes all its traffic to the alternate co-located PE-PSTN. As already pointed out, the TE LSP between a pair of PE-PSTNs is determined based on the peak load between the two PE-PSTNs. This does not account for the potential rerouting of traffic from other VoIP gateways upon a failure of their primary PE-PSTN. This is because this would result in drastically overestimating all the TE LSPs, potentially leading to suboptimal routing of the TE LSP in steady state. Thus, in case of a PE-PSTN failure, the TE LSP of the PE-PSTN used as a backup carries more traffic (during the period of the PE-PSTN failure), but there are several aspects to consider.

Each TE LSP is sized for peak load. Hence, if the PE-PSTN failure does not occur during busy periods, it is quite likely that the TE LSP will actually carry no more traffic than it has been sized for. That said, even if it turns out that a TE LSP carries more traffic than its actual bandwidth, this does not have any severe consequence. In steady state, the MPC network has been designed such that each TE LSP follows its shortest IGP path (or the shortest path satisfying the color constraints when those are used). Thus, although the traffic carried on those TE LSPs might temporarily exceed the signaled bandwidth, the proportion of PSTN traffic stays below some desirable threshold guaranteeing the QoS. The only case where this might not be true is when PE-PSTN and catastrophic failure are combined in the network. However, TK considered this scenario extremely unlikely and felt it was outweighed by the advantages of the current design rules.

IPv6 Internet Access Service Design

Several large customers in Kingland needed a service to interconnect IPv6 networks and for IPv6 Internet access. For example, Kingland's national academic and research network runs regional IPv6 networks and therefore required high-speed IPv6 interconnection across these networks, along with IPv6 Internet access. In response to this demand, TK launched an IPv6 Internet access service.

Because it is absolutely essential to protect the stability of the MPC, TK decided to use the IPv6 Provider Edge (6PE) approach described in the section "Deploying IPv6 Over an MPLS Network" in Chapter 1. This allowed TK to introduce an IPv6 service incrementally on the edge without any software upgrade or configuration change in the core, which remains purely IPv4/MPLS.

Because the number of IPv6 services is fairly small today and requires pure IPv6 connectivity only, TK decided to support the IPv6 services on dedicated 6PE routers. This isolates the mPE routers supporting IPv4 Internet and Layer 3 MPLS VPN services from any faults or problems that could occur with the IPv6 and 6PE technologies. These newer technologies have been subjected to less-extensive testing and validation, and TK has less production experience with them. 6PE routers have been located in every Level 1 POP as well as in four Level 2 POPs where customers also requested IPv6 services. Two 6PE routers are deployed in each Level 1 POP to support dual-homing of IPv6 customer sites. This represents a total of 16 6PE routers.

As illustrated in Figure 4-39, 6PE routers are dual-attached to the two P routers in the POP. They are generally attached with STM-1 PoS interfaces, but a few of them are attached with STM-16 PoS interfaces so as to support very high-speed IPv6 customer connections.

Figure 4-39   *6PE Design in a Level 1 POP with IPv6 Route Reflection and IPv6 Internet Peering*

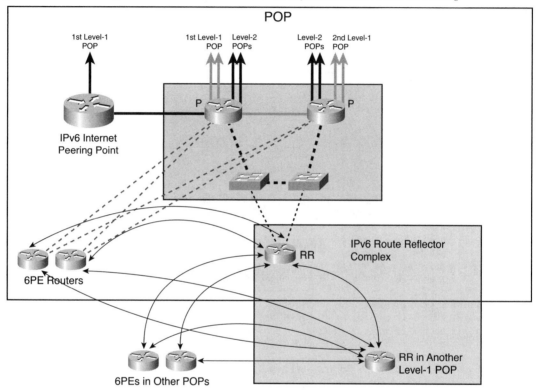

```
------ STM-1 or STM-16
◄──► VPNv4 Peering
```

TK uses a separate set of route reflectors dedicated to the IPv6 Internet service. This is for the same reasons TK elected to use separate sets of route reflectors for IPv4 Internet and for Layer 3 MPLS VPN. Namely, doing so avoids contention across the different services in terms of control-plane convergence in network failure situations. Because the number of 6PE routers involved in the IPv6 route reflection is currently quite small, TK deployed only two IPv6 route reflectors. They are located in two different Level 1 POPs (Center POP and South POP). These are also the POPs that support native IPv6 peering to the IPv6 Internet.

The IPv6 route reflectors contain the full IPv6 Internet routing table, which currently contains about 1000 routes.

As the number of IPv6 Internet access services grows and operational experience is developed, TK plans to migrate the IPv6 Internet service onto the shared mPE routers in line with its overall network evolution strategy.

For routing between the 6PE router and the IPv6 CE routers, TK uses static routes as well as BGP.

TK uses a configuration template for the 6PE routers. It is shown in Example 4-13.

Example 4-13   *6PE Router Configuration Template*

```
! interface to Site Y of Customer X
interface POSx/y
 no ip address
 ipv6 address IPv6-address-of-interface
ipv6 enable
!
router bgp 32764
!peering with first v6 RR
 neighbor IPv4-address-of-first-v6-RR remote-as AS-number-of-TK
 neighbor IPv4-address-of-first-v6-RR update-source Loopback0
 no neighbor IPv4-address-of-first-v6-RR activate
!peering with second v6 RR
 neighbor IPv4-address-of-second-v6-RR remote-as AS-number-of-TK
 neighbor IPv4-address-of-second-v6-RR update-source Loopback0
 no neighbor IPv4-address-of-second-v6-RR activate
!v6 native peering with customer
 neighbor IPv6-address-of-CE remote-as AS-number-of-v6-customer
!
 address-family ipv6
 neighbor IPv4-address-of-first-v6-RR activate
 neighbor IPv4-address-of-first-v6-RR send-label
 neighbor IPv4-address-of-second-v6-RR activate
 neighbor IPv4-address-of-second-v6-RR send-label
 neighbor IPv6-address-of-CE activate
 redistribute connected
 no synchronization
 exit-address-family
```

TK offers the same QoS support for the IPv6 Internet access service as for the IPv4 Internet access service. A single CoS is supported on the access links; it is identical to the Standard CoS of the Layer 3 MPLS VPN service. In the core, the IPv6 Internet traffic is handled together with the IPv4 Internet traffic and the Layer 3 MPLS VPN Standard CoS. To that end, TK takes advantage of the default behavior of the IOS 6PE implementation, which sets to 0 the EXP field of the label stack entries pushed by the ingress 6PE router. This ensures that the IPv6 traffic receives the desired treatment in the MPC (namely, that it is scheduled in the DF queue) without having to modify the QoS core service policies described in the "Quality of Service Design" section. Note that because the 6PE approach uses two labels, use of Penultimate Hop Popping

(PHP) in the core does not create a problem. PHP will expose the second label stack entry, which also contains an EXP field set to 0.

Design Lessons to Be Taken from Telecom Kingland

A number of conclusions can be drawn from Telecom Kingland's design:

- An IP/MPLS packet core can be used as the multiservice core to integrate current and future services (including Internet, Layer 3 VPN, enterprise voice within a Layer 3 VPN, PSTN telephony trunking, and so on).

- Multiple services may be offered by the same edge devices, although extra consideration is necessary in terms of security and scale.

- Load balancing of Layer 3 MPLS VPN traffic can be achieved through the combination of iBGP Multipath functionality and different route distinguishers per VRF.

- Carrier's Carrier may be used as an effective tool to help scale large routing requirements, or for customers that require service separation within their own network environments.

- PSTN telephony trunking can be carried over the packet core with extremely strict QoS and resiliency both during normal situations and upon link/SRLG/node failure. This involves a tight combination of a dedicated, strict priority queue and the call admission control, Constraint-Based Routing, and Fast Reroute capabilities of MPLS Traffic Engineering.

- Internet and Layer 3 MPLS VPN traffic can be efficiently rerouted in case of link, SRLG, or node failure within a few seconds in the worst case with an appropriate OSPF design.

- Multiple CoS on access links is very useful for multimedia VPN. This involves sophisticated QoS service policies and requires careful fine-tuning (particularly on lower-speed links).

- Where capacity can be easily and economically provisioned, multiple CoSs can be handled together as a single class in the core (all the VPN CoSs plus the Internet in TK's case). Appropriate levels of QoS can be ensured via capacity planning. However, it's a good idea to isolate essential control traffic (routing, signaling, management) to protect network stability even in the worst, unexpected situations.

- IPv6 Internet services can be offered in an incremental fashion over an existing MPLS core without any upgrade or change in the core and thus without any impact on existing services.

CHAPTER 5

Global Service Provider Design Study

Globenet is a fictitious international service provider with 77 points of presence (POPs) all around the globe—namely, in North and South America, Europe, the Middle East, Africa, Asia, and Australia/New Zealand. Network density varies from country to country. Globenet's network expansion strategy consists of building presence in more than 60 countries while limiting the number of POPs in each country (with some exceptions, such as in the U.S.).

For customers that require a large number of connections spread over many locations in a specific country, Globenet relies on interconnection with regional service providers and establishes tight agreements with them to provide seamless service. Recently, Globenet also started deploying virtual POPs (VPOPs) in some countries. The main concept behind VPOPs relies on the co-location of some of the routers in regional service providers' premises. Such VPOPs are then connected to the Globenet core network by means of a guaranteed bandwidth service across the regional service provider network. This effectively allows Globenet to establish a POP in a particular country without extending its own core network to reach the corresponding parts of the world.

NOTE   A regional service provider may be either a national telco (such as Telecom Kingland, discussed in Chapter 4, "National Telco Design Study") or a service provider having deployed a dense network in a particular region of the world.

Typically the profile of Globenet's customer base is medium-to-large international enterprises with sites in multiple countries and a requirement to rely on a unique service provider for their telecommunications services rather than dealing with a plethora of national and international carriers. Furthermore, for such enterprises, the cost of international leased lines is still very significant (although more affordable than a few years ago, at least in some regions). Therefore, purchasing the necessary international capacity to build a private network is typically a costly proposition, leaving aside the complexity of having to deal with a large set of regional connectivity providers.

Globenet's network is made up of a broad range of links that differ significantly in terms of speed and technology in various regions.

This chapter's objective is to discuss the current Globenet network design that illustrates an international service provider with respect to the set of objectives and network characteristics of such networks. In particular, this chapter details the following key design aspects:

- Layer 3 Multiprotocol Label Switching (MPLS) virtual private network (VPN) scalability

- Inter-autonomous system (AS) and interprovider operations of Layer 3 VPN and quality of service (QoS)

- Virtual POP involving interprovider MPLS Traffic Engineering (TE)

- Fine-grain QoS control in some parts of the core combining DiffServ and MPLS DiffServ-aware Traffic Engineering

- Asynchronous Transfer Mode (ATM) pseudowire deployment for trunking of ATM infrastructure over MPLS

- Introduction of IPv6 Layer 3 VPNs

Globenet Network Environment

Several characteristics are specific to international service provider networks. Typically they rely on a very broad set of physical link types and related Layer 2 technologies. This is primarily because of the wide range of pricing per Mbps of bandwidth (for instance, link costs are significantly higher in Asia than in the U.S.). Consequently, this unavoidably results in limited capacity in certain regions, such as Asia and intercontinental links.

This led Globenet to carefully optimize the design in some parts of its network using various technologies such as QoS, MPLS Traffic Engineering, and ATM to efficiently engineer its network and reduce the recurrent bandwidth costs. Specifically, Asia takes advantage of ATM with Private Network-Network Interface (PNNI) routing and signaling protocol. POPs are interconnected through Globenet's ATM switches with carefully sized and carefully routed ATM variable bit rate-real time (VBR-rt) virtual circuits (whose size is determined based on traffic requirements). Conversely, high-speed SONET-DWDM links (OC-3 and OC-48) have been deployed between the POPs in the U.S.

Globenet does not own any fiber. Instead, it leases every circuit (protected and unprotected SONET-Synchronous Digital Hierarchy (SDH) circuits, dense wavelength division multiplexing (DWDM) links, time-division multiplexing (TDM) circuits, and ATM permanent virtual circuits (PVCs)) around the world and has to deal with many other carriers and service providers.

In larger POPs, Globenet uses separate PE routers and P routers, just like the service providers described in earlier chapters. However, in smaller POPs, Globenet has a number of routers that play the role of both P router and PE router, without any separation between the two functions. Shared PE routers are used to support all IP services, including Internet access and IP VPNs.

Connectivity between Internet and Layer 3 MPLS VPN customer sites and Globenet POPs is provided via Frame Relay, ATM, leased line, or SONET-SDH, with access speeds ranging from 56 kbps to OC-3.

With respect to collaboration with other service providers, Globenet must address multiple scenarios to provide a seamless service to its international customers:

- Customer sites may be directly connected to a Globenet POP (using Layer 1 or Layer 2 connectivity services provided by a regional service provider).

- Customer sites may be connected to the POP of a regional service provider with whom Globenet has an interprovider agreement.

- Customer sites may be connected to a Globenet virtual POP that is interconnected to the Globenet core network through the backbone of another service provider offering international guaranteed bandwidth. This is described in detail in the section "Virtual POP Design."

This highlights the level of complexity required by such international networks in terms of interoperations with regional and sometimes international service providers. This entails elaborate arrangements at the commercial level, at the technical level, such as those necessary to provide tight Service Level Agreements (SLAs) and high availability in all regions, and at the operational level, such as appropriate interactions across network management systems from different providers. The Network Operations Centers (NOCs) have to deal with many other service providers while continuing to be the single point of contact. Moreover, the operational arrangements also involve sophisticated monitoring and troubleshooting tools to quickly and efficiently determine a problem's root cause in case a failure occurs in some part of the world.

Globenet Service Portfolio

Globenet has developed a broad data service portfolio over the years. Originally it offered X.25, Frame Relay, and ATM international services. The X.25 and Frame Relay traffic has significantly decreased over the last three years, and Globenet actively encourages its X.25 and Frame Relay customers to migrate toward other VPN services such as Layer 3 MPLS VPN. Nevertheless, ATM traffic continues to increase slightly, especially in Asia. Therefore, Globenet continues to provide native ATM services.

Internet access services have been offered for many years and continue to increase at a rate of approximately 40 percent a year. Internet connectivity occurs via private and public peering in Network Access Points (NAPs) as well as transit providers.

Layer 3 MPLS VPN service has undoubtedly been the most successful service over the last three years. Globenet has a current installed base of 16,000 dedicated VPN ports grouped into 500 VPNs. It has a traffic growth rate of 80 percent per year and increases its number of customer sites by 120 percent per year. It also offers multicast and voice VPN services.

Moreover, Globenet supports a rich set of five classes of service (CoSs) in the context of the Layer 3 MPLS VPN offering.

Remote access to both VPN and Internet services has been very successful, primarily because of the high population of mobile workers in international companies.

Recently, Globenet started expanding its Layer 3 MPLS VPN service offering to support IPv6 VPNs in addition to the existing IPv4 VPNs.

Globenet POP Network Structure

Globenet POPs are of four different types—Type 1a, Type 1b, Type 2, and Type 3—based on the density of customer access and aggregated traffic throughput.

Type 1 POP Structure

Type 1 POPs are located in large cities and are made up of a set of two P routers and multiple PE routers. P routers are connected to other Type 1 POPs via E3, OC-3, or OC-48 links and to the Type 2 POPs via n * 2 Mbps and OC-3 links. In Asia, they are connected via ATM PVCs supported over Globenet's ATM switches. The multiple PE routers are connected to the P routers via Gigabit Ethernet switches, as shown in Figure 5-1. Furthermore, several virtual LANs (VLANs) are used for separation:

- One VLAN connects the Network Access Server/Broadband Access Server (NAS/BAS) to the various PE routers in their respective VRFs.
- One VLAN connects the core-facing interfaces of the PE routers to the P routers.

Figure 5-1 *Globenet Type 1a POP Design (Every Region Except Asia-Pacific)*

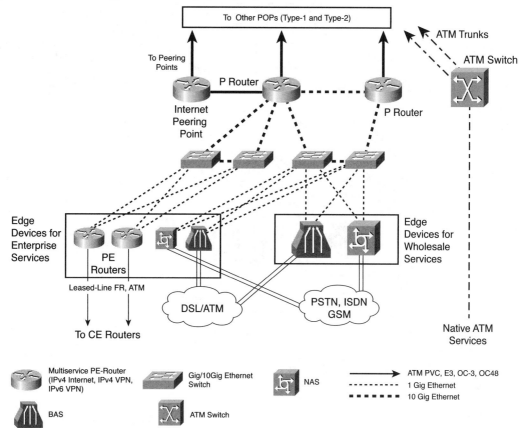

P routers connect PE routers as well as NASs. In the Type 1 POPs located in countries where asymmetric digital subscriber line (ADSL) service is offered, BASs are also connected to the P routers.

Figure 5-2 shows the Type 1a POP design in the Asia-Pacific region (AsiaPac). The difference with the Type 1a POP in other regions is that connectivity to Type 2 POPs in AsiaPac is supported through ATM PVCs provided by Globenet ATM switches.

Figure 5-2 *Globenet Type 1a POP Design for the AsiaPac Region*

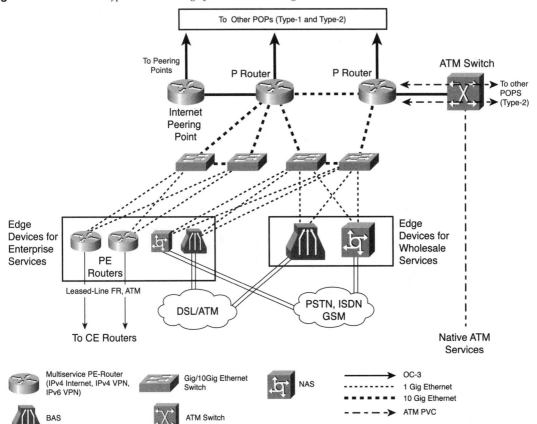

Figures 5-1 and 5-2 show one of two subtypes of Type 1 POP (called Type 1a). The other subtype is Type 1b (shown in Figure 5-3). It is similar to Type 1a, except that Globenet ATM switches are connected to the PE routers and are trunked over MPLS using ATM pseudowires. (Pseudowire service is discussed in Chapter 1, "Technology Primer: Layer 3 VPNs, Multicast VPNs, IPv6, and Pseudowire.") Such Type 1b POPs are deployed in the North America and Europe–Middle East–Africa (EMEA) regions. Here, Globenet decided to carry its ATM traffic over its MPLS infrastructure because of the dominance of IP traffic over native ATM traffic in these regions. The transport of the ATM traffic by means of pseudowire service is illustrated in Figure 5-4.

Figure 5-3   *Globenet Type 1b POP Design*

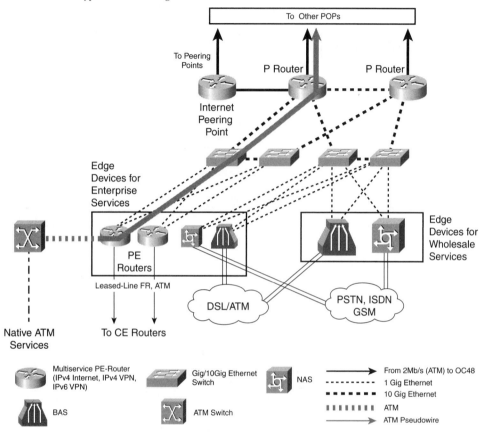

Figure 5-4   *Transport of ATM by Means of Pseudowire Service in Type 1b POPs*

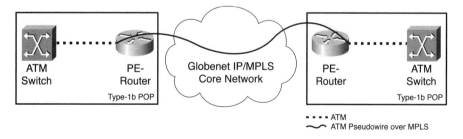

Type 2 POP Structure

Smaller POPs are classified as Type 2. They have only a single set of routers that act as both P routers and PE routers and are called P/PE routers. There are at least two such P/PE routers per POP, each connected to other Type 1 or Type 2 POPs. P/PE routers are also connected to CE routers, NASs, and occasionally BASs. The interconnection between devices is identical to a Type 1 POP and relies on Layer 2 Gigabit Ethernet switches. The structure of a Type 2 POP is shown in Figure 5-5 (all regions except AsiaPac) and Figure 5-6 (AsiaPac).

Figure 5-5   *Globenet Type 2 POP Design (All Regions Except AsiaPac)*

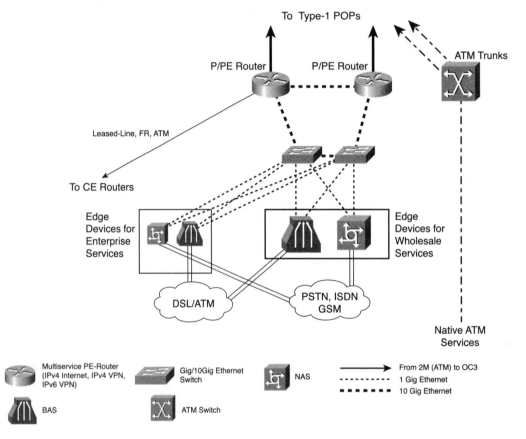

Figure 5-6   *Globenet Type 2 POP Design for the AsiaPac Region*

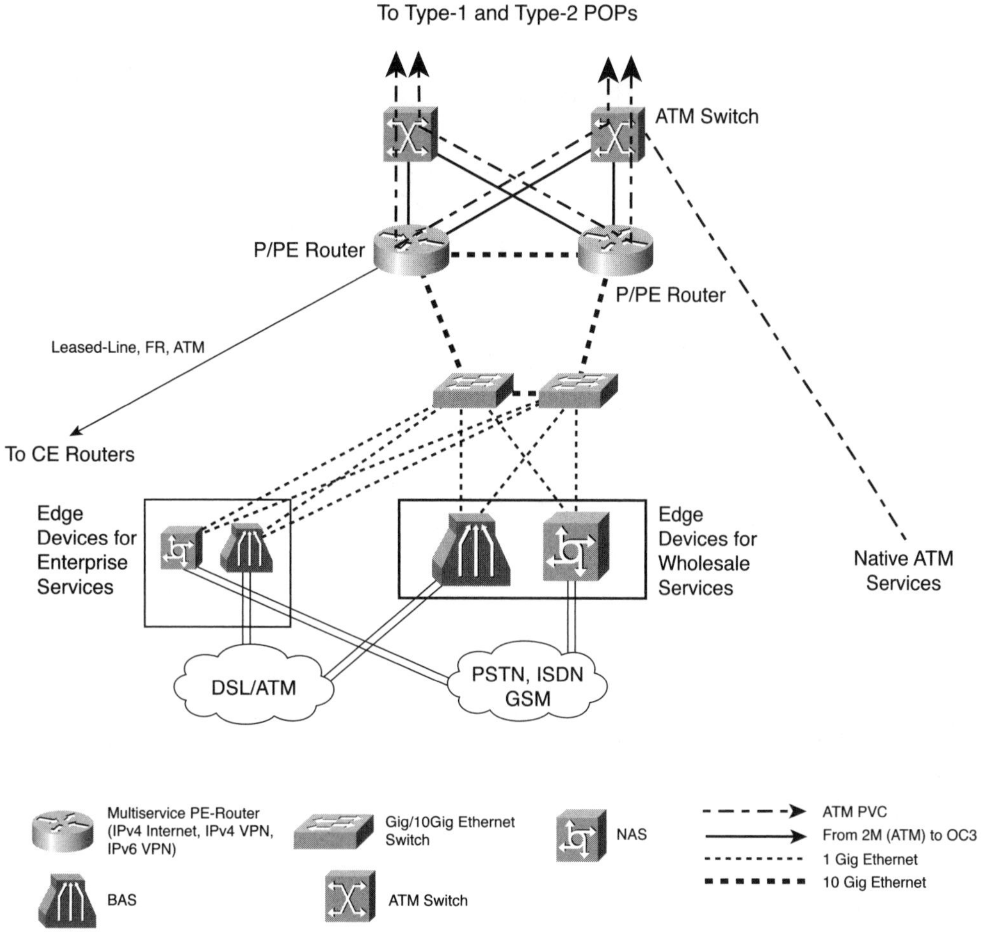

Type 3 POP Structure

In Asia, Globenet has very small POPs limited to one P/PE router connecting the NAS and several CE routers. Such Type 3 POPs are interconnected to the closest Type 1 or Type 2 Globenet POP by means of ATM PVCs provided by its ATM network or leased from a regional service provider. The structure of a Type 3 POP is shown in Figure 5-7.

Figure 5-7 *Globenet Type 3 POP Design (Only in Asia)*

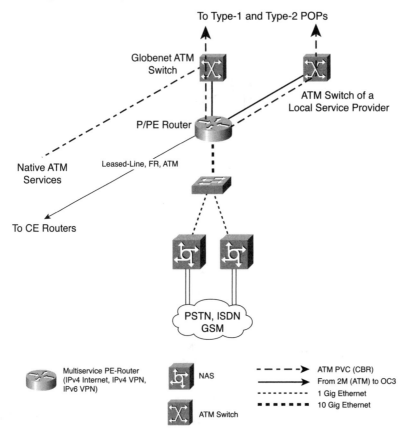

Globenet Worldwide Network Architecture

The total number of routers residing within the 77 POPs run by Globenet worldwide slightly exceeds 250, including 200 PE routers sharing the Layer 3 MPLS VPN and Internet services.

To help illustrate the overall network architecture, the next few sections describe the network topology built by Globenet on a per-region basis.

NOTE   For the sake of simplicity, for the regions with a large number of POPs, just a subset of representative POPs is shown in each figure.

EMEA Region

The Europe–Middle East–Africa (EMEA) network consists of 25 POPs, mostly Type 1 POPs interconnected with protected STM-1 and STM-16 links (leased from different regional service providers). A few smaller Type 2 POPs (mainly in Eastern Europe) are connected to the Type 1 POPs with $n * 2$ Mbps bundled links. n is determined by the traffic demand from the POP and varies in value from 1 to 4. In this case, multilink PPP (see [MLPPP]) is used. The structure of the EMEA region is shown in Figure 5-8.

Figure 5-8   *Globenet Network Design for the EMEA Region*

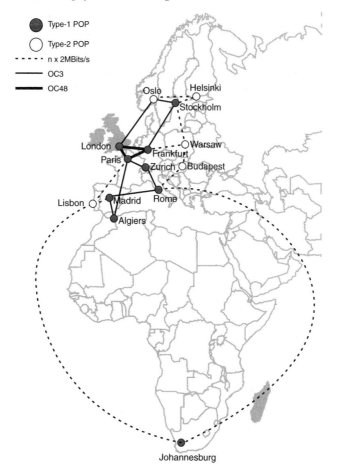

References Used in This Book

Throughout this book you will see references to other resources. These are provided in case you want to delve more deeply into a subject. Such references appear in brackets, such as [L2VPN]. If you want to know more about this resource, look up the code in the "References" appendix to find out specific information about the resource.

In EMEA, the IP network and the ATM network (deployed earlier for support of native ATM services) operate using either of two models in different parts of the network:

- In "ships in the night" mode, the ATM network and the IP/MPLS network each have their own dedicated bandwidth capacity and operate independently of each other.

- In "inverted overlay" mode, in some cases, ATM switches are trunked over the IP/MPLS core network via MPLS pseudowires. In this mode, all the bandwidth is managed by the IP/MPLS network, and the bandwidth needed by ATM is provided by the IP/MPLS network through the MPLS pseudowires.

Globenet's strategy in EMEA is to migrate toward a full inverted overlay mode in the long run considering the increasing IP/ATM ratio in this region.

Asia-Pacific Region

The total number of POPs in Asia is 30, with two additional POPs in Australia—one in Sydney (Type 1) and another in Perth (Type 2). The network topology is (partially) shown in Figure 5-9.

Figure 5-9 *Globenet Network Design for the AsiaPac Region*

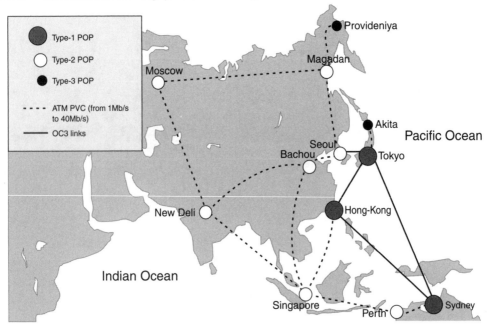

Only a few of the POPs in Asia are Type 1 POPs, and they are interconnected with unprotected OC-3 links. The rest are predominantly Type 2 POPs with a few Type 3 POPs.

Because of significant bandwidth costs in this region, Globenet recognized the need for careful bandwidth dimensioning and for tight traffic engineering. This is why it decided to interconnect the Type 2 and Type 3 POPs in this region via ATM virtual circuits (VCs) supported over Globenet's ATM switches instead of via separate dedicated links (as is done in EMEA). This allows Globenet to make fine-grain optimization of bandwidth usage, because VCs can be individually sized to match current demand without any granularity limitations that come with direct links.

Hence, in Asia, Globenet effectively uses an overlay model in which all the capacity is used to interconnect the ATM switches and where Type 2 POPs are interconnected by ATM VCs supported off of the ATM switches. The ATM VC sizes vary between 1 Mbps (for the smallest POP, such as the Type 3) and 40 Mbps. Above such rates it is usually more cost-effective to interconnect routers by means of dedicated leased lines.

For operational and cost reasons, Globenet resizes each ATM VC only once every six months (based on measured load multiplied by an overbooking factor). Because of this low frequency, Globenet elected to use an additional traffic engineering technique (MPLS-based TE) on top of its ATM PVCs to further optimize the use of the bandwidth provided by the ATM network between ATM VC resizing periods. Moreover, as explained in detail in this chapter, MPLS TE allows for the use of dynamic TE LSP dimensioning every two hours, which could not be easily achieved by means of ATM PNNI.

North America Region

There are 15 POPs in Globenet North America region (the U.S. and Canada). The majority of those are Type 1b, interconnected by unprotected OC-48 (based on leased DWDM links). The rest are Type 2 POPs connected to Type 1 POPs via unprotected OC-3 links. The North America topology is shown in Figure 5-10.

Because Globenet's ATM switches are interconnected via ATM pseudowires over the MPLS network in North America, you see that Globenet uses the inverted overlay model in this region. In this model, all the capacity is managed by the IP/MPLS network, and ATM switches are interconnected via MPLS pseudowires supported off of the IP/MPLS network.

Figure 5-10 *Globenet Network Design for the North America Region*

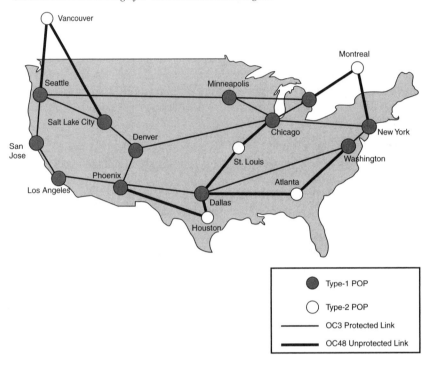

South America Region

Globenet has six Type 2 POPs in South America located in Caracas (Venezuela), Bogota (Columbia), Rio de Janeiro (Brazil), Santiago (Chile), Buenos Aires (Argentina), and Lima (Peru).

Until recently, all these POPs were interconnected via ATM PVCs supported over the ATM switches using the overlay model (as deployed in the Asia region). However, a recent upgrade changed this topology to dedicated 34-Mbps links directly connecting the POP routers, thereby migrating from the overlay model to the "ships in the night" model also used in parts of the EMEA region. The topology for this region is shown in Figure 5-11.

In South America, because of the high cost of terrestrial links, a couple of satellite links are used. Use of such satellite links is attractive to Globenet because they result in additional bandwidth at lower cost. They also allow easier long-distance connections within the region because their tariff is distance-independent. Special considerations with these satellites are discussed in the sections "QoS Design in the Core Network in the EMEA, AsiaPac, and South America Regions" and "MPLS Traffic Engineering in the AsiaPac, EMEA, and South America Regions."

Figure 5-11   *Globenet Network Design for the South America Region*

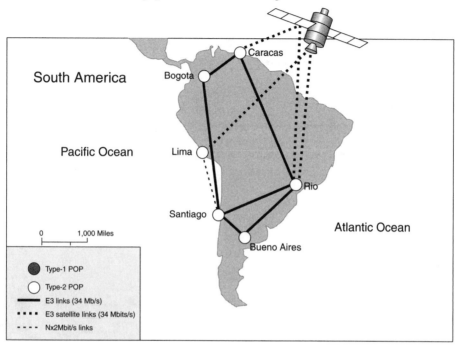

It is worth observing that because of each region's specificities in terms of bandwidth service costs and availability, Globenet ended up using three different models for IP/MPLS and ATM interworking:

- A "ships in the night" model was chosen in some places in EMEA as well as in South America, where IP/MPLS and ATM run independently of each other.

- An overlay model was chosen in AsiaPac, with IP/MPLS running over ATM.

- An inverted overlay model was chosen in North America and in some places in EMEA, with ATM running over IP/MPLS.

The ratio between the IP and ATM traffic was a key decision-making factor for selecting the appropriate model for IP/MPLS and ATM interworking. Indeed, in places where the majority of the traffic is IP, the inverted model is the most appealing and cost-effective. Conversely, in regions where such a ratio is in favor of ATM, the overlay model is perfectly adequate. Finally, the "ships in the night" model adopted in some places in EMEA and in South America is motivated by a situation in which neither the IP/MPLS traffic nor the ATM traffic is predominant. In the future, Globenet foresees a general trend toward generalizing the inverted overlay model considering the considerable growth of the IP traffic.

Intercontinental Connectivity

All the previously described regions are interconnected via a mix of protected E3 and OC-3 links, as shown in Figure 5-12.

Figure 5-12 *Globenet Network Design for Interregion Connectivity*

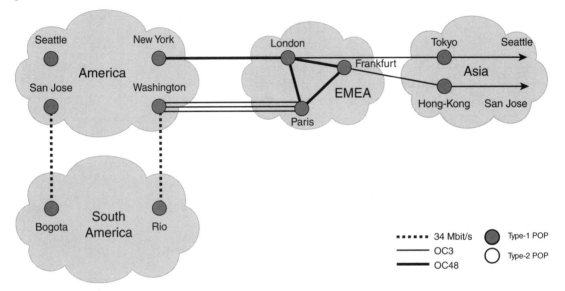

Globenet Routing Architecture

Globenet elected to use a multi-AS routing architecture in which each region constitutes a separate autonomous system. The rationale for this was primarily driven by scale, where regional routing information could be bounded. Within each AS the routing protocol of choice is Intermediate System-to-Intermediate System (IS-IS) with a single IS-IS Level 2 topology.

Internet routes are distributed to the P routers. However, this is purely a failsafe procedure so that Internet traffic may continue to be forwarded in the event of a label-switching failure. The design of Globenet's Internet route reflection is as discussed in Chapter 4. However, each region is an independent autonomous system. Internet access is provided locally within each region, as well as through the distribution of IPv4 routes between different regions.

The total number of Interior Gateway Protocol (IGP) routes varies from AS to AS but never exceeds 1000 in any given AS. For IPv4 Internet, Globenet currently carries approximately 140,000 routes. For its Layer 3 MPLS VPN service, the total number of VPNv4 routes worldwide is 80,000, including routes that are received from regional inter-AS partners. Because of the increasing number of VPNv4 routes, Globenet chose to filter routes between regions, even though in terms of number of routes the current savings at the Autonomous System Boundary Routers (ASBRs) is minimal.

Interoperator Partnerships

Globenet does not have sufficiently dense network coverage in all regions of the globe to always cost-effectively connect customers with many locations in a given country. Therefore, its strategy is to connect such customers to a regional service provider partner and then use the inter-AS VPN solution set between its network infrastructure and that of the regional service provider. This interoperator connectivity is provided through at least two exit point ASBRs. For instance, Telecom Kingland (covered in Chapter 4) is one example of a regional service provider with whom Globenet is partnering for seamless Layer 3 MPLS VPN service.

In some countries, however, Globenet is either unable (because of local regulations) or unwilling (because of a large number of customers) to use any of the connectivity models in the inter-AS VPN solution set to extend its network. In these cases, Globenet might use a virtual POP (VPOP) in which one of its routers is colocated in the POP of a regional service provider. The router is connected to Globenet's main network by means of inter-AS traffic-engineered label-switched paths (TE LSPs) providing bandwidth guarantees for transit through the regional service provider. Such interconnection is discussed in detail in the "Virtual POP Design" section.

Link Types and Protection Details

Table 5-1 shows the different link types and characteristics in the Globenet network.

Table 5-1   *Link Types and Characteristics in the Globenet Backbone*

Link Type	Speed	Protection	Localization
OC-48 DWDM	2.5 Gbps	None	North America and EMEA: Type 1 to Type 1 POPs
OC-3	155 Mbps	Protected and unprotected, depending on the region	All regions: Type 1 to Type 1 POPs Type 1 to Type 2 POPs
E3	34 Mbps	Protected	In South America: Type 2 to Type 2 POPs
ATM	From 1 Mbps to 40 Mbps	Via ATM PNNI	Asia Pacific: Type 1 to Type 2 POPs Type 2 to Type 2 POPs Type 2 to Type 3 POPs
$n * 2$ Mbps	From 2 Mbps (n=1) to 8 Mbps (n=4)	Protected	EMEA: Type 1 to Type 2 POPs Type 2 to Type 2 POPs
Gigabit Ethernet	1 Gbps/10 Gbps	None	All regions: Within POPs

<table>
<tr><td>**NOTE**</td><td>In general, Globenet always tries to deploy unprotected OC-3 links (and to rely on MPLS Traffic Engineering Fast Reroute functionality to provide fast local protection). However, there are several regions where only protected OC-3 links are available. This explains the mix of protected and unprotected OC-3 links.</td></tr>
</table>

During the past ten years, Globenet has gathered various network failure statistics that vary greatly within each region in terms of both frequency and duration. The results are summarized in Table 5-2. These statistics have greatly influenced the routing and MPLS Fast Reroute network design.

Table 5-2   *Link Failure Statistics in the Globenet Network*

Failure Type	Link/Router Type	Occurrence	Duration
Link failure	OC-48 links (EMEA and U.S.)	Unknown	Unknown
Link failure	OC-3 SONET links (unprotected)	Between once a week (EMEA) to several times a day (South America)	From a few seconds to several days (fiber cut) or even weeks for the transatlantic links
Link failure	ATM	On average, twice a week	From 1 second to 1 minute
Router interface failure	Edge+core	Negligible	A few hours
Unplanned router failure (such as power supply, router software failure with traffic impact)	Edge+core	Once every 3 months	Variable
Router reboot (planned failure)	Edge	Once every 10 months	10 minutes
Router reboot (planned failure)	Core	Once a year	10 minutes

Design Objectives for the Globenet Network

The design objectives for the Globenet network include the following considerations:

- Offer a rich set of Layer 3 MPLS VPN services to Globenet's international customers, including data (Unicast and Multicast), voice, and video with sophisticated QoS features and IPv6 support.

- Ensure that Globenet's network design can cope with the expected growth of its Internet and VPN traffic and will scale appropriately.

- Provide a highly available network that can provide fast convergence with minimal traffic impact on single network element failures such as links or nodes without any additional expense.

- Minimize the recurring bandwidth cost and provide differentiated services by deploying various network optimization techniques where justified, such as traffic engineering and DiffServ, while maintaining reasonable network management and operational complexity.

- Use the available bandwidth on the IP/MPLS network to carry ATM traffic with an equivalent quality of service where the traffic ratio of IP to ATM is high.

The rest of this chapter describes the design Globenet chose in terms of IPv4 and IPv6 Layer 3 MPLS VPN, ATM pseudowires, QoS, traffic engineering, network recovery, and VPOP. Special emphasis is given to the inter-AS and interprovider aspects of the design as far as VPN, QoS, and TE are concerned.

Layer 3 MPLS VPN Service Design

The design of the Globenet Layer 3 MPLS VPN service caters to both "managed" and "unmanaged" access. The managed service allows Globenet to supply and manage the customer access equipment. The unmanaged service just provides connectivity to the Layer 3 MPLS VPN service; no management of the customer access equipment is deployed. The vast majority of Globenet customers use the managed service, with only a few large Enterprises taking the unmanaged service.

Many aspects of the MPLS VPN design (such as PE router engineering guidelines, load-balancing support, naming conventions, and so on) are as detailed in previous chapters. Therefore, we will not cover them again here. Unless otherwise stated, Globenet uses all the Layer 3 MPLS VPN design best practices we have already detailed. Because Globenet is an international service provider, providing a worldwide service portfolio, this chapter concentrates on the aspects of the design that are specific to these types of providers.

Shared-Edge Internet and MPLS VPN Services

Globenet chose to use the same PE routers to terminate all services, including Internet and Layer 3 MPLS VPN, as well as for ATM pseudowires used to trunk their ATM switches. However, Internet routes are distributed only to PE routers that have customer sites attached that require Internet access or that need more than just a default route. You will see later in this chapter how Globenet provides Internet access.

The implication of shared services on the same edge routers was taken into consideration when designing the network. The main areas of concern were identified as security and scale. Both of these topics are discussed later in this chapter.

Globenet decided it did not want to run a Border Gateway Protocol (BGP)-free core (unlike Telecom Kingland, which was reviewed in the preceding chapter). The primary reasons for this decision were that Globenet had been running an Internet network with BGP in the core for a number of years and saw no compelling reason to change, and it also wanted to provide a failsafe mechanism for Internet traffic in case of LSP failure. Therefore, BGP-4 is delivered to all P routers for Internet routes. All traffic (including VPN and Internet) is label-switched across the network by means of RSVP-TE LSPs between P routers and LDP between PE/P routers.

NOTE	LDP is enabled on the RSVP-TE tunnel interfaces between P routers. This is an important part of the design, because it allows the Layer 3 MPLS VPN traffic to maintain a complete end-to-end LSP between ingress and egress PE routers.

Connectivity Between Globenet Regions

Because the Globenet Layer 3 MPLS VPN service caters primarily to large Enterprise connectivity, routes belonging to different customers frequently need to be distributed between different regions of the worldwide network. Because of this requirement, Globenet needed to choose an inter-AS solution to provide connectivity across its different autonomous systems.

For scalability reasons, Globenet chose to evaluate only options B and C of the inter-AS solution for its internal connectivity requirements. For detailed discussions of these two solutions, refer to the section "Layer 3 MPLS VPN Services Across Autonomous System Boundaries" in Chapter 1 and also to section 10 of [2547bis]. As a reminder, the three main inter-AS solutions are as follows:

- **Option A** — Back-to-back Virtual Routing/Forwarding instances (VRFs)
- **Option B** — VPNv4 route exchange between ASBRs
- **Option C** — VPNv4 route exchange between route reflectors (RRs) with next hops exchanged between ASBRs

Having reviewed options B and C, Globenet chose to deploy the inter-AS option B solution on all its internal interconnection points between its various autonomous systems.

Globenet chose direct exchange of VPNv4 routes between regions as the right solution for a number of reasons:

- Filtering at the autonomous system boundaries can be easily deployed so as to distribute only necessary routes.
- The ASBRs do not require any VRFs (as they would with option A). They simply populate their Label Forwarding Information Base (LFIB) with VPNv4 forwarding information that is more scalable.
- Each autonomous system does not need to carry the Interior Gateway Protocol (IGP) routes of the PE routers located in other regions.

Figure 5-13 provides an overview of how the option B connectivity is deployed between the different worldwide regions.

Figure 5-13   *Globenet Internal Inter-AS Connectivity*

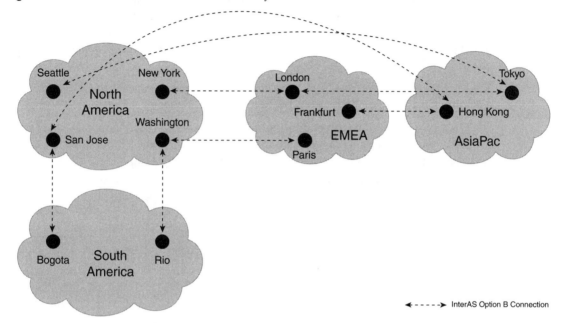

Filtering VPNv4 Routes at the ASBRs

Globenet uses dedicated P routers within the POP to provide ASBR functionality. These P routers are attached to the core P routers within the POP using OC-3 or OC-48 links.

The default behavior of a PE router or ASBR when receiving VPNv4 routes is to keep only the routes that carry a route target extended community for which the receiving router has a corresponding "import" statement configured within a particular VRF. This functionality is commonly called Automatic Route Filtering (ARF).

The use of inter-AS option B at the ASBRs means that no VRFs are necessary. Therefore, by default, an ASBR never keeps any VPNv4 routes it receives. To overcome this issue, and therefore provide connectivity between different autonomous systems, the default ARF functionality must be disabled. Globenet achieves this using the configuration template shown in Example 5-1.

Example 5-1   *ASBR Configuration Template to Disable ARF*

```
router bgp 32763
 no bgp default route-target filter
```

Having enabled the ASBRs to keep all VPNv4 routes, Globenet realized that the overall number of routes that would need to be advertised between autonomous systems would be a subset of the overall number of routes within a given region. For example, it found that only 20 percent of the routes within the EMEA region needed to be advertised toward the North America region. This was because only a small percentage of its overall customer base has a presence in more than one region. However, without some kind of filtering at the ASBRs, all VPNv4 routes would by default be distributed to all regions. This behavior was not an acceptable long-term design practice for Globenet.

To overcome the distribution of all VPNv4 routes to all regions, Globenet chose to implement a filtering scheme at the ASBRs. It evaluated two primary options:

- **Reserved range route target filtering**—Filter at the ASBRs based on a route target value taken from Globenet's reserved range, and add this value to any VRF during export of its routes if those routes need to cross autonomous system boundaries

- **Customer-specific route target filtering**—Filter based on customer-specific route target values at the ASBRs

---

NOTE   Just as you saw with Telecom Kingland in the preceding chapter, Globenet reserves the first 100 route target values for its own internal use.

The main advantage of the first option of filtering based on a reserved route target value is that the filters at the ASBRs do not need to be changed whenever an existing VPN needs to expand across regions or a new VPN needs to be added. This is because with this option only a few fixed filters are necessary because the route target values used for filtering never change. This helps prevent a misconfiguration of the filters affecting multiple customers.

A further important advantage of this scheme is that it prevents the ASBRs from having to request routing updates from the route reflectors whenever local policy changes. Whenever a filter is changed at the ASBR, it must attract routing information it previously discarded. For example, if the filter originally denied route target value 32763:921, all routes carrying this value would have been discarded. However, if at a later date a customer is added that uses this route target value, the route reflector must reobtain the routes. This is achieved by sending a route refresh message to the route reflector(s), which causes a download of the entire Multiprotocol BGP (MP-BGP) table for the VPNv4 address family to the ASBRs. [Route-filter] proposes a change to this behavior in which the route reflector downloads only the relevant routes based on route target values. However, at the time of the initial design, this option was unavailable to Globenet.

Although the reserved route target option has the previously described advantages, it does not completely eliminate configuration changes. Consider the case in which an existing VPN is regional in terms of connectivity but wants to add sites in other regions of the worldwide network. Changes to the PE router configurations need to be made so that the reserved route target value may be added to the VRFs of that VPN so that their routes may be advertised between regions. This is not an issue for new customer deployments, because the PE routers need to be touched anyway. A further disadvantage of this approach occurs when multiple autonomous systems exist. This means that several route target values need to be assigned to provide the relevant filtering on a per-AS pair basis. This can quickly become very complex and difficult to manage.

Although the majority of changes to the Globenet network configuration involve the addition of new customers rather than to existing ones (who move from regional connectivity to multi-regional connectivity), they decided to utilize the second option of using the customer specific route-target values and apply filters at the ASBR-routers only. The main reason for this was that each autonomous system could select its own import/export policy (as you will see in the next section). This essentially forced Globenet to rewrite the route target values at each AS boundary. Rewriting these attributes requires ASBR-specific configuration changes; therefore, the advantages of using reserved route target values were significantly diminished. Furthermore, Globenet did not want to touch multiple points in the network to apply filtering policy, even if this was unlikely to be a regular occurrence.

The risk of filter misconfiguration was deemed minimal because all provisioning is achieved through the use of a centralized tool rather than at the router itself. Also, the number of VPNv4 routes held by the route reflectors was not believed to be an issue in terms of route refresh at this time. Therefore, a download of the full table when changing the filters was not a major concern. The configuration shown in Example 5-2 shows how this filtering is applied.

Example 5-2 *ASBR Configuration Template to Filter VPNv4 Routes*

```
router bgp 32763
 no bgp default route-target filter
 neighbor Globenet_RR-address remote-as 32763
 neighbor Globenet_RR-address update-source loopback0
 !
 address-family vpnv4
 neighbor Globenet_RR-address activate
 neighbor Globenet_RR-address route-map asbr-routes-in in
 exit-address-family
!
ip extcommunity-list 1 permit rt InterAS-client-RT-value/s
!
route-map asbr-routes-in permit 10
 match extcommunity 1
 !
```

Route Target/Route Distinguisher Allocation Between Regions

Option B inter-AS provided Globenet with the opportunity to deploy its own IGP domain for each region, and also its own filtering and route distribution policies. But from a Layer 3 MPLS VPN service provisioning aspect, this left Globenet with a dilemma as to how the route targets (RTs) and route distinguishers (RDs) for a given customer VPN should be allocated. It essentially had two options to choose from:

- **Cross-regional values**—Use the same values for a given VPN across all regions

- **Region-specific values**—Use values that are specific to a given region

Although the use of cross-regional values had some benefits in terms of troubleshooting and network provisioning, it was rejected as a viable solution. The main reason was that it would have forced Globenet to coordinate the RT/RD value assignments for all Layer 3 MPLS VPNs (regardless of whether the VPN had interregional connectivity requirements) between all regions to avoid any conflict between value selection. From a service management perspective, this was unacceptable. Therefore, the choice to use specific values for a given region was selected. This allowed the local region to use its autonomous system number value within the RT/RD structure, thus making each assignment unique across regions.

Using region-specific values provides the desired autonomy between regions but introduced a coordination issue at the autonomous system boundaries. Because each region uses its own RT/RD values, if it wants to exchange routes with another region, it must know what values are in use for the same VPN by other regions in the worldwide network. Although this is a service management issue, it is not as large a problem as using cross-regional values. Only the VPNs that cross regional boundaries need to have their RT/RD assignments coordinated, and only so that the relevant values can be entered into the filters at the ASBRs. Furthermore, the issue is isolated to the ASBRs because Globenet rewrites the route target values to the local regional values when accepting routes from another region. This is achieved using the **RT-rewrite** functionality. Example 5-3 shows the configuration template used.

Example 5-3 *ASBR Configuration Template for* **RT-rewrite**

```
ip extcommunity-list 1 permit rt incoming-rt-value
!
route-map Inter-Region-RT-rewrite permit 10
match extcommunity 1
set extcomm-list 1 delete
set extcommunity rt local-rt-value additive
```

Figure 5-14 shows a customer (SoccerOnline) that has presence in the North America and EMEA regions, as well as its RD/RT assignments with the relevant ASBR **RT-rewrite** filters.

Figure 5-14 *Globenet* **RT-rewrite** *for SoccerOnline*

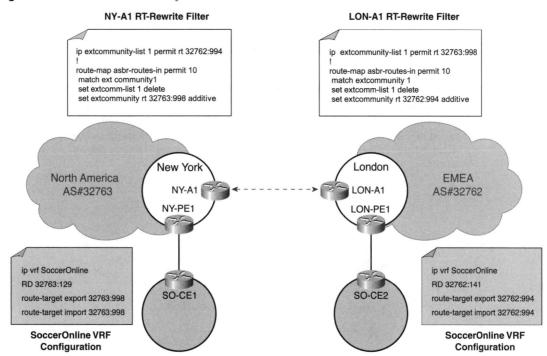

NY-A1 RT-Rewrite Filter

```
ip extcommunity-list 1 permit rt 32762:994
!
route-map asbr-routes-in permit 10
  match ext community1
  set extcomm-list 1 delete
  set extcommunity rt 32763:998 additive
```

LON-A1 RT-Rewrite Filter

```
ip  extcommunity-list 1 permit rt 32763:998
!
route-map asbr-routes-in permit 10
  match extcommunity 1
  set extcomm-list 1 delete
  set extcommunity rt 32762:994 additive
```

North America
AS#32763

New York

NY-A1

NY-PE1

London

LON-A1

LON-PE1

EMEA
AS#32762

SO-CE1

SO-CE2

```
ip vrf SoccerOnline
RD 32763:129
route-target export 32763:998
route-target import 32763:998
```

**SoccerOnline VRF
Configuration**

```
ip vrf SoccerOnline
RD 32762:141
route-target export 32762:994
route-target import 32762:994
```

**SoccerOnline VRF
Configuration**

Connectivity with Regional Service Providers

Globenet has a number of VPNv4 peering agreements with various local Layer 3 MPLS VPN service providers in different parts of the globe. Thus, it can provide seamless VPN services to customers that can be attached through these local operators. Globenet co-locates its equipment with the regional service provider whenever possible and uses Gigabit Ethernet as the preferred connectivity medium. In some cases Frame Relay is used for this purpose.

When assessing the design requirements for these connections, it was clear that they were different from those considered for connectivity between the various Globenet regions. Several issues were identified with the option B and C inter-AS solutions:

- Coordination of RD/RT assignments with regional service providers was considered too complex.

- Security from label spoofing, intrusion, and denial-of-service (DoS) attacks was difficult to achieve with 100 percent accuracy.

- Forwarding is based on the global LFIB rather than a VRF-specific Forwarding Information Base (FIB) and therefore is arguably more open to abuse.

- Exchange of Globenet IP address space would be necessary if inter-AS option C were chosen.

- Certain services such as Multicast and IPv6 are more complex to deploy and require functionality beyond that which is needed within a single Globenet region.

Considering these issues, Globenet chose to deploy option A inter-AS (back-to-back VRFs, as discussed in Chapter 1) for all regional service provider connectivity. This model, although less scalable than the other inter-AS solutions in terms of memory allocation, number of interfaces, and so forth, allows Globenet to easily deploy inter-AS VPNs and overcome the issues introduced by the other solutions. Figure 5-15 shows each of the current peering connections.

Figure 5-15 *Globenet Inter-AS Connectivity with Regional Service Providers*

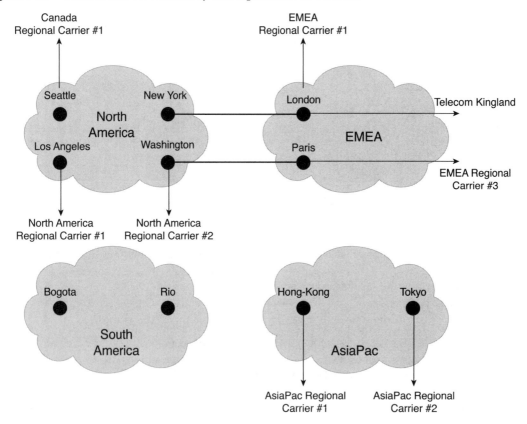

Using this inter-AS option, Globenet can treat all regional service providers as if they are just another VPN client. At the ASBRs, a VRF is enabled for each inter-AS VPN that needs connectivity to the regional service provider. Furthermore, a separate logical interface is required for each VPN. Hence, Gigabit Ethernet and Frame Relay are needed, because both of these technologies provide this functionality through VLANs and PVCs, respectively.

BGP-4 is enabled within each VRF context, and routes are exchanged using this protocol.

The same set of configuration parameters are enabled as used for normal VPN customer VRFs—maximum routes, maximum prefix on the BGP-4 session, and so forth.

Figure 5-16 shows an example of a customer (Candy International) that needs connectivity with Globenet and a regional service provider and how this type of connectivity is used.

Figure 5-16   *Candy International Regional Service Provider Connectivity*

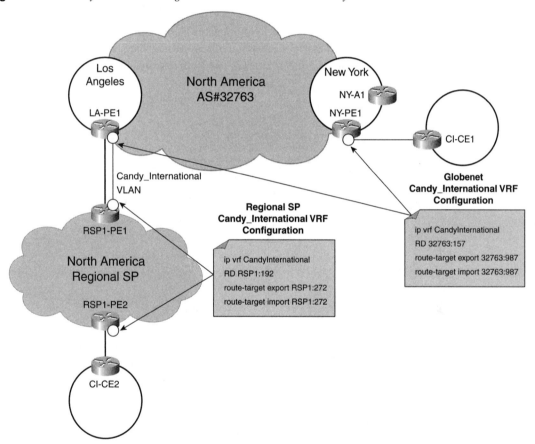

Providing Internet Services to MPLS VPN Customers

Internet access is bundled with Layer 3 MPLS VPN services. Several connectivity options are available, depending on the customer's requirements. Access to Internet services may be obtained via the global routing table at a given Globenet PE router, or it may be via a default route within a specific customer VRF.

Each region in the Globenet worldwide network provides its own Internet access using local peering sessions with other Internet service providers in its region. This means that each region, with the exception of South America, receives an adequate number of routes from its local peering sessions to prevent it from needing any transit services.

Local IPv4 routes received from Globenet customers attached within that region are exchanged across the autonomous system boundaries of the Globenet network. A customer may also get Internet access via its own VRF via a backup default route from other regions. This is leaked across the regional boundaries, but it remains in the customer's VPN context.

Figure 5-17 shows how Internet connectivity is established across the Globenet network. The North America region is used as a transit autonomous system by the South America region. The North America, AsiaPac, and EMEA regions all have direct connectivity between them.

Figure 5-17 *Globenet Worldwide Internet Connectivity*

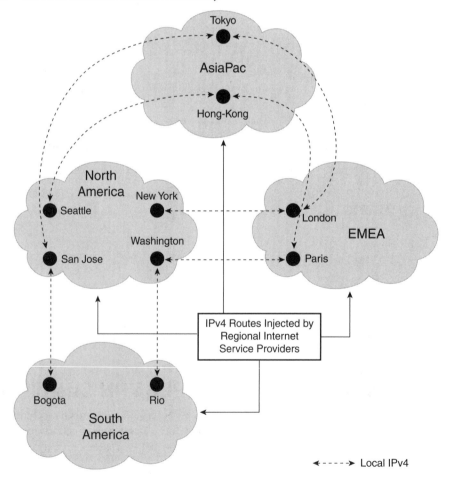

Internet Via the Global or VRF Routing Table

Globenet evaluated whether to carry the Internet routes within the global routing table or within a specific "Internet" VRF.

Carrying routes within a VRF had some attractive properties:

- A higher degree of security is provided without the need to deploy access control lists (ACLs). This is because all outside access (except routing protocols) to the PE router from attached customer sites (such as Telnet, Simple Network Management Protocol (SNMP), and so forth) is disabled by default in a VRF.

- The core infrastructure is totally isolated and therefore protected from outside intrusion. Furthermore, the edge of the network is also protected from outside intrusion because routes cannot be leaked from a VRF into the global routing table unless explicitly configured.

However, a number of disadvantages were also noted:

- Scaling properties are at best a challenge if both Internet and Layer 3 MPLS VPN services are needed at the PE router. Scaling at the PE router is a challenge because of the large number of IPv4 routes that become VPNv4 routes (because they are included in a VRF) and therefore consume more resources such as memory and label space. This leaves little room for additional Layer 3 MPLS VPN attachments on Globenet's older router platforms.

- All current and future IP features necessary for Internet traffic need to be supported on a per-VRF basis; in other words, they need to be "VRF-aware."

Consequently, Globenet decided to deploy Internet within the global table and apply the right filters at the edge of its network to help mitigate the risk of intrusion or DoS attacks.

Internet Access Following the Default Route

As mentioned earlier, the typical profile of a customer accessing Globenet Layer 3 MPLS VPN services involves large corporations that have a presence in various regions around the world. These types of customers have tended to follow a hub-and-spoke configuration in the past. This means that they have several central sites/data centers scattered across various regions and a large number of satellite premises.

For VPN connectivity, the any-to-any nature of a Layer 3 MPLS VPN service is very attractive, especially for applications such as voice over IP (VoIP). However, for Internet service it is still typical to access the full set of Internet routes at the central sites and just follow a default route from the satellite sites toward the central site. The central site normally houses Network Address Translation (NAT), caching, and firewall services for the corporation.

A default route may be injected into a particular VPN in a number of ways. In some cases the VPN client receives Internet connectivity from an ISP other than Globenet. In this case the default is advertised as part of the routing information within the VPN context, and therefore to all attached sites in the VPN. This is independent of the Internet services that Globenet provides. The only service Globenet provides to this type of customer is VPN connectivity.

If Globenet provides the Internet access, the customer has various options. The easiest type of access to deal with is the case in which the end customer has registered IP address space or provides its own NAT/firewall services. In this case Globenet doesn't need to provide NAT or firewall services; it only needs to generate a default route for these customers. Figure 5-18 shows a typical topology for this type of customer.

Figure 5-18   *Internet Access Via the Default Route Generated from the Customer Hub Site*

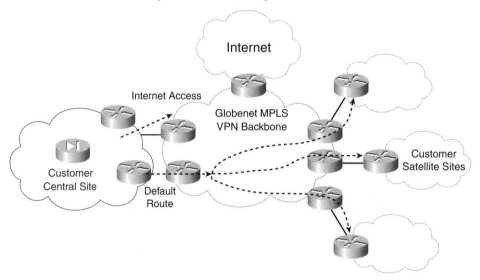

Figure 5-18 shows that the customer central site, from where Internet access is obtained, generates a default route to the VPN. This default is advertised across the Globenet network for import into the VRFs of remote satellite sites. If Globenet manages the customer CE router, it generates a default route on the central site CE router. It points a static route toward the customer's firewall (which typically resides on a local LAN) and uses the **default-information originate** command within the customer BGP process that faces the Globenet PE router. If the CE router is unmanaged, either the customer generates the default from the CE router, or Globenet generates it from within the VRF at the PE router.

If a customer does not use a central location to provide access to the Internet, and if the customer uses registered IP address space, Globenet provides the facility to access the Internet via one of its Internet gateways using a default route injected into the customer VPN at the PE router closest to this Internet gateway. Figure 5-19 shows an example of this type of connectivity.

Figure 5-19   *Internet Access Via the Default Route Generated from the Globenet Exit Point*

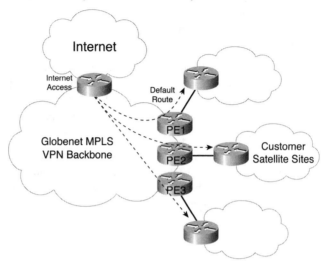

Globenet uses the template shown in Example 5-4 to generate a static default route into the customer VRF at the PE router close to one of the Internet exit points.

Example 5-4   *Static Default Route Template*

```
ip route vrf customer-vrf-name 0.0.0.0 0.0.0.0 Internet-exit-point-IP-address global
ip route customer-site-IP-addresses netmask outbound-interface-address
```

Example 5-4 shows that a default is injected into the customer VRF (configured on PE1, PE2, and PE3 in Figure 5-19) with a next hop pointing toward one of the Globenet Internet exit points. The **global** keyword is used on the static route configuration to indicate that the next hop for this route is held in the PE router's global routing table rather than the VRF itself. The second static route points to a route held within the attached customer site. This configuration is necessary so that these IP subnet addresses can be advertised toward the Internet so that return traffic can be routed back toward the originating VPN site.

Full Internet Access Via the PE-CE Access Link

Globenet also provides Internet services to customers that need to announce and receive routes directly to and from the Internet. An example of this type of customer is one that requires dual attachment with the Internet.

Globenet assessed the possibility of injecting Internet routes into each customer VRF, which requires Internet access. However, this solution was quickly rejected. With more than 150,000 Internet routes injected into each VRF requiring Internet access, it was clear that this was not a scalable solution and that Globenet would very quickly run out of memory at the PE routers.

Instead, Globenet decided to advertise Internet routes to all its P routers in the core network and to any PE routers that require Internet routes. (In other words, Globenet has Internet clients attached, which is not true of all PE routers.) These routes are held in the global routing table of the P/PE routers.

As the Internet routes are held in the global routing table, a separate connection must be provided to each VPN site that wants to advertise and receive Internet routes to and from the PE router. This additional connection is often provided via a Frame Relay PVC between the PE router and CE router. This means that each VPN site (that wants to obtain partial or full Internet routes) has two Frame Relay PVCs—one for the VPN service and another for the Internet service.

The PE router is configured to redistribute Internet routes toward the customer CE routers via a BGP-4 session. Conversely, any BGP-4 routes received from an attached CE router are injected into the global routing table at the PE router and are advertised toward the Internet using the IPv4 address family. Figure 5-20 illustrates this solution.

Figure 5-20   *Full Internet Route Access Between PE/CE Routers*

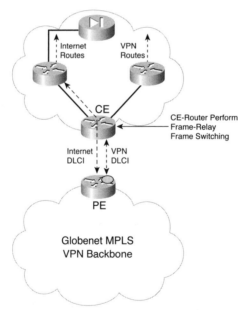

Figure 5-20 shows that the customer CE router can terminate the VPN Frame Relay PVC directly but use frame-switching functionality to offload the Internet PVC to another router in the site. This router then can inject Internet routes into the site via a firewall so that all Internet traffic from the site travels via the firewall and over the Internet PVC to the PE router. This PVC is terminated in the PE router's global table; therefore, the PE router can forward the traffic as normal. The VPN PVC is terminated within a VRF, and the PE router uses the MPLS VPN forwarding mechanisms for any packets received across this connection.

Internet Access Via Globenet NAT/Firewall Services

The entire Internet solution set described so far relies on the end customer providing its own NAT/firewall services. However, many of Globenet's customers do not want to run their own cache engines, firewalls, and NAT services. Instead, they want to obtain these from Globenet.

Globenet provides these services at common gateway points within the Type 1 POPs in each region. Figure 5-21 shows the POP structure.

Figure 5-21   *Type 1 POP Internet with NAT/Firewall/Cache Facilities*

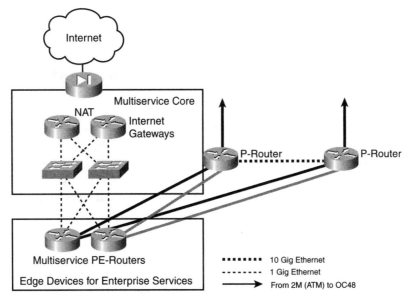

Each Internet gateway generates a default route that is imported into every subscribing customer VRF. To that end, the default route is carried within an "Internet" VRF whose export route target is imported by subscribing customers into their local VRFs. Conversely, corresponding customer routes are imported into the Internet VRF and are advertised toward the Internet for reverse traffic forwarding.

At an incoming PE router, for traffic that does not match an intranet destination in the customer VRF, the default route is followed toward the Internet gateway. This gateway is configured to perform NAT to translate the customer address space to a registered address from an available pool of IP addresses. The packet is then passed through the Globenet cache engine(s) and firewall. Globenet has several Internet gateways so that if it has customers that use the same address space, it can perform NAT translation via different gateways so as not to create a clash between VPN clients.

mVPN Service Design

Globenet provides an intra-AS multicast VPN (mVPN) service. The details are similar to those discussed in the preceding chapter, including the use of Protocol-Independent Multicast Sparse Mode (PIM SM) in the core and Protocol-Independent Multicast Source-Specific Multicast (PIM SSM) at the edge. However, because Globenet caters to large international enterprises, this service may extend across two or more of its regional networks. The implications of this are that the service needs to operate within an inter-AS environment. Currently Globenet has no requirements to run an mVPN service with any of its regional service provider partners.

As mentioned earlier, Globenet chose to use option B for inter-AS connectivity between all its worldwide regions. This model requires the exchange of VPNv4 routes directly between ASBRs. A number of observations may be made with this type of connection:

- **MP-BGP next-hop rewrite**—Because each connection between ASBRs is an external MP-BGP session, every route's next hop is rewritten to the ASBR interface address that is used for the session source.

- **Receiving ASBR next-hop rewrite**—A receiving ASBR may or may not rewrite the next-hop IP address. This is achieved by configuring next-hop-self at the receiving router.

- **Original next-hop IP addresses are unavailable to the receiving autonomous system**—IGP routes are not exchanged between different autonomous systems. Therefore, the original PE router next-hop addresses cannot be reached from an adjacent region.

These observations introduce a number of problems when extending mVPN service between different autonomous systems:

- **The default multicast distribution tree (MDT) for each inter-AS mVPN cannot be established**—The default MDT relies on the ability of the PE routers to join the default Multicast group. The source of the group is the originating PE router address used for MP-BGP peering. This address cannot be reached between regions because no IGP routes are distributed across autonomous systems.

- **Reverse Path Forwarding (RPF) checks fail on P routers**—When a PE router sends a PIM join {PE router source, MDT group} for the default MDT, each P router in the path between the source and destination PE routers must perform an RPF check on the source. Because IGP routes (such as PE router source addresses) are not leaked across autonomous systems, the receiving regional P routers are unable to perform an RPF check.

- **RPF checks at adjacent-region PE routers fail**—When a PIM join is received in an mVPN, an IP lookup is performed in the VRF to find the next hop toward the destination. This destination must be a PIM neighbor that can be reached via the MDT tunnel interface. However, because the ASBRs change the next hop of the originating PE router for a given MDT group, the originating source address is lost, and the RPF check at the PE router cannot succeed.

Because of these issues, the mVPN solution needs to be modified to work with inter-AS option B.

MP-BGP Support of Inter-AS mVPN

The intra-AS mVPN solution deployed by Globenet originally provided the ability to learn the source address of a given MDT tunnel through a VPNv4 routing update. This update was of the format {2:RD:PE-router-loopback-address} and was carried in an extended community attribute with the MDT group address for each locally attached mVRF. This solution worked within the intranet of each region in the global network. However, because the extended community attribute was nontransitive, MP-BGP was unable to advertise the route across autonomous system boundaries. This prevented Globenet from extending its mVPN solution across different regions.

To overcome this issue, Globenet chose to introduce a solution [MDT-SAFI] that defined a new subaddress family (SAFI) that carries the address of the source PE router to which a join should be sent for the MDT group contained in the PIM join. The format of the NLRI carried in this SAFI is {RD:PE-IP-address}. Each MDT group is carried in the MP_REACH attribute using the format shown in Figure 5-22.

Figure 5-22 *MDT SAFI*

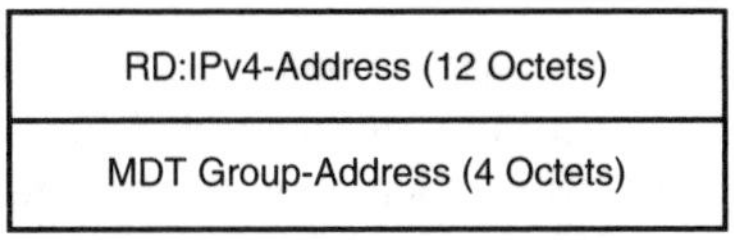

RD:IPv4-Address (12 Octets)
MDT Group-Address (4 Octets)

RD: Route-Distinguisher of the VRF to which the MDT attribute belongs.

IPv4-address: IP-v4 address of the originating PE-router.

MDT Group-address: Group-address of the MDT-group that a given VRF is associated with.

In an adjacent autonomous system, a PE router that wants to join a particular source of the default MDT for a given mVPN must know the originator's address of the source PE router. As previously discussed, this presents some issues because the originator next hop for VPNv4 routes is rewritten at one or more points in the network. Therefore, each VPNv4 route that is originated by the PE routers in each autonomous system must carry a new attribute (the connector) that defines the route's originator. The format of this attribute is shown in Figure 5-23.

Figure 5-23 *Connector Attribute Format*

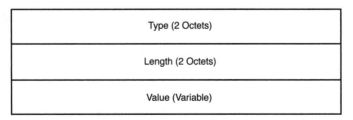

Type (2 Octets)
Length (2 Octets)
Value (Variable)

Type is the Type of the data contained in this TLV.
Length is the Length of the Value portion in the TLV.
Value is a variable length field defined by the AFI/SAFI carried in this tuple, which would be used by the AFI/SAFI in this tuple.

When the connector attribute is used for the inter-AS mVPN solution, the type is set to a value of 1, the length of the value field is set to 4, and the value field contains the IPv4 address of the originating PE router.

To support this new functionality, Globenet added the new SAFI to all PE routers, route reflectors, and ASBRs that need to support inter-AS mVPN functionality. This configuration is added using the template shown in Example 5-5.

Example 5-5 *Inter-AS mVPN SAFI Template*

```
router bgp 32763
 neighbor remote-PE/ASBR/RR-address remote-as 32763
 neighbor remote-PE/ASBR/RR-address source-update loopback0
 !
 address-family ipv4 mdt
 neighbor remote-PE/ASBR/RR-address activate
 neighbor remote-PE/ASBR/RR-address send-community extended
```

Establishing mVPN MDT Groups Between Globenet Regions

As already established, normally PIM sends join messages containing the IP address of upstream PE router(s) that is/are sources of a given MDT group. To be able to perform RPF checks, IPv4 reachability to the PE router in another autonomous system must be available to the P routers. This is not the case with option B inter-AS because the autonomous systems do not exchange any of their IGP routes, including those of their local PE routers. However, the P routers do have reachability to the BGP next hop of the BGP MDT update received within the MDT SAFI at the PE routers. Therefore, if the PE routers add the remote PE router IP address (as received within the MDT SAFI) and the BGP next-hop address of this address within the PIM join, the P routers can perform an RPF check on the BGP next-hop address rather than the original PE router address. This allows the P router to forward the join toward the ASBR that injected the MDT SAFI updates for an adjacent autonomous system. This functionality is called *RPF vector*.

Having received the join, an ASBR can determine that the next-hop address is in fact itself. Having determined this, the ASBR performs an RPF check based on the originating PE router address carried in the join.

Inter-AS mVPN System Flow

Having established the technical additions to allow mVPN to extend across autonomous system boundaries, this section provides an end-to-end flow (using the Globenet North America and EMEA regions) to help solidify the concepts.

Figure 5-24 shows a PE router (NY-PE1) in the Globenet New York POP and a PE router (LON-PE1) in the London POP. Both of these run the same mVPN instance (m1), whose default MDT is y1.

Figure 5-24   *Globenet Inter-AS mVPN Example*

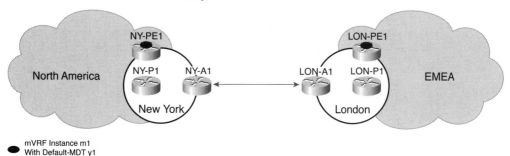

mVRF Instance m1
With Default-MDT y1

Using the sample topology shown in Figure 5-24, the following sequence of events occurs to establish mVPN connectivity between NY-PE1 and LON-PE1:

1   NY-PE1 advertises the default MDT information for the m1 mVPN instance using the MDT SAFI. This information has the format {RD1, NY-PE1, y1} with a next hop of NY-PE1.

2   NY-A1 receives {RD1, NY-PE1, y1} and advertises this information to LON-A1 with a next hop of NY-A1.

3   LON-A1 advertises {RD1, NY-PE1, y1} to LON-PE1 with itself as the next hop.

4   LON-PE1 does not have reachability to NY-PE1 but does have reachability to LON-A1.

5   LON-PE1 sends a join using the RPF vector mechanism mentioned previously to {LON-A1, NY-PE1, y1} via LON-P1.

6   LON-P1 performs an RPF check on LON-A1 and forwards the join to LON-A1.

7   LON-A1 removes the vector LON-A1 and performs an RPF check on NY-PE1. Then it sends the join to {NY-PE1, y1} via NY-A1. (These steps also happen in the reverse order.) At this point an MDT tunnel interface between NY-PE1 and LON-PE1 is successfully established.

MPLS VPN Security and Scalability

While designing its MPLS VPN service, Globenet recognized that security was a fundamental requirement that must be met to protect its network infrastructure and its customers' network facilities.

It was clear that the decision to use MPLS as the service-enabling technology provided a number of inherent security capabilities that were built into the technology from its inception:

●   **IP address space and routing separation**—The use of a route distinguisher enables uniqueness of IP addresses in the core of the Globenet network, and the use of VRFs and routing contexts provides routing separation.

- **No visibility of the core network**—This is enabled using the command **no mpls ip propagate-ttl forwarded**.

- **Resistance to MPLS label spoofing**—The default behavior of an incoming IP interface (such as the PE-CE links) is to drop packets that carry MPLS labels.

Although these capabilities provide basic security protection, intrusion or DoS attacks may be possible in a number of other areas. For example, even though the core IP addressing is hidden from attached customers, the same cannot be guaranteed for the subnet used on the PE-CE link. Visibility of this link address might allow an attached customer to intrude or perform a DoS attack on the PE router. For this reason, Globenet does not redistribute the PE-CE link addresses at the CE router into the IGP of a managed customer. For unmanaged customers, the default configuration is to disable the redistribution of connected interfaces (such as the PE-CE link) into MP-BGP for advertisement to other sites of the VPN. For customers that want to receive these addresses, Globenet makes sure that their inbound packet filters at the PE routers are updated to deny the local PE router addresses. (Filters are discussed later in this section.)

To help identify all the areas that should be addressed in the MPLS network design, Globenet broke the problem into the following three functional areas:

- Operational security
- Control plane protection
- Data plane protection

VPN Operational Security

Operational security may be defined as the steps necessary to protect unwelcome or unauthorized access to the Globenet network resources (such as routers and servers) and the blocking of service exploitation (such as DoS attacks).

Globenet evaluated all the services and protocols it uses at its routers. It noticed that a number of the default configuration settings were enabled for services or protocols it did not actually use in production. Using this information, Globenet built a configuration template to disable all the services and protocols that were deemed unnecessary. This template is shown in Example 5-6.

Example 5-6 *Configuration Template to Disable Unused Services and Protocols*

```
no service pad
no ip source-route
no ip bootp server
!
interface interface
 no ip redirects
 no ip directed broadcast
 no ip unreachables
 no ip proxy-arp
!
no ip http server
!
no cdp run
```

NOTE   Disabling IP unreachables is advisable, because a worm may attempt to send packets to random IP addresses, some of which may not exist. When that occurs, the router replies with an "ICMP unreachable" packet. In some cases, replying to a large number of requests with invalid IP addresses may result in degradation of the router's performance. An alternative option is to restrict the number of IP unreachables using the command **ip icmp rate-limit unreachable**.

A number of other services are enabled on all routers. These are used to enhance troubleshooting effectiveness and fault isolation, restrict access to the routers, and provide authentication/authorization of users. The configuration template shown in Example 5-7 enables these services.

Example 5-7   *Configuration Template to Enable Various Security Services*

```
service password-encryption
!
aaa new-model
aaa authentication login default group tacacs+
enable secret password
!
ip ftp username username
ip ftp password password
ip domain-name Globenet.com
exception protocol ftp
exception dump ftp-server-IP-address
!
logging source-interface loopback0
logging syslog-server-IP-address
access-list 20 remark SNMP ACL
access-list 20 permit snmp-host
access-list 20 deny any log
!
tacacs-server host Globenet-tacacs-server-IP-address
tacacs-server key key
!
snmp-server community community RO 20
line vty 0 4
 transport input ssh
 login tacacs
```

NOTE   [MPLS-Security] provides a more detailed analysis of security for MPLS-based VPNs and also a set of best-practice guidelines.

NOTE   SSH provides an encrypted channel between a remote console and a network router. If SSH is enabled on a router, Telnet access can be disabled to force all administrative sessions to run over the encrypted channel that SSH provides. In this case, attackers cannot find open Telnet ports.

VPN Control Plane Protection

Control plane security may be defined as the steps necessary to protect and authenticate the distribution of routing and forwarding information within the Globenet network.

Globenet deploys a number of control plane protection mechanisms. You saw in Chapter 3, "Interexchange Carrier Design Study," the use of the **maximum routes** command within VRFs. This command is enabled on all Globenet PE routers. It is set to a customer-specific value with a warning threshold set to 75 percent of the route maximum. In addition to this basic protection scheme, Globenet also restricts the number of routes at the routing protocol level.

You saw in Chapter 4 how to achieve protection from the OSPF protocol in terms of restricting the maximum number of LSAs that a particular process may receive. Globenet uses these protection mechanisms whenever it deploys an OSPF customer. In addition, it uses the **maximum-prefix** command on a per-session basis for BGP-4 and on a per-process basis for EIGRP.

RIPv2 does not require any additional configuration. The Routing Information Protocol (RIP) database will be populated only by routes that are present in the VRF. Because these are restricted based on the **maximum routes** command, the RIP database population is also limited.

Globenet also extensively deploys neighbor authentication for routing protocols. Neighbor authentication allows a receiving router to authenticate the source of the routing update using a shared key that only it and the neighboring router know. Globenet chose to use MD5 authentication so that the authentication key was not carried between routers. MD5 provides the ability to create a message digest by using the key and the message as a hash to MD5. This prevents its routers from receiving unauthorized updates from a routing peer. Globenet also uses this mechanism to verify updates it receives from label distribution peers.

Globenet enables routing authentication in three different segments of the network: PE-CE, PE-PE, and PE-P/P-P/P-PE. [MPLS-VPN-Vol2] provides details of how MD5 authentication works with RIPv2, EIGRP, OSPF, and BGP-4, and LDP.

VPN Data Plane Protection

Data plane protection is concerned with protecting packets that are forwarded across the network. Because the majority of Globenet customers use its managed service, Globenet decided to deploy access list filters at the CE routers. These filters protect the Globenet infrastructure, including the ASBRs, P routers, PE routers, and CE routers.

The filter is applied at the CE routers on ingress from the attached customer site and performs the actions listed next. The configuration template used to apply this policy is shown in Example 5-8; it does the following:

- It prevents the redistribution of the PE-CE link subnet into the attached customer site.

- It prevents ICMP traffic from the CE router toward the PE router except for a designated address (which is the outbound interface address used by the CE router for connectivity with the PE router). This address cannot be reached from the attached customer site and belongs to the Globenet address space.

- It allows only the BGP-4 protocol (in this case) to run on the PE-CE link. This is achieved by denying routing updates from any other routing protocol.

- It blocks any traffic addressed toward the Globenet backbone.

- It allows site-to-site traffic to flow.

Example 5-8   *Configuration Template for PE-CE Data Plane Protection*

```
ip access-list extended Globenet-CE-filter
 permit icmp host CE-interface-address host PE-interface-address
 permit tcp host CE-interface-address host PE-interface-address eq bgp
 deny ip any Globenet-backbone-addresses
 permit ip any any
```

Scaling and Convergence of the Layer 3 MPLS VPN Service

Globenet investigated what elements would affect the overall scaling of the MPLS VPN service. Although many factors were identified, the main concerns fell into the following broad categories:

- Control plane design
- Edge router capabilities

The control plane design covers all elements of routing and forwarding, including interior routing protocols, exterior routing protocols, label distribution protocols, and so forth. The Layer 3 MPLS VPN service incorporates all these elements and therefore is subject to the scaling limits of each. Many questions and areas of discussion arise when evaluating the scaling properties of each protocol, but in terms of the Layer 3 MPLS VPN service, Globenet was primarily concerned with the following:

- How do the various protocols interact, and how large can each grow? For example, what factors will increase the network deployment size?

- Because MP-BGP is used as the major routing distribution protocol in the backbone network, how many sessions can be successfully deployed? Are tools required to increase the protocol's scalability?

- Because BGP-4 is used at the edge of the network, and MP-BGP is used in the core, do these need to be tuned for optimal performance?

- How is routing and forwarding convergence affected from customer site to customer site when compared to an intranet built over a Frame Relay network?

Protocol Interaction

Globenet deploys a number of protocols to support its service portfolio, including RSVP, LDP, IS-IS, and MP-BGP. Clearly the interaction between these protocols is an important consideration.

IGP-LDP synchronization functionality is deployed (this was discussed in the preceding chapter) to ensure appropriate synchronization between LDP and IS-IS in case of topology changes. Tuning the IS-IS protocol for fast convergence is also deployed. This is described in the section "IS-IS Routing Design."

MP-BGP Scaling Considerations

All the MP-BGP features (and their tuning) that you have seen described in previous chapters are deployed on the Globenet network. These include update groups, route reflectors, path maximum transmission unit (MTU) discovery, hold queue tuning, Selective Packet Discard (SPD) queue optimization, and so on.

The route reflector design is also the same model described in previous chapters. It consists of a single level of hierarchy in each autonomous system (rather than a more-complex multihierarchy design, which would be unnecessary given the current amount of routing state for Globenet's Layer 3 MPLS VPN service). PE routers are required to maintain an MP-BGP session with at least two separate route reflectors, and all route reflectors are fully meshed. Any routes that need to cross autonomous system boundaries are held by the ASBRs.

In addition to the route reflector design described, Globenet chose to attempt to restrict VPNv4 routes from reaching the parts of its network where no customer sites were attached with interest in the said routes. For example, in the North America region, Globenet has several customers that are local to the California region. Therefore, distribution of their routes to the route reflectors in the East Coast region is unnecessary. This is illustrated in Figure 5-25.

You can see from this figure that California has local routes, as does New York. Because the route reflectors are fully meshed, and it is assumed that no filtering was adopted, all sets of route reflectors hold all the California and New York VPNv4 routes. Given this, Globenet chose to deploy enhanced route filtering, as described in [rt-constrain], to restrict distribution of routes based on extended community attributes.

Figure 5-25   *Regional Customer Attachment Example*

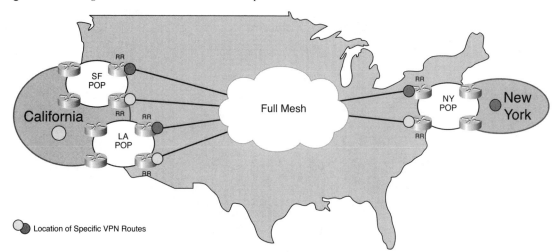

Location of Specific VPN Routes

[rt-constrain] provides a new SAFI (RT filter) that is used to advertise the route target extended community attributes used at the PE routers for import/export policy. For example, consider Figure 5-26. Globenet has a customer called ABC Inc. in California and another customer called XYZ Inc. in New York. Each PE router advertises the route target values used by these VPNs to the route reflectors using the RT filter SAFI. Using this information, the route reflectors can filter the advertisement of the routes to unnecessary regions of the network.

Figure 5-26   *RT Filtering for ABC Inc. and XYZ Inc.*

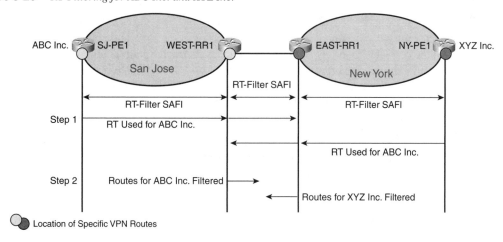

Location of Specific VPN Routes

As illustrated in Figure 5-27, this filtering results in the route reflectors in California not storing the routes that are used only on the East Coast. Likewise, the route reflector in New York doesn't store the routes that are used only in California.

Figure 5-27 *Regional Customer Attachment with RT Filtering*

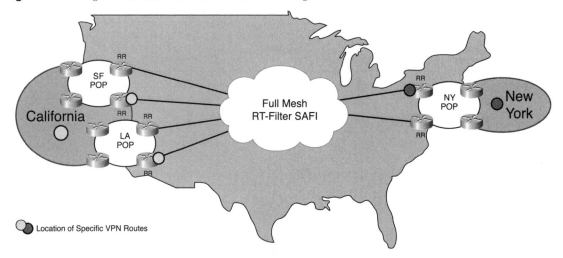

In the case of ASBRs that have no VRFs configured, an extended community list filter may be used to generate the updates to the RT filter SAFI.

Globenet Routing Convergence Strategy

Convergence can be defined as the time taken for routers in a particular routing domain to learn about the complete topology and to recompute an alternative path (assuming that one exists) to a particular destination after a network change has occurred. This process involves the routers adapting to these changes by synchronizing their view of the network with other routers in the same domain. Because Globenet uses a number of protocols that all interact, it was important within the design to define a routing convergence strategy that covered both its backbone and its services' convergence.

Broadly speaking, convergence may be split into two subcategories:

- **Convergence of the internal infrastructure**—This category includes backbone IGP convergence and MP-BGP control plane convergence.

- **Convergence of external services**—This category includes convergence of routing information between external customer sites, such as between sites using the Layer 3 MPLS VPN service.

Globenet identified that the convergence of its backbone network was dependent on which protection mechanisms it deployed at different layers. The strategy chosen was to combine MPLS fast reroute and fast IGP convergence, as detailed in the "Network Recovery Design" section later in this chapter.

Layer 3 MPLS VPN Service—Routing Convergence

The Layer 3 MPLS VPN architecture uses the services of BGP (with multiprotocol extensions) to distribute VPN routing information between the edges of the network. BGP was essentially invented to solve a route distribution problem in a very scalable manner and to provide a mechanism to achieve a loop-free routing topology. Because of its distance vector-like behavior, and the features implemented to provide stability, BGP by its very nature does not converge as quickly as a link-state IGP. Interaction between MP-BGP and the IGP can have a significant effect on routing convergence. For this reason, additional implementation timers have been added to speed up the default routing convergence times. These timers may be adjusted to provide an optimal deployment of a Layer 3 MPLS VPN service.

From a backbone network perspective, Globenet tunes its IS-IS timers to gain subsecond IGP convergence. However, because the Layer 3 MPLS VPN service relies heavily on the MP-BGP protocol for route distribution, subsecond IGP convergence is insufficient to ensure fast failure detection affecting a set of VPN routes. Instead, next-hop reachability of all routes is checked, by default, every 60 seconds (this is driven in IOS by the "scanner" process and is a configurable timer). If a particular link fails in the backbone network, the IGP can detect this very quickly. However, the MP-BGP process may take up to 60 seconds to determine that a given next hop is no longer available. Therefore, the routes previously learned via that next hop are invalid. For this reason, Globenet chose to deploy the next-hop tracking (NHT) feature on all its PE routers.

The NHT feature is enabled by default in the IOS version deployed at the Globenet PE routers. It allows MP-BGP to register next-hop addresses (PE router loopback interface addresses) for MP-BGP routes with the RIB Address Tracking Filter (ATF) feature. This feature provides an efficient routing update notification service and monitors all route changes in the PE router's Routing Information Base (RIB). When a route changes in some way (for example, it becomes unreachable, or the metric changes) the ATF immediately notifies MP-BGP so that it has current routing information and therefore can react to the change. If a next hop for a given set of VPNv4 routes changes, the router can react immediately rather than waiting for the periodic "scanner" process as previously described.

Although backbone convergence clearly was important, Globenet noted that it needed to define convergence characteristics of its Layer 3 MPLS VPN service from its customers' point of view. It defined this as site-to-site convergence. To this end, it wanted to make sure that convergence times (in terms of route distribution from customer site to remote customer site(s)) were as close as possible to those obtained by the customer when Globenet was using its previous Layer 2 overlay technology. To achieve this goal, Globenet realized that a certain amount of protocol tuning would be necessary, primarily within MP-BGP.

To understand each of the components of the overall site-to-site convergence time, Globenet analyzed in the laboratory how a routing update was sent from one site to another (including new and withdrawn routes). Using this information, Globenet defined eight individual convergence points in the total end-to-end convergence time. These are illustrated in Figure 5-28, as highlighted by T1 through T8.

Figure 5-28   *MPLS VPN Service Convergence Points*

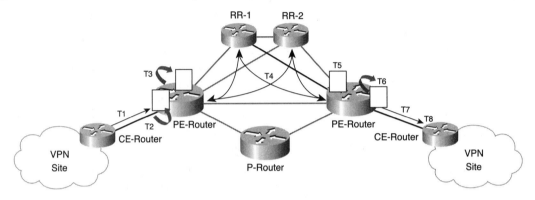

These are defined as follows:

- **Convergence point T1**—PE router receipt of a routing update from an attached customer site.

  This convergence point is very dependent on the routing protocol used on the PE-CE link. However, the most noticeable figure relates to the case in which BGP-4 is used on the PE-CE link because it relies on a timer to advertise routes, the maximum value of which is 30 seconds.

- **Convergence point T2**—Import of local routing information received at point T1 into the corresponding ingress VRF(s).

  This value is typically close to 0, except in the case of OSPF where an SPF-delay timer is used, the default of which is 5 seconds.

- **Convergence point T3**—Receipt of local routes received at point T1 into MP-BGP on the local PE router.

  This value is always close to 0 because routes are placed into MP-BGP immediately on receipt.

- **Convergence point T4**—Advertisement of newly inserted VPNv4 routes to MP-BGP peers (the Globenet route reflectors).

  This convergence point is driven by the MP-BGP advertisement-interval timer for internal BGP. By default it is 5 seconds, although this timer is initiated only when an update is sent. Therefore, if no updates have been sent in the last 5 seconds preceding the receipt of another route, the update for this route is sent immediately. Because Globenet deploys VPNv4 route reflectors, this timer is always 10 seconds. Convergence point T4 is relevant to the initial PE router that first advertises a route plus the route reflector that subsequently advertises it between the edge of the network.

- **Convergence point T5**—Processing of advertised VPNv4 routes from point T4 on a remote PE router.

  MP-BGP updates are processed immediately; therefore, this convergence point is always close to 0.

- **Convergence point T6**—Import of newly received routes at point T5 into local VRF(s).

  In IOS the PE router runs a timer called the import scanner every 15 seconds by default (although this can be configured). This timer is not applied in case of route withdrawals because these are processed immediately, or for next-hop accessibility checks. However, it is relevant in terms of when newly received routes are imported into interested local VRFs.

- **Convergence point T7**—Advertisement of routes received from the MPLS backbone to CE routers.

  The value of this convergence point is the same as for T1. Assuming that the Globenet customer uses BGP-4 on the PE-CE link, it uses the same advertisement interval default of 30 seconds in BGP-4.

- **Convergence point T8**—Processing of incoming updates by the relevant attached CE router(s).

  Generally this is close to 0 except in the case of OSPF on the PE-CE link, which uses an SPF-delay timer with a default of 5 seconds.

Using these convergence points, Globenet determined that the default theoretical convergence times, depending on the PE-CE protocols, were as detailed in Table 5-3.

Table 5-3   *MPLS VPN Convergence Times Depending on the PE-CE Protocol*

Static	BGP-4	OSPF	EIGRP	RIPv2
25 seconds	85 seconds	35 seconds	25 seconds	85 seconds

These convergence times were clearly the worst-case figures and therefore were likely to be substantially lower in practice. They were also based on intra-AS connectivity. If the routing information needed to cross AS boundaries, these times would increase based on the additional BGP-4 convergence. However, Globenet felt that some parameter tuning was necessary to reduce these figures, especially in the case of external BGP on the PE-CE links.

Having decided to tune protocol timers, Globenet realized that the values set would depend on a number of factors (such as the number of routes, total number of VRFs, total number of BGP-4 sessions, and so on) because of their potential processing impact. Globenet also realized that careful validation of the settings was necessary. After various lab tests, Globenet noted that the biggest gains in terms of convergence time reduction could be obtained by tuning the operation of the BGP protocol, both within the backbone network and on the PE-CE links (assuming that BGP-4 was in operation on these links).

Tuning the BGP Protocol

The main delay in route convergence with the BGP protocol is the time taken to advertise a new or deleted VPN route. This time is primarily driven by the *advertisement interval* timer. This is set by default to 5 seconds for internal BGP (convergence point T4) and 30 seconds for external BGP (convergence points T1 and T7).

Globenet chose to reduce the internal BGP timer to 1 second and the external BGP timer to 5 seconds. These new timer values allow routes to be distributed across the backbone network more quickly. They also provide a small delay for the advertisement of these routes to external peers to allow a certain amount of packing of routes into the updates.

Using these new timer values, Globenet was able to drop the theoretical maximum convergence time (when BGP-4 is used on the PE-CE links) to 27 seconds. (This is the default theoretical maximum of 85 seconds minus twice a 4-second saving for internal BGP and twice a 25-second saving for external BGP.) This time is more inline with the other routing protocols. Globenet monitors the routers' available resources on a regular basis to make sure that these new timer values do not negatively affect its routers' scalability.

Edge Router Capabilities

Clearly the edge router capabilities are a major factor in scaling the Layer 3 MPLS VPN service. The main components that drive the edge router's scalability are processing power and available memory space.

When reviewing the CPU and memory characteristics, Globenet noted several points that affected the overall scale. In general, it found that CPU usage is driven by a number of factors, including (but not limited to) the following:

- **Amount of provisioned QoS**—Some PE router platforms deployed by Globenet use hardware forwarding, and some do not. For the ones that do, the route processor CPU is unaffected by QoS features. However, on the PE router platforms that are unable to perform hardware-based forwarding, the number and complexity of QoS features activated can significantly affect the route processor CPU. Therefore, these features need careful consideration before deployment. As discussed in the "Quality of Service Design" section, Globenet minimized the QoS features to be supported on the PE routers in the following ways:

In the case of managed CE routers, the classification, marking, and policing functions are currently entirely performed by the CE router's completely offloading this task from the PE router. This greatly facilitates scaling. It is much easier for each CE router to support the QoS functions relevant to a single site than for a PE router to support the QoS function for all the sites attached to it.

Globenet chose a DSCP/EXP value scheme such that EXP values get automatically marked correctly based on the Differentiated Services Codepoint (DSCP) values via the IOS default mapping so that no DSCP-to-EXP mapping needs to be performed by the PE router.

In the case of unmanaged CE routers, a relatively light input policy is applied because traffic classification doesn't involve any fancy packet inspection and is based only on the DSCP field.

In a nutshell, Globenet ensured that the QoS features on the input side have no, or minimal, impact on the PE router performance. Hence, the QoS features to be considered for PE router performance impact are primarily the ones related to scheduling on the egress (when forwarding packets onto the PE-CE link). These features really cannot be avoided, because they are essential to the enforcement of Globenet's five classes of service over this congestion point. They also have been designed as light as possible because they also only rely on DSCP-based classification.

- **"Managed" or "unmanaged" service**—For customers that use the "managed" service (they have managed CE routers), the CPU requirement may be distributed between the PE router and the attached CE routers, as just discussed for the specific aspect of QoS. This helps scale the overall system to a greater extent. This is not possible for unmanaged CEs.

- **PE-CE protocol connectivity type**—Each routing protocol has different requirements and therefore needs more or fewer processing cycles. For example, OSPF requires the processing of initial LSA generation but may remain relatively quiet assuming no routing changes, except for database refresh every 30 minutes. In contrast, RIP sends periodic updates at regular intervals.

- **Number of attached VPNs and associated VRFs**—Clearly the number of VRFs at the PE router drives CPU requirements because the amount of routing information to be processed and stored increases with the number of VRFs.

From a memory perspective, Globenet noted that the amount of memory required at the PE router increases based on the following:

- **Number of VRFs/routes**—Each VRF and every route within the VRF requires memory. As the number of VRFs and routes increases, so does the required memory. Note that a VPNv4 route requires more memory than an IPv4 route.

- **Internet routes at the PE routers**—Because Globenet stores Internet routes at some of its PE routers, the amount of memory available to store VPN routes is clearly reduced. This may be quite significant on some of its older router platforms that have limited memory.

- **OSPF/RIPv2 connectivity**—OSPF and RIPv2 both rely on databases to store their routing information. This memory is in addition to that used to store the routes in the VRF and forwarding tables. Globenet therefore restricts the number of these types of customers that may be deployed on any given PE router.

- **BGP paths**—The number of remote sites for a given VPN increases the number of routes and paths received from remote locations at the local PE router. Given this, Globenet chose to use the **maximum routes** command in each VRF to restrict the number of routes and to be able to engineer the routers appropriately.

Globenet has several different edge router platforms, each of which had its maximum scale characterized during lab verification testing in terms of the maximum number of services it can support (assuming typical service distribution and associated features). The parameters used to determine the maximum scale were based on the typical split of Internet/Layer 3 VPN customer attachments, typical access speeds, typical CoS portfolio, maximum continuous CPU load of 50 percent, and so on. Based on this, Globenet defined provisioning rules for each platform it specified as 70 percent of the maximum scale tested.

IPv6 VPN Service Design

In response to requests from some customers with important VPN sites located in countries with early adoption of IPv6, Globenet introduced an IPv6 VPN service. The most fundamental customer requirement behind the need for an IPv6 VPN service to enable the construction of its IPv6 intranet, as opposed to an IPv6 global reachability service, is the need for the same isolation and security as provided in the IPv4 VPN service. In the future, when access to the IPv6 Internet is also required from these IPv6 intranets, another key benefit of the VPN service will be its ability to route IPv6 Internet traffic independently within each intranet. This is essential, because customers often want to ensure that all the traffic to and from the public IPv6 Internet is forced to transit via one of their own central sites providing IPv6 firewall services.

Globenet offers a very similar VPN service for IPv6 as for IPv4. Its objective is to ultimately offer exactly the same VPN services for IPv4 and IPv6. For example, although Globenet initially offered a more restricted QoS service to the IPv6 traffic, it planned to later extend the full QoS services to IPv6.

A given VPN site may request IPv4-only support, IPv6-only support, or both IPv4 and IPv6 support. Even when both IPv4 and IPv6 support are required, the site needs only a single (physical or logical) access link to the Globenet POP.

Customer requests for IPv6 VPN service have been identified to date in only the Asia Pacific and EMEA regions. Therefore, the IPv6 VPN service is currently offered only within these two regions, as well as across these two regions because a few customers have VPNs with sites spanning both regions. Globenet currently supports 15 IPv6 VPNs, for a total of 500 IPv6 VPN routes.

IPv6 VPN Design Within a Globenet Region

Globenet supports its IPv6 VPN service using the 6VPE approach that was described in the section "IPv6 VPN Provider Edge" in Chapter 1. This approach involves activating an additional address family (VPN-IPv6) in MP-BGP on the PE routers to advertise the IPv6 routes belonging to the VPNs and then relying on the same mechanisms as used for IPv4 VPNs for route distribution and control such as VRFs, route distinguishers, and route targets. A key characteristic of the 6VPE approach is that it can operate over an IPv4 MPLS backbone that remains entirely IPv6-unaware and, even more generally, completely unaware of the IPv6 VPN service. So Globenet did not need to carry an upgrade or configuration change on its P routers that keep operating as pure IPv4 MPLS P routers.

In line with its shared PE router philosophy (in which all PE routers support all Globenet's services), and because most IPv6 VPN customers also need IPv4 support in the VPN anyway, Globenet supports IPv6 VPNs from the same PE routers as IPv4 VPNs and IPv4 Internet access.

However, because the number of POP locations where there is currently a demand for IPv6 VPN service is quite low, Globenet decided to deploy this service incrementally. This means that the 6VPE functionality is activated only on the subset of PE routers that actually need to support the service today. This saved additional configuration on the many PE routers that do not need to support that service. Also, this considerably reduced the MP-BGP meshing level for the VPN-IPv6 address family so that only two route reflectors (located in two different Type 1 POPs) are used to reflect this address family within a region. Globenet elected to use a dedicated mesh of route reflectors for IPv6 VPN prefixes mainly for the same reason it used a separate route reflection mesh for IPv4 Internet and IPv4 VPN in the first place—isolation across services from a convergence viewpoint. The incremental deployment of the 6VPE functionality on selected PE routers as well as the dedicated set of route reflectors for IPv6 VPN is illustrated in Figure 5-29.

To support IPv6 VPN as per the 6VPE approach, the concept of VRF used for IPv4 VPN was extended in Cisco IOS into the concept of "multiprotocol VRF," which applies to both IPv4 and IPv6. The multiprotocol VRF can now comprise routing and forwarding tables for both IPv4 and IPv6. Also, it lets Globenet naturally define VRF attributes that are independent of the protocol (such as the route distinguisher, which can be used by both the VPN-IPv4 and the VPN-IPv6 address families). Globenet also can define, where applicable, policies that are intended to apply to all protocols (such as RT import/export rules when the same VPN topology is sought for both IPv4 and IPv6 in the considered VPN). At the same time, this concept allows Globenet to define, where needed, policies that are specific to a protocol (for example, when a hub-and-spoke topology is required for both IPv4 and IPv6 in the VPN but where the hubs for IPv4 and IPv6 are located in different VPN sites).

Figure 5-29 shows two multiprotocol VRFs on the PE router PE-Tokyo1. Customer1 VRF attaches a VPN site that runs IPv6 only, and customer2 VRF attaches a VPN site that runs both IPv6 and IPv4.

Figure 5-29 *6VPE Deployment in Globenet's AsiaPac Region*

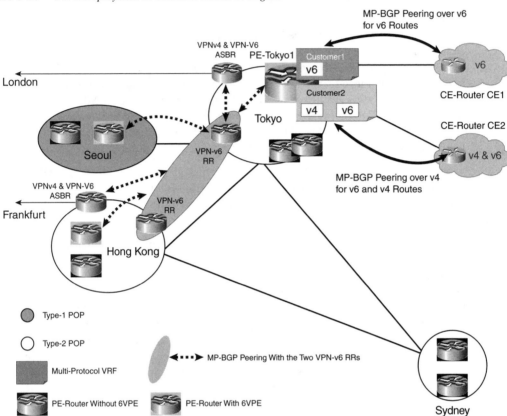

Example 5-9 shows the corresponding configuration for PE-Tokyo1. For customer1 VRF, which is used only for IPv6 traffic, the RT import and export policy is applied at the level of the multiprotocol VRF. Hence, in case IPv4 support was added later at the customer's request, this policy would also apply to IPv4 (unless a different policy is needed for IPv4, in which case an IPv4-specific policy would be configured under the IPv4 address family). For the customer2 VRF, it is assumed that the customer requires different RT import and export policies for IPv4 and IPv6. Globenet applied those at the level of the address family.

Example 5-9 *PE Router Configuration Template for IPv6 VPN Service*

```
hostname PE-Tokyo1
!
vrf definition customer1
rd 32761:customer1-and-PE-Tokyo1-specific-value
  route-target import 32761:customer1-specific-value
  route-target export 32761:customer1-specific-value
  address-family ipv6
!
```

Example 5-9   *PE Router Configuration Template for IPv6 VPN Service (Continued)*

```
vrf definition customer2
rd 32761:customer2-and-PE-Tokyo1-specific-value
  address-family ipv4
    route-target import 32761:customer2-specific-value-for-v4
    route-target export 32761:customer2-specific-value-for-v4
  address-family ipv6
    route-target import 32761:customer2-specific-value-for-v6
    route-target export 32761:customer2-specific-value-for-v6
!
router bgp 32761
!
!BGP configuration for exchange of IPv6 VPN address family with Route
!Reflectors (over IPv4)
  neighbor IPv4-address-of-v6-VPN-RR1 remote-as 32761
  neighbor IPv4-address-of-v6-VPN-RR1 update-source loopback0
  neighbor IPv4-address-of-v6-VPN-RR2 remote-as 32761
  neighbor IPv4-address-of-v6-VPN-RR2 update-source loopback0
  address-family vpnv6
    neighbor IPv4-address-of-v6-VPN-RR1 activate
    neighbor IPv4-address-of-v6-VPN-RR1 send-community extended
    neighbor IPv4-address-of-v6-VPN-RR2 activate
    neighbor IPv4-address-of-v6-VPN-RR2 send-community extended
  exit-address-family
!
!BGP configuration for exchange of v6 address family with CE1 of
!Customer1 (over IPv6)
address-family ipv6 vrf customer1
  neighbor IPv6-address-of-CE1-of-customer1 remote-as CE1-Site-AS
  neighbor IPv6-address-of-CE1-of-customer1 update-source loopback0
  neighbor IPv4-address-of-CE1-of-customer1 activate
  no synchronization
  exit-address-family
!
!BGP configuration for exchange of v4 address family with CE2 of
!Customer2 (over IPv4)
address-family ipv4 vrf customer2
  neighbor IPv4-address-of-CE2-of-customer2 remote-as CE2-Site-AS
  neighbor IPv4-address-of-CE2-of-customer2 update-source loopback0
  neighbor IPv4-address-of-CE2-of-customer2 activate
  no synchronization
  exit-address-family
!
!BGP configuration for exchange of v6 address family with CE2 of
!Customer2 (over IPv4)
address-family ipv6 vrf customer2
  neighbor IPv4-address-of-CE2-of-customer2 remote-as CE2-Site-AS
  neighbor IPv4-address-of-CE2-of-customer2 update-source loopback0
  neighbor IPv4-address-of-CE2-of-customer2 activate
  no synchronization
  exit-address-family
```

continues

Example 5-9   *PE Router Configuration Template for IPv6 VPN Service (Continued)*

```
!
!attachment of customer1 vrf on the PE-CE interface to CE1 of customer1
int serial0/0.1
  frame-relay interface-dlci 1001
  description "to CE1 of customer1"
  vrf forwarding customer1
  ipv6 address IPv6-address-of-interface-towards-CE1/length
!
!attachment of customer2 vrf on the PE-CE interface to CE2 of customer2
int serial0/0.2
  frame-relay interface-dlci 1002
  description "to CE2 of customer2"
  vrf forwarding customer2
  ip address IPv4-address-of-interface-towards-CE2 mask
  ipv6 address IPv6-address-of-interface-towards-CE2/length
```

The configuration presented in Example 5-9 shows the configuration of MP-BGP for peering PE-Tokyo1 with the two IPv6 VPN route reflectors, as well as the MP-BGP configuration for peering with Customer1 and Customer2. For the sake of simplicity, it does not show the MP-BGP configuration for peering with the IPv4 VPN route reflectors or the IPv4 Internet route reflectors, but those are, of course, included in the actual configuration of the shared PE routers.

NOTE   Before the introduction of IPv6 VPNs in Cisco IOS and the associated extension of VRFs into multiprotocol VRFs, configuration of VRFs in IOS involved slightly different commands (to create the VRF and attach it to an interface). These commands assumed IPv4 only, so they are called the IPv4 VRF commands. These commands have been used everywhere else in this book to illustrate IPv4 VPN PE router configurations. These commands can be used whenever a VPN supports only IPv4 traffic. However, when a VPN needs to support IPv6 or both IPv6 and IPv4, the multiprotocol VRF and its associated commands must be used. Those are the ones used in Example 5-9.

NOTE   The majority of VPN sites that required an IPv6 VPN service were already using Globenet's IPv4 VPN service beforehand. Hence, these sites were attached to a VRF that had been configured using the IPv4 VRF commands instead of the multiprotocol VRF commands. To convert those into multiprotocol VRFs and add IPv6 support, Globenet used a specific IOS command (**vrf upgrade-cli**) that automatically converts the IPv4 VRF commands into multiprotocol VRF commands without any service impact. Then Globenet only had to add the IPv6-specific configuration inside the existing VRF. Details and example of such migration scenario are further discussed in [IPv6-DEPLOY].

Globenet currently does not have a specific offer for IPv6 Internet access from IPv6 VPNs because it has not received any customer request for this to date. However, all the same methods currently offered for IPv4 Internet access from IPv4 VPNs (and described previously in the section "Layer 3 MPLS VPN Service Design") could also be offered for IPv6 Internet access from IPv6 VPNs as customer demand materializes for those. Specifically, Internet access via injection of a default route inside the VRF from the CE router of a customer hub site, as well as injection of a default route toward an IPv6 Internet gateway into a customer VRF, would operate in exactly the same way for IPv6 as for IPv4. Internet access via Globenet firewall services would also operate for IPv6 as for IPv4, with the exception that NAT generally is not applicable to IPv6 and that Globenet firewall services would, of course, have to support IPv6. Full Internet access via the PE-CE access link could be supported in the same manner. The full IPv6 Internet routes could be stored in the PE router's global routing table. Also, a separate (physical or logical) connection between PE router and CE router could be used to advertise the IPv6 Internet routes to the CE router from the connection used for the VPN traffic. The same connection would be used for both IPv4 and IPv6 traffic inside the VPN, and the other connection would be used for IPv4 and IPv6 Internet traffic.

One difference between IPv4 and IPv6 operations with respect to Internet routes is that in IPv4, the full Internet routes are stored by all P routers in the core. In IPv6 the P routers would not participate in the MP-BGP exchange of Internet IPv6 routes. Only the PE routers that actually have to offer full IPv6 Internet access would participate in the MP-BGP exchange of those routes. They would do so in accordance with the 6PE approach presented in the "IPv6 Provider Edge" section in Chapter 1. This approach allows the exchange of global IPv6 reachability information among PE routers interconnected by an IPv4-only MPLS core and accordingly forwards IPv6 traffic over this core.

IPv6 VPN Design Across Globenet Regions

Globenet supports IPv6 VPNs that have sites spanning both its EMEA and AsiaPac regions. Just as with IPv4 VPNs, it uses inter-AS option B for IPv6 VPN operations across regions so that the ASBRs of the two regions exchange (labeled) IPv6 VPN reachability information. To support interregion IPv4 VPNs across AsiaPac and EMEA, Globenet uses MP-BGP sessions between the two pairs of ASBRs supporting the direct intercontinental links—namely, Tokyo/London and Hong Kong/Frankfurt. Globenet uses the same ASBRs for inter-AS operations for IPv6 VPNs.

With inter-AS option B for IPv6 VPNs, to exchange IPv6 VPN reachability, Globenet had a choice between using the peering between the ASBRs over IPv6 or over IPv4. Because Globenet ASBRs were already peering over IPv4 for IPv4 VPN inter-AS support, Globenet elected to also use the same IPv4 peering for the IPv6 VPN inter-AS support. The BGP next-hop attribute is encoded as an IPv4-mapped IPv6 address.

Disabling the ARF feature that you saw earlier for IPv4 VPN inter-AS operation directly applies to IPv6 VPNs. The inter-AS route filtering (based on customer-specific route target values), as well as the route target rewrite, configured on the ASBRs for IPv4 VPN routes (as described in the "Layer 3 MPLS VPN Service Design" section), has also been applied by Globenet to the IPv6 VPN routes.

ATM Pseudowire Design

As previously described, Globenet uses ATM pseudowires in its Type 1b POPs to trunk its ATM infrastructure over the IP/MPLS network in the parts of its network where IP traffic is the highly dominant traffic type (namely, North America and parts of Europe). It refers to this connectivity as an "inverted overlay" model, where ATM is overlaid on top of IP rather than the other way around.

The fundamental concepts of pseudowire technology were covered in Chapter 1, so we will not cover this again here. However, as explained in Chapter 1, a number of different media types may be carried across pseudowire, such as Frame Relay, Ethernet, ATM, and so forth. Globenet only had the requirement of connecting its existing ATM switches using trunks that were provided via ATM pseudowires that could be used to carry ATM cells over the IP/MPLS network directly between the switches.

To achieve this, Globenet chose to deploy the ATM Transparent Cell Transport service (see [PWE3-CELL-TRANSPORT]). It emulates full connectivity between two remote ATM switch ports whereby all cells (with the exception of idle/unassigned cells, which are discarded) are mapped to a single pseudowire provisioned across the IP/MPLS network. With Transparent Cell Transport mode, a single pseudowire is necessary between each pair of ATM switches that need to be interconnected via the IP/MPLS core.

This mode of operation provides absolute transparency for interswitch connectivity so that Globenet can run PNNI between its switches. Globenet also can support any traffic classes of ATM connections (CBR, VBR-rt, VBR-nrt, and so forth), as well as both VCs and virtual paths (VPs). These are necessary because they offer VPs as native services to end customers and have to maintain this functionality.

Globenet chose to use the "cell-packing" functionality that allows for the encapsulation of multiple ATM cells coming into an ATM interface inside a single MPLS packet for transport over the IP/MPLS network. The cell-packing feature is more efficient than single-cell relay in terms of overhead because the same pseudowire encapsulation overhead is then used to transport multiple ATM cells instead of just one. The pseudowire encapsulation overhead is composed of the link layer overhead (for example, HDLC and PPP over POS), the MPLS label stack, and the pseudowire control word. Assume in a given environment that this amounts to 24 bytes. In single-cell mode, this means 24 bytes of overhead for 52 bytes of payload, which represents a 46 percent overhead. When cell packing is used and ten cells are packed into a single MPLS packet, the overhead is still 24 bytes but the payload is now 520 bytes, which translates into a reduced overhead of 5 percent. Clearly, the more cells are packed together, the higher the efficiency. However, packing more cells means that the first received cell has to wait until all the other cells are received by the pseudowire ingress PE router before being transmitted. In turn, this translates to induced delay and jitter for the transported ATM traffic. To finely control this trade-off, the IOS implementation supports the configuration of both a maximum number of cells to be packed (so that delay and jitter impact is minimized when cells arrive at a fast rate) and a maximum cell-packing timer. This timer triggers transmission of cells even if the maximum number of cells to be packed hasn't been received after some controlled time (so that delay and jitter are also kept under a controlled bound in case of cells arriving at a relatively low rate). Globenet wanted to keep very low delay and jitter for its ATM pseudowires, which carry all types of ATM connections, including CBR, and yet achieve reasonable bandwidth efficiency. Therefore, Globenet elected to configure a maximum timer for cell packing of 20 microseconds and a maximum number of cells to be packed of five cells.

A sample configuration of the ATM pseudowires, including cell packing and the corresponding QoS configuration, is given in the later section "Pseudowire QoS Design for ATM Trunking."

Quality of Service Design

Globenet believes that mission-critical and multimedia applications can be supported cost-economically in an intranet that spans multiple continents and regions where bandwidth is expensive only if the network provides quality of service levels that are finely optimized for the different types of traffic. One of the reasons for this is that the very significant propagation delays involved in very long-distance transmission leave very little room in some application delay budgets for network-induced delay and jitter. To meet the requirements of its global customers, Globenet adopted an aggressive market positioning toward high QoS and SLAs and elected to offer a rich QoS offering.

In particular, Globenet supports five classes of service on the access links to its Layer 3 MPLS VPN service:

- VPN Voice
- VPN Video
- VPN Business Latency
- VPN Business Throughput
- VPN Standard

A separate queue is used to schedule each of these classes on the access links between CE routers and PE routers. Routing traffic and management traffic between CE routers and PE routers is handled in the VPN Business Throughput CoS.

For the Internet service, a single CoS is supported on the access that is equivalent to the VPN Standard CoS of the Layer 3 MPLS VPN service.

Globenet also supports one queue for each of the five CoSs in the core network in all regions (except in North America, where these CoSs are aggregated into three queues) for the following reasons:

- Because of the relatively tight bandwidth provisioning policy in Globenet's core network in many parts of the world
- Because of long propagation delays involved in cross-continental or intercontinental transmission
- Because of the resulting requirement for fine control of QoS

The queue carrying VPN Voice is optimized for real-time operations. It is called the Expedited Forwarding (EF) queue. This queue is also used to schedule the traffic from the ATM pseudowires that support trunking of ATM switches over the IP/MPLS core in North America and EMEA. When Globenet offers a virtual IP leased-line service in the future (for example, to Africa Telecom so that it, in turn, can build its VPOPs through Globenet's network), the corresponding traffic will also be scheduled in the EF queue.

Table 5-4 details the mapping between each type of traffic, the DSCP values, the queues on the access links, the EXP/DSCP values in the core, and the queues in the core.

Table 5-4 *QoS Mapping of Classes, DSCP, EXP, and Queues*

Class of Service	DSCP on Access	Queue on Access	EXP/DSCP in Core	Queue in Core (Except North America)	Queue in Core (North America)
VPN Voice	46	EF	EXP=5	EF	EF
ATM pseudowires	—	—	EXP=5		
Future: virtual IP leased line	—	—	EXP=5		
VPN Video	34	AF4	EXP=4	AF4	AF2
VPN Business Latency	26	AF3	EXP=3	AF3	
VPN Business Throughput	16 (in-contract) 8 (out-of contract)	AF2	EXP=2 EXP=1	AF2	
Management on access	16		EXP=2		
Routing on access	48		—*	—*	—*
Control in core (routing, management, signaling)	48	—	DSCP=48 EXP=6	AF2	AF2
VPN Standard and Internet	0	DF	EXP=0	DF	DF

*As per the Layer 3 MPLS VPN model, the routing traffic carried on the access links is purely between CE router and PE router.

For example, the VPN Business Latency CoS is marked with DSCP 26 on the access links between CE routers and PE routers and uses the AF3 queue on these links. In the core, it is marked with EXP 3. It is scheduled into the AF2 queue in North America (along with VPN Video and VPN Throughput) and in the AF3 queue (separately from any other traffic) in all other regions.

Note that for the VPN Business Throughput in-contract and out-of-contract, Globenet decided to use two precedence-based DSCP values (DSCP=16 of CS2 and DSCP=8 of CS1) instead of the more obvious AF21 (DSCP=18) and AF22 (DSCP=20) values, which share the same setting for the 3 precedence bits. This is to make sure that those automatically get mapped into different EXP values (EXP=2 and EXP=1) on the PE routers with the default IOS DSCP-to-EXP mapping, which automatically copies the 3 precedence bits into the 3-bit EXP field. This is the same rationale discussed in the "mPE Router Ingress Policy" section in Chapter 4. It led Telecom Kingland to select DSCP values that directly map by default to the appropriate EXP scheme.

We will now review in detail the SLA offered by Globenet, the QoS designs used in various parts of the core network, and the QoS designs used on the edge to achieve the SLA commitments.

VPN and Internet SLA

Globenet offers a very rich QoS service to ensure optimum performance for its end customers. First, Globenet includes POP-to-POP SLA commitments for each of its five classes of service in the customer contract. Globenet also offers a "consultative" QoS design service that involves investigating its customers' applications, their respective requirements to address their stated business objectives, and their operations for current infrastructure (using specialized network analysis tools). This leads to recommendations on the optimum use of Globenet's QoS services for the customer, such as site access rates, respective ratio across the five CoSs for each site, and mapping of applications to CoS. Finally, on request, Globenet also offers site-to-site SLA commitments for each CoS.

Table 5-5 provides sample POP-to-POP commitments for each CoS. Each cell of the table lists commitments for each VPN CoS (VPN Voice, VPN Video, VPN Business Latency, VPN Business Throughput, and VPN Standard). These are specified in terms of one-way delay, jitter, and packet loss. Delay and jitter are expressed in milliseconds, and packet loss is expressed as a percentage of total transmitted packets for that CoS. (A dash [—] indicates that the particular field is not applicable.)

Table 5-5   *Extract of Globenet Per-CoS POP-to-POP SLAs*

POPs	Core Europe[1]	Sweden	U.S. East Coast[2]	U.S. West Coast[3]	Tokyo	Hong Kong	Sydney
Core Europe[1]	20/10/0.1	30/20/0.1	65/20/0.2	90/30/0.2	100/30/0.2	100/30/0.2	170/40/0.2
	30/—/0.1	40/—/0.1	80/—/0.2	105/—/0.2	120/—/0.2	120/—/0.2	190/—/0.2
	30/—/0.3	40/—/0.3	80/—/0.5	105/—/0.5	120/—/0.5	120/—/0.5	190/—/0.5
	40/—/0.1	50/—/0.1	90/—/0.2	115/—/0.2	140/—/0.2	140/—/0.2	210/—/0.2
	50/—/0.5	70/—/0.5	105/—/1	135/—/1	160/—/1	160/—/1	250/—/1
Sweden	30/20/0.1	— —	75/30/0.2	100/30/0.2	110/30/0.2	110/30/0.2	180/40/0.2
	40/—/0.1		90/—/0.2	115/—/0.2	130/—/0.2	130/—/0.2	200/—/0.2
	40/—/0.3		90/—/0.5	115/—/0.5	130/—/0.5	130/—/0.5	200/—/0.5
	50/—/0.1		100/—/0.2	125/—/0.2	150/—/0.2	150/—/0.2	220/—/0.2
	70/—/0.5		125/—/1	155/—/1	180/—/1	180/—/1	270/—/1
U.S. East Coast[2]	65/20/0.2	75/30/0.2	25/10/0.1	45/20/0.1	110/30/0.2	110/30/0.2	180/40/0.2
	80/—/0.2	90/—/0.2	35/—/0.1	55/—/0.1	125/—/0.2	125/—/0.2	195/—/0.2
	80/—/0.5	90/—/0.5	35/—/0.1	55/—/0.1	125/—/0.5	125/—/0.5	195/—/0.5
	90/—/0.2	100/—/0.2	35/—/0.1	55/—/0.1	145/—/0.2	145/—/0.2	215/—/0.2
	105/—/1	125/—/1	45/—/0.5	65/—/0.5	165/—/1	165/—/1	255/—/1
U.S. West Coast[3]	90/30/0.2	100/30/0.2	45/20/0.1	25/10/0.1	90/30/0.2	90/30/0.2	160/40/0.2
	105/—/0.2	115/—/0.2	55/—/0.1	35/—/0.1	105/—/0.2	105/—/0.2	175/—/0.2
	105/—/0.5	115/—/0.5	55/—/0.1	35/—/0.1	105/—/0.5	105/—/0.5	175/—/0.5
	115/—/0.2	125/—/0.2	55/—/0.1	35/—/0.1	125/—/0.2	125/—/0.2	195/—/0.2
	135/—/1	155/—/1	65/—/0.5	45/—/0.5	145/—/1	145/—/1	235/—/1
Tokyo	100/30/0.2	110/30/0.2	110/30/0.2	90/30/0.2	— —	40/20/0.1	85/30/0.2
	120/—/0.2	130/—/0.2	125/—/0.2	105/—/0.2		50/—/0.1	100/—/0.2
	120/—/0.5	130/—/0.5	125/—/0.5	105/—/0.5		50/—/0.3	100/—/0.5
	140/—/0.2	150/—/0.2	145/—/0.2	125/—/0.2		60/—/0.1	110/—/0.2
	160/—/1	180/—/1	165/—/1	145/—/1		80/—/0.5	130/—/1
Hong Kong	100/30/0.2	110/30/0.2	110/30/0.2	90/30/0.2	40/20/0.1	— —	85/30/0.2
	120/—/0.2	130/—/0.2	125/—/0.2	105/—/0.2	50/—/0.1		100/—/0.2
	120/—/0.5	130/—/0.5	125/—/0.5	105/—/0.5	50/—/0.3		100/—/0.5
	140/—/0.2	150/—/0.2	145/—/0.2	125/—/0.2	60/—/0.1		110/—/0.2
	160/—/1	180/—/1	165/—/1	145/—/1	80/—/0.5		130/—/1

Table 5-5   *Extract of Globenet Per-CoS POP-to-POP SLAs (Continued)*

POPs	Core Europe[1]	Sweden	U.S. East Coast[2]	U.S. West Coast[3]	Tokyo	Hong Kong	Sydney
Sydney	170/40/0.2	180/40/0.2	180/40/0.2	160/40/0.2	85/30/0.2	85/30/0.2	—
	190/—/0.2	200/—/0.2	195/—/0.2	175/—/0.2	100/—/0.2	100/—/0.2	
	190/—/0.5	200/—/0.5	195/—/0.5	175/—/0.5	100/—/0.5	100/—/0.5	
	210/—/0.2	220/—/0.2	215/—/0.2	195/—/0.2	110/—/0.2	110/—/0.2	
	250/—/1	270/—/1	255/—/1	235/—/1	130/—/1	130/—/1	

[1] Core Europe consists of London, Frankfurt, and Paris.

[2] U.S. East Coast consists of New York and Washington.

[3] U.S. West Coast consists of Seattle, San Jose, and Los Angeles.

In general, the commitments are given from one POP to another POP. For example, you can see from Table 5-5 that Globenet commits to a one-way delay of 85 ms, a jitter of 30 ms, and a packet loss of 0.2 percent for the VPN Voice CoS between the Tokyo POP and the Sydney POP.

However, in the cases where a few POPs are meshed at very high speed, Globenet bundles this set of POPs from an SLA viewpoint (such as the Paris, London, and Frankfurt POPs bundled as "Core Europe"). This provides the following:

- SLA commitments applicable between any two POPs within this set of POPs

- SLA commitments between that set of POPs and other POPs (or other sets of POPs)

This reduces the combination of POP-to-POP commitments that would have to be expressed otherwise. For example, for the Voice VPN CoS, Globenet commits to a one-way delay of 100 ms, a jitter of 30 ms, and a packet loss of 0.2 percent for traffic from any POP in Core Europe (Paris, London, or Frankfurt) to the Tokyo POP.

The SLA commitments for Internet access services are the same as the ones for the VPN Standard CoS. However, these commitments apply only to traffic exchanged between two sites both subscribing to Globenet Internet access service (traffic that travels over the Globenet network end-to-end). Traffic exchanged between one site using the Globenet Internet access service and the rest of the Internet is not within the scope of the SLA commitments. This traffic transits over other Internet backbones, which are outside Globenet's control.

Because propagation delays are very significant when compared to the tight commitments Globenet offers, and because the level of meshing is low in some parts of the world, and because some links are low-speed so that queuing delay can be significant even with short queue occupancies, the POP-to-POP SLA commitments that Globenet can achieve are heavily dependent on some aspect of the current core network:

- **The link speeds**— Upgrading a regional link from 2 Mbps to 34 Mbps or from 34 Mbps to 155 Mbps will noticeably affect the queuing experienced by the various CoSs at the corresponding hop.

- **The core topology and underlying infrastructure path**—If a POP needs to transit via some location away from the shortest geographic route, or if it has some direct connectivity to that POP (perhaps allowed by some new submarine cable route), this affects QoS commitments because of different propagation delays (as well as the impact of the potential additional hop).

Because of this significant dependency on actual underlying core link topology and speed, Globenet reserves the right to update the SLA commitments on a monthly basis. Note, however, that such updates generally improve the commitments as a result of upgrades in the core.

When the customer requests site-to-site commitments (CE router-to-CE router), Globenet establishes them by combining the following for each CoS and for each targeted pair of sites:

- The relevant POP-to-POP commitments listed in Table 5-5
- The QoS performance for the relevant access links from CE router to PE router and from PE router to CE router

In turn, Globenet has determined the QoS performance on the access links for each access technology (leased line, Frame Relay, ATM, and so on) and each access speed. Globenet used a methodology similar to the one followed by Telecom Kingland to support its custom SLAs for the access links. See the section "Layer 3 MPLS VPN and Internet SLA" in Chapter 4.

Generally in accordance with the recommendations established jointly with Globenet as part of the "consultative QoS design service," the customer selects the proportion of each CoS it wants on the access link for each site. This proportion applies to both directions of the CE-PE link. The customer does not have to use the five CoSs; it may use any subset of these CoSs for a given site. In the default service offering, Globenet imposes some constraints on the selected proportion across CoSs as deemed necessary to meet the corresponding QoS objectives. For example, the VPN Voice CoS is limited to 30 percent of the access link. Similarly, the VPN Voice and VPN Video CoS are collectively limited to 60 percent of the access link. A minimum of 4 percent of access speed must be selected for the VPN Business Throughput CoS because it is used to carry routing and management traffic.

The VPN Voice CoS is designed to transport IP telephony services. It provides the very low latency, jitter, and loss required by such applications. To ensure that such QoS objectives can be met end-to-end, traffic sent into the VPN Voice CoS is strictly policed on the access against the contracted rate, and the excess is dropped.

The VPN Video CoS targets videoconferencing applications. Although such applications have requirements for controlled delay, Globenet decided to handle them as a CoS separate from the VPN Voice CoS for a number of reasons:

- Video applications generally can tolerate higher levels of latency and jitter than telephony applications. Even when lip synchronization techniques are used on the destination system, an under-run of video packets (for example, packets from the video stream don't arrive in time for replay because of a sudden delay increase in the core) is more tolerable than an under-run of audio packets.

- Video applications use variable-size packets, including long packets. Carrying such long packets in the same queue as the voice traffic (which uses only short packets) would degrade the delay and jitter commitments that can be provided to voice traffic.

- Video applications use higher rates than voice and transmit at variable rates. Again, handling such traffic in the same queue as the voice traffic would jeopardize the voice traffic.

The VPN Video CoS is engineered to provide controlled rate and delay. To better control the delay in the VPN Video CoS, Globenet decided to drop the traffic sent to the Video CoS on the access into the network that was in excess of the contracted rate (instead of demoting it). Hence, the end customer needs to adjust the volume of videoconferencing traffic to the contracted rate for the VPN Video CoS. This may be achieved as part of the negotiation (using protocols such as H.323 and SIP) that takes place at the beginning of a multimedia session. In addition to authorizing the user/endpoint for establishing a videoconference, the admission procedure may also check that the new video stream fits within the engineered capacity of the VPN Video CoS (which might be configured by the operator as one of the multimedia system parameters). Conversely, the end user may adjust the contracted rate for the VPN Video CoS to satisfy the expected demand for the site.

In the future, Globenet will investigate enhancing the VPN Video CoS to accept some out-of-contract traffic. This traffic would then be demoted and subject to selective random drop in the access and in the core (using Weighted Random Early Detection (WRED)). This may play well with some videoconferencing end systems that can dynamically adjust their encoding rate based on the experienced packet loss. (For example, a loss of 1 percent results in the end system's reverting to the next-lower encoding rate.) However, this makes it more difficult to control the delay experienced by in-contract video traffic. The fraction of out-of-contract traffic that is not dropped by WRED goes into the same queue as the in-contract traffic and hence increases its delay and jitter. Note that scheduling the out-of-contract VPN video traffic in a different queue than the in-contract VPN video traffic generally is not an acceptable alternative because it would result in permanent reordering of packets in the video stream.

The VPN Business Latency CoS addresses requirements of responsive applications, typically client/server-based, with fairly low throughput but a requirement for controlled response time. A typical example is a mission-critical interactive application (such as a reservation or ordering system) in which a user clicks (or enters carriage returns) and then waits for the server response. Systems Network Architecture (SNA) terminal-to-host transactions; Enterprise Resource Planning applications such as SAP, Oracle, PeopleSoft, and Siebel; and financial wire transfers and credit card transactions are examples of applications that may be served by the VPN Business Latency CoS.

Traffic sent to the VPN Business Latency CoS is policed on the access against the contracted rate, and the excess is dropped. Because the corresponding applications generally do not transmit at a high rate, it is typically fairly easy to select a reasonable contracted rate for the

CoS that is never exceeded in practice by actual traffic. Still, as with the VPN Video CoS, Globenet will investigate in the future the opportunity to enhance the VPN Business Latency CoS to accept some out-of-contract traffic. However, an issue that Globenet is potentially facing for support of out-of-contract VPN video, out-of-contract VPN latency, and other additional QoS services is the shortage of EXP values. Globenet already uses seven of the eight available values.

The VPN Business Throughput CoS is configured to satisfy applications that require high throughput. More specifically, it optimizes throughput for long-lived TCP flows. Store and forward, file transfer, Lotus Notes, and Microsoft Exchange are examples of applications that can operate well over the VPN Business Throughput CoS. Although reasonable delay is provided for this CoS, the prime objective is to offer low loss to the in-contract traffic because this is what drives the throughput actually achieved by TCP. Out-of-contract traffic is accepted in the VPN Business Throughput CoS on the access but is demoted (in other words, marked differently) and is subject to more aggressive selective random drop than the in-contract traffic. Although accepting out-of-contract traffic tends to increase the latency for the in-contract traffic (which is not so important for the targeted applications), it allows smoother adjustment of TCP streams to the available bandwidth and ultimately better overall throughput.

The VPN Standard CoS is used for all the applications not classified into the other CoSs and that can be appropriately served with reasonable latency and loss commitments.

QoS Design in the Core Network in the EMEA, AsiaPac, and South America Regions

Globenet manages five separate queues in the core for the following reasons:

- Because of constrained bandwidth in the core, particularly in the Asia Pacific and South America regions
- Because of some relatively low-speed links that involve higher delay and jitter for a given queue occupancy
- Because of high-propagation delays of long-distance links
- Because of the need for very fine optimization to meet the tight SLA requirements presented earlier

Figure 5-30 illustrates the mapping of CoSs into these five queues.

This lets Globenet isolate the five types of traffic from one another, enforce different capacity planning policies, and apply different sets of QoS mechanisms to each.

Figure 5-30   *Usage of the Five Queues in EMEA, AsiaPac, and South America*

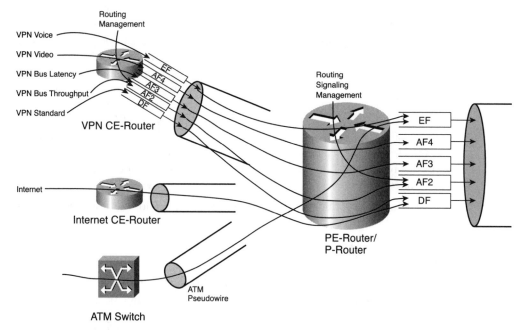

For the EF traffic, Globenet combines the following mechanisms:

- Use of strict priority queuing for the EF queue to achieve optimum delay and jitter in a short time.

- Use of DiffServ-aware MPLS Traffic Engineering (DS-TE) (which was presented in Chapter 2, "Technology Primer: Quality of Service, Traffic Engineering, and Network Recovery") to transport the EF traffic over separate tunnels that are "constraint-based routed" to keep the EF traffic load under 30 percent of link speed on any link. We call these tunnels the EF tunnels. This stringent 30 percent bandwidth constraint is deemed appropriate by Globenet to bound the delay, jitter, and loss through the core to the levels required by traffic transported in the EF queue (such as ATM pseudowire as well as VPN voice).

- Separate capacity planning for EF traffic and validation through a network simulation tool that the network has enough capacity so that the EF load remains below 20 percent of link capacity in normal operation (and hence is routed by TE along its shortest path. Also, validation that TE can route the EF load within the 30 percent limit (on shortest path or non-shortest path) during single-failure conditions.

- Conditional policing to 40 percent of the link rate. Although Globenet does not expect TE to route more than 30 percent of EF traffic, even in (single) failure situations, the conditional policer is configured to 40 percent (instead of 30 percent). This is to ensure that EF traffic is not dropped unnecessarily in transient periods where the actual load can temporarily exceed the expected load. Such transient periods can occur when the actual EF load surges and the corresponding dynamic tunnel size increase lags (through the auto-route mechanism, as discussed later, in the "MPLS Traffic Engineering Design" section). They also can occur during the interim period where tunnels carrying EF traffic have been fast rerouted because of a failure and have not yet been rerouted by their headend and thus have not yet been subjected to proper TE admission control. Clearly, Globenet expects the actual EF load to always be below 40 percent on core links. Therefore, it does not expect this conditional policer to come into action. It is configured as a safety precaution, in case of extraordinary unplanned situations, in order to prevent the EF traffic from hogging most, or all, of the bandwidth and thus deteriorating the QoS of other classes (such as the VPN Video, VPN Business Latency or VPN Business Throughput) or even potentially affecting network stability in case the routing and Control traffic can no longer be transported appropriately.

For the rest of the traffic (which we call the "non-EF traffic"), Globenet combines the following mechanisms:

- Use of a separate DiffServ queue for each CoS to ensure isolation and appropriate levels of QoS

- Use of DS-TE to transport all the non-EF traffic together (but separately from the EF traffic) over tunnels that are "constraint-based routed." The sum of all tunnels admitted on a link is limited to 100 percent of link capacity. (This is adjusted by an overbooking factor on higher-speed links, as discussed in detail in the section "MPLS Traffic Engineering Design.") We call these tunnels the non-EF tunnels.

- Aggregate capacity planning across EF and non-EF traffic and validation through a network simulation tool that the network has enough capacity so that the following are true:
  - Both EF and non-EF traffic is routed on its shortest path by DS-TE and the total aggregate load remains below 80 percent of link capacity in the absence of failure. (Sometimes the aggregate load can reach 100 percent of the link even in the absence of failure, resulting in a small percentage of tunnels being routed on their non-shortest path even in the absence of failure.)
  - Both EF and non-EF traffic can be routed (on its shortest path or on a non-shortest path) by DS-TE within the bandwidth limits just specified (30 percent for EF tunnels and 100 percent plus overbooking for non-EF tunnels) during single-failure conditions.

- Each CoS is allocated individual scheduling parameters based on its respective QoS requirements and expected traffic load.

With this approach, you can observe the following:

- Under normal conditions, Globenet operates below congestion, but possibly at fairly high utilization at peak time, such as 80 percent link utilization (or even nearing 100 percent for the few exceptions just mentioned). Operating at high utilization while maintaining strict quality of service for demanding applications allows Globenet to minimize its use of very expensive international links. Hence, this is a key element in Globenet's strategy to offer high-quality services at competitive prices.

- Under failure, Globenet operates close to congestion, with utilization nearing 100 percent. Some links may even temporarily operate under congestion (with an aggregate packet load exceeding 100 percent link occupancy). This may happen because the traffic load surges and the corresponding dynamic tunnel size increase through the auto-route mechanism lags. This could also happen during the interim period when EF tunnels and non-EF tunnels have been fast-rerouted and have not yet been rerouted by their headend and thus have been subjected to proper TE admission control. However, such periods are very short in duration, as discussed in the "Network Recovery Design" section later in this chapter.

- As detailed later, the default (DF) queue (carrying VPN Standard CoS and Internet traffic) is allocated only a small fraction of the bandwidth. This is to ensure that this CoS will suffer most during potential congestion periods, hence protecting all the other more-important CoSs.

You see that this approach, which handles the EF traffic from all the other CoSs differently, clearly calls for differentiated admission control of EF tunnels and non-EF tunnels, whereby

- The EF tunnels are limited to some EF-specific engineered levels (30 percent in the case of Globenet).

- All the tunnels (the non-EF tunnels and the EF tunnels) are collectively limited to some aggregate engineered levels (100 percent plus overbooking in the case of Globenet).

This matches perfectly with the Russian Dolls Model (RDM) of DS-TE (discussed in Chapter 2), which limits Class Type 1 to Bandwidth Constraint BC1 and then limits Class Type 0 (CT0) and Class Type 1 (CT1) together to Bandwidth Constraint BC0.

RDM also allows Globenet to achieve maximum sharing of bandwidth across EF tunnels and non-EF tunnels. If the EF tunnels currently are not reserving their full 30 percent, whatever is left over can effectively be reserved by the non-EF tunnels so that the link can be used up to 100 percent (plus overbooking). This avoids any capacity wastage.

Moreover, by using a higher TE preemption priority for the EF tunnels (CT1) than for the non-EF tunnels (CT0), the EF tunnels will always be able to reserve up to their full BC1 bandwidth should they need it, no matter how many non-EF tunnels have been established before (or will need to be established in the future). In other words, by using preemption priorities in conjunction with the RDM, Globenet can fully protect the EF tunnels from bandwidth starvation even if the EF tunnels (CT1) share a common bandwidth constraint BC0 with the non-EF tunnels (CT0). This is sometimes referred to as achieving "isolation" across Class Types.

Hence, Globenet elected to use the RDM with

- EF tunnels belonging to Class Type 1 and using a higher preemption priority

- Non-EF tunnels belonging to Class Type 0 and using a lower preemption priority

Another benefit of using the RDM with such a preemption policy is that the control plane bandwidth allocation of DS-TE matches very accurately DiffServ's data plane bandwidth allocation. DS-TE always allows the EF tunnels to reserve as much bandwidth as they need (up to their own bandwidth constraint, BC1=30 percent). The scheduler always grants the corresponding EF packets as much bandwidth as they need (up to the conditional policing rate) because they are scheduled in a strict priority queue. The non-EF tunnels always can reserve all the bandwidth from BC0 left unused by the EF tunnels. The scheduler effectively gives the queues carrying the non-EF packets (AF4, AF3, AF2, and DF queues) all the physical link bandwidth left unused by the EF queue. This ensures that no matter what proportion of EF tunnels and non-EF tunnels is currently established, the corresponding EF and non-EF traffic actually receives the corresponding proportion of scheduling resources. Thus, both types of traffic are protected from QoS degradation.

Figure 5-31 shows how the CoSs are mapped onto tunnels from Class Types CT0 and CT1. This figure also illustrates the strong separation of the control plane (path selection) and the data plane (scheduling) in DiffServ-aware MPLS TE. You can see that the path a packet follows is exclusively controlled by the TE tunnel into which it is encapsulated, while the scheduling of that packet is controlled by the packet CoS marking (MPLS EXP bits). For example, while an Internet packet and a VPN video packet going beyond P router P2 are encapsulated into the same non-EF tunnel (and hence follow the exact same path through the core), these packets are scheduled into different queues at every hop—namely, the DF queue and the AF4 queue. Conversely, while a VPN video packet going beyond P router P2 and a VPN video packet going beyond P router P3 are encapsulated into different non-EF tunnels, on the considered hop (P router P1), these packets are scheduled in the same AF4 queue.

Figure 5-31 *Usage of Five Queues and Two Class Types in EMEA, AsiaPac, and South America*

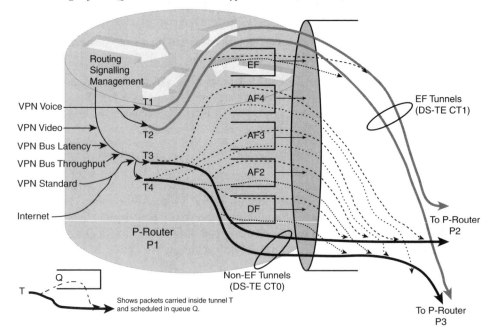

Globenet also considered a bandwidth constraints model that would constrain the EF tunnels and the non-EF tunnels independently, as with the Maximum Allocation Model (MAM) (also discussed in Chapter 2). But, in Globenet's environment, this would lead to either some bandwidth wastage or some unacceptable congestion risks. For example, if the EF tunnels were limited to 30 percent of link capacity, and the non-EF tunnels were limited independently to 70 percent of link capacity, clearly the aggregate load would be kept below 100 percent so that congestion would be prevented. However, if the EF tunnels currently have only 10 percent of link capacity reserved, the non-EF tunnels would not be able to reserve more than their 70 percent, unnecessarily leaving 20 percent of link capacity wasted. Conversely, if the EF tunnels were limited to 30 percent of link capacity and the non-EF tunnels to 90 percent of link capacity, clearly the non-EF tunnels could reserve up to 90 percent so that no capacity is wasted when the EF tunnels actually use only 10 percent. However, the non-EF tunnels could also establish up to 90 percent of link capacity even if the EF tunnels have indeed reserved their full 30 percent. This would result in an aggregate load of 120 percent on the link and a level of congestion that is unacceptable to Globenet. Hence, it rejected a model with independent bandwidth constraints.

In the future, Globenet may investigate the use of a third Class Type with the RDM. For example, this may be used to create a third mesh of TE tunnels to carry separately the interactive traffic (VPN Video CoS and VPN Business Latency CoS), which also has some delay constraints but less stringent than voice VPN CoS. The tunnels in that third mesh are called the interactive tunnels. In that case, RDM would be used to

- Limit the EF tunnels to 30 percent
- Limit the EF tunnels and interactive tunnels together to a limit specifically engineered for the VPN Video and VPN Business Latency traffic (say 50 to 60 percent)
- Limit the EF tunnels, interactive tunnels, and non-EF-noninteractive tunnels together to 100 percent (plus overbooking)

Globenet uses a number of satellite links in South America. They are attractive to Globenet because they result in additional bandwidth at lower cost and allow easier long-distance connections within the region because their cost is distance-independent. However, these links involve a propagation delay on the order of 300 ms (the amount of time the signal takes to travel to the satellite and back to Earth). This makes them unsuitable to transport voice traffic. This is another important application of DS-TE for Globenet. In South America, it uses DS-TE to make sure that the Voice VPN CoS is never routed onto satellite links.

NOTE   Although satellite services generally are offered as unidirectional services, Globenet always combines two such unidirectional services into a single link that behaves as a bidirectional link to the routers.

The details of the current DiffServ-aware MPLS Traffic Engineering design for the EF traffic and non-EF traffic are provided later, in the "MPLS Traffic Engineering Design" section.

Cisco's Modular QoS CLI (MQC) supports independent control of three scheduling attributes for each queue:

- **Minimum bandwidth**—This attribute defines the minimum bandwidth that is guaranteed to the queue by the scheduler.

- **Excess bandwidth**—This attribute defines how to allocate excess bandwidth to a queue beyond its minimum bandwidth (which may be 0 in cases where a minimum bandwidth is not also configured). The excess bandwidth is expressed as a percentage of the bandwidth not allocated to any queue (or allocated to a queue but currently left unused).

- **Priority**—This attribute specifies that any offered load in this queue is to be serviced ahead of all other queues (up to the optionally configured policing bandwidth on the priority queue).

In a very similar way, Globenet felt that some of its CoSs required absolute allocation of bandwidth. (The amount of bandwidth allocated to the queue must reflect very closely the expected peak traffic based on the contracted rates.) This was necessary to meet the delay/jitter/bandwidth requirements associated with the CoSs:

- EF traffic (VPN Voice as well as ATM pseudowires and virtual IP leased line in the future)
- AF4 traffic (VPN Video)
- AF3 traffic (VPN Business Latency)

The other CoSs needed only relative bandwidth allocation (the amount of bandwidth allocated to the queue must primarily reflect a relative level of service versus some other classes):

- AF2 traffic (VPN Business Throughput)
- DF traffic (VPN Standard as well as Internet)

Consequently, on the queues corresponding to the CoSs that need only relative bandwidth allocation, Globenet elected not to configure a minimum bandwidth. Instead, it configured an excess bandwidth. This way, Globenet would not need to modify the configuration for these queues if it decided to modify the minimum bandwidth of a CoS requiring absolute bandwidth allocation. This decision also would be advantageous if Globenet decided, in the future, to introduce an additional CoS with its own absolute bandwidth allocation requirement.

Example 5-10 illustrates the core QoS egress service policy for an OC-3 Packet over SONET (PoS) link. Globenet configured the following:

- A conditional policing bandwidth of 40 percent of link bandwidth on the EF queue (which is configured with the priority attribute).
- A minimum bandwidth on the AF4 queue of 20 percent of link bandwidth.
- A minimum bandwidth on the AF3 queue of 5 percent of link bandwidth.

- An excess bandwidth on the AF2 queue of 83 percent of the remaining bandwidth.
- An excess bandwidth on the DF queue of 17 percent of the remaining bandwidth. Globenet selected the percentage values of 83 percent and 17 percent to allocate roughly five times more excess bandwidth to the AF2 queue than to the DF queue.

This bandwidth allocation is illustrated in Figure 5-32.

Example 5-10 *Core QoS Egress Service Policy on an OC-3 Link in EMEA and AsiaPac*

```
!
class-map match-any class-RealTime
  match mpls exp 5
class-map match-any class-Video
  match mpls exp 4
class-map match-any class-Latency
  match mpls exp 3
class-map match-any class-Throughput
  match mpls exp 2
  match mpls exp 1
  match dscp 48
  match mpls exp 6
!
policy-map Core-QoS-OC3-policy
  class class-RealTime
     priority percent 40
     queue-limit 3060 packets
  class class-Video
     bandwidth percent 20
     queue-limit 3875 packets
  class class-Latency
     bandwidth percent 5
     queue-limit 3875 packets
  class class-Throughput
     bandwidth remaining percent 83
     random-detect precedence-based
     random-detect exponential-weighting-constant 9
     random-detect precedence 6 214 1425 1
     random-detect precedence 2 214 1425 1
     random-detect precedence 1 72 214 1
     queue-limit 3875 packets
  class class-default
     bandwidth remaining percent 17
     random-detect
     random-detect exponential-weighting-constant 7
     random-detect 45 298 1
     queue-limit 3875 packets
!
int pos0/0
  service-policy output Core-QoS-OC3-policy
```

Figure 5-32 *Bandwidth Allocation in the Core in EMEA, Asia Pacific, and South America*

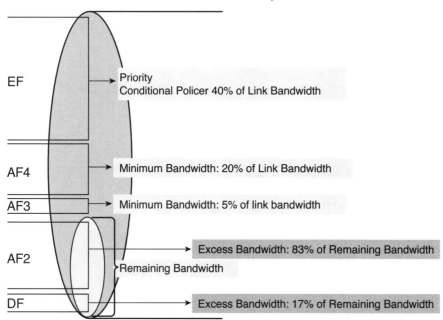

Because the VPN Business Throughput CoS is expected to carry a majority of TCP traffic, Random Early Detection (RED) is applied to the AF2 queue for optimum interaction with TCP flow-control mechanisms.

Globenet decided to handle control traffic, as well as management traffic, in the same queue as the VPN Business Throughput CoS (AF2 queue) because it offers appropriate transport commitments. The control traffic is identified based on the following:

- DSCP value 48 (which corresponds to precedence 6). Cisco routers automatically set the DSCP to this value when generating routing packets (OSPF, BGP) as well as other essential control traffic (LDP, RSVP-TE, Telnet, and so on).

- EXP value 6 for routing packets that are MPLS encapsulated over the core, such as BGP packets.

The management traffic originated by the Management System toward any network element is marked with DSCP=16 on the network management system side. Hence, it is marked with the appropriate EXP=2 value when encapsulated in MPLS and can be classified based on this criterion. For the traffic originated by the P router or PE router, the device must be configured to set the DSCP to the same DSCP=16 value (which then gets mapped to EXP=2). Cisco IOS supports the concept of local policy. This allows classification and marking to be applied to locally generated traffic (while usual QoS service policies are applied to logical or physical interfaces). As shown in Example 5-11, Globenet uses such a local policy to identify traffic going to the management system and marks it with DSCP=16.

Example 5-11 *Core QoS Local Policy Template for Marking Management Traffic in EMEA, AsiaPac, and South America*

```
!
!local route map (applies on locally generated traffic)
ip local policy route-map LocalTraffic
!
!identifies Management Traffic
Access-list 101 permit ip host loopback-address management-subnet mask
!
route-map LocalTraffic permit 10
  match ip address 101
  set ip dscp 16
!
```

NOTE   Globenet uses IS-IS as its IGP in the core. Because IS-IS is not encapsulated in IP, the DiffServ mechanisms cannot be directly applied for preferential treatment of IS-IS packets, as is done for BGP, for example (or OSPF when it is used). For example, IS-IS traffic obviously is not captured by the classification criteria (match on IP DSCP=48 and MPLS EXP=6) used to classify routing traffic such as OSPF and BGP. To protect the IS-IS traffic, Globenet takes advantage of mechanisms supported by its routers specifically for locally generated traffic. For example, locally generated traffic identified as essential (such as some IS-IS messages) can bypass any dropping mechanism on egress. In some cases it can be scheduled into a dedicated queue, which operates in parallel to the DiffServ queues, and with a minimum bandwidth allocated to it to provide appropriate protection to that traffic.

Globenet needs to ensure that the out-of-contract traffic (accepted in the VPN Business Throughput CoS beyond the contracted rate) cannot steal significant resources in case of congestion in the AF2 queue. Therefore, it uses WRED inside the AF2 queue. More precisely, Globenet elected to

- Apply a regular RED random drop profile to the important traffic (VPN Business Throughput in-contract as well as control and management traffic)

- Apply a much more aggressive drop profile to the VPN Business Throughput out-of-contract traffic

To configure the RED regular drop profile, Globenet used the same formulas as Telecom Kingland that were presented in the "QoS Design in the Core Network" section in Chapter 4. Hence, for the important traffic, Globenet computed the RED parameters in the following way:

- The exponential weighting constant n is such that

  $2^{-n} = 10 / B$, where B = queue bandwidth / (MTU $*$ 8)
  (with MTU = 1500 bytes)

- The minimum and maximum thresholds are set to 15 percent and 100 percent of the pipe size, respectively, where

  pipe size = RTT * queue bandwidth / (MTU * 8)

- The maximum drop probability is set to 1.

The AF2 queue is allocated 83 percent of the remaining bandwidth. Consider the following:

- The EF queue is expected to carry at most 30 percent of link capacity in a steady situation. DS-TE is configured to route up to only 30 percent worth of EF traffic on any link (despite the fact that the conditional policer is configured to 40 percent of link capacity to cope with transient situations).

- The AF4 queue is allocated 20 percent of link capacity.

- The AF3 queue is allocated 5 percent of link capacity.

Thus, the normal service rate of the AF2 queue taken into account by Globenet for WRED fine-tuning is 83 percent of (100–30–20–5) percent, which is about 37 percent of link bandwidth. On an OC-3 link, this means the queue bandwidth of the AF2 queue to be taken into account for RED fine-tuning is 57 Mbps. With this queue bandwidth and assuming a round-trip time (RTT) of 300 ms, these formulas yield the following values, which appear in Example 5-10:

- An exponential weighting constant of 9

- A minimum threshold of 214

- A maximum threshold of 1425

For the VPN Business Throughput out-of-contract, Globenet elected to apply a maximum threshold that equals the minimum threshold of the in-contract traffic. Therefore, out-of-contract traffic is discarded very aggressively (if needed, to the point where 100 percent of the out-of-contract packets get dropped) before the in-contract traffic has to enter its own random drop mode. The minimum threshold is set to a third of the maximum threshold, which is 72. The maximum drop probability is also set to 1.

Figure 5-33 illustrates these WRED drop profiles for the AF2 queue.

NOTE The WRED profile in the class-Throughput class is configured in Example 5-10 with the keyword precedence-based. This syntax indicates that WRED applies to the EXP field of MPLS packets (in addition, of course, to the Precedence field of IP packets).

Figure 5-33 *WRED Drop Profiles in the AF2 Queue in the Core*

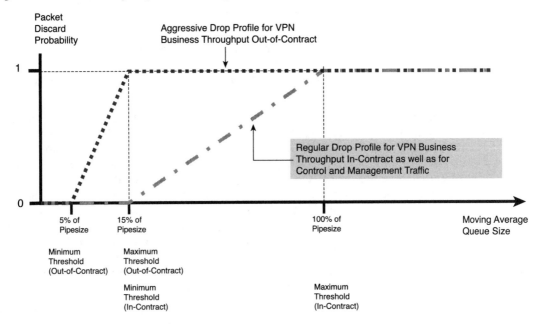

Globenet also activated RED in the DF queue to smooth adjustment of TCP flows (which are expected to be dominant in that queue because it carries Internet traffic as well as VPN Standard) to the available capacity in that queue. For fine-tuning of RED in the DF queue, Globenet also used the formulas detailed previously for regular RED drop profile. Because the DF queue is allocated 17 percent of the remaining bandwidth, the normal service rate of the DF queue taken into account by Globenet for RED fine-tuning is 17 percent of (100–30–20–5) percent, which is 7.65 percent of link bandwidth. On an OC-3 link, this means a queue bandwidth of about 11.9 Mbps. This results in

- An exponential weighting constant of 7
- A minimum threshold of 45
- A maximum threshold of 298
- A maximum drop probability of 1

Globenet did not activate RED in the VPN Voice, VPN Video, or VPN Business Latency CoSs because those are not expected to carry a dominant proportion of TCP, or TCP-like, elastic traffic.

Finally, like Telecom Kingland, Globenet decided to place a limit on the instantaneous queue size for each of the three queues. This avoids unexpected hogging of buffers by one queue and places a hard bound on absolute worst delay and jitter through that hop.

For the EF queue, the queue limit is configured so that it corresponds to an absolute worst queuing delay through that hop of 30 ms for the real-time traffic. On an OC-3 link where the

EF queue can use up to 40 percent of link bandwidth and with a packet size of 76 bytes (assuming G.729 codecs at a 30-ms sampling interval, which means a payload of 30 bytes plus an IP header of 40 bytes and a PPP header of 6 bytes), this means an EF queue limit of 3060 packets.

For all the other queues, to make sure that the queue limit does not result in unnecessary tail drops, Globenet configured a queue limit such that it could buffer up to 100 ms worth of traffic in the queue, assuming an average packet size of 250 bytes and assuming that the queue is currently granted 50 percent of the link capacity. This represents 3875 packets.

The default behavior of a TE tunnel headend in the Cisco IOS implementation is to copy the EXP field received in the outmost label stack entry to the EXP field of the pushed MPLS TE tunnel label entry. Similarly, the default behavior of a label switch router at disposition of the TE tunnel label stack entry (the penultimate hop router when PHP is used on TE tunnels, as is the case in Globenet's network) is to leave the EXP field of the exposed label entry untouched. Hence, the EXP marking scheme is entirely preserved through MPLS TE tunnels. In the core, packets from any Layer 3 MPLS VPN CoS, or from the Internet access service, have the exact same EXP value in the outmost label stack entry whether they are currently transported in a TE tunnel (for instance, at an intermediate hop of the P router-to-P router TE tunnel) or not (for instance, on the hop from the PE router to the first P router). This means that the same QoS egress policy relying on classification of packets based on the outmost EXP field value can be used independent of whether, and where, MPLS TE is used.

As shown in Example 5-10, Globenet elected to use the concept of class default (which captures all the traffic that hasn't been classified into other classes) to classify traffic that needs to go into the DF queue. This is an efficient way to ensure that if some packets with an unexpected marking end up in the core (for example, through a security hole temporarily opened by misconfiguration), they will always be scheduled in the DF queue. This protects more-important traffic from denial of service.

Also, as explained in the section "Layer 3 MPLS VPN Service Design," the Internet traffic normally is label-switched through the Globenet core. However, it could be forwarded natively as IP traffic in some exceptional situations where MPLS connectivity between PE routers is temporarily lost. In this case, the Internet traffic is still scheduled in the DF queue, even without any explicit classification on the DSCP of 0 in the QoS egress policy, because this traffic is naturally captured by the class default.

Globenet applies a core QoS egress service policy such as the one described in Example 5-10 on all core-facing interfaces of PE routers as well as on all P router interfaces. Because a few parameters, such as WRED fine-tuning and maximum instantaneous queue size, depend on the interface bandwidth, a different service policy is created for every interface type (OC-3, OC-48, and so on). The rest of the service policy (including definition of classes and scheduling configuration) is the same, independent of the interface bandwidth.

QoS Design in the Core Network on ATM PVCs

In the Asia-Pacific region, Globenet uses ATM PVCs supported on its own ATM infrastructure to interconnect some of its P routers and P/PE routers. Several models are conceivable for QoS interworking between the IP/MPLS layer and the ATM layer. Globenet selected a simple QoS interworking model whereby each ATM PVC is seen and used by the IP/MPLS layer exactly as if it were a point-to-point link, only it can be of any arbitrary speed:

- At the IP/MPLS layer, the DiffServ mechanisms are applied independently over each ATM PVC exactly as if it were a point-to-point link.

- At the ATM layer, to make sure that the ATM VC is closely emulating a point-to-point link, Globenet uses a number of techniques. First, on the ATM switches, Globenet provisions the ATM PVC with an ATM traffic class of VBR-rt and with a Sustainable Cell Rate (SCR) equal to the targeted IP bandwidth (taking into account the ATM cell header and cell packing overhead). The VBR-rt ATM traffic class ensures that ATM cells are switched through the ATM infrastructure with very low delay and jitter. The provisioned SCR ensures that, as long as the router transmits at the SCR rate or below, enough resources will be reserved in the ATM infrastructure to carry the offered traffic on the PVC with negligible cell loss. Finally, on the routers, Globenet activated ATM-level traffic shaping so that traffic is shaped in accordance with the provisioned SCR. Three configurable parameters control the detailed behavior of each per-VC ATM shaper on Globenet routers: SCR, Peak Cell Rate (PCR), and a committed burst (which defines the size of the burst that the shaper can transmit in excess of SCR but at, or below, PCR). Globenet configured the ATM shapers with a PCR and an SCR, both equal to the SCR provisioned on the ATM PVC and with a very small burst. This ensures that routers shape traffic very smoothly against the ATM PVC SCR and that absolutely all the cells transmitted are within the ATM PVC traffic contract. Hence, all the transported IP/MPLS traffic is guaranteed to experience very low delay/jitter and negligible loss.

With this model, the congestion problem is effectively completely pushed out of the ATM layer (which provides a fixed-rate pipe). It is dealt with entirely at the IP layer, which is responsible for adapting the aggregate IP rate to the fixed rate supported by the ATM PVC. This is very attractive to Globenet because it provides a very simple operational demarcation point between the IP/MPLS layer and the ATM layer. Also, congestion can be dealt with very selectively in the IP/MPLS layer because it has full awareness of the CoSs. Finally, this model allows Globenet to apply virtually the same IP/MPLS QoS service policies over ATM PVCs and hence have a consistent QoS approach regardless of the underlying transport layer.

Globenet elected the VBR-rt traffic class instead of CBR because it offers delay/jitter and loss levels that are perfectly satisfactory for the IP/MPLS traffic (including the demanding VPN Voice CoS) while monopolizing fewer resources on the ATM network.

Globenet also considered a more complex QoS interworking model involving a variation of the VBR traffic class where the ATM switches accept ATM traffic with some level of burstiness. For example, Globenet considered allowing the router to send some traffic in excess of the SCR router and marking the less-important IP traffic (VPN Business Throughput out-of-contract, VPN Standard, Internet) as CLP=1 (with the Cell Loss Priority bit set). This had the potential benefit of effectively allowing the IP/MPLS traffic to take more advantage of statistical gains inside the ATM network and make use of excess capacity on a best-effort basis while ensuring that the less-important traffic is dropped first by the ATM switches (through the CLP bit) in case of congestion inside the ATM network. However, Globenet considered risks of QoS degradation for the important CoSs. For example, in case there is currently only a very small rate of less-important IP/MPLS traffic, the important traffic would effectively be allowed to burst beyond the SCR. Then it would potentially be subject to remarking of the CLP bit and eventually to discard in case of temporary congestion within the ATM network. Also, the operational demarcation point is less clear between the IP/MPLS layer and ATM layer and would make troubleshooting in case of unexpected QoS degradation more difficult. Finally, Globenet generally expects discard at the IP/MPLS layer to interact more smoothly with elastic IP traffic than discard at the ATM layer. The main reason for this is that random discard mechanisms such as RED/WRED applied at the IP/MPLS layer are specifically designed and are fine-tuned to optimize their interaction with transport protocols' congestion control mechanisms.

To implement the simple QoS interworking model selected by Globenet, the egress QoS policy applied on ATM interfaces involves the following:

- Defining a QoS service policy that is the same as the one used on other types of links, only with fine-tuning of the rate-dependent parameters (RED/WRED profiles and queue limits) according to the range of PVC rates.

- For each ATM PVC, activation of per-VC ATM traffic shaping at that VC's SCR.

- For each ATM PVC, application of the QoS service policy at the VC level. This relies on the router support of per-VC queuing whereby a logical separate scheduler effectively runs independently for each ATM VC and schedules the packets according to the service policies and supply packets to the ATM per-VC shaper. Operation of such per-VC queuing and per-VC shaping is illustrated in Figure 5-34.

A short first-in, first-out (FIFO) buffer (called the Tx-ring on a Cisco router) is used on Globenet routers to hand over to the transmission logic the packets selected by the scheduler. As discussed in the "CE Router Egress Policy" section in Chapter 4, this Tx-ring may introduce a small additional delay/jitter component that applies indiscriminately to any traffic (including the VPN Voice traffic in that case). Although this is always negligible on high-speed links, it can be noticeable on lower-speed links if the Tx-ring size is too large. Hence, Globenet felt that fine-tuning of the Tx-ring size was justified on ATM PVCs considering that optimum delay/jitter is sought for the VPN Voice CoS. In the context of ATM, there is a separate logical Tx-ring buffer for each PVC that controls how packets from the multiple VCs are handed over to the ATM Segmentation and Reassembly (SAR) logic and that enforces isolation across VCs. This per-VC logical Tx-ring is illustrated in Figure 5-34. Its fine-tuning obeys the same trade-offs as over the point-to-point link. The smaller the Tx-ring size, the smaller the introduced delay/jitter. However, the Tx-ring size must not be too small, because this could result in under-run of the Tx-ring buffer and an inability to achieve the targeted ATM rate. For example, on an ATM PVC with a rate of 20 Mbps, assuming a 1500-byte MTU, a Tx-ring size of four packets as selected by Globenet results in a worst-case delay/jitter contribution of 2.4 ms.

Figure 5-34   *Per-VC Queuing on ATM PVCs in the Globenet Core*

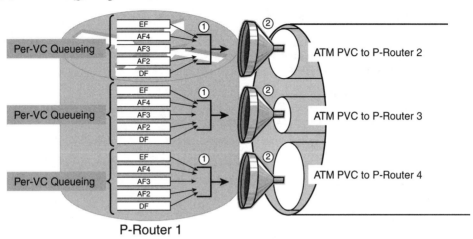

① Per-VC Logical Tx-Ring
② Per-VC ATM Shaping

A QoS egress policy applied on an ATM PVC in the Globenet core is provided in Example 5-12.

Example 5-12   *Core Egress QoS Service Policy Template on ATM PVC in EMEA and AsiaPac*

```
!
class-map match-any class-RealTime
  match mpls exp 5
class-map match-any class-Video
  match mpls exp 4
class-map match-any class-Latency
  match mpls exp 3
class-map match-any class-Throughput
  match mpls exp 2
  match mpls exp 1
  match dscp 48
  match mpls exp 6
!
policy-map Core-QoS-ATM-policy
  class class-RealTime
    priority percent 40
    queue-limit 395 packets
  class class-Video
    bandwidth percent 20
    queue-limit 500 packets
  class class-Latency
    bandwidth percent 5
    queue-limit 500 packets
  class class-Throughput
    bandwidth remaining percent 83
    random-detect precedence-based
```

continues

Example 5-12 *Core Egress QoS Service Policy Template on ATM PVC in EMEA and AsiaPac (Continued)*

```
              random-detect exponential-weighting-constant 9
              random-detect precedence 6 28 184 1
              random-detect precedence 2 28 184 1
              random-detect precedence 1 10 28 1
              queue-limit 500 packets
          class class-default
              bandwidth remaining percent 17
              random-detect
              random-detect exponential-weighting-constant 7
              random-detect 6 39 1
              queue-limit 500 packets
     !
     vc-class atm Core-20Mb
       vbr-rt 24000 24000 10
       oam-pvc manage
       encapsulation aal5snap
     !
     interface ATM8/0/0.1 point-to-point
        ip address interface-prefix mask
        pvc Singapore-to-NewDeli 0/112
        class-vc Core-20Mb
        tx-ring-limit 4
        service-policy out Core-QoS-ATM-policy
      !
```

MPLS DiffServ-aware TE operates over ATM PVCs exactly as it operates over point-to-point links. Like those, MPLS DS-TE sees each PVC as a link with configurable bandwidth constraints (BC0 and BC1) and other MPLS TE attributes. Each PVC is used in the exact same way for constraint-based routing and admission control. Clearly, the bandwidth constraints configured by Globenet reflect the rate of the individual ATM PVC. More precisely, BC0 is set to the estimated bandwidth achievable at the IP layer, taking into account the Layer 1 and Layer 2 overheads. This also includes the ATM overhead of the ATM cell header as well as the overhead of partial fill of the last cell used to carry a packet. As mentioned in the later section "Setting the Maximum Reservable Bandwidth on Each Link," Globenet systematically took into account the lower layers' overhead when configuring the reservable bandwidth on a link, should it be a PoS link with PPP, ATM PVCs, and so on.

QoS Design in the Core Network in North America

Because high-speed links are more readily available and have a much lower cost in the North America region, Globenet deployed a simpler and coarser-grain QoS design in North America than in other regions.

First, Globenet decided to aggregate several CoSs in the core and hence to manage only three queues. Figure 5-35 illustrates the mapping of CoSs into these three queues in North America.

Figure 5-35   *Usage of the Three Core Queues in North America*

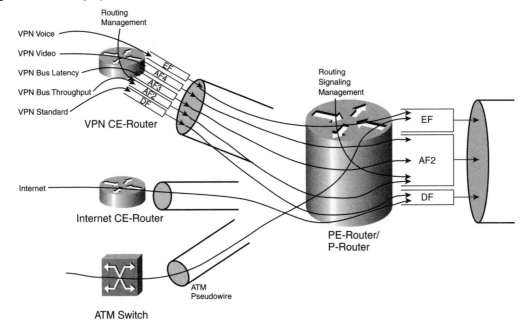

Secondly, Globenet elected to simply rely on capacity planning with some level of overengineering to ensure that adequate service rate is granted by each queue to its transported traffic to meet its respective QoS requirements. Hence, neither MPLS DiffServ-aware TE nor regular MPLS TE is used in North America to perform constraint-based routing or admission control of traffic.

As in the other regions, Globenet uses a strict priority queue as the EF queue to offer optimum delay and jitter to the EF traffic. It also applies a conditional policer to 40 percent of link bandwidth as a safety measure to protect the rest of the traffic. In North America, the AF2 queue is used for traffic scheduled in the AF2, AF3, and AF4 queues in other regions. Therefore, it needs to be allocated a higher proportion of the remaining bandwidth than in other regions. Conversely, the DF queue, which carries the same CoSs as in other regions, needs to be allocated a smaller share of the remaining bandwidth. Thus, Globenet allocated 89 percent of the remaining bandwidth to the AF2 queue and 11 percent of the remaining bandwidth to the DF queue. Globenet selected these relative allocations to ensure the same relative share of the bandwidth to the DF queue as in other regions:

- In North America, assuming a maximum sustained load in the EF queue of 30 percent, the remaining bandwidth is 70 percent. 11 percent of this 70 percent represents 7.7 percent of the link bandwidth.

- In other regions, also assuming a maximum sustained load in the EF queue of 30 percent, and because the AF4 and AF3 queues are allocated 20 percent and 5 percent of the link bandwidth, respectively, the remaining bandwidth is 45 percent. The 17 percent of this 45 percent remaining bandwidth represents 7.65 percent of the link bandwidth.

Similarly, the AF2 queue receives the same relative share of bandwidth in North America as the AF2, AF3, and AF4 queues collectively receive in other regions.

In addition to granting a different share of the link capacity to each queue, Globenet enforces an aggregate capacity planning policy to trigger provisioning of additional link capacity whenever

- The aggregate load across all traffic reaches 55 percent of the link capacity, in the absence of failure, as determined by the monitoring of interface counters.

  or

- The aggregate load across all traffic would reach 90 percent of the link capacity, should one of the links or nodes fail, as determined by a centralized simulation tool collecting current network topology, estimating traffic matrix, and assessing the theoretical load on all links resulting from any single-failure situations.

QoS Design in the Core Network Across Regions

As explained in the "Layer 3 MPLS VPN Service Design" section, inter-AS option B is used for Layer 3 MPLS VPN operations across regions of the Globenet network. Hence, the VPN packets are label-switched by the ASBRs and are encapsulated with an MPLS header on the links between ASBRs. By default, the label-switching behavior in the IOS implementation is to copy the received EXP value in the transmitted MPLS header. This means that all the VPN packets transmitted on the link between ASBRs naturally have their EXP field set according to Globenet policy.

Thus, Globenet simply applies similar QoS egress policies on the links between ASBRs across regions, as it does on core links in a region. On the OC-48 link between North America and Europe, a QoS egress policy with three queues (as used within North America) is applied at both ends of the link. On all other links, which are OC-3 or E3, QoS egress policies with five queues (as used within EMEA, AsiaPac, and South America) are applied.

As explained in the "Layer 3 MPLS VPN Service Design" section, traffic going from an Internet CE router to a destination that is in another region of the world and that is not also attached to Globenet's network exits the Globenet network in the ingress region because each region has its own local Internet peering point(s). This means that traffic going to the rest of the Internet never travels over the interregion links. The only Internet traffic Globenet carries over the interregion links is the traffic directly exchanged between two Internet CE routers attached to Globenet in different regions. The proportion of Internet traffic on the interregion links is then somewhat smaller than within each region. For this reason, Globenet allocates a smaller proportion of the remaining bandwidth to the DF queue on these links than within the regions.

More importantly, it allocates a larger proportion of the remaining bandwidth to the AF2 queue to maximize the QoS of the corresponding traffic on these constrained links.

The Internet traffic is carried in native IP packets (non-MPLS encapsulated) on the interregion links. However, no additional classification configuration is required in the egress QoS policies applied on the interregion links. The traffic going into the DF queue is classified using the concept of class default, which captures not only MPLS packets marked with EXP=0 but also IP packets marked with DSCP=0 because those are not explicitly classified into the other queues.

QoS Design on the Network Edge for Layer 3 MPLS VPN and Internet

The QoS design on the edge of the Globenet network is made up of QoS mechanisms on the CE routers (when managed by Globenet) and on the user-facing interfaces on PE routers.

CE Router Egress Policy

The key elements of the CE router egress policy are the same as those discussed for Telecom Kingland in the "CE Router Egress Policy" section in Chapter 4. In particular, assuming again Frame Relay access, the same hierarchy applies across

- The physical interface bandwidth
- The Committed Information Rate (CIR) enforced via Frame Relay traffic shaping
- The bandwidth allocated to each queue by the scheduler operating over the Frame Relay traffic shaping

Globenet also uses fragmentation and interleaving (FRF.12 in the case of Frame Relay) as well as fine-tuning of the Cisco Tx-ring to optimize delay and jitter for real-time traffic on low-speed accesses. Globenet also configures its egress QoS policy so that the policing actions enforced for each CoS do not apply to the Service Assurance Agent (SAA) sample traffic that is used to measure performance for that CoS.

Of course, one difference with the design of Telecom Kingland is that Globenet supports five CoSs instead of three. Another difference is that Globenet handles routing traffic and management traffic on the access link in the same queue as the Layer 3 MPLS VPN Business Throughput CoS instead of handling it in a dedicated user-hidden queue. To that end, as in the core, Globenet uses a local policy to set the DSCP of locally generated traffic destined for the Network Management System to the DSCP=16 value of the Layer 3 MPLS VPN Throughput CoS.

To further protect routing and management traffic, Globenet excludes this traffic from the scope of the policing applied to the rest of the VPN Business Throughput in the same manner as it excludes SAA traffic. This is achieved by applying policing through a child policy whose class explicitly excludes the routing and management traffic in addition to the SAA traffic. Otherwise, in case of high load in the Layer 3 MPLS VPN Business CoS, some routing and management traffic could be remarked as out-of-contract and then subject to aggressive WRED discard by the CE router or further downstream in the network.

Example 5-13 details a QoS service policy applied on a CE router. The customer contracted a 512-kbps CIR on a Frame Relay access and elected to allocate 25 percent of the CIR to the VPN Voice CoS, 10 percent to the VPN Latency CoS, and 50 percent to the VPN Throughput CoS. This customer does not use the VPN Video CoS.

Example 5-13 *CE Egress QoS Service Policy Template for a VPN Site with Four CoSs*

```
!identifies Routing Traffic
access-list 100 permit tcp any eq bgp any
access-list 100 permit tcp any any eq bgp
!
!identifies Management Traffic
access-list 101 permit ip host CE-loopback-address Management-subnet mask
!
!identifies VPN Voice traffic
access-list 102 permit classification-criteria-provided-by-customer-for-Voice
!
!identifies VPN Business Latency traffic
access-list 104
    permit classification-criteria-provided-by-customer-for-Business-Latency
!
!identifies VPN Business Throughput traffic
access-list 105
    permit classification-criteria-provided-by-customer-for-Business-Throughput
!
!identifies SAA Traffic
access-list 106 permit ip host CE-loopback-address
    host SAA-shadow-router-address
access-list 106 permit ip host CE-loopback-address
    host remote-CE-SAA-responder-router-address
!
!local route map (applies on locally generated traffic to
!mark management traffic)
ip local policy route-map LocalTraffic
!
route-map LocalTraffic permit 10
  match ip address 101
  set ip dscp 16
!
!class-map used below to exclude SAA traffic (from traffic to be policed)
class-map match-all class-NotSAA
  match not ip access-group 106
!
!class-map used below to exclude SAA, Management, and Routing traffic
!(from traffic to be policed)
class-map match-all class-NotSAAManagementRouting
  match not ip access-group 106
  match not ip access-group 101
  match not ip access-group 100
!
class-map match-any class-VPNVoice
  match dscp 40
  match dscp 46
```

Example 5-13 *CE Egress QoS Service Policy Template for a VPN Site with Four CoSs (Continued)*

```
   match ip access-group 102
!
class-map match-any class-VPNLatency
  match dscp 26
  match ip access-group 104
!
class-map match-any class-VPNThroughput
  match dscp 16
  match ip access-group 105
  match ip access-group 100
  match ip access-group 101
!
policy-map police-VPNVoiceNotSAA
  class class-NotSAA
    police cir percent 25 bc 30 ms conform-action set-dscp-transmit 46
    exceed-action drop
!
policy-map police-VPNLatencyNotSAA
  class class-NotSAA
    police cir percent 10 conform-action set-dscp-transmit 26
    exceed-action drop
!
policy-map police-VPNThroughputNotSAAManagementRouting
  class class-NotSAAManagementRouting
    police cir percent 50 bc 400 ms conform-action set-dscp-transmit 16
    exceed-action set-dscp-transmit 8
!
policy-map CE-to-PE-QoS-policy
  class class-VPNVoice
    priority
    service-policy police-VPNVoiceNotSAA
  class class-VPNLatency
    bandwidth percent 10
    service-policy police-VPNLatencyNotSAA
  class class-VPNthroughput
    bandwidth percent 50
    random-detect dscp-based
    random-detect exponential-weighting-constant 3
    random-detect dscp 16 66 198 1
    random-detect dscp 8 22 66 1
    service-policy police-VPNThroughputNotSAAManagementRouting
  class class-default
    bandwidth remaining percent 100
    set ip dscp 0
    random-detect
    random-detect exponential-weighting-constant 3
    random-detect 22 66 1
!
map-class frame-relay map-class-CE-to-PE
  frame-relay cir 512000
  frame-relay mincir 512000
```

continues

Example 5-13 *CE Egress QoS Service Policy Template for a VPN Site with Four CoSs (Continued)*

```
    frame-relay bc 5120
    frame-relay fragment 320
    service-policy output CE-to-PE-QoS-policy
!
int serial0/0
    tx-ring-limit 2
    frame-relay traffic-shaping
!
int serial0/0.1
 ip address CE-interface-prefix mask
 frame-relay interface-dlci 100
 frame-relay class map-class-CE-to-PE
!
rtr responder
!
```

Assuming a G.729-30 ms codec, each VoIP call represents about 20 kbps of traffic at the IP layer. This means that the VPN Voice CoS contracted rate (25 percent of the 512-kbps CIR) can accommodate six simultaneous VoIP calls. The burst tolerance configured in the VPN Voice policer is set to 30 ms so that it can accommodate the simultaneous burst of one packet from each of the six simultaneous calls. The packet size with G.729-30 ms calls is 76 bytes so that the maximum burst could be 6 * 76 = 456 bytes, which fits within 30 ms at a rate of 25 percent of 512 kbps.

The burst tolerance in the policer for the VPN Business Throughput CoS is configured so that it can accommodate one RTT-worth of traffic. Globenet tests demonstrated that this setting generally allowed effective interactions with TCP flows. Therefore, Globenet can collectively achieve a global transfer rate that is close to the contracted rate at all times (and more when spare capacity is available to accommodate out-of-contract traffic).

For fine-tuning of the regular RED profile on low-speed links, Globenet uses the same formulas as the ones used by Telecom Kingland and presented in the "CE Router Egress Policy" section in Chapter 4:

- The exponential weighting constant n is such that

  $2^{-n} = 1 / B$, where B = bandwidth / (MTU * 8)
  (with MTU = 1500 bytes)

- The minimum and maximum thresholds are equal to 100 percent and 300 percent of B, respectively. The maximum drop probability is set to 1.

However, unlike Telecom Kingland, Globenet offers a VPN Business Latency CoS that specifically addresses mission-critical traffic with a low delay requirement. Therefore, Globenet is more interested in optimizing achievable TCP throughput in the VPN Business Throughput CoS than minimizing its delay. Consequently, Globenet took a different WRED fine-tuning approach than Telecom Kingland. Rather than using the regular RED minimum and maximum thresholds for the in-contract traffic and using smaller (and hence very aggressive) thresholds for the out-of-contract traffic, Globenet used the regular RED minimum and maximum thresholds for the out-of-contract traffic and larger (and hence more lenient) thresholds for the in-contract traffic. Specifically, it used a minimum and a maximum threshold for the in-contract traffic. These are equal to 100 percent and 300 percent, respectively, of the maximum threshold used for out-of-contract traffic. (In other words, Globenet used a minimum and maximum threshold set to 300 percent and 900 percent of the pipe size, respectively.) This means that the average and maximum delay experienced by the in-contract traffic may be somewhat increased. However, this allows end users to significantly increase the effective TCP throughput they can obtain from the VPN Business Throughput CoS, even beyond their contracted rate, when the data path has spare capacity. The subset of mission-critical traffic with tight delay requirements can still be handled optimally through the VPN Business Latency CoS. These WRED drop profiles for the AF2 queue are illustrated in Figure 5-36.

Figure 5-36   *WRED Drop Profiles in the AF2 Queue on the Edge*

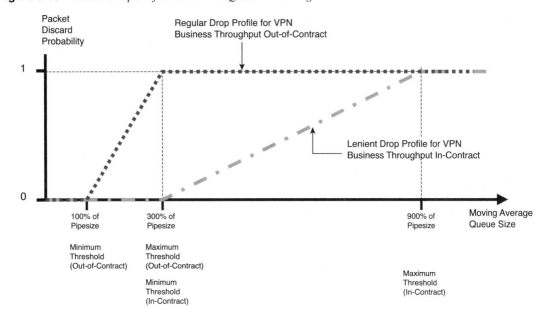

PE Router Ingress Policy

On interfaces attaching unmanaged Internet CE routers, it is essential that incoming traffic be remarked with the DSCP value of the Internet CoS so that it gets the appropriate treatment throughout the Globenet network. It also shouldn't be able to steal any resources destined for other CoSs, no matter what DSCP marking the Internet customer may be intentionally (or unintentionally) setting. To that end, Globenet applies a very simple QoS input policy over interfaces attaching unmanaged Internet CE routers. It systematically remarks the packet DSCP to 0 on all received traffic, as illustrated in Example 5-14.

Example 5-14 *PE Router Ingress QoS Policy for Unmanaged Internet CE Routers*

```
policy-map EdgeInInternet-QoS-policy
  class class-default
    set dscp 0
!
map-class frame-relay map-class-CE-to-PE
  service-policy input EdgeInInternet-QoS-policy
!
int serial0/0.1
  frame-relay interface-dlci 100
    class map-class-CE-to-PE
```

Similarly, on interfaces attaching unmanaged VPN CE routers, Globenet needs to police the traffic sent in each CoS against its contracted rate. In the case of unmanaged Layer 3 MPLS VPN service, it is the customer's responsibility to ensure that traffic sent by the unmanaged CE router toward the PE router has been marked according to Globenet's DSCP values for the five Layer 3 MPLS VPN CoSs. So, on the PE router, Globenet only needs to perform classification on the basis of the DSCP field based on Globenet's DSCP scheme. Example 5-15 shows an input QoS policy applied on an interface attaching an unmanaged Layer 3 MPLS VPN CE router.

Example 5-15 *PE Router Ingress QoS Policy for Unmanaged MPLS VPN CE Routers*

```
!
class-map match-any class-VPNVoice
  match dscp 46
!
class-map match-any class-VPNVideo
  match dscp 34
!
class-map match-any class-VPNLatency
  match dscp 26
!
class-map match-any class-VPNThroughput
  match dscp 16
!
policy-map EdgeInVPN-QoS-policy
  class class-VPNVoice
   police cir percent 25 bc 30 ms conform-action transmit exceed-action drop
  class class-VPNVideo
   police cir percent 25 conform-action transmit exceed-action drop
 class class-VPNLatency
    police cir percent 10 conform-action transmit exceed-action drop
 class class-VPNthroughput
    police cir percent 20 bc 400 ms conform-action transmit exceed-action set-dscp-
     transmit 8
```

Example 5-15   *PE Router Ingress QoS Policy for Unmanaged MPLS VPN CE Routers (Continued)*

```
   class class-default
     set ip dscp 0
 !
 map-class frame-relay map-class-CE-to-PE
    service-policy input EdgeInVPN-QoS-policy
 !
 int serial0/0.1
    frame-relay interface-dlci 100
    frame-relay class map-class-CE-to-PE
```

As a security measure against potential replacement or tampering with the Globenet managed CE router located on the customer premises, Globenet also applies per-CoS policing on interfaces attaching managed CE routers. The same type of input policies as for unmanaged CE routers (as shown in Example 5-15) are used for that purpose.

PE Router Egress Policy

The egress policy on the PE router to manage the link toward the CE router is very similar to the managed CE router egress policy (detailed in the "CE Router Egress Policy" section). The main differences is that classification can be performed directly on the DSCP values because all the traffic has already been classified and marked by the ingress CE router.

QoS Design for the Interprovider VPN with Telecom Kingland

One objective of the partnership with Telecom Kingland (discussed in Chapter 4) is to offer the same Layer 3 MPLS VPN service features to all sites of a customer, whether these sites are attached directly to Globenet or to Telecom Kingland. To that end, Telecom Kingland supports the Globenet QoS offering (including the five Globenet CoSs) on the access links attaching sites that belong to a Globenet VPN (instead of Telecom Kingland's regular QoS offering with three CoSs: VPN Real-Time, VPN Premium, and VPN Standard). Using this method, an end customer has to deal with only a single QoS offering for its VPN, even when the VPN contains some sites attached to Globenet and other sites attached to Telecom Kingland.

Figure 5-37 illustrates how consistent QoS is achieved end to end between two VPN sites—one attached to Telecom Kingland and the other attached to Globenet. It also provides the QoS markings and policies at every step of the path.

To facilitate end-to-end QoS operation, Telecom Kingland uses Globenet's DSCP values for marking by the CE routers. This allows support of five CoSs end to end and avoids the need to map, at the boundary between the two networks, from one DSCP value scheme to another. Thus, Telecom Kingland applies on the CE router an egress QoS policy based on both Globenet's DSCP marking scheme and its five-CoS offering.

Figure 5-37 *QoS Markings and Policies in the Interprovider VPN with Telecom Kingland*

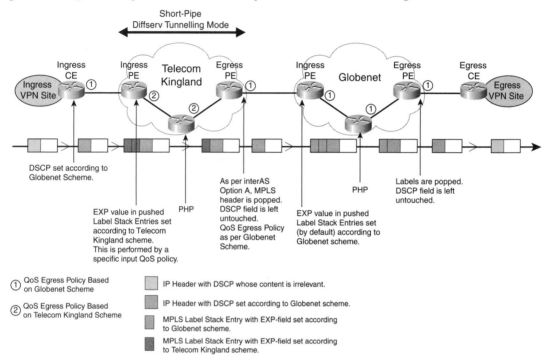

For transport over its backbone, Telecom Kingland wants to schedule all the VPN traffic, regardless of its CoS, in its DF queue, which is the one designed to carry all VPN traffic, including VPN voice traffic. So it needs to make sure that the PE router sets the EXP field of the label stack entries pushed by the ingress PE router to the value corresponding to the DF queue in Telecom Kingland's marking scheme, which is EXP=0. However, the PE router must not overwrite the DSCP value that was set by the CE router according to Globenet's marking scheme. It is preserved and can be used by Globenet downstream of Telecom Kingland to apply the corresponding QoS treatment. To that end, on the ingress PE router, Telecom Kingland applies a specific input QoS policy on interfaces attaching CE routers belonging to a Globenet VPN. It contains a sophisticated marking configuration that leaves the DSCP field untouched but that sets the EXP field of all the pushed label stack entries to 0. This input policy is illustrated in Example 5-16. Note that if Telecom Kingland didn't apply this policy, the traffic marked as VPN Business Latency for which the Globenet DSCP value is 26 and hence maps by default into EXP=3 would be scheduled in Telecom Kingland's AF3 queue. This queue is dedicated to transport of essential control and signaling traffic because EXP=3 is the value allocated to its telephony transit signaling traffic by Telecom Kingland. Of course, this would be unacceptable to Telecom Kingland.

You observe that Telecom Kingland effectively manages to apply its own QoS scheme through its MPLS backbone while preserving the Globenet QoS marking in the DSCP of the transported

IP packets. This optional capability of an MPLS DiffServ backbone is called QoS transparency. It can be very useful where multiple DiffServ administrative domains are interconnected, such as in the interprovider VPN scenario considered here with Globenet and Telecom Kingland. The specific method that Telecom Kingland uses to achieve QoS transparency is called the short pipe DiffServ tunneling model. It is characterized by the following:

- **On MPLS imposition**—Mark the imposed EXP value without modifying the QoS marking of encapsulated traffic (DSCP in the considered scenario).

- **On MPLS disposition**—Ignore the EXP value as received before the MPLS label pop, leave QoS marking of the exposed header unchanged (DSCP in the considered scenario), and use this QoS marking for egress scheduling.

A second DiffServ tunneling model called the pipe model supports QoS transparency. The only difference with the short pipe model is that, on MPLS disposition, egress scheduling is based on the EXP value as received before MPLS label pop. This is useful in environments where the MPLS network operator does not want to know the DiffServ policy of the transported traffic, even on the disposition router. Because Telecom Kingland is aware of the Globenet DiffServ policy and the Globenet policy is the one to be applied at the egress of the Telecom Kingland core, Telecom Kingland deployed the short pipe model.

Example 5-16 *Telecom Kingland's PE Router Ingress QoS Policy Template for Globenet's VPN*

```
policy-map EdgeInGlobenet-QoS-policy
  class class-default
    set mpls exp imposition 0
!
map-class frame-relay map-class-CE-to-PE-Globenet
  service-policy input EdgeInGlobenet-QoS-policy
!
int serial0/0.1
  frame-relay interface-dlci 100
    class map-class-CE-to-PE-Globenet
```

Because Layer 3 MPLS VPN inter-AS option A is used between Telecom Kingland and Globenet, the Telecom Kingland egress PE router pops the MPLS label stack and transmits the VPN packets as native IP packets over a link between back-to-back VRFs. As per the default operation of PE routers in the Cisco IOS implementation, the egress PE router leaves the exposed DSCP field untouched. Therefore, it contains DSCP markings as set by the ingress CE router according to Globenet's scheme.

As explained in the "Layer 3 MPLS VPN Service Design" section, the back-to-back VRF links are instantiated as VLANs over a Gigabit Ethernet link between the Globenet PE router and the Telecom Kingland PE router. For proper treatment of the Layer 3 MPLS VPN packets on that Gigabit Ethernet link, Telecom Kingland again applies a QoS egress policy based on Globenet's marking. This policy is similar to the three-queue policy applied by Globenet in the North America region. Note that there is no need to apply hierarchical QoS policies with some per-VLAN QoS policy on that interface. (An example is a first level of policy at the VLAN level enforcing per-VLAN shaping, with a second level of policy applying the three queues separately for each VLAN over its shaped rate.) Globenet is marketing a seamless QoS service through Telecom Kingland. Therefore, the user remains unaware of the interprovider boundary and does not subscribe to any contracted bandwidth specific to the interprovider boundary to be enforced by Globenet. Rather, scheduling is applied purely based on the three CoSs and irrespective of which VPN/VRF packets belong to.

Finally, Globenet receives packets and treats them in the exact same way as the rest of the Globenet Layer 3 MPLS VPN traffic, because they are received with their marking.

End-to-end QoS operations in the reverse direction (that is, for traffic from a site connected to Globenet toward a site connected to Telecom Kingland) are very similar. Globenet handles packets in the exact same way as it does for the rest of the Layer 3 MPLS VPN traffic. In this direction, Telecom Kingland needs to apply the following:

- An ingress QoS policy to set the imposed EXP to 0 on the PE router receiving the traffic from Globenet

- A three-queue egress QoS policy on the egress PE router that is based on Globenet's DSCP marking scheme, on the interfaces attaching Layer 3 MPLS VPN sites belonging to a Globenet VPN

QoS Design for Multicast Traffic

Globenet's mVPN service definition includes the following treatment of multicast traffic:

- All the multicast traffic is handled in the VPN Standard CoS. This ensures that multicast traffic cannot affect any of the other Layer 3 MPLS VPN CoSs.

- The aggregate multicast traffic generated by each site is limited to an agreed-upon rate that is smaller than the access link speed. This provides some basic protection against one site's sending multicast traffic at full access link speed. In turn, this provides some basic protection to the unicast traffic sharing the VPN Standard CoS with the mVPN traffic.

On its managed CE routers, Globenet classifies the multicast traffic as belonging to the VPN Standard CoS based on the multicast address prefix range. Then, as part of the existing VPN Standard CoS policy, the multicast packets have their DSCP field set to DSCP=0, just like unicast packets do. At the ingress PE router, it is worth remembering that multicast packets do not get encapsulated in MPLS, but rather in a multicast Generic Routing Encapsulation (GRE) tunnel. As per the default behavior of PE routers in the Cisco IOS implementation, the Globenet ingress PE routers copy the DSCP of the received multicast packet to the DSCP of the imposed multicast GRE header. Because the DSCP of the multicast packet was set to DSCP=0 on the CE router, all mVPN packets are sent to the core with the same DSCP=0 value in their multicast GRE header. As mentioned, Globenet's current QoS policies in the core ensure that any non-MPLS encapsulated IP packets with DSCP=0 are captured in the class default and thus are handled as part of the VPN Standard CoS in the DF queue. Finally, on the egress PE router, for scheduling over the PE-CE link, multicast packets are automatically classified by the existing egress QoS policy as belonging to the VPN Standard CoS. Hence, they are scheduled in the DF queue because of their DSCP=0 field (which is captured by the class default).

Globenet enforces rate limiting of the aggregate multicast traffic via the ip multicast rate-limit command.

QoS Design for the IPv6 VPN

Globenet currently supports a single CoS for the IPv6 VPN traffic, which is the VPN Standard CoS. In other words, all IPv6 traffic within a VPN is handled in the VPN Standard CoS on the CE-PE link, in the core, and on the PE-CE links.

With respect to the CE-PE link, the IPv6 traffic is automatically classified in the class default of a managed CE router because it does not match any of the explicit classification criteria defined for IPv4 by Globenet. Thus, it is naturally handled in the DF queue of the VPN standard CoS.

For handling through the core, Globenet uses the default 6VPE behavior in IOS on the ingress PE router. This sets the EXP field to 0 for all label stack entries pushed on IPv6 VPN packets (regardless of the DSCP value in the IPv6 packets). Then, because of this EXP=0 marking, all MPLS packets carrying IPv6 VPN packets get automatically classified in the DF queue by the existing core QoS policy. (Classification, which operates on the outmost EXP field, is entirely unaware of what is actually carried inside the MPLS packet.) This applies to both managed and unmanaged CE routers.

Finally, on the egress PE router, for scheduling over the PE-CE link, IPv6 packets are again captured by the class default and scheduled in the DF queue.

In the future, after the corresponding operation has been validated, the exact same QoS offering as for IPv4 VPNs will be offered for IPv6 VPNs. Note that this does not mean that five CoSs will be supported for IPv6 in addition to the five existing CoSs for IPv4. Rather, it means that the existing five CoSs will then be useable indiscriminately by any subset of IPv4 and IPv6 traffic. Just as customers today can specify their arbitrary classification criteria for which subset of IPv4 traffic belongs to which CoS. Customers in the future will be able to add their arbitrary criteria for which subset of IPv6 traffic also belongs to which of the five CoSs. The definition of the five CoSs, as well as their associated SLA commitments, will remain unchanged. The QoS design will build on the existing IPv4 VPN design. It will have the additional abilities for CE routers to perform detailed classification of IPv6 traffic and to mark the DSCP field of IPv6 packets (in accordance with Globenet's DSCP scheme already defined for IPv4 VPN). Also, the ingress PE routers will be configured to apply to IPv6 VPN traffic the same default DSCP-to-EXP mapping as for the IPv4 traffic. The egress PE routers will be configured to classify IPv6 traffic based on their DSCP field (as they do today for IPv4 traffic). QoS operations in the core will remain unchanged.

Pseudowire QoS Design for ATM Trunking

In North America and EMEA, Globenet supports trunking of its ATM switches using ATM pseudowire. Transparent Cell Transport mode is used for the ATM pseudowires. This allows the ATM switches trunked over the ATM pseudowires to support ATM virtual circuits and ATM virtual paths of any ATM traffic classes, including CBR. Thus, Globenet must give these ATM pseudowires a QoS that is appropriate for all ATM traffic classes, including CBR. This is why the ATM pseudowire traffic is scheduled in the EF queue at every hop in the network, along with the Layer 3 MPLS VPN voice traffic. Globenet ensures this by applying on the PE router an input QoS policy on the ATM interface supporting the pseudowire service. This policy marks the EXP field of the MPLS label stack entries imposed by the PE router to a value of EXP=5.

Also, in EMEA, where traffic is transported over MPLS DiffServ-aware TE tunnels to benefit from constraint-based routing and admission control, the ATM pseudowire is carried in dedicated separate TE tunnels. The rationale for this and the corresponding design are detailed in the "TE Design for ATM Pseudowires" section.

Example 5-17 shows the configuration details of marking the EXP field of the pseudowire traffic and steering this traffic into the dedicated MPLS TE tunnels (using the preferred path feature).

Example 5-17 *PE Router Template for ATM Pseudowires*

```
!
policy-map EdgeInATM-QoS-policy
  class class-default
    set mpls exp imposition 5
!
pseudowire-class ATM-Trunk1
  encapsulation mpls
  protocol ldp
  preferred-path interface tunnel tunnel-Id1 disable-fallback
! where tunnel-Id1 is the tunnel Id of the "Pseudowire Tunnel" starting
! on this PE-router and terminating on the remote PE-router PE1
!
pseudowire-class ATM-Trunk2
  encapsulation mpls
  protocol ldp
  preferred-path interface tunnel tunnel-Id2 disable-fallback
! where tunnel-Id2 is the tunnel Id of the "Pseudowire Tunnel" starting
! on this PE-router and terminating on the remote PE-router PE2

interface ATM1/0/0
  encapsulation aal0
  atm mcpt-timers 10 20 60
  xconnect remote-pe-ip-address pw-class ATM-Trunk1
  cell-packing 5 mcpt-timer 2
  service-policy input EdgeInATM-QoS-policy
!
interface ATM1/1/1
  encapsulation aal0
  atm mcpt-timers 10 20 60
  xconnect remote-pe-ip-address pw-class ATM-Trunk2
  cell-packing 5 mcpt-timer 2
  service-policy input EdgeInATM-QoS-policy
```

The **mcpt-timers** command lets you allocate three possible timers per ATM interface that specify the maximum cell packing timeout (MCPT). These values give the cell packing function a limited amount of time to finish. If the selected timer expires before the maximum number of cells are packed into an MPLS packet, the packet is sent anyway. As shown in Example 5-17, Globenet configured timers of 10, 20, and 60 microseconds and uses the second of these values. It also configured the maximum cell packing at five cells so that the packet also is transmitted whenever five cells have been received and thus can be encapsulated together.

By default, the preferred-path feature ensures that the corresponding pseudowire traffic gets rerouted onto another path (an LDP-established LSP between the corresponding routers) in the event that the configured TE tunnel interface goes down. This behavior can optionally be changed (using the **disable-fallback** keyword) so that in case of TE tunnel failure, the pseudowire traffic is not rerouted on another path. Instead, the affected pseudowires are turned down, and the PE router generates an ATM Operations, Administration, and Maintenance (OAM) indication on the affected pseudowires. This behavior is useful, for example, in environments where the ATM devices attached to the pseudowire have backdoor connectivity among each other and can attempt to dynamically reestablish the affected ATM circuits using the backdoor connectivity thanks to PNNI. For this reason, Globenet elected to use the disable-fallback option. As explained later, in the section "Last Resort Unconstrained Option," all TE tunnels are configured with a last resort unconstrained option. This ensures that the TE tunnel should always be routable and established, regardless of a failure situation, as long as there is IP connectivity between headend and tail-end. Thus, the only case in which the TE tunnel carrying ATM pseudowire traffic goes down is if there is indeed a complete loss of connectivity between the corresponding two PE routers or if there is a failure of the MPLS TE control plane because of a bug or operational misconfiguration. Although these situations are expected to occur very rarely, Globenet preferred to ensure fast and predictable reaction, maximizing the chances of recovery in the ATM network.

NOTE   The PE router configuration includes disabling auto-route announce on the TE tunnels used to transport ATM pseudowire traffic to make sure that no other traffic is routed onto these tunnels.

SLA Monitoring and Reporting

Globenet performs ongoing active measurement using IOS Service Assurance Agent (SAA) in a very similar manner to Telecom Kingland. It too uses dedicated SAA routers in every POP and activates the SAA responder on all its CE routers. It generates different sample streams (with different packet size and different DSCP marking) for each of the five CoSs and for POP-to-POP measurement in EMEA, AsiaPac, and South America. Within North America only three different samples are generated, because only three queues are maintained in the core in that region.

Globenet also uses SAA to perform site-to-site measurement for the five CoSs when its customers request this service. For example, in large VPNs, these site-to-site measurements may be deployed among regional sites and headquarters sites, or among remote sites and the hub site(s) of the VPN.

Globenet collects and compiles this measurement data to provide end users with the monthly QoS metrics for each CoS (POP-to-POP and, where applicable, site-to-site within its VPN). These are used to validate the contractual SLA commitments. The details of this measurement method, including sample frequency, sample size, and aggregation formulas across samples, are clearly spelled out in the SLA because they condition the computed values.

For network engineering purposes, Globenet also polls, on every core interface, at 15-minute intervals the MIB counters providing statistics for each queue in the core. In particular, it tracks the following for every queue:

- The number of bytes and packets that were scheduled in the queue
- The number of bytes and packets that were dropped
- The current queue depth
- Where RED/WRED is used, the number of bytes and packets that were dropped (for each RED/WRED profile)
- For the EF queue, how many packets were policed by the conditional policer

Globenet uses this information to confirm that the respective allocation of bandwidth across the CoS is appropriate and possibly, over time, to refine these relative allocations. Globenet also uses this information to validate current capacity planning (or trigger capacity upgrade where needed).

On customer request, Globenet also polls similar counter information on interfaces supporting PE-CE links and CE-PE links and gives the customer reports summarizing that information. This helps the customer validate, and adjust where needed, its access rate, the percentage of bandwidth allocated to each CoS, and the distribution of customer traffic over these CoSs.

MPLS Traffic Engineering Design

Because of the significant bandwidth cost in Globenet's global capital expenditure (capex) budget, the ability to efficiently traffic-engineer the core network was a crucial aspect of the design. To that end, Globenet conducted a detailed study to evaluate the most appropriate bandwidth optimization technique to deploy in each region, taking into account the traffic matrix, current link utilizations, and traffic growth forecasts. The objective was twofold. Globenet wanted to efficiently optimize the bandwidth to delay any link upgrade. Also, as explained in the "Quality of Service Design" section, Globenet wanted to meet the strict QoS commitments of the five CoSs, both in steady state and under any single network element failure. It would do this through proper cooperation of traffic engineering admission control and constraint-based routing features with QoS mechanisms.

The cost of bandwidth significantly differs from one region to another. Hence, in North America, where bandwidth costs are relatively cheap compared to the AsiaPac region, Globenet could afford to overengineer the network core by deploying a network made of OC-3 and OC-48 links. This helped it maintain sufficient margin before reaching any point of congestion, even during failure. Because of the North America region's bandwidth-rich topology, traffic engineering generally was not required. However, when necessary, it could be achieved by means of IGP metric optimization.

In the South America, EMEA, and AsiaPac regions, more careful bandwidth provisioning could yield very significant cost savings. Hence, in those regions, Globenet elected to use DiffServ-aware MPLS Traffic Engineering (DS-TE) to ensure that the load of EF traffic is kept below 30 percent of link capacity. At the same time, the aggregate load is kept below 100 percent of link capacity (plus some overbooking on higher-speed links), even under single-failure situations. Hence, in these regions the EF traffic and the non-EF traffic are carried on separate meshes of DS-TE tunnels belonging to different DS-TE class types (CT1 and CT0, respectively) so that they can be subject to different bandwidth constraints. As discussed in the section "QoS Design in the Core Network in the EMEA, AsiaPac, and South America Regions," Globenet uses the Russian Dolls Model so that the EF tunnels (CT1) are limited to their own bandwidth constraint, BC1. The non-EF tunnels (CT0) are limited together with the EF tunnels (CT1) to a shared bandwidth constraint, BC0. Also, in South America, Globenet uses DS-TE to ensure that the EF tunnels are routed only over terrestrial links and not over satellite links.

Globenet considered using MPLS Traffic Engineering within each region or across all regions. Within each region, meshes of TE tunnels would be provisioned on a per-region basis. Across all regions, a global mesh of TE tunnels between routers residing in different regions would be set up. The number of TE tunnels in a mesh equals $n * (n - 1)$, where n is the number of routers (remember that TE LSPs are unidirectional). Therefore, a per-region MPLS TE mesh was considered the optimal compromise, allowing Globenet to efficiently engineer the traffic in each region without requiring a considerable number of TE tunnels.

In terms of TE tunnel provisioning and configuration, an important requirement was to rely on dynamic network-centric mechanisms to reduce any risk of human error. Furthermore, considering the traffic growth and potential increase in the number of routers in their network, the addition of new equipment was not considered a rare event. Consequently, there was a requirement to automate the creation of any new TE LSPs in the network.

In each region except North America, two full meshes of TE LSPs between the P routers are required because DS-TE is used. In North America, where MPLS Traffic Engineering is used for the sole purpose of fast protection, a single full mesh of TE LSPs is required between the P routers. All these meshes of TE LSPs are automatically provisioned by means of the auto-mesh feature [see AUTO-MESH].

Another key aspect of MPLS Traffic Engineering is the ability to effectively determine the required bandwidth for each TE LSP. An important property of such an international network is that each region span several time zones. This make a dynamic TE LSP sizing strategy quite attractive and efficient in terms of bandwidth consumption. Indeed, if the TE LSP sizes are dynamically adjusted based on the actual traffic demand, they will not have to be sized based on their peak demand but on the exact required bandwidth at any point in the day, rendering their overall placement significantly more efficient. Indeed, because the TE LSPs do not face their peak demand simultaneously because of the presence of different traffic types and multiple time zones, such a dynamic strategy allows for the avoidance of oversized TE LSPs, which leads to shortest TE LSP paths and consequently to a better QoS. Note that this also allows for more efficient network resource usage. This was one of the motivations for using some dynamic TE LSP size adjustment techniques for the TE LSPs (expect in North America, where zero-bandwidth TE LSPs are used for Fast Reroute purposes only). Another motivation was that this avoided the challenge of accurately predicting and tracking the traffic matrix, which is particularly difficult in some parts of the network that have a low and/or fast-growing customer base.

In terms of network recovery strategy, Globenet had a rich QoS service portfolio targeting telephony, videoconferencing, and mission-critical applications. Also, its IP/MPLS backbone in North America and some places in Europe carries ATM traffic. Therefore, Globenet decided to use MPLS Traffic Engineering Fast Reroute for all its services and networks in the various regions. Some statistics gathered during the last decade on its ATM and IP networks showed that more than 90 percent of its unplanned failures were link failures. Thus, Globenet decided to deploy Fast Reroute to protect against link failures only.

Setting the Maximum Reservable Bandwidth on Each Link

The first task when enabling DiffServ-aware MPLS Traffic Engineering is to configure the bandwidth constraints on each TE-enabled link. Note that when regular TE is used, the single bandwidth constraint is also called the Maximum Reservable Bandwidth. The operator can configure these to any arbitrary value. They do not have to be identical to the actual link speed.

In the case of North America, MPLS Traffic Engineering is used only for Fast Reroute. Thus, each TE LSP has a bandwidth of 0 and consequently follows the IS-IS shortest path. Although each link could have been configured with a Maximum Reservable Bandwidth of 0 (BC0=0), Globenet decided to set it to the actual link speed in case it needed to use nonzero-bandwidth TE LSPs in the future in that region.

By setting the bandwidth constraint above or below the actual link speed (or the allocated service rate of the DiffServ queue corresponding to the constrained class type), the operator can enforce overbooking or underbooking policies. This over/underbooking approach is called link over/underbooking. It allows over/underbooking ratios to be fine-tuned on a per-link basis (or on a per-type-of-link basis) but not on a per-LSP basis. Note that the operator can also enforce over/underbooking by factoring an over/underbooking ratio when determining the tunnel size in relation to the traffic demand. The latter approach is called LSP over/underbooking. In contrast, it allows over/underbooking ratios to be fine-tuned on a per-LSP basis but not on a per-link basis.

Because outside North America Globenet uses a dynamic TE LSP sizing strategy, the bandwidth reserved by any given TE LSP is usually close to the bandwidth consumed by transmitted traffic currently using that TE LSP. This means that bandwidth reservation is accurate because it reflects the actual traffic demand. Generally there is not much room for efficiency improvement in trying to take advantage of the statistical gain of reserving multiple tunnels on a given link. However, as explained later in this chapter, the dynamic resizing algorithm involves selecting the highest load over several successive measurement periods. For this reason, Globenet observed that, on higher-speed links, where the number of TE LSPs is higher, the actual load is consistently smaller than the reserved load (by a small proportion, though). Globenet decided to take advantage of this small statistical gain and decided to enforce some overbooking for the non-EF TE LSPs on the higher-speed links. Because this overbooking depends on the link speed (and in fact is negligible on lower-speed links), Globenet used the link over/underbooking approach and configured the bandwidth constraints as detailed in Table 5-6. As explained in the section "QoS Design in the Core Network in the EMEA, AsiaPac, and South America Regions," the bandwidth constraint (BC1) applied to the EF TE LSPs is configured to 30 percent of link speed, and no overbooking is applied on those.

Table 5-6   *Bandwidth Constraints Setting (with Link Overbooking)*

Actual Link Speed	BC0 (Reservable Bandwidth for CT0 + CT1)	BC1 (Reservable Bandwidth for CT1)
Less than 2 Mbps	1.0 * link speed	0.3 * link speed
2 Mbps to 40 Mbps	1.0 * link speed	0.3 * link speed
OC-3	1.05 * link speed	0.3 * link speed
OC-48	1.10 * link speed	0.3 * link speed

For example, an OC-3 link of 155 Mbps is configured with a BC0 of 163 Mbps. Therefore, the routers may signal TE LSPs for up to 163 Mbps (across both EF TE LSPs and non-EF TE LSPs), which provides a bandwidth overbooking factor of 1.05. Within this 163 Mbps, up to 46.5 Mbps can be reserved for TE LSPs using the bandwidth pool BC1 (that is, the EF TE LSPs) so that no overbooking is applied on the EF TE LSPs.

A configuration example is shown in Example 5-18.

Example 5-18   *OC-3 Configuration Template*

```
interface pos3/0
 ip rsvp bandwidth 163000 subpool 46500
!
```

For the sake of simplicity, all the configuration examples shown in this chapter mention raw link bandwidth. However, Globenet takes into account the available payload for each medium and uses this effective bandwidth for TE purposes. For instance, the link speed of an OC-3 link is equal to 155.44 Mbps, but because of the SONET overhead, just 149.76 Mbps is available for the traffic payload. Furthermore, additional protocol overheads must be taken into account (for example, the PPP overhead) to precisely evaluate the effective bandwidth available for the traffic on each medium.

Automatic Setup and Provisioning of a Full Mesh of TE LSPs

The auto-mesh mechanism, which allows for the automatic provisioning of full meshes of TE LSPs, was introduced in Chapter 2. As a reminder, this functionality consists of three main components:

- **Discovery process**—IGP extensions allow each router to discover the other members of the mesh or meshes it belongs to. Each mesh of TE LSPs is identified by a mesh group number.

- **Local template configuration**—For each mesh, a TE template is locally configured that specifies the set of TE LSP attributes for each TE LSP of the mesh.

- **Automatic TE LSP setup**—For every other member of the mesh the router belongs to, it triggers the automatic provisioning of a corresponding TE LSP whose characteristics are specified in the TE template.

A new generic IS-IS Type-Length-Value (TLV) named Router CAPABILITY is defined in [ISIS-CAPS]. It allows each router in a routing domain to advertise some of its capabilities within a single level or to the entire routing domain by means of a TLV leaking procedures. One use of such a TLV is to advertise the property of a router to participate in a TE LSP mesh. This is achieved by carrying an additional specific sub-TLV named TE-MESH-GROUP (defined in [ISIS-TE-CAPS]). The format of the Router CAPABILITY TLV and TE-MESH-GROUP sub-TLV are shown in Figure 5-38.

Because each Globenet region is composed of a unique IS-IS Level 2, each router advertises the Router CAPABILITY TLV with the S bit cleared. The allocation of the mesh group numbers is shown in Table 5-7.

Table 5-7 *Auto-Mesh Mesh Group Number Allocation Per Region*

Region	Mesh Group Number (Non-EF Tunnels)	Mesh Group Number (EF Tunnels)
North America	100	—
South America	200	201
EMEA	300	301
AsiaPac	400	401

Figure 5-38 *IS-IS Router CAPABILITY TLV and TE-MESH-GROUP Sub-TLV Format*

TYPE: 242
LENGTH: Variable (N*8 Octets)

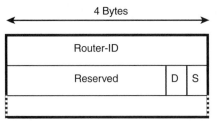

TYPE: 2
LENGTH: Variable (N*8 Octets)

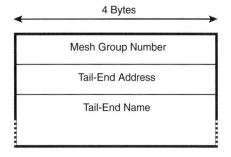

Sbit (0x01)—If the S bit is set(1), the IS-IS Router CAPABILITY TLV MUST be flooded across the entire routing domain. If the S bit is not set(0), the TLV MUST NOT be leaked between levels. This bit MUST NOT be altered during the TLV leaking.

D bit (0x02)—When the IS-IS Router CAPABILITY TLV is leaked from level-2 to level-1, the D bit MUST be set. Otherwise this bit MUST be cleared. IS-IS Router capability TLVs with the D bit set MUST NOT be leaked from level-1 to level-2. This is to prevent TLV looping.

Mesh-group-number—Identifies the mesh-group number.

Tail-end address—User configurable IP address to be used as a tail-end address by other LSRs belonging to the same mesh-group.

Tail-end name—32-bits string which facilitates the TE LSP identification.

Note that a single mesh of unconstrained TE LSPs is required in the North America region.

The configuration task of each router is then drastically reduced compared to if all the TE LSPs had to be manually configured on each router. For instance, a region made up of 30 routers interconnected by two meshes of TE LSPs would require the configuration of 60 TE LSPs on each of the 30 routers and a total of 1740 TE LSPs. Instead, thanks to the auto-mesh feature, a limited set of configuration steps are required, as shown in Example 5-19 for the South America region.

Example 5-19 *Configuration of Auto-Mesh TE on a Router*

```
Router(config)#mpls traffic-eng auto-tunnel mesh
Router(config)#router isis
!
!Configuration of the set of mesh-group the router belongs to (200 in this
!example)
Router(config-router)#mpls traffic-eng mesh-group 200 loopback0
!
!Create a template interface:
Router(config)#interface auto-template 1
!
```

continues

Example 5-19 *Configuration of Auto-Mesh TE on a Router (Continued)*

```
!Specifies a mesh-group that a template interface uses to signal
!tunnels for all mesh-group members
Router(config-if)#tunnel destination mesh-group 200
!
!Create the interface template for mesh-group 200
Router(config)#interface auto-template 1
Router(config-if)#ip unnumbered loopback 0
Router(config-if)#tunnel mode mpls
Router(config-if)#tunnel mpls traffic-eng autoroute announce
Router(config-if)#tunnel mpls traffic-eng priority 4 4
Router(config-if)#tunnel mpls traffic-eng auto-bw
Router(config-if)#tunnel mpls traffic-eng path-option 1 dynamic
!
!
```

A similar configuration is adopted for the mesh group 201.

On a Cisco router, the addition of a new member is automatically detected by every other member of the same mesh group, and the mesh of TE LSPs is adjusted accordingly. Similarly, when a member leaves the mesh group, the corresponding set of TE LSPs is removed from the mesh without requiring any manual intervention.

Dynamic Traffic Engineering LSP Bandwidth Adjustment

Because of the presence of multiple time zones in some regions, sporadic traffic patterns, and the need for efficient bandwidth usage, Globenet elected to use a dynamic TE LSP size adjustment mechanism. (Bandwidth adjustment does not apply to the North America region, where zero-bandwidth TE LSP is used.) As explained in Chapter 2, the basic principle of such a mechanism is to dynamically adjust the required bandwidth of each TE LSP based on the actual traffic demand. This is determined by the observed amount of traffic sent onto the TE LSP in question. The router monitors the amount of traffic sent onto each TE LSP every X minutes (where X is configurable). Then it automatically computes the average bandwidth for that TE LSP (this is also called a bandwidth sample). A second parameter called resizing frequency determines how often a TE LSP is resized. For instance, if the resizing frequency is set to Y minutes, every Y minutes each router evaluates the new bandwidth that must be signaled for each TE LSP. The current algorithm used on a Cisco router consists of selecting the highest-bandwidth sample over the elapsed period of Y minutes and resizing the TE LSP accordingly should the new computed bandwidth be different from the current one.

NOTE   If no path satisfying the new bandwidth constraint can be found, the current TE LSP bandwidth is maintained, and the TE LSP is not modified. Instead, the bandwidth is reevaluated at the next resizing period.

There is, of course, a delicate trade-off between accurate sizing and signaling frequency. Indeed, each router can be configured to collect samples and resize each TE LSP very frequently. Setting X to a small value has the effect of carefully monitoring the amount of bandwidth used on each TE LSP. (Note that in this case, every traffic peak is not really averaged and would be reflected in the sample.) If a small value is chosen for Y, each TE LSP is resized on a frequent basis. Thus, small X and Y values allow for an accurate bandwidth reservation of each TE LSP, reflecting the actual traffic pattern.

The downside of such parameter settings is the signaling overhead and potential network instability. Consider a region composed of two meshes with 50 routers. This leads to a total of approximately 5000 TE LSPs. If X and Y are configured to 1 minute and 10 minutes, respectively, each sample is collected every minute, and every TE LSP is resignaled with the new bandwidth value every 10 minutes. Every router then resignals on average ten TE LSPs per minute, leading to an average of 500 TE LSPs per minute (about eight TE LSPs resignaled per second). Furthermore, each router resignals all its TE LSPs every 10 minutes with some possible global synchronization and its well-known network effects (there would unavoidably be bursts of TE LSPs resignaling, leading to various undesirable race conditions). This highlights the fact that more-conservative timer values should be chosen. On the other hand, these values should not be too large, because they would result in TE LSP oversizing compared to the actual demand. This might lead to tunnels following non-shortest paths, thus affecting the delay for the traffic forwarded onto those TE LSPs. Furthermore, this may also lead to TE LSP undersizing, where more traffic may flow on TE LSPs than their reserved bandwidth. That said, even if the resizing period is set to a large value, such a strategy is significantly more efficient than any other LSP sizing strategy based on the absolute or 95 percentile peak.

Moreover, another benefit of such a dynamic TE LSP adjustment mechanism is that it allows traffic growth to be taken into account (which is different for the two class types) without requiring any manual intervention. Thus, Globenet made various simulations to evaluate the trade-off between sample collection frequency, resizing frequency, and bandwidth utilization efficiency and signaling load.

Three sets of values for X and Y were studied, as shown in Figures 5-39, 5-40, and 5-41. The graphs in these figures show the actual bandwidth used by a TE LSP compared to the reserved bandwidth as well as the total number of TE LSPs signaled in the network.

Figure 5-39 shows the first set of values: X = 5 minutes, and Y = 15 minutes.

With such parameter settings, the ratio between the average reserved bandwidth and the actual traffic equals 1.10. The graph shown in Figure 5-39 clearly shows that the reserved bandwidth is pretty close to the actual traffic demand, which was expected considering the small values of X and Y. The number of resizes per minute, considering that the computed bandwidth value is almost always different from the current bandwidth, equals T / 15, where T is the total number of TE LSPs in the region. For instance, if T equals 400 (a mesh of 20 routers), the average number of resizes per minute is 26.

Figure 5-39   *Reserved Versus Actual Bandwidth on a TE LSP with X = 5 Minutes and Y = 15 Minutes*

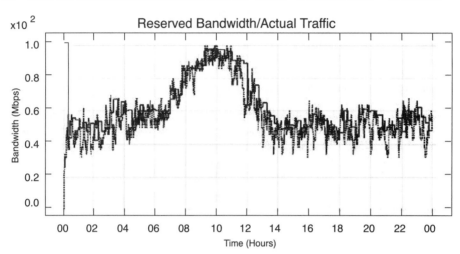

Figure 5-40 shows the second set of values: X = 10 minutes, and Y = 60 minutes.

Figure 5-40   *Reserved Versus Actual Bandwidth on a TE LSP with X = 10 Minutes and Y = 60 Minutes*

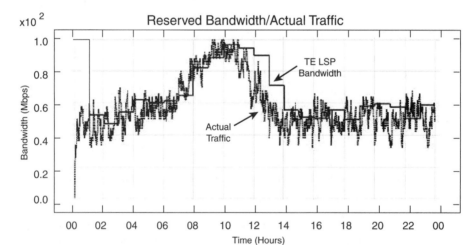

In this second case, the ratio between the average reserved bandwidth and the actual traffic is 1.18. Although the reserved bandwidth reflects less accurately the actual traffic demand, such parameter settings are still quite satisfactory for the non-real-time traffic and allow for a reduction in the number of resizes by a factor of 4.

Figure 5-41 shows the last set of values: X = 10 minutes, and Y = 120 minutes.

Figure 5-41 *Total Resizing Frequency in the Network with X = 10 Minutes and Y = 120 Minutes*

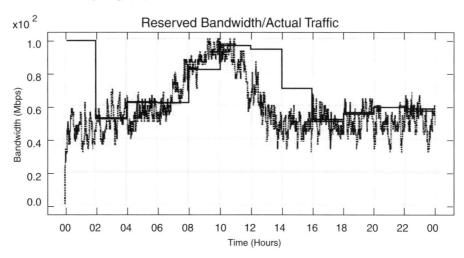

In this last case, the ratio between the average reserved bandwidth and the actual traffic is 1.28. Although the amount of resizing is still reduced by a factor of 2 compared to the previous case, the reserved bandwidth is considered too inaccurate compared to the actual traffic demand.

Consequently, Globenet chose a sampling frequency of 5 minutes and a resizing frequency of 15 minutes for the real-time TE LSPs. A more conservative resizing frequency of 60 minutes was chosen for the non-real-time TE LSP.

NOTE	The graphs shown in Figures 5-39, 5-40, and 5-41 were generated by a simulator for representative traffic patterns and a similar network size.

Additional Resizing Parameters

Example 5-20 shows how both the sampling and the resizing periods can be configured on a Cisco router. It is worth mentioning that other parameters exist, such as the minimum and maximum bandwidth a TE LSP can be dynamically resized to. Globenet decided not to configure these parameters to keep its TE LSP size as close as possible to the actual load.

Example 5-20 *Configuration of a TE LSP with Auto-Bandwidth*

```
!
Router(config)#interface auto-template 1
Router(config-if)#ip unnumbered loopback 0
Router(config-if)#tunnel mode mpls
Router(config-if)#tunnel mpls traffic-eng autoroute announce
Router(config-if)#tunnel mpls traffic-eng priority 4 4
```

continues

Example 5-20 *Configuration of a TE LSP with Auto-Bandwidth (Continued)*

```
Router(config-if)#tunnel mpls traffic-eng sub-pool 10
Router(config-if)#tunnel mpls traffic-eng auto-bw frequency 900
Router(config-if)#tunnel mpls traffic-eng path-option 1 dynamic
!
Router(config)#mpls traffic-eng auto-bw timers frequency 300
!
```

In this example, the sampling and resizing frequencies equal 5 minutes (300 seconds) and 15 minutes (900 seconds), respectively.

Additional Advantages of Dynamic TE LSP Resizing

In addition dynamically adjusting the reserved bandwidth to the actual traffic demand to efficiently use the network bandwidth, Globenet developed some internal scripts that gather the set of bandwidth samples on a few representative TE LSPs. This way, accurate traffic matrices could be collected, which helped further adjust the network parameters and make accurate forecasts. Note that such scripts could also have been developed without the use of the auto-bandwidth feature, but because auto-bandwidth computes such samples, the scripts simply have to collect the sample values.

TE LSP Path Computation

The path taken by TE LSPs is computed by means of a dynamic CSPF algorithm on every headend router. Based on various experiments, Globenet discovered that the CSPF computation time was negligible (on the order of a few milliseconds). Thus, having to perform path computation for every CT1 TE LSP once every 15 minutes and once an hour for the CT0 TE LSPs (in addition to unpredictable network element failure events) did not have any noticeable impact on Globenet's router's CPU cycles. It also allowed for a high degree of flexibility.

MPLS Traffic Engineering in North America

As mentioned, the motivation for deploying MPLS TE in North America was exclusively for the fast restoration capability upon link failure. Because MPLS TE was deployed for Fast Reroute only in this region, Globenet had the option of choosing between using one-hop tunnels (as described in Chapter 3) and using a full mesh of unconstrained TE LSPs. The latter option was chosen. This decision was motivated by the following:

- Considering a nonnegligible traffic growth in the North America region, Globenet did not want to preclude the use of MPLS for bandwidth optimization in case it needed to deal with network resource optimization in the future. Thus, in this case, the use of a full mesh of unconstrained TE LSPs offered an easy migration path.

- A full mesh of TE LSPs allowed Globenet to easily gather traffic matrix information among its POPs.

Consequently, the chosen TE design in North America consisted of deploying a full mesh of unconstrained TE LSPs between Globenet's set of P routers (30 in total because each of the 15 POPs had two P routers). Auto-mesh was used for the provisioning of those TE LSPs with the TE template shown in Example 5-21.

Example 5-21 *TE Template Used for Mesh Group 100 in North America*

```
Router(config)#mpls traffic-eng auto-tunnel mesh
Router(config)#router isis
Router(config-router)#mpls traffic-eng mesh-group 100 loopback0

!Create a template interface:
Router(config)#interface auto-template 1

!Specifies a mesh-group that a template interface uses to
!signal tunnels for all mesh-group members
Router(config-if)#tunnel destination mesh-group 100

!Create the interface template for mesh-group 100
Router(config)#interface auto-template 1
Router(config-if)#ip unnumbered loopback 0
Router(config-if)#tunnel mode mpls
Router(config-if)#tunnel mpls traffic-eng autoroute announce
Router(config-if)#tunnel mpls traffic-eng priority 7 7
Router(config-if)#tunnel mpls traffic-eng bandwidth 0
Router(config-if)#tunnel mpls traffic-eng path-option 1 dynamic
!
```

These TE LSPs systematically follow the IS-IS shortest path because no constraints are applied during the TE LSP path computation. IS-IS then dynamically routes all the traffic, independent of the CoS, onto these TE LSPs using **autoroute announce** command.

MPLS Traffic Engineering in the AsiaPac, EMEA, and South America Regions

In the AsiaPac, EMEA, and South America regions, MPLS traffic engineering is used not only for fast protection but also for bandwidth optimization. As explained in the "Quality of Service Design" section, Globenet decided to deploy MPLS DiffServ-aware Traffic Engineering (DS-TE) using the Russian Dolls Model (RDM) and using two class types (CTs):

- CT1 for the EF traffic (VPN Voice, ATM pseudowire, and IP virtual leased line). BC1 is set to 30 percent of the actual link speed. This allows for the limitation of the proportion of EF traffic so as to bound the delay, jitter, and loss of the EF queue.

- CT0 for the rest of the traffic (VPN Video, VPN Business Latency, VPN Business Throughput, VPN Standard, and Internet). For each link, BC0 equals the link bandwidth (plus overbooking on higher-speed links, as discussed earlier and as summarized in Table 5-6).

As discussed in the "Quality of Service Design" section, Globenet enforces isolation between class types by using different preemption values for the two class types. TE LSPs belonging to CT1 (EF TE LSPs) have a higher preemption priority (value 3 or 4), whereas the TE LSPs belonging to CT0 (non-EF TE LSPs) have a lower preemption priority (value 7).

Two full meshes between the P routers of each region are provisioned by means of auto-mesh TE: one for the EF traffic and the other for the rest of the traffic. The corresponding TE templates are provided in Examples 5-22 and 5-23.

Example 5-22 *TE Template Used for the Mesh of EF TE LSPs in AsiaPac, EMEA, and South America (Mesh Groups 201, 301, and 401). Example for Mesh Group 201.*

```
Router(config)#mpls traffic-eng auto-tunnel mesh
Router(config)#router isis
Router(config-router)#mpls traffic-eng mesh-group 201 loopback0
Router(config-router)#exit

!Create a template interface:
Router(config)#interface auto-template 2
!Specifies a mesh-group that a template interface uses to
!signal tunnels for all mesh-group members
Router(config-if)#tunnel destination mesh-group 201
Router(config-if)#exit

!Create the interface template for mesh-group 201
Router(config)#interface auto-template 2
Router(config-if)#ip unnumbered loopback 0
Router(config-if)#tunnel mode mpls
Router(config-if)#tunnel mpls traffic-eng autoroute announce
Router(config-if)#tunnel mpls traffic-eng priority 4 4
Router(config-if)#tunnel mpls traffic-eng sub-pool 10
Router(config-if)#tunnel mpls traffic-eng auto-bw
Router(config-if)#tunnel mpls traffic-eng path-option 1 dynamic
!Configure CBTS on the tunnel so that it carries traffic marked with EXP=5
Router(config-if)#tunnel mpls traffic-eng exp 5
!
!
```

Example 5-23 *TE Template Used for the Mesh of Non-EF TE LSPs in AsiaPac, EMEA, and South America (Mesh Groups 200, 300, and 400). Example for Mesh Group 200.*

```
Router(config)#mpls traffic-eng auto-tunnel mesh
Router(config)#router isis
Router(config-router)#mpls traffic-eng mesh-group 200 loopback0

!Create a template interface:
Router(config)#interface auto-template 1

!Specifies a mesh-group that a template interface uses to
!signal tunnels for all mesh-group members
Router(config-if)#tunnel destination mesh-group 200
```

Example 5-23   *TE Template Used for the Mesh of Non-EF TE LSPs in AsiaPac, EMEA, and South America (Mesh Groups 200, 300, and 400). Example for Mesh Group 200. (Continued)*

```
!Create the interface template for mesh-group 200
Router(config)#interface auto-template 1
Router(config-if)#ip unnumbered loopback 0
Router(config-if)#tunnel mode mpls
Router(config-if)#tunnel mpls traffic-eng autoroute announce
Router(config-if)#tunnel mpls traffic-eng priority 7 7
Router(config-if)#tunnel mpls traffic-eng global-pool 10
Router(config-if)#tunnel mpls traffic-eng auto-bw
Router(config-if)#tunnel mpls traffic-eng path-option 1 dynamic
!Configure CBTS on the tunnel so that it carries traffic marked
!with all EXP values which are not carried by other TE tunnels to
!the same destination
Router(config-if)#tunnel mpls traffic-eng exp default
!
```

NOTE   In the Cisco IOS command-line interface (CLI) used in the previous examples, a tunnel is associated with CT1 by configuring it to reserve bandwidth from the sub-pool (which corresponds to BC1). A tunnel is associated with CT0 by configuring it to reserve bandwidth from the global-pool (which corresponds to BC0).

In South America, Globenet uses the concept of affinities defined by MPLS TE (discussed in the "TE LSPs Between PE-PSTN1 Routers" section in Chapter 4). Globenet uses one of the 32 bits associated with every link to indicate whether a link is a satellite link. Then, an additional command is included in the mesh group for EF tunnels in South America to ensure that the path computation for EF tunnels excludes all the links advertised with the "satellite" bit.

To dynamically route packets to the right tunnel from the EF tunnel mesh or the non-EF tunnel mesh, depending on the packet CoS, Globenet uses the CoS-Based Tunnel Selection (CBTS) feature. For a given TE tunnel, CBTS allows the operator to configure, on that tunnel's headend, which EXP bit values that tunnel is meant to transport. Then, on the headend router, autoroute takes into account that information to perform CoS-aware routing over the set of TE tunnels. In turn, this results in autoroute's populating extended forwarding tables operating on the basis of <prefix, CoS> pairs (instead of simply on the basis of <prefix>, as per usual routing and forwarding). A <prefix, CoS> entry points to a given tunnel when

- That tunnel is the best path toward that destination prefix (according to the usual auto-route routing algorithm)

   and

- That tunnel is configured to carry that CoS (more specifically, the EXP value for that CoS)

Operation of CBTS in Globenet for dynamic routing of traffic over the EF TE LSP mesh and the non-EF TE LSP mesh is illustrated in Figure 5-42.

Figure 5-42 *CBTS Operations Over the EF Tunnel and Non-EF Tunnel Meshes*

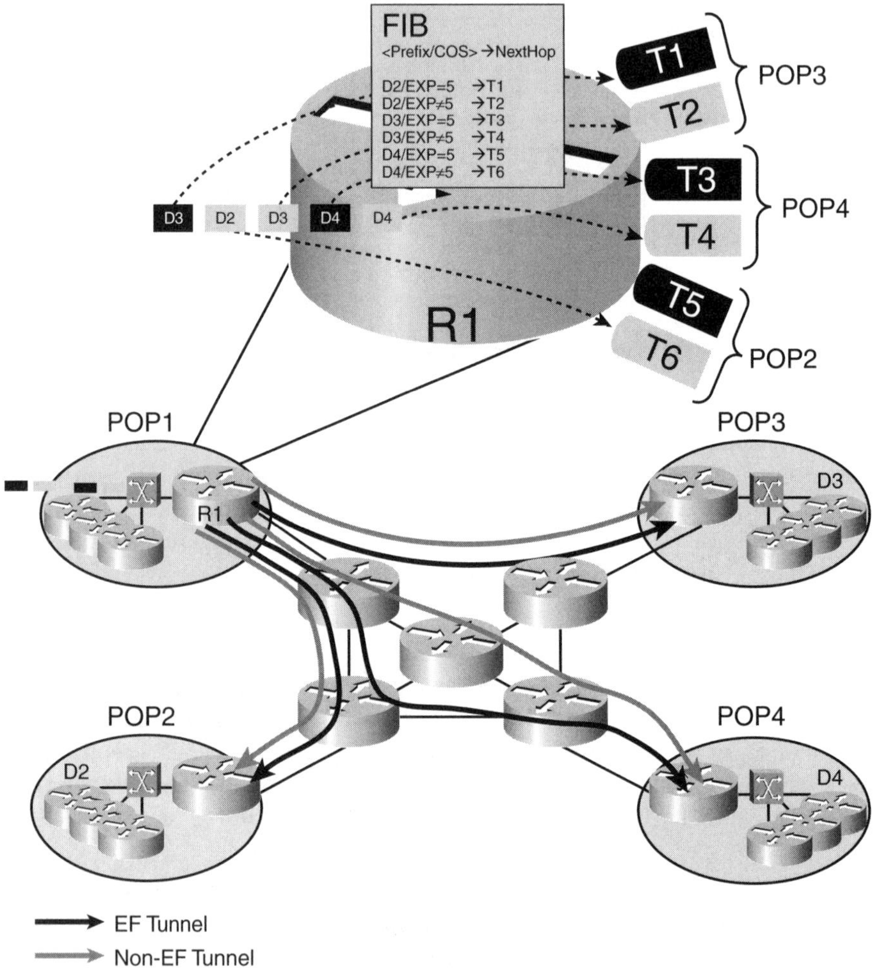

As shown in Example 5-22, because Globenet wants the EF traffic to be dynamically routed over the first mesh of TE LSPs, it configures CBTS in the corresponding mesh group template so that these TE LSPs carry packets with EXP=5. As shown in Example 5-23, because Globenet wants the rest of the traffic to be dynamically routed over the second mesh, it configures CBTS in the corresponding mesh group template so that these TE LSPs carry packets marked with all the other EXP values.

This is all that is required to ensure that all the traffic is dynamically routed over the two meshes of TE LSPs based on its CoS, as desired by Globenet. No additional configuration or any static routes are necessary.

Reoptimization of TE LSPs

To determine the most appropriate reoptimization strategy, Globenet decided to conduct a study on the placement of the TE LSPs on a per-region basis. By its nature, a distributed CSPF computation leads to some degree of unpredictability in terms of TE LSP placement because of the unsynchronized TE LSP path computation by each headend router. That said, several simulation runs were performed based on predictive bandwidth requirements analysis during peak hours to get an estimated value of the number of TE LSPs that would not follow their IGP shortest paths. As expected, the simulations showed that this ratio was a function of the network utilization but would stay below 5 percent during steady state. This number would be multiplied by a factor of 1.5 during single-element failure. Furthermore, in an international network such as Globenet's, propagation delays may not be negligible and may have a significant impact on SLAs. Because the network density is not very high in some regions, a TE LSP that does not follow the current shortest path available (satisfying its constraints such as bandwidth) is highly undesirable.

NOTE	Of course, the ratio is equal to 0 in the case of North America, because all the TE LSPs have 0 reserved bandwidth and thus follow the shortest IS-IS path.

In light of these simulation results and considering the network topology and committed SLAs, Globenet decided not to delay any reoptimization should a more optimal path become available (such as following the restoration of a link). Consequently, each router has been configured to perform both timer-based and event-based reoptimization. The reoptimization timer has been set to 5 minutes. A reoptimization evaluation is triggered upon any link restoration in the network (signaled by IS-IS).

Because unstable links are not uncommon in some regions of the world, event-driven reoptimization is required to be used in conjunction with a dampening mechanism. The aim of such a dampening mechanism is to ensure that an unstable link does not often trigger the origination of new IS-IS LSPs. In addition to triggering successive IS-IS shortest path first (SPF) recomputation, this would also trigger multiple MPLS TE reoptimization actions (CSPF computation and TE LSP signaling in the network). Moreover, a too-aggressive reoptimization strategy in the absence of a dampening mechanism would lead to successive traffic disruptions. Indeed, consider the case of a link experiencing a state change once every second (a situation that could happen with an unstable DWDM laser, for instance). If a new IS-IS LSP is originated upon every single link state change without dampening, every router in the network would trigger a reoptimization evaluation of all its TE LSPs. Potentially, a nonnegligible number of TE LSPs would be rerouted onto the restored link (especially if the link in question is a high-speed link). One second later, all those TE LSPs would be rerouted onto their respective backup tunnels by MPLS TE Fast Reroute, followed by a reoptimization, and so on.

This shows the importance of using a dampening mechanism in conjunction with any event-driven reoptimization strategy. On a Cisco router, such a dampening mechanism could be configured at either the link or the IS-IS level. Globenet decided to use the IS-IS LSP origination dampening feature, which is discussed later in this chapter. Figure 5-43 shows the IS-IS LSP origination frequency when using an origination LSP dampening mechanism. Note that this frequency corresponds to the reoptimization evaluation frequency for each router in the network because a TE LSP reoptimization is triggered when a new IS-IS LSP reporting a link-up event is received.

Figure 5-43   *Reoptimization Evaluation Frequency Upon a Flapping Link with IS-IS Dampening*

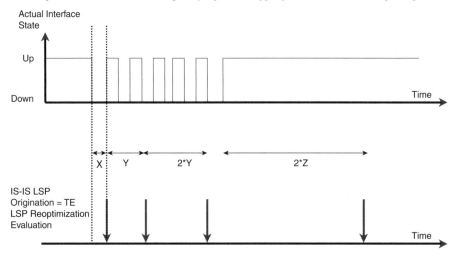

X: Amount of time the router waits before originating the a new LSP when the first topology change occurs.
Y: Amount of time the router waits before originating the a new LSP when the second topology change occurs.
Z: Maximum amount of time between the origination of two successive LSPs.

Note that when a reoptimization evaluation is triggered, a headend router evaluates whether a more optimal (shortest) path can be found for each of its TE LSPs. If so, each TE LSP to be reoptimized is signaled along the new path in a nondisruptive fashion using the make-before-break procedure.

This highlights that combining event-driven reoptimization with an IS-IS origination dampening mechanism allows for the immediate reuse of new or restored bandwidth resources. This optimizes TE LSP paths while preserving network stability in case of unstable network resources.

Traffic Engineering Scaling Aspects

Scaling aspects are always important criteria to consider when deploying any technology. As far as MPLS TE is concerned, the main parameter of interest is the total number of TE LSPs per headend and midpoint router, which affects the routers' memory consumption. (Note that the signaling processing overhead is usually negligible, especially with refresh reduction, which is what Globenet elected to use.) Therefore, Globenet estimated the total number of TE LSPs per midpoint and headend router on a per-region basis both in steady state and under network element failure conditions.

Because the total number of routers in a single mesh never exceeds 50, the maximum number of TE LSPs to manage is 100 for a headend (which is negligible). Globenet estimated that the total number of TE LSPs per midpoint would be in the worst case no greater than 1000, even under failure conditions. Both numbers are far from reaching the scalability limit on most modern router platforms, including the routers deployed by Globenet.

Thus, Globenet felt that the TE design did not pose any scalability issues.

Use of Refresh Reduction

Because of the low degree of connectivity in some regions, the number of TE LSPs per midpoint could potentially be nonnegligible (although quite far from raising any concern). Hence, Globenet chose to activate refresh reduction in its network to reduce the signaling refresh overhead. Moreover, because some links may not be very reliable with a nonnegligible bit error rate, the reliable messaging feature delivered with refresh reduction (see [REFRESH-REDUCTION]) was also beneficial.

Monitoring TE LSPs

Globenet decided to use dynamic and automatic mechanisms whenever possible to optimize the bandwidth usage (with auto-bandwidth) and minimize the risk of configuration errors (with auto-mesh). That said, such mechanisms must be appropriately tuned. Therefore, a network monitoring tool is required to adequately adjust the related parameters.

Globenet decided to gather various sets of monitoring data:

- **Network element failures**—In addition to the SNMP generic traps originated upon link and node failures, Globenet decided to produce scripts collecting the MPLS TE SNMP traps sent when a TE LSP reroute is performed because of a failure or reoptimization (because a better path has been discovered). Note that some scripts perform event correlation to determine the root cause of each failure (link versus node). For the case of an inter-AS TE LSP, the set of data exclusively relies on SNMP variables (or on any variable available via show commands) collected on a regular basis on each router originating an inter-AS TE LSP. Such information is indeed very useful to monitor the network availability for the VPOPs with respect to Globenet's availability SLA with Africa Telecom. (The design of Globenet VPOPs is discussed in detail later in this section.)

- **TE LSP resizing**—As discussed in the section "Dynamic Traffic Engineering LSP Bandwidth Adjustment," parameters must be adjusted to determine the sampling and resizing frequencies. A compromise must be found between optimal bandwidth usage provided by an accurate bandwidth reservation and network stability with reasonable MPLS TE signaling overhead and traffic shift in the network. Because gathering the relevant data for all the TE LSPs and links would be nontractable, Globenet decided to select for each region a set of representative TE LSPs and links to monitor.

For each selected TE LSP, the following set of variables is collected:

- Counters such as the number of transmitted bytes over the TE tunnel interface are collected every 2 minutes

- Bandwidth samples computed by auto-bandwidth

- How often a TE LSP is resignaled

- The number of TE LSPs that do not follow the shortest IS-IS path

This set of data helps Globenet determine whether the bandwidth sampling frequency is appropriate (compared to the actual traffic pattern). Then, the ratio of reserved bandwidth to actual traffic is computed to observe the accuracy of the bandwidth reservation, which is determined by the resizing frequency.

For each selected link, the ratio between the reserved bandwidth on the link and the aggregated traffic is computed (counters are collected every 10 minutes). This last parameter, in conjunction with the number of TE LSP resizes and the proportion of TE LSPs that follow the IS-IS shortest path, is used to determine whether the TE LSP resizing frequency should be adjusted. For instance, suppose that the ratio between reserved bandwidth and actual traffic is 1.5. Suppose also that 60 percent of the TE LSPs do not follow the IS-IS shortest path and that each TE LSP is on average resized once a day. This would indicate that the sampling and resizing frequency could be increased without compromising the network stability and would allow for more optimal bandwidth usage. Furthermore, a higher proportion of the TE LSPs would likely follow the IS-IS shortest path, thus resulting in shorter propagation delays. Conversely, if the reserved bandwidth/actual traffic ratio is 1.1, and 5 percent of the TE LSPs follow the IS-IS shortest path, and the number of TE LSP resizes is too high, the sampling and resizing frequencies should probably be decreased.

Note that examples of these graphs were provided in the section "Dynamic Traffic Engineering LSP Bandwidth Adjustment."

It is worth reemphasizing that such analysis is conducted on a small set of representative TE LSPs and links in each region because gathering and analyzing the data just discussed requires time and network resources.

Last-Resort Unconstrained Option

Globenet's network has been dimensioned to survive any single failure without significant QoS degradation. In other words, upon any single-element failure in the network, such as a link or router failure, simulations have been done to ensure that any TE LSP can find an alternate path with the same bandwidth requirements. That said, a safe approach to cope with any unexpected multiple failures is to configure each TE LSP with a last-resort option in which the bandwidth constraint is relaxed. This guarantees that any TE LSP will get a path in any condition should the connectivity be preserved between the source and destination. In this case the TE LSPs simply follow the shortest IGP path.

TE Design for ATM Pseudowires

Globenet uses ATM pseudowires in North America and EMEA to interconnect its ATM switches. It paid specific attention to the design of MPLS TE for optimum transport of this traffic.

As discussed, Globenet's network in North America relies on overprovisioning and does not require the deployment of call admission control techniques (by means of MPLS Traffic Engineering) in addition to QoS. Indeed, capacity has been provisioned (and, where necessary, the IS-IS metrics have been fine-tuned) to always limit the proportion of EF traffic (including the pseudowire traffic) below a desired ratio. Hence, in North America, the pseudowire traffic does not need any specific handling as far as MPLS TE is concerned. The pseudowire traffic is routed along the IGP path from the PE router to the next P router. Then it gets forwarded to the unconstrained TE LSP going toward the right egress P router along with the rest of the traffic.

However, the case of EMEA is vastly different, so MPLS DS-TE has been deployed to ensure QoS guarantees and network resource optimization. One option would have been for IGP to route the pseudowire traffic between P router and PE router and to carry such traffic onto the DS-TE LSP for EF traffic, in the exact same way as the rest of the EF traffic is routed. The downside of such an option would have been the constraint of using shared engineering rules for the pseudowire traffic as well as for the rest of the EF traffic. More specifically:

- The pseudowire traffic would have been routed on the same TE LSPs as the rest of the EF traffic.

- The bandwidth computed for the tunnel carrying the pseudowire traffic would have been dynamically adjusted by auto-bandwidth and based on the aggregate load measured across all the EF traffic.

This was not considered entirely satisfactory by the engineering team in charge of the ATM network and making use of the ATM pseudowire service. They decided that they would rather have dedicated TE LSPs whose bandwidth is computed based on their own bandwidth requirement and constantly reserved through the core.

Consequently, Globenet decided to carry the pseudowire traffic between PE routers onto dedicated TE LSPs. The bandwidth of these TE LSPs is determined based on the known port utilization between ATM switches. For instance, if two ATM switches used to be interconnected by means of a leased line of capacity B Mbps, whose peak load was estimated at X percent, the corresponding TE LSP would be signaled with a bandwidth of

X percent * B * some margin considering the traffic growth

Furthermore, such a scheme allows for the configuration of higher preemption priority for the TE tunnels carrying pseudowire traffic than the DS-TE TE LSPs carrying the rest of the EF traffic.

Therefore, EMEA actually has three types of TE LSPs, as shown in Figure 5-44:

- **EF tunnels**—These carry the VPN Voice CoS (and, in the future, the virtual IP leased-line CoS). They belong to class type 1 (so they reserve bandwidth from the subpool) and use preemption priority 4. Their bandwidth is automatically adjusted by means of the auto-bandwidth feature. They run P router-to-P router.

- **Pseudowire tunnels**—These carry the ATM pseudowire traffic. They belong to class type 1 (so they reserve bandwidth from the subpool) and use preemption priority 3. (As a reminder, the priority of a TE LSP increases when its preemption value decreases.) Their bandwidth is statically configured on the headend router. They run PE router-to-PE router.

- **Non-EF tunnels**—These carry the rest of the traffic, including the VPN Video, VPN Business Latency, VPN Business Throughput, and VPN Standard CoSs and the Internet traffic. They belong to class type 0 and use preemption priority 7. Their bandwidth is dynamically adjusted by means of auto-bandwidth. They run P router-to-P router.

Figure 5-44 *Three Types of TE LSPs in EMEA*

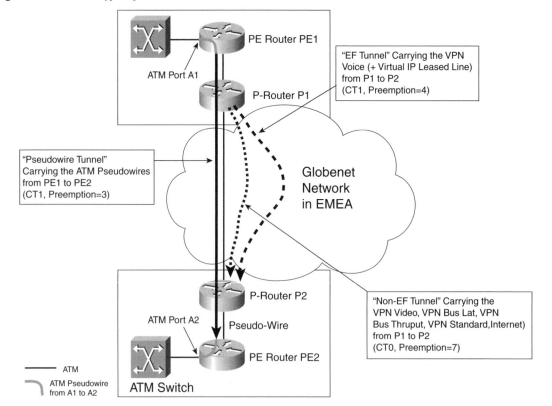

The use of higher-priority TE LSPs for the ATM pseudowire traffic increases the chance that such traffic will follow its shortest path if contention occurs in the network because of an unexpected traffic increase or network element failure.

The mechanisms used to steer the ATM pseudowire traffic to the specific TE tunnels established by Globenet in the EMEA region for that purpose were discussed in the "Pseudowire QoS Design for ATM Trunking" section.

Network Recovery Design

As with any network recovery design, you must first determine the requirements in terms of availability SLAs should a network element failure occur in the network. Therefore, Globenet conducted a detailed analysis covering several years of failure statistics. It turned out that the vast majority (more than 90 percent) of the failures had been link failures (fiber cut, local leased-line failures, and router interface failure to a much lesser extent). Unexpected router failures resulting in traffic loss were insignificant. On the other hand, planned router failure so as to perform software or hardware upgrades were handled by scripts that isolated the traffic from the elements to upgrade by increasing the attached link metrics of the router in question. Such operations have always been done during maintenance windows. During these times, the traffic load was low enough that all the traffic usually routed through the router in question could be rerouted to an alternate path while offering an equivalent QoS.

Globenet's requirement was primarily to protect the traffic from link failures, with an objective of rerouting the traffic within a few tens of milliseconds whenever possible. Unexpected router failures were considered sufficiently rare to tolerate longer rerouting times. Moreover, upon single-link failure, the equivalent QoS along the alternate path must be provided at least to all important CoSs (ATM pseudowire, VPN Voice, VPN Video, VPN Business Latency, and VPN Business Throughput).

NOTE	In contrast to Telecom Kingland (discussed in Chapter 4), Globenet leases its circuits. This leads Globenet to always require diversely routed links from its leased-line providers or to lease capacity from different providers to increase its chances of having diverse links. Thus, SRLG protection was not required. Note that in the past, multiple links provided by different service providers simultaneously failed because of a shared network element failure (such as a transatlantic fiber). Such a shared risk is usually outside Globenet's knowledge and thus is impossible to protect against. However, such an event is rare.

Based on the considerations just discussed, Globenet adopted the following network recovery design:

- Use MPLS Traffic Engineering Fast Reroute as its network recovery technology of choice on unprotected SONET-SDH circuits, protected SONET-SDH circuits (in case of router interface failure), unprotected DWDM links, and Ethernet links (intra-POP). This protects against any single-link failure. Note that both inter-POP and intra-POP links are protected by means of Fast Reroute, although most of the failures relate to inter-POP link failures.

- In the AsiaPac region, where routers are interconnected by means of ATM PVCs, link failures are handled by both PNNI and MPLS TE Fast Reroute. Upon ATM VC failure, both PNNI and MPLS TE Fast Reroute trigger some recovery actions but operate at different time scales. As discussed later, a design that triggers recovery actions at both layers was Globenet's preferred option. When (or if) the ATM VC is restored, MPLS Traffic Engineering starts reusing it by means of MPLS TE reoptimization.

- Tune the IS-IS parameters to achieve 5 seconds of rerouting time in case of unexpected node failure or multiple link failures that could not be handled by MPLS TE Fast Reroute.

MPLS TE Fast Reroute Design Within Globenet Regions

This section presents the detailed design of Fast Reroute as deployed in all regions of the Globenet network.

Failure Detection

Considering the broad set of link types, Globenet had to adopt different strategies in terms of failure detection mechanisms based on the Layer 2 protocol in use:

- **SONET-SDH links**—The SONET-SDH layer provides a very efficient failure detection mechanism whereby an alarm is usually received within a few milliseconds (usually less than 10 ms). Thus, for Globenet's network in North America, OC-3 and OC-48 link failures are detected within a few milliseconds.

NOTE   Note that in some cases, link failure may take significantly more time for example in the case of rings that spread across multiple countries because of incompressible propagation delays due to the speed of light.

- **Leased line (n * 2 Mbps bundles)**—2-Mbps leased lines are usually provided by means of a SONET-SDH or Plesiochronous Digital Hierarchy (PDH) infrastructure that provides efficient failure detection mechanisms. Failure detection times for such leased lines are usually on the order of a few milliseconds.

- **ATM VCs**—The case of ATM VC is more complex. Indeed, ATM VCs are routed and signaled by means of PNNI. Thus, upon a link or ATM node failure in the ATM network, PNNI first must detect the failure. This can take from a few milliseconds in case of a SONET-SDH link failure to up to several seconds should an ATM switch node fail. PNNI then must converge (compute another path for the set of affected VCs and resignal such VCs along an alternate path if a path is found). Hence, the overall restoration time upon ATM VC failure varies from several seconds to a few tens of seconds. Note that sometimes ATM VCs might not be restored because of a lack of resources in the network.

Globenet's ATM network has been dimensioned to restore 100 percent of its ATM VCs in case of single failure. However, there are a few identified links and nodes whose failure would provoke a small proportion of the set of affected VCs to not be restored. Although the ATM layer provides failure indication mechanisms by various means, the failure detection may be too slow and thus requires the use of hello-based liveness mechanisms at the IP/MPLS layer. After careful consideration, Globenet decided not to tweak the IS-IS hello protocol so as to limit the CPU router impact because IGP hello messages require nonnegligible processing. Globenet decided instead to use the Bidirectional Forwarding Detection (see [BFD]) protocol with a hello period of 100 ms and a dead timer (hold time) of 400 ms. Thus, a failure will be detected within at most 400 ms regardless of the failure's root cause.

- **Gigabit Ethernet links**—When two pieces of equipment are interconnected by point-to-point Ethernet links, failure detection times similar to SONET-SDH can be achieved. Conversely, the use of Layer 2 Gigabit Ethernet switches drastically increases the failure detection time if a router port fails since failure detection is performed by means of IGP hello-based protocol. Similar to the ATM case, Globenet elected to use BFD as its failure detection mechanism of choice for its Gigabit Ethernet links with the same set of parameters.

- **Router failures**—Various router failure types can lead to different failure detection times and have different impacts on the forwarding traffic. For instance, the case of a power supply failure on a router is equivalent to the simultaneous failures of its entire set of attached links. Therefore, the failure detection time is similar to the link failure case. A control plane failure on a distributed router architecture has no impact on the traffic forwarding. The routing protocol detects the failure, and the traffic is smoothly rerouted to an alternate path without any traffic disruption. Conversely, a route processor failure on a centralized router architecture affects both the control and forwarding planes. In turn, this provokes a traffic disruption until the routing protocol converges, because MPLS TE Fast Reroute is just used for link protection. Globenet considered the latter case sufficiently rare to not justify any particular special measures to handle such failures.

Set of Backup Tunnels

Because MPLS TE Fast Reroute protects the traffic from link failures, just next-hop backup tunnels are required in the network. Furthermore, as mentioned previously, the Globenet network does not contain any SRLG. Because the vast majority of the links are leased, Globenet managed to lease its circuit to different regional providers to get diverse links.

Backup Tunnel Constraints

The first constraint that backup tunnels must meet is, of course, to be diverse from the protected link.

The second backup tunnel constraint is related to the bandwidth. When a backup tunnel path must be computed to protect a facility such as a link, the backup tunnel can be provisioned with bandwidth equivalent to the protected link. (Another example is a specific bandwidth pool (such as BC1) if the decision is made to provide an equivalent QoS to the TE LSPs of class type CT1.) Although quite efficient in terms of QoS, such an approach would require the use of a sophisticated backup tunnel path computation tool to maximize the bandwidth sharing between backup tunnels that protect independent links. As a reminder, the backup tunnel is used during rerouting times—in other words, from the time the node immediately upstream of the failure triggers Fast Reroute to the reoptimization of the TE LSP by its headend router. In the case of the Globenet network, such rerouting times have been evaluated to likely be less than 1 second in the worst case. This means that such a backup tunnel would be used for at most 1 second. The second aspect of the study consisted of evaluating for each link failure the potential congestion that may occur along a backup tunnel provisioned with zero bandwidth. The simulations showed that even in Asia, where links (ATM VCs) are sized upon the traffic demands (with some margin) and link utilizations are pretty high, worst-case scenarios implied getting up to 80 percent of real-time traffic and 120 percent of non-real-time traffic onto some links during the rerouting period (less than 1 second). Globenet considered this satisfactory with respect to its SLAs. Thus, it chose to provision the set of next-hop backup tunnels with zero bandwidth. (The backup tunnels would then follow the IGP shortest path that avoids the protected link.)

Figure 5-45 shows the set of configured backup tunnels for the node of Washington. It shows a set of next-hop backup tunnels configured to protect the traffic from the failure of any of the attached links of the Washington node. Note that two backup tunnels are required for each protected link (one in each direction), although just one of them is shown in Figure 5-45 for the sake of clarity.

Figure 5-45   *Set of Next-Hop Backup Tunnels to Protect the Attached Links of the Washington Node (One Direction Is Shown)*

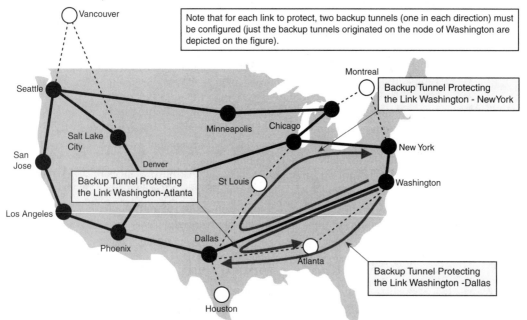

Such backup tunnels would protect any TE LSPs from a link or router interface failure in the core. But what about the intra-POP links (between PE routers and P routers)? Although such failures are less frequent compared to the long-distance links in the core, Globenet wanted to use Fast Reroute in case a router interface failed (PE router or P router). Because the mesh of TE LSPs is between the P routers, Globenet had to choose a specific network design for the intra-POP links protected by Fast Reroute.

The solution was to configure unconstrained one-hop primary TE LSPs between each PE router and P router, along with an appropriate diversely routed tunnel. Consider the Paris POP, shown in Figure 5-46 (a Type 1a POP).

Figure 5-46   *One-Hop Tunnel Used to Protect the Intra-POP Link with Fast Reroute*

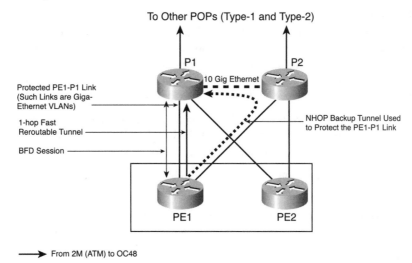

Such a configuration (with USCom) was detailed in Chapter 3. In a nutshell, for each link to protect, a one-hop TE LSP (in each direction) is configured to protect the intra-POP link. For example, as shown in Figure 5-46, a primary TE LSP is configured between PE1 and P1 as a fast reroutable TE LSP. Note that because of the PHP operation, no additional label is added to the traffic forwarded along such a link. In addition, a next-hop backup tunnel is configured that avoids the protected link (the next-hop backup tunnel shown in Figure 5-46).

In case of a PE-P link failure, upon failure detection by means of the BFD protocol (because such links are Gigabit Ethernet VLANs), the affected traffic is rerouted onto the backup tunnel. (An additional label corresponding to the backup tunnel is pushed in case of failure.)

Provisioning the Set of Backup Tunnels

Globenet elected to use automatic provisioning for its next-hop backup tunnels. Such mechanisms are described in detail in Chapter 3 and therefore are not described again here. As a reminder, very few commands are configured on each router for the automatic configuration of unconstrained one-hop and next-hop backup tunnels. This dynamically determines the set of next hops by means of the IGP (the set of active routing adjacencies). It also automatically computes a diversely routed backup tunnel path for each link to protect, should at least a fast reroutable TE LSP traverse the protected link in question.

Configuring a Hold-Off Timer

Hold-off timers are sometimes required when network recovery mechanisms coexist at different layers, as explained in detail in Chapter 2. The aim of such a hold-off timer is to increase the chance of restoring a failed resource at Layer n before triggering any restoration at Layer n + 1. Although this may lead to increased rerouting times, should Layer n fail to restore the failed resource, this avoids race network recovery attempts, which may lead to unpredictable and undesirable results (see [NET-RECOV] for detailed explanation on this topic).

In the case of unprotected links (2-Mbps leased lines, OC-3 and OC-48 links (North America and EMEA), and Gigabit Ethernet links), MPLS TE Fast Reroute must be triggered as soon as the failure is detected. Thus, no hold-off timer is required.

Conversely, there are various situations in which hold-off timers are required in the Globenet network:

- **Protected OC-3 links (by SDH)** — Because such links are protected by means of SONET-SDH, a hold-off timer must be set to a value slightly larger than the worst-case recovery time by the SONET-SDH layer. Indeed, the objective is first to rely on SONET-SDH protection to recover the failed resource without attempting to reroute the traffic by means of Fast Reroute. In the vast majority of the cases in the Globenet network, such rerouting times do not exceed 100 ms. Thus, Globenet decided to set the hold-off timer to 120 ms.

NOTE   The use of a hold-off timer implies that an interface failure (which cannot be recovered at the SONET-SDH layer) will not be restored before 120 ms plus the Fast Reroute rerouting time.

- **ATM VCs (AsiaPac)** — As already pointed out, ATM VC recovery is first handled by PNNI, which usually converges within a few seconds. This leads to the two following possibilities:
  - Set the Fast Reroute hold-off timer to the PNNI worst-case rerouting time to give the ATM layer a chance to recover the affected VCs before triggering any action attempt at the Fast Reroute level. The advantage of such an approach

would be to rely on the restoration of the affected ATM VC. This would provide an equivalent QoS at the price of a longer traffic disruption compared to a few hundreds of milliseconds with Fast Reroute.

— Do not use an FRR hold-off timer. With this approach, the traffic disruption would be minimized (limited to a few hundreds of milliseconds), but potential congestion may occur for the non-real-time traffic during the rerouting periods. This was the approach Globenet chose in combination with the use of appropriate timers so as to reuse the restored ATM VC as soon as possible. This can be achieved thanks to the combination of two mechanisms:

— The IS-IS LSP origination in case of a second new event is set to 20 ms to speed up the advertisement of a restored ATM VC.

— A reoptimization trigger in case of a link-up event.

IS-IS Routing Design

IS-IS handles node failures with the objective of achieving a rerouting time of 5 seconds, should a node fail or multiple failures occur that cannot be handled by FRR. To that end, IS-IS had to be tuned appropriately because the default configuration is usually to adopt a hello period frequency of 10 seconds and a hold time period of 30 seconds.

The first set of parameters to be adjusted is related to the IS-IS hello protocol. Globenet decided to set the hello and hold time timers to 1 second and 4 seconds, respectively.

The second parameter category is related to the SPF triggering and LSP origination. As explained in detail in Chapter 2, modern routers provide the ability to use dampening algorithms to allow for quick reaction in terms of LSP origination and SPF triggering while protecting the network in case of unstable conditions. To that end, Globenet decided to set the related parameters as shown in Example 5-24.

Example 5-24 *Fast IS-IS Configuration Example*

```
hostname Globenet.Newyork.P1
!
interface pos3/0
 isis hello-interval 1
 isis hello-multiplier 4
!
router isis
 lsp-gen 5 10 20
 spf-interval 5 80 20
 prc-interval 5 80 20
```

When a network element failure occurs, a router waits for 10 ms before originating a new IS-IS LSP. If a second state change occurs, a new IS-IS LSP is originated after 20 ms. The maximum time between the origination of two consecutive LSP originations will never exceed 5 seconds in case of an unstable link (according to the dampening algorithm described in Chapter 2).

Note that the initial waiting time before triggering an SPF has been set to 80 ms. The failure of a node (which is of a particular interest in this case, because traffic recovery exclusively relies on IS-IS to handle such failures) generates the origination of several IS-IS LSPs (by each neighbor of the failing router). Because the network is sometimes sparse in some regions of the world, the reception of such IS-IS LSPs by other routers may be spaced by several tens of milliseconds. Hence, waiting for 80 ms before triggering the first SPF allows for the increased likelihood of computing a new routing table based on an accurate topology.

Additionally, all the Globenet routers have been configured to prioritize the IS-IS LSP flooding against SPF triggering. They also provide the relevant QoS to IS-IS control packets to avoid loss of routing adjacency if a link gets congested. This reduces the failure notification time up to a rerouting node.

The use of incremental SPF was also considered. However, it would not have significantly reduced the overall convergence time compared to the other components, such as the failure detection time, LSP propagation, and so on.

Given this, the set of parameters shown in Example 5-24 allows for the achievement of the rerouting time target of 5 seconds, should an unplanned node failure occur in the network.

Failure of a PE Router Supporting ATM Pseudowires

PNNI handles the failure of a PE router supporting ATM pseudowires. First the failure detection can be determined by means of local signaling (alarm indication signal (AIS)) or switch-to-switch ATM OAM flow (cells F4 and F5), which are transparently carried onto the pseudowire.

As soon as the failure has been detected, PNNI converges and appropriately reroutes the set of affected ATM VCs along some alternate paths. In some cases, these alternate ATM paths may themselves transit via interswitch trunks that are supported as other pseudowires. An interesting consequence to note is that such traffic shifts caused by rerouting may imply that some pseudowires receive some unexpected peak load, at least for the duration of the failure. But because all the TE LSPs carrying the pseudowires have been dimensioned on the expected ATM peak load, this should not pose any problem unless such failures occur during busy hours. Furthermore, even in this case, although such TE LSPs would carry more traffic than they have been dimensioned for, the real-time EF queue would be able to absorb the extra traffic without any severe QoS degradation.

Network Recovery for IPv6 VPN

Because the 6VPE approach relies on recursion over the IPv4 BGP next-hop address of the PE routers, the exact same IPv4 LSPs are used to transport IPv6 VPN traffic over the core (from PE router to PE router) as those used to transport the IPv4 VPN traffic or IPv4 Internet traffic. This means that the IPv6 VPN traffic automatically inherits the benefits of core features applied to these IPv4 LSPs. In particular, the IPv6 VPN traffic is automatically protected in Globenet's network by MPLS Fast Reroute (and fast IS-IS convergence) exactly like the IPv4 VPN traffic without any additional mechanisms or configuration needed.

Virtual POP Design

In parts of the world where Globenet had customers but did not have the possibility or the desire to extend the Globenet network, it elected to deploy virtual POPs (VPOPs). A VPOP is a POP managed by Globenet but colocated in the premises of another service provider. It is connected to the rest of Globenet's network via inter-AS TE LSPs providing bandwidth guarantees. More specifically, not only do such TE LSPs span multiple AS boundaries, but those autonomous systems belong to different service providers, which requires close cooperation.

This section, which describes the VPOP design, is one of the most specific aspects of the Globenet network design.

The motivation for relying on an inter-AS TE LSP to connect the VPOP to the rest of the network is as follows:

- **Fast convergence in case of inter-ASBR link failures**—When interconnecting two autonomous systems via a pair of ASBRs, the failure of such an inter-ASBR link usually provokes a traffic disruption that may last for a few tens of seconds or sometimes a few minutes. This is especially true when the pair of ASBRs is interconnected by means of a single link, because in this case the link failure requires that BGP converge (with a change of BGP next hop). One of Globenet's requirements was to be able to offer equivalent service availability to the end customers that are connected to a VPOP.

- **Bandwidth and QoS guarantees**—The second motivation for the use of inter-AS TE LSPs was to get bandwidth guarantees between the VPOP and the rest of the network. You will see in the rest of this section that MPLS Traffic Engineering was an ideal candidate to reach that objective.

Globenet managed to establish agreements with several regional service providers, including Africa Telecom, involving a private inter-AS TE peering. The case of Africa Telecom is covered in detail in this section.

Africa Telecom is a regional service provider with tens of POPs in Africa and three POPs in Europe (in Paris (France), London (UK), and Frankfurt (Germany)), interconnected with links from 2 Mbps to OC-3. MPLS Traffic Engineering has been deployed in Africa Telecom's core (ATC) for fast recovery with Fast Reroute for link protection.

Globenet had already deployed two POPs in Africa: Algiers (Algeria) and Johannesburg (South Africa). For the Johannesburg POP, the decision was made to convert it to a VPOP.

Conversion of the Johannesburg POP to a VPOP

Figure 5-47 shows the Johannesburg POP before its conversion to a VPOP (when the POP was part of Globenet's network).

Figure 5-47 *Johannesburg POP Before It Is Converted to a VPOP*

Globenet followed these migration steps:

Step 1 Globenet installed a new Type 2 POP within the ATC premises. The two PE routers are locally connected to two P routers of the ATC network, as shown in Figure 5-48.

Step 2 As shown in Figure 5-49, a set of two counterdirectional inter-AS TE LSPs have been provisioned between each PE router of the VPOP and the Globenet ASBRs located in Paris. The details are discussed later in this section.

Figure 5-48   *Local Connectivity of the Johannesburg VPOP to the ATC Network*

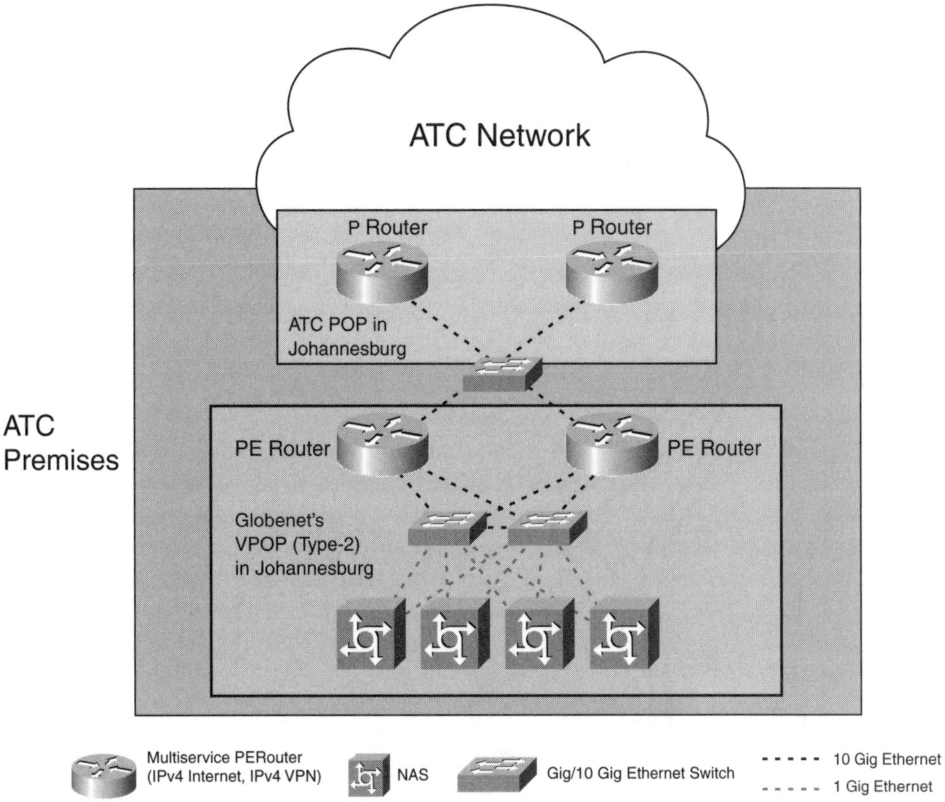

Step 3   Globenet's customers previously connected to the old POP were migrated to the new VPOP. The old POP and the two leased lines, Lisbon-Johannesburg and Rome-Johannesburg, were decommissioned.

Globenet's customers are connected to the VPOP via leased lines or Frame Relay PVCs provided by Africa Telecom.

Figure 5-49 *Inter-AS TE LSP Connecting the Johannesburg VPOP to Globenet's Network*

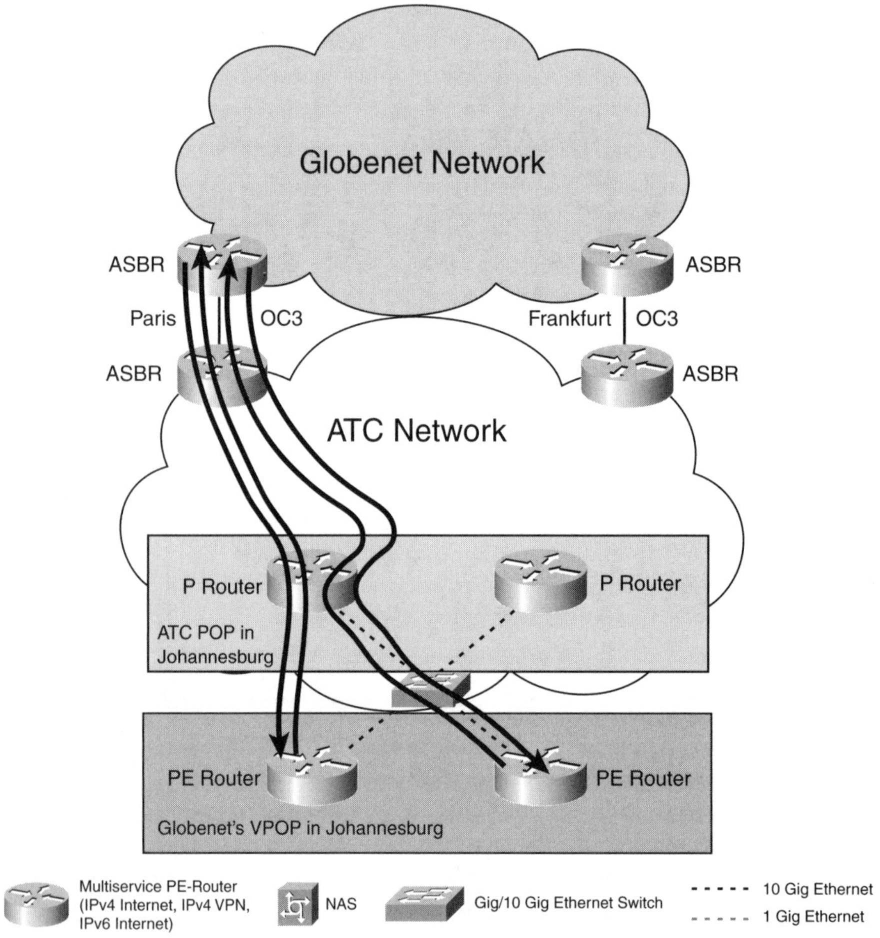

Attributes of the Inter-AS TE LSPs

As with any other TE LSP, several attributes must be determined for an inter-AS TE LSP:

- **Inter-AS TE LSP types**—Various types of inter-AS TE LSPs exist. A *contiguous TE LSP* is by definition an end-to-end TE LSP that traverses multiple domains (IGP area, AS). A *stitched TE LSP* is made of multiple segments in each domain that are stitched at the domain boundaries. Globenet and Africa Telecom decided to deploy contiguous TE LSPs so that Globenet could keep strict control of their inter-AS TE LSPs. Indeed, with a stitched TE LSP, each domain is in charge of its own segment. This implies that the headend router of such inter-AS TE LSPs loses control of the LSP reoptimization, for instance. Considering that such TE LSPs are really critical to Globenet because it carries all the traffic for each VPOP, contiguous TE LSPs were much more appropriate. Moreover, stitched TE LSPs have several limitations in terms of Fast Reroute. (See the IETF relevant documents for more details).

- **Bandwidth**—Although Globenet elected to use a dynamic bandwidth adjustment mechanism in each of its regions, such a model would have been difficult to apply for the case of inter-AS TE LSP because TE LSP costs are determined by their bandwidth. Hence, the agreement made with Africa Telecom was to statically define the inter-AS TE LSP bandwidth with the possibility to revisit each TE LSP bandwidth requirement once a month at Globenet's request. Consequently, Globenet developed some internal scripts gathering the amount of traffic sent to each inter-AS TE LSP once every 10 minutes. Each bandwidth sample is collected and the TE LSP bandwidth is adjusted monthly to the 95th percentile by Globenet.

- **TE/DS-TE Class Type**—Because the ATC network uses MPLS TE only for Fast Reroute and not for constraint-based routing, regular TE and its single class type (CT0) can be used in the ATC network to perform admission control and constraint-based routing of the inter-AS TE LSPs. Hence, these are signaled as CT0 LSPs, and ATC need not deploy DS-TE. The section "VPOP QoS Design" has more details on the mechanisms involved in the ATC network to guarantee appropriate levels of performance to the traffic carried over the inter-AS TE LSPs.

- **Recovery**—Each inter-AS TE LSP is configured as fast reroutable to benefit from Fast Reroute in case of a network element failure within the ATC network or at AS boundaries. More details related to network recovery of inter-AS TE LSPs are discussed later in this section.

Globenet VPOP Migration Strategy

There were two main motivations for converting the Johannesburg POP into a VPOP:

- The two leased lines Johannesburg-Lisbon and Johannesburg-Rome could be cancelled, leading to substantial cost savings. They were instead replaced by inter-AS TE LSPs whose cost per Mbps was significantly lower and whose bandwidth could be adjusted as needed with a significantly finer granularity.

- This provided an opportunity for Globenet to get its equipment hosted in the Africa Telecom POP and hence decommission the premises it was running in Johannesburg. The costs there were very high, considering the need for power supply protection, air conditioning, and so on.

Four additional VPOPs were deployed in Africa following the same interconnection model as for the Johannesburg VPOP: Brazzaville (Congo), Cairo (Egypt), Khartoum (Sudan), and Abuja (Nigeria).

For instance, the two Globenet PE routers of the Brazzaville VPOP have been connected by means of inter-AS TE LSPs to Globenet's Algiers POP, as shown in Figure 5-50.

Figure 5-50 *Globenet VPOPs in Brazzaville and Johannesburg*

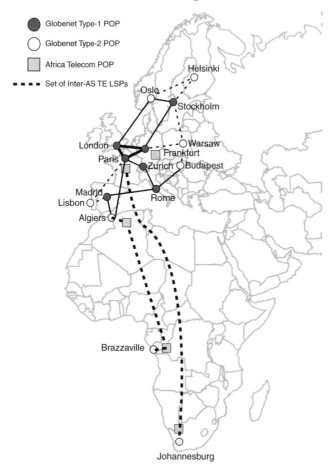

When the number of customers in a specific area gets large, Globenet can decide to deploy an additional VPOP so as to connect those customers to a closer VPOP, thus reducing the cost of the access lines. However, this requires adding and managing a new VPOP. Such economic analysis is conducted on a case-by-case basis.

Path Computation for Inter-AS TE LSPs

An inter-AS TE LSP path can be computed through various techniques that differ in terms of optimality. In a nutshell, the first method is called *loose hop routing* or *per-domain routing*. It consists of configuring the path on the headend router as a set of loose hops where each hop is an ASBR and the last hop is the final destination. Upon receiving the RSVP-TE Path message, the ASBR computes the shortest path in its AS, obeying the set of constraints to reach that hop. (This operation is sometimes called the ERO expansion.)

Although it's quite simple, the limitation of such an approach lies in its inability to compute a shortest path end to end. Indeed, when configuring the set of loose hops, the network administrator does not know which set of loose hops will provide the shortest path to reach the destination. The network topology in the other AS is unknown and might change as links and nodes are added in the future and network element failures unavoidably occur.

Consider the case of the inter-AS TE LSP between Globenet's Paris POP and Johannesburg VPOP. As shown in Figure 5-51, in steady state, the shortest inter-AS path between the two is via Paris' ATC ASBR (the solid line).

Figure 5-51   *Inter-AS Shortest Path Selection*

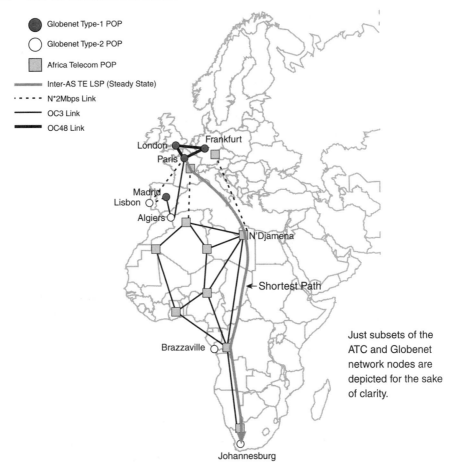

Let's now consider various failure cases.

In the first case, the link between Paris and N'Djamena fails. As shown in Figure 5-52, with the simple loose hop routing approach, Globenet's Paris router would retry along the same ATC ASBR of Paris. This would lead to the traversing of traffic across the 2-Mbps link between Paris and Algiers within the ATC network. Such a path would, of course, be suboptimal. However, Globenet's Paris ASBR could not have detected such suboptimality because of its lack of visibility to the available resources and topology in the ATC network.

Figure 5-52 *Inter-AS Shortest Path Selection After a Link Failure in the ATC Network with Loose Hop Routing*

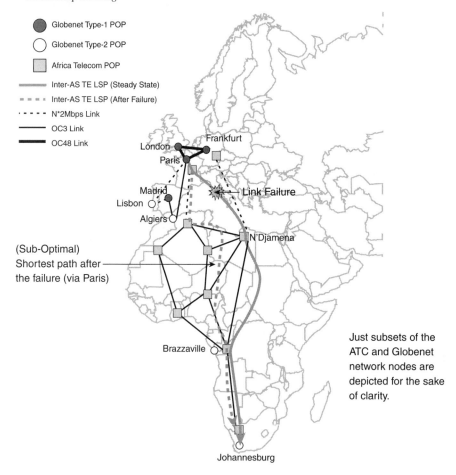

Now consider the case of ATC router failure in Paris. Because of the lack of visibility on the ATC network topology and state, Globenet tends to configure on the Paris ASBR a backup loose path through the closest ASBR connected to the ATC network. Doing so reroutes the affected inter-AS TE LSPs—in this case, to the Frankfurt ASBR connected to the Paris POP by means of an OC-48 link. Unfortunately, as shown in Figure 5-53, such a choice is not optimal because the Frankfurt ASBR of the ATC network is in fact connected to the N'Djamena node by a 2-Mbps link. In this failure case it would be more desirable to route the inter-AS TE LSP via Algiers (by means of OC-3 links in Globenet's network) so as to follow a path in the ATC network exclusively made of OC-3 links.

Figure 5-53   *Inter-AS Shortest Path Selection After a Node Failure (Paris) in the ATC Network with Loose Hop Routing*

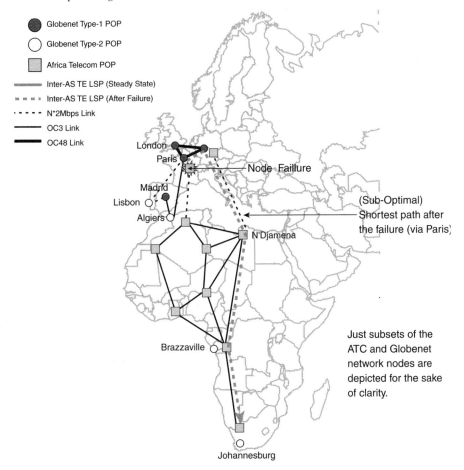

The two previous failure examples highlight that the loose hop routing path computation method cannot guarantee the selection of the shortest end-to-end path. Furthermore, even if a static configuration can be performed to get an optimal path in the majority of cases, this would require constant adjustments to cope with network upgrades, failures, and reoptimization within both networks.

Globenet conducted a detailed analysis to determine whether being able to compute the shortest path was a strict requirement. Globenet concluded that because Africa is a large continent and, more importantly, because the ATC network is made up of links having significantly different link speeds, there were many situations in which the difference in propagation delays and bandwidth (and consequently QoS) between the shortest path and an alternate path would be significant. Hence, it was required to select the end-to-end shortest path whenever possible.

Moreover, considering the number of peerings between Globenet and Africa Telecom (four for the moment, with plans to increase that number), any manual solution would be cumbersome and ineffective in handling dynamic and unpredictable changes (such as network element failures).

Consequently, Globenet and Africa Telecom elected to use a path computation element (PCE)-based computation approach for their inter-AS TE LSP path computation. One of the main advantages of the PCE-based computation approach described here of a PCE lies in its ability to compute the path of a TE LSP for which it is not the headend. In some cases, as shown next, the computation of an end-to-end path requires the cooperation of multiple PCEs. Ideal candidates for PCE are ASBRs (or ABRs in the case of interarea MPLS TE). The path computation algorithm consists of using a backward recursive approach whereby each PCE computes a set of shortest path(s) to the destination in its own domain. These are passed to the requesting upstream PCE, which itself computes a set of shortest paths to the destination, and so on.

In the Globenet-Africa Telecom case, two autonomous systems are involved. Let's discuss how such optimal paths are computed in this environment. Figure 5-54 shows Steps 1 and 2 in the computation of the inter-AS TE shortest path using a PCE-based approach between Globenet and Africa Telecom.

This example considers the case of an inter-AS TE LSP between the Globenet ASBR in Paris and a PE router residing in the Johannesburg VPOP. Note that a similar procedure applies to the case of the inter-AS TE LSP between a Globenet PE router residing in a VPOP and one of Globenet's ASBRs.

As shown in Figure 5-54, all the ASBRs of Globenet and ATC act as PCEs (Paris, Frankfurt, and Algiers).

For the sake of illustration, assume the following link metric assignment in both networks:

- OC-192—Cost = 1 (currently there is no OC-192)
- OC-48—Cost = 4
- OC-3—Cost = 16
- 2 Mbps—Cost = 1232

Figure 5-54   *PCE-Based Computation of an Inter-AS TE Shortest Path, Steps 1 and 2*

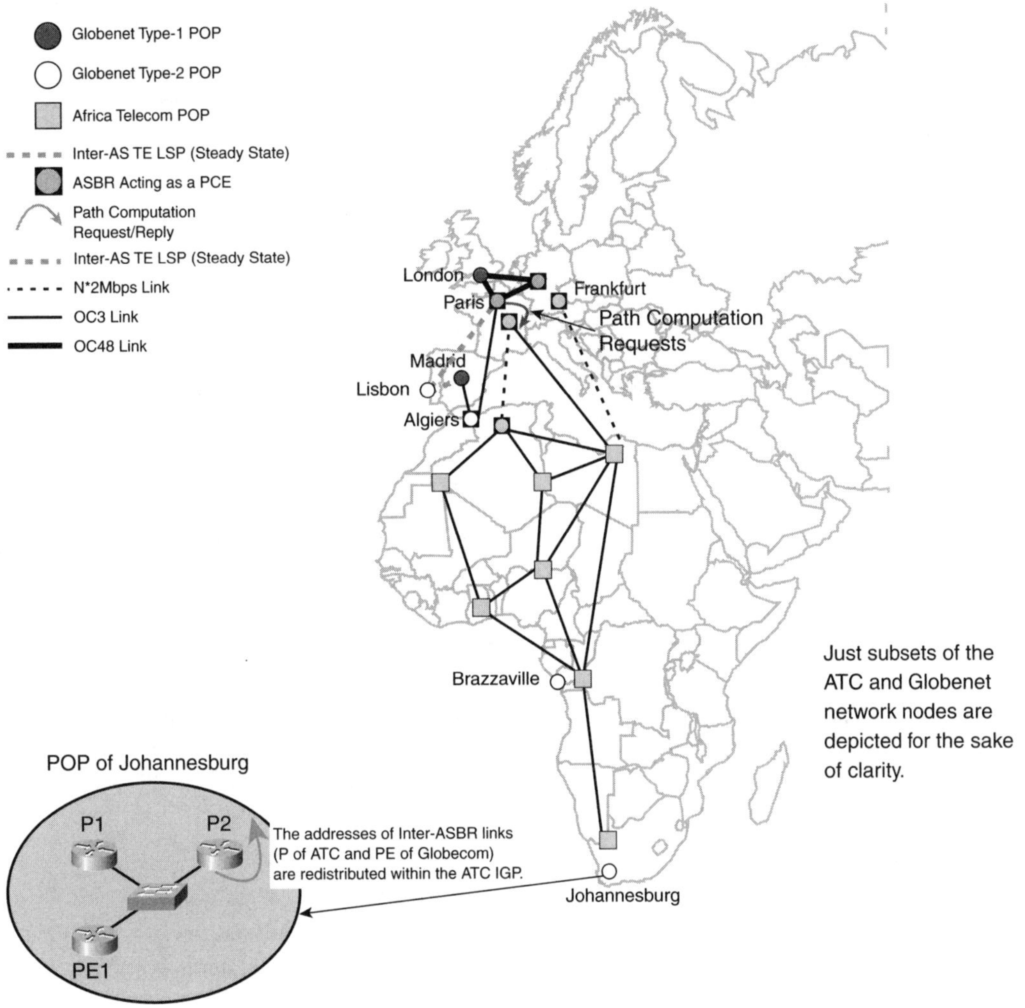

Legend:
- ● Globenet Type-1 POP
- ○ Globenet Type-2 POP
- ▢ Africa Telecom POP
- ▪▪▪▪ Inter-AS TE LSP (Steady State)
- ◉ ASBR Acting as a PCE
- ⌒ Path Computation Request/Reply
- ▪▪▪▪ Inter-AS TE LSP (Steady State)
- ····· N*2Mbps Link
- ——— OC3 Link
- ▬▬▬ OC48 Link

London
Paris
Frankfurt
Path Computation Requests
Madrid
Lisbon
Algiers
Brazzaville
Johannesburg

Just subsets of the ATC and Globenet network nodes are depicted for the sake of clarity.

POP of Johannesburg

P1   P2

The addresses of Inter-ASBR links (P of ATC and PE of Globecom) are redistributed within the ATC IGP.

PE1

Figure 5-55 *Inter-AS PCE-Based Shortest Path Computation, Steps 3 and 4*

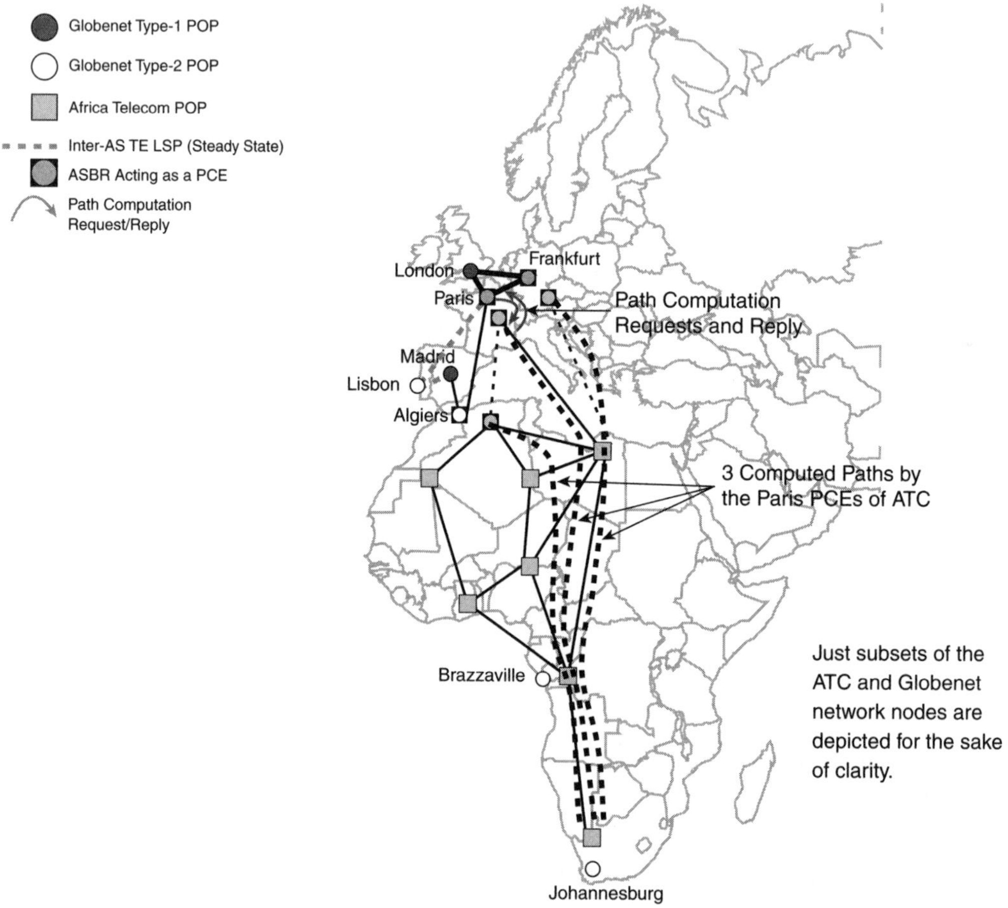

Let's now review the PCE-based inter-AS TE LSP path computation process step by step.

Step 1 As shown in Figure 5-54, the headend router (the Globenet ASBR) must first select a PCE to send a path computation request to.

NOTE The IETF PCE (Path Computation Element) working group is responsible for the standardization of the LSP-PCE protocol.

The PCE discovery process can be performed by means of local or static configuration (where multiple PCE addresses can be specified) or via IGP discovery. In the latter case, the PCE addresses and capability are advertised in the Router CAPABILITY

TLV by means of various PCE-related sub-TLVs defined in [ISIS-TE-CAPS]. In the case of Globenet, considering the limited number of PCEs and the fact that Globenet currently has a few TE peering points only with ATC, it chose to use static PCE discovery. On each ASBR that can originate an inter-AS TE LSP, Globenet statically configured the PCE's address (in the ATC network) to send the path computation request to.

Step 2 A path computation request is sent to the selected PCE, which in turn analyzes the request. (In this example, as shown in Figure 5-54, Globenet's ASBR in Paris sends its path computation request to Paris' ATC ASBR.) Paris' ATC PCE determines that the TE LSP destination can be reached by one of its P routers in Johannesburg. (Remember that this is because of the redistribution of inter-ASBR links within the IGP. Hence, the VPOP's PE router addresses are redistributed by the ATC IGP.)

Step 3 As shown in Figure 5-55, the ATC ASBR in Paris computes the shortest path which obeys the set of specified constraints (bandwidth and so on) from every ATC ASBR (Algiers, Paris, and Frankfurt) to the destination (the destination PE router of the Globenet VPOP in Johannesburg). This example assumes that at least one path satisfies the set of constraints from each of the three ASBRs to the destination. The three paths are then returned to the requesting PCE (Globenet's PCE in Paris) along with the corresponding path costs:

— From the ATC ASBR in Algiers to the destination, cost = 48.

— From the ATC ASBR in Paris to the destination, cost = 48.

— From the ATC ASBR in Frankfurt to the destination, cost = 1264.

An important consideration is preserving confidentiality. To preserve confidentiality, the entire path is not returned to the requesting PCE. Instead, the three computed paths returned to the requesting ASBR are made up of two hops: the entry ASBR (ATC ASBRs in Algiers, Paris, and Frankfurt) and the destination (Globenet's PE router in the Johannesburg VPOP, specified as a loose hop). Note that knowledge of the actual path within the ATC network is not required to compute the shortest path end to end. Only knowledge of the cost of each of these paths is required and is passed to the requesting PCE.

Step 4 Upon receiving the set of shortest paths between each entry ASBR of the ATC network and the destination, the requesting PCE (Globenet's ASBR in Paris) can compute the shortest path end to end. This is because it gets the network topology and resource information about the Globenet network from the MPLS TE topology database advertised in IS-IS. Such a computation is identical to a CSPF computation where the tree root is the destination node. This leads to the following computed path:

— Path 1 (via Paris)—Cost = 49 (the inter-ASBR links have a cost of 1)

— Path 2 (via Frankfurt)—Cost = 1264 + 4 + 1 = 1269

— Path 3 (via Algiers)—Cost = 16 + 1 + 48 = 65

Step 5   The Globenet ASBR in Paris then signals the inter-AS TE LSP along the computed shortest path (via the ATC ASBR in Paris) up to the destination. The first hop is specified as a strict hop and refers to the first entry (the ASBR of the ATC network in Paris). The other hops (to the final destination) are listed as a loose hop in the corresponding RSVP Path message. The ATC entry ASBR finally expands the path to the final destination on receipt of the RSVP-TE Path message. Such a mechanism guarantees the computation of the shortest end-to-end path.

Let's now go back to the failure case of the link between Paris and N'Djamena. Upon receiving the failure notification by means of an RSVP-TE Path Error message, the Globenet ASBR in Paris would reinitiate a path computation request. ATC's ASBR in Paris would return the following set of three paths:

- From the ATC ASBR of Algiers to the destination—Cost = 48
- From the ATC ASBR of Paris to the destination—Cost = 1280
- From the ATC ASBR of Frankfurt to the destination—Cost = 1264

Thus, when the Globenet ASBR in Paris computes the shortest path from itself to the destination, it finds three possible paths:

- Path 1 (via Paris)—Cost = 1 + 1280 = 1281
- Path 2 (via Frankfurt)—Cost = 1264 + 4 + 1 = 1269
- Path 3 (via Algiers)—Cost = 16 + 1 + 48 = 65

Hence, the best end-to-end path is via Algiers, not Frankfurt (although this is the closest ASBR from Paris from the Globenet ASBR viewpoint).

This example demonstrates that the PCE-based path computation method always allows for the computation of the shortest end-to-end path across multiple domains.

NOTE   A shortest path end-to-end can be computed only if the two networks use consistent metrics. Indeed, because the end-to-end shortest path is computed thanks to the computation of two disjointed path segments performed by two distinct PCEs, you must ensure that both PCEs use consistent metrics. Globenet and Africa Telecom were using consistent metrics based on bandwidth, so the use of the IGP metric was perfectly adequate. That said, it is worth mentioning that in cases where IGP metrics are computed based on nonsimilar criteria, the solution is to use the TE metric as a path cost indication that both service providers can use consistently. [SECOND-METRIC] specifies the possibility of using either the IGP or the TE metric for the path computation. Every computed path cost returned by the PCEs would then be based on the TE link metric, thus ensuring the computation of the shortest end-to-end path.

NOTE	Such a PCE-based path computation approach can also be used in a context where the headend router is located anywhere in the originating AS. In such a case, a very similar procedure is used, whereby the headend router first initiates the request to the PCE residing in its domain. For example, consider a TE LSP that originates on a node X in the Globenet network and terminates on a PE router in Johannesburg. Then, there would just be an additional phase corresponding to the sending of the path computation request to the PCE in the Globenet network. The rest of the procedure would be identical.

Reoptimization of Inter-AS TE LSPs

In contrast with intra-area TE LSPs, where the triggers for reoptimization can be either timer- or event-driven, Globenet chose to elect a timer-based-only reoptimization approach for its inter-AS TE LSP. Globenet decided to trigger the reoptimization of its inter-AS TE LSPs every 2 hours. The reoptimization process is similar to the computation of an inter-AS TE LSP path. The only difference is that the path of the active TE LSP is provided in the path computation request to the PCE to avoid double booking of bandwidth when evaluating the existence of a better path. If a more optimal (shorter) path exists, the headend router resignals the TE LSP using the nondisruptive make-before-break procedure. We must highlight a very important aspect of PCE-based path computation concerning reoptimization. Consider again the case of failure of the link between Paris and N'Djamena in the ATC network. With a loose-hop routing path computation, there is no way to discover whether the initial preferred path (because the set of loose paths has to be manually configured) has been restored (if the current path does not go through the same set of ASBRs) other than by resignaling the TE LSP and seeing whether it succeeds. Of course, this is very undesirable. Conversely, the PCE-based path computation allows the headend to issue a new path computation request mentioning that such a request is related to a reoptimization. The headend router thus reroutes the inter-AS TE LSP if and only if a shorter path exists.

Routing onto Inter-AS TE LSPs

Routing the traffic onto inter-AS TE LSPs requires a bit of extra configuration. Indeed, an automatic mechanism so as to use such TE LSPs when computing the routing table is not currently available (but is being investigated at the time of writing). By definition, routing protocols hide some information across domains so that the headend of an inter-AS LSP does not have topology information about the domain in which the TE LSP's destination belongs. Note that this generally applies to interdomain MPLS Traffic Engineering, where a domain may be an IGP area or an autonomous system.

Consider the example shown in Figure 5-56. From the Globenet VPOP to Globenet's ASBR1, several static routes are required on PE1:

- A static route pointing to LSP1 for the ASBR1 loopback address (destination of the inter-AS TE LSP)

- A static route pointing to LSP1 for the loopback addresses for the set of PE routers and route reflectors residing in the Globenet network (just one route reflector is shown in Figure 5-56)

Figure 5-56 *Routing onto Inter-AS TE LSPs*

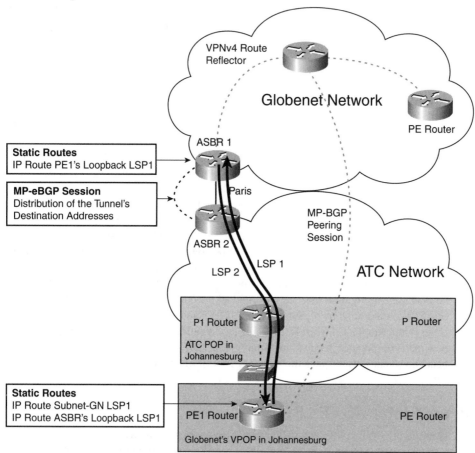

Note that PE1 learns Globenet's IPv4 and VPNv4 routes by means of the MP-BGP sessions between PE1 and the relevant set of Globenet route reflectors.

From the Globenet core network to VPOP, just one static route to the PE1's loopback address pointing to LSP2 is required on ASBR1. Note that such a static route is then redistributed into IS-IS.

The aim of the MP-BGP session is for ASBR2 to learn the inter-AS TE LSP's destination addresses and for ASBR1 to learn the inter-ASBR link addresses for management purposes. At this point, the regular BGP route recursion is applied to steer the traffic to the appropriate inter-AS TE LSP.

VPOP QoS Design

Globenet wanted to offer to customers connected to a VPOP the exact same QoS services, including support for its five VPN CoSs and the associated comprehensive SLA commitments. To allow this, Africa Telecom uses the inter-AS TE LSPs discussed earlier to give Globenet a service of Virtual IP Leased Line (VLL). Such a VLL service is characterized by the following:

- Packets carried over the inter-AS TE LSPs experience a delay that is comparable to the delay provided by a classical leased line. (In other words, it is dominated by the propagation delay.)

- Packets carried over the inter-AS TE LSPs experience a very small jitter (say, 30 to 50 ms). This is compatible with the jitter objectives that Globenet wants to commit to for its most demanding CoS (VPN voice) over that route.

- Packets carried over the inter-AS TE LSPs experience a negligible loss.

- QoS marking transparency is provided to the packets carried over the inter-AS TE LSPs. In other words, Globenet can set the packets' QoS markings according to its scheme on one side of Africa Telecom and can be sure that these markings will be preserved when the packets reenter Globenet on the other side.

To provide such a service, Africa Telecom decided first to handle the VLL traffic separately from the rest of its traffic from a scheduling perspective. At every hop of the ATC network, Africa Telecom activated a new queue dedicated to the VLL traffic. Because Africa Telecom was not using the EF queue to schedule its own traffic, it decided to use the EF queue for the VLL traffic and instantiate it as a strict priority queue to optimize delay and loss. A new EXP value of 5 is also dedicated to the VLL traffic.

Then, Africa Telecom takes full advantage of the TE capabilities to perform admission control and constraint-based routing of the inter-AS TE LSPs within its network. It configured BC0 to 50 percent on its OC-3 links and to 30 percent on the lower-speed links. First, this ensures that the load of VLL traffic routed on any link is sufficiently low so that the strict priority EF queue can guarantee the targeted delay/jitter/loss. Also, this ensures that sufficient capacity is kept for the rest of Africa Telecom traffic.

Should Africa Telecom need to schedule some of its own traffic into the EF queue in the future, it would carry the corresponding traffic onto appropriately sized TE tunnels. This would ensure that consistent admission control is performed across the inter-AS TE LSPs used for the VLL service and the intra-AS TE LSPs used for its own EF traffic.

To make sure that packets received from Globenet in the inter-AS TE LSPs can be classified easily in the ATC network, Africa Telecom applies an input QoS policy on its ASBRs on the interfaces attaching the Globenet routers. This policy unconditionally remarks the EXP field of the outmost label stack entry (the one containing the label for the inter-AS TE LSP) to EXP=5 (the VLL value in the Africa Telecom network). It leaves all the other QoS markings untouched (the EXP field of LDP and MP-BGP labels applied by Globenet as well as the DSCP of carried packets). This way, the packets entering Africa Telecom have EXP=5 in the outmost label stack entry but carry the Globenet marking in all the QoS fields. At the egress of Africa Telecom, the ASBR performs penultimate hop popping, which, by default, leaves the EXP value of all the exposed label stack entries untouched. Hence, when reentering Globenet's network, packets arrive with the regular Globenet QoS marking. Also, at the egress of Africa Telecom, the ASBR applies an egress QoS policy specified by Globenet and based on Globenet's EXP scheme. The QoS marking and QoS service policies at every step across the operators are illustrated in Figure 5-57 from the Globenet VPOP to the Globenet core.

Figure 5-57   *QoS Policies*

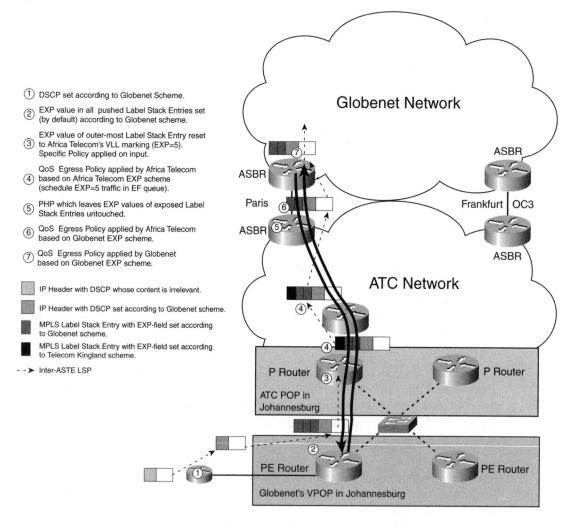

You should recognize the "short pipe" DiffServ tunneling mode, which was discussed in the section "QoS Design for the Interprovider VPN with Telecom Kingland." Telecom Kingland used this mode for very similar purposes: to be able to apply their QoS scheme to the Globenet traffic transiting through their network while preserving QoS transparency of the Globenet QoS markings.

Africa Telecom decided not to apply a very strict input policing of traffic sent to the inter-AS TE LSPs to the agreed-upon rate for the VLL services. Instead, Africa Telecom and Globenet agreed to operate in a more flexible model. In this way, Globenet can send more traffic than the agreed-upon rate but then receives an additional charge based on the measured excess over the agreed-upon rate. This way, Globenet can much more easily cope with growth in traffic demand, and Africa Telecom gets additional revenue. Also, in that case, Globenet can readjust the inter-AS TE LSP bandwidth monthly.

Note that for security reasons, Africa Telecom still applies some raw policing over all the traffic received on the interfaces attached to Globenet to protect against denial-of-service (DoS) risks. A policing rate is chosen that is expected to be higher than what Globenet would normally ever need. Although it is somewhat lenient, such a policing eliminates the most serious risks of DoS considering the very high speed of the interfaces attaching Globenet routers (Gigabit Ethernet). Also, to protect its own traffic, Africa Telecom applies a policer on the EF queue at every hop whose rate reflects BC0 (with some margin). This ensures that no matter how much VLL marked traffic may end up in the network, it will not be able to hog all the bandwidth despite the fact that it is using a strict priority queue.

Recovery of Inter-AS TE LSPs

The ability to provide fast recovery for the inter-AS traffic was undoubtedly a major motivation for the adoption of such an inter-AS TE model. Indeed, providing fast recovery (on the order of a few tens or even hundreds of milliseconds) by means of BGP interconnection is quite challenging, if not impossible. This is particularly true in case of failure of inter-ASBR links, IPv4, and VPNv4 route reflectors.

The case of inter-AS TE LSPs is in that respect quite different. Consider the case of the inter-AS TE LSP between the Globenet ASBR in Paris (G2 in Figure 5-58) and the Johannesburg VPOP, shown in Figure 5-57.

The recovery of an inter-AS TE LSP, should a failure occur within an AS, is identical to the case of an intra-AS TE LSP. As a reminder, both Globenet and Africa Telecom elected to use FRR for link protection in their network.

Figure 5-58 *MPLS TE Fast Reroute Design for the Paris ASBRs (Routers A2 and G2)*

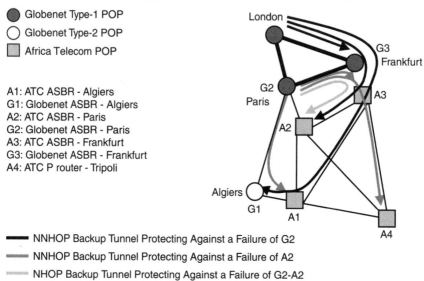

- NNHOP Backup Tunnel Protecting Against a Failure of G2
- NNHOP Backup Tunnel Protecting Against a Failure of A2
- NHOP Backup Tunnel Protecting Against a Failure of G2-A2

On the other hand, inter-ASBR link failure and ASBR failure have specificities in the case of inter-AS TE:

- **ASBR link failure**—The only requirement is to configure a next-hop backup tunnel originated on one ASBR and terminating on the next-hop ASBR. Note that because no IGP is usually running between ASBRs (which is also the case for Globenet and Africa Telecom), the path of such backup tunnels must be explicitly configured and cannot be dynamically computed by path computation algorithms such as CSPF.

- **ASBR node failure**—Protecting against the failure of an ASBR requires, for each upstream neighbor of the protected ASBR, the configuration of one next-next-hop backup tunnel per ASBR next hop. Similar to the next-hop backup tunnel case, next-next-hop backup tunnel paths have been manually configured. For instance, to protect against the failure of the ASBR A2, three next-next-hop backup tunnels must be configured: from G2 to A3, from G2 to A4, and from G2 to A1. Similarly, protecting against the failure of the exit ASBR G2 requires the configuration of three next-next-hop backup tunnels: from London to G3, from London to A2, and from London to G1.

There is one important fact to highlight here. Although Globenet chose to use Fast Reroute for link protection only, it elected to use Fast Reroute for both link and node protection (protecting against ASBR failure) in the specific case of inter-AS TE LSPs. Such ASBRs concentrate all the inter-AS traffic to their VPOPs.

As explained in Chapter 2, the inability to differentiate a link failure from a node failure implies systematically using the next-next-hop backup tunnel, should both a next-hop and a next-next-hop backup tunnel exist, regardless of the failure type (inter-ASBR link or ASBR failure). In other words, if both a next-hop and a next-next-hop backup tunnel are configured and operational, the failure of an inter-ASBR link or an ASBR triggers the use of the next-next-hop backup tunnel. That said, configuring a next-hop backup tunnel in addition to the next-next-hop backup tunnel has some benefit in case of double failures. If the next-next-hop backup tunnel fails (for instance, because its destination node fails), it is still useful to use the next-hop backup tunnel if the inter-ASBR link also fails. For this reason, Globenet decided to systematically configure a set of next-hop and next-next-hop backup tunnels.

NOTE	Note that in all these examples, TE LSPs are shown in one direction. The primary and backup TE LSPs must be configured in both directions.

Policy Control at ASBR Boundaries

Such interprovider private TE peering requires some level of policy control to ensure that the set of signaled TE LSPs does not violate the agreements.

This actually requires the configuration of signaling control mechanisms. Several TE LSP characteristics can be checked at ASBR boundaries upon signaling, such as the signaled bandwidth and preemptions. Furthermore, being able to control the number of signaled TE LSPs is of the utmost importance. Indeed, each inter-AS TE consumes resources on a router (memory and CPU for signaling processing). Thus, Globenet and Africa Telecom decided to control the maximum number of inter-AS TE LSPs in addition to the sum of their bandwidths. Currently, on a Cisco router, both the total amount of bandwidth and the number of TE LSPs can be part of the interprovider policy. Globenet and Africa Telecom wanted to control another TE LSP parameter: the origin AS. Thus, for each signaled inter-AS TE LSP, the receiving ASBR checks the origin AS that the TE LSP headend belongs to. If the headend router does not belong to a specified set of Globenet autonomous systems, the inter-AS TE LSP is rejected. RSVP Path Error messages are originated upon TE LSP rejection because of policy violation. They are subject to specific logs in the NMS system so as to track potential DoS attacks.

Africa Telecom VPOP

Thanks to the private TE peering agreement, VPOPs can be deployed by both service providers. The preceding example showed how Globenet could deploy four VPOPs in Africa by means of inter-AS TE LSPs traversing the ATC network. Similarly, Africa Telecom decided to extend its reach in Europe in the future by deploying various VPOPs using the same model as in the case of Globenet's VPOPs.

Design Lessons to Be Taken from Globenet

A number of observations can be made from the design choices Globenet made:

- Delivering multiple services from the same edge platforms is possible, although a number of areas, such as scale and security, require close attention.

- Layer 3 MPLS VPN services may be delivered seamlessly across multiple autonomous systems, either of the same provider or of different operators cooperating closely.

- Where a simple overprovisioning strategy cannot be adopted in the core because of high bandwidth cost in many regions of the world, careful network optimization techniques can be deployed. By combining traffic engineering and a rich set of QoS mechanisms in a concerted way, strong QoS differentiation can be achieved in the core. You also can achieve tight SLAs while operating at relatively high link loads and thus minimize recurring bandwidth cost.

- The use of DiffServ-Aware MPLS Traffic engineering (DS-TE) allows for optimum traffic distribution in the network on a per-class basis using differentiated call admission controls and constraint-based routing. These take into account the resources actually granted to each class by DiffServ scheduling as well as per-class engineering constraints defined by the operator.

- Where the end customer's intranet spans very large geographic distances such as multiple continents, bandwidth is scarce, and significant incompressible propagation delays eat up most of the delay budget for sensitive applications. A rich set of classes of service lets you address in a cost-effective way the specific requirements of various customer applications.

- Where access to the Layer 3 MPLS VPN service is supported through another service provider, consistent CoS offerings may be supported for the end customer, even when the two service providers have deployed different QoS policies in their core. This is achieved through appropriate QoS mapping functions at service provider boundaries.

- Layer 3 MPLS VPN services can be extended to support IPv6 in an incremental fashion. The upgrade for IPv6 support can be localized to the subset of the edge routers that actually need to offer that service. The core needs no upgrade or configuration changes.

- In parts of the network where there is much more IP traffic to carry than native ATM traffic, the ATM network can be trunked over the multiservice MPLS infrastructure. This involves support of pseudowire services on the edge routers and an appropriately engineered core to guarantee appropriate QoS and reliability.

- A service provider can extend its reach to other regions via other service providers' IP/MPLS networks by deploying virtual POPs (VPOPs). The VPOP model relies on the combination of various technologies. These include inter-AS MPLS Traffic Engineering with dynamic computation of shortest interprovider constrained paths, interprovider QoS, and Fast Reroute. This provides a service equivalent to any other "regular" POP, with strict SLAs in terms of QoS and network availability. It offers a cost-effective alternative to service providers that want to extend their footprint. It also allows a very fine granularity as well as rapid adjustment in terms of interconnection bandwidth offered to the VPOP.

- Automatic provisioning features can be used to ease the deployment of a full mesh of MPLS Traffic Engineering LSPs with minimal configuration.

- MPLS Traffic Engineering LSPs can be automatically resized by headend routers to dynamically adjust the TE LSP bandwidth to the actual traffic demand and consequently to find the shortest path for the requested bandwidth and optimize network resources.

Large Enterprise Design Study

This chapter is devoted to the study of a fictitious large European holding of banks called EuroBank. EuroBank was initially a large bank called MainBank in the United Kingdom (UK). Several years ago it acquired EnterBank, a bank in the UK that specialized in providing services to business customers. It also acquired a small insurance company called UK Insurance (UKI), which provided services for consumers and enterprises. EuroBank continued its expansion into other parts of Europe via acquisitions of local banks in Germany (GerBank) and Spain (SpainBank) that had a national branch network. Spainbank also owned two offices in Germany.

Recently, EuroBank acquired a brokerage office in New York City because of its proximity to the New York Stock Exchange. EuroBank's presence in the U.S. is currently limited to that brokerage office, and no banking services are offered at this location. EuroBank plans to continue its expansion via internal and external growth (through acquisitions in other countries).

From a networking perspective, EuroBank's primary objective was to consolidate its multiple subsidiary networks into a single infrastructure to achieve significant cost reductions and enhance communications through a higher-speed network. While doing so, a paramount requirement for EuroBank was to provide strict isolation between its various subsidiaries because each of them operates in strict autonomy. For example, an EnterBank branch location in the UK should not be able to establish any connectivity with a branch location from UKI, and vice versa. In other words, EuroBank needed to support the various subsidiaries in separate partitions. It chose to achieve this through the use of Layer 3 network-based Virtual Private Network (VPN) technology.

More recently, EuroBank decided to take advantage of the chosen VPN technology to also enforce isolation between various departments within one of its subsidiaries—MainBank. For example, MainBank's accounting department should not have any connectivity with the brokerage service, and vice versa.

EuroBank has a number of data centers. Unlike the intersubsidiary connectivity requirements, each data center needs to be accessed by all the subsidiaries of the EuroBank group, because they host applications from all the subsidiaries/departments. More specifically, some servers are dedicated to specific subsidiaries/departments, whereas other servers must be accessed by all the locations of EuroBank. Furthermore, communication is needed between different data centers (for example, for backup between servers located in different data centers).

EuroBank took advantage of the transition to a more advanced IP infrastructure to migrate its telephony and video applications to this IP infrastructure to achieve the cost reduction objectives it was pursuing. EuroBank elected to outsource its telephony to a telephony service provider (TSP) offering a complete managed voice over IP (VoIP) service. This includes installation and operation of IP phones and all the necessary call processing devices on EuroBank premises.

Because of the mission-critical applications as well as these voice and video applications now carried over the IP network, tight quality of service (QoS) and reliability were absolutely required while keeping bandwidth costs down. Moreover, new emerging applications requiring more flexibility in terms of voice/data integration for various banking applications (for example, click-to-talk applications or monitoring of remote equipment by video over IP) reinforced these requirements.

The objective of this chapter is to discuss the current EuroBank network design, which is illustrative of a large Enterprise that has deployed its own MPLS infrastructure. In particular, this chapter reviews how the Managed Voice Service integrates and operates in EuroBank's network. Also, because the TSP uses the Layer 3 MPLS VPN technology as a building block in its own infrastructure to implement EuroBank's Managed Voice Service for different customers, this chapter briefly discusses the Layer 3 MPLS VPN design used by the TSP.

It is worth noting that the network design presented in this chapter also applies to many other industry sectors, such as insurance, energy, and manufacturing. Indeed, such companies generally share similar requirements in terms of cost reduction by servicing all their subsidiaries over a single network infrastructure. They also have requirements for secure and controlled communication between different subsidiaries and departments in a given business, as well as integration of telephony services over the shared network. The same challenges are also often faced as a result of the dynamics of mergers, acquisitions, and international expansion.

EuroBank's Network Environment

Across all its subsidiaries, EuroBank has more than 1100 branches across Europe (which we call *branches*). In addition, EuroBank runs more than 40 large office sites (which we call *offices*) across the UK, Spain, and Germany. Each office has tens to hundreds of employees working in different departments (front and back office).

EuroBank built a private core network composed of nine points of presence (POPs): five in the UK (including three in London), two in Germany (Berlin and Frankfurt), and two in Spain (Barcelona and Madrid).

All branches and offices are connected to the EuroBank core network. For the branches, this connection is provided in the UK and Germany by means of a managed Layer 3 MPLS VPN service provided by local service providers in these countries. In Spain this connection is achieved through a managed Frame Relay network provided by a local service provider. In all countries, offices are directly connected to the core network via one of the nine POPs using private leased lines (34 Mbps or 155 Mbps), ATM PVCs, Metro Ethernet connections, or, when co-located within the POP, using local Fast Ethernet or Gigabit Ethernet connections.

EuroBank core POPs are also attached to the Layer 3 MPLS VPN service and to the managed Frame Relay-based service of their local service providers in their respective country.

Each office usually is composed of server farms hosting various applications accessed by branch locations. As already pointed out, each branch also accesses applications hosted in the various data centers in Europe.

EuroBank has four data centers—two in London, one in Frankfurt, and one in Madrid. These are interconnected to the local POP(s) by means of redundant high-speed links, Fast Ethernet or Gigabit Ethernet (wherever such metro services are available in that particular city), or 155-Mbps leased lines otherwise. Data centers are usually close to the core network POPs but are never co-located for availability reasons (thus keeping a power supply failure, for instance, from affecting both the POP and the data center). Such data centers host many applications on UNIX servers and mainframes that are accessed by the various branches and offices in the EuroBank group. In other words, although the branches usually connect to remote applications hosted in an office of their subsidiary, they also access applications hosted in the various data centers. Likewise, offices access applications hosted on servers located in other offices or within the data centers.

In the past, EuroBank operated nine data centers, but it reduced that number to four over the last two years to meet its cost-reduction objectives. This was made possible because the company's high-speed MPLS infrastructure offers the necessary performance levels, allowing transparent access to a remotely located data center and because of the Layer 3 MPLS VPN technology, which allows strict control of access to different resources in the same location.

Description of the Branch Office

Branch offices are small-to-medium locations with regular front-office banking services. They do not require the support of multiple VPNs. They are located in various towns and cities across the UK, Germany, and Spain.

Table 6-1 indicates the number of branches per subsidiary and per country.

Table 6-1   *Number of Branches Per Subsidiary and Per Country*

Subsidiary	Country	Number of Branch Office
MainBank	UK	400
EnterBank	UK	120
UKI	UK	200
SpainBank	Spain	300
GerBank	Germany	100

As previously stated, in the UK and in Germany, the branches are not attached directly to the EuroBank core network. Instead, they are connected by means of a Layer 3 MPLS VPN connection that is provided by a regional service provider. The rationale for such an approach was essentially driven by cost, because financially appealing agreements were made with local service providers that had a large national presence. Taking advantage of a managed service was substantially cheaper both in terms of capital expenditure (capex) and operational expenditure (opex) when compared to the cost of deploying a separate network and an operational support organization for national coverage throughout each country.

In these countries, the branches are connected to the Layer 3 MPLS VPN local service provider, each via a single CE router that is managed by that service provider. The access link from the CE router to the service provider's PE router is typically an SDSL link offering a bidirectional connection at a rate ranging from 512 kbps to 2 Mbps.

In Spain, EuroBank used the Frame Relay managed router service established with a local service provider by SpainBank before its acquisition by EuroBank. SpainBank's branch and office locations, as well as the EuroBank core POPs in Spain, are all connected to this managed router service via a CE router managed by the service provider using Frame Relay permanent virtual circuits (PVCs). The exact set of Frame Relay PVCs across these locations was determined based on each location's bandwidth requirement and the traffic matrix between locations. In particular, the CE router of each branch or office is connected to two managed CE routers located in either the Madrid POP or the Barcelona POP. One Frame Relay PVC is connected to a central CE router and is used as a primary PVC. A second Frame Relay PVC of the same capacity (called a shadow PVC) is connected to the second central CE router located in the same POP and is used if the primary central CE router fails. The detailed structure of a POP in Spain is described in the section "Description of a Core Network POP." SpainBank has two offices in Germany that used to be connected to the rest of its national network by means of international Frame Relay PVCs. These offices are now connected to the EuroBank POP in Germany via leased line and are attached to the SpainBank VPN.

The EuroBank access links in the branches in every country are backed up by the service provider via multiple ISDN bearer channels. These channels are dynamically established by way of a floating static route in case the connection between the branch and the service provider PE router fails. In such a failure case, the appropriate number of bearer channels is aggregated using multilink PPP (see [MLPPP]) to provide an equivalent bandwidth until the service is restored and the traffic is switched back to the local access link. Note that such backup technology is deployed both in the case of access to a Layer 3 MPLS VPN service provider core and in the case of the Frame Relay managed service used in Spain.

References Used in This Book

Throughout this book you will see references to other resources. These are provided in case you want to delve more deeply into a subject. Such references appear in brackets code, such as [L2VPN]. If you want to know more about this resource, look up the code in the "References" appendix to find out specific information about the resource.

Figure 6-1 shows the structure of a branch, as well as its connectivity to the EuroBank core network.

Figure 6-1 *Branch Location and Interconnection to the EuroBank Core*

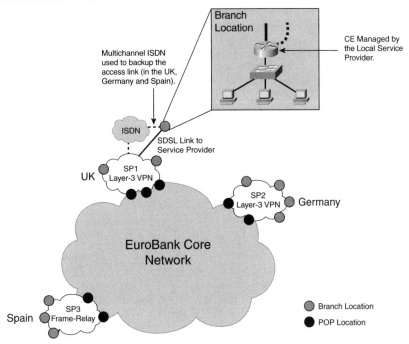

Description of an Office Location

As discussed, EuroBank offices potentially host hundreds of employees from different subsidiaries. They include all back-office processing in addition to the front-end applications. Outside the UK, the offices in Spain, Germany, and New York each support staff from a single subsidiary.

From a networking infrastructure perspective, the only difference between the UK offices and the offices outside the UK is how the CE routers are connected and how many VPNs each CE router needs to support. In the Spanish and German offices, two CE routers are connected to the EuroBank core network by means of leased lines or metro connections. This is also true for smaller office locations in the UK.

The office locations in the UK, an example of which is shown in Figure 6-2, are composed of two multi-VRF-capable CE routers. (Multi-VRF functionality is explained in detail in the section "UK Office Location Layer 3 MPLS VPN Design.") These CE routers attach to PE routers in the local POP via leased lines or metro connections. Hosts and servers are attached to the office network via Gigabit Ethernet switches dual-attached to the multi-VRF CE routers.

A separate virtual LAN (VLAN) is configured on the Ethernet switch for each VPN supported at that location. That VLAN is attached to the corresponding VRF in the multi-VRF CE routers. Finally, each host port at the switch is configured to be in the VLAN that corresponds to its VPN.

Figure 6-2 *Office Locations in the UK and Interconnection to the EuroBank Network Core*

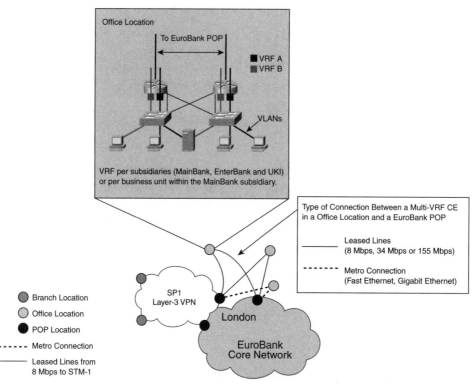

The CE routers of larger offices in the UK are generally connected to the EuroBank core network POPs (whose structure is described in the next section) via 34-Mbps (and sometimes 155-Mbps) leased lines. In large cities such as London, the larger office CE routers are connected to the core POPs via a metro Fast Ethernet or Gigabit Ethernet connection provided by a local service provider. For the smaller office locations, the medium used to connect these sites to the core network is leased lines from 8 Mbps to 34 Mbps.

When possible, EuroBank leases protected circuits from its local service provider. In the absence of such protection, it relies on its Interior Gateway Protocol (IGP) (OSPF) convergence to reroute the traffic in case of a leased line failure. EuroBank also relies on IGP convergence to handle CE router or PE router failure.

Observe that full redundancy is supported in the office locations by doubling all the network equipment. This redundancy is provided by two CE routers (dimensioned so that each can single-handedly deal with all the traffic to and from the location), dual Gigabit Ethernet switches, and dual connections to the core network via two different POPs (or, where not possible, via two different routers of one POP).

Description of a Core Network POP

The core network is composed of nine POPS: five in the UK (three in London, one in Manchester, and another in Newcastle), two in Germany (Berlin and Frankfurt), and two in Spain (Barcelona and Madrid).

The POP structure is shown in Figure 6-3. Each POP has two P routers connected to two PE routers via two Gigabit Ethernet switches. To ensure full redundancy, each P router and PE router is attached to the two switches.

Note that the POP structures in the UK, Germany, and Spain differ slightly:

- In the UK, the EuroBank PE routers are directly connected to the PE router of their local service provider by means of multiple Frame Relay PVCs (one for each VPN) multiplexed over dedicated STM-1 links. Effectively, the EuroBank MPLS network and the service provider MPLS VPN can be seen as using the inter-AS option "A" case that was described in the "Inter-AS Back-to-Back VRFs (Option A)" section in Chapter 1, "Technology Primer: Layer 3 VPN, Multicast VPNs, IPv6, and Pseudowire." The EuroBank PE routers are also connected to the offices by means of metro connections, leased lines, and ATM PVCs.

- In Germany, the Frankfurt POP structure is identical to that of the UK, except that the PE routers support only a single VPN. In the case of the POP in Berlin, the POP structure is slightly simpler because only two PE routers also act as P routers. This is justified by the fact that the POP in Berlin is not connected to any data center. Having two sets of PE routers and P routers is not justified.

- In Spain, the PE routers are connected via a point-to-point Gigabit Ethernet link to each of the two central CE routers that are managed by the local service provider and that aggregate the traffic coming from the branches. Also, as in the case of the POPs in Germany, the EuroBank PE routers handle only a single VPN. Note that for similar reasons as in the case of Germany, EuroBank decided to have two PE routers (also acting as P routers) for its POP in Barcelona. The company has two P routers and two PE routers in its POP in Madrid (connected to its data center in Spain), as shown in Figure 6-3.

EuroBank decided to locate each of the nine POPs in the same premises as a large office. Therefore, the location infrastructure shown in Figure 6-3 actually covers both the POP and the co-located office. The PE routers in this case are used to attach the remote CE routers of other office locations as well as to support the VPN(s) for this location.

Figure 6-3 *EuroBank POP Infrastructure*

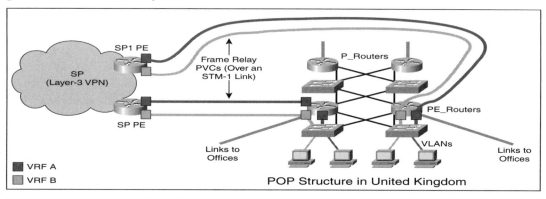

POP Structure in United Kingdom

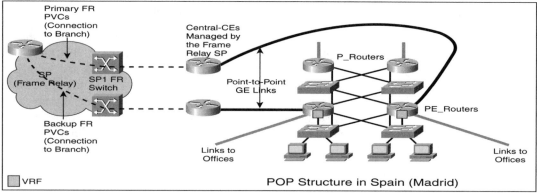

POP Structure in Spain (Madrid)

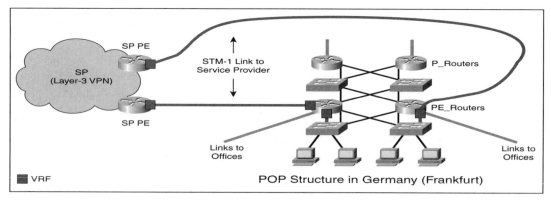

POP Structure in Germany (Frankfurt)

Just as in the other regular office locations, VLANs over the Gigabit Ethernet switches are used to propagate the VPN connectivity to the hosts in the co-located office.

The long-distance links interconnecting the POP locations are a mix of E3 (34-Mbps) links and ATM PVCs provided by international service providers (see Figure 6-4). The only exception is the case of the UK, where the three long-distance inter-POP links are Fast Ethernet. The three POPs of London are interconnected by Gigabit Ethernet (full rate). You'll read more about the metro connections in the section "Description of the Metro Connections in the UK."

Figure 6-4   *EuroBank Core Network Topology*

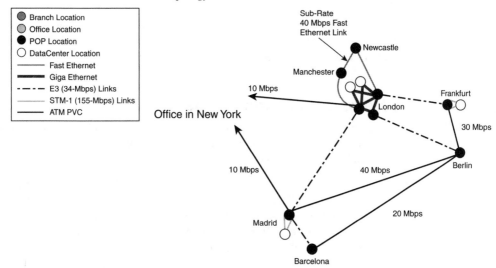

Description of the Data Centers

A data center has two PE routers connected to two different POP locations wherever possible or otherwise to two different routers of the closest POP. A data center location is shown in Figure 6-5.

Figure 6-5   *DataCenter Infrastructure*

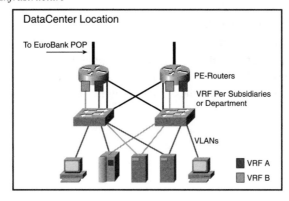

The PE routers in each data center support a VRF for each VPN of the EuroBank group (whether VPNs per subsidiary or VPNs per department, as is the case for MainBank). As in offices and POPs, VLANs are used to distribute the VPN connectivity to the hosts and servers. Scalability in terms of number of MAC addresses and so forth was not of concern, because the number of hosts and servers located in a data center is minimal.

The servers located in such data centers host a large set of applications, such as legacy IBM mainframe applications, brokerage applications, and various intranet applications. During the night, 60 percent of the traffic is related to backup data transfer.

Description of the Metro Connections in the UK

In the UK, metro connections are used to interconnect large offices to a POP, to interconnect data centers to POPs, and for POP to POP connections. EuroBank elected to use two different metro services for such interconnections:

- **Fast Ethernet**—This is deployed between some offices and their attachement POPs, between the Manchester POP and the Newcastle POP, and to connect each of the Manchester POP and the Newcastle POP to a London POP. In the latter case, a redundant managed service is provided by EuroBank's metro service provider. Two SDH Network Termination Units (NTUs) that deliver Fast Ethernet interfaces (copper) are located in the EuroBank office and the metro service provider POP, respectively. The two NTUs are interconnected by means of an SDH Multiplex Section-Shared Protection (MS-SP) ring. Because the Fast Ethernet connection is mapped to a protected SDH VC4, such links can be used at full line rate (100 Mbps).

  Fast Ethernet is used between the Manchester POP and the Newcastle POP, with a guaranteed subrate of 40 Mbps. In this case, high network availability is achieved by doubling the equipment, as shown in Figure 6-6. Note that input policing is performed on the Ethernet switch located in the metro service provider POP. This implies the configuration of output shaping on the P routers. The details of this process are discussed in the "Quality of Service Design" section.

- **Gigabit Ethernet**—This is deployed between EuroBank's data centers and the POPs in London, and between the three POPs in London. In contrast with the previous Fast Ethernet cases, P routers residing in two EuroBank sites are interconnected by means of two Gigabit Ethernet switches managed by EuroBank's metro service provider. Each

Gigabit Ethernet switch located in the EuroBank premises is connected to another Gigabit Ethernet switch that resides in the metro service provider POP. They act as metro provider edge equipment and are locally connected to a EuroBank P router by means of a point-to-point Gigabit Ethernet link, as shown in Figure 6-7.

Figure 6-6   *Subrate Fast Ethernet Connection Between the POPs of Manchester and Newcastle*

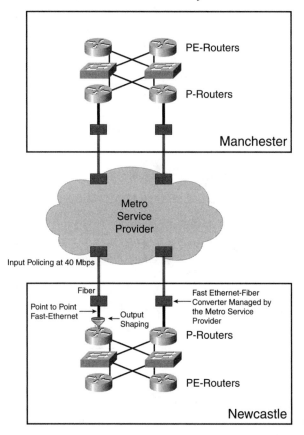

EuroBank decided to buy metro Gigabit Ethernet connections with rates ranging from 300 Mbps to 600 Mbps based on its traffic estimates, which are reevaluated each month based on the traffic statistics provided by the service provider. Note that input traffic shaping is configured on the service provider's ingress Ethernet switch. High network availability is achieved by means of complete redundancy. Two Ethernet switches are installed in EuroBank locations and are connected to the metro service provider core network via fully diverse fiber paths.

The metro service provider provides statistics related to port usage via a web interface (daily, weekly, and monthly usage).

Figure 6-7 *Gigabit Ethernet Metro Connection*

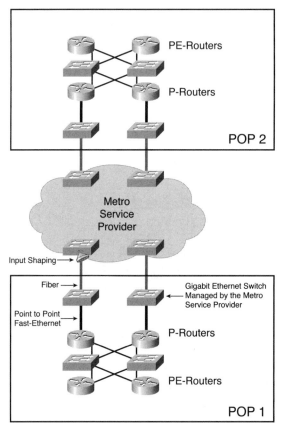

EuroBank Design Objectives

The design objectives for the EuroBank network included the following considerations:

- Offer a rich set of Layer 3 MPLS VPN services to the various subsidiaries and departments. Isolate subsidiaries and departments. Control access to shared applications.

- Support the levels of QoS required by mission critical banking applications, telephony over IP and videoconferencing applications.

- Provide the ability to support encrypted Layer 3 service for specific services such as the brokerage traffic, which requires a high level of confidentiality.

- Ensure that the network design is sufficiently flexible so as to easily handle the internal expected growth of traffic as well as the expansion of the network because of further acquisitions.

- Try to optimize the network's opex/capex by limiting the size of EuroBank's core network to the main branches/offices and data centers. Rely on the managed Layer 3 services provided by local operators for their small offices.

- Integrate the Managed Voice Service outsourced to the TSP in the EuroBank environment, allowing any-to-any telephone connectivity without compromising the subsidiary/department isolation.

- Provide a highly available and redundant network that can provide a total routing convergence bounded to 5 seconds in case of core link or P router failure.

The rest of this chapter describes the design EuroBank chose in terms of routing, Layer 3 MPLS VPN service design, Layer 3 MPLS VPN design for VoIP, and QoS.

EuroBank Network Core Routing Design

The total number of routers in the EuroBank network core is 140. This includes P routers, PE routers, and multi-VRF CE routers located in the offices, POPs, and data centers (the branches, of course, are not part of the IGP routing domain). The number of internal routes does not exceed 500, and no external routes are advertised into OSPF (the OSPF link-state database consists of only router and network LSAs—LSA of type 1 and 2). Hence, EuroBank adopted a simple routing design consisting of a single OSPF backbone area.

EuroBank conducted a detailed analysis of the required convergence time to satisfy the requirements of its applications in terms of network availability (including its Systems Network Architecture (SNA) application via data-link switching (DLSw), interactive applications, and so on). The conclusion was that the rerouting time should be at most 5 seconds should a core link or P router fail.

As already pointed out, EuroBank systematically elected the use of protected circuits (whenever possible). For instance, all the STM-1 links are protected, and the ATM PVCs are also dynamically rerouted in the service provider core. In the former case, the convergence time is on the order of a few tens of milliseconds, and in the latter case, ATM PVCs are restored in the service provider core within 2 to 3 seconds.

In the case of the metro connections, Fast Ethernet links rely on the SDH NTU (thus, tens of milliseconds of convergence time are achieved thanks to SDH protection). In the case of the Gigabit Ethernet switches used in metro connections, they can propagate any link failure caused, for instance, by a failure within a few milliseconds. As soon as the switch detects the failure, the LAN port on the customer side is turned off, thus propagating the failure notification to the routing neighbor. Note that the Gigabit Ethernet links used for metro connections are not themselves protected; their failure is handled via OSPF rerouting.

When links cannot be protected by means of lower-layer network recovery mechanisms (such as in the case of 34-Mbps leased line, router failures, and so on), the core network exclusively relies on OSPF to converge and restore the affected traffic. As already pointed out, the network is fully redundant both in terms of equipment (dual routers, dual Gigabit Ethernet switches, and so forth) and network paths (no single point of failure).

To meet the 5-second convergence time, EuroBank decided to modify the default OSPF hello timer from its default 10-second value to 1 second and the OSPF *RouterDead* timer from its default 40-second value to 3 seconds. Such parameter settings have proven not to generate any unreasonable control plane overhead on the routers. Thus, in any failure case, the worst failure detection time is bounded to 3 seconds. This gives OSPF 2 more seconds to complete its convergence. Upon failure detection, each routing neighbor originates a new LSA that is propagated across the network to reflect the topology change. Note that the time for each router to receive the updated OSPF LSA is composed of several components:

- The link propagation delay
- The queuing delay on each traversed hop
- Serialization delay

EuroBank determined that the worst-case delay for each router to receive an LSA update was always less than 500 ms.

The last step of the recovery cycle is the routing table computation, which is on the order of 200 ms for the EuroBank network. This shows that a convergence of 5 seconds can be achieved (including the LSA origination time).

NOTE   EuroBank decided to use Nonstop Forwarding (NSF) techniques in the future on its PE routers.

Host Routing

Each host in the EuroBank network can access the network by means of at least two routers. However, a protocol is required to select the appropriate router and redirect the traffic to the other one should the primary router fail. Hence, EuroBank elected to use Hot Standby Router Protocol (HSRP) with a hello timer of 1 second and a hold time of 3 seconds.

In case a PE router (in an office) or CE router (in a branch) fails, the slave router starts receiving the traffic within 3 seconds, which meets the EuroBank routing convergence target. Because HSRP relies on the election of a master and a slave, in steady state, the master receives all the traffic from the various hosts to be routed onto the network core. To take advantage of the two leased lines connecting the two routers to the network core, it is desirable for the master to reroute part of the traffic toward the slave router. In the branch office case, the master router load-balances the traffic by means of an appropriate BGP configuration. In the case of the servers and mainframes located in the data centers, this is achieved by means of multigroup HSRP so that both routers play the role of master but for a subset of the hosts.

NOTE	EuroBank elected to use Gateway Load Balancing Protocol (GLBP) in the future for its branches and offices. GLBP is similar to HSRP in many respects but offers a superior solution in terms of traffic load balancing. It is particularly suitable in environments that have a large number of hosts. In a nutshell, the principle consists of load-balancing the traffic from the hosts to the routers by using a single virtual IP address (as in the case of HSRP) and multiple virtual MAC addresses. This way, the traffic is balanced across the multiple routers rather than electing one master router that receives all the traffic and is responsible for load balancing. Consequently, in steady state the traffic is balanced between the two routers. Of course, such a protocol is well suited for environments that have a large number of hosts. Indeed, load balancing is less accurate if the number of hosts is limited. This is particularly true with mainframes that generate and receive large amounts of traffic. In the case of data centers where a few hosts generate most of the traffic, it is more appropriate to use HSRP, where the master router performs the load-balancing function.

Layer 3 MPLS VPN Service Design

EuroBank adopted Layer 3 MPLS VPN technology to provide a scalable method of separating its different subsidiaries into its own VPN. It also wanted to provide multiple "departmental" VPNs within one of its subsidiaries without having to maintain separate logical connections in the core network. Before this technology was available, it was typical for an Enterprise to use Ethernet VLANs and/or Frame Relay PVCs to achieve the same goal. Clearly this method was less flexible for connectivity across the WAN and less cost-efficient than that offered by the Layer 3 MPLS VPN solution. Also, this approach in general required physically separate routers per VPN, or the use of complex filters to provide the necessary separation.

EuroBank enabled MPLS on all its core links and within every POP, including any P routers and the interfaces facing the core network at the PE routers. There was no requirement to run label switching within the office sites or the data centers, except on the interfaces that face the core network. MPLS labels are distributed using Label Distribution Protocol (LDP). Figure 6-8 shows the core network and where the LDP protocol is deployed.

Figure 6-8 *EuroBank LDP Deployment*

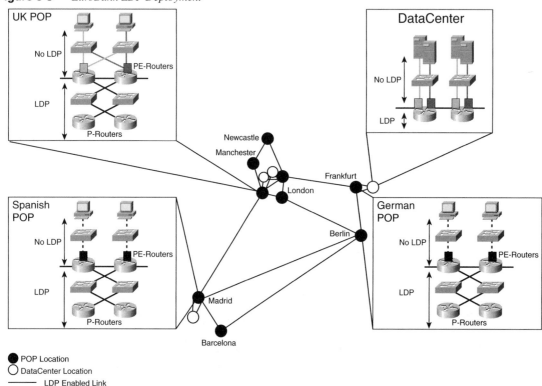

Intersubsidiary and DataCenter Connectivity Requirements

As previously mentioned, the EuroBank holding company consists of five subsidiaries: MainBank, EnterBank, UKI, GerBank, and SpainBank. Isolation across subsidiaries was an important aspect of the design. This meant that direct connectivity between subsidiaries had to be prevented. The MainBank subsidiary was split even further into three separate departments: Accounting, Brokerage, and Branch.

Within each subsidiary other than MainBank, as well as within each MainBank department, every device must be able to communicate with every other device.

As well as the branch and office locations, the EuroBank group has four data centers that house various servers running multiple applications. Some of these applications belong to a specific subsidiary (or department) and must be accessible only to devices from that subsidiary (or department). Every subsidiary in the EuroBank group has at least one such centralized subsidiary/department-specific application hosted on one or more dedicated servers accessible via the data centers. Other applications running in the data centers are shared and must be accessible across all the subsidiaries.

Office Location Requirements

In the UK, an office location supports staff from multiple subsidiaries. Within the MainBank subsidiary, multiple departments are supported. Therefore, multiple VPNs are necessary in the UK office locations.

For office locations outside the UK, only employees from a single subsidiary are supported, so only a single VPN is necessary.

All offices and branches need access to the shared applications in the data centers.

EuroBank Group VPN Definitions

To achieve all the necessary communication and isolation requirements just described, EuroBank defined a number of VPNs:

- **EnterBank**—EnterBank VPN
- **UK Insurance**—UKI VPN
- **GerBank**—GerBank VPN
- **SpainBank**—SpainBank VPN
- **MainBank**—Accounting VPN
- **MainBank**—Brokerage VPN
- **MainBank**—Branch VPN
- **Shared Applications**—EuroBank Shared VPN (or Shared VPN for short)

With the exception of the Shared VPN, each VPN contains routing information from the branches, offices, and subsidiary/department-specific data center application of that specific subsidiary/department, as well as any shared data center application. The Shared VPN contains routes from all the shared applications hosted in data centers and supports connectivity among those, such as for backup purposes. This model allows for easy advertisement of routes to and from private VPNs into a common VPN with shared access.

Within the Brokerage VPN, EuroBank runs sensitive applications that need their data encrypted as it passes between different brokerage locations. EuroBank used [IPSEC-ARCH] to achieve this. The details are explained in the section "EuroBank Brokerage Encryption Deployment and Design."

Route Target and Route Distinguisher Allocation

EuroBank chose to use a private autonomous system number, 65001, to support the allocation of route target and route distinguisher values. This same autonomous system number is used for EuroBank's MP-BGP process as well as for BGP-4 peering with regional MPLS VPN service providers that provide connectivity on behalf of the branch locations. The VPNs have no specific load-balancing requirements. Therefore, the same route distinguisher is used for all the VRFs in a given subsidiary/department VPN.

Table 6-2 shows the chosen values for each VPN.

Table 6-2 *Route Target and Route Distinguisher Allocation*

VPN	Route Target	Route Distinguisher
MainBank Accounting	65001:11	65001:10
MainBank Brokerage	65001:21	65001:20
MainBank Branch	65001:31	65001:30
EnterBank	65001:41	65001:40
UKI	65001:51	65001:50
SpainBank	65001:61	65001:60
GerBank	65001:71	65001:70
EuroBank Shared VPN	65001:1	65001:1

Data Center Layer 3 MPLS VPN Design

Each of the data centers in the EuroBank group houses subsidiary/department-specific servers from each of the previously defined VPNs. Access to these servers from within a VPN is direct. In other words, there is no requirement to pass through a firewall or Network Address Translation (NAT) device. Each server that belongs to a given subsidiary/department VPN is configured at the switch to belong to the relevant VLAN, as defined in Table 6-2.

Each VPN that accesses the data centers does so via a VRF connection at the data center PE routers. Example 6-1 shows the data center PE router configuration (with only two VRF definitions).

Example 6-1 *Data Center PE Router VRF Configuration Template*

```
ip vrf Accounting
 rd 65001:10
 route-target export 65001:11
 route-target import 65001:11
!
ip vrf Brokerage
 rd 65001:20
 route-target export 65001:21
 route-target import 65001:21
!
interface GigabitEthernet 1/0.1
 encapsulation dot1q 11
 ip vrf forwarding Accounting
 ip address address-from-/24-subnet-for-the-Accounting-VPN
!
interface GigabitEthernet 1/0.2
 encapsulation dot1q 12
 ip vrf forwarding Brokerage
 ip address address-from-/24-subnet-for-the-Brokerage-VPN
!
```

As shown in Example 6-1, each VPN attaches to a local switch in the data center using Gigabit Ethernet VLANs. The VLAN assignments for each VPN are shown in Table 6-3.

Table 6-3   *VPN VLAN Allocation*

Subsidiary	VLAN
MainBank Accounting	11
MainBank Brokerage	12
MainBank Branch	13
EnterBank	14
UKI	15
SpainBank	16
GerBank	17
EuroBank Shared VPN	1

The physical layout of each data center is as presented in the earlier section "Description of the Data Centers." Figure 6-9 shows how each VPN is separated at the data centers using the various VLANs. It also highlights that access to the shared applications from each subsidiary is controlled via a firewall. The firewall is necessary so that the EuroBank groups can closely control who can access the shared applications.

Figure 6-9   *Data Center Physical Connectivity to VPN and Shared Applications*

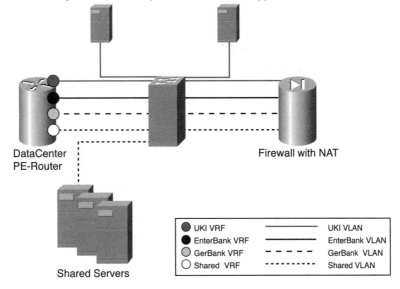

DataCenter
PE-Router

Firewall with NAT

Shared Servers

● UKI VRF	—————	UKI VLAN
● EnterBank VRF	—————	EnterBank VLAN
◐ GerBank VRF	– – – –	GerBank VLAN
○ Shared VRF	··········	Shared VLAN

In an environment of mergers and acquisitions, it is not unusual for one or more subsidiaries/departments of the same holding company to use private IP addresses (see [PRIVATE]). In this case NAT functionality is necessary before the shared applications are accessed so as to avoid any address conflicts.

Access between subsidiary/department VPNs and the shared servers is restricted through the use of a virtual firewall instance for each subsidiary/department VPN. Traffic entering the data center switch that is destined for one of the shared servers is sent to the virtual firewall instance for the specific VPN. Then it is bridged onto a VLAN that attaches to routing and NAT functionality for access into the shared server VLAN. This is achieved using transparent mode on the firewall, which allows for the definition of virtual firewalls that have only two ports where traffic is transparently bridged between these two ports. Figure 6-10 shows the virtual firewall instances and how they interconnect, as well as the inside/outside interfaces for NAT.

Figure 6-10 *NAT and Virtual Firewall Connectivity*

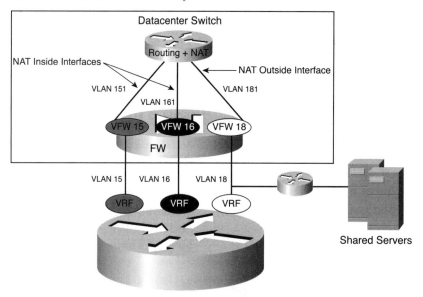

Each server that hosts shared applications must have reachability information for its IP address injected into each of the subsidiaries/department VPNs. The shared servers are housed on the same /24 Ethernet segment. Therefore, only the subnet address needs to be advertised rather than all the specific shared server /32 addresses. In addition, to allow for successful routing of return traffic coming from the shared servers, the pool of "outside" addresses used by the NAT function at the switch is injected into the shared VPN.

Advertisement of this routing information is achieved through the use of Routing Information Protocol (RIP), which is configured to run between the routers inside the Shared VPN and the virtual firewalls. Each shared server uses a default gateway address that, through the use of HSRP, sends traffic to either of the exit routers in the shared VPN. Figure 6-11 shows how this routing is achieved for shared servers located on subnet 164.27.23/24.

Figure 6-11   *Routing Between the PE Router and Shared Servers*

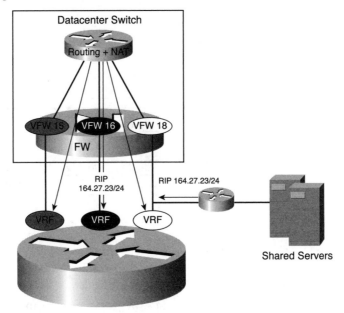

Datacenter PE-Router

Using this infrastructure, EuroBank can maintain the use of IP addresses from the [PRIVATE] range and still keep separation between subsidiaries/departments. Figure 6-12 shows how packets can flow between the Accounting VPN in an office site and the shared server with address 167.27.23.1, which belongs to the Shared VPN and is located in one of the data centers.

Figure 6-12 *Traffic Flow Between the Office and the Shared Server*

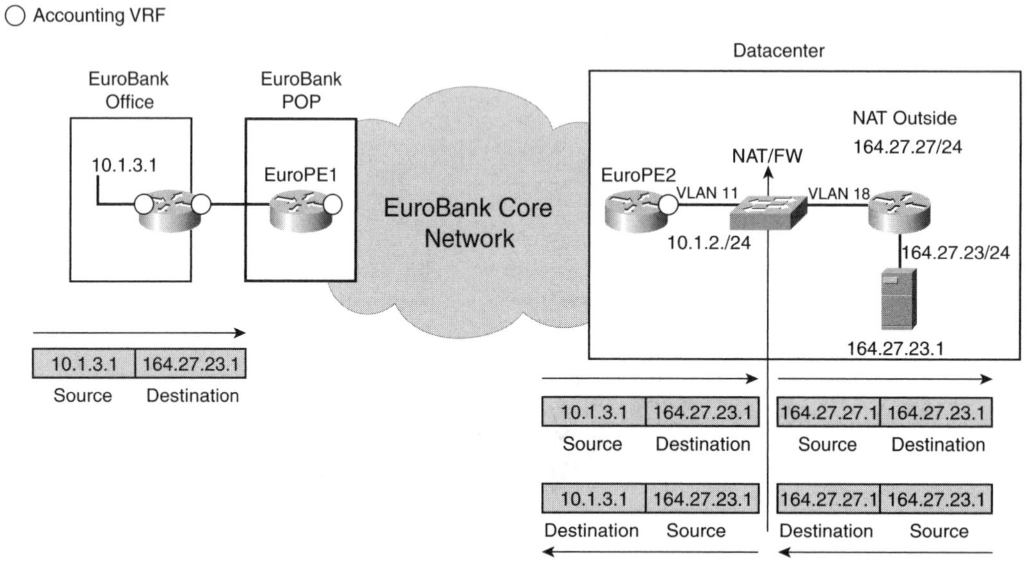

POP Layer 3 MPLS VPN Design

The branches of each of the subsidiary banks attach to either a Layer 3 MPLS VPN service provider or, as in the case of Spain, a Frame Relay provider.

As previously described, if the branch attaches to the EuroBank POP via Frame Relay, the circuit terminates on routers that are managed by the Frame Relay service provider. These are attached directly to a EuroBank PE router via a point-to-point Gigabit Ethernet interface that is associated with the relevant VRF. However, for branches that connect via a Layer 3 MPLS VPN service provider, EuroBank decided to use Inter-AS Option "A" (back-to-back VRFs) and present itself as a CE router to each service provider. This way, EuroBank could learn routes from branches attached to these service providers and also advertise routes from the relevant VPNs into the service provider MPLS VPN network. Figure 6-13 shows this connectivity.

The number of back-to-back VRF connections between the MPLS VPN service provider and EuroBank differs, depending on whether the connection is from a UK or German POP. In the case of the UK, three separate VPNs are needed: UKI, EnterBank, and MainBank Branch. However, in the case of Germany and Spain, only one VPN is necessary for the GerBank and SpainBank subsidiaries.

EuroBank runs BGP-4 on the inter-AS links to exchange the necessary routes with the MPLS VPN service provider. The connectivity from branch offices to the MPLS VPN backbone is via static routes, with floating static routes providing backup through ISDN.

Figure 6-14 shows how the shared server subnet is advertised into the UKI and MainBank Branch VPNs at a UK POP and then subsequently is advertised across the Inter-AS links.

Figure 6-13   *InterAS Option "A" with MPLS VPN Service Providers*

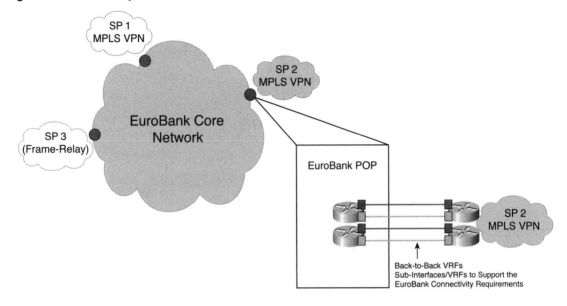

Figure 6-14   *Advertising VPN Routes Across Inter-AS Links*

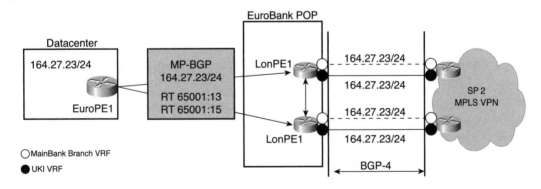

Core MP-BGP Design

With nine POPs and four data centers, EuroBank has a total of 26 PE routers (two in each location). With just over 1100 VPN routes (which consist of branch and office location subnets) and a small number of PE routers, EuroBank decided that it was not necessary to deploy MP-BGP route reflectors in its initial deployment. Instead, EuroBank ran direct MP-BGP sessions in a full mesh between all PE routers.

UK Office Location Layer 3 MPLS VPN Design

As described earlier, EuroBank chose to use multi-VRF functionality in its UK office locations. This technology provides a cost-effective option for the deployment of multiple VPNs using a single CE router. In this case a CE router that is located at the UK office location can provide independent routing and forwarding tables (through the use of VRFs), as illustrated in Figure 6-15.

Figure 6-15 *CE Router FIB/RIB Separation Using Multi-VRF*

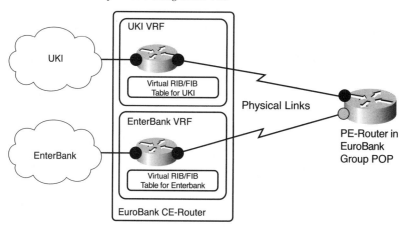

The use of multi-VRF functionality lets EuroBank reduce its acquisition costs as compared to other implementation options by not having to deploy multiple CE routers in the office locations (one CE router for every subsidiary). Instead, two multi-VRF-capable CE routers (which are necessary for redundancy in case one of the routers fails) are deployed and can support all the necessary VPNs.

As mentioned, the connectivity of an office location to a EuroBank POP depends on size and where the office is located. In some cases Ethernet technology is used, and in other cases, leased lines are used.

When Ethernet technology is used, each subsidiary VPN has a VLAN connection between the POP PE routers and the office CE routers, as shown in Figure 6-16.

If leased-line access is used, Frame Relay encapsulation is used on the link between the PE router and the multi-VRF-capable CE routers to separate the different VPNs. Each VPN is allocated a separate Data Link Connection Identifier (DLCI). Within the office location, VLANs are still used.

Figure 6-16   *PE Router-to-CE Router Connectivity with Multi-VRF*

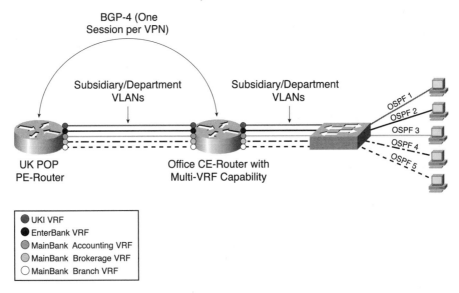

The configuration of a multi-VRF-capable router contains a number of significant differences from the usual configuration of a [2547bis] PE router:

- Multi-VRF capability does not require the configuration of MPLS forwarding on its outbound interfaces facing the core network. This is because labels are not imposed when packets are sent from the multi-VRF CE router toward the PE router in the POP.

- The multi-VRF CE router does not need MP-BGP configured. It simply uses a standard routing protocol (such as BGP-4, OSPF, RIP, and so on) on the link with the PE router.

- The incoming interface at the CE router is associated with a VRF, as is the CE router-to-PE router link. A normal PE router does not associate any upstream links with a particular VRF.

Routing Within Each Multi-VRF VRF

EuroBank decided to run external BGP on the multi-VRF CE router-to-PE router links and use the same BGP autonomous system number for all the VPNs. The use of a single autonomous system number was possible because each VPN is placed in a separate BGP VRF context, one for each VPN accessible via the multi-VRF CE routers. Furthermore, EuroBank had no requirement to leak routes between different VPNs. Therefore, it was not possible to have a routing conflict (such as an AS-path mismatch) between VPNs.

Within each office and data center site, a separate OSPF process was configured for each VPN so that all subnets for that VPN could be learned from the site. Example 6-2 provides the configuration of an office PE router (with only two of the VPNs shown) and the corresponding multi-VRF CE router.

Example 6-2 *Office PE Router/CE Router VRF Configuration Template with BGP*

```
hostname office-PE1
!
ip vrf Accounting
 rd 65001:10
 route-target export 65001:11
 route-target import 65001:11
!
ip vrf Brokerage
 rd 65001:20
 route-target export 65001:21
 route-target import 65001:21
!
router bgp 65001
!
 address-family ipv4 vrf Accounting
 neighbor multi-vrf-CE-address remote-as 65002
 neighbor multi-vrf-CE-address as-override
!
 address-family ipv4 vrf Brokerage
 neighbor multi-vrf-CE-address remote-as 65002
 neighbor multi-vrf-CE-address as-override

hostname multivrf-CE1
!
ip vrf Accounting
 rd 65001:10
!
ip vrf Brokerage
 rd 65001:20
!
router bgp 65002
!
 address-family ipv4 vrf Accounting
 redistribute ospf 100
 neighbor PE-router-address remote-as 65001
!
 address-family ipv4 vrf Brokerage
 redistribute ospf 200
 neighbor PE-router-address remote-as 65001
```

EuroBank Multicast Deployment and Design

EuroBank currently runs only Multicast traffic in its large office sites in the UK. This is restricted to run within the EnterBank subsidiary only. EuroBank has no requirement for Multicast applications at the branch offices of any subsidiary and does not deploy it in Germany or Spain either.

Because its Multicast deployment is limited to the EnterBank VPN in large UK offices only, EuroBank chose to run Multicast in the EnterBank routing instance (as opposed to in all VPNs). At the multi-VRF CEs, EuroBank deploys the Multicast VPN (mVPN) solution (which you read about in previous chapters) to isolate the multicast from other subsidiary VPNs. Having said this, EuroBank is beginning to see some signs that isolated Multicast might be necessary between its different subsidiaries. If this happens, it will consider deploying mVPN inside other subsidiary VPNs.

EuroBank Brokerage Encryption Deployment and Design

The brokerage location in MainBank and the New York brokerage office must be able to exchange information that, based on its sensitivity, must be encrypted. To provide this service, EuroBank chose to use [IPSEC-ARCH] tunnel mode between the CE routers in a brokerage location to which any servers and clients that need encryption are attached.

Because of the relatively small number of endpoints that need encryption, the configuration of [IPSEC-ARCH] is statically defined with relevant source/destination prefixes that may be matched using a crypto-map. If a packet matches one of the destinations configured in the crypto-map, it is encrypted using the information exchanged with the gateway attached to that destination.

Figure 6-17 shows how a host with address 10.7.1.1 sends traffic across an IPSec tunnel if it is destined for any host on remote subnet 10.8.1/24.

Figure 6-17   *IPSec Between the New York Office and MainBank Brokerage VPN*

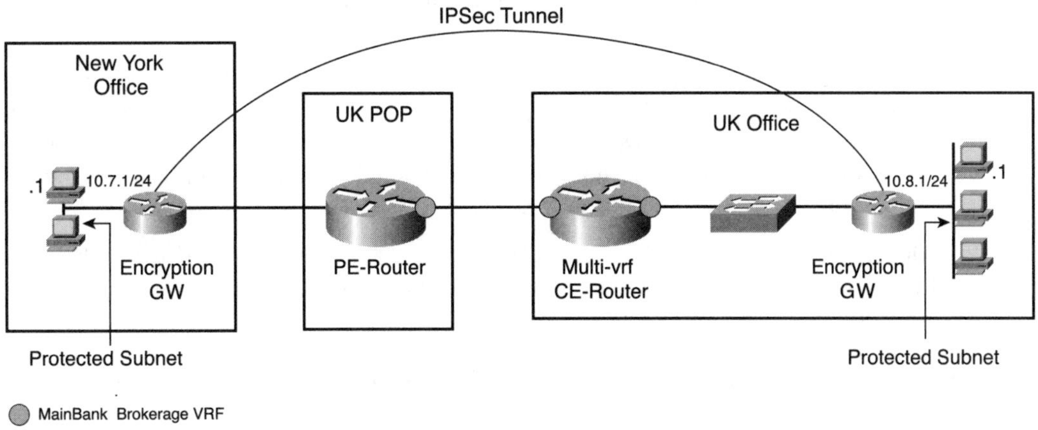

Layer 3 MPLS VPN Design for VoIP

EuroBank elected to move to a pure voice over IP (VoIP) solution for its telephony needs. The primary objective was to reduce costs through the transport of all the intra-holding voice calls (national as well as international calls) over the EuroBank MPLS infrastructure. Another objective was to take advantage of new services such as online access to a corporate telephone directory from the telephone and "follow-me" numbers. With these numbers, a mobile worker can log onto a telephone in any location and be reached at his or her regular phone number.

EuroBank decided to outsource its telephony services to a Telephony Service Provider (TSP) called PhoneNet. PhoneNet is a global TSP whose Managed Telephony Service covers all EuroBank locations (UK, Germany, Spain, and the U.S.). EuroBank's decision to rely on a Managed Telephony Service instead of running it itself was driven by the following motivations:

- EuroBank did not have in-depth expertise with the VoIP technology.

- Installation, operation, and maintenance of telephony devices across the many EuroBank locations would require a very heavy operational structure. (This is the same reason that drove EuroBank to use Managed CE routers in its branches.)

- A TSP with many connection points to the Public Switched Telephone Network (PSTN) worldwide can offer efficient off-net call routing for both incoming calls (someone outside EuroBank calls someone inside EuroBank) and outgoing calls (someone inside EuroBank calls someone outside). Doing so minimizes international call costs.

- Using a single TSP worldwide allows for the use of a uniform dial plan and consistent voice services throughout the EuroBank holding.

Because of these factors, PhoneNet could offer a feature-rich Managed Telephony Service at an attractive price.

The objective of this section is to describe how PhoneNet's Managed Voice Service operates within EuroBank's Layer 3 MPLS VPN design. It also briefly digresses from the EuroBank design to discuss how PhoneNet uses the Layer 3 MPLS VPN technology inside its own network to offer Managed Telephony Services to multiple customers. This is a very interesting application of the Layer 3 MPLS VPN technology on its own.

Although the low-level details of the VoIP design are outside the scope of this book, let's start by reviewing the high-level architecture of the Managed Voice Service design.

Architecture of the Managed Telephony Service

As part of the Managed Telephony Service, PhoneNet supports both on-net calls (between two EuroBank telephones) and off-net calls (between a EuroBank telephone and a telephone outside EuroBank).

PhoneNet provides and operates the following:

- IP phones in every location of every EuroBank subsidiary.

- Centralized call managers located in two London data centers. In each of these two data centers, PhoneNet runs a cluster of call managers. Each cluster has one to N processors (such as Windows or Linux servers) running the call manager application. Each cluster is provisioned and seen by the rest of the network as a single atomic call manager.

NOTE   Call managers are centralized devices involved in VoIP signaling with IP phones. For example, the call manager is responsible for converting the telephone number that the user dials into the IP address of the called IP phone. You'll read more about the call manager's involvement in VoIP signaling later.

To support off-net calls, PhoneNet also provides IP interconnections of the EuroBank intranet to PhoneNet's VoIP backbone. The backbone is interconnected in many places to the PSTN as well as to other VoIP telephony service providers.

Figure 6-18 illustrates how the Managed Voice Service provided by PhoneNet integrates into EuroBank VPNs.

Because every IP phone in every VPN needs to be able to communicate with the call managers for VoIP signaling, the call managers are placed in the EuroBank Shared VPN. Then the mechanisms described in the "Data Center Layer 3 MPLS VPN Design" section (including NAT and virtual firewalls, as well as redistribution of reachability across shared and nonshared VPNs) ensure that, as with the shared servers, the call managers can communicate with devices in any VPN.

For the same reasons, the IP links attaching the EuroBank intranet to the EuroBank VPN on PhoneNet's VoIP backbone (which provides support for off-net calls) are also attached to the EuroBank Shared VPN.

Figure 6-19 shows the equipment deployed in EuroBank data centers by PhoneNet for the Managed Voice Service. It also shows how this equipment attaches to the EuroBank Shared VPN.

Figure 6-18 *Architecture of the Managed Voice Service Provided by PhoneNet*

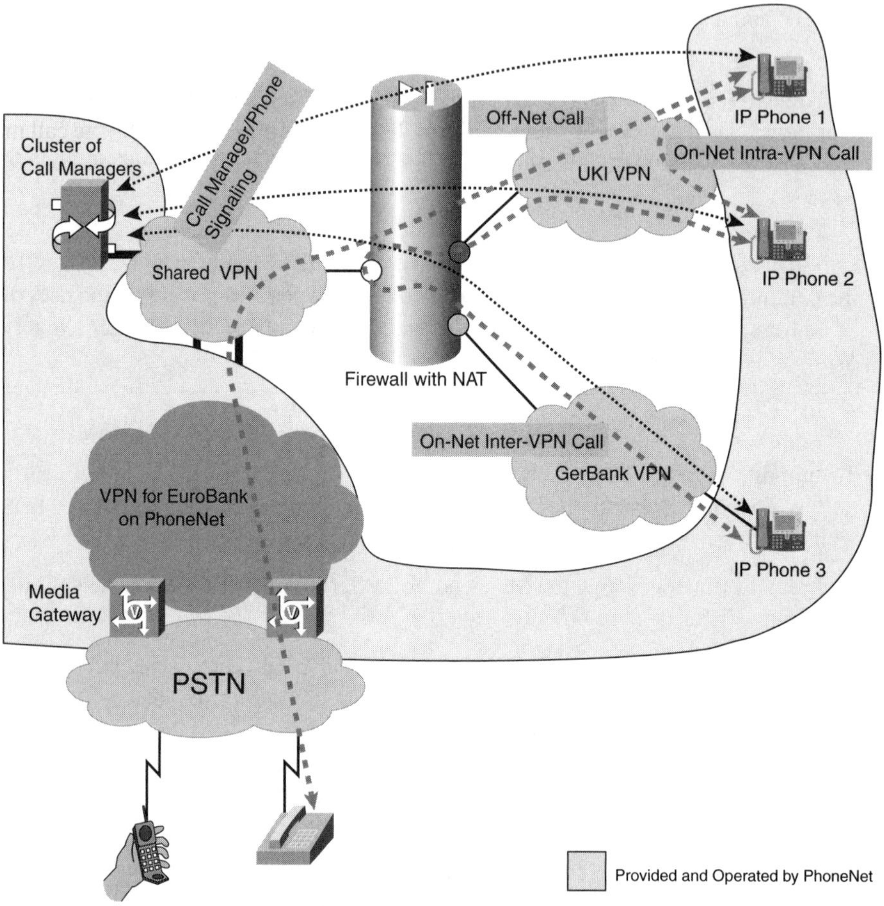

The call manager is located on one side of the NAT and virtual firewall entity, but most IP phones are located on the other side. As explained in the section "Data Center Layer 3 MPLS VPN Design," the NAT and virtual firewall entity can ensure basic connectivity among the call managers and IP phones. However, this is insufficient to ensure proper VoIP signaling operations. VoIP signaling protocols encode IP addresses and port numbers inside the body of their messages to communicate those to other entities involved in VoIP signaling. (For example, the call manager tells an IP phone the IP address of the remote IP phone to transmit the voice stream to.) Although regular NAT operations would translate address and port information inside the IP packet headers, they would not automatically translate address and port information buried inside the VoIP signaling. That information would be received as sent and thus would be meaningless to the entity receiving the VoIP signaling message. This NAT-traversal problem is not specific to VoIP signaling. It is generic to any application involving signaling of address and port information. A common solution to this problem involves activation of an application-level gateway (ALG) on the NAT device. This ALG understands the specific protocol involved and performs the necessary translation of address and port information wherever it may appear inside the protocol messages. In the context of EuroBank, such an ALG has been activated on the NAT and firewall device to ensure proper VoIP signaling operation. This ALG supports the specific VoIP signaling protocol used by the call manager and IP phones in EuroBank.

Figure 6-19   *Managed Voice Service Deployment in Data Centers*

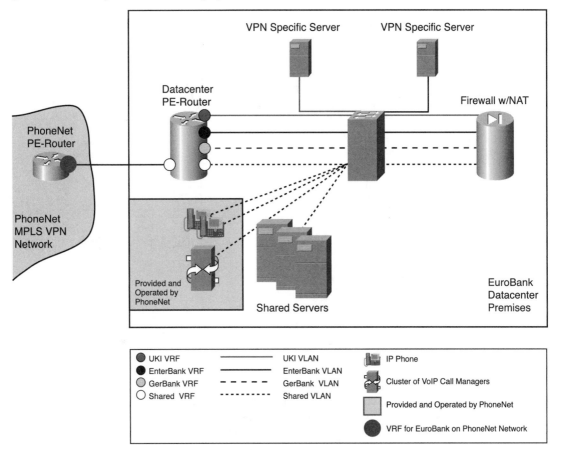

We will now discuss in more detail how the VoIP Signaling ALG operates in conjunction with the call manager and VoIP signaling to achieve proper call handling in a EuroBank VPN as well as across VPNs.

On-Net Voice Call Within a EuroBank VPN

The exact signaling exchanges depend on the actual VoIP signaling protocol used between the call manager and IP phones. (Examples are Skinny Client Control Protocol (SCCP); see [SCCP] and Session Initiation Protocol (SIP); see [SIP].) However, the key conceptual steps generally include the following, as illustrated in Figures 6-20 and 6-21:

- **IP phone registering phase**—This is shown in Steps A and B in Figure 6-20. This phase happens whenever an IP phone boots. It contacts the call manager to indicate its presence and IP address.

Figure 6-20   *IP Phone Registering Phase*

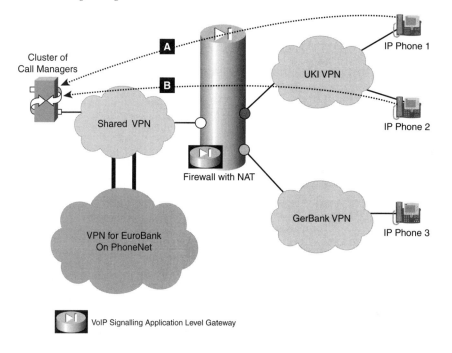

When doing so, the IP phone encodes its "inside" address. The ALG intercepts this signaling message and replaces the inside IP address with a dynamically allocated outside IP address. The NAT and virtual firewall device stores the corresponding address/port translation state. The signaling messages finally reaches the call manager, which sees only an outside address for the registering telephone and which populates those outside addresses in its telephone number translation table.

- **Call signaling phase**—This phase happens when a user dials a telephone number on an IP phone.

  The calling telephone conveys via VoIP signaling to the call manager the called telephone number as well as the (inside) IP address and port number it will use for the media stream (Step 1 in Figure 6-21).

Figure 6-21   *On-Net Intra-VPN Voice Call*

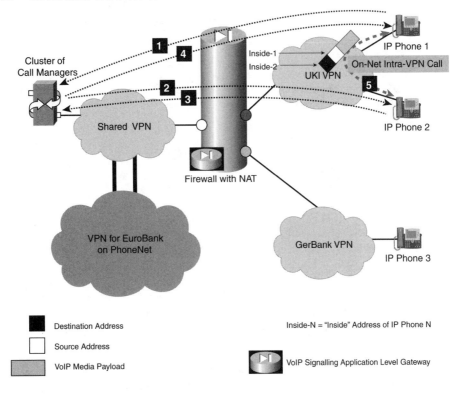

The call manager looks up the called telephone number in its telephone number translation table, which returns the outside address of the called IP phone. (The translation table was populated in synchronization with the NAT and virtual firewall device, as discussed in the registering phase.)

The call manager sends a VoIP signaling message to the called IP phone (Step 2 in Figure 6-21), which includes the IP address and port as signaled by the calling telephone in Step 1 (hence, in inside format).

The ALG intercepts this message. Because it realizes that both the calling and called telephone are in the same "inside" domain, the ALG does not translate the IP addresses and port numbers in this signaling message.

The called telephone returns its inside IP address and port number to the call manager (Step 3 in Figure 6-21), which eventually signals those to the calling phone (Step 4 in Figure 6-21). Similarly, the ALG does not translate the (inside) IP address and port number encoded by the called telephone, because the calling telephone is in the same "inside" domain.

At this stage, both IP phones have been provided with the "inside" IP address and port number of the remote telephone. They can exchange the voice media streams directly with each other using those (Step 5 in Figure 6-21).

Hence, although signaling messages are exchanged between the shared VPN and a nonshared VPN (the UKI VPN in Figure 6-21) and they transit through the NAT and virtual firewall device (and its VoIP signaling ALG), the media stream travels directly from telephone to telephone inside the VPN without transiting through the NAT and virtual firewall device.

On-Net Voice Call Across Two EuroBank VPNs

Figure 6-22 illustrates the steps involved in establishing a voice call from IP phone 2 in the UKI VPN to IP phone 3 in the GerBank VPN.

The same signaling steps occur as those described previously for a call in a VPN. The key difference in the case of a call across VPNs is that the VoIP signaling ALG in the NAT and virtual firewall device realizes that the two telephones are not in the same VPN. Thus, it translates the "inside" address and ports signaled to the remote telephone in the body of the signaling messages into "outside" address and port. The net result is that each IP phone believes it is talking to an IP phone located in the Shared VPN, and the NAT and firewall device is responsible for performing the corresponding NAT function on the media stream. Note that the virtual firewall device allows communication only between two nonshared VPNs for flows explicitly recognized as properly signaled voice calls.

So, in the case of a voice call spanning multiple nonshared VPNs, signaling messages are again exchanged between the shared VPN and a nonshared VPN (the UKI VPN and GerBank VPN in Figure 6-22). They transit through the NAT and virtual firewall device (and its VoIP signaling ALG). However, the media stream travels between two nonshared VPNs via the NAT and virtual firewall device. This is how calls can be established between telephones located in different VPNs and using incompatible (and potentially overlapping) "inside" addresses and also without compromising the fundamental EuroBank requirement to isolate devices in different nonshared VPNs.

EuroBank considered another approach to integrate the Managed Telephony Service inside its environment. The idea was to create an additional VPN (a "voice VPN") in which to attach all the IP phones and call managers and that would be isolated from all the other devices. However, EuroBank dismissed this option because it could not cope with telephony applications that are not based on dedicated telephone hardware (such as softphone applications running on PCs, which EuroBank was considering deploying). Also, extending an additional VPN to every location raises serious issues for some locations, such as the branches connected via a managed VPN or Frame Relay network.

Figure 6-22   *On-Net Inter-VPN Voice Call*

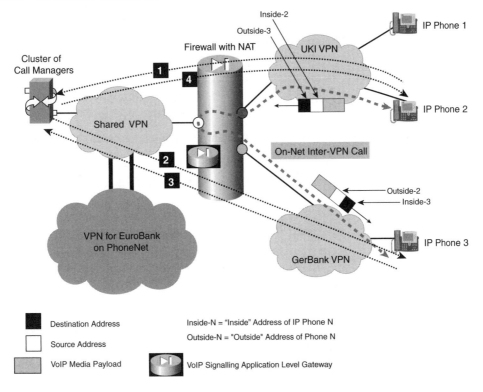

Layer 3 MPLS VPN Design Within PhoneNet and EuroBank Off-Net Voice Calls

Let's leave the EuroBank intranet environment for a moment and consider the infrastructure PhoneNet uses to build its Managed Voice Services for EuroBank as well as many other customers. PhoneNet chose MPLS and Layer 3 MPLS VPN technology as the basis for its VoIP infrastructure because it easily addresses PhoneNet's requirement for isolation across its many Voice Services customers. This technology also allows all these customers to access some PhoneNet shared resources such as media gateways and media gateway controllers providing interconnection to the PSTN.

This is achieved using the well-known rainbow VPN design. Rainbow VPN ensures that devices attached to that VPN can communicate with devices attached to VPNs of any "color"—in other words, with devices attached to any VPN. In this design, the following rules are followed:

- Each managed voice customer belongs to a separate VPN over the PhoneNet Layer 3 MPLS VPN network (such as EuroBank being supported as its own dedicated VPN over the PhoneNet network).

- All the shared PhoneNet resources (PSTN media gateways and media gateway controllers) are attached inside a rainbow VPN.

- All the routes in the rainbow VPN are redistributed into every Voice Services customer VPN.

- All the (necessary) routes in every Voice Services customer VPN are redistributed into the rainbow VPN.

The two last points are very easily achieved through appropriate additional route target import and export statements at the PE routers.

Figure 6-23 shows the VPNs PhoneNet uses to support its managed Voice Services in this manner.

Figure 6-23 *PhoneNet Layer 3 MPLS VPNs and Off-Net Voice Call*

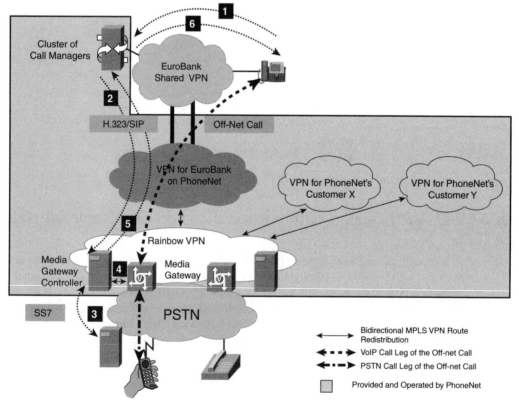

Note that from PhoneNet's viewpoint, the only visible part of EuroBank is its Shared VPN. In reality, an IP phone may actually be located in any EuroBank VPN. However, this is hidden from PhoneNet by the NAT and virtual firewall device located in the EuroBank network and its ALG through the mechanisms explained earlier.

In the case of an off-net call initiated by an IP phone in the EuroBank network, the following conceptual steps occur:

- VoIP signaling happens as for on-net calls between the calling phone and the call manager (Step 1 in Figure 6-23).

- This time, because it has been configured that way by PhoneNet, the telephone number translation table indicates to the call manager that it needs to signal this call establishment to a given media gateway controller. This media gateway controller is directly reachable to the call manager because it is reachable from the VPN dedicated to EuroBank on the PhoneNet network and to which the EuroBank intranet is attached.

- Using SIP (see [SIP]) or H.323 (see [H323]), the call manager signals call establishment to the media gateway controller, including the IP address and port for the media stream on the calling side (Step 2 in Figure 6-23).

- In turn, the media controller does the following:
  - It performs signaling to the PSTN signaling control point using Signaling System 7 (SS7) (see [SS7]) (Step 3 in Figure 6-23).
  - It programs (for example, via a Media Gateway Control Protocol such as [MGCP] or [MEGACO]) the media gateway for the corresponding media stream on its IP side (Step 4 in Figure 6-23).
  - It tells the call manager the IP address and port number for the media stream (Step 5 in Figure 6-23).

- The call manager eventually returns this IP address and port number to the calling telephone (Step 6 in Figure 6-23).

- Finally, media streams can be exchanged directly between the calling IP phone and the PSTN media gateway.

The details of these steps and their relative sequencing depend on the actual signaling protocols used at the various steps and on voice features activated for the call.

With off-net call establishment, the call manager can select which media gateway controller to signal. In turn, the media gateway controller can select which of the media gateways it manages to route the voice call through. Thus, PhoneNet can achieve very efficient voice routing to maximize transport of the call over its MPLS packet infrastructure and hence minimize its use of PSTN on long distances. For example, if a user in a UKI branch in Manchester calls an external telephone in Los Angeles, PhoneNet can ensure that this call is carried to the U.S. over its MPLS network and only enters the PSTN through one of its media gateways in California (say, in Los Angeles). This ensures that only the cost of a local call will be charged by the destination PSTN operator, which eventually translates into significant savings for EuroBank.

For off-net calls initiated from the PSTN toward a EuroBank phone, the PSTN SS7 signaling network recognizes the dialed telephone number as being managed by PhoneNet. (This is true either because that telephone number was allocated by PhoneNet to EuroBank from PhoneNet's number range or because the telephone number was allocated by another telephony operator but was handed over to PhoneNet through number portability.) Accordingly, the PSTN SS7 signaling network signals the call establishment to the media gateway controller that PhoneNet identified as responsible for that number or number range. Then steps similar to those just described take place, but this time in the reverse order.

Quality of Service Design

The EuroBank network carries a multitude of applications with very different quality of service (QoS) requirements and very different importance to EuroBank's business. At one end of the spectrum, the network will be carrying traffic from a user casually browsing the Internet. At the other end of the spectrum, the network will be carrying brokers' instructions with extremely tight latency constraints as well as the whole company's telephony traffic and its associated tight delay and jitter constraints.

Another interesting challenge is that the EuroBank network is made up of a mix of routinely congested links, occasionally and moderately congested links, and completely uncongested links. This stems from the great variations in bandwidth costs depending on the link span and location, which forces EuroBank to apply different approaches in different parts of the network. For example, the high cost of international bandwidth resulted in EuroBank provisioning bandwidth very carefully on the international POP-POP routes (in the 10–40 Mbps range) and having to deal with periods of congestion on those. On the other hand, reasonable costs of Fast Ethernet and STM-1 links in a metro area or sometimes even on long distance within a country allow EuroBank to provision bandwidth more generously on the corresponding POP-POP and POP-office links and having to cope with only occasional moderate congestion on those. Finally, attractively priced metro Gigabit Ethernet services allow EuroBank to overprovision capacity among the London POPs and to never expect congestion on these links.

Another important consideration was that EuroBank did not have experience in how some applications behaved and needed to be handled in the network from a QoS perspective. Hence, it wanted to have some flexibility to nimbly adjust the QoS treatment given to some applications, as proven necessary in practice. As a result, EuroBank adopted the following approach:

- It defined service classes that group applications with similar QoS requirements as well as similar levels of importance with respect to EuroBank's business mission. Those are defined independent of the bandwidth management policies (and their associated queues), which actually get deployed in different parts of the network. EuroBank defined nine such service classes.

- There is no QoS policy on Gigabit Ethernet-based POP-POP and POP-data center links because those links are overprovisioned.

- It adopted a mid-grain three-queue QoS policy on the 100+ Mbps POP-POP, POP-office, and POP-data center links.

- It adopted a fine-grain six-queue QoS policy on the sub-100 Mbps POP-POP and POP-office links.

- It used the three classes of service available from the managed Layer 3 MPLS VPN and managed Frame Relay service providers, which provide connectivity for the branches.

- It mapped the nine service classes into the various QoS policies. Specifically, a mapping is defined for those nine service classes onto the six queues of the fine-grain QoS policy. Another mapping is defined for mapping the service classes onto the three queues of the mid-grain QoS policy. Finally, a mapping is defined to the three classes of service for the managed router services.

This QoS approach applies finer-grain mechanisms in the core than on the edge because links tend to be higher-speed in the edge than in the core, which is thus the primary bottleneck. This is quite characteristic of Enterprise MPLS networks with large geographic coverage (particularly international). This is the opposite of the typical situation in service provider MPLS networks (such as the one for USCom and Telecom Kingland, described in Chapters 3 and 4, respectively). In that case, links tend to be much faster in the core than on the access. Hence, finer-grain QoS mechanisms are deployed on the access, which constitutes the primary bottleneck, rather than in the core.

Recall the N/M/P QoS model defined in the "QoS Models" section of Chapter 2, "Technology Primer: Quality of Service, Traffic Engineering, and Network Recovery." In that model, N is the number of queues on the access, M is the number of queues in the core, and P is set to 0 if MPLS Traffic Engineering is not used. The EuroBank MPLS network adheres to an N/6/0 model. In this model, N=1 for some access scenarios such as Gigabit Ethernet links to data centers, N=3 for some access scenarios such as branches or Fast Ethernet links to offices, and N=6 for some access scenarios such as 8–34 Mbps leased-line access to offices. In comparison, where its "PE-to-CE" QoS option is used, USCom follows a 3/1/0 model.

EuroBank's Service Classes

Table 6-4 lists the service classes defined by EuroBank. It also lists application examples, the DSCP value used to identify each service class, and the EXP value used in the MPLS core.

Table 6-4   *EuroBank Service Classes*

Service Class	Application Examples	DSCP	EXP in EuroBank MPLS Network
Network Control	Routing	48	6
Voice	VoIP on-net and off-net	46	5
Video	Videoconferencing	34	4
Mission-Critical Interactive	CITRIX interactive, bank transactions with mainframe, Automatic Teller Machine (ATM), web-based mission-serving transactions, voice signaling	26	3
Mission-Critical Batch	CITRIX print jobs	18	2
Intranet Interactive	Web traffic that is not mission-serving	10	1
Multicast	Multicast applications	8	Not applicable because Multicast traffic is encapsulated in GRE as per the mVPN solution
Intranet Batch	File transfers, e-mail	2	0
Default	Anything else	0	0

EuroBank picked DSCP values such that they automatically map to the desired EXP values using the default DSCP-to-EXP mapping of the IOS PE router implementation. (This copies the 3-bit precedence field into the EXP field of the imposed MPLS label stack entries.) However, Table 6-4 shows that DSCPs from two different service classes are mapped to the same EXP value. Both DSCP=2 of Intranet Batch and DSCP=0 of Default map to EXP=0. This is because EuroBank decided not to use the EXP=7 value and leave it as reserved for future use. Being left with seven EXP values while eight service classes are transported over MPLS (Multicast traffic is not encapsulated in MPLS), EuroBank decided to allocate the same EXP value to the Intranet Batch and Default service classes. This was decided because these two service classes are always grouped in the same queue in all the various QoS policies deployed by EuroBank and thus don't need to be distinguished inside the MPLS core. Note that if in the future these two service classes need to be scheduled in different queues, EuroBank can easily do so by activating the necessary DSCP-to-EXP mapping on PE routers. For example, suppose the Intranet Batch service classes need better treatment and need to be grouped with the Mission-Critical Batch service class. The PE router could be configured to make sure that the EXP value of all imposed label stack entries on packets arriving with DSCP=2 were marked with EXP=2 (without rewriting the IP header's DSCP value). The necessary configuration is shown in Example 6-3.

Example 6-3 *PE Router Input Policy for DSCP-to-EXP Mapping*

```
!
class-map match-any Intranet-Batch
  match dscp 2
!
policy-map PE-input-DSCP-to-EXP
  class Intranet-Batch
    set mpls exp imposition 2
    ...
interface pos0/0
  service-policy input PE-input-DSCP-to-EXP
```

Traffic Classification in Offices and Data Centers

EuroBank elected not to perform fine traffic classification on the PE routers or CE routers. Instead, it distributed the classification function further toward the edge and performed it on the router closest to the end systems and upstream of the PE router. In particular, this allows EuroBank to very easily identify and classify traffic coming from a particular server. Also, it allows the operational teams in charge of the networking infrastructure within the sites to adjust the classification configuration without having to involve the operational team in charge of the MPLS network. Moreover, this helps maintain high performance on the PE routers and CE routers by distributing these tasks to other devices on the periphery of the network.

To be able to classify into different service classes different types of transactions of the same application, EuroBank relies on deep packet inspection. Here, the classification device actually looks inside the packet payload at application-specific information to determine what type of transaction this packet belongs to. EuroBank uses the IOS Network-Based Application Recognition (NBAR) feature (see [NBAR]) as well as some of its application-specific extensions to perform the deep packet inspection necessary to support classification of its service classes.

EuroBank uses the CITRIX Independent Computing Architecture (ICA) protocol to support banking transactions with servers located in data centers. As shown in Table 6-4, some CITRIX flows need to be classified as mission-critical interactive, and others need to be classified as mission-critical batch. Example 6-4 shows the configuration EuroBank uses to classify differently the CITRIX ICA background transactions from the other CITRIX transactions using NBAR. It also shows EuroBank's ability to interpret the ICA tag, which reflects the priority of the CITRIX ICA transaction.

Example 6-4 *Classification of CITRIX ICA Transactions Using NBAR*

```
!
class-map match-any Mission-Critical-Interactive
  match protocol citrix ica-tag "0"
  match protocol citrix ica-tag "1"
  match protocol citrix ica-tag "2"
  match protocol http url "/transact/*"
  match ...
  match ...
class-map Mission-Critical-Batch
  match protocol citrix ica-tag "3"
```

EuroBank also relies on NBAR to identify web transactions to specific URLs (such as the ones under the "/transact/*" branch, as shown in Example 6-4). This means that the corresponding traffic should be classified as mission-critical interactive instead of regular intranet interactive.

Bank transactions to mainframes also need to be classified as mission-critical interactive. In the case of EuroBank, these are a subset of the SNA traffic that is carried over IP using DLSw+ (see [DLSw]), which places all SNA traffic inside TCP packets. Multiple methods exist to classify different types of SNA traffic and mark it accordingly. EuroBank elected the method that involves establishing multiple TCP connections for the DLSw+ traffic, each using a well-known port number and corresponding to a required level of priority. It also involves steering different SNA flows (for example, depending on the SAP or MAC address) into the appropriate TCP connection. Then, EuroBank can easily classify DLSw+ traffic based on the well-known TCP port and can mark it with the EuroBank DSCP of the corresponding traffic class.

The traffic from Automatic Teller Machines (ATMs) that needs to be classified in the Mission-Critical Interactive service class is classified based on the fact that it is encapsulated as X.25 over TCP (XOT) (see [XOT]). Example 6-5 shows the configuration of a local QoS policy that is used to apply a QoS policy to traffic generated by the router itself, as is the case here for the XOT traffic carrying flows from the ATMs.

Example 6-5   *Classification and Marking of ATMs Using a Local Policy*

```
!
ip local policy route-map XOT
!
route-map XOT permit 20
  match ip address 141
  set dscp 26
!
access-list 141 permit tcp any any eq 1998
access-list 141 permit tcp any eq 1998 any
!
```

PhoneNet uses call managers and IP phones to support the Managed Voice Service offered to EuroBank. The call manager controls which DSCP value the IP phones use in packets carrying VoIP media streams. It also controls which DSCP value the IP phones use as well as the call manager itself in voice signaling packets. This is achieved by first configuring the DSCP values to be used on the call manager. Then the call manager instructs the IP phones, via signaling, to use those values. EuroBank indicated to PhoneNet that DSCP 46 and DSCP 26 are to be used for media stream and voice signaling traffic, respectively. The IP phones and call manager automatically mark those as belonging to the EuroBank Voice and Mission-Critical Interactive service classes without EuroBank's having to classify this traffic.

EuroBank routers automatically mark routing traffic with precedence 6, which corresponds to the DSCP=48 used by EuroBank for the Network Control service class. In the MPLS core, routing traffic is automatically marked with EXP=6 because the 3-bit precedence field gets copied by default into the EXP field at MPLS imposition.

If, based on observations, EuroBank realizes that a given application is not getting appropriate treatment, it can move that application to a different service class. This simply requires that the classification function be adjusted to mark the DSCP of the corresponding flows to the DSCP value of the new service class. As soon as this is done, the corresponding traffic is automatically granted the DiffServ treatment for that service class.

Sub-100-Mbps QoS Policy

EuroBank applies a fine-grain QoS policy involving six queues to manage the congestion that occurs fairly routinely on sub-100-Mbps links. Table 6-5 lists these six queues, the service classes that are mapped into each queue, and the queue parameter configuration.

Table 6-5   *EuroBank Six-Queue Policy*

Queue	Service Classes Mapped into the Queue	Queue Configuration
EF	Voice	Priority Conditional policer at 20 percent of link speed (Maximum expected voice load is 10 percent)
AF4	Video	Allocated minimum bandwidth of 10 percent
AF3	Mission-Critical Interactive, Network Control	Allocated minimum bandwidth of 30 percent (Maximum expected load of 10 percent)
AF2	Mission-Critical Batch	Allocated minimum bandwidth of 20 percent
AF1	Intranet Interactive, Multicast	Allocated minimum bandwidth of 15 percent
DF	Intranet Batch, Default	Allocated minimum bandwidth of 5 percent

The corresponding QoS policy is illustrated in Figure 6-24.

It is worth remembering that the router packet scheduler enforcing this QoS policy has a property called work-conserving. This means that bandwidth never gets wasted. As a consequence, if a class does not use all its allocated minimum bandwidth at one time, the unused fraction can be used by other classes that have more to transmit than their own allocated minimum bandwidth. This is why a generous allocation of 30 percent to the Mission-Critical Interactive service class (while the expected maximum load is about 10 percent) is not a wasteful approach. If there happens to be more mission-critical interactive traffic than expected (say 20 percent instead of 10 percent), the corresponding queue has enough capacity to maintain the required high levels of service. If there is no more than the expected load of mission-critical interactive traffic, the bandwidth allocated but unused by the corresponding queue can be reused by the other queues anyway.

Figure 6-24 *EuroBank Six-Queue QoS Policy for Sub-100-Mbps Links*

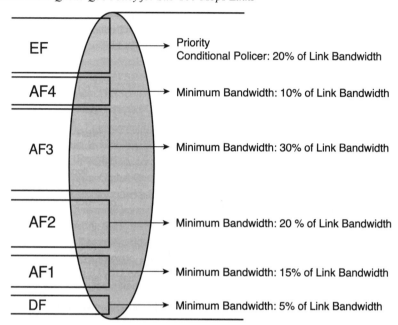

This policy is applied in the EuroBank network on all the links whose rate is strictly less than 100 Mbps:

- POP-to-POP links based on ATM PVC in the 10–40-Mbps range, on E3 links as well as on subrate (40-Mbps) Fast Ethernet links
- Office-POP links based on leased line in the 8–34 Mbps range

The configuration for the six-queue sub-100-Mbps QoS policy is shown in Example 6-6 in the case of a leased-line link.

Example 6-6 *Six-Queue Sub-100-Mbps QoS Policy for Leased Line*

```
!
class-map match-any class-EF
  match mpls exp 5
class-map match-any class-AF4
  match mpls exp 4
class-map match-any class-AF3
  match mpls exp 3
  match mpls exp 6
  match dscp 48
class-map match-any class-AF2
  match mpls exp 2
class-map match-any class-AF1
  match mpls exp 1
```

Example 6-6   *Six-Queue Sub-100-Mbps QoS Policy for Leased Line (Continued)*

```
   match dscp 8
!
policy-map 6Q-policy
  class class-EF
     priority percent 20
  class class-AF4
     bandwidth percent 10
  class class-AF3
     bandwidth percent 30
  class class-AF2
     bandwidth percent 20
  class class-AF1
     bandwidth percent 15
  class class-default
     bandwidth percent 5
!
int serial1/0/0
 service-policy output 6Q-policy
```

In the case of the subrate 40 Mbps Fast Ethernet POP-POP link in the UK, EuroBank needs to shape the traffic against the contracted 40 Mbps. (This is because, as indicated in the section "Description of the Metro Connections in the UK," input policing is performed by the operator of the subrate Fast Ethernet service.) This is achieved using hierarchical service policies, which allow a service policy to invoke another service policy as the action to perform on one of its classes. As illustrated in Example 6-7, EuroBank first applies a top-level policy enforcing the aggregate shaping to all the traffic collectively. Then it calls a lower-level service policy that is the same as in Example 6-6 and enforces the six-queue scheduling over the shaped rate.

Example 6-7   *Six-Queue Sub-100-Mbps QoS Policy for Subrate Fast Ethernet*

```
!
policy-map 6Q-policy-with-40Mbps-shaping
  class class-default
     shape average 40000000
     service-policy 6Q-policy
!
interface fastethernet0/0
 service-policy output 6Q-policy-with-40Mbps-shaping
```

In the case of ATM PVCs, the QoS policy first needs to apply ATM-level traffic shaping in accordance with the contracted ATM traffic class (VBR-nrt) and the contracted sustainable cell rate and peak rate. Then it needs to apply the scheduling policy independently within each ATM PVC. Examples of application of QoS policies over ATM PVCs can be found in the section "QoS Design in the Core Network on ATM PVCs" in Chapter 5, "Global Service Provider Design Study."

100+ Mbps QoS Policy

A simpler three-queue policy is applied on 100+ Mbps interfaces. On these interfaces, congestion is rare, not very heavy, and relatively short. Thus, it isn't necessary to fine-tune the congestion management mechanisms for each service class. The key objectives during the short congestion periods are simply to ensure that the voice traffic remain completely protected and that the applications that can afford to be slowed down are indeed squeezed to make room for all the interactive and important applications. This is achieved through the policy whose queues, service class mapping, and queue configuration are presented in Table 6-6.

Table 6-6   *EuroBank Three-Queue Policy*

Queue	Service Classes Mapped into the Queue	Queue Configuration
EF	Voice	Priority Conditional policer at 20 percent of link speed (Maximum expected voice load is 10 percent)
AF4	Video, Mission-Critical Interactive, Network Control, Mission-Critical Batch, Intranet Interactive, Multicast	Allocated bandwidth of 75 percent
DF	Intranet Batch, Default	Allocated bandwidth of 5 percent

This policy is applied in the EuroBank network on all the links whose rate is in the 100–155 Mbps range:

- POP-to-POP full-rate Fast Ethernet and STM-1 links
- Office-POP STM-1 links
- Data center-POP full-rate Fast Ethernet and STM-1 links

The three-queue QoS policy is illustrated in Figure 6-25.

Gigabit Ethernet Link QoS Policy

Because subrate (300–600-Mbps) Gigabit Ethernet links are completely uncongested, EuroBank decided not to implement any QoS mechanisms on these links. It might revisit that decision in the future should congestion and noticeable QoS degradation appear on those links.

QoS Design on the Access for Branches

EuroBank branches are connected to the EuroBank core through a managed Layer 3 MPLS VPN service or a managed Frame Relay-based router service. Therefore, EuroBank service classes need to be mapped onto the classes of service supported over each of these services. This section details the case of interoperation with the managed Layer 3 MPLS VPN service used to access branches in Germany, but a very similar approach is followed in Spain and the UK.

Figure 6-25   *EuroBank Three-Queue QoS Policy for 100+ Mbps Links*

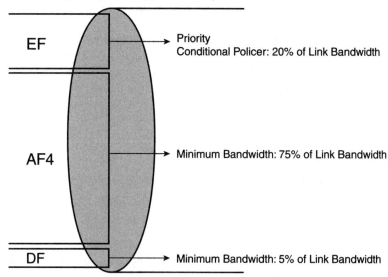

The Layer 3 MPLS VPN operator supports three classes of service (CoSs). These classes of service are listed in Table 6-7, along with their DSCP values as per the service provider scheme, with the EuroBank service classes that are mapped into each CoS and their associated EuroBank DSCP values.

Table 6-7   *Layer 3 MPLS VPN Service Provider CoS and EuroBank Service Class Mapping*

Layer 3 MPLS VPN Service Provider CoS	Layer 3 MPLS VPN Service Provider DSCP	EuroBank Service Classes Mapped into Service Provider CoS	EuroBank DSCP
Real-Time	40 (precedence 5)	Voice	46
Premium	In-contract: 24 (precedence 3) Out-of-contract: 16 (precedence 2)	Mission-Critical Interactive	26
		Network Control	48
		Mission-Critical Batch	18
		Intranet Interactive	10
Standard	0	Intranet Batch	2
		Default	0

NOTE	When the customer of a service provider sends traffic to a Layer 3 MPLS VPN service provider at a rate exceeding the contracted rate for the corresponding class of service, the service provider may drop the excess or may accept the excess traffic but mark it as such. In the latter case, the traffic in excess is said to be marked as out-of-contract, and the traffic that is within the contracted rate is said to be in-contract. For example, Telecom Kingland supports the concept of out-of-contract traffic in its VPN Premium class of service. More details can be found in the "Quality of Service Design" section in Chapter 4.

Traffic Flowing from a Branch

This section considers traffic flowing from a branch toward the EuroBank core.

Because the LAN within the branch is exclusively based on Fast and Gigabit Ethernet switching that is overprovisioned compared to the current load, no QoS mechanisms need to be activated within the branch itself.

Traffic leaving the branch is first classified and marked by the service provider managed CE router. EuroBank used the web-based interface provided by the service provider to configure the classification criteria that need to be applied by the CE router. This is done on EuroBank's behalf to classify traffic into the three service provider classes of service in accordance with the mapping of Table 6-7. For instance, EuroBank indicated that the CE router needs to identify packets carrying the CITRIX protocol and classify those in the Premium CoS. As another example, because VoIP media streams as well as VoIP signaling messages are premarked by the IP phones, EuroBank indicated to the service provider that the packets arriving with DSCP=46 (EuroBank's DSCP value for voice) need to be mapped to the Real-Time CoS. Packets arriving with DSCP=26 (EuroBank's DSCP value for Mission-Critical Interactive, which includes VoIP signaling) need to be mapped to the Premium CoS.

When marking traffic after classification, the service provider uses its own DSCP values (as opposed to EuroBank's DSCP values).

This classification and marking, as well as the subsequent QoS steps involved in proper end-to-end QoS handling in the case of traffic flowing from a branch, are illustrated in Figure 6-26.

The service provider relies on the DSCP field being marked to its own values to apply its corresponding QoS mechanisms. These QoS mechanisms are applied on the CE router located in the branch for transmission onto the access link, as well as at every hop in the service provider's network, including eventually on the PE router for transmission onto the link toward EuroBank. This ensures that traffic experiences QoS performance levels in accordance with the SLA commitments provided by the service provider for each of its three classes of service from the CE router in the branch to its delivery point into the EuroBank network (on input into the EuroBank PE router).

Figure 6-26   *End-to-End QoS Across the Service Provider Network for Traffic Flowing from a Branch*

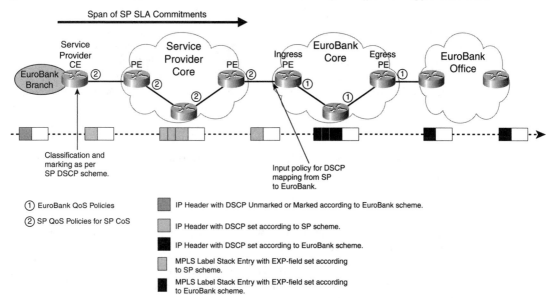

Because the EuroBank PE router receives packets from the service provider network marked as per the service provider DSCP scheme, EuroBank applies an input policy on that interface that maps the DSCP values back to EuroBank's DSCP values. This mapping is based on Table 6-7 and is illustrated in Example 6-8. The packets received and marked as Premium are mapped into EuroBank's Mission-Critical Interactive service class regardless of whether they were marked by the service provider as in-contract or out-of-contract. The fact that some packets crossed the policed contract rate enforced by the service provider does not mean that such packets are less important to EuroBank.

Example 6-8   *DSCP Mapping Policy from the Service Provider to EuroBank*

```
!
class-map match-any class-RealTime-SP
  match dscp 40
class-map match-any class-Premium-SP
  match dscp 24
  match dscp 16
!
policy-map DSCP-Mapping-SP-to-EuroBank
  class class-RealTime-SP
    set dscp 46
  class class-Premium-SP
    set dscp 26
  class class-default
    set dscp 0
!
int pos0/0
  service-policy input DSCP-Mapping-SP-to-EuroBank
```

Because the service provider supports only three classes of service, the traffic from the branch is mapped into only three of the nine EuroBank service classes.

EuroBank considered performing fine-grain classification on all the traffic received from the service provider (instead of just based on the received DSCP). It needed to be able to classify the traffic into its full range of service classes (instead of into only three of those). However, EuroBank did not retain that approach for a number of reasons. First, it may have a performance impact because it applies to the aggregate traffic received from all the branches in that country. Second, the branches run only a subset of the EuroBank service classes because, for example, multicast and videoconferencing are not currently used in branches. Finally, a coarse differentiation of voice, mission-critical, and default addresses the essential QoS requirements.

As soon as packets have their DSCP marked according to EuroBank DSCP values, they are handled accordingly by the QoS policies applied inside the EuroBank network.

Traffic Flowing to a Branch

This section considers traffic flowing from the EuroBank core toward a branch through the service provider Managed Router service.

This time packets get classified and marked by EuroBank. Therefore, they are initially marked with DSCP values from EuroBank scheme and experience the corresponding treatment throughout the EuroBank network.

For the packets to be handled appropriately through the service provider network, EuroBank applies an egress policy on its egress PE router. It remarks the packet DSCP according to the service provider DSCP values, as illustrated in Example 6-9. This egress policy is also the one applying the three-queue QoS policy on the link toward the EuroBank Layer 3 MPLS VPN network.

Example 6-9   *DSCP Mapping Policy from EuroBank to the Service Provider*

```
!
class-map match-any class-EF
  match dscp 46
class-map match-any class-AF4
  match dscp 26
  match dscp 48
  match dscp 18
  match dscp 10
!
policy-map 3Q-policy-with-DSCP-Mapping-EuroBank-to-SP
  class class-EF
    set dscp 40
    priority percent 20
  class class-AF4
    set dscp 24
    bandwidth percent 75
  class class-default
    set dscp 0
    bandwidth percent 5
!
int pos0/0
 service-policy output 3Q-policy-with-DSCP-Mapping-EuroBank-to-SP
```

The application point for this DSCP mapping policy, as well as the subsequent QoS steps involved in proper end-to-end QoS handling in the case of traffic flowing to a branch, are illustrated in Figure 6-27.

Figure 6-27   *End-to-End QoS Across the Service Provider Network for Traffic Flowing to a Branch*

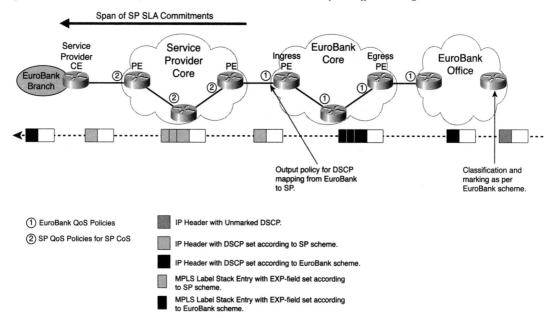

After being received with appropriate DSCP marking by the service provider PE router, packets are handled according to the three classes of service scheme by the service provider. This includes corresponding scheduling by the service provider PE router onto the access link toward the branch.

Finally, packets are forwarded by the CE router onto the branch LAN. Because no QoS mechanisms are used inside the LAN, it does not matter that packets are transmitted with DSCP values according to the service provider scheme instead of the EuroBank scheme. If EuroBank were to apply QoS policies within the branch, one approach could be to get the service provider CE router to map back the DSCP values into EuroBank values. (This is very much like the DSCP mapping performed by the EuroBank PE router for traffic flowing from the service provider into the EuroBank core, as shown in Example 6-8.)

Design Lessons to Be Taken from EuroBank

A number of lessons can be drawn from the EuroBank design discussion:

- Enterprise networks with requirements such as integration of multiple separate networks, isolation of subsidiaries, selective communications with shared resources, overlapping addresses, and consolidation of data centers can address these issues very effectively by deploying Layer 3 MPLS VPN technology in their intranet.

- Where they are more cost-effective, Layer 3 MPLS VPN services from service providers can be used to attach some of the locations. These can be seamlessly integrated with the Enterprise's own Layer 3 MPLS VPN service.

- The concept of multi-VRF CE routers can be used to extend the reach of multiple VPNs to a location that does not run MPLS.

- If encryption is required in the Enterprise, IPSec may be used in combination with Layer 3 MPLS VPN service to provide secure connectivity to the VPN.

- VoIP telephony services, whether operated by the Enterprise itself or managed by a TSP on behalf of the Enterprise, offer any-to-any voice connectivity across VPNs. They do this through the use of VPN-aware Firewall (FW)/NAT techniques including voice-specific ALG and thus without compromising VPN isolation. These telephony services also offer significant cost savings for off-net calls through optimum voice routing, minimizing the use of the PSTN.

- Layer 3 MPLS VPN is a key enabling technology for TSPs themselves. It allows them to securely isolate all the telephony service customers from one another while allowing each of those to access shared telephony resources such as gateways. This allows off-net connection to and from the PSTN.

- Layer 3 MPLS VPN offers a flexible way for a VPN to access dedicated servers while allowing a set of VPNs to access applications hosted on shared servers.

- Flexible QoS approaches can be used to address the great variety of application requirements over a mix of highly congested, moderately congested, and completely uncongested links that may be found in an Enterprise network. For example, a large number of classes (nine in this example) can be defined. Then these classes can be grouped into a smaller number of queues, depending on the link type (six queues on sub-100-Mbps links, three queues on 100+ Mbps links, and one queue on Gigabit links in this example).

- Simple routing design allows for convergence of a few seconds (5 seconds in this example) to handle the cases of router and unprotected link failures.

- Protocols such as HSRP and GLBP allow for dynamic rerouting in case of router failures within a few seconds as well as load balancing the host-to-POP traffic. In some cases, such as the office locations in the EuroBank network, these protocols need to be VRF-aware. In other words, they must be able to run in a VRF context.

APPENDIX A

References

Throughout this book you will see references to other resources. These are provided in case you want to delve more deeply into a subject. Such references appear in brackets, such as [L2VPN]. If you want to know more about this resource, look up the bracketed code in this appendix to find out specific information.

[2547bis] Rosen, E. et al. "BGP/MPLS IP VPNs." draft-ietf-l3vpn-rfc2547bis-03. Work in progress.

[6PE] De Clercq, et al. "Connecting IPv6 Islands Over IPv4 MPLS Using IPv6 Provider Edge Routers (6PE)." draft-ooms-v6ops-bgp-tunnel. Work in progress.

[6VPE] De Clercq, et al. "BGP-MPLS VPN Extension for IPv6 VPN." draft-ietf-l3vpn-bgp-ipv6. Work in progress.

[ADDR-ARCH] Hinden, et al. "IP Version 6 (IPv6) Addressing Architecture."

[AF] Heinanen, J. et al. "Assured Forwarding PHB Group." RFC 2597.

[AUTO-CONF] Thomson, S. et al. "IPv6 Stateless Address Autoconfiguration." draft-ietf-ipv6-rfc2462bis. Work in progress.

[AUTO-MESH] "MPLS Traffic Engineering Auto-tunnel mesh-group." www.cisco.com.

[AUTOROUTE] "MPLS Traffic Engineering Autoroute." www.cisco.com.

[BFD] "Bidirectional Forwarding Detection." http://www.ietf.org/html.charters/bfd-charter.html.

[BGP-IPv6] Marques, P. and F. Dupont. *Use of BGP-4 Multiprotocol Extensions for IPv6 Inter-Domain Routing.* RFC 2545.

[BGP+Label] Rehkter, Y. and E. Rosen. *Carrying Label Information in BGP-4.* RFC 3107.

[DHCP-IPv6] Droms, R. et al. *Dynamic Host Configuration Protocol for IPv6 (DHCPv6).* RFC 3315.

[DIFF-ARCH] Blake, S. et al. *An Architecture for Differentiated Services.* RFC 2475.

[DIFF-TERM] Grossman, D. *New Terminology and Clarifications for Diffserv.* RFC 3260.

[DLSw] Wells, L. and A. Bartky. *Data Link Switching: Switch-to-Switch Protocol AIW DLSw RIG: DLSw Closed Pages, DLSw Standard Version 1.0.* RFC 1795.

[DS-FIELD] Nichols, K. et al. *Definition of the Differentiated Services Field (DS Field) in the IPv4 and IPv6 Headers.* RFC 2474.

[DSTE-MAM] Le Faucheur et al. "Maximum Allocation Bandwidth Constraints Model for Diff-Serv-aware MPLS Traffic Engineering." draft-ietf-tewg-diff-te-mam. Work in progress.

[DSTE-MAR] Ash. "Max Allocation with Reservation Bandwidth Constraints Model for DiffServ-aware MPLS Traffic Engineering & Performance Comparisons." draft-ietf-tewg-diff-te-mar. Work in progress.

[DSTE-PROTO] Le Faucheur et al. "Protocol Extensions for Support of Differentiated-Service-aware MPLS Traffic Engineering." draft-ietf-tewg-diff-te-proto. Work in progress.

[DSTE-RDM] Le Faucheur et al. "Russian Dolls Bandwidth Constraints Model for Diff-Serv-aware MPLS Traffic Engineering." draft-ietf-tewg-diff-te-russian. Work in progress.

[DSTE-REQ] Le Faucheur, F. et al. *Requirements for Support of Differentiated Services-aware MPLS Traffic Engineering.* RFC 3564.

[ECN] Ramakrishnan, K. et al. *The Addition of Explicit Congestion Notification (ECN) to IP.* RFC 3168.

[EF] Davie, B. et al. *An Expedited Forwarding PHB (Per-Hop Behavior).* RFC 3246.

[EXTCOM] Tappan, D. et al. "BGP Extended Communities Attribute." draft-ietf-idr-bgp-ext-communities-07. Work in progress.

[FRF.12] *Frame Relay Fragmentation Implementation Agreement—FRF.12.* Editor A. Malis. Frame Relay Forum Technical Committee. December 1997.

[FRR] Pan, P. et al. "Fast Reroute Techniques in RSVP-TE." draft-ietf-mpls-rsvp-lsp-fastreroute. Work in progress.

[G114] "One-way Transmission Time." ITU-T Recommendation G.114.

[GMPLS] Berger, L. *Generalized Multi-Protocol Label Switching (GMPLS) Signaling Resource ReserVation Protocol-Traffic Engineering (RSVP-TE) Extensions.* RFC 3473.

[GRE] Hanks, S. et al. *Generic Routing Encapsulation (GRE).* RFC 1701.

[H323] "Packet-Based Multimedia Communications Systems." H.323. International Telecommunication Union (ITU) Telecommunication Standardization Sector (ITU-T).

[IF-MIB] McCloghrie, K. et al. *The Interfaces Group MIB.* RFC 2863.

[INT-SERV] Braden, R., D. Clark, and S. Shenker. *Integrated Services in the Internet Architecture: an Overview.* RFC 1633.

[INTER-AREA-AS] Vasseur et al. draft-vasseur-ccamp-inter-domain-path-comp.

[INTER-AS-TE-REQS]   Zhang, R., J. Vasseur, et al. "MPLS Inter-AS Traffic Engineering Requirements." draft-ietf-tewg-interas-mpls-te-req. Work in progress.

[INTER-DOMAIN-PATH-COMP]   Vasseur, J. and A. Ayyangar. "Inter-domain Traffic Engineering LSP Path Computation Methods." draft-vasseur-ccamp-inter-domain-path-comp. Work in progress.

[INTER-DOMAIN-SIG]   Ayyangar, A. and J. Vasseur. "Inter-domain MPLS Traffic Engineering—RSVP Extensions." draft-ayyangar-ccamp-inter-domain-rsvp-te. Work in progress.

[IPPM-DELVAR]   Demichelis, C. and P. Chimento. *IP Packet Delay Variation Metric for IP Performance Metrics (IPPM).* RFC 3393.

[IPPM-LOSS]   Almes, G. et al. *A One-way Packet Loss Metric for IPPM.* RFC 2680.

[IPPM-OWDELAY]   Almes, G., S. Kalidindi, and M. Zekauskas. *A One-way Delay Metric for IPPM.* RFC 2679.

[IPPM-RTDELAY]   Almes, G., S. Kalidindi, and M. Zekauskas. *A Round-trip Delay Metric for IPPM.* RFC 2681.

[IPSEC-ARCH]   Kent, S. and R. Atkinson. *Security Architecture for the Internet Protocol.* RFC 2401.

[IPv6]   Deering, S. and R. Hinden. *Internet Protocol, Version 6 (IPv6) Specification.* RFC 2460.

[IPv6-DEPLOY]   Popoviciu, Ciprian, Eric Levy-Abegnoli, and Ole Troan. *Deploying IPv6 Networks.* Cisco Press. ISBN 1587052105.

[IPv6-DISC]   Narten, T., E. Nordmark, W. Simpson. *Neighbor Discovery for IP Version 6 (IPv6).* RFC 2461.

[IPV6RIR]   APNIC, ARIN, RIPE NCC. *IPv6 Address Allocation and Assignment Policy.* Document ID: ripe-267. www.ripe.net/ripe/docs/ipv6policy.html

[ISIS]   ISO. "Intermediate system to Intermediate system routing information exchange protocol for use in conjunction with the Protocol for providing the Connectionless-mode Network Service (ISO 8473)." ISO/IEC 10589:1992.

[ISIS-CAPS]   Vasseur et al. "IS-IS extensions for advertising router information." draft-vasseur-isis-caps. Work in progress.

[ISIS-GMPLS]   Kompella, K., Y. Rekhter, et al. "IS-IS Extensions in Support of Generalized Multi-Protocol Label Switching." draft-ietf-isis-gmpls-extensions. Work in progress.

[ISIS-TE]   Smit, H. and T. Li. *Intermediate System to Intermediate System (IS-IS) Extensions for Traffic Engineering (TE).* RFC 3784.

[ISIS-TE-CAPS]   Vasseur, Le Roux, et al. "IS-IS MPLS Traffic Engineering Capabilities." draft-vasseur-isis-te-caps. Work in progress.

[ISIS-V6]   Hopps. "Routing IPv6 with IS-IS." draft-ietf-isis-ipv6. Work in progress.

[ISP-security]   Greene, Barry Raveendran and Philip Smith. *Cisco ISP Essentials.* Cisco Press. ISBN 1587050412.

[L2TPv3]   Townsley, M et al. "BGP/MPLS IP VPNs over Layer 2 Tunneling Protocol ver 3." draft-townsley-l3vpn-l2tpv3. Work in progress.

[L2VPN]   Rosen, E et al. "Framework for Layer 2 Virtual Private Networks (L2VPNs)." draft-ietf-l2vpn-l2-framework. Work in progress.

[LDP]   "LDP Specification." draft-ietf-mpls-rfc3036bis. Work in progress.

[local-scope]   Meyer, D. *Administratively Scoped IP Multicast.* RFC 2365.

[LOOSE-PATH-REOPT]   Vasseur, Ikejiri, and Zhang. "Reoptimization of an Explicit Loosely Routed MPLS TE Path." draft-ietf-ccamp-loose-path-reopt. Work in progress.

[LSP-PING]   Kompella, K. et al. "Detecting MPLS Data Plane Failures." draft-ietf-mpls-lsp-ping. Work in progress.

[MDT-SAFI]   Nalawade, G. et al. "MDT SAFI." draft-nalawade-idr-mdt-safi. Work in progress.

[MEGACO]   Groves, C. et al. *Gateway Control Protocol Version 1.* RFC 3525.

[MGCP]   Arango, M. et al. *Media Gateway Control Protocol (MGCP) Version 1.0.* RFC 2705.

[MLPPP]   Sklower, K. et al. *The PPP Multilink Protocol (MP).* RFC 1990.

[MP-BGP]   Bates, T. et al. *Multiprotocol Extensions for BGP-4.* RFC 2283.

[MPLS-DIFF]   Le Faucheur, F. et al. *Multi-Protocol Label Switching (MPLS) Support of Differentiated Services.* RFC 3270.

[MPLS-MGT]   Nadeau, Thomas D. "MPLS Network Management MIBs, Tools, and Techniques." Morgan Kaufmann, 2002.

[MPLS-Security]   Behringer, M. "Analysis of the Security of BGP/MPLS IP VPNs." draft-behringer-mpls-security. Work in progress.

[MPLS-STACK]   Rosen, E. et al. *MPLS Label Stack Encoding.* RFC 3032.

[MPLS-TE]   Osborne, Eric and Ajay Simha. *Traffic Engineering with MPLS.* Cisco Press. ISBN 1587050315.

[MPLS-VPN-Vol1]   Pepelnjak, Ivan and Jim Guichard. *MPLS and VPN Architectures, CCIP Edition.* Cisco Press. ISBN 1587050811.

[MPLS-VPN-Vol2]   Pepelnjak, Ivan, Jim Guichard, and Jeff Apcar. *MPLS and VPN Architectures, Volume II.* Cisco Press. ISBN 1587051125.

[mVPN] Rosen, E. Et al. "Multicast in MPLS/BGP IP VPNs." draft-rosen-vpn-mcast. Work in progress.

[NBAR] "Network-Based Application Recognition." www.cisco.com/warp/public/732/Tech/qos/behavioral/traffic

[NET-RECOV] Vasseur, Jean-Philippe, Mario Pickavet, and Piet Demeester. *Network Recovery: Protection and Restoration of Optical, SONET-SDH, IP, and MPLS.* Morgan Kaufmann. ISBN 012715051X.

[OSPF-CAPS] Lindem et al. "Extensions to OSPF for Advertising Optional Router Capabilities." draft-ietf-ospf-cap-04.txt. Work in progress.

[OSPF-GMPLS] Kompella, K., Y. Rekhter et al. "OSPF Extensions in Support of Generalized Multi-Protocol Label Switching." draft-ietf-ccamp-ospf-gmpls-extensions. Work in progress.

[OSPF-IPv6] Coltun, R., D. Ferguson, and J. Moy. *OSPF for IPv6.* RFC 2740.

[OSPF-TE] Katz, D., K. Kompella, and D. Yeung. *Traffic Engineering (TE) Extensions to OSPF Version 2.* RFC 3630.

[OSPF-TE-CAPS] Vasseur et al. "OSPF MPLS Traffic Engineering Capabilities." draft-vasseur-ospf-te-caps. Work in progress.

[OSPFv2] Moy, J. *OSPF Version 2.* RFC 2328.

[PMTU] Mogul, J. and S. Deering. *Path MTU Discovery.* RFC 1191.

[PREEMPT] De Oliveira et al. "LSP Preemption Policies for MPLS Traffic Engineering." draft-deoliveira-diff-te-preemption. Work in progress.

[PRIVATE] Rehkter, Y. et al. *Address Allocation for Private Internets.* RFC 1918.

[pwe3-atm] Martini, L. et al. "Encapsulation Methods for Transport of ATM Over MPLS Networks." draft-ietf-pwe3-atm-encap. Work in progress.

[PWE3-CELL-TRANSPORT] Martini, L. et al. "PWE3 ATM Transparent Cell Transport Service." draft-ietf-pwe3-cell-transport. Work in progress.

[pwe3-cp] Martini, L. et al. "Pseudowire Setup and Maintenance Using LDP." draft-ietf-pwe3-control-protocol-10. Work in progress.

[pwe3-eth] Martini, L. et al. "Encapsulation Methods for Transport of Ethernet Frames Over IP/MPLS Networks." draft-ietf-pwe3-ethernet-encap. Work in progress.

[pwe3-fr] Martini, L. et al. "Frame Relay Over Pseudo-Wires." draft-ietf-pwe3-frame-relay. Work in progress.

[pwe3-req] Xiao, X. et al. *Requirements for Pseudo-Wire Emulation Edge-to-Edge (PWE3).* RFC 3916.

[pwe3-sonet] Malis, A. et al. "SONET/SDH Circuit Emulation Over Packet (CEP)." draft-ietf-pwe3-sonet. Work in progress.

[QoS-CONF] *Cisco IOS Quality of Service Solutions Configuration Guide. A* vailable on www.cisco.com.

[QoS-REF] *Cisco IOS Quality of Service Solutions Command Reference.* Available on www.cisco.com.

[QUEUING1] Gross, Donald and Carl M. Harris. *Fundamentals of Queueing Theory, Third Edition.* Wiley-Interscience. ISBN 0471170836.

[QUEUING2] Kleinrock, Leonard and Richard Gail. *Queueing Systems: Problems and Solutions.* Wiley-Interscience. ISBN 0471555681.

[RED] Floyd, S., and V. Jacobson. "Random Early Detection Gateways for Congestion Avoidance." IEEE/ACM Transactions on Networking, Vol. 1, No. 4, August 1993, pp. 397-413.

[REFRESH-REDUCTION] Berger, L. et al. *RSVP Refresh Overhead Reduction Extensions.* RFC 2961.

[RIP-IPv6] Malkin, G. and R. Minnear. *RIPng for IPv6.* RFC 2080.

[Route-filter] Chen, E. and Y. Rekhter. "Cooperative Route Filtering Capability for BGP-4." draft-ietf-idr-route-filter. Work in progress.

[RSVP] Braden, R. et al. *Resource ReSerVation Protocol (RSVP)—Version 1 Functional Specification.* RFC 2205.

[RSVP-TE] Awduche, D. et al. *RSVP-TE: Extensions to RSVP for LSP Tunnels.* RFC 3209.

[rt-constrain] Marques, P. et al. "Constrained VPN Route Distribution." draft-ietf-l3vpn-rt-constrain. Work in progress.

[RTP] Schulzrinne, H. et al. *RTP: A Transport Protocol for Real-Time Applications.* RFC 3550.

[SCCP] "Skinny Client Control Protocol." See Cisco CallManager System Guide, Release 4.0(1)—Understanding IP Telephony Protocols. www.cisco.com/en/US/products/sw/voicesw/ps556/products_administration_guide_chapter09186a00801ec5cc.html

[SECOND-METRIC] Le Faucheur, F. et al. *Use of Interior Gateway Protocol (IGP) Metric as a Second MPLS Traffic Engineering (TE) Metric.* RFC 3785.

[SIP] Rosenberg, J. et al. *SIP: Session Initiation Protocol.* RFC 3261.

[SLA] Filsfil and Evans. "Deploying Diffserv at the Network Edge for Tight SLAs."

Part 1: Internet Computing, IEEE, January/February 2004, Vol. 8, No. 1

Part 2: Internet Computing, IEEE, March/April 2004, Vol. 8, No. 2

[SS7]   "Introduction to CCITT Signalling System No. 7." Q.700. International Telecommunication Union (ITU) Telecommunication Standardization Sector (ITU-T).

[TRAFFIC1]   Bonald et al. "Statistical Performance Guarantees for Streaming Flows Using Expedited Forwarding."

[TRAFFIC2]   Yao et al. "Diffserv on High Speed Links."

[TRAFFIC3]   Bennett et al. "Delay Jitter Bounds and Packet Scale Rate Guarantee for Expedited Forwarding."

[TRAFFIC4]   Telkamp et al. "Internet Traffic Is Not Self-Similar at Timescales Relevant to QoS."

[UNIQ-LOCAL]   Hinden et al. "Unique Local IPv6 Unicast Addresses." draft-ietf-ipv6-unique-local-addr. Work in progress.

[VPLS]   Lasserre, M., V. Kompella, et al. "Virtual Private LAN Services Over MPLS." draft-ietf-l2vpn-vpls-ldp. Work in progress.

[XOT]   Forster, J. et al. *Cisco Systems X.25 over TCP (XOT). RFC 1613*. www.ietf.org/rfc/rfc1613.txt

INDEX

Numerics

100+-Mbps QoS policy, 470
6PE routers, 274
6VPE functionality, 327

A

ABRs (Area Border Routers), 91
AC (Attached Circuit), 42
access. *See also* remote access
    dial-in, 14
    DSL, 15
    Internet
        following default routes, 305, 307
        via NAT/firewall services, 309
        via PE-CE links, 307–308
    IPv6, 272
    via NAT/firewall services, 309
    POP network structure, 280, 284–285
    provisioning, 131
    QoS, 470
    VPN, 3–5
        autonomous system boundaries, 19–22
        Carrier's Carrier architecture, 16–18
        CE routers, 7
        components, 5
        IPv6, 30–41
        label allocating (PE routers), 8–9
        Layer 2, 41–45
        multicast, 22–30
        packet delivery, 12–13
        PE routers, 6–7
        remote, 14–15
        route target formats (PE routers), 10
        VPNv4 prefix creation (PE routers), 9–10
        WRED drop profiles, 238
Add/Drop Multiplexers (ADMs), 118, 270
addresses
    autoconfiguration, 33
    IPv6, 32
    multicast allocation, 216
    NAT, 30
    SAFI, 311
adjacencies, 28, 82–85
ADM (Add/Drop Multiplexer), 118
advertisements
    inter-AS VPNv4 exchanges, 20
    interval timers, 324
AF (Assured Forwarding), 59
affinities (traffic engineering), 70
Africa Telecom, VPOPs, 421
agents, SAA, 371
aggregation
    core QoS engineering, 65
    traffic engineering (DiffServ), 86–89
algorithms
    Dijkstra, 74
    exponential back-off, 102
    load balancing, 82. *See also* load balancing
allocation, 300
    labels (PE-routers), 8–9
    MAM, 345
    multicast address, 216
    names (VPN), 132
    RD, 132, 201
    routes, 300
"Always-on" connectivity, 31
American Registry for Internet Numbers (ARIN), 119
anycast addresses, 33

D

F

G

M

R

S

V

W–Z

Cisco Press

FUNDAMENTALS SERIES
ESSENTIAL EXPLANATIONS AND SOLUTIONS

CISCO SYSTEMS

Voice over IP Fundamentals

A systematic approach to understanding the
basics of Voice over IP

Jonathan Davidson, CCIE® No. 2560
James Peters

When you need an authoritative introduction
to a key networking topic, **reach for a Cisco
Press Fundamentals book**. Learn about network
topologies, deployment concepts, protocols,
and management techniques and **master
essential networking concepts and solutions**.

Look for Fundamentals titles at your favorite bookseller

802.11 Wireless LAN Fundamentals
ISBN: 1-58705-077-3

**Cisco CallManager Fundamentals:
A Cisco AVVID Solution**
ISBN: 1-58705-008-0

Data Center Fundamentals
ISBN: 1-58705-023-4

IP Addressing Fundamentals
ISBN: 1-58705-067-6

IP Routing Fundamentals
ISBN: 1-57870-071-X

Voice over IP Fundamentals
ISBN: 1-57870-168-6

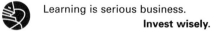

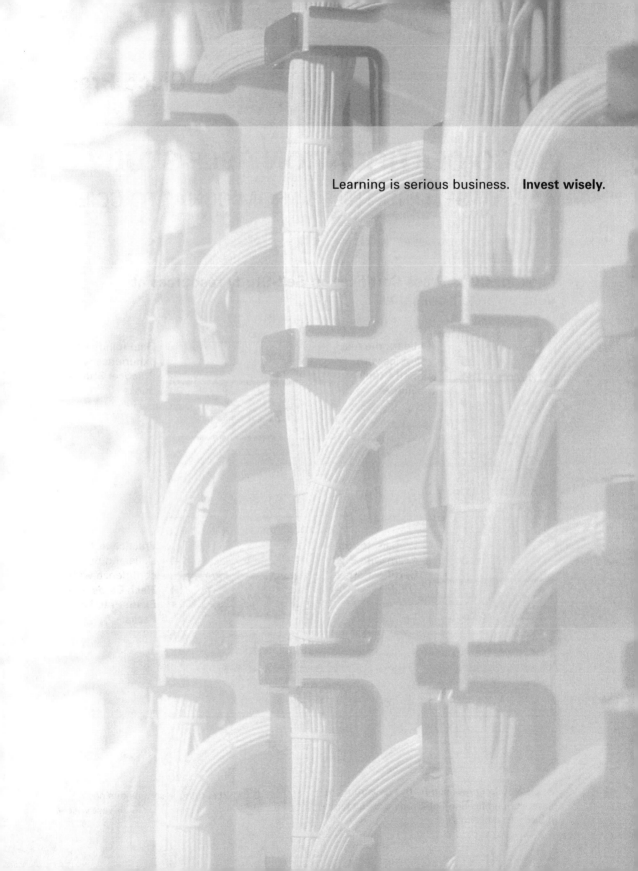

Learning is serious business.　**Invest wisely.**

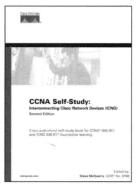

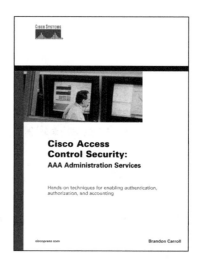

DISCUSS
NETWORKING PRODUCTS AND TECHNOLOGIES WITH CISCO EXPERTS AND NETWORKING PROFESSIONALS WORLDWIDE

VISIT NETWORKING PROFESSIONALS
A CISCO ONLINE COMMUNITY
WWW.CISCO.COM/GO/DISCUSS

CISCO SYSTEMS

THIS IS THE POWER OF THE NETWORK. now.

SEARCH THOUSANDS OF BOOKS FROM LEADING PUBLISHERS

Safari® Bookshelf is a searchable electronic reference library for IT professionals that features more than 2,000 titles from technical publishers, including Cisco Press.

With Safari Bookshelf you can

- **Search** the full text of thousands of technical books, including more than 70 Cisco Press titles from authors such as Wendell Odom, Jeff Doyle, Bill Parkhurst, Sam Halabi, and Karl Solie.

- **Read** the books on My Bookshelf from cover to cover, or just flip to the information you need.

- **Browse** books by category to research any technical topic.

- **Download** chapters for printing and viewing offline.

With a customized library, you'll have access to your books when and where you need them—and all you need is a user name and password.

Cisco Press

3 STEPS TO LEARNING

STEP 1　　　　　**STEP 2**　　　　　**STEP 3**

First-Step　　　　Fundamentals　　　Networking
　　　　　　　　　　　　　　　　　　Technology Guides

STEP 1　**First-Step**—Benefit from easy-to-grasp explanations.
　　　　No experience required!

STEP 2　**Fundamentals**—Understand the purpose, application,
　　　　and management of technology.

STEP 3　**Networking Technology Guides**—Gain the knowledge
　　　　to master the challenge of the network.

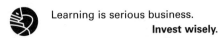